Memoirs of Pancho Villa

THE TEXAS PAN-AMERICAN SERIES

MARTÍN LUIS GUZMÁN

Memoirs of

————◆►————

TRANSLATED BY VIRGINIA H. TAYLOR

UNIVERSITY OF TEXAS PRESS : AUSTIN

The Texas Pan American Series is published with the assistance of a revolving publication fund established by the Pan American Sulphur Company and other friends of Latin America in Texas. Publication of this book was also assisted by a grant from the Rockefeller Foundation through the Latin American translation program of the Association of American University Presses.

International Standard Book Number 0–292–73301–1 (cloth)
0–292–75028–5 (paper)

Library of Congress Catalog Card Number 65–11146
Translation copyright © 1965 by Martín Luis Guzmár
Fifth Printing, 1975

First Paperback Printing, 1975

Publisher's Foreword

This account does not carry Pancho Villa to the end of his life. It ends in 1915 as he was preparing for new battles in the internecine warfare among the Revolutionary generals which followed the triumph of the Revolution. Martín Luis Guzmán, author of this volume, has the necessary materials and records at hand and plans to complete the story at some future time.

The Spanish version of these *Memoirs* has been somewhat condensed in translation by eliminating, with no indication of ellipses, some of Villa's repetitions and redundancies.

The University of Texas Press wishes to express its great appreciation to the El Paso Public Library and to Walter N. Babbitt, director of the Library, for making available extensive files of pictures of the Villa period. The Press is especially indebted to C. L. Sonnichsen, dean of the Graduate Division of Texas Western College, El Paso, for valuable assistance in locating and identifying pictures.

The Press, the author, and the translator are extremely grateful to Robert C. Stephenson, of the University of Puerto Rico, for his careful review of the manuscript.

Preface

Two fortuitous events are responsible for the existence of this book and its title. One was the incident that brought a number of documents from the archives of General Francisco Villa into my hands. I have had them published in full as *El hombre y sus armas* (The Man and His Arms). The other was my participation in the military activities of the Revolution in 1913 and 1914.

General Villa's archives provided me with a mass of papers, absolutely authentic historically and autobiographically, and organized in the following manner: 1) The service record of Pancho Villa, an official document relating to the Madero Revolution of 1910 and 1911, consisting of 40 typed pages; 2) A manuscript account in pencil, consisting of 103 pages of various kinds and sizes; and 3) Five large books of manuscripts, in excellent penmanship, the title page of which reads, "Gen. Francisco Villa, by Manuel Bauche Alcalde, 1914."

The service record states what Villa did from November, 1910, the beginning of the Maderista movement, to April, 1911, when Villa retired to the town of San Andrés in the state of Chihuahua after the taking of Juárez and the triumph of Francisco I. Madero. The notes in pencil begin with Villa's flight to the sierra in 1894—the future guerrilla was then fifteen or sixteen years old—and end in 1914, a few days after Villa, general in chief of the Northern Division, had taken the plaza of Ojinaga. The five manuscript books contain a narrative in autobiographical form, interspersed with political comment and historical and social analysis. It begins, as does the account in pencil, with the family incident of 1894 and extends to Pancho Villa's entrance into the United States on January 2, 1913, after his escape from the military prison Santiago Tlaltelolco.

It is evident from the context of the papers that the service record was written under Villa's direction from data furnished by him; that the notes in pencil were written while Villa was relating (to Bauche Alcalde probably) the important events of his life; and that the five manuscript books represent Bauche Alcalde's version of one part of the notes (from their beginning to Villa's arrival in the United States in January, 1913) and of the service record, to which he has added his thoughts on Porfirismo and the Revolutionary movement.

Half of the notes in pencil appear to have been lost; but undoubtedly they were at one time complete. This conclusion is reached by comparing the existing portion with the contents of the manuscript books and observing that there are one and one-half pages, attached at the end of the notes relative to the first advance of Villa's troops to the south, under the heading "To be added to the taking of Torreón." It can be firmly maintained that Villa gave a complete report to Bauche Alcalde, or to whoever was taking the notes in pencil, on the period of his life preceding the Revolutionary campaign of 1910–1911 (this campaign is covered in the service record) and the period between that campaign and the events of February, 1914.

Having dealt with Villa personally and somewhat intimately; having heard him relate the story of his persecutions and experiences in the Revolution; having, especially, committed myself to the greatest possible exactness in writing down all that he said in my presence, I am definitely of the opinion that neither the service record, nor the notes in pencil, nor the version of Bauche Alcalde are texts written in Villa's own language. It appears that the typist who wrote the first of these documents, like the one who took down the notes while Villa was talking, considered the guerrilla's manner of speaking too unrefined and wished to give his statements a more cultured form, to rid them of archaic words and rustic terms, to improve the construction of his sentences, and to omit his parallelisms and redundancies. In the manuscript books Bauche Alcalde devoted himself to converting Villa's natural expressions into the language of a man from Mexico City. In fact, in the notes there is seldom an appearance of the diction, the grammar, and the expressive purity of Villa's habitual speech except when reference is made to things he learned in the cities or to strictly military subjects.

Thus, to write this book, I have had to do the following things with regard to language and style: a) To set the standard of Villa's speech as far as possible without altering the existing text, the notes in pencil, and the service record, even leaving the narrative as it appears in the greater part of the passages from pages 3 to 16, 23 to 53, and 88 to 132 of this book (I say "the greater part of the passages" because there are gaps which I had to fill, one of which was very long, beginning on page 98 and ending on page 111); b) To put in the same language the authentic and strictly autobiographical part of the manuscript books, which is now

found from pages 16 to 23 and 53 to 88, with exception of the existing gaps; and c) To write directly and without the links of the previous
texts—but flexibly only to a certain degree—everything following
page 132. This portion is an original narration made, insofar as my ability permitted, according to the manner in which Villa was able to tell
things in his own language, the Castilian of the sierras of Durango and
Chihuahua. It is excellent Castilian, popular but neither vernacular nor
archaic, and in Villa, who was speaking it with no culture other than
that of his untamed predecessors, although with a great natural understanding of the beauty of the word, it was full of repetition, highly expressive redundancies, recurring parallelisms, and other peculiarities.
Thus I was confronted with the problem of not departing from the
language I always had heard Villa use, and at the same time remaining
within the limits of the literary.

A numerical estimate will perhaps give an idea of what I had to do
with the preceding texts. The 6,500 words contained in the first sixty-
one pages of the notes in pencil have been converted into the narrative
appearing in the first eleven pages of this book. The 15,300 words in the
service record have been transformed into pages 23 to 53.

These statements explain the form of this work. With respect to its
basis, or rather the facts that are narrated and their historical value, a
few lines should suffice. The contents of the gaps filled in as far as page
132 and the facts stated in the remaining pages constitute historical material based on documents or on reports furnished to me by firsthand
witnesses.

I do not know whether I have achieved my purpose. No one is less
competent than the author himself to judge works of this nature. They
are difficult for anyone to evaluate outside of the historical perspective
which develops only with the passage of years. But I am indeed sure of
the truth of my intention, and to such degree that if I had fully undertaken the subject of Pancho Villa under other circumstances, I would
have followed some procedure analagous to the one employed here,
even if I had no papers such as those which came into my possession in
this case. Always, for various reasons, I was fascinated by the project of
writing the life of Pancho Villa in autobiographical form, as I indicated
in my book entitled *El águila y la serpiente* (The Eagle and the Ser-
pent). Purely aesthetic motives required me to say, in the language and
with the concepts and ideas of Francisco Villa, what he had been able
to say about himself in fortune and in adversity; political motives required me to make a more eloquent defense of Villa in the face of the

iniquity with which the Mexican Counter-Revolution and its allies have unburdened themselves of their sins by setting him up as a target; and lastly, motives of a didactic and even satirical nature required me to bring into greater relief the way a man born of Porfirian illegality, entirely primitive, entirely uncultured and devoid of schooling, entirely illiterate, could rise—an inconceivable fact without the assistance of an entire social order—from the abyss of banditry to which his environment had driven him, to the heights of great victory, of the greatest victory over the system of exalted injustice, which was a regime incompatible to him and to his brothers in grief and misery.

Martín Luis Guzmán

Contents

Illustrations

Following page 192

All pictures are from the collection of the El Paso Public Library

Enriqui Banda, Pancho Villa, Javier Hernández
Eugenio Aguirre Benavides, Pancho Villa, Alvaro Obregón, Rodolfo Fierro, Dr. Raschbaum, José Ruíz

Troops firing from mountainside
Máximo Castillo

Revolutionary bugler
Gun emplacement on mountainside

Emilio Campa and José Inés Salazar
Revolutionaries at battle of Juárez

Revolutionaries boarding train
Revolutionaries beginning attack at Juárez

Pancho Villa in civilian dress
Felipe Angeles

Victoriano Huerta
Eulalio Gutiérrez

José Isabel Robles
Don Luis Terrazas
Raúl Madero
Antonio Rojas

Venustiano Carranza
U.S. General Hugh L. Scott and Pancho Villa

Francisco I. Madero
Pascual Orozco, Jr.

Pancho Villa in dress uniform
Juan N. Medina
Eduardo Hay
Guiseppe (José) Garibaldi

BOOK 1 *The Man and His Arms*

CHAPTER 1

At Seventeen Years of Age Doroteo Arango Becomes Pancho Villa and Begins His Extraordinary and Eventful Career

Gogojito Hacienda. Don Agustín López Negrete and Martina Villa. The San Juan del Río Jail. Félix Sariñana's Men. The *Acordada* of Canatlán in the False Corral. Ignacio Parra and Refugio Alvarado. The Lead Mare at the Hacienda de la Concha. Don Ramón. The First Three Thousand Pesos. Sr. Amparán's Horse.

In 1894 I was sixteen years old, living on the Hacienda Gogojito in the municipality of Canatlán in Durango and farming on halves with the Sres. López Negrete. Besides my mother and my brothers, Antonio and Hipólito, I had with me my sisters—Marianita, fifteen years old, and Martina, twelve.

On September 22 I returned from the field, where I had nothing but grass to cut. I found Martina clinging to my mother, who stood on one side of her, with Don Agustín López Negrete on the other. My mother wept but spoke firmly, "Leave my house, Señor. Have you no shame?"

I went to my cousin Romualdo Franco's for the pistol I kept there and returned and fired at Don Agustín and hit him three times.

He called out to the five boys who had come with him. They came running with their carbines but he said, "Don't kill the boy; just carry me home." They lifted him into his coach and took him to the Hacienda Santa Isabel de Berros, a league from Gogojito.

Seeing I was still free, I got on my horse and headed for the Sierra de la Silla, opposite Gogojito.

The next day I went down to my friend Antonio Lares' and asked, "How is Don Agustín?"

"He's in a bad way. They've sent after you from Canatlán."

"Tell my mother to take the family to the house at Río Grande."

I went back to the sierra. From that moment on I was pursued, wanted dead or alive in every district. I spent months in slipping back

and forth from the Sierra de la Silla to the Sierra de Gamón, living off
anything I was lucky enough to find—usually meat without salt—since
I dared not enter a town.

Because of my inexperience, three men did finally catch me and put
me in jail in San Juan del Río one night. The next morning, before shooting me, they took me out to grind a barrel of *nixtamal*. I killed one of the
guards with the pestle of the metate and headed for the Cerro de los
Remedios nearby. By the time they notified the police it was too late:
they could not possibly catch me. By the river I found a wild colt,
mounted, and rode upstream. After a couple of leagues the horse tired
and I let him go. I walked home at a good pace, upstream to Río
Grande. One of my cousins gave me his horse and saddle and food
enough for several days. With this I returned to the Sierra de la Silla
and the Sierra de Gamón and stayed there until the following year.

I was then known as Doroteo Arango. My father, Agustín Arango,
was the natural son of Don Jesús Villa and because of his origin took his
mother's name, Arango, instead of his father's. My brothers and sisters
and I, legitimate children of a legitimate marriage, also received the
name Arango, the only one by which our family was known.

I adopted my grandfather's surname as some protection against pursuit, calling myself Francisco Villa, a name I still carry and consider my
own. To the world I became and remain Pancho Villa.

I hid out in the Sierra de la Silla and the Sierra de Gamón until 1895.
In early October of that year a certain Pablo Martínez betrayed me to
the authorities. Seven men found me asleep in a field at La Soledad be-
neath the Sierra de la Silla. When I woke seven carbines were leveled
at me and seven men were ordering me to give up. I could only answer,
"I surrender," but I added, "What's the hurry, Gentlemen? Why don't
we roast some ears of corn before we go wherever you are taking me?"

Their leader, Félix Sariñana, said "Why not? We'll roast some corn,
have a meal with him, and then take him back to town."

What they didn't know was that my horse was grazing some four
hundred meters away, my saddle was out of sight in the furrows, and my
pistol under the blanket I was lying on. When two of them went to cut
the corn and two others to fetch wood, I grabbed the pistol and made
for the three that remained. They panicked and hit the dirt in a gulch.
I ran for my horse and by the time they had got together to pursue me
was already taking it easy on the way to my hideout. I could see them
watching from down on the flat.

Two or three months later they sent the *acordada* of Canatlán after me. They knew where I was hiding and almost trapped me in the False Corral, but they were unfamiliar with the lay of the land and I led them into ambush. When they came into full view I killed three *rurales* and some horses. This slowed them down, and while they were milling around I made off and escaped by the only possible exit, which they knew nothing about.

Wanting to hole up in the Sierra de Gamón but having nothing to eat, I took twelve head of cattle with me and made for a ravine called Quebrada del Cañon del Infierno. In this solitude I killed the cattle by myself. I dried the meat, and it supplied me well for five months. Part of it I sold to lumbermen friends who were felling trees in Pánuco de Avino. They brought me coffee, tortillas, and other provisions. I spent five months there.

At the end of this time I returned to the Sierra de la Silla. One night I visited the Hacienda Santa Isabel de Berros. At the house of a friend, Jesús Alday, I asked, "Is there any news?" He replied, "Plenty. And your part of it is they're still after you. Brother"—he called me his kid brother—"I have a couple of friends for you. Join up with them and you won't get into so much trouble. I'll have them here tomorrow night if you say so."

That's the way it was. The two "friends," dead now, were Ignacio Parra and Refugio Alvarado, fugitives like me. When they saw me they said, "Why, he's just a kid and you've been talking him up big."

Ignacio turned to me: "Do you want to join up with us, young fellow?"

I said, "I'd like to, Señor, if I can help out."

That same night we left for the Hacienda de la Soledad and the next day for Tejame, near the Hacienda de la Concha.

Before dark my compañeros said, "Listen, young fellow, if you go with us you will do what we say. We kill and rob. We are telling you so you won't be frightened."

"Señores," I said, "I am ready for anything. The law is after me and I'll defend myself. Just give the orders and I'll carry them out."

They said, "You see that herd of mules in the stubble?"

"I see it, Señores."

"Well, we are going to make off with it tonight. Get rid of the bell on the lead mare and bring her in, leading the mules."

I did as they ordered about eleven that night. I brought the lead mare, Ignacio took charge of her, and Refugio and I drove the herd. With the mules we made for the Promontorio spring and by dawn had the whole herd there. We moved on that night whenever we could and morning found us opposite Las Iglesias. Traveling by night only we next came to a little ranch at one side of the Hacienda de Ramos where my compañeros had friends. From there we reached Urique, near Indé, and from Indé got to Agua Zarca, where my compañeros had other friends. One more night and we were in the sierra Cabeza del Oso, opposite the Hacienda de Canutillo and Las Nieves. Next morning it was the Sierra del Amolar and a final night brought us to Ojito. The owner of the pasture there, Don Ramón, was an old friend of Ignacio and Refugio's. We left the herd there, and as it was a secluded spot we rested in the old man's house. It was elegant. We had everything we needed.

Eight days later we turned our mules over to buyers, and on the day afterward Ignacio led me aside and said, "I'm delivering your share of the money, young fellow."

"Very good, Señor." He gave me three thousand pesos—a great surprise, for I had never had even a hundred pesos in my hands at one time. I went and bought some clothes.

Not long after, I asked Ignacio when we were leaving. I still wanted to be back in my own part of the country. He said, "Day after tomorrow night, and listen, young fellow, buy yourself a good horse and saddle. That's your best friend."

On my way to a saloon I saw a black horse with a fine new saddle standing at the door. As I calmly mounted, the owner shouted, "Hey, man, where are you going?"

It was too late to stop me. I rode the horse away and hid it where we had left the mules, the only place I knew in that country.

Years later I learned that it had belonged to a certain Ramón Amparán.

When we were ready to leave and my compañeros saw what a magnificent horse I was riding they wanted to know how much it had cost. I replied, "Only the effort to mount it when a drunk left it at the saloon door." After that they greatly respected me.

CHAPTER 2

Still a Boy, Pancho Villa Prefers Being the Number One Bandit in the World to Seeing His Family Dishonored.

Pancho Villa's Mother. Ignacio's *Aguamiel*. Two Friends at Pueblo Nuevo. The Mule's Packsaddle. How Villa Uses His First Fifty Thousand Pesos. Félix Sariñana's Commission. Death of the Three Deer Hunters. Refugio's Bad Disposition. Delivery by Simón Ochoa. The Inspector Jesús Flores. The Foreman of the Medina Farm. The Little Old Man with the Bread.

We returned to our country and first of all I went to visit my family. My mother received me with her usual affection. I gave her what money I had. At this she called me aside and asked, "My dear son, where did you get so much money? These men are leading you into evil ways. You are committing crimes and it will be on my conscience if I fail to make you understand."

I answered, "Mama dear, it is my fate to suffer. You know how it began. I only wanted to defend the honor of my family. I'll be the Number One bandit in the country before I'll see my family dishonored. Give me your blessing, commend me to God, and He will know what to do."

The next night we went on toward Canatlán as far as the Cañada de Cantinamáis, a ranch where the family of Ignacio Parra lived. His mother and little sisters, only half-civilized creatures, welcomed us warmly. We would have stayed there a second day, but they sent about two hundred men from Canatlán to arrest us. Ignacio was a brave man. When they told him all those people were after us he said, "Don't worry, Little Sister. I still have time to drink my *aguamiel*."

And so it was. He had just finished when the men fell upon us. The firing began at ten in the morning. We sustained it, withdrawing to the Cerros de las Cocinas. On the way they shot Refugio's horse from under him, and Ignacio ordered me to take him up behind me. I did this safely and we got away so fast that no one was following us when we started climbing the hills.

Soon afterward we went down the other side to the Cabañada de las Cocinas, a farm belonging to the Hacienda de la Sauceda. There Ignacio said to the foreman, "Bring me some horses for these." They brought up the remuda, we changed horses and went on to the Hacienda de Alisos.

By dark we had reached a house some distance from the hacienda. A friend gave us something to eat. My compañeros ordered him to carry supplies to the sierra and leave them at a place called Magueyitos. The next day he brought three bags of provisions. We took what we needed and started across the sierra to Maguey; from there we reached Pueblo Nuevo, about thirty leagues away.

Pueblo Nuevo is on a mountainside. There my compañeros had good friends—one of them a rich miner. With them we went up and down the slopes of Pueblo Nuevo dancing and carousing, not because we liked to drink—except for Refugio—but because we had plenty of money.

Some two months after this Ignacio said, "Get ready, we are leaving."

The fact was that the miner had delivered 150,000 pesos to a man, and he and Ignacio planned for us to hold him up on the road.

Climbing up the ravine we came to a level place in the sierra and were there two days without Ignacio's saying anything. At last he said, "A man will come by leading a mule. We must waylay him but not kill him. He is carrying money."

About noon we saw him coming. At the sight of us he was too frightened to reach for his guns. Don Ignacio told him to hand them over. We searched him thoroughly but found only four hundred pesos in his jacket pocket and let him go.

Some two hundred meters on our way I said to Ignacio, "Why wouldn't he carry the money under the packsaddle?"

"Go get it, boy," he said.

I did, for a fact. I overtook him and found the money where I expected. Ignacio and Refugio respected me for that.

We cooked dinner. The man ate with us and afterwards we turned him loose. When we divided the money, there were fifty thousand pesos for each of us.

We returned to our own country. I gave my mother five thousand pesos and among my close relatives distributed four thousand more. I bought a tailor shop for a man named Antonio Retana who had very poor eyesight and a large and needy family. I hired a man to run it and gave him the same amount of money. And so it went. In eight or ten months I had given away all that was left of the fifty thousand pesos.

The following year I visited my mother again. I had not fixed on a day to leave, but the justice of the peace sent a report to San Juan del Río and the next morning a posse of sixty men arrived. My compañeros and

I were having breakfast when one of my sisters came to the door and said, "Here comes a crowd of men."

We grabbed our rifles, went out to face them, and began shooting. From behind a boiler near the kitchen I picked off the chief, who was no other than Félix Sariñana, whom I have mentioned. The rest ran, and we mounted our horses and rode at a good pace to the Sierra de Gamón. There one morning three deer hunters found us asleep at the entrance of the Cañon del Infierno. We woke to a rifle pointing at each of us. When we drew our guns they shot Refugio in the leg, but you can be sure that fifteen minutes later the deer hunters were dead.

In that encounter I was shot in the chest but only a slight mark remains.

In the Sierra de la Silla we stayed in the False Corral for three months till Refugio's leg was well. When he could ride we made for the Sierra de la Ulama near Santiago Papasquiaro, where a friend of my compañeros was going to help us with some slaughtering. We rounded up three hundred head of cattle from the plains of Papasquiaro. We slaughtered them and when the meat was dry Ignacio said, "Boy, you and Refugio take the meat to Tejame. Don Julio has already arranged for a buyer."

We set out, but on the way down a canyon one of my mules rolled over a cliff with his entire load. Refugio, a blasphemous man, cursed me and the mother that bore me. I reached for my rifle and began shooting. One shot hit his horse in the forehead and there went Refugio and his horse rolling two hundred meters downhill. Lost without his rifle and his horse, he pleaded, "Don't shoot, Boy. Don't be hard-hearted."

I left him with the load and returned to Ignacio. When I told him what had happened he went in search of Refugio. I do not know what passed between them, but when he returned three days later he informed me that Refugio would no longer be our compañero, and in fact we never again joined up with him.

Turning over to Don Julio what was left, we went to Canatlán, to Don Pablo Valenzuela, a friendly and respected man. We stayed several weeks in his house. From there we set out for Durango, to Ignacio's. A lady was living there with him. She was well educated and treated us with great consideration.

Fifteen days later we were betrayed, this time by a man named Simón Ochoa. At the door one day we found two mounted men, an officer and Jesús Flores, the inspector general of police, waiting for us. As we were going out, Flores said, "Who are you, Señores?"

Ignacio replied, "We are the landlords."

Flores said to the officer, "Dismount and search them."

Ignacio looked at me and winked and asked, "Are you afraid to do it, Inspector?"

The three of us drew at the same time. Standing at the door we fired at close range, and Flores fell dead. The others ran down the street for help.

Losing no time, we saddled and were just leaving when we saw more mounted men coming in pursuit. We moved down the street at a trot. Out of town we stopped at Cerro del Mercado. Ignacio said, "We will shelter our horses in the arroyo." We did, and began firing, and after a few shots they returned to Durango.

Remounted, we traveled all that night and by morning reached the Sierra de Ocotlán, near the Sierra de la Silla. The next day we climbed the sierra and at the top found the foreman of the Medina farm, which belonged to the Hacienda de San Bartolo. He was an acquaintance and we asked him for news. He said, "The news is that they killed Refugio Alvarado and Federico Arriola in Malpaíses de Ocotlán."

That night we went down to the Hacienda de San Bartolo. Friends told us how Refugio was killed. They said it was the foreman, a man named Luis, who caught him. We left the hacienda in search of the foreman. Coming upon him and some cowboys out on the prairie we halted to discuss the situation and the result was that we got into a gunfight. Luis was severely wounded in the arm; if he is still alive, his arm is missing.

It was only right to avenge our compañero, even though we had parted company with him because of his obstinate nature.

In those days we were staying in the Sierra de la Silla. José Solís joined us. He was a friend of Ignacio's from a little town the other side of Durango. I did not know him or the circumstances of their friendship.

We set out for Canatlán to buy ammunition. On the road, opposite the Las Cocinas farm, we met a poor old man with a burro loaded with two boxes. He told us it was bread. When we asked him to sell us a little, he said he could not because he was taking it to the owners of the Hacienda de Santa Isabel. Solís said, "Sell us the bread or I'll take it from you."

The old man answered, "In my affairs only I command."

Solís shot him twice and killed him. I protested, but Ignacio said that Solís was in the right since the old man had refused to sell us bread.

I said, "No, Señor, he was not in the right. It was unnecessary to kill the old man. If this goes on, I will be leaving you."

Ignacio answered, "Leave any time you like, but in the end you will be unable to get along without me."

I left them then and there and went to San Juan del Río.

CHAPTER 3

Pancho Villa Tries in Vain to Lead an Honorable Life: The Representatives of Justice Seem Determined To Make Him Rob and Kill.

The Slaughter of a Few Cattle. "If He Had Given Me No Cause, I Would Not Have Killed Him." Catarino Saldaña's Ten Thousand Pesos. The Owner of the Hacienda de Piedras. Luis Orozco. El Verde. Gangrene. The Charitable Don Santos Vega. A Judge's Warrant. Death of Pancho Villa's Mother.

In San Juan del Río I remained hidden for a month in Antonio Retana's house. He was the tailor for whom I had provided the means of making a living. Afterward I went to the Hacienda de Santa Isabel de Berros and got two friends to give me some *gordas* for a few days in the sierra. Up there I devoted myself to slaughtering. I planned to get money by selling the meat.

I killed about twenty-five head of cattle, dried the meat and the hides, made up my bundles, and then left them in the care of a friend while I went to Canatlán, back to the home of Don Pablo Valenzuela. I hoped he would buy the meat. We agreed on a price and the bundles were carried to Canatlán.

Don Pablo being a good as well as a rich man, I took only two hundred pesos and left the balance on deposit with him. Then I returned to visit my dear mother, but finding the house watched, I left after only two hours.

From there I was on my way to the Sierra de Menores; to make it I had to pass by the Rancho de Valdés, owned by Don Eulogio Veloz. Since everyone there knew me, I crossed a pasture some distance from the house. Before I got back on the road a man rode up and in an insulting tone accused me of trespassing and said he was going to carry me before the owner.

I answered, "I am doing no harm."

He rode his horse against mine and struck me twice. My anger boiled up. I spurred my horse, drew my pistol, fired, and killed him instantly. I dismounted for his pistol and cartridge belt. Looking at the body a moment, I thought to myself, "If he had given me no cause, I would not have killed him."

I remounted and followed the dead man's horse, which had run off and stopped behind some rocks. It would not let me catch it so I shot it, took the saddle and rifle, and went on toward the Hacienda de Menores.

At the hacienda there were friends who had known my grandfather from the age of seven but were unaware of my present occupation or the life I was leading. I stayed with them five days. In the house was an agreeable fellow named Manuel Torres. To him I explained my circumstances and hardships and I invited him to go with me.

Manuel Torres had guns and a horse and had spent the best part of his life in colleges. He was a person of intelligence but I succeeded in persuading him. He explained how we would have to conduct ourselves. He liked anything that was different.

We made a trip to San Andrés de la Sierra. The manager there was a friend of mine. He informed me of ten thousand pesos he was going to dispatch by a certain Catarino Saldaña.

On the road we took the money away from Saldaña but did not kill him. He even traveled quite contentedly with us for a couple of days. We handcuffed him at night so as not to have to watch him while he slept, but the chain was long and didn't bother him much. When we came near the ranches we decided to free him. One morning we took leave of him and went on to Durango.

As Manuel Torres was fond of *tertulias* and fiestas, he devoted himself to having a good time. Whether he spent all the five thousand pesos he had I cannot say, but he knew I had money on deposit in the house where we were staying, since I trusted the family, and he presented a letter which he said I had written. This was false. At the time I did not even know how to read. He requested the money in my name, took the two horses, saddles and all, and, already having my permission to leave, abandoned me there on foot.

I provided myself with another saddle and a horse. A friend who lived at the Hacienda de la Tinaja near Durango brought me one which was always rearing, but I saddled it and set out for the Hacienda de Santa Isabel with the intention of pursuing the traitor.

Before reaching San Bartolo I came to the Rancho de Los Cerritos. My horse began rearing and when I got off it ran away to a pasture with the rope and saddle. I had my pistols, since I carried them in my belt.

In the morning a number of ranchers came to cut corn. One of them was riding a dark bay. When he reached his field he unsaddled and went to work in the furrows. He had his back to me and even if he turned round could not see his horse. I quietly saddled it. When he missed it I would be a league away.

I rode off untroubled, reflecting that even if its master was poor he had his land, while I was an outcast, pursued and always in danger.

Thus mounted I reached the Hacienda de Menores, the home of Manuel Torres. He had gone to San Luis de Cordero. At San Luis de Cordero I was informed that he had gone to live in Torreón. So I went on. After a short time on the road I was overtaken by a man of good appearance, well armed and mounted, who wasted no words. "That's a fine horse you are riding, my friend. Horses like that are ridden only by bandits or the owner of the Hacienda de Piedras—me, that is."

In reply I put my pistol to his breast and said, "Hands up." He put them up.

I took his pistol and cartridge belt and caught the reins of his horse. Half a league along an arroyo I had him dismount and sit down while I retired some fifty steps to unsaddle the horses. He was carrying a satchel full of excellent food. I built a fire, heated the food, and gave him something to eat. Then, since it was already getting dark, I took him to the vicinity of the Hacienda de Piedras and said, "There it is. Get going."

When he had ridden off, I went on my way toward the Las Labores ranches near El Rodeo and on to La Gotera, a place below Yerbabuena. Luis Orozco lived there and as far as I know still does. Since he received me cordially, I invited him to join me, which some five days later he did, though he was a man of good standing. Perhaps our friendship prevailed upon him.

At the Sierra de la Ulama, halfway between Santiago Papasquiaro and Tejame, we stayed to help our friend Don Julio with his planting. We were there three months.

From there we went to Tejame and while building a tannery were questioned by authorities. They decided to put us in prison. When they came to arrest us we killed two policemen and left for Durango, and so lost all we had invested in making stone troughs for the tannery.

After six days in the sierra we reached the house of one of Luis Orozco's friends in Durango. But he was more of a fugitive than we were. An hour after we arrived we were having a gunfight with the police, and left the family with added trouble.

On the way to La Gotera, passing through Menores, the home of Manuel Torres, we heard that he was chief of the *acordada* at that hacienda. We looked for him, to shoot it out with him. When we encountered him, we fired, and although we missed, we frightened him so he begged us not to kill him.

Leaving the hacienda at a half trot, with him up behind me on my horse, we entered a barren stretch. In the most solitary spot we got ready to shoot him, but he begged for his life, promising to give up his office and retire. At first we were inclined to doubt him, but when he signed a document we set him free. And it is true that he retired and ceased to be our enemy. Not only that but knowing everything that happened he kept us well informed.

One day I said to Luis Orozco, "Hombre, we can't live like this. Let's go to Chihuahua and look for work."

We got as far as Hidalgo del Parral, but Luis began to think of home and said, "If you aren't going back I am."

I answered, "Well, I'm not. I mean to find work. I'm tired of dodging bullets in the hills."

He went home and I stayed on. Without knowing the trade I went to work in the Del Verde mine. I had been working a month when I bruised my foot on a stone. Out of inexperience I neglected it and gangrene set in. To have it treated I sold my horse, saddle, rifle, and even my blanket. When I could no longer pay, the doctor left me unattended. I had to cure my foot myself but was so poor I hadn't even a place to sleep. I stayed on a hillside near the arroyo La Cruz, spending my nights in holes from which lime was extracted. Sometimes the holes were so dirty that I had to burn matches to clean the ground before I could get inside. I got up each morning with the six-o'clock whistles and, walking with a great deal of pain, dragged myself to the market, though without a centavo to pay for the food I needed.

A mason there, Santos Vega, was engaged in some projects that required a lot of work. One morning he asked, "Do you want work?"

"Yes, Señor."

"Have you had breakfast?"

I was not accustomed to revealing my poverty and did not answer, but you can be sure I had not had breakfast and for a good reason.

"Take this and get some breakfast, and over there, on the way to the station, is where I'll put you to work."

I got a cup of *atole* but wasn't really able to work. I could hardly walk, and that with great pain.

Seeing me limp, Sr. Vega said, "Is your foot bothering you?"

"Yes, Señor." And then I asked, "Will you please look at it?"

He untied the bandages and looked. "Hombre, have you no family?"

"No, Señor."

"Sit down and break bricks for riprap and every day I will give you a peso." And I did that.

Some old women sheltered me down below the station. Each day I gave them the peso I earned, and they fed me and took an interest in me. When Maestro Vega brought a doctor who wanted to cut off my leg they would not permit it. They said, "Señor, stay away from here: we will cure him."

And so they did. With nightshade and hot-water compresses they stopped the gangrene and cured me. I didn't miss a single day of work, for I needed the peso. But I was ashamed of my clothing and I carried it every week to the hill above Parral and washed it myself.

Maestro Vega grew fond of me. Now that I had improved and was stacking adobes like the rest of the peons I said one afternoon, "Señor, I can use the trowel now and won't ask any more for doing it."

"If you work like the others, you will earn what they earn. What tools do you need?"

"A trowel, a hammer, two picks, a plumb, and string."

He gave me twenty pesos for tools and the next day I went to work as a mason. When I had been working with the trowel for three months, the maestro said, "I am going to give you an interest in a couple of my jobs so you can supervise the masons."

Each week the accounts showed between three and four hundred pesos profit, which we divided. But one afternoon the chief of police dropped in, and when he had gone Vega came over to me and said, "They are asking who you are and whether you're from Durango. They say there are warrants out for you but they are holding off out of consideration for me. What shall I tell them?"

"Señor, there must be some mistake. Tell the chief I work wherever I find it convenient."

"All right, I will tell him."

That afternoon I took my departure. With a horse, a rifle, and a pistol I returned again to my old and troubled life.

As before, I headed for the sierra. At the Hacienda de Guadalupe de la Rueda I told Eleuterio Soto of my departure from Parral and he said, "I'll go to Durango with you." He was well armed, had a horse, and was one of the bravest men I had ever known. We set out for Río Grande, where my dear mother lived. On the way I met one of my brothers at Santa Isabel de Berros. The first thing he said was, "Our mother is very ill. I came to bring Martina."

"Take Martina then and tomorrow night I will be there."

I started the next night, but on the way stopped at a small house, where I learned that my mother was dead. I could see the lights in the house where they were watching over her body. I looked for a long time and then turned off toward Chihuahua. I wept as I rode away.

CHAPTER 4

Villa Finally Re-establishes Himself in Chihuahua, but Exploitation by the Rich Forces Him To Return to His Sorrowful Life.

Pineida's Horses. The Encounter at the Oak. Eleuterio Soto's House. Don Aurelio del Valle and His Hacienda de la Rueda. A Judge of the *Acordada*. The Armed Service. The Revenge of Compadre Eleuterio Soto. Villa Sells Meat. The Terrazas and Juan Osollo. La Mina Vieja. "If You Want a Horse, I'll Tell You Where to Get One." Villa Disguises as a Servant.

At the Hacienda de San Bartolo we changed horses. Gregorio Pineida, the judge of the *acordada* there, had two very good ones. We arrived before dawn. I led the two horses out by the halter; we saddled them quietly and went on. The first thing Pineida did when he woke that morning was to visit the stable, and finding the horses gone and seeing our tracks, he followed.

By dawn we were opposite the Hacienda de Lajas, about two leagues from San Bartolo. There we went to sleep in an arroyo and slept until nearly noon. I had been awake some twenty minutes when I heard Pineida and his men approaching. From our elevated position I recognized him and his *acordada* through my field glasses. As quickly as possible we saddled, and without losing time headed for the Coneto spring, but the ground was rough. They reached it before we did. On the slope of the sierra at Coneto I asked Paulino Villa, a very distant relative, "What is the news?"

"Pineida is coming for his horses. I saw him in Coneto with all his men."

"Well, don't worry. Bring me a couple of sets of shoes for the horses."

So it was. He brought horseshoes and nails. It took us until dark to shoe the animals. Then we mounted other horses that Paulino was taking care of for me. Leading the two we had been riding, we set out for Iglesias.

About four in the morning we reached a small ranch about three leagues below Iglesias. We went to sleep, and when the sun came up we woke and had breakfast. Feeling weak, I said, "I am going to take another nap. All right?"

"Sure, Compadre. I'll climb up on these big rocks and watch."

It was not difficult for Pineida to follow us: our tracks were very plain in the damp ground. Between ten-thirty and eleven I heard my compadre calling.

"Stay behind the tree, Compadre. They are close."

Eleuterio fired. One of Pineida's men fell from his horse. The battle began. From behind an oak I picked off horses and men, and my compadre was not missing a shot from his stone fortress.

Pineida's forces were made up of some twenty *rurales* and about ten others—thirty-five, more or less, against the two of us. But with at least fifty cartridges each we could protect ourselves. After we had killed nine men and fourteen horses, Pineida and his forces broke and ran. My compadre shouted joyfully, "Get the horses from the arroyo and saddle them, Compadre."

I chose Pineida's, which were the best. I saddled them and we rode to the top of the ridge our enemies had abandoned. They were getting into formation behind the next ridge. In their flight some had gone over a side of the embankment and others had gone over places it would have seemed impossible to cross. My compadre dismounted and leveled his rifle, and when he killed another horse with the first shot they fled again, this time not to stop.

We were free and we mounted and headed for the Hacienda de Ramos. All that day and night we traveled and morning found us at Tres Vados on the Sestín River, quite a long way from where Pineida and his men had discovered us. We stopped to buy provisions and then quietly took the road to Indé, which we reached the next day. Three leagues from town we halted to rest the horses and prepare something to eat, and then, back on our horses, we headed for the Cabeza del Oso and the next night emerged upon the Hacienda de Guadalupe de la Rueda.

Eleuterio Soto lived here. Señor, what news we learned, too. In his absence false charges had been made against him. Crimes committed by others had been blamed on him, and his enemies were searching for him everywhere.

I said, "This is what they call justice, Compadre."

"Yes, Compadre, this and the suffering they cause you."

As I remember, they accused Eleuterio of stealing some mules from the hacienda of Don Aurelio del Valle and his brothers. Don Aurelio was a cunning, evil man, a cruel landlord, and his brothers were still worse than he was.

My compadre, by character incapable of such crimes, determined to confront his accusers and contest the charges. Since these were false, he was certain nothing could be proved against him. But he, and I too, underestimated the wickedness in the souls of those men. Don Aurelio bribed the chief of the *acordada* of Indé, who, bowing to the will of his landlord, seized Eleuterio and very coolly prepared to shoot him. Only because my compadre had rendered valuable service in the river region and had a good name there did they finally relent and reduce the sentence to serving in the army. This often happened. A landlord would use the army to rid himself of men when he feared them or desired to quietly enjoy the little sister or the wife or the sweetheart of the poor fellow he persecuted.

My compadre was consigned to the ranks and carried off to jail. Soon he was in uniform in Mexico City enduring harsh treatment. Seeing so much corruption and evil, how could one still his resentment? I saw to it that my compadre's family were in need of nothing and I sent him two thousand pesos to Mexico City, certain that with that much he could buy his way out of the army.

So it was. He was able to pay a substitute and have enough money left over to return, and one day he was back and looking for me. When he saw me he said, "Compadre, I am on my way to the hacienda. Don

Aurelio has wronged me and I mean to kill him. His money won't help him. In two days he'll be a dead man."

"Do as you see fit, Compadre."

Two days later I heard that Don Aurelio had been killed. A special train carrying a doctor came from the capital, and they put Don Aurelio on it, but it is inconceivable that he was able to recover from the three wounds inflicted by my compadre, for they were mortal ones. Still, they do say that he is alive in Chihuahua today.

The night after I heard the news, my compadre appeared in Parral. He said, "Well, Compadre, I killed him for the suffering that, God knows why, he caused me. Here I am again.

"Good, Compadre." And so we were together once more. Lacking a means of livelihood and hounded from employment, we headed for the Sierra de Matalotes. There we slaughtered three hundred cattle and, having contracted for the sale of the meat in Parral, collected our profits on delivery. With the money we went to the city of Chihuahua, where I intended to open a market. We hoped no one would recognize us and we could work in peace, and truly we wished for no more than that, except that my compadre wanted to bring his family along.

We opened the market. I took charge. Eleuterio returned for his family. And thus a year passed.

But I was killing cattle in the city slaughterhouse and selling the meat in my market in name only. Each time I went to slaughter a cow or two I always met an employee named Terras and a certain Juan Osollo. I would present myself at the slaughterhouse with my papers in order— for I was no longer so ignorant as before—but there was always some difficulty. The brand was not the one in the papers, or the description did not fit; something was lacking, or things were not clear enough. There was no scarcity of reasons why I should not do my slaughtering, and I did not get to do it. Then this Juan Osollo would come up to me and say, "Don't lose heart, Panchito. If you need meat, I am your friend." And he would offer me the meat from the cows that I had already sacrificed to settle with his bosses, knowing I could close my market or accept his offer; and then they would bring the meat to my office as a favor and the next day come and collect.

I was indignant on my own account, and when I found out that they were doing the same thing everywhere in Chihuahua I quit the slaughterhouse and the city where my labor had brought so little return. I turned the business over to a Sr. Nicolás Saldívar, who was to make a go of it if he could.

In the mining town of Santa Eulalia I found work in the Mina Vieja, but after a painful year and a half I was still in need, and my pursuers from Durango tracked me down again. Again I went wandering through the mountains, an empty-handed outlaw. I had neither horse nor pistol nor rifle—nothing. From a friend whose name I do not remember I finally secured a pistol. Thus armed I went to Chihuahua to talk with Saldívar, to whom I had left my business. I told him how destitute I was and said, "Amigo, furnish me a horse and saddle."

Looking at me with an amused smile he answered, "I thought you were a gamecock. Can't you find a horse for yourself? But if you like, I'll tell you where to get one."

"All right, Señor, tell me where."

"There are a lot of horses, fine, sleek ones, at the slaughterhouse. Get one of them if you aren't afraid to. The dark one with the white tail is the best."

"What time are they there?"

"If you know how to tell time, go between two and four in the afternoon."

At three in the afternoon, in front of all the butchers, I got the white-tailed horse and galloped off. They shouted and pursued me. About a thousand meters ahead, I reached the road to Cerro Grande and turned down an arroyo. There I dismounted and loosened the cinches, and the butchers passed by at full gallop without seeing me. When they were out of sight I mounted and rode very peacefully toward the Rancho de La Boquilla. I reached Parral by way of Satevó. Disguised as a servant I hid in the house of Miguel Baca Valles, who treated me with great consideration; but I could not stay long, for talk of my return got round, and again I had to return to my wanderings.

CHAPTER 5

Pancho Villa Meets Don Abraham González and Joins the Madero Revolution To Fight for the People.

José Sánchez. Villa's House in Chihuahua. Patriotic Sentiment. Don Abraham. Don Francisco I. Madero. The Death of Claro Reza. Villa Unites His Forces in the Sierra Azul. The First Fifteen Men. Don Abraham names Cástulo Herrera. Villa's Discourse. On with the Revolution.

Without rest I wandered about with José Sánchez and Eleuterio Soto. We went from Chihuahua to San Andrés to Ciénaga de Ortiz, back to San Andrés, and once again to Chihuahua. Always pursued, always in hiding, I distrusted everyone and everything. At each turn I feared surprise or ambush.

Since we stopped so often in Chihuahua I bought a house to stay in while there. It was an old one, but large, at No. 500, Tenth Street. It had three adobe rooms whitewashed with lime, a very small kitchen, and a large pen for my horses. I myself thatched the roof of the corral and built the stables, the water trough, and the hayrack.

I would not exchange that house, which I still own and have rebuilt in a modest manner, for the most elegant palace. There I had my first talks with Don Abraham González, now a martyr to democracy. There he asked me to join the Revolution and fight for the oppressed people. There I learned one night how my long struggle with the exploiters, the persecutors, the seducers, could be of benefit to others who were persecuted and humiliated as I had been. There I felt the anxiety and hate built up in my soul during years of struggle and suffering change into the belief that the evil could be ended, and this strengthened my determination to relieve our hardships at the price of life and blood if necessary. I understood without explanation—for nobody explains anything to the poor—how our country, which until then had been for me no more than fields, ravines, and mountains to hide in, could become the inspiration for our best actions and the object of our finest sentiments. I heard the name of Francisco I. Madero for the first time. I learned to love and revere him for his unshakable faith, for the Plan of San Luis, because he, a rich man, was devoted to the struggle for the poor and oppressed.

And it happened that once when I had an appointment with Don

Abraham at my house, while José and Eleuterio were there, we were besieged by a force of twenty-five *rurales* under Claro Reza. I must tell you about Reza. He was counted my friend and compañero, and was indebted to me for favors and assistance. But once when he was in jail for stealing burros, he bought his way out by sending a letter to Juan Creel offering to deliver Pancho Villa into the hands of justice— Pancho Villa, the notorious criminal from Durango. But I had friends and one of them, a *rural* named José (I do not remember his last name), warned me and I was able to escape.

I avoided capture but could not keep Reza from besieging Eleuterio, José, and me in my house, and this made me very angry. We stayed on guard every night until one morning, about four, we prepared to fight, determined to kill or be killed. To our surprise our besiegers had retired quietly and left us in peace.

Eleuterio said, "This is how he repays us. Let's go after him."

I answered, "Yes, Compadre. We'll go and look for Reza, but on one condition. We kill him wherever we find him, even in the Palacio de Gobierno. Are you willing?"

He said, "Yes, Compadre, I am."

Early in the morning, well mounted, armed, and supplied with ammunition, we set out to search for him, beginning on Zarco Avenue. We were lucky, for there, at a meat market opposite "Las Quince Letras," where we least expected it, we spotted him. We poured bullets into him. It was daytime in a busy place, and, hearing the shots, some people ran, others gathered and crowded round to see the corpse. In the mood to kill anyone who crossed our path, we went slowly through the crowd, which was increasing every moment, without anyone's daring to stop us. Soon afterward, when we were farther away, soldiers came in pursuit, but they must have been calling upon God to save them from overtaking us, for at no moment did we have to push our horses.

Up the Sierra Azul we made for La Estacada. There we began to recruit fighters for the Madero Revolution. Without much effort we enlisted fifteen of the best men. One afternoon, Feliciano Domínguez, a recruit, spoke to me privately. He said, "Chief, my uncle, Pedro Domínguez, is back from Chihuahua where he went to be appointed judge of the *acordada*. He says that he will never stop pursuing us, and I think it is dangerous for him to become a judge. I regret it, since he is my uncle and a good and brave man, but he must be killed for the good of our cause. He lives at the Rancho del Encino."

I replied, "You are right. We must destroy the enemies of the people.

We will take eight men to the ranch and rid your uncle of his ideas."

So it was. With nine men I went to the ranch, leaving the rest of the forces in camp at La Estacada. When Pedro Domínguez saw us coming he got ready to defend himself. We stormed the house, but being a very good shot he fired from behind a fence and killed two of our horses. Seeing one of our men in the kitchen door he killed him with a shot under the eye. Then my compadre and I went over the fence after him, and just as one of his shots went through my compadre's hat I put a bullet through the middle of his body.

He ran to the road. My compadre hit him twice, but he had the strength to jump another fence before he fell. I went to secure his rifle, which he was now too weak to fire. When I came in reach he bit me. Eleuterio shot him in the head with a pistol. As we finished with him an old man came out of the house. Running toward us and shaking his fists, he cried, "Bandits, bandits!" until one of our boys raised his rifle, aimed, and killed him with the first shot. Thus ended that episode. We were free from Domínguez' threat to our plans.

I wanted to be sure of the fifteen men who had joined me. When I knew their minds, what they were worth, and how they could serve, we took the road to Chihuahua and stopped at the Rancho de Montecillo, about three leagues from the capital. That night I entered the city to talk with Don Abraham about plans for an insurrection. He said, "Pancho, I want you and your men to hide in a house in the city, to protect me from there. The police will be watching me, and any day they may arrest me and put me in jail."

I replied, "Very well, Señor. My men will be in my house on Tenth Street. Two of them will guard you at all times. The rest will be ready, and if the police get you we will rescue you wherever you are and take you to the sierra."

And so it was. The next day, October 4, 1910, I installed myself with my first young Revolutionaries in the house at No. 500. I list their names: Francisco Villa, Eleuterio Soto, José Sánchez, Feliciano Domínguez, Tomás Urbina, Pánfilo Solís, Lucio Escárcega, Antonio Sotello, José Chavarría, Leonides Corral, Eustaquio Flores, Jenaro Chavarría, Andrés Rivera, Bárbaro Carrillo, Cesáreo Solís, and Ceferino Pérez.

All of us were well armed and well mounted. We had sufficient ammunition. I paid for everything out of my own pocket; it was my duty as chief to see that my men lacked for nothing. I knew from riding through the sierra with the enemy at my back how useless troops are unless well equipped. Day and night we watched over Don Abraham, ready to defend him against any threat. We ourselves were in as great danger. Reza's death had rid us of our worst enemy but was not enough to insure our safety.

Eleuterio said, "We have to be more cautious now. The risks are greater because there is less we can do."

I replied, "Yes, Compadre, now that we are ready to fight for the people, I realize how little we can do."

One day Don Abraham and Cástulo Herrera came to the house on Tenth Street. My compadre Victoriano Avila had recommended me, but having dealt with me for so short a time, Don Abraham hardly knew me well enough to entrust the campaign to me. It did not surprise me to learn that I was not to be chief.

Deeply moved, Don Abraham said, "The time has come to begin. I am going up north, to Ojinaga, and you, Pancho, are going south. You will organize forces in San Andrés, and everyone will recognize Cástulo Herrera here as chief. You will obey his orders and do your duty until the end."

I replied, "Señor, you can count on me to obey and fight as a willing Revolutionary in the name of the people. My men will obey Cástulo Herrera to the last moment of their lives."

Don Abraham embraced us, one by one. And we began the march to the Sierra Azul that night of November 17, a memorable date to every Mexican. I shed tears as we left Chihuahua. Never since I watched from afar the house where my mother lay dead have I felt so much like weeping. It was an effort to remain silent. I wanted to shout and have my compañeros shout in reply, "Viva el bien de los pobres. Viva Abraham González. Viva Francisco I. Madero."

CHAPTER 6

Under Cástulo Herrera, Villa Takes Command and Serves His Apprenticeship as a Great Guerrilla Fighter.

The First 375 Men. "Not Another Shot." The Revolution in San Andrés. Death of Lieutenant Colonel Yépez. Villa Takes Santa Isabel. The March on Chihuahua. The Action at Tecolote Flat. Death of Compadre Soto. Villa Enters Chihuahua Incognito. Pascual Orozco. The Battle of Cerro Prieto.

We stayed five days in the Sierra Azul, eating only meat and tortillas. There we recruited 375 men, some from San Andrés and others from Santa Isabel and Ciénaga de Ortiz. I was well known to the people in the district, whom I invited to fight in the Revolution. But my task of enlisting men meant no more than choosing among the volunteers who came well mounted, well armed, and well supplied with ammunition, all from their own resources.

When we considered our force ready, Herrera ordered an attack on San Andrés. We left the sierra that same night and at dawn besieged the town without meeting resistance, for the few *rurales* garrisoned there had already fled. It was now our first duty to appoint authorities, so everyone would know we were there neither to riot nor to plunder.

It was hardly eight in the morning when our forces were assembled in the plaza. Elated over their easy success, they began to fire into the air. I waited for Herrera to stop the useless waste of ammunition, but when he did nothing, I ran over and shouted, "Not another shot. We need our ammunition for the enemy. What makes you think the rest of our fighting will be as easy as this? We haven't begun to fight yet." The shooting ceased, I ordered the people to quarter the troops, and everyone obeyed me.

About nine-thirty that same morning Herrera ordered me to take an escort and see if the ten-o'clock train was bringing passengers from Chihuahua. I chose the fifteen who had come with me from my house on Tenth Street, and set out for the railroad. When we reached the station we heard the whistle of the locomotive, but I had no time to organize my attack. I formed my men into a firing line, protected in the best way possible, and had just done this when we saw Federal soldiers detraining. I recognized them as the troops of the 12th Battalion under Lieutenant Colonel Pablo Yépez.

We opened fire without waiting. At the outset the Colonel and some of his soldiers were killed, but I forget how many. What happened was that when the battalion captains saw the people coming to my assistance they had the engineer start the train. They withdrew as far as the Hacienda de Bustillos with their dead and wounded. They had fought bravely. I marched back to town. There Herrera and I posted advance troops, as they are called in the army, and took other precautions in case the battalion should return and attack. But this did not happen.

We stayed in San Andrés two more days, and the fourth day after our arrival I marched to Santa Isabel and besieged it the same night. At daybreak I tightened my lines and I took the place without resistance. On entering, I appointed authorities as we had done in San Andrés. I devoted two days to organizing our forces better. We increased our numbers to five hundred, some of the new men bringing their own arms, of different kinds and calibers. With this force I decided to march on Chihuahua. I say that I decided because the truth is that Herrera, although considered the chief, did not actually take command and I was the one who carried on the campaign.

On the first day's march we reached the Rancho de Escuderos about four leagues from Chihuahua. We posted our advance in the customary manner and waited until dawn, when I ordered twenty men to go out under Guadalupe Gardea and Antonio Orozco, first and second captains respectively, and reconnoiter as far as Cerro Grande. At the same time I selected twenty-three men to explore the Los Carrejones area, where there were several ranches by that name. I approached within half a league of the capital. On the top of some hills I stopped to observe the town through field glasses.

Feliciano Domínguez, serving as captain and my aide, came up and said, "My Colonel, I think I hear shots near Tecolote."

It was true. Shots could be heard from the direction of Tecolote about three-fourths of a league away. I ordered my men to mount and without losing a second rode toward the flat. Opposite the Rancho de las Escobas, Eleuterio Soto, now a lieutenant colonel and the second in command of my forces, said, "With your permission, my Colonel, we will halt. You see what is going on."

I did see. There were Federal troops opposite Tecolote, the brigade commanded by General Juan J. Navarro, and the number of soldiers, according to my calculations and information I received afterward, was about eight hundred from all three branches.

Being little skilled in war and considering only my duty, I decided to engage the brigade, something a person of my scant knowledge should never have risked. In truth, my boldness can be considered utter recklessness. The result was that while I was taking possession of the north side of the flat, the 12th Battalion fell upon us. The battle began with such fury that we found ourselves within ten steps of each other, and I learned how my inexperience had misled me. They killed several of my boys and all our horses, and began to surround me.

Seeing them on all sides, I decided to retreat before we all perished with nothing gained. I threw my forces against them and broke through on the north. Nine of my twenty-three men were killed, but I was able to save the rest, two of whom were wounded. I myself was shot in the leg and Jesús José Fuentes in the arm. The rest of us made our escape thanks to the poor judgment of the enemy. If they had sent a squad of cavalry to pursue us, none of us would be alive. When we were out of danger, a boy took me up behind him on his horse. We rejoined the body of troops I had left at the Rancho de los Escuderos. With my forces together, I moved into the Sierra Azul, where we spent the night.

In the encounter at Tecolote Flat, which began at ten in the morning of November 27 or 28 and ended about twelve, my compadre Eleuterio Soto was killed. He had kept his word and stayed with me to the death. Also killed were José Sánchez and Leonides Corral, two of the fifteen who had left Chihuahua with me to begin the campaign.

After two days in the Sierra Azul I went incognito to the capital for necessary supplies such as sugar and coffee. In spite of my wound I was able to do this at night on the third day after the fight, accompanied by two dependable men, Feliciano Domínguez and Eustaquio Flores. We returned with several mules loaded with what we needed most. The next morning I organized my forces, and in good order set out to San Andrés, where we arrived without incident about three in the afternoon. The citizens were sympathetic and considerate. They provided lodging for officers and troops, forage for the horses, and provisions for the entire force. We stayed there only a few days, since I had received a telegram from Pascual Orozco, Jr., in Guerrero, saying, "I have just taken this place. Come and I will give you some ammunition." A three-day march took us to Guerrero.

In Ciudad Guerrero I received an even better welcome than in San

Andrés. The people were well disposed to the Revolution, and Pascual Orozco and his forces were friendly. The townspeople wanted to give us good quarters, but seeing that families were leaving their homes and putting up campaign tents for shelter in order to do this, we unanimously decided that part of our forces would camp on the outskirts of the town, to be less trouble to such hospitable people. Our Revolution was in the hands of men who loved order and respected the rights of others.

The next day Pascual Orozco wanted to have a talk with the rest of us. We met that same night at nine. The following chiefs were present: Pascual Orozco, Jr., Francisco Salido, Cástulo Herrera, José de la Luz Blanco, and I, Francisco Villa. We discussed a plan to attack General Navarro's column. According to all information he had spent the previous night in San Nicolás de Carretas. We agreed that at dawn on the next day, which was December 11, we would advance in the same direction at different times, with each chief at the head of his forces and in communication with each other.

Francisco Salido and I led the column with our troops. At brief intervals we received couriers who advised us of the position of the enemy. We marched in this manner until about eight in the morning, when we learned that Navarro was entering Cerro Prieto. We ordered our forces to take the hill on the southeast which overlooked the town. Hardly had we taken our positions when firing broke out and a fierce battle began between the vanguard of our column and that of the Federal column under Navarro. The battle lasted three hours and a half, more or less, and at the end we were badly pressed. Federal artillery was bombarding our positions while infantry was moving up the hill and causing us many casualties. But just when we were most discouraged, Orozco's cavalry appeared on the plain and the Federals retreated in order. Hearing the trumpet and seeing the Federals fall back, Francisco Salido left the shelter of a large rock. He was urging his troops on when a shell shattered his breast and killed him.

From the hill I could see that Orozco had lost his horse in the hand-to-hand combat between his cavalry and that of Navarro under Trucy Aubert. This engagement too lasted about three and a half hours, and I, Francisco Villa, the only chief left standing at the top of the hill, was unable to assist because my horses were down on the south side and I had to organize a defense against the Federal infantry and artillery. Señor, I had so many dead and wounded and my forces were in such disorder that if Orozco had not arrived the Federals would have routed us completely.

After heavy casualties in the long encounter, Orozco's forces finally dispersed along the slope of the Sierra de Picachos. Taking advantage of the respite I gathered my wounded and the guns of those who were dead, and retired in moderate order as it began to grow dark. The field remained in possession of the Federal troops. The lights that my compañeros kept burning in the sierra guided our retreat.

CHAPTER 7

Although He Could Commandeer Everything, Villa Takes Only What Is Necessary To Sustain His Troops.

At La Capilla Ranch. Campaign Plans. The Widow of Santos Estrada. Villa Is Surprised in San Andrés. Captain José Chavarría. Remedios Paz. The Remudas of the Sres. Cuilty. Guerrillas Riding Bareback. The Huahuanoyahua Ranches. Entrance in Satevó. El Sauz. Santa Gertrudis. Ciudad Camargo. La Boquilla.

About twelve that night I joined Pascual Orozco at the Rancho de la Capilla on the slope of the sierra. We greeted each other affectionately and grieved over our defeat and the losses. But as it was not my duty to grieve, I went at once to attend to the unsaddling. Later, when we were discussing the way to continue, a courier arrived from Santa Isabel with a letter advising Pascual that a convoy of fifty men and ten mules loaded with ammunition had left Chihuahua for Navarro's camp. We read it—by that time I knew how to read—and planned to intercept the ammunition. I would do this, and Pascual would stay on, for sympathizers were joining our ranks daily.

And that's how it was. I saddled, and with my forces in good order left camp about twelve in the morning. We took a short cut to where we calculated the convoy would be and soon we were approaching Santa Isabel. I learned that the convoy was already there. But instead of being destined for Navarro, the ammunition had been sent for the defense of the town. Consequently I went on to San Andrés, where I quartered my troops. Most of them were from this town and had friends there. They all asked permission to visit family or friends. Horses and saddles were all that remained at headquarters and the only force was the troops on guard.

That day I received a note from Julia R., widow of Santos Estrada. She had lost her husband in the fight at El Tecolote. She told me that Federal troops were marching toward San Andrés and I should be ready to meet them. But the only forces I had been advised of were the fifty men in charge of the ammunition at Santa Isabel, so I thought the lady was referring to them, and was glad I would have an opportunity to attack the convoy outside the town, where I would be certain to get the ammunition.

This time I was mistaken. A Federal force had entered the town secretly by way of an arroyo. They were guided by José Liceaga, who lived in the town and was a tax collector for the Porfirio Díaz government. Taken by surprise, I tried only to save the guard at my headquarters. It would have been reckless to attempt resistance. When his forces are scattered and cannot face an attack, it is a commander's duty to save the men he can. I mounted my horse and retired to the station, where I held out all afternoon and protected the soldiers who had come to join me when they heard shots.

A sergeant in command of a squad which was keeping up a sustained fire came through the streets in pursuit of José Chavarría, first captain of my forces. On reaching a wire fence that closed off a street, Chavarría rolled under it and began to shoot from the ground. He killed the sergeant, and the squad retired; in this manner he escaped unhurt and succeeded in reaching us.

We held the station until nightfall. Then under cover of darkness we retreated southward to the ranch called La Olla. We reached it without incident. Picking up supplies we continued to the sierra, where we arrived late at night and in bad shape—on foot and without blankets, since our equipment had been left at our quarters with the horses and saddles. We had saved only our arms, for each soldier, on receiving my permission to leave, had carried his gun and ammunition with him. In a campaign one must always take this precaution against surprise, lest equipment fall into the hands of the enemy.

The surprise at San Andrés was costly, but my troops went to the sierra, man for man, in spite of snow and bitter cold. What more can be said for loyalty to the cause we were defending? My men and officers came without any covering against the snow, faithful to their oath. Being poor, they knew what it was to suffer and they accepted their lot.

Thus the night was spent. In the morning I went to La Estacada ranch to ask the owner, Remedios Paz, to furnish me with two saddled horses. On these I sent Captain Jesús José Fuentes and the soldier Lucio Jiménez to the Hacienda del Corral de Piedra, owned by the Sres. Cuilty, to fetch the horses in their remudas. The captain was familiar with these pastures. This done, I returned to my forces. I had brought them to the highest part of the sierra, where we had water and cattle to sustain us and would be safe from another surprise. We stayed six days. All we had to eat was beef, which the troops roasted on coals and ate without seasoning. At the end of this time Captain Fuentes arrived with more than 400 horses. We divided them. Some soldiers used halters from the ranches, some used palm ropes they had woven, and most of them used leather cords made from the hides of the cattle we had eaten.

So my guerrillas, ragged and riding bareback, started down the sierra to Ciénaga de Ortiz. On the way we came to the Huahuanoyahua River. On both sides there were ranches, and sometimes we took two saddles, sometimes five, and even ten if we found that many. When we left, very few of our men were riding bareback. I equipped these in Satevó, where I surprised a detachment of fifty state *rurales*. I took their guns, horses, and saddles. Some of them were killed in this action, and others joined my ranks. I spent eight days in Satevó, reorganizing. I was able to find some food there, but to supply flour and forage I had to start operating a mill. Finally, when my troops had recovered and were well supplied again, I marched seventeen leagues to the Hacienda del Sauz. We spent the night there and I got the owner to give us food, forage for the horses, and five thousand pesos for expenses. The next day we went to Ojo del Obispo, a ranch where they treated us kindly and gave us everything we needed. After a couple of days there, we left for the Hacienda de Santa Gertrudis, about eighteen leagues away.

At this hacienda we were treated more cordially than anywhere else. We reached it about noon the day after leaving Ojo del Obispo. The foreman had the granaries, containing large quantities of corn, put at my disposition. He ordered the cowboys to slaughter some of the best cattle to feed our troops. He also had *nixtamal* brought to the houses on the quadrangle of the hacienda and ordered the women to make tortillas. Finally, he invited my officers to sit at his table because he wanted to have the pleasure of entertaining us personally.

We stayed for three days before setting out for the mining town of Naica, seven leagues away, which we reached at eleven in the morning. The miners received us with sympathy, and the general manager gave me twenty-five hundred pesos unasked, a third of the sum in clothing, and furnished forage and rations.

After this we went on our way. I planned to attack Ciudad Camargo at dawn on the following day, before Federal troops on the way from Chihuahua could reinforce it. By morning I had my men in position and ready but, wishing to avoid bloodshed if possible, I sent a courier to the commandant and the principal business men to say: "Señores, I give you an hour and a half to decide. Surrender or I will storm the town. You will be responsible for any blood that flows."

They replied, "If Pancho Villa can take Ciudad Camargo, let him."

The attack began about twelve, and after several hours and great difficulty I reduced the town and all but one of the barracks, which still held out. By five in the afternoon the forces from Chihuahua were close. We would be defeated if we remained. I therefore withdrew after collecting about sixty rifles and the ammunition we had taken. In this action, which occurred on February 7, 1911, I lost very few men.

Outside the town I reassembled and marched about three leagues up river. At nightfall I ordered a halt, men and horses being worn out. The enemy could not surprise me there, but I took the usual precautions. There was forage but no food for the troops, except that the owner of a herd of cows had them milked for me. Seeing how the milk revived my men I paid him the thirty-five pesos he asked.

At daybreak I marched to La Boquilla, where a company was constructing a dam and three thousand men were employed. In the company village, garrisoned by twenty-five men and a commandant—all paid from company funds—there was a good market and clothing stores.

Since I took them by surprise, they offered no resistance. I commandeered their arms and took charge. The manager had forage spread for my horses, and by his order the troops ate in the hotels with the officials. Some of my officers and I stayed in his house. We were treated with great consideration and had whatever we needed. Finally, he directed that I be given four thousand pesos in clothes, with which I supplied such of my troops as had not been equipped.

We stayed in La Boquilla three days. When ready to march I asked what our expenses had been, wanting to sign an IOU, collectible if our cause was victorious. But the manager said we owed nothing and the company was glad to help. I thanked him in the name of the Revolution and set out for El Valle de Zaragoza, some thirty leagues away.

CHAPTER 8

Villa Spies on Parral in Person. He Escapes and Returns to Camp but Cannot Find His Troops.

El Valle de Zaragoza. Santa Cruz del Padre Herrera. Duties of a Military Chief. The Camp at El Durazno. Juan Ramírez. El Rancho de Taráis. The Burros with a Load of Charcoal. The Godmother Librada Chávez. The Quarters at Parral. The Surprise. Albino Frías. La Sierra de Minas Nuevas. Santos Vega. Jesús Orozco. Las Cuchillas.

The day after leaving La Boquilla I was just outside El Valle de Zaragoza. We reached it about twelve but found so many troops protecting it and the fortifications so strong that I decided not to enter. I invited the enemy to come out and fight, saying, "It is a duty in war to save towns from devastation whenever possible. Come out and meet Pancho Villa and his Revolutionaries." But they refused, knowing they were out of our reach.

I retired to the Hacienda de la Jabonera, three leagues away. There I spent the night and was supplied with forage and everything necessary. In the morning I proceeded toward Santa Cruz del Padre Herrera, a march of some twenty leagues. We reached it about two the next afternoon. Here too there was a garrison, but a small one, made up of only citizens of the town. Not wanting to cause bloodshed I summoned them to surrender. They answered with bluster, saying that if I was a man I would attack and drive them out. So, deploying my troops to converge on the town from four directions and seizing the church, which was defended as the dominating point, I began the assault. Realizing they could gain nothing by resistance, they parleyed, and came out to deliver their arms and ammunition. I entered the town and appointed new authorities, with Gilberton in charge as commandant.

In Santa Cruz del Padre Herrera I got supplies and then marched six leagues farther to Sierra del Durazno. There I camped. My plan was to leave the troops for several days while I went in person to size up the military installations at Parral. In this campaign certain risks were to be assumed by the leader himself, not his subordinates. I called a meeting of my officers to consider this step and they approved, except for my being the one to reconnoiter. They said that I might be detected and would certainly be killed. The troops, left without a leader, would have to disband. But I insisted on seeing for myself and that same night rode away across the Sierra de las Cuchillas, accompanied by Captain Albino Frías and Captain Encarnación Martínez.

To get to the Rancho de Taráis we had to cross the sierra. It was a thirty-five–league ride but by six in the morning we had reached it. The owner was Juan Ramírez, a friend of mine, who put us up for the rest of the day. That night I asked him to keep our fine horses, whose appearance might attract attention. I asked him to take us to Parral on less conspicuous ones.

We went armed with pistols only. The next day Ramírez' son would follow with burros loaded with charcoal, and our rifles would be hidden in the burro packs. The burros were to unload at the home of Librada Chávez, a godmother of mine, with whom we were going to stay. The same wretched horses were to return for us in four days.

That is how I entered Parral, where I had grown to manhood and where the justice of the rich had so many times prevented me from earning an honest living. Ramírez sent his son with the burros and the rifles, and I soon learned what I wanted about the enemy forces and their quarters. There were three locations inside the city, one near the railroad station, one at the slaughterhouse, and a third at the Hospital de Jesús. On the hill at Mina Prieta there was still another detachment under Alberto Díaz.

But it happened that the appointment we had made for the fourth day could not be kept. Ramírez aroused suspicion where he was waiting with the horses. He was apprehended and carried to the commandant for questioning. He said he had come to see his daughter who was ill in Parral, and the chief of the plaza, believing him, let him go. To avoid further suspicion, he had to visit his daughter, who really did live there. Not finding him where we had agreed, we thought he had been unable to come, and returned to Parral to the home of my godmother.

The next day he told us what had happened. The horses were at his daughter's house, to which we went at once as it was already late in the afternoon. Soon we were on the road to Piedra Bola, skirting the hill till beyond the orchard and then to Rancho de Taráis and our own horses. At the orchard, however, we had met a rider who reported having seen three men on magnificent horses, one of which he thought he recognized as belonging to Pancho Villa, who was operating in that area.

On hearing this, the commandant sent 150 dragoons of the 7th Regiment to capture us. When they reached the Rancho de Taráis I was in the house, a stone one with only one room and one exit, the door by which we entered. Albino Frías was with me, and the other captain had gone after forage. It was easy for him to flee, which he did as soon as he heard firing and saw in the semidarkness that we were surrounded. We were almost lost this time, but we led the dragoons to believe that we would defend ourselves to the last and then ran out with a pistol in the right hand and a carbine in the left, intent on killing as many as possible before they killed us. What happened was that we broke through and fled, and in spite of the heavy firing at such close quarters I suffered only a grazing wound over my right eyebrow.

Seeing I was safe, I made for the Sierra de Minas Nuevas just above the Rancho de Taráis, walking all night through a heavy snowstorm. As I was without word of my compañeros I hid in the rocks and stayed there the rest of the day without food, waiting to return to Parral for a horse. At dark I took the road to the city, and about two in the morning reached the hills near the station. There I stayed until five. I entered the town through the district of La Viborilla and went to the house of Santos Vega, the master mason who helped me and gave me work when I was suffering from gangrene. In his house I hid till nightfall, when I went to the home of Jesús Herrera, another friend, who let me have a horse without a saddle, and, riding bareback, I reached Los Obligados, Jesús José Orozco's ranch about nine leagues from Parral. Orozco gave me lodging from two in the morning, the hour I arrived, until the time I left, a period of two days. We spent the time in treating the wound on my forehead. When I left he supplied me with a good horse, saddled and bridled, and fifty pesos in money.

It was dark when I set out for camp, by way of the Rancho de Taráis to learn what happened to Ramírez and my compañeros. Ramírez and his son had been seized by the 7th Regiment and carried to Parral, but no one had word of the two captains. With this sad news I climbed the sierra by a short cut to where I had left my troops, and thus at daybreak

I was near Santa Cruz del Padre Herrera and only a short distance from Las Cuchillas. I decided to rest there, since my horse was exhausted. In a ravine I unsaddled it and staked it out where it could find grass. Secure against surprise in that familiar territory, I lay down and slept for several hours.

When I woke, more or less about twelve by the sun, I saddled and set out at a good pace toward camp. There, at seven that night, I had a surprise: the place was deserted; my men had disappeared.

What could have happened? Where were they? Why had they gone? Fear and doubt made me feel utterly lost. I shouted out the names of my officers, believing at least one must have waited, but not a single soul was there to answer. I searched, and there, in the half darkness, found the remnants of beeves my men had killed. Nothing else.

Weary of shouting and searching, I accepted it as perhaps my destiny to find myself abandoned in the lonely night of the sierra when I should have been amongst my troops, and the feeling grew more acute as my breath and that of my horse united in a single whisper. I staked my horse, spread out my saddle, and resting my head on it lay down to sleep, resolved not to worry any more until the next day, which would surely offer an explanation of the mystery.

CHAPTER 9

Villa Meets Francisco I. Madero and Thinks that if All the Rich Men of Mexico Were Like Him There Would Be No Revolution.

Villa's Troops. Natividad García. Satevó. Compadre Fidel Avila. Javier Hernández. Feliciano Domínguez. Encarnación Márquez. Lucio Escárcega. José Chavarría. The Fight at La Piedra. Sr. Madero. Bustillos. Madero in San Andrés. The Conference at Bustillos. On to the Frontier.

Yes, on finding myself alone in the sierra, I lay down and went to sleep.

At dawn I saddled and started for San José, about nine leagues away.

One of my captains, Natividad García, was from that town. I went to his house and found him in. He and four soldiers came running to meet me. They lifted me from my horse and led me into the house. They embraced me and began to explain what had happened. When Albino Frías reached camp and told them how the dragoons had us surrounded at the Rancho de Taráis and we had broken out, he thought I had been killed, and my long absence served to confirm this. Without their chief, the officers took counsel and decided to abandon the campaign and retire to their towns and ranches. All had gone their separate ways.

I asked Natividad if they wanted to return to my command. Offended, he answered, "My Colonel, we will stay to the death. We disbanded thinking you were dead. But now you have only to command and we will obey."

Rising and embracing him I said, "Natividad, I expected nothing less, and I say the same of your men. Recall your troops and have them ready to leave at daybreak." Within two hours they were reunited and greeted me with rousing assurances of devotion and loyalty.

Early the next morning we marched toward Satevó, about twenty-five leagues from San José. There I planned to wait for Captain Fidel Avila. On the way past Los Zancones, where he lived, I left word that the dead had come to life and Pancho Villa would meet him in Satevó. And so it was. The next day he appeared with his men. I set up headquarters there and sent out couriers, one to Ciénaga de Ortiz for Captain Javier Hernández, another to Santa Isabel for Captain Feliciano Domínguez, and another to San Andrés for Captain Encarnación Márquez, Lucio Escárcega, José Chavarría, and others.

Meanwhile I started operating the local mill, so that when reinforcements arrived there would be flour on hand. It took little time for the officers to gather their men and bring them in. Each of them, on receiving word that I had returned, reorganized and quickly marched to headquarters.

With my troops together, some seven hundred men, I marched to San Andrés. We carried four hundred sacks of flour and spent the first night at the Rancho de San Juan de la Santa Cruz. There a courier informed me that the Federals were coming down the Chihuahua road to attack me.

This was about two in the afternoon. I deployed my forces to meet them at La Piedra, about a league away. In the pitched battle that lasted three hours, against one hundred fifty cavalrymen under a lieutenant colonel, we killed the colonel and many of his men. The rest, fewer than fifty, scattered toward El Terrero. I had taken horses, arms, and ammunition. Twenty-three of my soldiers were dead and fourteen wounded.

In Ciénaga de Ortiz I spent four days taking care of my wounded and those of the enemy. I housed them at the Rancho de Almagre in the Sierra de la Silla, where nobody would look for them. With these arrangements made, we started for San Andrés, stopping on the way at Santa Isabel, where the people received us with cheers. The next day we went to San Andrés, about nine leagues farther. We arrived at one in the afternoon. The people came out to welcome us, conducted us to quarters already prepared, and provided forage and rations. They were ready to bestow whatever they possessed upon the Revolutionaries. We stayed there for eight uneventful days. At the end of this time Provisional President Francisco I. Madero summoned me to meet him in Bustillos without my forces—first taking every precaution against surprise. I did so. Within two hours I was at the Hacienda de Bustillos.

I will never forget my welcome. He had words of high regard for me, but even when not speaking he put his friendship into the way he looked at me. I thought to myself, "Here is one rich man who fights for the people. He is a little fellow, but he has a great soul. If all the rich and powerful in Mexico were like him, there would be no struggle and no suffering, for all of us would be doing our duty. And what else is there for the rich to do if not to relieve the poor of their misery?"

These were my thoughts as he said, "Why, Pancho, you're only a boy, and I expected you to be an old man. I wanted to meet you and embrace you, for what you have already done and what you are doing. How many men do you have?"

"Seven hundred men, poorly armed, Sr. President."

But our talk was brief. I explained how easy it would be for the Federals to come from Chihuahua in one night and said I should return to avoid surprise and concentrate on fighting.

"Very well, Pancho, go. Tomorrow I will visit you by train. I will be in San Andrés from ten to twelve in the morning." When we parted he gave me a warm embrace.

I started back at once and reached San Andrés late in the afternoon. That night I called a meeting of my officers and arranged for a formal review the next day. I wanted to receive the President with my troops mounted and ranged from the station to the center of town. So it was. When the President got off the train, I was waiting with the principal authorities. We welcomed him with "Hurrah for Madero, hurrah for the

Leader of Democracy, hurrah for Liberty, down with Dictatorship!" which he acknowledged with friendly reply. I accompanied him when he entered a buggy which was waiting, and together we reviewed my forces. He went over each section between the station and the town, and man for man observed the condition of the troops.

From the Municipal Palace we went to the kiosk. There he addressed my forces in the plaza. Hearing him, I understood how he could command and guide and why the Revolutionaries felt it a duty to win or die with him. My men listened quietly and then shouted his name with wild enthusiasm. This done, we returned to the station while my troops continued to cheer. In a humble house nearby we ate with him, and the troops stood at attention to show their respect. When he left the little house for the station they broke into cheers once more. He seemed to love everyone, and returned the friendliest greeting to every man. Before entraining he had an order for me. "Pancho, tomorrow I expect you in Bustillos at exactly ten in the morning. Bring only a small escort."

In Bustillos he said, "Pancho, I want to confer with you and Orozco." The conference took place immediately. We were to consider whether to attack Chihuahua. I opposed the plan and stated my reasons. I said, "Sr. President, in my opinion we should not attempt it since we haven't the ammunition to maintain ourselves there. We do have men enough, and they are brave. But we are doomed to fail, Señor, if we exhaust our ammunition. In my humble opinion we must continue with guerrilla warfare, keeping close to the frontier, where we can get arms and ammunition. If we do, we will suffer no setbacks."

Saying, "Pancho, I am of the same opinion; I believe these tactics will bring success," he turned to Pascual Orozco and asked, "What do you think, Don Pascual?"

Pascual answered, "It seems wisest, Sr. President."

Since we were all in agreement, Sr. Madero informed us that we were to use the railroad for rapid attacks. My forces would leave San Andrés the next day on two trains he was going to send me. The next day I put horses and troops aboard the trains and proceeded to the Hacienda de Bustillos, where the rest of the forces joined us. We left for San Pedro but failed to make it, lacking the power to pull such heavily loaded cars. We spent the night at San Antonio de los Arenales, five leagues from our destination.

The next day we solved our problem. With the convoy divided, the engines should be able to haul us in two trips to Pedernales, where the difficult part of the road ended. It is uphill to that point and downhill from there on. Beyond, the entire convoy could be carried from Temósachic, where we would find additional locomotives, for which we telegraphed. It worked out.

CHAPTER 10

Pancho Villa Becomes Sr. Madero's Righthand Man.

Las Varas. Chiefs Salazar, García, and Alaniz. An Order from Madero. "Boys, Now is the Time." José Orozco's Fight at Bauche Station. Raúl Madero. A Train from Ciudad Juárez. Breaking Camp. Madero's Serape. Villa's One Hundred Horses. Giuseppe Garibaldi and His One Hundred Filibusters.

In Temósachic we hooked up the nine locomotives and continued to Las Varas, where we detrained to give troops and horses a day of rest. The next morning we marched on foot to Pierson, where more trains were waiting. Beyond Pierson we had orders to stop at Guzmán and wait for the rest of the column. They arrived three days later. One or two days later the President summoned me to his lodgings at the station. There he took me by the arm, and we walked along the track until we were out of earshot. He said, "I don't know what to do, Pancho. I cannot eat or sleep. Salazar, García, and Alaniz are sending me arrogant letters. They dispute my authority and undermine the loyalty of the troops. More than once I have ordered Orozco to disarm these troops, but he tells me there will be bloodshed if he does. What shall I do, Pancho?"

I replied, "Sr. President, I obey your orders. If you tell me to disarm the leaders, I will disarm them and their troops. No more than eight or ten will be killed at most."

"There is no other remedy, Pancho. Do it."

After seeing him to his quarters, I returned to camp. There I chose five hundred of my best men, with a first and second captain at the head of each hundred. When they were ready, I informed them of what we were going to do. There are times in war when such warning is wise. When men know what to expect, they go into danger with less chance of being demoralized. I said, "Compañeros, the President orders me to disarm the forces of Salazar, García, and Alaniz. I know I can depend on you in this. I expect his wishes to be carried out and my orders to be executed to the letter." They answered, "They will be."

In files, two abreast, I led them to the other camp. Entering, pistol in hand, I shouted, "Boys, now is the time," which was our countersign.

We rushed forward and surrounded the forces of Salazar, García, and Alaniz. In four minutes we had their arms and ammunition without a single casualty, although a few blows were exchanged with those who resisted. When this was done I led the commanders to the President as prisoners. I told him his orders had been executed without casualties except for a few blows; their arms and ammunition were in my possession. At his direction I delivered the arms and ammunition to Orozco and retired with my troops.

The next day Sr. Madero ordered Orozco to take one hundred fifty men to Bauche station. Orozco alighted there and engaged in a battle with troops sent from Ciudad Juárez. When the fight had lasted all afternoon and he was hard pressed, he called for reinforcements. Madero sent me to his assistance. I entrained my troops and one hundred of my best horses, leaving ten men to take the rest of the horses to Casas Grandes. At twelve the next day I reached Bauche station and immediately took part in the second day's battle. As I unloaded them I detached my troops in columns, to enter action with Orozco's. The firing grew steadily from one till five in the afternoon, and at times there was hand-to-hand fighting. But at five we threw them back in disorder and drove them toward Ciudad Juárez, where they probably reassembled. It was growing dark, and it was impossible for us to break camp, although we could collect the arms and ammunition the Federals had lost in their flight. For the moment we were ignorant of the casualties on either side, since we had taken only five prisoners, but we occupied such good positions that we remained till the next day. Raúl Madero took part in the battle on April 16, 1911, and fought bravely.

That night about ten we saw a train approaching from the north. Believing it to be the main body of the Federals, which might have left Ciudad Juárez to assist the forces we had defeated, we decided to hold our positions and wait. By morning light we saw our mistake. What we had taken for a strong column was only an escort of fifty men carrying a cannon and a section of machine guns. Seeing the condition of the camp, they hastened to retreat, but if we had known their exact strength we could have taken them.

We broke camp and buried our dead and the enemy's. Forty-nine Federals had been killed and we had nine dead and some twenty odd wounded. An advance detachment of Federals approached as we were at our task, and we left without burying several of the bodies.

When our main forces arrived we marched on foot to the Rancho de Flores, near the Río Bravo. There we were kindly received, although Sr. Madero was not with us. The President was following, on foot like the troops, part of whom were alternating as his escort in marches kept brief to avoid tiring him. The next day he reached the ranch. He was wrapped in a colored serape, and one would have taken him for a regular soldier instead of the Citizen President of the Republic.

That day he and his column rested at the ranch. At night the leaders came to report on the day. We informed him that our water supply, at a dam nearby, was exhausted. It was the only available source, and it had been consumed by the troops and my one hundred horses. We could not stay; on his suggestion, with which we agreed, it was decided to proceed the next day and camp on the banks of the Río Bravo. That move was completed about noon. The forces of the chiefs who were accompanying Sr. Madero arrived first. My men had waited until I returned from a reconnaissance. Leading them in regular formation, I was the last to reach the second camp. As I remember, that was April 20, 1911.

I presented myself for orders and was sent just north of Ciudad Juárez, down the river and below the main body of the column, almost at the edge of the city. There I issued instructions and took all precautions, every two hours sending a report to headquarters. Our situation was both dangerous and difficult, and if it had not been for my one hundred horses we would have had to retire in search of supplies, for not one staple article was allowed to cross from the United States. Seeing this, I proposed to the President and Orozco a rotation of four escorts, each of twenty-five horses, to fetch flour, corn, sugar, coffee, cattle, and so on from Bauche station, going the ten leagues by a roundabout way to avoid surprises. We did this and so succeeded in maintaining ourselves, though not without difficulty.

It was then I had a quarrel with Giuseppe Garibaldi, an Italian filibuster, who had brought one hundred men, filibusters like himself, some of them Italians and the rest North Americans. What happened was that I was resting one day in the shade of my tent when one of my soldiers came up to me. He said, "My Colonel, while I was passing through Colonel Garibaldi's camp, he required me to give up my arms and now he will not return my rifle and ammunition."

I questioned him as to Garibaldi's reasons and he insisted that his only offense was in passing through the camp. I sent Garibaldi this message: "Sr. Garibaldi, kindly return my soldier's rifle and ammunition. If you have a complaint against him, come and state it. I interfere with no troops of yours, and you will not interfere with mine. Francisco Villa."

The soldier delivered the note himself, and Garibaldi answered on the back of it, "Sr. Francisco Villa, I will deliver no rifle and no ammunition. Come and get them if you like. Giuseppe Garibaldi."

His words angered me. My note was polite and should have given no offense. Apparently he wished to quarrel. It made me even angrier to consider that I was dealing with a filibuster who meddled in our affairs and insulted me, a thing I resented not merely as a man of honor but as a Revolutionary, too. With thirty of my best men I promptly rode to his camp.

CHAPTER 11

Villa and Pascual Orozco Provoke the Attack on Ciudad Juárez against the Advice of General Viljoen. They Make Their Plans without Madero's Knowledge and Obtain a Definite Triumph for the Revolutionary Army.

Garibaldi's Reply. A Mexican Soldier. An Embrace before Madero. Pascual Orozco. Villa's Secret Meetings. General Viljoen. The President's Orders. The Secret Plan. "Esmelda." Orozco's Fifteen Men. The Battle Begins.

At the head of my men I met him about fifty paces from his camp. I called a halt. I accosted him, saying, "I have nothing but contempt for your whole troop, Señor. You see I have brought only

thirty of my own men along. Quite enough, though, to recover my soldier's rifle and ammunition and your arms and ammunition too and
those of every last filibuster with you. I propose to teach you, Sr. Garibaldi, the difference between a man and a blusterer."

He was warning me that he too was a man when I rode at him and
gave him a blow on the head with my pistol and jolted him somewhat.
I added, "Hand me your gun, Don So-and-So."

The panther of a moment before turned quiet as a lamb, and without
a word handed over his pistol, along with his sword and rifle. I demanded his soldiers' arms. He moved back the few steps between him
and his camp, formed his one hundred men and ordered them to hand
over their arms to my thirty, who all this time stood waiting for my
orders. When the arms were surrendered without incident, I said, "Sr.
Garibaldi, let this be a warning to you and every other foreigner to treat
a Mexican soldier with respect." I left him with that, and he must have
been thankful I did not shoot him.

We marched off, my troops carrying the arms taken from the filibusters, one of whom was trying to pass as a direct descendant of a
great Italian liberal. Some hours later, one of the President's aides appeared in my tent and told me that Sr. Madero wished to see me. Accompanied only by my aide, I presented myself to the Citizen President. When we were alone, he asked, "Pancho, why did you disarm
Garibaldi?" In answer I gave him the paper with my message on one
side and Garibaldi's on the other.

He read both sides. He read them again, and his face cleared. I saw
that Garibaldi must have invented a story to curry favor and give me a
bad name. But the President had the proof, written and signed, that
once again Pancho Villa had only stood up for his rights and the honor
of his country. He clapped me on the shoulder and said, "Pancho, I
want you and Garibaldi to make it up. You obey my orders, don't you?"

I replied, "Yes, Señor, I do whatever you order."

He went on, "Well, then, I am going to call Garibaldi in. You two will
give each other an embrace and after that you will return his arms."

I replied, "Very good, Sr. President."

Garibaldi and I embraced in the presence of Sr. Madero. We returned to camp together, where I handed over his arms and ammunition, and that was the end of it.

In several meetings the possibility of taking Ciudad Juárez was considered. The President thought it was too risky and always deferred to
Viljoen, a Boer general, who said it was impossible since the city was so

strongly fortified. This was the decision although Orozco and I insisted that for dignity's sake at least we ought to take the risk. It was shameful to retire without an effort.

Orozco asked me privately, "Compañero, what do you think we should do?"

I replied, "We ought to send some of José Orozco's troops to provoke the Federals into exchanging shots with us. When we hear them we can pretend to be surprised and detail more troops to help under pretense of reconnoitering. Then the Federals will send reinforcements in their turn. Step by step, we can build up the tension until we can no longer restrain our troops. Once they get out of hand, what can we do? We will explain that there is no remedy except to proceed in earnest and win. What do you think, Compañero?"

Orozco answered, "I think it will work."

Then we brought José Orozco in on our plans. He would have fifteen men swim down the river to provoke the Federals, not entering the town but luring the Federals out. To keep out of it, we ourselves crossed the river at the Esmelda foundry and spent the night in El Paso.

It worked the way we intended. The next day, at the hour set, we heard shots. Innocently we asked what was happening, and they said, "It looks like your men and the Federals are fighting." We each hired a car to hurry to Esmelda and arrived together and crossed the river. In our sector we found Sr. Madero there to meet us. Keeping up our pretense we asked what was happening. He said, "The only thing that could happen. Some of our boys are skirmishing with the Federals. Recall them immediately."

We answered, "Very well, Sr. President," but with no intention of withdrawing the men. Instead we sent fifty to help the fifteen.

Soon Sr. Madero reappeared and said, "What are they doing now? Haven't you withdrawn them?" We replied, "No, Señor. The men are scattered and can't be reassembled under such heavy firing."

"Well, find out how they are doing, but withdraw them as soon as possible."

To which we replied, "Very well, Señor. We will send help, to get them back." We did send help but to keep things going.

It was nearly dark when Sr. Madero returned. He spoke in vexed tones, "Well, what has happened now? Are they withdrawing, or not?"

Then we made the answer we had agreed on. We said, "Sr. President, a withdrawal is impossible. The troops are in a fighting mood. They won't listen. It would be risky to stop them. There is no remedy but to order an all-out attack. Otherwise those who are already fighting will die one by one. And if they do we incur the ill will of the whole army, who will look on our indecision as cowardice."

"Then what must we do?"

That was the moment we were waiting for, and at once we drew up the plan of attack as follows: Orozco would enter by the river with five hundred men and take the Customs House; José Orozco would advance with two hundred to where our men were already fighting; and last, I would attack from the south, from the railroad station. That day, May 8, 1911, will not be forgotten by Revolutionaries. We contrived to launch our attack by military logic, circumventing Sr. Madero, who was President but no military man. We were creating the opportunity to win a great victory or die in the attempt. In war, duty may require this. Sometimes a civilian chief is unable to see what is plain to the eyes of his military subordinate. If the success of a campaign or a revolution is at stake, that subordinate must be guided by his own judgment.

CHAPTER 12

Villa Plays an Important Part in Taking Ciudad Juárez and Can Act as the Noble and Generous Victor along with Madero.

The Cemetery of Ciudad Juárez. The "Cowboys' Corral." The Railroad Station. A Powerful Column. General Navarro. Surrender. Viljoen's Opinion. Casualties and Prisoners. Bread for the Troops. El Paso. Villa as Host. The Honor of the Federal Officers.

My route led past a hill above the cemetery. There I spent the night, with my forces crowded into one of the arroyos. According to plan, at four in the morning I worked close to the Ketelsen warehouses and began firing. Forces in the school across the way challenged us with a machine gun, which caused me some losses and broke my line. I tried to proceed, but found myself flanked. From the shelter of the "Cowboys' Corral" cavalry were firing and at the street intersection, barricaded with beams and sandbags, I encountered still more concealed fire. Between them they kept me from advancing, and I fell back upon the railroad station.

In the station yard were piles of crossties. From behind these, I could increase my fire upon the school and the other two points. I concentrated on the first of these, important for its strategic position. The enemy there could get no reinforcements or food and would be unable to replace their ammunition. By nightfall I had dislodged them, and ten of my men held this new position and poured telling fire on the Cowboys' Corral and the street defenses. The Federals, outflanked in their turn, withdrew toward their headquarters. We followed, advancing through the interiors of houses which served to hide and protect us. From wall to wall and house to house we moved ahead. That night and into the morning hours of the next day the struggle continued, until about ten, when the Federals, in full retreat, abandoned their wounded and the prisoners they had taken the day before.

Close on their heels we occupied their former positions, believing we had won, but a strong column emerged from the market plaza, under their commander in chief, General Navarro. It appeared to consist of some sixty infantrymen, several hundred dragoons, two mortars, and a battery of machine guns. They advanced as if resolved to break through. But they failed. As they came into sight we received them with steady fire, and although their artillery razed houses, neither that nor anything else discouraged my men. By the open passages between houses we could attack from different directions and often from close up. Seeing this they retired in good order. My troops, enheartened, charged after them but they held us off. I could see Navarro exhorting his men and leading them back to headquarters.

After the retreat, which was heroic but costly, Navarro saw that he could undertake no offensive and chose to parley, doubtless considering further resistance useless. In my opinion he acted wisely. We were determined to take the plaza. It would have done them no good to resist, the more that they did not have their hearts in it, while we, the liberating army, as they called us, were inspired and invincible. A soldier must accept unavoidable defeat.

The surrender took place at three in the afternoon of May 10, 1911. Lieutenant Colonel Félix Terrazas, with part of my troops, was the first to enter Navarro's quarters. On my arrival I saw that he and my men were receiving the General's sword. Terrazas said, "What do we do now, my Colonel?"

I replied, "Put the officers under escort. Assemble the prisoners, and collect the arms and ammunition; and while this is being done, march the soldiers to the jail, where they will be at the disposal of our leader." Having dictated these measures, I mounted and cantered off, followed only by an aide, to tell the President that Ciudad Juárez had fallen, General Viljoen's opinion notwithstanding.

Although he heard me, Sr. Madero seemed to doubt what I had said. He asked, "What is that you are saying, Pancho?"

I replied, "We are entering the city, Sr. President. The place is ours; General Navarro is a prisoner in the custody of Lieutenant Colonel Terrazas."

Giving me a warm embrace, he said, "We will go at once. You are returning to organize your troops? I approve. See that the soldiers do not steal or get drunk."

I returned to the city, where I ordered my officers to assemble the troops and quarter them without loss of time. That was done, and by five in the afternoon our men were quartered in the school building and in nearby *quintas*. I sent ten men to the cemetery to dig a grave for our dead while another fifteen men and I were busy gathering the bodies and putting them in carts. When this was done, I went to José Muñiz' bakery. I ordered him to set his bakers to work baking as much bread as possible. He did so, and as he told me I could have warm bread by four in the morning, I was there to get it at that time. I packed it in ten *malva* sacks and carried it with me. At five I went to the jail. There I distributed my sacks of bread and barrels of water among the Federals, although these were the only provisions on hand and my own forces were in the same need as the Federals, if not worse. In war the victor endures privation in good spirit, but for the vanquished, and even more for the prisoner, every privation aggravates the bitterness of defeat, which is the most bitter thing of all.

The Federal prisoners were grateful to me.

Lastly I carried bread to my own soldiers, but there being too little for all, I organized escorts under their respective officers to search for provisions and return quickly.

I had many duties that day. I visited Navarro and the imprisoned officers. I embraced the General. He had done us much harm, but victory had been beautiful and was not to be abused. I said, "Sr. General, I am going to take nine of your officers to El Paso to dine with me. We are in wretched shape here."

He answered, "They are your prisoners, Colonel."

In a couple of automobiles from El Paso I carried nine officers, whose names I do not remember, across the river. We ate together at the Hotel Ziegler on the friendliest of terms. No one seeing us would have dreamt that I was the victor and these were my prisoners. When it came time to pay, some of them attempted to do it, but I said, "No, Señores, you are my guests. I appreciate your offer but you must not deprive me of my right." Then, when we had drunk a beer, I added, "Now, Señores, if it is agreeable, we will return."

One of them then said to another, "Wouldn't you like to stay in Texas?"

I thought he had meant this for a joke. We soon saw he had not, but before I could speak up, one of the captains reproached him, saying, "Señores, the Colonel brought us here trusting in our honor. We cannot abuse his confidence. Pancho Villa is no less a gentleman than any one of us."

They agreed, and we returned to Ciudad Juárez. Some of my companions had predicted that the Federal officers would not return. They looked at me with increased respect when they saw that they were wrong.

CHAPTER 13

Villa Is Led into Insubordination by Pascual Orozco. Upon the Triumph of the Revolution He Retires to His Own Private Business.

A Visit from Orozco. The Secret Conference. A Conspiracy against the President. Villa's Shame and Regret. Raúl Madero. The Ten Thousand Pesos. Five Men as an Escort. San Andrés.

That afternoon at about five Pascual Orozco came to my quarters. He said, "Compañero, if I bother you, it is because I have a serious matter to discuss with you."

I replied, "Come in."

But he answered, "No, Compañero. I will wait for you in my quarters.

It is something we must discuss in private. The consequences may be great."

Mystified, I offered to go at once. He spurred his horse and rode away. I followed him on foot, but lost no time. He led me to his rooms and when we were alone said, "Compañero, you will not have forgotten that General Navarro shot some members of our families. Do you agree that if the President objects to his execution, we should disobey and shoot him anyway?"

In was true that Navarro had committed excesses. In the elation of victory I had forgotten. I replied, "I understand. My men and I will support you in executing him."

He said, "Good. And since you agree, we will see the President at ten in the morning to tell him what we want and consider his answer, but always in agreement with what we have said. No?"

I replied, "Yes, Compañero."

At the appointed hour I presented myself with fifty men. Orozco was there with his troops. He called me aside and said, "I am going to ask them to deliver Navarro to us. If the answer is no, disarm the President's guard."

I answered, "Very well."

He entered the office and after a moment appeared at the door and shouted, "Disarm them." I consequently understood that Sr. Madero was opposed to the execution, but had no recourse except to keep my word. I gave the order to disarm the guard, and it was executed. Sr. Madero rushed out and saw what I had done.

"So, you are against me too, Pancho?"

I made no answer but waited for orders from Orozco. All he did, however, was to come out behind Sr. Madero and say, "No, Señor, let's understand each other."

They went on speaking. I could not hear what they were saying for the whispering of the troops, but I saw them embrace, and this naturally surprised me at first. One of two things must have happened. Either Orozco had lacked the courage to order the execution of Navarro in opposition to the President, or Sr. Madero had dissuaded him. As in either case Orozco owed me an explanation, I rearmed the guard and returned to my quarters.

There I waited but Orozco neither came to see me nor sent anyone else. But I never lack for friends, and after three days in my quarters, I learned the black story. Orozco, expecting a sum of money from Don Porfirio's agents, promised to assassinate Sr. Madero and wished to involve me. Having disobeyed the President's order I would have to go along with the rest, or at least I would have difficulty in proceeding in any other way, as I now understood.

At the last moment Orozco lacked the courage to go through with it, or to go all the way, and knowing my violent character, planned for me to disarm the guard so that I would appear to be the principal instigator of the shooting and the President would challenge me face to face, and I would draw my gun and kill him, and everything would be done, with Pascual Orozco uninvolved and me, Pancho Villa, apparently the true and only assassin.

It was a devious plot. But Orozco was deceived in me. In my ignorance I did nothing except to request the execution, and after my military conscience, which obeys well as it commands well, I subordinated myself to Orozco, who had assumed responsibility. Therefore, seeing that he took no step to consummate the execution, I rearmed the guard, though I had only fifty men and Orozco had all his troops. I returned to my quarters without a word, and I think Orozco's plans may have been frustrated by this.

Word of the conspiracy leaked out and became notorious in Ciudad Juárez. I have stated the facts, and by them must be judged. I do not justify myself. Certainly, after our victory in Ciudad Juárez, which was great and beautiful, I felt no desire for vengeance and had no wish to darken our triumph with bloody executions. But it is true that Orozco awakened my desire to deal with Navarro as he had dealt with our people; I forgot our embrace and the spirit of forgiveness. It is also true that I agreed to Orozco's plan and went along to insist on the President's approving the execution. But I did this without repudiating him as President. I understand now that I was mistaken and had let Orozco mislead me. But to me Sr. Madero was untouchable, and I disarmed the guard thinking only to ensure the execution—not in order to attack him personally or allow anyone else to attack him. Thinking about it now, I believe this also: if we had succeeded in the plan I was told about, not Orozco's secret plan, and Sr. Madero had intervened between Navarro and my forces or between Navarro and Orozco's forces, I, Pancho Villa, at the head of my troops would have supported Sr. Madero.

This is a true account of what happened at the time.

Three days after our insubordination, Raúl Madero, the President's brother, came to my quarters. He asked, "What has happened to you? Why haven't you been to see Pancho?" By "Pancho" he meant his brother.

I replied, "I am ashamed. Don't you know what Orozco was going to do, and how I came close to helping him do it?"

He answered, "Yes, but we have the story straight and no one doubts your innocence."

We embraced and wept, getting each other wet with our tears.

He said, "Let's go to the Customs House. I'll talk to Pancho."

I waited while Raúl spoke with him. After a moment he came out and said Sr. Madero was waiting for me. When I entered, Sr. Madero rose and came to greet me. He took me by the arm, as he had done months before when he asked me to disarm Salazar. He said, "You have something to tell me, Pancho? Come." Without turning my arm loose, he took me with him.

I said, "Sr. President. I want to resign. I am overcome with regret and shame."

He replied, "Good, Pancho, good. Should we put Raúl in charge of your troops?"

"Yes, Señor, on condition that my troops accept him as their leader. They must not know that I am leaving them for good. If you permit, I will tell them that you have sent me on a mission and Raúl is to be in command while I am absent."

"Good, Pancho. Do that. And I will assign you twenty-five thousand pesos for your needs."

I answered that I had not fought for money but only for the victory of the people, and would retire to work for my living if the guarantees he had made were honored now that the Revolution had triumphed.

He said, "Pancho, you will see them honored, and so will the people. I promise. But now if you are unwilling to take all I offer you, accept at least a small amount. I will have ten thousand pesos turned over to you."

I declared that it would be better to give me a draft for that amount dated two months ahead, which he did at once under his own signature. He called Raúl and said, "Give Pancho any train he wishes. Take over his command and furnish him with ten thousand pesos. You will take him to the station."

The President wanted me to have an escort but I would take only five men. Raúl and I went to get the money, which I consented to draw at once in obedience to the President's wishes, and then we went to the barracks. There I told my soldiers my mission would keep me away from five to twenty days and until I returned they were to respect Raúl as their leader.

They promised to do so. I took the five men who were to accompany me. We went to the train with arms, saddles, and an allotment of seven thousand cartridges each. Saying goodbye to Raúl, I left for Pierson by way of Casas Grandes. From there we proceeded to Las Varas and by another train on to San Andrés, where the wives and widows of soldiers who had fallen in my campaign came to see me; and as they had nothing to eat, being from a town that had given everything to the Revolution, I had 1,500 hectoliters of corn brought from the Hacienda de Ojos Azules and distributed.

I reported the distribution of supplies to the governor of the state, Don Abraham González, and this ended my campaign from 1910 to 1911. I then devoted myself to private business.

CHAPTER 14

Loyal to Madero, Villa Unmasks Orozco and Enters the Struggle against Him

A Call from Madero. Lunch at Chapultepec. Orozco Becomes Suspect. Villa's Promise. The Attack on the Penitentiary at Chihuahua. Faustino Borunda and His Sixty Men. Governor Aureliano González. At the Southern Pacific Station. A Letter from Pascual Orozco. Five Hundred Men Again. Orozco's Father. His Traitorous Son.

In Chihuahua, near the end of 1911, I received a message from Sr. Madero, who was then already President. He summoned me to the capital. I was then engaged in private affairs but, still thinking of him as my chief, I obeyed. When I presented myself to receive his orders, he greeted me affectionately and said, "Pancho, come by the Castle and have lunch with us."

At noon that day I was in the Castle of Chapultepec. There I had lunch with his family, who were all considerate and friendly. The President said, "Pancho, I have sent for you to learn what Pascual Orozco is doing. I hear bad reports of him."

I answered, "Sr. President, Orozco consorts with Don Juan Creel and Alberto Terrazas, and you know them. That's all I can say."

Madero reflected and then, fixing his eyes on me, asked, "Pancho, if Orozco betrays the Revolution, where will you stand?"

I replied, "Sr. President, you can rely on me."

Laying his hand on my shoulder, he said, "Pancho, I was sure of it. Go back to Chihuahua and watch Orozco and keep me informed of whatever occurs."

Now Orozco, under the title of chief of the Military Zone, had made himself king of Chihuahua. He forgot our cause. He had elegant secretaries and advisors and devoted himself to society in the company of our enemies.

Two months later they again called me to the capital. Madero said, "Pancho, the reports on Orozco grow worse. How is it with you?"

I answered, "Sr. President, what I said once, I say again. I will die for your government. I no longer have troops, but I have friends who will be ready when you need them. You need only arm them."

Embracing me and bidding me goodbye with more affection than ever, the President added, "Return to Chihuahua, Pancho, and keep on watching Orozco. When the time comes, recruit men. I will give you the equipment you need."

On the morning of February 2, 1912, at five o'clock the State Penitentiary in Chihuahua was attacked by Orozco's orders. Since he was in charge, with all the military forces under his command, the attack could have no object except to uncover the designs of those who were against him.

I was in my house on Tenth Street when the shooting began and remained there, waiting for events to determine my attitude. If my suspicions were well founded, prudence would argue against taking the opportunity Orozco was offering. At about ten o'clock, sixty armed men came to me under the command of Faustino Borunda, now a lieutenant colonel in the Constitutionalist Army. He said, "My Colonel, we cannot find General Orozco. He ordered us to take the Penitentiary, but we couldn't. Will you take command?"

I answered, "I don't understand, boys. Have a bite to eat, wait a bit, and I think you will soon get your orders."

They came in, they ate, and when they were ready to go, I said, knowing Faustino was a man I could count on, "Don't leave, Compadre. Let the others search for Orozco, but you stay here."

Minutes later, the government office telephoned that the interim Governor, Sr. Aureliano González, needed me. I reported at once, and found José Orozco present with his men, and Pascual Orozco at the Governor's side. The Governor said, "The General and I offer you a chance to aid us. Will you go after Antonio Rojas, who has escaped from the Penitentiary?"

Orozco interrupted him to add, "It was Rojas who stirred up a part of the garrison against us."

I was angry but answered calmly, "Señores, I am always ready to serve the government, only first, Sr. Governor, I have a few words to speak and I want Compañero Orozco to give me a straight answer." With my eyes on Pascual Orozco, I continued, "Compañero Orozco, do you expect me to betray the government, yes or no? Weigh your words well and be on your toes."

"I'm on my toes all right." But he turned pale and would not face me. "Will you go after Rojas?"

"Yes, Señor."

"What do you need?"

"A hundred men, armed and mounted."

"But Rojas has more than two hundred."

"No matter, one hundred is enough."

"Good. I'll give you one hundred of José's men and have a Southern Pacific train ready to carry them."

"All right. I'll wait at the station."

He left, believing I had fallen into his trap. But once alone with Sr. González I began to develop plans of my own.

I said, "My friend, you are in a bad fix and must listen to me. Authorize me to raise troops and find money and arms any way I can." He gave me the authorization at once, for he was loyal to the government, though dominated by Orozco.

At home I mounted and equipped eleven of the men from my slaughterhouse business, and at their head started for the station, letting the horses set the pace. Orozco's troops were already there, with a message from him: "Compañero Villa, proceed with the troops. Inspect Rojas' position but don't open fire."

Understanding what was behind these words, I thought, "Pascual is unmasking, but not very bravely." It was time to end the game, and I wrote bluntly on the back of his note, "Sr. Orozco, not being absolutely without shame, I leave your troops where they are, and I return to the desert and the life of an honorable man." With my eleven men I left the city, where the traitor was all-powerful, and started for Huahuanoyahua, resolved to gather troops and fight against him.

In Huahuanoyahua the same day and at Ciénaga de Ortiz the following one I told old friends how things were and what was to be done. In from the ranches came 150 men to join me, almost all of them armed but few with ammunition. Farther along, in Satevó, my compadre Fidel Avila joined me with 100 men. It was the same everywhere. I recruited in San José del Sitio and other places and within a few days raised an effective force of 500, almost all of them mounted and armed at their own expense.

Late one afternoon when we were camped at the Rancho de San Juan de la Santa Vera Cruz, Pascual Orozco, Sr., drove up in an automobile. He greeted me and added, "So you have troops, Colonel."

I replied courteously, "Yes, sir."

"I have private business to discuss with you."

"Let us eat first and afterwards talk all you like."

We shared a friendly meal at the house of Cosme Hernández and then retired to private rooms, where Orozco, Sr., said, "My son and I have always respected you, Colonel, and in his name I ask you to withdraw your support from Madero, who has broken his promises. My son has instructed me to give you 300,000 pesos, with which you can retire to private life, here or in the United States."

I replied, "Sr. Madero is the choice of the people. We promised him our support. Whether his government is good or bad it is too early to judge. You may think one way and I another, but in any case, tell your son that I am not for sale at any price, and although we were once friends, we will now have to shoot it out."

With this the conference ended. When we left the house it was snowing. Orozco's father had no overcoat. I gave him the blanket I was wearing; he accepted it, climbed into the automobile, and drove off to Chihuahua. Watching him depart, I thought a man's worst fate is to have a traitor for a son.

Villa Seizes Parral from José de la Luz Soto and Decides To Wait for the Attack of the Orozquistas under Emilio P. Campa.

Bustillos. Orders from Abraham González. Braulio Hernández. Emilio Vázquez Gómez. A Letter from Villa. At the Gates of Chihuahua. Satevó. El Valle de Zaragoza. Sixty Choice Men. Ciénaga de Olivos. Juan Bautista Baca. José de la Luz Soto. Maclovio Herrera. Jesús M. Yáñez. A Loan of Fifty Thousand Pesos. Emilio P. Campa.

I marched my forces to the Hacienda de Bustillos, where I established my quarters and waited for orders, which came in a letter from Don Abraham González, who had again taken over the government of Chihuahua. He asked me to approach the capital without fighting to see if he could not get safely out and join my men, and then we would all start recruiting in the south.

Two hours after this letter, I received another, from Braulio Hernández, the greatest traitor in Chihuahua. It enraged me but made me laugh, too:

Colonel Francisco Villa:
Esteemed Friend, I hope you are supporting General Pascual Orozco and Don Emilio Vásquez Gómez. Come to my field of operations to receive your orders. Our motto is "Land and Justice." Expecting you and your forces in the near future.

Colonel Braulio Hernández
Coyame, March, 1912

It filled me with loathing to see what this once honorable man had become, and I answered:

Sr. Braulio Hernández:
Unmask and bid Pascual unmask, you pair of traitors. I will join neither you nor anyone so degraded.

Francisco Villa

In obedience to Don Abraham I started for Chihuahua in two trains. That night at twelve, as I unloaded my forces at Las Animas station, I learned that Orozco was preparing an ambush on the outskirts of the city at the Southern Pacific station. He must have paid little attention to my former operations if he imagined I would walk into one of his ambushes. At dawn I ordered my cavalry to saddle. In road formation I started for Chihuahua without communicating my plans or giving any battle orders, but religiously observing Don Abraham's instructions.

Orozco naturally anticipated my advance and dispatched forces to attack me. Even without orders I would have had to retreat, for I was short of ammunition. I brought my men away in good order, under fire that killed not a single man, but though I was conscious of doing my duty and acting wisely, it was difficult to check the impulses of the men who wanted to punish Orozco right then.

I returned to Satevó, and from there continued on to El Valle de Zaragoza, and as the Orozquistas would send troops to attack me or cut off my passage, I went to meet them at La Boquilla, near the big dam. There I gave them a fight of little importance. Watching the route they would take from Santa Rosalía, I saw clouds of dust which must have been raised by a force of some five hundred. When the Orozquistas came close I had most of my men retiring in perfect order. But some of them had not recognized the assembly call and failed to respond. They stayed in their houses and were taken prisoners. For the rest of us, that action had the advantage of supplying us with the horses and ammunition of Orozco's casualties, and when the fight was over some of my men had two horses each.

I retired to El Valle de Zaragoza, where we camped outside the town. My soldiers were in low spirits; as it happens in all armies, I had some cowardly men who were infecting others with their fears. What with the desertions of that night I was left with only sixty men. I was not discouraged. I thought, "Those who do not leave will be the best." And truly, the sixty who stayed were the best I had. With them I set out by way of the Balleza River to Ciénaga de Olivos, intending to turn the people against the traitors, though, as things were going, I, being loyal to the established authorities, was proceeding as a rebel, and they, the conspirators and traitors, were acting in the name of true authority.

One day I received a letter from Parral signed by Juan Bautista Baca. He informed me of José de la Luz Soto's suspicious attitude and his constant communication with Pascual Orozco. Although my force was reduced to sixty men and Parral was garrisoned with four hundred, I planned to take it and supply myself with materials of war. My men were in favor of this, and we marched that night. At dawn we were at the gates, unsuspected. But, unwilling to devastate the town by a surprise attack, I sent an ultimatum: "If you are loyal to the government, come out to receive me, and if you are an enemy, come out to fight. I shall take the town in any case. Francisco Villa."

Receiving no answer I went ahead. As it was growing dark, I entered unhurriedly and once inside, with my horses in a big corral, approached one of the barracks on foot, and entered without anyone stopping me. That part of the garrison was commanded by Maclovio Herrera (today a general in the Constitutionalist Army), whom I had the good fortune to encounter by accident. I explained why I was there and how I had entered. He answered, "Your forces are equal to ours. Call on the commander to yield. I will help you to disarm him."

I collected the extra rifles and ammunition in the barracks and then looked for lodging for my men. The next day, still doubtful of Luz Soto's attitude, I repeated my questions to Maclovio Herrera. He said, "These commanders are traitors. Seize whatever they have and use it in defense of the government. My men and I will follow you and execute your orders."

I answered, "Then go and disarm Jesús M. Yáñez' troops; I will disarm Luz Soto's."

But it occurred to me to try a ruse, and I added, "If we wait a while, I think we can avoid a battle." I sent the following communication to Yáñez: "Sr. Major Jesús M. Yáñez, Come for half of my ammunition. I have twice as much as I need. Francisco Villa." Twenty minutes later, Yáñez came to my barracks and asked for the ammunition.

I replied, "Amigo, what I have for you is the disagreeable news that you are my prisoner. Order your quarters to be turned over to Maclovio Herrera."

Submissively he replied, "Very well," and did as I commanded.

My troops now had control of the armament and troops in Parral, and we increased the number of our forces to five hundred, since I was able to arm volunteers who joined us. I took other steps. I called on the wealthy men of the town for a loan of 150,000 pesos. With the money I began to pay my troops and supply them with what they needed. Everything was bought and always paid for in the town. I was organizing and equipping my troops when a courier arrived to warn me that troops were coming to attack me. When I verified this and found that some 1,500 men were coming from El Valle de Zaragoza, I decided to remain and defend myself.

The next day about three in the afternoon I received a telephone call from Emilio P. Campa, who claimed to be speaking from Sombreretillo. He said, "I will be there tonight to teach you a lesson."

I answered, "Come on man, come on. We will receive you as you deserve."

I took measures, placing my troops in two strategic positions, supplied with food, water, and other necessities. Thus prepared I could defend Parral against Campa's 1,500 men.

CHAPTER 16

Villa, in Combat with Orozco, Receives Orders To Join the Northern Division Commanded by Victoriano Huerta.

Martiniano Servín. La Mina Prieta. Victory at Parral. A Letter from Campa. Five Thousand Orozquistas. The Rich Men of Parral. Santa Bárbara. Francisco Lozoya. Los Obligados. Las Catarinas. El Amolar. Las Nieves. Tomás Urbina. Mapimí. Raúl Madero. Bermejillo. Trucy Aubert. Huerta. The Northern Division. Gómez Palacio. An Order from Huerta.

We waited that night, and about four in the morning saw the enemy's horses. By five they had drawn a cannon in place opposite La Mina Prieta hill and the firing began. Part of my forces were at El Caracol, and I was with the rest at the station.

They gave us a hard fight. At seven in the morning they were already on the hill. I called Martiniano Servín and said, "Martiniano, take the hill, any way you can. I will hold the station with these twenty-five."

At the head of one hundred men he began the climb. From below, through a fence, I watched his riflemen advance, and twenty minutes later heard them sounding the *diana*. They were announcing success. Servín had taken the hill, a cannon, and two machine guns, and turned one of the guns on the cavalry. We redoubled our own fire and the cavalry began to break. I mounted twenty-five men and at their head charged in hand-to-hand combat. They fled in disorder. Without losing a second I regrouped my forces and made a flank attack on the troops fighting against Maclovio Herrera. They were unable to resist; they fled and left us horses, saddles, arms, ammunition, and over a hundred prisoners, whom I put in the public jail. After this I quartered my forces to prevent excesses and dispatched scouts to follow the disorderly retreat of the enemy to Jiménez.

The next morning a milkman brought me a note: "Your luck has run out. In four days I will be back to take you down a peg. Emilio P. Campa." Two days later a courier warned me that four trains were coming and an army was advancing on Parral by way of El Valle. Some said there were six thousand men, others, over eight thousand. I waited and found that the actual number was five thousand.

Landowners and merchants in Parral were not politicians or very brave. They were interested in business only, and it made no difference to them whether they lived under traitors or loyalists. Fearful in the face of the approaching forces and knowing I had only 560 men, poorly armed and equipped, they begged me to deliver the place and spare their interests, saying, "Consider the number of the enemy and the certainty of defeat." They were right about the numbers, but I could not retire without at least a trial of strength, considering that we had just defeated many of these men.

I replied, "Señores, I cannot abandon the place. Let the enemy drive me out if they can."

They did. They arrived at exactly twelve noon. The battle began at the edge of town, where my troops were distributed in small groups. Until eleven that night, when they had me surrounded on all sides, I held out. Then, under cover of a counterattack at one point, I saved my forces. There are times in war when determination counts more than superior arms, or greater numbers, or skill. We broke through and reached the Hacienda de Santiago.

After a night's rest we left for Villa de Santa Bárbara at dawn the next day. There I bought horses and saddles for the men who had left Parral on foot with only part of their equipment. They had saved arms and ammunition. At dark I received a telephone call. A voice informed me, "This is Francisco Lozoya. I am a prisoner at La Boquilla. Wait for me and I will escape tonight." I knew it was Orozco and not Lozoya but I answered calmly, "Escape. I will wait for you." We mounted and quietly rode to the Rancho de los Obligados, about five leagues away. There I slept without worries while the enemy rode all night, only to reach Santa Bárbara without finding me. After spending the next night at the Hacienda de las Catarinas, we crossed the Sierra del Amolar and in

Las Nieves met my compadre Tomás Urbina, now a general in the Constitutionalist Army, with four hundred men.

I said, "Compadre, let's go to Torreón for equipment and supplies." He agreed and with our combined forces of nine hundred men we marched for six days, to reach Mapimí. There we met Raúl Madero with a force of railroad men.

The people of Mapimí were happy at the arrival of loyal troops.

I wired news of my whereabouts to General Huerta, who was in Torreón in command of the Northern Division, and received instructions to leave my forces and report for orders. I left at once, with only a part of my staff. On passing through Bermejillo, I found General Trucy Aubert. He and his troops welcomed me warmly. In Torreón General Huerta greeted me cordially and said, "Move your forces to Gómez Palacio and we'll see what you need." Up till then I had been paying all expenses with the 150,000 pesos I had collected in Parral. This was not enough and it was about time for our needs to be considered.

I took leave of the General and did as ordered. There the entire town of Gómez Palacio, men and women, the old and the young, joined in welcoming us. I was content. I thought, "Orozco, who was all-powerful, succumbed to ambition. Men know now what he is and they will always consider him the greatest of traitors. But I, Pancho Villa, though I was in disgrace because of an innocent error, am restored to the position which is my due. Men will not forget that Pancho Villa was loyal to the cause of the people."

While quartering my troops in Gómez Palacio, I received a letter from Sr. Madero which made me very happy. He said: "Pancho, I congratulate you. Go on as now. Ask General Huerta for whatever you need. It pleases me to know you are cooperating with him. Francisco I. Madero." I understood Sr. Madero was detailing me to Huerta's command. Though I had other plans for sweeping the traitors from Chihuahua, I obeyed. The next day I presented myself, saying, "As the President wishes, Señor, I am at your command." He replied that he would review my men at ten the next morning.

At the time agreed on he did so. Afterwards he said, "Amigo, I congratulate you. Your troops are well trained. Now tell me what you need."

"Señor, I need three hundred Mausers and ammunition for all my men. For the sake of uniformity I want to get rid of the 30-30's. I need clothing, too."

He gave me an order for the three hundred guns and the ammunition, and as nothing was said about clothing, I proceeded to buy it with what was left of the 150,000 pesos. When this was done, I received orders to go to Bermejillo and wait for the division. I camped at the Hacienda de Santa Clara, a short distance from Bermejillo. Six days later the Northern Division arrived. Huerta came in the morning. At three in the afternoon as I was returning from a reconnaissance, he called me and said: "Go to Tlahualilo and attack the rebels there."

He was drunk. Seeing this, I started to explain that it was inconvenient to leave immediately. I said, "Sr. General . . ." Interrupting me in loud and arrogant tones he said, "Do as you are told."

I withdrew to obey but went in search of General Rábago. When I found him, I said, "Compañero, explain to Huerta why I want to wait till dark. I will attack at dawn but if I start now the dust will give me away and the enemy will escape."

General Rábago was able to persuade Huerta, who summoned me when I was on the point of leaving and said, "Good, Amigo. Leave at dark as you wish. Take the 7th Cavalry with you and be fighting at dawn."

"Many thanks, my General. With your permission, I will withdraw and carry out your orders."

CHAPTER 17

Villa Is Promoted to Brigadier General and Plays an Important Part in Huerta's Campaign against Orozco.

The 7th Cavalry. Tlahualilo. Military Experience. Rábago. An Embrace from Huerta. Villa's Rank as General. The Chills. Conejos. Villa's Charge. García Hidalgo. Emilio Madero. Compadre Urbina. Escalón. To Rellano. A Mine. Cástulo Martínez. Navarrete's Artillery.

At dark I departed and marched all night. At two in the morning, knowing we were possibly approaching outposts, I entered the chaparral, always going in the direction of Tlahualilo. I took short cuts and avoided the advance lines as I had planned. I had no military background but I knew by experience that the principal talent of a leader lay in his skill in planning beforehand and his determination in executing his plans. At dawn a party of advance troops was returning, probably to report that there was no news. My troops attacked it, and four of the six men were killed. The enemy sallied out at the noise. Firing began on both sides, and the fighting became general.

From before six it lasted until eleven, when the enemy, confused and disorganized, left the town in our possession and began a disorderly retreat. General Rábago, coming up with artillery at that moment, unlimbered his guns and with only four shots dispersed them. I took six hundred horses, ten cars of supplies, saddles, and a lot of rifles and ammunition. When the fight was over, Rábago and his troops returned on the train on which they had come and I remained in the town. The next day, with my forces and horses and carts, I went to join the division, which was on the way to Peronal station. While I was reporting on the number of dead and wounded in the 7th Regiment, the horses taken from the Orozquistas could be seen coming toward us in an immense herd, and Huerta said, "What animals are those, Amigo?" "Some six hundred I took from the Orozquistas, my General." "*Caramba*, come here."

He embraced me and asked, "What are you going to do with them?"

"Whatever you say, my General. I expected to give them to the 4th and 7th cavalries unless you ordered otherwise."

"Dispose of them as you see fit."

I left him and went to notify the chiefs of the 4th and 7th cavalries that any soldiers with weak horses were to receive replacements from my herd. When I had furnished them with remounts there were still two hundred or more left.

On the way to Conejos we reached Peronal but did not stop, for the water there was exhausted. When we could see the Sierra de Conejos in the distance I asked Lieutenant Colonel Rubio Navarrete, "Señor, if the enemy was in the mountains over there, how should a good leader advance?" Whereupon this man of great military knowledge ordered the following: the artillery proceeded in a formation called a column of batteries, with my forces flanking it on the right, those of Raúl Madero on the left, and in the front a vanguard and a squadron of guides. We all rode at a gallop to raise a cloud of dust which would keep the enemy from knowing we had no infantry. Seeing the vanguard and guides marching in line as foragers, I asked him if my forces should march in the same way. He sent word that we should not, that it would be best for me to continue the reconnaissance to the right as much as possible, in case the hills were occupied. As it happened, when my men and I arrived within range of the hills, gun and cannon fire broke out everywhere. The Orozquistas were there, and what had begun as practice finished in earnest.

In my opinion it was a mistake for the Orozquistas to betray their presence before learning our strength; traveling without infantry as we were, they could have caused us serious trouble if they had let us advance further. We did not even return their fire. We limited ourselves to carrying out our reconnaissance and reporting to Huerta, who ordered us to spend the night there and wait for the infantry. That afternoon Huerta summoned me before the hour I usually reported. On arriving I found Generals Téllez, Rábago, Emilio Madero, and Trucy Aubert present and waiting for me. By that time they had made me a brigadier general, much against my wishes, for I knew how the regular army would laugh, but I endured it with patience. I was not fighting for them but for my country.

Huerta addressed me as follows, "Sr. General, the battle begins at daybreak. Your men form the right wing, and you will hold without a single backward step until you win or you are killed. Rábago will take over in case you do not survive."

I only said, "Very well, Sr. General, I have my orders, and with your permission I will retire."

General Huerta perhaps considered me one of those who are impressed by threatening words, but I only thought, "He wants me to win his battles."

Shortly after four in the morning we were eating breakfast and by seven I had drawn up my cavalry for action. The fighting began on my wing. I had 800 men and the enemy some 1,600. I was supported by Rubio Navarrete, whose batteries broke the Orozquista lines and caused them serious damage. Unfamiliar with such an attack I thought at first that he was making a mistake. The shells were whistling very low over our heads and threatening to destroy our own lines. I sent word to him several times. He replied that his fire was accurate and I should keep on. I did, and as we continued to advance I saw that the fire reached farther ahead and the shells always fell on the enemy and never on us. I understood then the work of a true artilleryman like Rubio Navarrete and how he would support us.

Things quickened, with the cavalry engaged on both sides and no more than three hundred meters between. My officers were to engage at close quarters, and under no circumstances to retreat, even if we all died. With so much force did our advance begin, and with so much dash, that the enemy lost heart and little by little gave way. Seeing that they were weakening and some turning back, I charged and broke their lines. We were pistoling them down point-blank. I had about eighty prisoners in two parties, most of their horses, and saddles from the dead animals, and I had the satisfaction of seeing them completely routed. The prisoners, which I sent to Huerta, were shot.

Since early that morning I had been feeling ill. At three in the afternoon, when the battle was over and the enemy had withdrawn half a league to hills to the right of the Sierra de Conejos, I fell to the ground, burning with fever, but would not retire with the enemy in front of me. At this moment Lieutenant Colonel García Hidalgo rode up and shouted with an insolence no man should tolerate in another—and least of all a general in a lieutenant colonel—"What are you doing there, sprawled out on the ground while your forces are scattered like this? Don't you know the battle is over?" Speechless, I could only point to the Orozquistas in the hills. But he smiled sarcastically and said, "Those? They're Emilio Madero's troops."

Very calmly I replied, "No, Señor, that is the enemy I have dislodged after fighting all day."

He retorted more insulting than ever, "What enemy? I tell you those are Emilio Madero's troops. You've done nothing at all—except, perhaps, to loaf."

His words stung me so I could no longer restrain myself. Forgetting I was ill, I mounted and shouted, "Not another word, you insolent loudmouth. Come along with me if you are looking for Orozquistas. I'll teach you the difference between fighting and showing off."

"Señor, I am General Huerta's chief of staff."

"What you are is a so-and-so, and you had better get out of my sight in a hurry. I've had enough."

He sang a different tune after that and left very meekly. I remained in camp until six that afternoon, when I lost consciousness as a result of high fever, and my boys carried me away. I could not even make my report. My compadre Tomás Urbina gave me an alcohol rub. Then he wrapped me in blankets, and I went to sleep under a cart, so as to breathe the open air without suffering from changes in the weather. Feeling better the next day, I went to headquarters. When Huerta had heard me out, he rose and came to me, saying, "Come here, Amigo. I must embrace you. General Rábago has already told me of your part in the battle." I couldn't help thinking, "It's too bad that Lieutenant Colonel García Hidalgo is not here to get a surprise."

The doctors prescribed medicine for me. I kept up the alcohol rubs and the treatment turned out very well. Feeling better the next morning, I reported that there was nothing new at the outposts.

Huerta ordered me to form the right flank of the trains, five hundred meters ahead of the convoy, with my cavalry deployed as marksmen, on the march from Conejos. Thus we advanced to Savalza and from there to the dam at Escalón. That ended the day's journey. There Huerta cautioned me about the outpost, expressing himself as he had in Conejos on the eve of battle, saying, "Sr. General, the enemy is in Escalón. If they attack tonight, I will hold you personally responsible."

I replied, "My General, you can be sure they will not surprise us, and if they attack, it will cost them dearly."

My outpost was usually effective, but I increased my vigilance that night. In addition to three cavalry groups at suitable points, a quarter-league from the division, I scattered guards at every serviceable point. And though I was still ill, I went in person to superintend until three in the morning, when Urbina relieved me. On going to bed I posted an aide as sentinel and ordered him to gather reports every quarter-hour and wake me at the least bit of news.

The next day I informed Huerta that nothing unusual had occurred during the night. As if he had not heard me, he gave me my orders: "At one this afternoon you and General Rábago will take Escalón, with your forces on the right and Don Emilio Madero's on the left."

We did, or rather, would have done this. But seeing us advancing, the enemy abandoned the place without fighting, and we occupied it. That afternoon, as usual, I stationed my outposts, and the next day when I went to report that nothing had occurred Huerta ordered me to reconnoiter as far as Rellano (The Landing), so called because it was the place where you began to climb El Escalón (The Stairway).

I took two hundred of my men. Near the Rellano dam I noticed something suspicious on the railroad track. Under the rails was a mine loaded with thirty-two boxes of dynamite, and the batteries to set it off were half a league from the road. I had eight inches of wire cut and the ditch where the batteries were hidden covered up again; then I advanced to the dam, where I exchanged a few shots with the enemy and killed seven Federals. I lost First Captain Cástulo Martínez and two soldiers. When I gave General Huerta an account of my exploration he noted where the mine was and ordered Rábago to remove it the next day. Then he said, "Sr. General, since you know this region, accompany the artillery and support them, and on the way give Lieutenant Colonel Navarrete all necessary information for emplacing his cannons for the attack." I saw with satisfaction that once again they were assigning me the lead.

CHAPTER 18

Villa Thinks the Regulars Do Not Like Him, and Huerta Confirms This by Treating Him Unfairly.

Manuel García Santibáñez. "Where is my General Villa?" Lunch with Huerta. Huerta Knew How to Command. The Seven Dead Men in the Well. Regulars and Revolutionaries. The Imprisonment of Urbina. Téllez, Rábago, and Emilio Madero. Flowers at El Valle de Allende and Parral. The Russecks' Mare.

Navarrete got his artillery into place and Huerta then ordered me to form the right flank. My forces were to establish contact with the enemy and protect the artillery, which was firing with great accuracy.

In midafternoon, when the main body of troops was reaching the field, the battle was nearly over. I had taken all my objectives and the rest of the forces had done equally well, except for the regulars, who were unsuccessful in taking the dam. As I was contemplating the advantage of artillery support, a battery under Captain Manuel García Santibáñez, today a colonel in the Constitutionalist Army, was set up in the positions I had taken. It outflanked Orozco completely. But Huerta ordered Rábago to attack on the left, and as his brigade was repulsed, along with Emilio Madero's forces, our whole action was endangered. In my opinion Huerta had made an error. It was not on their right that the Orozquistas were showing weakness but on the left. Fortunately, our artillery and the courage of my forces enabled the other brigades to hold the field that Rábago and Madero had abandoned.

That night I established my outposts with greater precaution than usual. I spread my men in firing line and protected the battery on the mountain with two machine guns and my choice troops. The night passed without incident. But at one in the morning a man appeared in my ranks, going from one side to another crying, "Where is my General Villa? Where is my General Villa?" None of my soldiers knew where I was and no one answered. Not suspecting he was an enemy they let him pass. When finally he met a captain of the 15th Battalion he became frightened, fired at him, and vanished in the darkness.

At dawn the firing was renewed. By eight my forces had driven the enemy from their positions. I ordered Urbina to make arrangements for breaking camp and went to report to Huerta. I said, "My General, it is all over. The victory is ours."

He answered, "I must embrace you, Sr. General. I have already informed the President of your exploits. Don't go. We must have lunch together. I have some *gorditas.*" We ate in a very friendly spirit. I had two *gorditas* with *frijoles* and they tasted very good in spite of my illness.

When my soldiers had broken camp I led them to a small ranch where we camped and buried our dead. We sent the wounded to the hospital and by four that afternoon I went to receive my orders. Huerta asked, "Sr. General, are we in danger?"

"No, my General. We do not even need outposts now. But you will order what is best."

He said, "If we are in no danger, you know what to do. And if we are, take steps against it."

Considering his words, I thought, "The man is drunk, but he does know how to command and if his judgment is sometimes at fault it is only because be begins to drink by seven in the morning and is hardly ever at his best." Not once in all the times I spoke with him was he altogether sober, for he drank morning, afternoon, and night. His talents must have been very great. Otherwise Sr. Madero, knowing his vice, would never have entrusted him with the campaign against the Orozquistas, who, if they won, would reverse the Revolution.

The next day we began our march to the north in the following order: my brigade was the extreme vanguard, as usual; Rábago's brigades and those of Don Emilio Madero came next; and finally the trains and artillery. Beyond Rellano we stopped at a well for the troops and the horses to drink. As it happened we exhausted the water in the well and so let a soldier down to fill the water coolers. While he was busy below, Rábago, Madero, and I began to drink with great satisfaction. All at once we heard him yell, "Let me out. Let me out. Pull me up." When he reached the top he explained in great fright, "There are seven dead men down there. I won't go down any more."

All of us except Don Emilio laughed heartily. He turned pale and said, "I believe I am going to throw up."

General Huerta had treated me kindly. Even so, I saw that neither he nor his friends looked on Sr. Madero's Revolutionaries with approval, though I could not understand why. We were loyal and dutiful. We performed the most difficult and exhausting assignments. We must have deserved praise. If not, why so many embraces? I sometimes wondered if the dislike came of our having humbled their pride in taking Juárez in 1910 or whether it was due to our having no military background other than our brief record as Revolutionaries. Whichever it was, many of the regulars, as well as Huerta, accepted us with reservations and constantly baited us.

We marched beyond Rellano. When we were opposite Rancho Colorado and Rancho de los Acebuches I learned that they had seized Tomás Urbina, then a colonel and now a general in the Constitutionalist Army, and had sent him under guard to headquarters. Assembling my brigade and withdrawing about a league from the other troops, I sent a message to Generals Téllez, Rábago, and Madero: "If anything happens to my compadre I will retire with my brigade and report to the President of the Republic as soon as possible."

They answered: "General, don't be alarmed. Your compadre will be with you by eight in the morning. We have already conferred with General Huerta." I do not know what arguments they may have used, but Urbina was with me at the hour named. One attempt having failed, they released him, I think, in order to deal with me directly.

We continued our march to Jiménez, my brigade always in the lead. There Huerta sent for me and said, "Send Colonel Urbina for some cattle for the division. Give him a small escort." I did so, specifying, "Compadre, take twenty men to the Hacienda de San Isidro and bring us five hundred head of cattle." He left at once to carry out that mission.

About ten that night General Huerta sent for me and said, "Go with General Rábago to Parral. Install authorities there and return immediately." In obedience to those orders, Rábago and I set out for Parral with our cavalry brigades. My forces made up the vanguard, and as the people of El Valle de Allende knew by telephone that I was going to pass through, they prepared a cordial welcome. Women and girls, old men, young men, and boys walked along with my troops carrying garlands. The flowers were for me, but I had no wish to arouse the jealousy of the Regulars and asked the people to save their offerings for Rábago, who was bringing up the rear. I said, "If you do, I will be better pleased than if I myself received them."

"But they are for you, Pancho Villa, all for you."

However, they did finally yield to my request, and when Rábago arrived his brigade entered the town on carpets of flowers. We remained there that night. At my suggestion Rábago quartered his troops in the town, and I moved with my brigade to a small ranch nearby. The next day we set out at dawn. Being in the lead, I stopped on the outskirts of Parral. Since I was well known in the town I thought there might be a reception and sent a secret commission to find out. I said, "If there are to be honors and entertainment, arrange them for General Rábago."

It was done. How could there fail to be entertainments for Pancho Villa in Parral! They greeted me with music and ovations, and there were so many flowers that Rábago had to pass them on to his officers as he received them. The demonstration made me happy, for the people, I could see, understood my sentiments and, what was most important, supported our cause.

When we had installed authorities, we returned to the division. In Jiménez half a day before Rábago, I quartered my troops and went to advise Huerta of my arrival. He received me with his usual cordiality. But in my own quarters I learned that when I was in Parral a captain had seized a mare of mine. Men by the name of Russeck claimed the mare belonged to them. I say now as then that they were enemies, conspiring with Orozco.

That afternoon when I went to receive my orders, I said, "My General, a captain in the Regular Army has seized a mare that I captured. Please give me an order for her return."

He may not have understood clearly, for he answered with an arrogance I was little inclined to tolerate. For a few moments our words were heated; as leader he would brook no question, and as a subordinate, though I was obedient, I had my self-respect to maintain. But the air cleared and he lowered his voice. He said, "You need no order for that. Tell whoever has your mare to return her."

I did so. I dispatched one of my aides with this communication to the offender: "To whom it may concern: By order and without protest return the mare that belongs to my troops. Francisco Villa."

They returned her, but the intrigue went on.

CHAPTER 19

In Spite of Villa's Brilliant Record in the Campaign against Orozco, Huerta Attempts To Shoot Him.

Villa's Sweat Bath. A Greeting from Huerta. Colonels Castro and O'Horán. The Xico Battalion. The Walls at the Station. Villa in the Square. "Why are They Going to Shoot Me?" Villa's Tears. "It is by Higher Order." Lieutenant Colonel Navarrete. Huerta's Honor. Antonio Priani. Villa's Farewell. Torreón. Monterrey. Blas Flores. Encarnación Márquez. San Luis Potosí. The Penitentiary. Octaviano Liceaga.

I was still suffering from fever, and that night they gave me an alcohol rub. In the Charley Chi Hotel they heaped blankets on me. Just as I began to sweat heavily a major and a second captain of the Regular Army came looking for me. They said, "General Huerta requests you to come at once to headquarters."

I replied, "Tell my General that I am taking a sweat bath. If the business is urgent, I will come, but if not, I will see him tomorrow."

They left and did not return. But as I was to learn later, Huerta had wished to confirm an order to march to Santa Rosalía. He considered my reply an act of insubordination. I went back to sleep. After a little, I was awakened by a noise. Lieutenant Colonel Navarrete had entered the room. As I was to learn, his forces had surrounded my quarters and ranged their cannon opposite my door by order of Huerta, who believed I was going to revolt. But my state was reassuring.

At sunrise next morning, wrapped in my blanket, I went to headquarters accompanied by an aide. Huerta rose and spoke in his usual manner.

"Good morning, Sr. General."

"Good morning, my General."

He left the car, his quarters, and I sat down to await his return and receive my orders. Two minutes must have passed when Colonels Castro and O'Horán entered and said, "Hand over your arms."

Without quite understanding what was happening, I saw two large escorts taking up their positions on both sides of the car. Even so I remained calm and made no resistance. I said only, "Very well, Señores, here they are." I unbuckled my pistol and handed it and my dagger over.

They took them and said, "Out here." Outside I was surrounded by files of the Xico Battalion, which was on the right or east side of headquarters. A few minutes later, still between the files of the battalion, the colonels placed me in the middle of an escort and led me to the other side of some walls, about 150 steps from the tracks. I was dizzy, either because of my heavy sweating throughout the night or because of what had just happened. But I felt no great uneasiness, thinking that it was all the result of some error which would soon be cleared up.

As we skirted the wall I saw what for the first moment I could not believe. They had formed a square and I was to be shot. The dizziness left me. Anger possessed me. I had given my fellow soldiers no reason for wishing my death, but apart from that, it was contrary to all regulations for them to shoot me without a hearing. I was not a traitor or an enemy, or even a prisoner. Why did they do this? But my indignation was brief. It changed to sorrow. I thought, "These are the men for whom I have been fighting, and as they are the ones who are going to kill me, I see that the interests of the people are not in the hands of their defenders but in the hands of their enemies instead."

As I stood in the square the first sergeant of the platoon went up to the wall and made a cross on it with a mattock. That cross is still there. The sergeant ordered me to stand at the foot of that mark. Unable to restrain myself, I asked Colonel O'Horán, "Sr. Colonel, why are they going to shoot me? If I am to die, I must know why. I have served the government faithfully. I demand it as my right to know."

I could not continue for the tears that choked me. At the time I hardly knew whether I was weeping from fear or from mortification, but I see now it was because of the wrong they were doing me. In my opinion I have never shown any signs of cowardice or avoided danger, however great, though there have been times when death was so near I was sure I was performing my last act.

When Colonel O'Horán made no answer, I turned to Colonel Castro and said, "Sr. Colonel, permit me to give you a last embrace. The National Army, if it has any honor, will repudiate this act."

I wanted him to understand that my crime would have had to be very great to warrant such an execution. Embracing me with great emotion, Colonel Castro replied, "It is by higher order."

I looked at him as if to divine who issued the order when suddenly, just as I was taking a step forward, Colonel O'Horán said, "One moment, Compañero. Wait till I have spoken with Huerta." And he left.

In a few minutes he returned, troubled, and said "The order is to be carried out."

Again the sergeant ordered me to stand at the foot of the cross, and again, with tears in my eyes and my dizziness returning, I demanded to be told why they were shooting me. As the sergeant tried to force me to the wall I threw myself to the ground, pretending to beg but only fighting for time. Navarrete appeared, looking anxious, and said, "One moment, Señores, one moment. Let me speak to Huerta."

He went away to add one more effort to theirs, but I had little hope left. I had started to hand my watch and money to the soldiers who were going to execute me when he returned and shouted from a distance, "Stop, by order of the General." He took me by the arm and led me into the presence of Huerta.

Weeping again, I do not know whether because they weren't going to shoot me or because there were after all some who protested against injustice, I said, "My General, why did you order me shot? Have I been disloyal? Have I ever done anything but my duty?"

To words that deserved an honest answer, he replied, "It was a question of honor." He turned his back and left.

I felt sad again. They said they were taking me to Mexico City before a court martial. I paid no attention. I only wondered, from curiosity rather than interest, what the crime would be on which they passed judgment. I asked myself again, "What act can they allege to justify this?"

When I saw they were putting me on the train I considered what it would mean to my soldiers. Humbly I asked Antonio Priani, then serving as Huerta's chief of staff, for permission to say goodbye to my troops. In truth it was a very sad thing to have to beg permission to see the men who had fought at my side. Priani, like his commander, only got drunk, while I was winning honor in the service of my country. When Priani returned from speaking to Huerta, he said, "They will draw up the troops in formation facing the car, and you can tell them goodbye from the steps." And so it was. Some of my troops came and lined up opposite the car. Their grief, I believe, was greater than mine, and perhaps one word from me would have caused them to fall upon those who had made me a prisoner.

When I appeared on the steps, surrounded by officers who were there to observe, I saw anger in the soldiers' eyes. I said, "Comrades, my gratitude exceeds words. You have faced hardships with me and fought in the name of the people. You have been good soldiers and loyal friends. Whatever fate awaits me, I urge you to be loyal to Sr. Madero, as that is the path I have taught you to follow. And remember that I love and embrace you all."

I could add no more, for Prianí interrupted, saying, "Enough, Señor, enough. Enter." And he took me by the arm and led me into the car.

In gratitude to Navarrete, who had saved my life, I had my horse saddled and presented to him. I gave him my sword too, which was precious to me. But as it all seemed very little, I wanted to give him my house in Chihuahua and told him that as soon as possible I would send him the deed. Señor! If I am alive today, I owe it to him and to no one else. And as he belonged to the Federation, whereas there were several Revolutionary chiefs in the Northern Division, I thought, "How strange, after fighting against so many Regulars, to owe my life to one of them and not to a Revolutionary!"

Twenty minutes after bidding goodbye to my soldiers I was traveling south, a prisoner with a large escort. The journey was a hard and melancholy one. In Torreón the next morning the escort delivered me to headquarters. Between twelve and one that same day they took me to another train, which was already made up. With another escort I set out for Monterrey. There they carried me to one of the barracks. I was confined in an unfurnished cement room, where I slept with no cover but my jacket, while my first captains, Blas Flores and Encarnación Márquez, accompanying me, slept on the floor.

The next morning I requested an interview with the battalion chief. He came to my room and I said, "These two captains who are accompanying me are not prisoners, as the consignment will inform you. I beg you to clarify this point and grant them the freedom of the street and the barracks." He agreed to this.

At six or six-thirty that afternoon an escort took me from the barracks to the station. A large crowd gathered, attracted by curiosity to see me. When I passed, a voice cried, "*Viva* Pancho Villa! Down with the rascals!"

Other voices answered the *vivas* and repeated them. I ignored them. I said no word and let no single smile cross my face; and I maintained this attitude, even though the shouts continued, until the chief of the escort told me to get on the train. The same thing happened in San Luis Potosí, to which the news of my arrival must have been wired, for the station was full of people of all classes. But I was humiliated by being conducted like a prisoner, and would not even approach the window to face the crowds that were asking for me. Someone cried, "Death to the traitor Pancho Villa!" At this there was a rumble of anger, or affection.

The train left San Luis Potosí. The next day we reached the capital of the Republic. When my escort left the train, a number of reporters surrounded me. They asked me questions, but I had nothing to tell them. I said nothing either on leaving the station or on the way to the office of the commandant.

From this office, after taking information about me and putting my name on many papers, they sent me to the Federal Penitentiary. There I was received by the director, Don Octaviano Liceaga, who likewise recorded personal data and then sent me to one of the great wings. They put me in a cell of cement and iron, with only an open toilet and an iron cot for furniture.

Thus confined, I thought, "In other years, in my struggle with the representatives of so-called justice, I killed many men to save my life and defend my honor. Then I was fighting against everybody because they would not let me earn a living in peace. At that time my enemies never succeeded in putting me in jail, as these have done now that justice is on my side, thanks to the Revolutionary struggle."

It was a sad but true thought.

CHAPTER 20

Villa Is Carried from the Penitentiary to Santiago Tlaltelolco, and Carlos Jáuregui Suggests that He Escape.

Don Santiago Méndez Armendáriz. Insubordination, Disobedience, and Stealing. *The Three Musketeers*. Villa's Plan. Santiago Tlaltelolco. Rosita Palacios. Carlos Jáuregui. The Caution of Villa.

Four days after my confinement in the penitentiary a young officer from the military court, Don Santiago Méndez Armendáriz, came to take my declaration. On entering, he said, "You are accused of many crimes, Sr. General."

I answered, "Señor, I can't believe it's a crime to fight for one's country."

When he went on to ask me questions I gave him the details of my arrest and the near execution. He listened calmly, and two days later when I was expecting to hear that I was free, he formally assented to my imprisonment.

As far as I could see, he was an honorable man, but he had to treat General Huerta's accusations with respect for political reasons, and he had accepted orders from above. I even asked myself, seeing how civilized and decent a man he was, "Have I perhaps committed crimes without knowing it?" But my answer was, "If I have, why does the judge treat me with such consideration?"

Six days later he returned. He greeted me kindly. His first question was why I had sacked Parral; and then he asked me to explain the moment when I was ready to throw my troops against the Army. He added that there were proofs of my having stolen 150,000 pesos in Parral, of which I was to give him a detailed accounting.

I saw they were trying to destroy me and answered, "Sr. Judge, I did not steal the money. It was a loan which I imposed on the merchants of Parral for war expenses, with authorization from the government of Chihuahua. I will render an accounting to the governor of Chihuahua, or perhaps to the Supreme Court of that state. The Sr. Judge has no reason to know, but if he inquires, he will learn that once when I was a boy I had five thousand pesos, and distributed it all to the poor. I have never taken money that was not mine except when I was in need of the most urgent necessities, and as for the rest, the insubordination and disobedience, it is not true, Señor. Unpleasant words sometimes passed between General Huerta and me, but that is not insubordination. The ill will of my enemies has to be supported by such tales of disobedience.

"Was I disobeying when I was entrusted with the biggest assignments in the campaign? It is true, though, and I do not deny it, that I considered myself subject to the direct orders of the President only, and when my troops were unjustly treated I wanted to receive my instructions directly from him. But who calls that disobedience? Does the Sr. Judge take only General Huerta's word, who is my enemy, and believe the officers under him who are enemies of the Revolution? As for sacking Parral, that is a fabrication like the rest. We had to have money for our troops. I gave orders to search for it, and if a banker resisted, he was threatened, after the military way, and then he agreed to aid the cause of the people. That is not sacking. How could I sack Parral, the town where I grew up, to which I owe so much? No, Sr. Judge, there is money in the banks, and when our cause is in danger, that money is offered voluntarily or we take it."

Four months were needed to prove that I had been authorized to impose the loan and that my campaign cost the treasury half a million pesos instead of the 150,000 which I obtained through the Supreme Court of Chihuahua and the governor of the state, Don Abraham González.

When this charge was dismissed, which made me appear different from what I was, there remained what they called "having been insubordinate" and "having disobeyed." The judge asked me questions, led me back and forth, and hemmed me in.

Tired out, I said one day, "I think, Sr. Judge, that you ask too many questions. You know perfectly well that there was no insubordination and no disobedience. Are you here to uncover the truth, or to represent my enemies? I ask no favors but I do demand justice."

His face exposed his true thoughts as he replied, "Friend Villa, I am sorry your case has come into my hands."

"Do not be sorry, Señor. Do your duty." But seeing that hidden influences were moving against me, I made no effort to defend myself. What hurt me most was the ingratitude.

They were holding me incommunicado. This I endured with resignation, wishing to leave a good record in jail, as I had done in war. But I suffered, not from the solitude, for I was accustomed to that, but from confinement and the silence. There is a difference between the solitude of the sierra, with the arroyos and the mountains all around, and that of a jail, where the walls let you see no one but yourself, and each day's rest is more exhausting than the most dangerous action.

One day I asked the judge if it was true that some books can hold us under a spell when we read them. He answered yes. I said, "Sr. Judge, if you can get me one of those books, I will be grateful, especially if it is about soldiers or war." He brought a book called *The Three Musketeers*, and I found great consolation in it.

Still, the seclusion exhausted me. One day on my way back from my bath, I said to the hall guard, "I am not going to enter my cell."

"Why?"

"Because no law or ordinance authorizes jailers to hold a man incommunicado for more than three months when he is awaiting trial. I am not a condemned criminal. I am subject to due process of law and I have had enough of this."

"So you won't go in?"

"No, Señor, I won't."

"Well, now, we'll see about that."

He went away, to return in a few minutes with four jailers armed with pistols and clubs.

"Are you going in or not?"

"That is what I said. I will not enter of my own free will."

After deliberation they took the case to Sr. Liceaga, who came in person and spoke to me kindly, "Why won't you obey the rules, Villa?"

"Because I refuse to believe there is a law which authorizes jailers to hold an innocent man like this. Show me your legal justification so that I can make a legal protest."

After a moment's reflection, he answered, "Remain in the hall while I consult the Department." They withdrew.

That afternoon Sr. Liceaga returned. He said, "The Secretary of the Interior will permit you to stay in the hall, without further isolation. But I must request you not to talk with the common criminals." After that morning they no longer kept me locked in a cell. I could walk through the hall in the sunshine I had missed. But the relief was a short one. Four months later they transferred me to the military prison Santiago Tlaltelolco.

There they gave me a room of my own in the upper corridors. It was no more than a dustbin, too foul to occupy. With my own money I had it cleaned, whitewashed, and coated with oil. Then I had a bed and a mattress brought in, and bought a rug, some chairs, and other pieces of furniture. Each day I devoted thought to obtaining one small thing, as previously I had devoted it to achieving great things, and it was not long before I marveled at my quarters. I thought, "Is it my destiny to find my greatest comfort in jail?"

At first the officer in charge, Colonel Sardaneta, and later Colonel Mayol who replaced him, had orders to allow me no visitors. This was a piece of rank discrimination, for the other prisoners, of whatever rank, could see anyone. But soon things changed and I too began to see people from the outside. My privileges were extended, and a girl named Rosita Palacios was allowed to visit me. She was a great comfort in those lonely days and became the object of my most amiable attentions.

With these interests weeks and months passed by, but justice overlooked me. I decided to learn to type and to keep books, two things which are useful in the world of business. I thought of writing on the typewriter because my lawyer, Bonales Sandoval, had me buy one for making copies of the records in my case. He said he needed these and I wanted him to have them at once. One morning when I went to the court to fetch the machine I found the clerk there alone. He was a courteous young man, Carlos Jáuregui, with whom I liked to talk.

"Good morning, Amigo. How is our business?" I was speaking about the typewriter, but he thought I referred to the case, a topic we often discussed. It was going badly, he said, because of influences determined to hold me a captive.

"Listen, my General, why don't you escape? Believe me, you are in danger and the way your case is going you will never be released. If you like, I'll help you. Look, I'll file the bar on the grill here and we can walk out together."

I saw that he meant it and thought, "Why shouldn't I be frank with him?" But I merely replied, "Come, come, what are you saying," and added, "We'll see. I'll think it over." I returned to my room without mentioning the typewriter.

CHAPTER 21

Villa Rejects the Offer of Madero's Enemies and with Carlos Jáuregui's Help Plans To Escape.

A Letter from Madero. Duplicate Keys. The Typewriter. A Hundred-Peso Bill. Jáuregui's Visits. The Lawyer José Jesús Martínez. Two Pistols and a Hundred Cartridges. Ranch Music. Hipólito Villa. Antonio Tamayo. General Bernardo Reyes. A Proposition. Tomorrow at Three.

That afternoon and the next day I did nothing but think of how to escape. I said to myself, "Jáuregui is right. The judge cannot render justice, Huerta's persecution continues, and Sr. Madero's government has left me in the hands of my enemies." On the judge's advice I had written Sr. Madero a letter explaining the trouble and the origin of my hardships. I reminded him that it was within his power to have a military indictment dismissed. I could hardly believe the answer and saw that my enemies were deceiving Sr. Madero.

Thereupon I took steps to escape. After a few weeks I was in possession of duplicate keys to the doors opening from my rooms to the roof of the jail. If I could reach the roof it would be easy to drop to the street.

But meanwhile I had not forgotten Carlitos' offer. It had certain advantages and I determined to explore his mind. One morning I found him alone again and said, "My boy, I have come for the typewriter."

"Here it is, my General, but you cannot have it without an order from the judge." Then, joking, he added, "Do you know what I would do with it if I could?"

"What?"

"Carry it to a pawnshop."

"You would be doing well. Youth without money is no youth, and it is unfair for some to have a lot when others have nothing. The poor who work but earn too little have a claim on the wealth of the rich. Or didn't you know that this is why we are fighting?" I handed him a hundred-peso bill saying, "Take this and buy yourself something. And come to my room this afternoon. We'll talk over that business of the other day." He came, and as we talked I was further convinced of his sincerity. I told him how I intended to escape. But he disapproved of my plans, which he thought risky and difficult. He said his method was the best, and assured me he could land me in the street unnoticed.

We came to no agreement that day. I continued to visit him when he was alone, at the hour when the judge and the secretary were in conference. And he continued to visit me in my room. Thus we strengthened our bonds of friendship.

One morning I said, "You are right. File the bar, and we will go out through the court and the main door. But do you think they will take me for a lawyer?"

"Yes, my General."

"Good. I will be the lawyer Jesús José Martínez. How is that?"

In another conversation we agreed on the following plan of action: I would go through the grill to the court some afternoon; there I would dress as the lawyer Martínez and go to the street with Carlitos. We would be discussing cases as we passed by the guard; outside I would meet Tomás Morales, Blas Flores, and my brother Hipólito, who would come to the capital to accompany me to Chihuahua on horseback. I told Carlitos to get me two pistols and a hundred cartridges, as well as clothes for my disguise as a lawyer. He convinced me however of the danger in leaving Mexico City on horseback; so we decided that first I would go to Toluca by automobile and there make whatever arrangements seemed best.

I was beginning to have great confidence in Carlitos, but when he brought the pistols and the cartridges and I had them in my hands, doubt assailed me and I said, "Understand one thing, boy; at the first sign of treachery, you will be the first to die."

He gave me the answer that reassures a man: "If I betray you, my General, you will have good reason to kill me."

What went slowly was the filing of the grill. The saws were jagged and squeaked, even though he had oiled them. There was danger of discovery if anyone in the corridors heard.

I asked, "Can't you close the corridor door, Carlitos?"

"It must not be closed, my General." But he was clever. He then had the idea of working while the band was playing ranch music. At such times the corridors were deserted.

The grill was almost cut. It must have been the eighteenth or twentieth of December when my brother Hipólito came to see me. He had visited me several times before and was in Mexico City with Blas Flores. He said, "I have considered your plan and even gone over the road to Toluca with Jáuregui. I don't like it. You are running great risks." After a further conversation between my brother and Carlitos, the latter assured me that Hipólito was wrong, and I said, "Good. If you are sure, send my brother and Blas Flores to Chihuahua and arrange our escape for the twenty-fourth."

So it was. My brother and Blas Flores left. Carlos had my fare paid from Veracruz to Havana for the twenty-fifth. Everything was ready for the twenty-fourth at three in the afternoon, when on that same day they notified me of the visit of a lawyer friend, Antonio Tamayo, and we had to risk a delay. I had let slip a hint of my intentions in conversations with General Bernardo Reyes, and that prisoner, who had many visitors and loved to gossip, might have told others what I had intimated to him. My fears were not unfounded. One day General Reyes had called Jáuregui, who was his protégé, and asked him why he visited me so much, and years later I learned that a friend of the General's, Espinosa de los Monteros, was saying I owed my escape to General Reyes.

That afternoon Antonio Tamayo gave me a friendly embrace and said, "Pancho, I have an offer that will interest you. I am fully authorized to make it. The Madero government cannot and should not last. Only if it falls can the country be saved. Pancho, I want you to be prepared for this. Important men in the army and in politics are agreed. I come with authority to invite you to join them. Give us your word and in six days you will be free again."

I was indignant and ashamed but I knew by experience that there are times for dissembling and I pretended to listen with sympathy, and replied, "I am grateful for the offer. Give me three days to think it over and decide without haste. There are steps in life which must be considered in the light of all the consequences, and a man must not take them without careful consideration."

"Three days then, Pancho. I will come back with a paper for you to sign, and six days afterward you will be absolutely free."

He left, with another embrace, and when he was gone, I shut myself in my room and began to weep. It was the enemies of the government who were offering me my liberty, and it was the government that was holding me prisoner to placate the men who would destroy it. I thought, "Yes, Señor, I will regain my liberty, but at my own risk, and to fight for Sr. Madero, not to join his enemies."

The next day I told Jáuregui, "We leave tomorrow at three. Are you ready?" He assured me that he was. The automobile would be waiting near the prison to carry the lawyer Jesús José Martínez to Toluca.

The next day, when it was nearly time, I concealed the pistols under my shirt; I put the cartridges in a handkerchief, wrapped in a serape. Luckily it was cold. I walked down the corridor as I usually did. To avoid attention I had changed my good shoes for canvas ones, as Carlos had recommended; and I had put on navy blue trousers such as a lawyer might wear.

As I passed down the hall I came to the lieutenant colonel's room. I spoke from the door, "Good afternoon, Sr. Lieutenant Colonel."

"Good afternoon, my General. You surprise me at this hour."

"Ah, yes, a little visit to pass away the time."

He got up from the cot where he was resting and I took him by the arm and guided him out in the corridor. Walking back and forth with him, I reached the place where the guards were stationed. I took out my watch and said in a loud voice, "With your permission, Sr. Lieutenant Colonel, it is time for me to go to court now."

He replied, "Do so, Sr. General."

When he left, the guards had no need to be concerned about me.

CHAPTER 22

Villa Escapes from Santiago Tlaltelolco and Gains the Liberty that Madero's Government Could Not Give Him.

The Courtroom Grill. "Do I Look Like a Lawyer?" The Automobile. *Rurales* at the Inspection Station. Shooting at a Target. Villa's Mustache. The Girls. Palmillas. The Train from Acámbaro. González. Celaya. Guadalajara. Colima. Manzanilla. Aboard the *Ramón Corral*. José Delgado. The Steward's Stateroom. Medical Examination.

I closed the courtroom door softly and said, "Good afternoon, my friend. Is everything all right?"

"Everything, my General."

And I added in a low voice, "Which is the right bar?"

"This one, my General."

I threw my blanket on the floor, handed Carlitos the cartridges, and grasping the bar with both hands succeeded in bending it out. I put my shoulder against it and pushing with all my might made the opening wide enough.

Once I was through the grill, Carlos produced an overcoat, a black hat called a *bombín,* and some dark glasses. These were to change me into a lawyer. I put them all on and left my cap on the judge's table. With the cartridges distributed in the pockets of my overcoat and the two pistols stuffed in where they would not look bulky, I sat down comfortably in my new clothes.

"Amigo, can I really pass for a lawyer?"

"Yes, my General. Only turn up your lapels, and don't forget to cover your mouth with a handkerchief as if you had a cold."

I did as he said. Beyond the next room we went down a winding stairway. The officer of the guard was reading or writing. I remember there were some other officers there. I began to blow my nose and coughed a little.

Very calmly, Carlitos said, "You see, Señor? When you make up your mind, you finish quickly. Today we have finished much earlier than ever before."

I nodded and went on mumbling and wiping my mouth. I wanted to hurry, but Carlitos said, "Don't go so fast, my General."

Señor! That boy was so sure of himself he was giving me lessons. We reached the door of the Santiago Customs House. I saw no automobile and disturbed, asked, "Where is it, Carlitos?"

"On the other side, my General."

"On the other side! Why so far away?"

"It could not be brought any closer, my General. Be calm. There it is."

As we climbed in, I said to the chauffeur, "Let's go, Friend. I am not a man who likes to waste time."

Carlitos had already engaged the car to take us to Toluca and it was unnecessary to say anything more. I felt more insecure than at any other moment in my life. What could I do there, even with pistols in my hands? In an automobile the bravest man can be killed.

"Listen, Carlitos, don't you think we ought to exchange the car for some horses?"

"No, my General."

At the Inspection Point two *rurales* stopped us. I reached for my pistols, but Carlitos caught my arm. They asked us who we were, where we were going, and if we were carrying arms or ammunition.

Carlos answered, "The lawyer Martínez and I are going to Toluca on an errand."

"Let's have a look."

They ordered us out and looked under the cushions. Then they let us go. I felt uneasy and asked Carlitos why they did this. He told me that the *rurales* were there to keep the Zapatistas in the state of Mexico from getting arms and ammunition.

"Why didn't you tell me? And why did you choose this road? Don't you see they will soon be shooting at us?" We were already going through the mountain passes, and I began to think of what could happen. I ordered the driver to stop for a while. We got out. We walked away from the car, and I said to Jáuregui, "How are you with a pistol, my friend?"

"Very bad, my General."

"Well, we'll see."

We chose a target and began to shoot; after that we went on our way.

In Toluca I said to the chauffeur, "Friend, leave me your card. Day after tomorrow I may need you to take me back."

On Carlitos' recommendation, the first thing I did in Toluca was to go to a barber shop and have my mustache shaved off. From there we went to eat. We looked for beds and found a rooming house.

I said, "Tell me, Lady, is the house safe?"

"Yes, Señor, you can feel secure. A major has the room in front. He leaves his pistol on the table, and up to this time no one has ever taken it."

I thought we had better leave, but we decided against it. We did, however, keep out of the major's sight, and since it was too early to go to bed, I said, "How are you with the girls, Amigo?"

"With the girls, my General?"

"Yes, my friend, with the girls."

"I do not know, my General."

"Well, we'll find out." We went in search of them. Now that I was free, I was invigorated and felt a need of this natural relief.

Next morning at four we left on foot for Palmillas station, about five kilometers from Toluca. We were to take the train there. It arrived about eleven, after we had had our breakfast. We got into the first car and bought tickets for Acámbaro but with the intention of getting off on the way, at Crucero González.

Soon afterward two old men who were reading a newspaper began talking about my escape, that is, Pancho Villa's escape. I feared someone might recognize me, but Carlitos assured me that I really looked like a lawyer suffering from a cold. I had my collar turned up to my ears and hardly ever took the handkerchief away from my nose. In Crucero González we took the train for Celaya. There, in a car on our way to the hotel, I noticed a couple of men approaching on horseback. I reached for my pistols, but they passed by without trying to stop us.

After supper at the hotel, we left the dining room for the office, which was near the entrance. We intended to wait there for the train for Guadalajara, but near the door I saw a man watching us suspiciously and I said, "My friend, let's take a walk." We returned to the station where I mingled with the crowd while Carlitos bought tickets and reserved Pullman berths for Guadalajara. When he had the tickets, I said, "Now find us a place to stay." A woman selling drinks in front of the station offered to rent us a bed until train time for fifty cents.

I said, "Lady, here is the fifty cents, but who will wake us when the train comes?"

"My husband will, Señor; he is the policeman here."

I asked Carlitos, "What do you think, my friend?"

"It's all right, Señor."

And it was, too. At one in the morning the station policeman waked us, and at nine we were in Guadalajara. I walked on over to the Colima train while Carlitos was buying our tickets.

We reached Colima at seven that night and stayed at the best hotel. Before eating supper, I said, "My boy, I can't stand this dirt any longer. I need a bath. Get me some clothes."

Since the day of my escape from Santiago I had not changed. I slept with my clothes on to be ready for whatever might happen. But the heat at Colima was intense, and I was sweating under the lawyer's overcoat which hid my pistols. I would be sick if I went on like that.

Bathed and clean, we went to the plaza. The overcoat no longer bothered me. I had found a way to carry it on my arm and still conceal my pistols. But Carlitos had brought me a hard-collar shirt, the kind a lawyer should wear, and the points were so uncomfortable I could not move my head. Carlitos had his eye on me. Seeing that he was laughing, I asked him sternly, "What are you laughing at, my boy?" My words must have offended him, for he said nothing more while I was getting accustomed to the collar.

The next day we went on to Manzanillo. There they informed Carlitos that the *Ramón Corral* was ready to sail for Mazatlán. That made me happy. Once we set foot in Mazatlán, it would be easy to cross the sierra to Durango. There were no tickets left, but they offered us passage on the "upper deck." We accepted and went to sit on a high bench on the poop. It was almost time to leave when I saw José Delgado, the telegrapher of the Northern Division, on the ship. He knew me and Huerta. As at that moment he was coming toward us, I thought he had recognized me, but seeing this was not the case, I got up with great unconcern and said to Carlos in a low voice, "Let's go, boy. Let's get away from here." We got off the ship and lost ourselves in the streets of the town.

Having little time to spend in Manzanillo and knowing of no other ship that would be leaving, I urged Carlos to return to the *Ramón Corral* and secure a stateroom at any price. He was to say that the lawyer Martínez was ill and in need of a private room. The arrangements were made, and for fifty pesos the steward let me have his stateroom for the twelve-hour voyage. On the ship again, I retired to the little room and Carlitos remained on the upper deck, with orders to keep José Delgado in view and communicate with me every half-hour. But he became seasick, and could not do his part, and I spent anxious hours in the stateroom. Then something unforeseen occurred. We reached port not the night announced but the following day, and that presented a complication. I had to appear on deck with the other passengers for medical inspection. The last thing in the world I wanted to do was to meet José

Delgado, who would certainly recognize me. I exaggerated my illness and laid out money to get the doctors to visit me in the stateroom.

Happily, when they saw I could pay for consideration, they asked whether I wished to disembark before the others, and as I answered yes and gave them a few pesos for a good boat, I left the ship under their protection while José Delgado and the others were detained by I know not how many regulations.

CHAPTER 23

Villa Escapes to the United States and Again Offers His Services to Madero.

Mazatlán. To the United States. Guaymas. The Immigration Agent. Nogales. An Embrace. Tucson. El Paso. Don Abraham González. The Insurrection. Horses and Arms. José Muñiz. Don José María Maytorena. The Agency's Horses.

In Mazatlán I concealed myself as best I could at the waterfront and waited for Carlitos. When he joined me, I said, "This is a country I know, my boy, and I know the right hotel for us. While I am getting a room, follow José Delgado. See where he stays and what he does."

I took a room with an exit on two streets. In a little while Carlitos arrived with his report, "Delgado is resting. I know what he is doing and where he is going. Now I want to go out and see Mazatlán."

"Which hotel is José Delgado staying in?"

"This one, my General."

"This same one?"

"Yes, my General."

"My friend, this Delgado is following me. He has recognized me and is figuring how he can gain a reward. If he finds me, I am lost. So I have a plan. Invite him to take a walk on Las Olas Áltas. I will meet you there, and we'll shoot it out."

"My General, if Delgado was following you, your plan would be a good one. But you should not go so far on a mere supposition. Up till now everything has turned out well, thanks to our prudence, which we must not abandon. Leave Delgado alone and keep out of sight." With Carlitos' good judgment and calm mind, he convinced me he was right. I was not looking for trouble and decided to let José Delgado go his own way as long as he did not cross ours.

"Very well, my boy, and where is he going?"

"He says he is going to Hermosillo to take charge of the telegraph office."

Since it was my intention to go on horseback from Mazatlán to Durango, Delgado's trip in the other direction relieved me of my worries. But Carlitos could not find my friend's butcher shop. I was expecting this friend to furnish me with horses and saddles for the trip. As it then seemed less dangerous to go north by railroad than to get horses and saddles in some other way, I decided against Durango. At four the next morning I left the hotel and had breakfast in the market district, where I was lost in the crowds. When I joined Carlitos at the station, the train was ready to leave. We got on the Pullman at once, and I shut myself in a compartment. We made the trip in a couple of days without serious incident. Carlitos was watching Delgado, who was on the train, and observed nothing suspicious from Mazatlán to Guaymas, where the fellow left us.

In Magdalena the immigration agent boarded the train. When he knocked I let him into the compartment. Seeing an official before me, I started to reach for my pistols, but thought better of it and kept quiet.

"Where are you from, Señor?"

"From Mazatlán."

"A native of Mazatlán?"

"No, Señor, I was born in Durango and raised in Mazatlán."

"Occupation?"

"Farming and cattle raising."

"You own property?"

"A hacienda."

"The name of it?"

"Santa Susana, Señor."

"I have heard of it. And your name, Señor?"

"Jesús José Martínez."

"Sign here, with your mark." I wrote the name "Jesús José Martínez" and made the first mark that occurred to me.

At Nogales, I said to Carlitos, "We are going to get off before the train stops. Just follow me." There was no need to respect international regulations. It was cold and snowing a little and I could wrap myself up. According to my memory it was January 2, 1913. After a few meters we crossed the street they call the International Line. I stopped, looked at Carlitos, and said, "We are in the United States." He looked surprised; I continued, "Yes, my friend, in the United States. You see those streets over there? That is Mexico. You see these? This is the United States. I am safe and secure now. Come, an embrace!"

After four days in Tucson we went to El Paso, where six days later I wrote to Don Abraham González: "Don Abraham: I am safe and sound in El Paso, Texas, where I am at your orders. I am the same Pancho Villa as ever. Give the President a report on my actions. If my presence is harmful to my country, I will remain in the United States. But I am ready to serve him."

Don Abraham replied: "Be patient, do not come to Mexico. It would compromise us. I am expecting all the President's friends to meet him at the Río Bravo."

Seeing that they were living in a dream, I begged Don Abraham to send someone to talk to me in person. Sr. Aurelio González came with authority to discuss whatever I wished. When I told him what was happening, he advised me to stay out of Chihuahua, saying, "I have instructions to pay your salary according to your rank."

I replied, "Good. If you will, just make me a loan of 1,500 pesos. The salary you give me would quickly come to an end, but the 1,500 pesos will last longer than you can hold Chihuahua."

They gave me the 1,500 pesos, and Don Aurelio González returned to Chihuahua. In a few days there were rumors of Huerta's coup in Mexico City. Expecting a like upset in Chihuahua, I bought rifles, saddles, and horses with the money and 3,000 pesos more that I borrowed from my brother. When I had everything ready, I learned of the overthrow of Chihuahua. To José Muñiz, who had my horses in Ciudad Juárez and to whom I had given 300 pesos to pasture them, I said, "Bring me the horses now."

He replied that he would send them that afternoon, but he sent nothing and the next day came and said that the colonel had him under surveillance and it would be impossible to deliver the horses. "Very well, Don José. In view of what you tell me, I will have to go to work. Give me back the 300 pesos." I added, "I am going to California to work on the railroad." He said, "I will bring you the money." But naturally he didn't return.

In Tucson I talked with Don José María Maytorena, who had just arrived from Sonora and at that time was one of the good Revolutionaries. He gave me one thousand Mexican pesos with the understanding that his men would move in Sonora and mine in Chihuahua. In El Paso, where I could buy only nags for the money I had, and lacking three of the nine we needed, I told Darío Silva and Carlitos Jáuregui, "We have to have three horses. Go to the agency, hire them for two days, and pay in advance."

They did. For three days they paid without delay. At the end of that time, I said, "Hire them for four in the afternoon. We cross the river at dark."

The rest of the horses were on the other side, and everything was ready for our march.

BOOK **2** *Battlefields*

CHAPTER 1

Villa Crosses the Frontier with Eight Men and Prepares for the Conquest of Chihuahua, Now Ruled by Rábago.

The First Nine Men. Encarnación Enríquez. Fidel Avila. The Ambush at Chavarría. Isaac's Telegrams. Sonoloapa. Bachiniva. Casas Grandes. Corralitos. La Ascensión. Juan Dozal. Juan N. Medina. Juan Sánchez Azcona. Alvaro Obregón. Villa's Reasoning. Respect for Women. Cannons at Hermosillo.

At Los Partidos I crossed the river. The nine of us, armed and mounted, crossed about nine at night. We were: Manuel Ochoa, now a lieutenant colonel; Miguel Saavedra, now a major; Darío Silva, now a second captain; Carlos Jáuregui, now an ensign: Tomás N., now deceased, shot by the Federation; Juan Dozal, now a colonel; Pedro Sapién, killed in taking Torreón; another whose name I do not remember, and Pancho Villa, chief of the Northern Division.

We had breakfast at Ojo de Samalayuca. At seven that night we stopped near Las Amarguras. In three days we reached the Hacienda del Carmen; in five, the Hacienda del Jacinto, near Rubio; and in seven, San Andrés. When Encarnación Enríquez, the president of the town, wanted to know what was happening, it was because I was already in his office. He saw me before him, armed and seconded, and got up to give me a hearty greeting.

I said, "You were appointed by Don Abraham González. Do you support Huerta?"

"No, Señor. I am ready to help you as much as I can." Trusting him, I went on to Chavarría. But I was to find that he broke his promises. At Chavarría I enlisted Andrés Rivera with fourteen men, well armed and mounted, among them my two brothers. With them I went to Santa Isabel, where I sent a telegram to General Rábago: "Sr. General Rábago: Knowing that the government you represent was preparing to extradite me, I have saved them the trouble. I am now in Mexico, ready to make war upon you. Francisco Villa."

From Santa Isabel we proceeded to San Juan de la Santa Veracruz.

There about sixty men from Ciénaga de Ortiz and nearby ranches joined me. I went to Satevó and from Satevó sent for Colonel Fidel Avila who, being a loyal friend, came at once.

I said, "Compadre, the struggle begins again. I need your help. Gather troops in San José and Santa María de Cuevas while I see how many I can recruit in Pilar de Conchos and Valle de Rosario." I got 250 men, and when I returned to join him, he had 180.

I said, "Stay here with the men, Compadre, and keep on recruiting. I will go to Carretas and San Lorenzo." I scouted these towns and enlisted 400 men.

While in search of troops, I encountered a passenger train below Chavarría; as the circumstances were favorable I ambushed and took it without trouble. In the baggage car I found 122 bars of silver; and in a passenger car Juan Dozal recognized a certain Isaac, whose last name I do not remember. His brief case contained telegrams from General Rábago ordering him to report with the armament in his possession. We took him off the train and I had him shot. To protect the silver I brought the train back to San Andrés. But the municipal president was no longer a friend. He had a large force under his orders, and seeing me arrive with only twenty-five men, he attacked. Undiscouraged, we answered in kind, pushed him back into the town, and were able to hold. His defended position stopped our advance, but I would not abandon the field without further effort against a man who only a short time before was professing friendship and now was betraying it.

The night passed in hard fight, in which their numbers offset our spirit. They might get reinforcements and I would lose the silver. They had already killed seven of my men, whereas we had killed only three of theirs; I decided to withdraw. We made it to a mountain called Sonoloapa, each soldier carrying a bar of silver.

On the road from there to Bachiniva one of the men wounded at San Andrés died and we buried him before continuing to Valle, unencumbered, for we had buried the silver, too. In Casas Grandes, our next halt, we came upon a part of José Inés Salazar's forces, about four hundred men. When they fired I laid siege to the place, expecting to make a violent assault that night. After dark, I said, "Boys, not one step back. We won't stop until we are inside." Within two hours we took the railroad station and some corrals they had fortified. I lost several of my compañeros, but forty of Salazar's men were killed, and we took sixty prisoners. The rest fled under cover of the night.

When we broke camp the next day we saw that Colonel Azcárate, their chief, was among the dead. I formed the sixty prisoners in files three deep and had them shot in that formation, to save ammunition by killing three with one shot. We threw the hundred-odd bodies into a well at the edge of town.

When we had done this a young lady appeared and said to Juan Dozal, "I am Colonel Azcárate's daughter. Is my father dead, Señor?"

Dozal replied, "Yes, Señorita."

"And my brother?"

"Yes, Señorita."

"Did they die in action?"

"Yes, Señorita."

"Then, they died honorably. Adios, Señores," and she left without another word.

We marched to Ascensión, which we reached by way of Corralitos. As there was not a single soul in sight, we thought it deserted. The inhabitants were Pascual Orozco's supporters. But after a couple of days they began to return, first the men, then the women, and finally the young ladies. They came to trust us so unquestioningly that before long the women were cooking for us.

I was organizing and equipping my troops for future action. One day I said to Juan Dozal, "Juan, go to Agua Prieta. Arrange for Plutarco Elías Calles to send me what ammunition he can and I will pay for it with cattle." He replied that he was ready but wanted his brother to go with him. I said no, that I needed his brother and persuaded him to go alone. From Agua Prieta they sent me 35,000 cartridges, which only moderately supplied my forces. So I said, "Go back and see if you can get more, and tell them to send me one thousand men. Tell them I will take Ciudad Juárez."

"Let me take my brother."

"The other day I wouldn't let you take him because I thought you would not return."

"I am more of a man than that."

I permitted him to take his brother and one hundred men to bring me all the ammunition I needed. The result was that a few days later I received this letter: "I am here with my brother and family. You let your brothers command you and your subordinates deceive you. Therefore I am returning to private life. I renounce the Revolution. Your humble servant. Juan Dozal." Meditating on the duplicity of men, even of those who seem closest and most constant, I resolved to be less kind in the future.

Juan N. Medina came to join me in La Ascensión. He was an educated man and an officer with great knowledge of war. He had written
to say he wanted to join us, and I had replied, "Come quickly and bring
plenty of courage." These last words, it turned out, were unnecessary.
In truth, Medina, like a number of Federals, was braver than many
Revolutionaries. Not only did he know how to train armies but he was
also ready to risk his life. I learned to have great confidence in him, and
many times followed his advice. With his arrival many of the services
began to improve. When he was the officer of the day, I would say, "Tonight we can sleep with our shoes off."

To La Ascensión came also some men sent by Don Venustiano Carranza, now the First Chief of the Constitutionalist Army. I never could
understand why this gentleman was our chief and I understood it still
less since he had just shown in his own district that he knew nothing
about war. He had begun his action in the state capital but now had no
seat for his government and his forces were failing to make any concentrated efforts. Still, Don Juan Sánchez Azcona and Alfredo Breceda
maintained that I was wrong, "Unity is necessary to our purpose. If each
leader independently carries on his own movement, you in Chihuahua,
Carranza in Coahuila, Maytorena in Sonora, we will never re-establish
legality and justice, we will only lose ourselves in anarchy."

"Yes, Señor, I agree, but I think unity can be achieved without sub-
jecting my forces and other Revolutionary troops in Chihuahua to generals from other states." Sr. Carranza, with the rank of First Chief of
the Constitutionalist Army, named General Obregón, who is not from
Chihuahua, to command the forces in our state as well as his own in
Sonora. My chief was going to be a man quite ignorant of my movements and in no position to follow my action, which was as much of an
error as if I, with no knowledge of events in Sonora, should be appointed
as Obregón's chief.

Sánchez Azcona replied that my liberty of movement was a thing
that could be arranged; in his opinion they should consider the peculiar
problems of my campaign, but it must be clear that I recognized the
Plan of Guadalupe as the others did and accepted Carranza as First
Chief.

I replied, "Tell Carranza that I do accept the Plan of Guadalupe and
recognize him as First Chief; but I will not tolerate meddling in my
sphere of action, and if I need generals I will appoint them myself."

He said he would so inform Carranza. He added that we must all
honor the Revolution and in the name of Carranza he recommended

that I hold a tight rein on my troops, to bring atrocities to an end. I said, "Señor, that is a slander upon my troops. Here nobody robs. Whatever is taken is taken by my order, to support the campaign. We need horses, arms, saddles, cattle, and money, and we take them whenever we find them. But this is not robbery; it is war."

He answered, "We do not doubt the honesty or the authority of Pancho Villa. What the First Chief recommends is respect for women."

"That too is slander. Men and women naturally seek each other out. The women do what they do voluntarily. I admit that sometimes a man goes to excess, but that is no basis for condemning my troops. I invite you to visit the houses in the town and inquire whether any woman has been injured by my soldiers. You can add in your report that this is the enemy's town and when we arrived there was not a young woman who hadn't already belonged to some Orozquista or other."

My words persuaded him, and as I had received him cordially, and he was a good friend of Don José María Maytorena, and Sr. Madero had great confidence in him, we became the best of friends. I gave him and the man who accompanied him the best lodging possible and showed them every courtesy, since they were the representatives of the Commander in Chief.

When Sánchez Azcona was ready to leave, I said, "They tell me you have cannon you are unable to use in Sonora. Tell Maytorena to send them to me. I have artillerymen who can make good use of them." He replied that it was true, that they had left the cannon in Hermosillo, and that he and Maytorena would arrange some way to send them to me.

CHAPTER 2

The Revolutionaries of Chihuahua, Coahuila, and Durango Appoint Villa Chief of the Northern Division.

San Buenaventura. Toribio Ortega. José Eleuterio Hermosillo. Félix Terrazas. San Andrés. Juan N. Medina. Encarnación Márquez. Natividad Rivera. Santiago Ramírez. Santa Rosalía. Maclovio Herrera. Manuel Chao. Jiménez. Urbina. Fierro. Rueda Quijano. Assistance for Carranza. The Nazas River. Avilés. The Death of General Alvírez.

After a month and a half in Ascensión I had some seven hundred men, well mounted, well armed, and supplied with sufficient ammunition. I began the action I was planning by marching to San Buenaventura, where Toribio Ortega joined me with his forces from Cuchillo Parado. I appointed him second-in-command of my brigade and José Eleuterio Hermosillo my chief of staff. We left for Bachiniva in full force, intending to attack General Félix Terrazas in San Andrés. Terrazas' forces, as I knew from scouts, exceeded mine in number and equipment, but I thought, "We must succeed by valor, not numbers."

And so it was. After a march of a day and night, resting only when it was absolutely necessary, we were opposite San Andrés, having evaded Terrazas' advance troops. The action began against Orozquistas fortified in Puente de Aldama. I avoided devastating the town, for the inhabitants had favored the cause of the Revolution and of justice since the days of Sr. Madero. We fought until five that afternoon. At that hour, seeing the advantage they had in their strong position, I said to Colonel Medina, "Sr. Colonel, we cannot advance as long as the artillery keeps on bombarding us." He agreed, and I continued, "Then silence the cannon." He did as I ordered. The enemy were brave but so was Medina. He was skilful and had good men under him and daring officers, Benito Artalejo, his second-in-command, Captain Eduardo H. Marín, and another of English ancestry, a certain Hondall or Jontal. We took two cannons, and with the enemy thus weakened I was able to make a full-scale attack by dark and overcome them. By two in the morning, with his forces routed, Terrazas had fled in a locomotive, and San Andrés was ours, with several trainloads of provisions and other supplies.

In this action, on August 26, 1913, according to my memory, I lost

Encarnación Márquez, a close friend for whom I wept. Natividad Rivera and many other Revolutionaries were killed. Among the wounded was Santiago Ramírez, a member of my staff. But the victory was useful. It helped me to organize and supply my forces and raised their morale to a level that never afterwards declined.

We stayed in San Andrés only long enough to reorganize, since they were sure to send forces from Chihuahua against us. Part of the supplies we captured I distributed among the families in the town. I sent the wounded to Madera, to go on to Sonora under escort of Fidel Avila and seventy-five men. With the rest I prepared to turn south along the sierra. I was expecting to make gains that would lead the enemy astray; I wanted to entice them into following false leads. Such is the strategy of revolution, not to conquer territory first and then defend it, but to rout the armies of the government, weakened by the obligation to defend. There were different opinions as to our tactics. Medina said, "It doesn't seem wise, my General, to go into combat now. Remember, we have only 150 men in our artillery." But others, like Toribio Ortega, thought we could lie in wait for the enemy and defeat them. There was even someone who said that if the cannon were only going to impede some of the men, it was better to abandon them, which shows how ignorant some military men can be. Seeing that Medina was right, I confused the enemy by passing Bustillos and heading for Santa Rosalía de Camargo.

In this maneuver I again joined forces with Fidel Avila, who brought me 200,000 cartridges from Sonora; and in Camargo Maclovio Herrera brought four hundred men from Parral. Meanwhile I sent for Manuel Chao, but he did not come, insisting that an intelligent man was needed in Parral. The truth is that Carranza, who had passed through that region on his way to Sonora, had sown discord among the Revolutionaries, promising commands or posts to some when they rightly belonged to others. I thought to myself, "The man irritates everyone wherever he goes and then sends sermons on unity. By 'unity' he means obeying him and waiting upon his decisions."

I took advantage of my stop in Santa Rosalía to reorganize my brigade in line with our plans. Because of his military knowledge and aptitude for command, I promoted Medina to chief of staff in title, as he already was in fact.

We resumed our march south to Jiménez. There Tomás Urbina joined me, coming from Durango with six hundred well-equipped and well-organized men. He had taken Durango and sacked it and was loaded with gold. With him he brought Rodolfo Fierro, and he had appointed Rueda Quijano paymaster of these forces so well supplied with money. Urbina said, "You see, Compadre, how well provided I am. Well, then, Carranza asked me to contribute something to his trip to Sonora, and I could not refuse. I gave him sixty pesos and a saddle I had no use for. Did I do right, Compadre?" I had to laugh.

In Jiménez we organized for an advance on Torreón, where the government had a division under General Munguía. We proceeded by train to Bermejillo and then marched to La Goma, on the Nazas River, where the forces would cross that were to follow the right bank to Torreón. The river being at flood stage, I had the artillery and baggage carried across on a raft that we found. On one of the trips a cable broke and my automobile was carried away by the current.

After Urbina's forces and mine had crossed the river we encountered advance troops of the enemy on both sides. On the left bank they had a column of one thousand men under Emilio P. Campa and Argumedo, and another thousand on the right bank under Felipe J. Alvírez.

At the Hacienda de la Loma, on the right bank facing La Goma, we prepared to attack; but first I called a meeting of the principal commanders, for I thought, "This is not just my brigade. We likewise have the forces of Urbina, Maclovio Herrera, Calixto Contreras, Aguirre Benavides, Yuriar, and Juan E. García. Hereafter we must have a single chief for concerted action." Medina supported my opinion. He thought our forces should be organized into a division, and pointed out the chances of failure if we did not organize. At the meeting I asked him to draw up a plan. The result, after discussion, was that they agreed with him, and from that moment on I, Pancho Villa, was commander of the Northern Division, created in this manner.

This was on September 29, 1913. On that date I constituted the division according to Medina's principles. I surmised and soon learned for sure that it displeased Urbina for me to be commander instead of him. He was a man of courage and ability, but he would not have made a better chief than I. I had the true spirit of a Revolutionary and he did not, or, at least, I was more devoted than he was to the cause of the people.

While we were meeting, Campa's column began a bombardment and I ordered my forces into combat immediately. These were my orders: my brigade would march on Avilés along the right bank of the Nazas; Maclovio Herrera's forces, the Juárez Brigade, would advance on Lerdo and Gómez Palacio along the left bank of the river so as to cover me on that flank; the Morelos Brigade, under Tomás Urbina would march on my right, separated from me by some small hills, with orders to make for my objective, Avilés.

It all followed as planned. At ten in the morning the engagement began, and by one in the afternoon we were at Avilés, where we met General Alvírez with his sappers, *rurales,* and artillery. They were well fortified and protected, but our push was that of an army anticipating victory. They could not stop us. Within half an hour I took the town by fire and sword. They lost half of their men and almost all their officers, their artillery, and their General. That afternoon, as we were pouring into the plaza, I came upon General Alvírez' dead body, stripped of clothing. There was nothing to show he had commanded armies and fought bravely to the last. It grieved me to see how impossible it is in war for a chief to prevent the most wanton excesses.

That day the enemy lost about five hundred men, Federals and Orozquistas, besides the nineteen officers I took as prisoners and ordered shot immediately, according to the Law of January 25 issued by the First Chief of the Constitutionalist Army. Elías Torres also fell into our hands, along with officers of the artillery whom Medina saved from death when they agreed to join us. We needed them.

In Avilés we took 2 cannons, 600 guns, 150,000 cartridges, and 360 grenades, and meanwhile, on the left bank, Maclovio Herrera had driven Emilio P. Campa's forces all the way from the Hacienda de la Goma to Lerdo, and had taken their artillery.

CHAPTER 3

Villa Takes Torreón and Prepares for His Advance on Chihuahua and Ciudad Juárez.

El Cañón del Huarache. The Revolutionary Artillery. Blas Flores. Manuel Madinabeitia. A Night Attack. Pedro Sapién. Elías Uribe. José Díaz. Moments of Victory and Defeat. Lázaro de la Garza. Brothers of Freemasonry. Plot against the Life of Villa. General Cuder.

The next afternoon at three I headed for Torreón with the forces of Generals Calixto Contreras, Eugenio Aguirre Benavides, Benjamín Yuriar, and Colonel Juan E. García.

At five the fighting became general and we forced the enemy back to their fortifications in the Cañón del Huarache, an opening between the highlands and the Cerro de Calabazas. But we pushed on to a position for our artillery which, under the officers we had taken in Avilés, now began to damage the artillery in El Huarache. And while we were gaining ground on the right bank of the Nazas, Maclovio Herrera and his brigade, with the forces of Contreras and García, were pushing the Orozquistas under Argumedo and Campa back to La Pila on the other bank.

The enemy held El Huarache until three in the morning. Under cover of darkness we entered, leaving our horses outside and scaling the hillsides on foot. In the advance they wounded Blas Flores, who died soon afterward. He was my friend; he had accompanied me to Mexico City. Many others were killed, and many wounded, among them Manuel Madinabeitia, who was on my staff. The enemy were making a valiant defense. But by three they could resist no longer. They abandoned the canyon to us and dug in on La Cruz and in strong trenches at San Joaquín. This was the situation at daybreak. That day we merely held our gains and stopped all counterattacks. I wanted to learn their weak points.

In the afternoon we had to resupply our right wing, inspect their position, and encourage them. This was where resistance would be most stubborn. Medina even climbed the hillside to make sure of the terrain. In the final assault at nine that night I ordered the soldiers forward on foot, bareheaded, with right arms raised. On the night of October 1, 1913, then, my forces rushed forward in a furious enveloping movement and within half an hour the plaza was in our hands. In the darkness the enemy had abandoned their positions and left the town. But they would not have escaped a decisive defeat if the floodwaters had not prevented Herrera from following them eastward.

Pedro Sapién, who was killed, was one of the eight who had come back across the Río Bravo with me. Elías Uribe and José Díaz and many other Revolutionaries were killed, and there were so many wounded I cannot remember them all. We got possession of eleven cannons, three hundred grenades, the artillery piece called "El Niño" with its iron carriage and accessories, more than three hundred guns, half a million cartridges, six machine guns, forty engines, and much railway equipment.

The enemy losses in men were 800 dead, almost all Orozquistas; 120 prisoners; and a great many wounded. I had the officers shot according to the Law of January 25, which Sr. Carranza ordered us to observe, but I sent their wounded to our hospitals.

Taking Torreón was important, as it supplied us with materials and enabled me to prepare my forces for winning important towns later. I would soon have to abandon it but even so, my being there at all, when the Federals considered me incapable of such an effort, would undermine their confidence and encourage Revolutionary action. Seeing that I had taken Torreón by skilful marches from San Andrés, without any support on the frontier and with Chihuahua and Ciudad Juárez at my back, they would throw their greatest strength against me in the center of the Republic, and pressure on the Revolutionary troops in the northeast, who were suffering defeat after defeat under Pablo González, would be lessened. To my right, the forces of Obregón in the northwest and those of Iturbe in Sinaloa would find it easier to advance.

I entered on October 1, at ten at night. The people shouted for Sr. Madero, my troops, and me. But I had no time for celebrating and ordered Medina to provide for the safety and protection of the inhabitants. I had the troops of Aguirre Benavides, Yuriar, and Urbina cover the plaza and serve as advance guard. The main body of the troops I left in La Cruz until dawn. Though the enemy was in flight it was not time to relax. In war a general must be as watchful in triumph as in defeat. Carelessness may be more costly than the bloodiest battle.

While there I had my headquarters in the Hotel Salvador. The people followed me everywhere with demonstrations of affection. Not on account of this but as a Revolutionary I responded by visiting the poor and having clothing and food distributed. I sent aid to the nuns in the hospitals. I ordered supplies brought in from wherever they might be

found and required a loan of 300,000 pesos from the banks, and to receive it and manage it I appointed Lázaro de la Garza, who was said
to be experienced in such matters.

Injustices perpetrated by Huerta's forces I ordered corrected, and the
perpetrators punished. But in fear of punishment they had gone into
hiding, and now they sent Aguirre Benavides and Medina and a group
of Masons to treat with me. The Masons said, "Sr. General, we come in
the name of our great brotherhood, whose mission is charity and justice.
We help the poor and the destitute and consider all men our brothers,
and the fate of any one of them is our concern. Therefore, we ask you
to have mercy on our accused brothers. Consider, Sr. General, that even
if they committed an error they deserve mercy. The Great Architect and
Creator of the world put goodness into our hearts, and we must not
consent to let evil take over."

I replied, "Gentlemen, you are either lying or you mistake your duty,
and Masonry is either not what you assure me it is, or you are not practic-
ing it. Why, before my arrival, did you exert no influence to prevent the
death of our Revolutionary brothers? Why do you defend the rich and
not the poor? Why do you abandon those who support the people and
favor the party of tyranny and usurpation? Make no appeals in the
name of humanity unless you want to see your brothers receive firing-
squad justice." With that I ordered them out of my sight.

From Torreón I decided to return to Chihuahua at once and, the
other chiefs agreeing, I instructed Medina to arrange for the march to
the north. We had not yet decided whether to storm the capital or
merely to threaten it with part of our forces while the rest moved to
make a surprise attack on Ciudad Juárez. Contreras' brigade was to remain in Torreón, and I left him in command. Other troops, perhaps those
of José Isabel Robles, were to join him in a reconnaissance toward Saltillo. Those going north with me were Yuriar's men and Aguirre Benavides' Zaragoza Brigade. We were on the road to Jiménez for three or
four days, accompanied by the trains, full or empty, except one which
might be needed by Contreras. Huertistas from Chihuahua, who had advanced when we moved on Torreón, were now retreating northward as
we advanced in that direction.

In Jiménez Medina finally accepted appointment as chief of staff and
energetically began to organize a division. In him the chiefs of brigades
and the corps had a critic to follow their work in detail, not just in the
mass, which is all the general in chief sees. There would no longer be
such waste. Everything would be set down on paper, signed and carried

as records: so many leaders, so many officers, so many troops, so many horses—payment for so much and nothing more—without the omission of an item.

Some of the chiefs complained, "Papers, just like the Federation."

I answered, "No, my friends, not like the Federation. The Federation cannot keep its papers in order and loses battles. We can." They grew accustomed to it, although inwardly a little resentful.

While I was in Jiménez, Lázaro de la Garza telegraphed that the bankers in Torreón refused to deliver the full amount of the loan. I took an engine and returned. At a meeting at the Banco Nacional I reminded them that I was not playing games. The money belonged to the nation that produced it. The people could take it when they needed it, and I could seize not only the amount of the loan but everything in the banks and outside too, if necessary. There was no more trouble.

At the meeting there was a plot to take my life. Learning the details from trusted friends, I sent General Díaz Cuder and several others to Jiménez to be shot. But later, after investigation, it appeared that Díaz Cuder was innocent, a victim of the actual conspirators. My duties left no time for protracted trials. I only called my bodyguards and said, "Keep close watch, avoid incidents and false accusations. I want no disaffection in the ranks."

CHAPTER 4

Villa Tries To Take Chihuahua, Fails, and Prepares for the Attack on Ciudad Juárez.

Jiménez. Santa Rosalía. The Shooting of Yuriar. Urbina. Manuel Chao. Rosalío Hernández. Four Days of Fighting at Chihuahua. Dr. Samuel Navarro. Eduardo H. Marín. Santa Eulalia.

Four days in Jiménez were spent in resting the horses and troops and organizing for an advance on Santa Rosalía, which was part of my plan. From there I would proceed against Chihua-

hua, an attack about which my generals were divided in opinion. Medina was against it. "We ought not to try it, my General. Chihuahua is
not Torreón. In Torreón three-fourths of the enemy were inexperienced
Federals. In Chihuahua, three-fourths of them are Orozquistas, veterans
like our own troops. Chihuahua will not be taken without a siege and
we lack the men and the ammunition for that."

He was right. But I saw the enemy fleeing before me and his spirit
broken. I thought, "Even if we fail we will win respect for trying." I
considered the many times I had overcome forces that already had me
in their power and decided to attack whatever it cost.

When we were ready to set out, Medina said, "We should leave Tomás
Urbina behind, although he is brave and a good organizer. We need his
troops, but he is a troublemaker. We are close to the frontier, my General, and nothing must happen to turn the United States against us." I
saw that he was right and called Urbina and said, "Compadre, I must
take all my troops north, but someone like you must stay behind to
warn me of any danger."

He answered, "Very well, Compadre. I will remain here with an
escort. Take my troops and win victories for the cause." To keep him
content I left directions with a staff officer to supply him with money
and whatever else he required.

In Santa Rosalía I was joined by Rosalío Hernández with his "Loyalists of Camargo," and also by General Manuel Chao. It was there that
General Yuriar tried to rebel against me. I had him arrested and shot.
Medina had prepared an indictment against him, but I said, "Amigo, I
have no time for such papers. If a soldier or an officer is insubordinate,
I shoot him without delay. If you want to have a court martial, do so
and decide whether my act was good or bad according to military
policy."

It took us five days in Santa Rosalía to prepare for the advance on
Chihuahua. I was giving all my attention to this and what would follow.
I had planned for Jáuregui and my brother Hipólito to take 300,000
pesos across the frontier at Ojinaga and buy arms and ammunition in
the United States. But Major Trinidad Rodríguez informed me that he
had not brought the full amount from Torreón. He said, "General Urbina
stopped me and asked me what I was carrying. When I showed him the
300,000 pesos for you, he took 100,000 and sent me on with the rest."
On hearing this, I thought, "God help me! My compadre is always doing
these things," but it was an injury to the cause, and my anger boiled

over. I ordered Trinidad Rodríguez to return and fetch the 100,000 pesos even if he had to take it by force. This he did.

Just before our departure from Santa Rosalía, Ortega came to see me and said, "Medina wants to attack Juárez instead of Chihuahua because he is popular there and hopes to be considered the victor." On hearing this Medina said, "If that is what he thinks, my General, put him in charge of the staff and let me command your troops at Chihuahua."

Ortega had chosen a bad moment. I had wanted to promote José Rodríguez, Medina, and Ortega to brigadiers and had told them so. But thinking it would be bad to advance two from my brigade and none from others, Medina generously agreed to the postponement of his own promotion. So I replied, "Yes, Señor, you shall command my brigade at Chihuahua and Ortega shall occupy your post."

From Santa Rosalía we reached Ortiz in three days, and the next day, when we were in Consuelo, I addressed a letter to the defenders of Chihuahua, requesting them in the politest of terms to surrender within twenty-four hours, or if they preferred to come out and fight in a spot of their own choosing. Signing with me were Herrera, commander of the Juárez Brigade: Aguirre Benavides, commander of the Zaragoza Brigade; José Rodríguez, commander of the Morelos Brigade; Hernández, commander of the Loyalists of Camargo; Chao, chief of artillery; and Medina, my chief of staff.

On the fourth I approached Avalos, still on the railroad line. As the enemy had not surrendered or come out to fight, the next morning I prepared to attack. This was my plan: Herrera and Aguirre Benavides would enter by Chuvízcar dam; the Juárez Brigade, under José Rodríguez, and Hernández' brigade would advance on the right; on the extreme left the Villa Brigade, under Medina, would attack El Cerro Grande and El Cerro Colonel. The artillery, under Chao, would be placed in the center. One hundred meters away, with the rear guard, would be headquarters.

That morning Chao and Aguirre Benavides, influenced, I believe, by Medina, came to say it would be best to merely hold the enemy there by deceit and make a sudden advance on Ciudad Juárez. But though I was sure of taking Juárez whenever we attempted it, I said, "Even if we fail here it will be good for the cause." They agreed and approved.

In the late afternoon of November 5 we were facing Chihuahua. The enemy had three cannons on El Cerro de Santa Rosa, and infantry on Cerro Grande and Cerro Colonel. Commanding were Orozco, Caraveo,

Salazar, and Rojas, Revolutionaries turned traitors. The Federals, in addition to covering the artillery on Santa Rosa, were occupying other positions.

The battle began before seven. We invited counterattack, although we knew the struggle would be hard. The fighting spread and grew so violent that by ten that night we had already taken Cerro Grande and Cerro Colonel, and had broken their lines as far as Chuvízcar. We were able to do this because the moonlight was almost as bright as day and nothing could stop the onslaught of my brigade under Medina. In the moonlight I could see my men falling on the enemy positions and taking them. Thus we continued throughout the night.

The next day the artillery on Santa Rosa halted us at every point we had reached. By eleven, Herrera's advance was stopped when Orozco, Caraveo, and Salazar had him almost surrounded, and his losses were heavy. I sent Aguirre Benavides' brigade to save him, which weakened us and upset my plan. In the remaining daylight we could do no more than hold our own, and at nightfall it took all our strength to repel their efforts to dislodge us.

The third day we carried the fight through the morning. As we could not advance in the face of their cannon, I saw that nothing could be done except to fill them with fear of what might happen under less favorable circumstances, and to retire without further serious losses. That night, the third of the battle, we withdrew by sections to the south and pitched camp at Alberto and Santa Eulalia.

The next day at dawn the enemy bombarded the positions we had abandoned. Then, seeing that we no longer occupied them, they came out, certain that they could now fight us in the open field. But this was the change of circumstances I had been looking for, and we threw ourselves upon them with so much fury that within two hours we had driven them back into Chihuahua, not to come out again or make another effort to molest us.

In the battle at Chihuahua, which, as I remember, took place on November 5, 6, 7, 8 of 1913, Dr. Samuel Navarro was killed. Many other Revolutionaries were also killed, among them Eduardo H. Marín. Dr. Navarro died while he was talking to me. I had moved several steps away to receive a dispatch. A grenade exploded at his feet and would have killed Ortega also if he had not wanted to hear the dispatch and followed me from where the three of us had been sitting. Aguirre Benavides performed gallantly in leading his troops to the defense of Herrera, whom he saved from destruction. My brigade, under Medina, and

Hernández' brigade were the only ones to report "without incident" the second day of the combat, the day the fighting was hardest.

I was right to attempt the action. It inclined the enemy to risk disputing that victory with me at a time and place which gave me the opportunity for a death blow.

CHAPTER 5

In a Daring Move Villa Passes up Chihuahua and Takes Ciudad Juárez by Surprise.

The Plan of Attack. Chao, the Infantry, and the Women. The Copper Foundry. A Coal Train. A Telegrapher. El Sauz. "K." Laguna Station. Moctezuma. Samalayuca. Juárez. General Castro. Major Topete. Leonardo Samaniego.

One morning in Charco I said to my generals and colonels, "Amigos, now is our chance. We will pretend to attack Chihuahua again, approaching as it grows dark. Then, by night, we will make a forced march to the Hacienda del Sauz, or to the Copper Foundry, which is nearby. Leaving 1,500 men there to support the line and destroy the bridges, and with the cavalry, or some 2,000 in all, we can take Juárez without wasting a step. Then we will have more than enough force for another attack on Chihuahua. If we find a train at El Cobre or El Sauz you will see how we get into Ciudad Juárez before they even know it." They were all smiles at this, and I continued, "General Chao, you will retire to Hidalgo with the trains, infantry, and the women. Leave not a single one here."

At nightfall on November 13 I moved northward. Chao had taken the trains, the infantry, and the women, as I ordered. At ten that night we passed Chihuahua. Making a turn we circled the city and in the morning were at the Copper Foundry. Good luck brought me a coal train about five in the afternoon, and we knew it was coming in time to ambush it.

Overjoyed, I said, "Here is the train I was talking about. Juárez will be ours within twenty-four hours. Colonel Servín, have the mules un-hitched from the carts we got at the Terrazas' haciendas. Let them carry the ordnance and advance day and night up the line to Juárez. General Hernández, Colonel Ortega, Colonel Avila, and Colonel Granados, stay on the road with 2,500 men as reserves. If you can, get closer to Juárez, but no matter if you can't. General Herrera, General Rodríguez, and I, Pancho Villa, will take 2,000 men on the train. We will surprise Ciudad Juárez tonight and take it by storm."

These were my orders at eight the next morning. We took the train two hours after a telegrapher had fallen into our hands. We planned all of it thanks to reports from Timoteo Cuellar in Juárez and other Revolutionaries along the line, who kept us informed of both the move-ments of the enemy and the disposition of its forces. Señor! I even had a sketch of the barbed wire and other defenses around Ciudad Juárez.

I said to the telegrapher, "My boy, wire Juárez in your regular code. Our telegrapher will watch. If you add anything, I will know it and have you shot. Send this: 'Derailed. No line to Chihuahua. Everything burned by Revolutionaries. Send second engine and orders.'" The tele-grapher did as I said when the conductor had signed the message. I remember the conductor's last name was Velázquez.

In a few minutes Ciudad Juárez replied: "No engines. Find tools. Advise and wait for orders when back on rails."

The engine was not derailed, but had to unload coal and entrain troops. Two hours later, my two thousand men were aboard.

I told the telegrapher, "Send this: 'On tracks. No road or wire south. Big cloud of dust; perhaps Revolutionaries. Velázquez.'"

And the answer came at once: "Back in to Juárez. Wire at each station."

At El Sauz station I connected the apparatus and said, "Wire this: 'In El Sauz. Send orders. Velázquez.'"

Ciudad Juárez answered with the letter "K."

I reached Laguna station. Again I asked for orders. Juárez answered with the letter "K." My reply was: "All right." And I thought to myself, "Yes, indeed, Señores."

Three kilometers from the station in Moctezuma, I stopped the train and sent the engine on with an officer to seize the telegrapher before he could warn Juárez. At the station I wired for orders. They gave them, answering with the letter "K," and at Villa Ahumada the answer was once more "K."

At Samalayuca I issued my orders for the attack and gave the countersigns. We were to get off at the station. General Rodríguez would advance on the right and take possession of the quarters of the Orozquistas, the most dangerous, who were stationed from Zaragoza Street to the Hippodrome. Irregular forces under Major Topete had promised to help us enter eight days after we took Chihuahua, but now that we were arriving under other circumstances I could not be sure of them. I ordered Herrera to enter on the left, attack the Federals' quarters, and anchor that flank. Captain Enrique Santos Coy was to go to the center, seize the office, and close the international bridges.

Before leaving Samalayuca I placed one of my railroad men and several soldiers in the cab. I gave strict orders, saying, "Amigo, if for any reason this man does not pull into the station, kill him, take the controls, and keep the train moving."

Just before we arrived, I called Medina and said, "Amigo, you are my chief of staff. You will keep order, with an eye to international relations. And there is another thing. The Huertista chief in Juárez is General Francisco Castro. When Huerta wanted to shoot me in Jiménez, he befriended me. If he is taken, save his life and let him escape."

We reached the station about midnight. Detraining as planned, we entered single file, unstopped, and one by one gained our objectives. After two hours of fighting we were in possession of the place and had driven the enemy from their quarters and taken the bridges and the commander's office. We surrounded the forces at the jail and held them paralyzed.

When the fighting began I sent Rodolfo Fierro to go in search of our artillery. With two engines, and flatcars with supplies, he left to bring back the cannon. I remained at the station, which I converted into my headquarters. Medina, with assistants and soldiers, went to guard the banks and audit the gambling houses, which are important in Juárez for the large sums of money they handle. I can imagine the surprise of owners and players when the Revolutionary troops took over at that hour in the morning. Medina lined up employees on the right and the public on the left, and in addition to tables, equipment, and everything in the offices, took some 300,000 pesos in bills and silver.

In the morning Major Topete's forces joined me. The Orozquistas who had escaped when we entered returned a little after five to counterattack. But we now had everything under control and drove them back. They lost courage and retreated to Guadalupe. I had the dead cleared away and the wounded gathered up and sent to the hospital. At six the Federal garrison in the jail surrendered. Their bands were marched through the town to play the *diana,* not only to celebrate the victory but to calm the inhabitants and let the other side of the frontier know that quiet would follow upon our arrival.

This action, a great step forward in the Revolution, occurred November 15, 1913, a month and a half after the taking of Torreón. The fall of Juárez, at a time when I was supposed to be in central Chihuahua, broke the spirit of the enemy, and with control of that frontier I could supply my forces until the fall of the usurpers.

General Castro fled that morning to the home of the lawyer Urrutia. I gave orders not to molest him. That night he crossed the canal and went to Los Partidos to the home of Máximo Weber, the German consul. I knew this also and ordered that he be allowed to leave and go wherever he wished.

The first thing we did in Ciudad Juárez was to appoint authorities: federal, state, and city. I distributed among my troops the arms and munitions taken. I seized the money in the banks but respected private accounts. I made deals with commercial houses in El Paso to clothe and equip my forces. Revolutionaries handed me a list of 128 names. These were enemies, responsible for reprisals during the Huertista occupation. I pardoned them, since Medina and I thought best to keep our Revolution in good repute. For the same reason I had the bridges opened to anyone who wanted to leave, friend or enemy, and chose patrols unfamiliar with Juárez who would arrest or delay no one. But no merchandise or movable goods was to leave.

Herrera shot a certain Portillo because of some ancient grudge. I convinced him that he was in error here, but he was justified in killing a townsman, Ibabe, who, after the fighting had ceased, had, from the house of the Sres. Ugarte, shot two soldiers of the Juárez Brigade. Thanks to my precautions these were the only deaths, and our clemency went so far that I even extended safe-conduct to the man who had been chief of Social Defense in Ciudad Juárez—Leonardo Samaniego, as I remember.

CHAPTER 6

The Possession of Juárez Strenghens Villa, and He Prepares for His Triumphs in the South.

The Arrogance of the Three Federal Officers. Villa's Magnanimity. Mr. Kelly and Mr. White. Three Shootings. A Telephone Conversation with Carranza. Aid from the Chief. Paredes' Son. Villa and the Law. A Letter from Herrera. The Juárez Brigade. A Talk by Medina. Madero and Carranza. Rodolfo Fierro.

The artillery officers I captured in the battle of Avilés had deserted in Santa Rosalía and joined the Huertistas in Chihuahua. But they were in Ciudad Juárez when my forces took it and again fell into my hands. One was a captain whom I had promoted to major, one a lieutenant whom I had promoted to captain, and the third a second lieutenant whose rank I had also raised.

I had a talk with them. I said, "You were my prisoners. I pardoned you and promoted you. You agreed to fight for me. Then you deserted and joined my enemies. Do you consider this honorable conduct? If it is justice you want, your death is assured. But I prefer to show that Pancho Villa is merciful. I will conduct you to the International Bridge and let you go free in the United States. When you leave, I will hand each of you one thousand dollars. In return, take my advice and leave war to those who can keep their word. An officer should die before breaking parole."

I said this in the presence of some Americans who had come to see me, a Mr. Kelly, a Mr. White, and a third whose name I don't remember. Elías Torres, the prisoner of highest rank, answered arrogantly, "Keep your clemency, I don't want it."

His words angered me, as he intended. I replied, "So you don't want my mercy. Very well, Señor. What penalty is visited on traitors?"

"Traitors deserve death, but I am no traitor."

"That is what you say, but it's your actions that count. You have named the penalty. You will be shot at once."

I asked the Captain, "What do you say?"

"I agree with my Major."

"Very well, they will shoot you too."

I asked the other one, "And you, Sr. Lieutenant?"

"I go along with the Major and the Captain."

"They will shoot you too."

And so it was. They were shot at once.

On the day I entered Ciudad Juárez I had a telephone conversation with Carranza, who was in Nogales. I said, "Señor, here I am, in possession of Ciudad Juárez since early this morning. The place is at your orders, Señor."

At first he doubted me. He was not certain he was talking with Pancho Villa in Juárez, because Pancho Villa was supposed to be in southern Chihuahua; but when he recognized my voice he said, "This is truly a surprise. I congratulate you in the name of the people. Your victory is a great one."

"Many thanks, Señor. We owe our victory to Revolutionary luck, and sacrifices and valor. But even luck must be supported. So I call on you for what I need, Sr. Carranza. Nobody knows better than you what it would mean to abandon the place after taking it. I must have reinforcements and money. Send me 300,000 of the pesos you are printing, and in a month I will take Chihuahua and open the road to the south." He said he could send me 300,000 pesos but no more, since he had to supply Obregón and Pablo González.

I thought to myself, "If he does what he says, we can get along with each other." I was soon to learn that Sr. Carranza was not quite frank with me. Two days later he wrote about the money but excused himself from sending reinforcements, on the pretext that the Federals would not attack. What he did was to give me advice. He recommended cutting the road between Chihuahua and Ciudad Juárez, as if I needed such a suggestion, and spoke of moving troops from Sonora and Sinaloa, which showed either his ignorance of war or his desire to hold me inactive. I saw that he was only pretending he wanted to help me.

Our first night in Juárez we took a boy named Paredes a prisoner. The lawyer Neftalí Amador told me he was the son of an enemy who had betrayed some of our men, and several of the Revolutionaries thought he should be shot. Not knowing how to answer them but being little disposed to take the boy's life, I postponed things until the following day. The next morning I sent for Medina. I said, "You, Colonel Medina, who tell me so much about provosts and papers, take charge of this young fellow who was taken prisoner last night. The Revolutionary men here think he should be shot."

When he had talked with the boy, Medina returned and said, "My

General, the boy is only a child. Sons must not be made to pay for the sins of their fathers."

"And that is the law, my friend?"

"Yes, my General, that is the law."

I turned the boy over to his mother and sister, who were in tears. I even had my men give him two hundred dollars and send him to the International Bridge with an escort and set him free.

The day after taking Juárez I moved my headquarters to the Customs House. I was there one morning when I received a letter from Maclovio Herrera, who had gone to El Paso and did not wish to return. He wrote:

Sr. General Francisco Villa:

I have retired to private life. I have left you the money that was in my possession. I am no longer with the Revolution. Colonel Medina takes advantage of his position as chief of staff. He continually asks me for papers and vouchers. He wants my troops to serve without rest, and always on the front line, as if there were no soldiers except mine. I hope, Señor, that victory is yours. Goodbye.

Medina and I went to the Juárez Brigade. It was necessary to keep them from losing heart. I ordered them into formation and Medina exhorted them, telling them that Herrera's absence meant nothing, since he would return soon. Medina even went so far as to say that he considered Herrera largely responsible for our triumphs. He promised to bring him back, since the enemy was threatening us and we needed every able man.

Trouble was averted, and I sent a delegation to Maclovio, who persuaded him of his error and of how he misjudged Medina, who was only doing his duty in asking for vouchers. But Maclovio was right when he said Medina always sent the Juárez Brigade on the desperate assignments. Who but Maclovio did we have for that?

He could not have really intended to leave. His act was part of the discord spread by Carranza, and Maclovio merely wanted to see whether he could induce me to relieve Medina of his duties.

On November 20, 1913, in Ciudad Juárez we celebrated the anniversary of the Revolution. But, as I learned, that date was not celebrated in Nogales, for Carranza did not consider Sr. Madero the great leader that the people needed. This made he sad; I could not understand how there could be Revolutionaries without devotion to Sr. Madero. Wasn't Carranza with Sr. Madero? Didn't he know about the early struggles? How could he fail to know that we were fighting the same battle?

That same day, November 20, I learned that the enemy was making a rapid march from Chihuahua to attack me. When my couriers informed me that the advance forces were already in Samalayuca, I called Rodolfo Fierro and said, "My boy, you are a railroad man. Take an engine and an escort and delay the enemy. I need one more day to make my preparations. Give me that day, whatever it costs."

He left at once, taking Martín López and a crane to tear up the road beyond Candelaria. A few hours later he reported. He had gone close to the enemy lines and was shelled but in a daring run burned ten of the cars standing on the tracks, and succeeded in containing the advance.

CHAPTER 7

Villa Defeats the Huertistas at Tierra Blanca and with This Victory Opens the Way for the Revolution.

Review in Ciudad Juárez. The Lands of Tierra Blanca. Manuel Madinabeitia. Manuel Banda. Jáuregui. Darío Silva. Primitivo Huro. Preparations for a Battle. Night Reconnaissances. Landa and Caraveo's Cavalries. Alatorre and Salazar. Zach L. Cobb. Kiriacópulus. A Charge by Pancho Villa. Rodolfo Fierro's Heroism.

That afternoon, November 21, 1913, I ordered a review of my troops, armed, mounted and equipped, for the next morning. At ten they were facing the station. The purpose was not the review. With the brigades assembled and the chiefs present I would give orders to march immediately against the enemy.

I proceeded thus lest I alarm the peaceful people of the town. I wished to keep the frontier quiet and protect international business. Furthermore, it was desirable to keep my preparations a secret from the enemy. Knowing they were on the march I let them advance in order to meet them at a place I had chosen, the plain stretching from Bauche station to Tierra Blanca, where I would occupy a position on the high ground, leaving them a sandy tract to immobilize their artillery and slow their other movements. They would have no water there or way of getting it. Of all my men, only Medina and the officers of my staff knew my intentions. Medina, because he was the one with whom I talked things over; the officers, because of the task they had before them, which they performed with the utmost courage. I name them: Manuel Madinabeitia, Manuel Banda, Carlos Jáuregui, Darío Silva, Primitivo Huro, Enrique Santos Coy, and one other whose name I do not remember.

Considering the importance of the outcome, I left only fifty men in Juárez, with the paymaster Alfredo Rueda Quijano, who had custody of the funds in the Customs House.

I said to Medina, "Amigo, if you need troops, and you are going to need them, arm civilians to assist you. Juárez is my base and you are my principal support. Don't fail me. This is the decisive moment. While I am fighting, remain here to forward aid and supplies. I am going to need water, provisions, fodder, arms, and ammunition. Get it all and send it."

Medina replied, "My General, have no fear. You will get what you need, without a moment's delay."

I left Juárez at ten in the morning with 6,200 men. At Mesa I called a council of my brigade chiefs and gave them instructions. These were my orders: on the east—that is, on my left—the Morelos Brigade under José Rodríguez and five hundred Loyalists of Camargo under Rosalío Hernández; in the center, the artillery under Martiniano Servín, with the Villa Brigade under Toribio Ortega on its right and the González Ortega Brigade under Porfirio Ornelas on the other side; on my right wing, Herrera's Juárez Brigade and part of the Morelos Brigade. The center, I calculated, would be a little toward the north to keep the angle of my line from closing, and the reserves, at my personal disposition though under Manuel Madinabeitia and Porfirio Talamantes, would be placed to make it appear that my line was closed all across the center. The front was several leagues long, and, though unable to protect it at all points, I had the option of sending reserves wherever the action was threatening. I could do this without betraying my weak points, making them believe that I was weak where in reality I was strong.

I said, "Amigos, this battle determines the future of the Revolution. If we are defeated, we lose Juárez and the frontier, with access to arms and ammunition. We must win."

That same afternoon we saw the enemy trains four kilometers from our positions. According to my calculations there were some 5,500 men of the three branches, and the famous cannons called "El Rorro" and

"El Chavalito" on their platforms. A Federal general by the name of José Jesús Mansilla was commanding the force, and the brigade chiefs were Manuel Landa, also a Federal, and the traitors Marcello Caraveo, José Inés Salazar, and Rafael Flores Alatorre. I think they must have been surprised to see my troops covering such a long front, and have thought we were very numerous. There are many miles between a point opposite Valverde, Texas, where my left began, and the water tanks at Bauche station on the northeast road, where my right was anchored.

Thus passed the night of the twenty-second. In the morning I was expecting them to attack, but either because of the heavy mist or for other reasons, they stayed quietly in their positions, and we let them see we were waiting in ours. We faced each other like that for several hours. It must have been six in the afternoon when the headlights of the trains came on and cast their illumination as far as our lines. I went up and down my front line, giving the order to advance at nine within two kilometers of the enemy trains and be ready to attack at twelve. My men would enter on foot, and the horses, ten for each man, would remain in care of Hernández. But at ten several officers heard cavalry at various points on the advance line we had established, and being advised of this, I waited.

The battle began the next morning at five. My right wing, which Herrera and Eugenio Aguirre Benavides were covering, met the attack of Landa and Caraveo's cavalry. The enemy thought they could easily crumple that flank, when my center would soon give way. To let them know that a movement against any single point of my line would provoke an assault, I threw my center into action, and, seeing that they left their line uncovered on the west and only infantry protected their trains on the east, I ordered an advance. My center moved. Porfirio Talamantes, at the cost of his life, got up to the first enemy engine with part of the reserves. But the fire from the sandbanks at the right of their line caused many casualties. I ordered my line to retire, for my purpose, already accomplished, had been only to relieve my right wing. Besides, I wanted to see if, encouraged by my retreat, their infantry would abandon the only natural defenses I had left them.

They did not fall into the trap; they stayed sheltered as they were. Seeing that their two large cannon were attempting to advance, I ordered Servín's artillery to stop them, and he not only did so but drove them back. Now, with control of the center, I ordered Fidel Avila to take four hundred of the Villa Brigade horses and go to the aid of Herrera and Aguirre Benavides. We were frustrating Landa and Caraveo in their efforts to gain control of Bauche, which they desperately needed for the water tanks there. At eleven that morning Herrera, Aguirre Benavides, and Avila pushed them back to the trains, causing many casualties and taking many prisoners.

Meanwhile, Salazar and Flores Alatorre on my left were trying to break through the lines held by Rosalío Hernández and José Rodríguez. Their strength was great, and such was their determination that they upset my two brigades. But recovering their balance, my men cut off part of Salazar's troops, and as Hernández pursued and annihilated these, the main body of Salazar's forces withdrew in disorder, saved only by the protection of a cloud of dust on the Zaragoza road.

During the action I received supplies and other necessaries from Ciudad Juárez. Trains arrived with water, bread, and fodder, as well as ammunition and machine guns. Private automobiles from Juárez and El Paso brought medicine and nurses. The wounded who were strong enough I put on trains and sent to Ciudad Juárez. There were many, and the mortality was great.

In Ciudad Juárez, as I learned, families converted their homes into hospitals—families by the name of Stock Mayer, Membrila, and Contreras de Rojas, or Díaz de Rojas, I do not remember now. We even received aid from the American city of El Paso. Business houses there gave us blankets and medicine for the wounded, as did Sr. Zach Cobb, the administrator of Customs; a Revolutionary named Kiriacópulus; and a bakery belonging to someone whose name I cannot recall. Cobb, especially, was a source of great help. Many Mexicans in the American city of New York aided us. As I remember, Don Alfonso Madero sent Medina five thousand pesos, or five thousand dollars.

Daybreak on the twenty-fifth found Flores Alatorre's forces strong in their right-wing positions but far from their purpose of routing my left. The fighting spread. It increased on the line defended by Rodríguez and Hernández. The opposing forces were beginning to paralyze Rodríguez' movements when, obeying my orders, he advanced with all the daring of a Revolutionary. But he fell wounded, and Flores Alatorre, who had received reinforcements, charged and began to force us back to the Hippodrome.

Seeing that my left was being overwhelmed and that this threatened my whole position, I sent word to General Ortega and to Avila and other officers all along the line to order a general cavalry attack on the signal of two cannon shots; to give this signal I waited only for the moment that would ensure the success of the charge.

As I waited, Herrera came and asked what he was to do, since the enemy were almost crushing him. I answered, "On the signal all the cavalry will fall on the enemy. Have confidence, Señor. Do what we are all going to do, move forward, crowd them back against their trains, and annihilate them."

So it turned out. At the signal we fell on them with such fury that we had them defeated at every point before they could recover their balance. We caught them with their artillery bogged in the sand at a time when their infantry had left the protection of ridges. Their panic was so great that some tried to run, others tumbled into the sand, and hardly a one faced us or remembered to use his arms. We wounded or killed them with our pistols, and there were no less than two hundred casualties. We took many prisoners and several of their cannon. The entire enemy line was broken and at the mercy of my center, which had broken through toward the east and west as my two wings were closing in and forcing them to scatter.

At nightfall we attacked the trains. I think this worth recording because of its significance and daring. When some of the enemy were trying to get aboard and while Caraveo, Argumedo, and Salazar were falling back in defeat on both sides, Rodolfo Fierro, at the head of the Corps of Scouts, ran his horse at full gallop to overtake a trainload who were escaping. In a rain of bullets he leaped from his horse to the train and climbing from one car to another reached the brake cylinder, released the air, and stopped the train. A beautiful feat, Señor! Soldiers from the Corps of Scouts and my brigade then fell on the train, and the slaughter was horrible.

The battle of Tierra Blanca, according to my memory, began on November 23, 1913, and ended two days later at night. The enemy lost more than one thousand men and left me three trains and two pieces of artillery.

CHAPTER 8

Villa Starts Governing the Conquered Territory and Begins To Feel the Hidden Forces of Politics.

Newspapers of the World. The Government of Chihuahua. Orders from Carranza. The Lawyer Jesús Acuña. Manuel Chao. Medina's Fears. Luis Aguirre Benavides. Francisco Escudero's Bravery. Villa's Patience. Eliseo Arredondo, Alfredo Breceda, and Rafael Múzquiz. Dinner with Eugenio Aguirre Benavides. The Caravan of Death.

The next day I detailed two squadrons to stay and break camp, and had some of the prisoners dig graves. Then I ordered the rest of the troops into formation for the march to Juárez. It was best we present a good appearance to the eyes observing from across the frontier. We now had international relations, and would be watched by newspapers from all over the world. They would see that we were not only victorious but disciplined and orderly. I carried the problem of administration to Medina, saying, "Amigo, choose someone to act for you on the staff. I need you here and you must take charge of the state government when Chihuahua falls in a few days. But keep it a secret until I announce it."

He acted as if unwilling and perhaps he really was. It seemed unwise to him to place an outsider in a political post. But he was wrong. I, a man born in Durango, was respected as the leader in Chihuahua.

I said, "Amigo, in war and politics men are judged by their conduct, not by their place of birth. You will be the governor of Chihuahua because you can do it and the Revolutionaries wish it."

Then something happened that I was not expecting. Carranza sent a lawyer by the name of Jesús Acuña to tell me that he wanted me to put General Chao in as governor of Chihuahua and relieve Medina and even dismiss him from my service. According to Carranza, Medina was conspiring to betray me.

I did not believe it. But I noticed that the public knew of my intention and that in appointing men to serve under him he failed to consult my wishes. I ordered him to remove the authorities he had chosen. He told me he would, but when he delayed I found an excuse for complying to a certain extent with the orders of the Commander in Chief. Perhaps suspecting my intentions or having a guilty conscience, Medina went over to the American side and sent me a letter of resignation in which he said he was returning to private life, as I was surrounded by traitors.

This angered me. I began to hear, and for some time I believed, accusations against him. Sadly I thought, "I always considered Medina a good Revolutionary, but now that he is safe and sound, with enough money to drink chocolate for a while, he disavows my authority and abandons the cause."

I grew so angry that I requested the United States to arrest him and return him, but this was not done. Either he had friends to protect him in El Paso, or the authorities knew I was mistaken. It was probably the latter reason because after three or four months I found I had been mistaken. I sent for him, and he joined me again.

While I was in Juárez I received the 300,000 pesos Carranza promised me. A boy by the name of Luis Aguirre Benavides brought them. I knew him, as Gustavo Madero had sent him to visit me when I was in prison in Mexico City and asked him to serve as my secretary. In my conversations with him I saw he was a quiet competent young man and thought he would make me a good secretary. But he said he already had the post of secretary to Francisco Escudero. I replied that Carranza and his ministers had more than enough civil servants while I needed them badly. So he promised to see if he could be released.

We let it go at that, and one day Escudero came to speak to me in the name of the Commander in Chief. He was an intelligent man, and we talked to Sr. Madero, of the hopes of the Revolutionaries, and of the need to preserve unity until the end.

He preached to me, saying, "Since the time of Father Hidalgo the people of Mexico have struggled for a better existence. Then our Revolution began, and it is our duty to finish it." I said that I thought so too and added, "With respect to unity, you can tell Carranza that Pancho Villa is with him and will continue to be with him as long as he and those around him serve the cause of the people."

Seeing how cordial we were, General Eugenio Aguirre Benavides, chief of arms in Ciudad Juárez, gave a banquet for me and Carranza's representative. I attended in good faith but Sr. Escudero's behavior made me suspicious.

The guests were a lawyer named Eliseo Arredondo, and another Sr. Aguirre Benavides, also a lawyer, named Adrián, and Sres. Alfredo Breceda and Rafael Múzquiz, and Eugenio Aguirre Benavides and his brother Luis. At dinner Escudero, somewhat inebriated, began to try

my patience. He kept on drinking and talking about his valor. Finally
he said, "My General, I am a better man than you."

Going along with him, I answered, "Yes, Señor, why not?"

He continued, "You, General, have the courage of a savage, and I of
a civilized man. You do very well in war, I do not deny it. But I have
been together in a room with a cunning gringo, William Bayard Hale,
to discuss problems of importance to our country, and it takes more
courage to face and overcome arguments than to exchange fire on the
battlefield, as you must admit."

I continued to eat without answering. In my cheerful frame of mind
I did not understand why he should speak in this way before the other
gentlemen. I thought, "If he is drunk, I must be patient. He can not
know what he is doing. But why do not the others reprimand him?"

Perhaps thinking to antagonize me further he said, "They say you are
a killer, but I doubt whether you would try to kill me. I am a better man
than you in every respect."

I began to believe he might really be braver than I was, since no one
had ever before dared to affront me that way. But I saw too that his assurance, which truly was great, rested on the certainty of my self-
discipline.

Finally he thrust his face into mine and shouted into my very mouth,
"Yes, Señor, I am a better man than you, a better man than you, do you
hear? I'll tell you what I think, you are going to be another Pascual
Orozco."

I could keep calm no longer. I stepped up to him and said, "Señor,
you are nothing but a sot. And for all your valor in dealing with gringos,
if you were not Carranza's representative, I would shoot you on the
spot."

He answered, "Go ahead, then. Shoot me."

I withdrew, while I still had my temper under control. And, as I
learned, the others followed me. Escudero declared the field was his,
and remained there alone and continued to drink two or three hours
longer. When Carranza was informed of this, he relieved Escudero and
sent me many apologies. I accepted them without rancor. But there
were rumors. I was told that Escudero really was a brave man and not
a habitual drinker, but had deliberately got himself drunk to provoke
me. I do not know. Luisito, who was thus without a chief, entered my
service.

At the end of November I received reports of the panic which had
struck the rich men of Chihuahua when they learned of my victory at

Tierra Blanca. To discredit my forces, they spread rumors of crimes we were committing. But the discipline and good behavior of my troops had been demonstrated in Ciudad Juárez, where no one was killed or robbed, and no one was punished without cause. General Salvador Mercado, chief of the Huertista forces of Chihuahua, was responsible for the fears. When the battle of Tierra Blanca ended on November 25, he was in such a hurry to leave that he was already on the road to Ojinaga by the twenty-eighth, taking the principal families of the town along with him. Marcelo Caraveo, the last to leave, abandoned the city three days later, and after that—that is, after December 1, 1913—it was at my mercy.

I could have closed the Ojinaga road to Mercado and the "caravan of death," the name the people gave to the civil columns that fled with the troops. My plan had been to push them south, to catch them between my forces and those advancing from La Laguna, also mine. But the best way to rid the State of enemies was to leave the road to the frontier open to Mercado and oblige him to take refuge in the United States. I would then be through with his army without casualties.

CHAPTER 9

With Villa Absent, the Northern Division Fails in Ojinaga but He Goes Quickly to Their Aid.

The Chihuahua Road. Federico Moye. Villa, Conqueror. Hugh L. Scott. Lázaro de la Garza. Felícitos Villarreal. Riches and the People. Pánfilo Natera. Toribio Ortega. Villa's Measures. Villa Under the Cottonwood. Plan of Attack.

As I remember, I left Juárez December 3, and after five days of marching entered Chihuahua. We were met by a commission of civilians headed by a man named Don Frederico Moye, who said, "Sr. General Villa, we come in the interests of peace. General Mercado's troops have abandoned the place and it is at your orders. We hope for the treatment great conquerors give to peaceful towns. Your orders will be carried out, but respect our lives, Señor, and those of our families, and do not despoil us."

I listened calmly and answered without arrogance, but I knew the ways of people who were submissive when helpless but continued to work under cover as implacable enemies. I explained that the inhabitants of Chihuahua, rich and poor, would have to unite in aiding the cause of the people, saying, "Señores, my forces are not puffed up with their triumphs. They will not mistreat you. But don't deceive yourselves. There will be punishment for those who commit evil acts against us. No one shall withhold the supplies my troops need or engage in conspiracies against our cause. My soldiers are ready to inflict the death penalty for such acts."

My entrance made a great impression, perhaps because I had so many troops, for I had left only the Hernández and Zaragoza brigades in Juárez. Our enemies could hardly contain their fear, but the humble people received us with affection. On my arrival I found two hundred soldiers of the 6th Battalion, under three Federal officers: a captain, a lieutenant, and a second lieutenant. They were there to guarantee order but were no longer needed. I called the captain and said to him, "You are not afraid of Pancho Villa or deceived by the slanders about me. Well, you shall see you are right. I give you and your officers safe conduct to any place you wish. But as for your troops, who are from this town, don't reproach me if I keep them to fight on the popular side."

At first I assumed the office of governor of Chihuahua to stimulate public business. But after a few weeks of work I transferred it to General Chao in obedience to Carranza's orders and occupied myself with military affairs only. I made a trip to Ciudad Juárez in connection with financial arrangements and the international situation. The American general at Fort Bliss, Hugh L. Scott, wanted to talk to me. We had exchanged greetings in the middle of the Bridge at Ciudad Juárez, and now he wanted to visit me.

I appointed Lázaro de la Garza to attend to the collection of money. He had served me well after the taking of Torreón. As assistant collector I appointed an engineer, Felícitos Villarreal, who was also a financier. These appointments were needed because the loan we received in Torreón was getting low and the Torreón bankers were showing bad faith. They were hardly free of troops when they refused to pay the drafts which I had drawn on them. They said, "We signed under duress and are not obligated to keep the agreement." But they were wrong. It was not true that they had agreed under duress to honor our drafts. It was from fear of my troops, quite a different thing. I did not take them by the hand and compel them to sign. They signed of their own free will when I convinced them that otherwise the people would treat them as enemies. Furthermore, the money they gave me did not really belong to them. It belonged to the people, the true owners of all the money there is in a country. The people are the ones who produce it. I, the representative of the people, had the right to demand, and it was just for them to deliver, all the money necessary for the cause.

It was also necessary to settle the conflict and find all possible resources. I returned to Chihuahua and organized a column of three brigades to advance on Ojinaga. It numbered about three thousand men, counting artillery. My problem was to find a leader, since I had duties I could not leave. I summoned the generals and principal commanders to a meeting in the Federal Palace. I explained the importance of the operation and suggested that they choose a leader. Present were Tomás Urbina, Herrera, Hernández, Ortega, José Rodríguez, Chao, Trinidad Rodríguez, and a few others. Also present was General Pánfilo Natera, chief of the Central Division, who had been on his way to consult with Carranza but was returning from Juárez by way of Zacatecas because the United States had not allowed him to cross to Nogales. Taking advantage of his presence, I said, "My friends, the operation is of great importance. It can rid the state of Chihuahua of enemies and leave us the masters of our action on the march south. But I cannot go, and you should choose General Natera, who is here, or General Ortega, who is familiar with the region."

I expected Natera to be chosen. I was hoping to avoid rivalries and jealousies. As it happened, Natera declined, having little knowledge of the terrain and the troops, and spoke for Toribio. Not to be outdone, Toribio, though he wanted the command, responded with praise of Natera. He extolled Natera's ability and said he would gladly yield to him. The others quickly took him up on his offer, none of them wanting Toribio as his superior.

The column to take Ojinaga consisted of 500 men from the Villa Brigade, under the command of José Rodríguez; 550 from the González Ortega Brigade, under Toribio Ortega; 450 from the Morelos Brigade, under Faustino Borunda; 400 from the Cuauhtémoc Brigade, under Trinidad Rodríguez, then a lieutenant colonel; 300 from the Contreras Brigade, under Luis Díaz Cuder. Also, there were two batteries of 75-

and 80-millimeter cannon under the command of Martiniano Servín and a machine-gun regiment under Margarito Gómez.

They left Chihuahua on December 22, 1913, with munitions and equipment of all kinds. In San Sóstenes they found a great deal of railroad material, arms, ammunition, and clothing which the enemy had abandoned. Four days after their departure they were at the ranch La Mula. Two days later they were in Mulato. The next day they fought with Caraveo and Flores Alatorre, who were defeated and forced to flee. Caraveo was wounded, and 260 prisoners were taken. They got four machine guns and ten mules loaded with ammunition. Three days later, on January 1, 1914, they made contact with the enemy at Ojinaga. This time the enemy attacked, dismantled a piece of artillery, caused many casualties, and forced a retreat. The next day the battle continued, and the enemy killed 200 men. On the third day enemy cavalry came out, supported by artillery. There was a furious encounter resulting in great bloodshed, and although the enemy withdrew, driven back by Servín's cannon and the action of our troops, Ortega ceased fire during the combat, and 80 of our men were killed and 130 taken prisoner. Señor! Our forces saw the enemy withdraw without loss or damage, and the 130 prisoners were shot in Ojinaga.

Our action was paralyzed in spite of Natera's effort and ability. The trouble came of disputes and quarrels among brigade leaders, who were angry with Toribio because he was apparently unwilling to win under Natera. So, on the second day, in the heaviest fighting, our forces retired to rest; and two days later their weariness and discontent increased; and a day later, Martín López and Carlos Almeida wanted to return to Chihuahua and José and Trinidad Rodríguez and Borunda to withdraw to Jiménez. Failure demoralized them, and it was only because Servín would not follow that they decided either to wait one day longer and take Servín away by force or to keep fighting until the end if Natera would shoot Toribio, whom they held responsible.

On January 6, I was advised in Juárez of these events and took my measures. The news reached me at eight at night. At once I gave General Rosalío Hernández orders to march with his troops and horses, and by two we were on the road. By telegraph I ordered Herrera and the Juárez Brigade to advance by train toward Ojinaga. In this way, without preparation or supplies, I started to Ojinaga with two brigades. In three days we were in La Mula. Having nothing to eat, we began to kill cattle on the ranches and our food was roast beef without salt. I sent

General Hernández and General Herrera from La Mula to El Mulato to await my orders, and with an escort of twenty-five men, including my staff, I myself made a forced march to the Hacienda de San Juan.

I reached camp at four on the afternoon of January 10. There was a heavy frost, and the wind almost blew us from our mounts. I appeared at the moment when spirits were lowest, and as the news of my arrival spread, everybody began to feel better. I dismounted under a cotton-wood and stretched out on the ground. I sent for the chiefs. As soon as they came, I began to talk to them. Wanting to give them an impression of calm, I had picked a sprig of grass, and as I talked indulgently, nibbled at it.

I asked them, "How have you been doing, boys? The reports are bad. But the coyote has had his last hen from my henroost. I am to blame. Natera told me he wasn't familiar with conditions here. But nothing will happen now I am here. Don't worry, and get some sleep." That night I heard them all singing.

The next day I dictated the following orders for the attack: the troops would be divided in three columns; on the south Hernández and José Rodríguez with eight hundred men, supported by Servín's artillery; on the right, that is on the east between the Conchos and the Bravo, my headquarters and nine hundred men under Trinidad Rodríguez and Herrera; on the left, Toribio Ortega with seven hundred men and the Auxiliaries of San Carlos under Chavarría. All were to be ready by seven at night. The horses would be chained, guarded by one man for every ten, and at 7:30 we would advance on the city, with our hats on our backs for identification.

Before the generals and chiefs withdrew, I called Toribio Ortega and said, "Compañero, it seems that you forgot the instructions I gave you in Chihuahua and because of that many Revolutionaries like Onésimo Martínez are dead. Well, I won't pardon you a second time. Goodbye."

CHAPTER 10

Pancho Villa Comes, Sees, and Conquers at Ojinaga, and Then Returns to Juárez, Where William Benton Attempts To Kill Him.

Villa's Instructions. Forty-five Minutes at Ojinaga. Jesús Felipe Moya. The North American General John J. Pershing. "Don't Worry. Just Watch the Stars." General Angeles. The Incident Involving William Benton. Luisito's Advice. Rodolfo Fierro. Manuel Banda. How the Englishman Wanted His Grave Dug.

We were ready to take Ojinaga, and that afternoon I addressed my chiefs and soldiers: "Chiefs and soldiers of liberty, any man who turns back will be shot then and there. The password is 'Juárez,' the countersign is 'Faithful Ones.' When your gun is trained on a man, ask him 'what number,' and if he is one of us, he will answer, 'One'; if he does not answer or gives a different number, fire. Do you understand?" They shouted yes.

My right wing, under Herrera and Trinidad Rodríguez, defeated Antonio Rojas and Fernández Ortinel in fifteen minutes and gained their objective. On the south, Mansilla and Salazar offered hardly any resistance to José Rodríguez and Rosalío Hernández. And on the west, where the fighting was heaviest, Caraveo's troops, after battling for forty-five minutes, abandoned their position when told of our success elsewhere. The action was much shorter than I could have expected. We took Ojinaga, not in an hour and a half, as I ordered, but an hour and five minutes. When the firing was dying down in every sector, I advanced at a moderate pace and entered the streets. Everywhere I heard soldiers shouting my name and advancing without opposition.

That was all I had to do to take Ojinaga, but it was not my triumph, it was that of my officers and soldiers. Thirty-five of my men were killed, among them Jesús Felipe Moya, a Revolutionary whom I had just promoted to general and for whom I wept. Four hundred of the enemy fell. We secured their horses, saddles, rifles, machine guns, and cannons.

Salvador Mercado and Pascual Orozco, who had directed the battle from the Old Customs House, crossed the river and took refuge in the United States. Of the generals, chiefs, officers, and soldiers who crossed the frontier with them, only Marcelo Caraveo, with eighteen men as an escort, and Desiderio García, with three or four others, ventured back into Mexican territory and set out for the south.

The next day I gave orders to clear camp, after giving the inhabitants of the town assurances of safety. Colonel John J. Pershing, in command on the other side of the river, asked permission to visit me in our territory. We greeted each other courteously. He congratulated me on my successes and I praised him for sheltering the defeated troops, since this spared me from being responsible for further casualties. When he offered me his hospitals for my wounded I answered that I could take care of them with my own facilities, but told him that I was grateful for the offer and would have accepted it if necessary. In less than forty-eight hours I was ready to return to Chihuahua, leaving only the González Ortega Brigade behind as a garrison.

I made the trip by automobile, with Raúl Madero, Rodolfo Fierro, Luis Aguirre Benavides, and a chauffeur. That night, when we were crossing the sierra by starlight and in bitter cold, Fierro said, "It is all right for us to make this trip, my General, but not for you."

"And why not for me?"

"This is a district where Caraveo may try to surprise us. We would die in this box and your death would be a great loss to the Revolution."

Wishing to allay his anxiety, I replied, "No, Friend, no one will kill me before the Revolution has triumphed. I serve the Revolution and, the Revolution being the people, God, who governs those stars above us, will protect me. Don't worry. Just watch the stars."

As soon as my troops reached Chihuahua, I held the Zaragoza Brigade there, and sent the Hernández Brigade to Camargo and the Herrera Brigade to Jiménez. I organized new brigades and a corps of mountain troops. Then, considering how much strength a powerful artillery would add to our southern advance, I asked Carranza to send me General Felipe Angeles. I remembered how effective Rubio Navarrete's cannon had been against Pascual Orozco in 1912. General Angeles was the artilleryman I needed. Unlike Obregón, I was not afraid to have experts assist me or teach me what I did not know.

While waiting, I went to Ciudad Juárez for equipment and munitions. In Juárez one night I was visited by an Englishman—William Benton, the owner of a ranch called, as I remember, Hacienda de Santa Gertrudis. He had committed many crimes under the protection of the Terrazas, for which reason I had ordered his ranch confiscated at a fair price and ordered him to get out of Mexico, the only steps we dared take against foreign exploiters.

Now Benton entered my quarters and said, "I have come to get my land back."

I answered, "I cannot return your land, but since you are English and I wish to avoid international incidents, I intend to pay you what it is worth, or what you paid for it, after which you will stay out of Mexico."

In a sudden rage he shouted, "I will not sell at any price, and I will not let a bandit like you rob me." He drew his pistol but before he could fire I was on top of him and had him disarmed. Then Andrés L. Farías and my guards seized him and carried him away. I found out later that he had boasted he would tell me face to face I was the bandit responsible for the crimes and robberies of the Revolution and would rid the world of me and others like me.

The day before, an American friend of mine had come to complain that the guards at the Customs House were interfering with his trade. To Luis Aguirre Benavides I said, "Luisito, write him an order to shoot anyone who bothers him." Aguirre Benavides wrote an order which, contrary to my usual practice, I read before signing: "When the bearer complains of anyone, execute summary justice." I said nothing and signed. Later I went to his department and said, "Luisito, you have done well. I have no words with which to thank you. I wish everyone would save me mistakes this way. But there are few who would dare."

Remembering this, I called Aguirre Benavides after the encounter with Benton. I asked, "What do you advise me to do, Luisito?" and he answered, "Why, let's wait and see, my General."

He meant that he did not wish to advise me in so serious a matter. But Rodolfo Fierro, who was there, said, "In my opinion, he deserves no mercy. We must execute him on the spot, my General." I took Fierro's advice into careful consideration, asking myself, "Does Benton's being an Englishman free him from blame?" I ordered him carried down to Samalayuca that same night, to be taken out and shot.

Banda handcuffed him and at midnight they took him away in an engine and a caboose. But Fierro did not understand clearly, nor did Jesús M. Ríos who went along. On reaching Samalayuca, they did not shoot him as I had ordered but decided to kill him by a blow on the head. They went to the field, searched for a good place, and put four soldiers to digging a grave. Benton was watching and said, "Listen, Amigo, make a deeper hole. The coyotes will get me out of this one."

Fierro promised to dig deeper and, as the soldiers shoveled out more dirt with Benton watching them, Fierro came up behind Benton and gave him a blow on the head. He fell in the hole and remained there, handcuffs and all, because Banda, who had the key to the handcuffs, failed to do his duty.

CHAPTER 11

Villa Orders Benton's Body Disinterred and Shot and Learns about International Problems.

Foreign Scandal. Mr. Bryan. George C. Carothers. Juan N. Medina. Felipe Angeles. Máxima Esparza. Carranza's Experience with International Difficulties. The House of Commons. The Shooting of Benton and the Autopsy.

Two days after Benton's death it was said that I, Pancho Villa, had assassinated him to avenge a personal quarrel. The United States newspapers played the story up, and Pancho Villa, the villain, became the subject of conversation throughout the world. I learned that Huerta was proclaiming me a criminal and requesting all the nations to sell me no more arms.

The American consul in Ciudad Juárez questioned me. Mr. Bryan, the Secretary of State in Washington, was friendly, but Benton's death was a serious affair. I gave the consul the truth, that Benton had tried to kill me and had paid for it with his life.

The consul asked, "Who pronounced the sentence?"

"The Revolutionary Army, Señor, which represents the people."

"And where is the corpse?"

"It is buried, Señor."

"Can it be disinterred?"

"Yes, Señor, but it will take some time."

"Can the grave be located?"

"All my graves can be located, Señor."

A special representative of that government, Mr. George C. Carothers, came to see me. After a courteous greeting we spoke very frankly. When he saw that I was telling the truth, he asked for the official papers.

"Why do you wish to see papers, Señor, when I have told you the details?"

But Mr. Carothers wished to help solve the problem. He said, "It is best, Sr. General, that my government have a copy of the death sentence. I am confident that it was made in writing and in due form."

I was very grateful for these words and I recognized their wisdom. When he went away I called one of my lawyers and said, "The great nations have time to waste upon papers. I don't, but we will humor them in this case. See Farías, Fierro, and Banda, and bring me the official papers passing sentence upon Benton. Bring them, Señor, in legal form." While I was on the way to Chihuahua, to prepare the advance to the south, the lawyers delivered a copy of William Benton's sentence to Mr. Carothers.

Juan N. Medina, who was in El Paso, telephoned me before I left Juárez, "My General, you do not have to explain Benton's death. That is an affair that concerns only Sr. Carranza, the head of our government." I answered, "Of course, and you who know these things ought to be here to keep me informed. I am in more trouble than ever since you abandoned me."

I ordered a special anniversary ceremony in honor of Sr. Madero and had the remains of Don Abraham González brought to Chihuahua two days later, on the twenty-fourth, and placed in the Government Palace in a chapel with burning candles and a tombstone there in his honor.

In Chihuahua I learned that General Felipe Angeles had left Sonora to join my forces and, knowing the time of his arrival, I ordered a band to meet him at the station, along with my escort and other forces. By his smile I knew he was pleased. I said, "Sr. General, we need your services on the battlefield. Chance alone has made me a soldier, and your professional knowledge will help us."

He replied, "Sr. General, I can teach you nothing because you have nothing to learn. In my opinion you have had great success in this war. Battles like Tierra Blanca would be a credit to any professional soldier. I am happy to place myself under your orders." His words pleased but did not inflate me, and seeing that he spoke in all sincerity I responded in like manner. He approved of my plan for the push south.

The day after my return to Chihuahua, the representatives of England and the United States again brought up the subject of Benton's death. Both consuls said the body must be disinterred and delivered to the widow. I replied, "The widow is Máxima Esparza, a native of this country. She has no need of foreign consuls to request the body." But they answered that I was wrong, that being the wife of an Englishman, she too was English.

I informed Carranza of the case, and when Secretary Bryan asked him for an explanation and for the body, he replied, out of his experience in international disputes, that if Benton was English then England should present the claims to the ministers of the Revolution. Since England recognized Huerta's government and could not deal with Sr. Carranza's, and since Carranza would not discuss English affairs with the United States, no one could make a claim, not even the widow herself.

But the scandal did not die down. Newspapers abroad accused me and the Revolution of crime. Our American enemies asked for intervention and accused President Wilson of covering up the crimes of the Revolutionaries. The reporters who traveled with me said, "The House of Commons attacks you and asks the United States to protect all foreigners while the Mexicans are at war."

Considering it all, I said to the United States consul, "Señor, I will deliver Benton's body, as you requested."

He replied, "I am glad. That is all Mr. Bryan and Mr. Wilson want. An International Commission will leave El Paso to receive the body and make a formal examination."

When I told Rodolfo Fierro, he reminded me that they would discover Benton was not shot. There would be only the mark of a blow.

I replied, "My friend, I ordered him shot. If you and Banda killed him some other way, you must arrange it the best way you can. Dig up the body, bury it again in the Municipal Cemetery in Chihuahua, and when the Commission disinters it and makes the examination, they must find evidence of bullet wounds and a blow that was delivered as an act of mercy."

They obeyed. But I was to learn how ignorant men can be. Fierro told Luis Aguirre Benavides how he had shot the body according to my orders, and Luis told one of my doctors. The doctor came and said, "My General, when you shot Benton you made a great mistake. If the body is examined, they will know that you shot him after he was already dead."

"And how will they know that?"

"The autopsy will show it."

After a little thought, I said, "Señor, you will perform the autopsy and find that he was shot and then given a blow on the head as an act of mercy. And if there is a second autopsy, it must confirm the first one."

We agreed, but the First Chief informed me that the entry of such a Commission would violate our sovereignty as an independent nation. I was to make no more statements to newspapers nor mention the death of Benton. Everything I did should be subject to his knowledge and orders, and he would send a commission of Mexican doctors and judges to decide what should be done.

As Sr. Carranza was the commander in chief I obeyed. I advised the Commission that it could not enter Mexico and informed the consuls that anything pertaining to Benton should be referred to Sr. Carranza.

CHAPTER 12

On the Eve of the March on Torreón Villa Notices that His Glory Is Arousing Envy.

Carranza and Villa. A Smile for Thirty-eight Cannon. Obregón's Plans. A Remembrance for the First Chief. José Bonales Sandoval. Félix Díaz. Pablo González. Máximo García. José Isabel Robles. Villa's Money. The Poverty of the Terrazas. The Gold in the Banco Minero. Luis Aguirre Benavides.

For the sake of the cause I invited Carranza to install his government in Chihuahua under protection of my troops. I wanted him to know how badly General Chao was running the government and to be the one to set things in order. Carranza promised to come and settle everything.

"Señor, I have thirty-eight cannon I took from the enemy, and I hope they will win a smile from you."

"I congratulate you on them and hope Mexico City will be hearing them roar."

So our dialogue went. He told me he thought I should have pardoned fewer of our enemies. I answered, "Señor, it is a question of partial amnesty, which is good for the cause. I pardoned some because they would not harm us, being respected men, and others because I thought they would be useful. Among these were artillery officers who are already serving me well. But if I am wrong, give me your orders, and I will shoot them all."

Carranza then approved my amnesties, denying me only the right to pardon chiefs and generals without his consent. I think he wanted the latter to be grateful to him and not to me or my forces.

But I ignored such trifles; the important thing was that Carranza supported the main action. Obregón was growing jealous of my increasing triumphs and was scheming to take over command of our advance to the south. He offered to provide troops for the Laguna campaign, saying that he was my chief when he was not, and hiding his true intentions under the statement that Sr. Carranza would take over all command when the campaign began. But Carranza paid no attention to him; he only sent him to his line in Sinaloa and Tepic and left me in the center, which was most important and which I had established.

Since those days marked the anniversary of Carranza's opposition to Victoriano Huerta, I informed him of my friendly attitude by sending the message: "Señor, on this memorable date, you raised your banner against the usurpers. I pray we may soon win the struggle in which you are the commander."

José Bonales Sandoval came to Chihuahua at this time. He was the lawyer who had been my defender in Santiago Tlaltelolco. He had written me from the United States saying that he wanted to talk to me, and I had told him to come on. Since he had participated in the death of Gustavo Madero, I thought it would be a good idea for him to come to Chihuahua so he could be shot. Félix Díaz wished to come with him, to offer us the support of a part of the Federal army which was opposed to Huerta. It would be a good idea for him to come too, so they could both be shot.

But since this would be a serious matter, I decided to consult Carranza first. So I neither shot Bonales Sandoval that time nor told him whether to bring Félix Díaz along.

I had more than 3,500 men stationed from Camargo to Escalón and the greater part of my forces were being readied for my advance to the south. Knowing that the enemy was concentrating at La Laguna, I understood that I should also equip the forces in Durango and the Laguna district, as it would be useful to have them operate with me.

I had asked Pablo González, who was commanding the troops in the

northeast, to threaten Monterrey and Saltillo while I was taking Torreón, and I suggested to Máximo García and José Isabel Robles, at La
Laguna, that they isolate Torreón and its district, which was what Carranza was recommending from Sinaloa. In the preparation for moving
south, the principal hindrance was lack of money. If business was good,
I would have fewer difficulties; and seeing that the mining companies
and private enterprises could do nothing without money, I asked Carranza for five million in paper money, and when he could not send it
immediately, I printed my own in Chihuahua and had all I needed from
then on.

I was helped at first by the gold we found in the Banco Minero de
Chihuahua. I will tell how I got possession of it. When the Huertistas
left Chihuahua, not all the rich and powerful men fled with them. Some
remained, feeling sure they owed us nothing and thinking we would
not persecute them.

Among those who stayed was Don Luis Terrazas. Knowing how important he was and how much he could help us, I ordered him brought
to my quarters in the Federal Palace. I said, "Señor, you are rich and
must have money. But the money you have is what the poor have allowed you to keep until the Revolution and the time has come for you
to return it."

He answered, "You think I am rich, Sr. General? All that is left of my
wealth is a rumor. I have neither houses, haciendas, nor stock. My family has lost everything in what you call the Revolution. If you asked me
for one thousand pesos in exchange for my life, you would have to
hang me."

Knowing he could never be persuaded by reason, I sent Luisito to
convince him, but Luisito failed. I sent one of my officers, but he failed
too. Then I sent Rodolfo Fierro, who returned and said, "My General,
Don Luis Terrazas says that he has no money, but he knows where there
is some."

"And where does he say it is?"

"In one of the columns of the Banco Minero de Chihuahua. One of
them is full of gold, he doesn't know which, but if we find it we will
have enough."

Raúl Madero and Luisito examined the steel columns of the bank.
These two, with a mechanic and an electric drill, made holes in the
columns until they discovered what they were looking for. They split
the column, and in fifteen or twenty sacks gathered up the stream of
gold that poured out. It was all in ten-peso gold pieces. When they

were ready to bring it, they noticed that twenty or thirty more coins tumbled out of the column. They shook it, and still more came. Then they beat in the upper part of the column and another stream of gold poured out, and they filled fifteen or twenty more sacks.

That night the gold was carted to my quarters, and the next day I had Luisito count it. At noon he had not finished and I asked, "How much have you counted, Luisito?" He replied, "Six hundred thousand pesos, my General."

I said, "Good, Luisito, you can stop counting, and leave the extra pile for my friends."

So it was. As commanders and officers came to see me, I said to each in turn, "Compañerito, take whatever you need from the pile."

I did this not from indifference to the money we needed so much but to let them satisfy their own greed and have no reason to censure mine. Even if it was true that I was not going to take a single cent for myself, there were few who would have believed it. In the Revolution it had to be that way. Each useful man had to be humored in his inclinations: the generous in his generosity and the greedy in his greed, all within working limits. My chiefs and generals took what they thought was their part. Some took a great deal, others but a little, each after his fashion.

When I saw that Luis Aguirre Benavides had taken none of the gold after having had his hands on it day and night, I said, "Luisito, count out another ten thousand pesos." He counted them. Then I said, "Good. Those are for you and your family. When the money was counted, I sent Luisito to examine the other columns, which he did very carefully.

CHAPTER 13

Villa Knows that the Powerful Are Responsible for the Affliction of the Poor and Wishes to Keep the Revolutionary Men Undefiled.

The Selfishness of the Rich and the Suffering of the Poor. Forty Thousand Pesos at La Quinta Prieto. Juana Torres. A Letter from Villa's Wife. Villa Forgives. The Magi. Anacleto Girón. Manuel Bauche Alcalde. Federico and Roque González Garza.

Of the gold that came from the columns of the Banco Minero de Chihuahua I took not a single coin for myself. Furthermore, I had no inclination to take one. I could see that many Revolutionaries were straying from the path, and some were seeing the struggle, which was the battle of the poor against oppressors, as a chance to gain wealth and hoard it. I thought that I, Pancho Villa, and other Revolutionary officers should set an example of unselfishness.

The rich, before they become rich, have the thoughts and inclinations of the poor. But a little money blinds them with eagerness to have more, and they forget. I therefore thought it would be good to show that I was indifferent to the gold.

But something occurred that I had not expected. The last forty thousand pesos disappeared from the cabinet at La Quinta Prieto where I had put it for safekeeping. They would believe that I had taken for my own use money intended for our common expenses. In great anger I questioned my brother Hipólito, "What do you know about the money?"

"I know nothing about it."

I called Juana Torres, my wife, and said, "Juana, what do you know about it?"

She replied, "Nothing."

I called Luisito and said, "Luisito, what do you know?"

"I know nothing about it."

My anger increased, and I threatened every man and woman near me. Hipólito and I began to investigate and he discovered that Juana's mother and her sister were the thieves. I had them put in prison. Weeping, Juana said, "They are innocent. All this is the work of intrigue. There are men and women who hate me." Señor, how could she believe that her mother and sister would rob the army and the cause? I kept them in prison, and though Juana Torres went on weeping and swearing they were innocent, I never wavered. I said, "Your mother and sister will stay locked up until the money is put back in the cabinet."

One day Juana Torres passed a letter to her mother in a lunch basket. It did not reach the prisoner but came to me instead. The jailer brought it and I opened it and read it. It went: "Mama, I suffer very much from what has happened to you. But what can I do with this bandit? My life with him is torture. I would rather die than endure it. I beg him, I weep, but he is heartless; he will never yield until he is paid."

When I read the letter I considered going in search of her and killing her. Señor, couldn't Juana Torres understand my kindness to her and everyone? How could she call me a bandit? In my early life perhaps I had fallen into great errors through ignorance and inexperience. But I was now a Revolutionary man who won battles for the people. Did that make me a bandit? If my conduct was worse than death to Juana Torres, then death she should get. But I distrusted my impulses. I called Luisito and said, "You see what women are. Read this letter."

He read the letter, and I explained, "Juana Torres is my wife by affection and law. I could have taken her by force, and did not do it. I could have taken her by gifts and flattery and did not do that. In my desire for her, I understood her scruples and made her my wife; I gave her the protection of civil marriage. But what happens now, Luisito? This is the way she treats Pancho Villa, who lifted her high above her dreams. And then I added, "I loved her, Luisito, but that is over. What punishment should such a woman suffer?"

Luisito said, "My General, pardon her."

"Yes, Luisito, women must be forgiven; but there are offenses which call for punishment."

I went to Juana's room, and handing her the letter said, "Juana, read me this letter. You know how badly I read, and how badly I treat men and women."

When she saw it, she almost fainted. You could see in her eyes that she was afraid I was going to kill her; and I did want to kill her, but I said, "Go on, Child, read me the letter. I want to hear it."

She could not speak; she stood there terrified, her lips, her fingers, and her knees trembling. But I felt no pity. I said, "You don't recognize it, my child, and don't want to read it to me?" As I approached her, I saw that she shook with fright and wanted to read but could not. I thought, "How could a powerful man like me crush a woman, even though she had offended him?"

At last, unable to resist my authority any longer, she began to read, in a quavering voice. I did feel sorry for her then and was about to pardon her. But my anger returned on hearing from her mouth the offensive words she had written. When she had finished, I said, "I am only an ignorant man who does not understand. Read it again. Once more I want to hear what it says about me."

She read it again, still weeping and still terrified. But now my pity was really great. Señor, how we men are alike in our passion! When the woman we love offends us we take the same pleasure in making her suffer as we took in winning her affection. I left her and went to set her mother and sister free in return for her disloyalty and I gave them enough money to leave Chihuahua.

At this time, when many political figures had arrived in the territory held by my forces and continued to arrive, the First Chief sent three white-bearded old gentlemen to look into our financial situation: Nicéforo Zambrano, Don Manuel Amaya, and another whose name I forget. When apprized of their business, I thought, "The Magi sent by the First Chief do not come to offer any treasure, but to see what they can carry away."

They said, "Sr. General, it is not good to print so much paper money. It causes serious complications. Use the bills issued by the Commander in Chief and what you seize in the progress of your campaign."

I replied, "Señores, I began this war with nothing but nine men. As for money, I used only the few pesos I myself had, those my brother lent me, and those Don José María Maytorena kindly contributed. If I had worried about complications, I would not be in control of Chihuahua at this moment, nor would I be on the point of moving south. I know nothing about money, but I know what my troops need and will hear of nothing unless it relates to our victory. If you don't want me to print money, bring me what I need. And if you cannot bring me all I need, permit me to have accounts that will be paid when this war ends. Then we can see what the Republic has lost in the way of money and gained in other ways."

A lawyer by the name of Luis Cabrera also came to discuss that subject. He was intelligent and, seeing that I was right, promised to support my requests. His only recommendation was to print no more paper money than necessary and that in regular series.

A man by the name of Gustavo Padrés came from Sonora because of his enmity for Maytorena, and I appointed him municipal president of Ciudad Juárez. And there were others, persecuted by Obregón, like

Pedro Bracamontes, whom I made municipal president of Chihuahua, and Manuel Bauche Alcalde, who published a newspaper for me, and Anacleto J. Girón, who was given command of troops because he appeared to be brave and well versed in military affairs. The lawyer Federico González Garza and his brother Roque González Garza also came, good Revolutionaries, whom I liked because of their affection for Sr. Madero. I appointed the lawyer secretary and advisor to Fidel Avila, chief of arms in Ciudad Juárez, and I gave Don Roque, his brother, the presidency of the Council of War of my division.

CHAPTER 14

In Control of All the Resources of Chihuahua, Villa Makes His Second Advance on the Cities in the Lagunera District.

Miguel Trillo. Enrique Pérez Rul. Huerta's Preparations. Federico Cervantes. Adolfo de la Huerta. Pictures of Villa and Carranza. Rafael Zubarán. Martín Luis Guzmán's Newspaper. The Revolution Divided. "You Are the Hero of This War, Sr. General." Aguirre Benavides. Rodolfo Fierro. Raúl Madero. Santa Rosalía. Yermo.

Our secretarial work increased to where Luisito could not tend to it alone. He brought in a boy named Miguel Trillo, who was working in the office of the secretary general, and another, a professor by the name of Enrique Pérez Rul. With them he could carry on his own work as well as that of others who were in charge of bookkeeping, payment of troops, and the purchases I was making for going south. I knew of Huerta's preparations to defeat me at Torreón, and wanted every step taken under my own eyes.

Worried about our shortage of arms and ammunition, I asked Carranza for skilled personnel to make projectiles in the shops at Chihuahua. I even thought of trying airplanes and asked for an aviator.

Carranza sent me Major Federico Cervantes, a young man I at first disliked. But he soon became useful because of his knowledge of artillery, and I saw he was devoted to Sr. Madero and the cause.

In preparation for his trip to Chihuahua, Carranza set up his principal offices in Ciudad Juárez, to which he sent his political representatives in advance. A boy, Adolfo de la Huerta, appeared with a trainload of employees, among them Carlos Esquerro, who took over the Customs House, where he found a small picture of me on the wall. He removed it and replaced it with a large one of Carranza. When they came to me with the story I answered, "Señores, my picture is not needed in Ciudad Juárez. I and my forces took that place. They all know me there, in flesh and blood, and will always remember me."

The lawyer Rafael Zubarán, Carranza's Minister of the Interior, one of the new arrivals, was accompanied by a boy named Martín Luis Guzmán, who came to see me in Chihuahua and said he was to start a newspaper in defense of our ideals and asked me if I would help. I offered whatever amount Sr. Carranza would give him and I provided him with a letter instructing my financial agent in Juárez to deliver my contribution and Manuel Chao's. But the boy, quitting Carranza's service, wrote to say he would not go on with the project and had left my money on deposit with the firm of Roberto Pesqueira and Francisco Elías, to be delivered to my order if the paper was not established.

It is my belief that these men were becoming restless. Each who left Sonora, or stayed away from there, because of differences with Carranza or Maytorena or Obregón, came to Chihuahua with the idea of pursuing a better course. Many of them expected me to take them under my protection, but though I refused no one, I discouraged them in their purpose of sowing confusion. At best this would grow, for the causes were increasing, whether from secret designs of Carranza's, or because he, Obregón, and Maytorena were enmeshed at last in the intrigues of the chocolate drinkers and sweet-scented gentlemen who followed them.

In my judgment the dissensions originated in the fiestas and *tertulias* our First Chief was so fond of attending in Sonora. His intimates considered the Revolution almost won and were not so much concerned with the struggle as with dividing the spoils. They were jealous of one another and fought among themselves and wanted the rest of us to do the same.

A lawyer named Vasconcelos, who came to see me, then or earlier, said, "You are the hero of the Revolution, Sr. General, and the people of the world have never made more progress than under their heroes. With you we will win."

I knew he either considered me superior to Carranza and the other leaders or wanted me to consider myself so. But I was not deceived. I saw only that he was Carranza's enemy and a talkative fellow. I knew, too, that while we were getting killed in Mexico, he, with a woman companion, was waiting out our success in the United States. I answered, "Señor, the true heroes are my boys who die on the battlefields."

But the germs of division were spreading to the minds of my stoutest men. One of the victims was Eugenio Aguirre Benavides. I had ordered him to bring his forces to Chihuahua where, being from the Laguna district, he would be useful to me. Rodolfo Fierro, also in Chihuahua, was on bad terms with Aguirre Benavides over the death of the young Revolutionary García de la Cadena. And Fierro had a fight with an officer on Aguirre Benavides' staff and killed him. Aguirre Benavides complained, "Señor, Fierro has wantonly seized an officer of mine and killed him. I ask you to punish him." His words inclined me to agree with him, but I tried to calm him, knowing how useful Rodolfo Fierro was in battle and not wanting to lose him.

Aguirre Benavides, a stubborn fellow, would not yield to persuasion. He insisted on his demands. I said, "Perhaps you are right, but do you think I would have a useful fellow like Fierro shot for one death? When times change and I have to return to the sierra, Fierro and his compañeros will follow me while you and your officers abandon me." He made no reply. But the next day, when following the dead officer to the cemetery, his brigade made such a display of grief on the streets of Chihuahua that I was angered. I removed him from command of the Zaragoza Brigade, and gave it to Raúl Madero, who had been without troops since the taking of Ojinaga.

But when Aguirre Benavides decided to go to Sonora to see Carranza, Raulito persuaded me that the change in command was inadvisable. We therefore had an amicable discussion, Eugenio, Luisito, Raúl, and I, after which I put him back at the head of his brigade, with Raúl as his second. It turned out to be a bad arrangement. Eugenio, still resentful, talked against Fierro and me, and although I paid no attention to reports of this, I knew that from that moment his heart was not with me.

The time came for my move south, the middle of March, 1914, when Carranza had left Sonora on his way to Ciudad Juárez. On ahead by train went the forces of Maclovio Herrera, Toribio Ortega, Eugenio

Aguirre Benavides, Orestes Pereyra, José and Trinidad Rodríguez, Miguel González, and Martiniano Servín, followed by two artillery trains, with twenty-eight cannons and about two thousand grenades, and the hospital train, the latter in charge of Colonel Andrés Villarreal, a doctor of great energy and knowledge. My own train, with the car of the Council of War and the machine guns, the automobiles, and the armament, equipment, and ammunition cars, left Chihuahua about seven in the evening. With me were Sr. General Felipe Angeles—commandant of my artillery—and my escort, my staff, and Luisito and my office employees.

At dawn of the seventeenth we halted in Santa Rosalía de Camargo, where I reviewed Don Rosalío Hernández' troops, and on the following day continued south, with my advance troops under the tireless, impulsive, and impatient Maclovio Herrera. I had been too busy in Santa Rosalía to accept more than a dance and a meal of the many celebrations planned by the people.

I left the hospital train in Escalón. My train arrived about six that afternoon at Yermo. My brigades, concentrated here and ready to advance, were: The Villa Brigade with 1,500 under General José Rodríguez; the Benito Juárez Brigade with 1,300 under General Herrera; the Zaragoza Brigade with 1,500 under General Aguirre Benavides and Colonel Raúl Madero; the González Ortega Brigade with 1,200 under General Ortega; the Cuauhtémoc Brigade with 400 under Colonel Trinidad Rodríguez; the Madero Brigade with 400 under Colonel Máximo García; the Hernández Brigade with 600 under General Hernández; a part of the Juárez Brigade of Durango with 500 under Colonel Mestas; the Guadalupe Victoria Brigade with 500 under Colonel Miguel González; the artillery, under General Felipe Angeles, Colonels Martiniano Servín and Manuel García Santibáñez, and consisting of two regiments of three batteries each and the cannons El Niño and El Chavalito on their platforms.

Considering this array and those yet to join me at La Laguna, I thought to myself, "It is true that I have many well-organized men and good artillery under an artillerist who knows how to use it, but in Torreón Huerta has likewise accumulated a big force, with his best artillery and his best commanders." It was clear that there would be a violent struggle at La Laguna which could result in the fall of Huerta or in a check to our cause, and looking at all my trainloads of men I was considering the steps I should take to win a victory with the fewest losses.

CHAPTER 15

Villa Stops the Federal Advance at La Laguna and Prepares To Attack Sacramento and Gómez Palacio.

Tlahualilo, Bermejillo, and Mapimí. Aguirre Benavides and Tomás Urbina. Humanitarian Sentiment. Generals Velasco and Angeles. Colonel Borunda. Sacramento. Rosalío Hernández. Abdón Pérez. Summary Judgment. Fifteen Hundred Men Hidden in Fifteen Trains. Villa's Speech.

At dawn, with my troops in a widespread line, I began my advance, having decided to go as far as Conejos that day. We met with no resistance. We were in Conejos before five that afternoon, March 19, 1914, and that night, in spite of bad weather, the artillery reached us with the other rear trains. From the couriers I learned that the enemy's center outposts were in Peronal, on our road, and his left was in Mapimí and his right in Tlahualilo. I said to my brigade leaders, "Señores, we will advance at dawn. On the left, General Aguirre Benavides will advance with the Zaragoza, Cuauhtémoc, Madero, and Guadalupe Victoria brigades to take Tlahualilo; the rest will advance together at the center and the immediate right to drive the outposts from Peronal and continue to Bermejillo. On our far right, Tomás Urbina will bring the two thousand men of the Morelos Brigade from Las Nieves to take Mapimí."

The next morning at five the whole movement began. My own escort and my staff led the center. They pursued and annihilated the eighty or one hundred *rurales* holding Peronal, with casualties of only one wounded and six or seven lost, but a captain and two soldiers were killed soon afterward in a skirmish with the *rurales* garrisoning Bermejillo. Of about 300 *rurales,* 106 fell in the fight, and the rest dispersed in the direction of Gómez Palacio with my forces in pursuit. That afternoon we reached the Hacienda de Santa Clara, south of Bermejillo, where I established my headquarters, and since we had repaired the tracks as we advanced, the military trains overtook us that day.

While my center and part of my right were on the march, Aguirre Benavides and Urbina were carrying out their assignment. Aguirre Benavides took Tlahualilo in a sudden, and I think skilful, attack, since he killed about sixty and had only fourteen dead and wounded. Urbina's

forces passed Pelayo, Hornillas, and Cadena, and fell on Mapimí. When
the enemy saw that neither their center nor their right had stopped us,
they were afraid that the garrison at Mapimí would be cut off, so they
abandoned that place quickly and ordered the garrison to retreat to
Gómez Palacio, following the rims of the sierra.

That afternoon General Felipe Angeles said, "My General, to avoid
bloodshed we should ask General Refugio Velasco to surrender Torreón and the other towns of La Laguna." I shared his humane views and
accordingly communicated with General Velasco by telephone, and he
and Angeles had the following conversation.

"Good afternoon, Sr. General Velasco."

"Good afternoon, Sr. General Angeles. Where are you speaking
from?"

"From Bermejillo, Sr. General."

"Have you taken Bermejillo already?"

"Yes, Sr. General."

"I congratulate you."

"Thank you, Sr. General."

"Were there many casualties?"

"Hardly any, Sr. General. That is why I am calling you. You will save
the lives of many Mexicans by bringing your useless resistance to an end
and surrendering the places you occupy."

General Velasco replied, "Sr. General, permit me to take issue with
you."

"In what respect?"

"In what respect?"

"That is what I asked."

Velasco, not wishing to continue, handed the telephone to one of his
colonels, who explained that the Revolutionaries would be the ones to
surrender. A little while afterward the telephone rang, and this time I
answered.

"Who is speaking?"

"Francisco Villa, Señor."

"Francisco Villa?"

"Yes, Señor. Francisco Villa."

"Fine, because we are coming after you in just a moment."

"Come on, Señores, you will be welcome."

"Have supper ready for us."

"We'll have something warm for you."

"We'll be there."

"Good, Señor, but if it's too much trouble, we'll come and get you. We have traveled a long way just for the pleasure of seeing you, and we are getting tired of looking for you everywhere."

"Are there many of you?"

"Not so many, Señor. Just a couple of regiments of artillery and ten thousand men."

At dawn on March 21, 1914, I was preparing for the new advance. Urbina had occupied Mapimí with the forces of Colonel Borunda, and the rest of his troops were making a forced march to join him. My rail and telegraph communications with the north were in good order. This was the news I was waiting for. I dictated my new measures as follows: Urbina was to march with the Morelos Brigade in open formation to Santa Clara, where he would arrive on the following morning and join my center; Aguirre Benavides was to continue his advance on the left to the Hacienda de Sacramento and take it at any cost with the support of the mountain artillery. Having driven the enemy from his Tlahualilo-Bermejillo line, and with the ridges of the sierra at my right, I was going to break his new San Pedro de las Colonias–Sacramento– Gómez Palacio line.

We were encountering stiffer resistance: the attack on Sacramento began before six in the afternoon, and at midnight they were still giving us a hard fight. I learned that their strength was concentrated in the church and in the central part of town, and from there they were holding us back. They had been reinforced by Juan Andreu Almazán with the entire garrison from San Pedro de las Colonias, whereas my mountain artillery, under Aguirre Benavides, was not coming into play because of mechanical damages suffered on the march. I ordered Rosalío Hernández to help Aguirre Benavides at Sacramento. I knew he was too proud to ask for reinforcements, but I needed Sacramento in my attack on Gómez Palacio. With it I would have the central railroad line from Torreón to Monterrey, which could furnish reinforcements to the enemy or afford him a safe retreat. I had twice asked Pablo González to destroy the railway tracks, but, as I feared, he had not.

To Bermejillo came a Federal officer, Abdón Pérez. He had been paymaster to the Huertistas in Torreón. He told me he had deserted because of dislike for Huerta and devotion to the people. When I asked him why he had served the enemy until that moment, he answered, "My General, we do not always do what we wish, but only what is forced upon us." Remembering the many times I had wanted to do good but had had to do evil, I took him onto my staff.

He then added, "My General, there is something else. When I deserted I buried the money I had in my custody, a large sum in gold coins." He wanted to tell me or someone where he had hidden it, but I cautioned that it would be better to keep his secret until we took Torreón.

In Bermejillo my soldiers also captured a locksmith who had betrayed certain Revolutionaries to the enemy. I ordered the Council to try him summarily and shoot him immediately.

At five, the morning of March 22, my center continued its advance on the railroad line. The plan was for the main forces to be concentrated at Santa Clara, where my advance was already stationed. But I noticed, as the troops were leaving Bermejillo, that many seemed to be missing, and I wanted the mystery cleared up. I had my escort search the fifteen trains with an order to put all armed men they found into formation on the track. We found no less than 1,500 men, well armed and supplied with ammunition. When they were lined up I stood in front of them and said, "Muchachos, we are here to take Torreón. Did you come here under my command to waste my arms or to use them against the enemy? I drag nobody into battle, even in defense of the people's cause. But neither do I let anyone desert in the face of the enemy. You who are ready to fight will step forward. The rest of you will stay where you are. I promise you won't have to face the enemy because you will be shot on the spot."

They all stepped forward, for such are soldiers that many of them will fight more in fear of their officers than for love of the cause. I formed them into three battalions, one of which I left at Bermejillo to garrison the town. The others entrained for Santa Clara.

CHAPTER 16

Villa Takes Possession of Sacramento and Ciudad Lerdo and Prepares To Take Torreón.

Sacramento. Trinidad Rodríguez. Máximo García. Velasco's Forces. Measures That Failed. Abdón Pérez. Saúl Navarro. Herrera. Villa's Charge. Gustavo Bazán. El Vergel. The Taking of Lerdo. Domingo Arrieta. Calixto Contreras. Severino Ceniceros. José Isabel Robles.

At Sacramento, Hernández' troops had already joined those of Aguirre Benavides. According to reports the fighting there was hard, for the enemy, under Almazán, had received heavy reinforcements from Torreón and was attempting to break Aguirre Benavides' lines. Trinidad Rodríguez, who had just come from Sacramento with two bullets in his body, was saying, "I am sorry, my General, that these bullets have taken me out of the fight, but what troubles me most is the punishment my brigade is taking. Still, as things are, the place will be ours before the day is over." Máximo García confirmed his prediction. They brought him back in worse condition than Rodríguez, with a bullet in his stomach. To judge from the wounded, Aguirre Benavides had no easy task, but he would accomplish it.

I left for Santa Clara well informed of the Federals' actual strength but without exact knowledge of their positions. With Refugio Velasco at their general headquarters were Generals Ricardo Peña, Eduardo Ocaranza, and Benjamín Argumedo, three men of great valor, and another, Federico Reyna, equally qualified, was there in command of volunteers. Their soldiers numbered no less than ten thousand. They had twelve cannons, an enormous number of grenades, and plenty of supplies. They had machine guns mounted on permanent emplacements and many good officers to direct them.

On my arrival I dictated orders for the attack on Gómez Palacio, the point where the enemy, spread out in front of my advance, had concentrated his entire left and center, after destroying the track south of Noé, toward which my trains were approaching. My right wing, the forces of Herrera and Ortega, would advance in a firing line on a five-kilometer front; my center, formed by the artillery and the two battalions I had just organized in Bermejillo and placed under the command of Lieutenant Colonel Santiago Ramírez, would follow the railroad line; my left wing, composed of the Villa Brigade and the Juárez Brigade from Durango, would advance in a firing line on another five-kilometer front. I ordered the trains transporting my general headquarters, the Health Service, and provisions to stop at Noé until the track was restored. Four kilometers from the town I ordered my troops to dismount and chain their horses. They would continue as infantry under the protection of our cannon.

At six that afternoon we saw the enemy on the outskirts of the city, in prepared positions. Part of our forces were delayed for an hour and the enemy artillery opened fire from concealed positions before we could put my orders into operation. That infuriated my troops, and it was impossible to contain them. Without dismounting or waiting for new orders, and first at a trot, then at a gallop, and then at a dead run, my brigade rushed forward in a frenzied assault which carried them through the fire of the enemy cannon and machine guns to the first line of houses in Gómez Palacio.

That was the beginning of a struggle that caused the enemy many casualties but caused us more, since we were advancing without protection and many of the soldiers of my center, knowing little about war but driven by fury, did not even obey the order to spread out. The first Federal grenade killed Abdón Pérez, the paymaster who had left the gold hidden in Torreón. The second grenade wounded Saúl Navarro, lieutenant colonel of the Villa Brigade, and several soldiers near him. Our casualties were increasing every minute because the enemies were firing accurately and their directions were well concerted, but the fighting grew all the more furious because my troops were undaunted. Our cannon could not even fire since some of my men, in their innocence, were already running between the houses and making themselves targets for our own pieces.

In the first encounter my center and wings had seventy dead and about two hundred wounded, and we had more dead and wounded that night. This happened because Herrera and his forces were so anxious to attack that for several hours they faced bombardment from La Pila hill. The hill was a natural defense and the firing was skilfully directed. Maclovio lost his horse and almost lost his staff, most of whom were killed or wounded.

The fighting became just as violent on the following morning. We had no less than 125 dead and 315 wounded, among them the chief of Herrera's staff, Lieutenant Colonel Triana. But by then General Angeles had drawn up our artillery at San Ignacio, a hill to the right of the railroad below El Vergel. He had batteries there under the command of Martiniano Servín and another commanded by Manuel García Santibáñez, and he himself was in charge of cannon located on the left side of the track nearer the enemy.

Seeing how strong the enemy positions were at Gómez Palacio, I said to Herrera, "Sr. General, while we hold the front here and our artillery bombards La Pila, La Jabonera, La Casa Redonda, and the entrenchments north of the city, extend your line on the right, attack Ciudad Lerdo, and take it." Herrera, not unaware of the danger of the maneuver, bravely left to carry out my orders. But I had made a mistake when I dictated this measure. Our fire, although accurate, was not containing that of the enemy, and the action of my center, which I myself was directing, was not blocking their movements. They therefore moved out to meet Maclovio's attack instead of waiting for it, their forces were superior in numbers, and I saw that they intended to outflank him and thus put our artillery in great danger. To correct my error I could think of nothing but to fall on the enemy cavalry, followed by Jesús Ríos and my entire escort. I charged with such fury that their fire could not stop me. We reached them and routed them. They scattered in flight, and Herrera was able to go on toward Ciudad Lerdo.

In the charge we killed Colonel Federico Reyna, leader of the Huertista volunteers. And why not, Señor, in an encounter in which officers were heroically exposed like the soldiers? Our charge was worth seeing. Throughout the morning the fighting was bloody, and as it seemed that the enemy were getting reinforcements on that front, I ordered my lines to spread out as far as El Vergel. Maclovio had to be able to take Lerdo that night; and the action at Sacramento had to be decided so the troops of Aguirre Benavides and Rosalío Hernández could come to my assistance.

I saw a boy walking behind my horse. The heat was so stifling and our thirst was so great that I felt sorry for him. I said, "Who are you, my boy?"

"I am Major Gustavo Bazán, my General."

"Which are your forces?"

"I belong to those of General Felipe Angeles."

"Señor! And what are you doing here?"

"I came from Sonora this morning to join him at El Vergel, my General."

"And why didn't you join him there?"

"He was at the front reconnoitering, and it was my duty to find him."

"Very well, my boy, but don't wear yourself out. Jump up behind and ride."

And I stopped to let him get on.

Soon after we concentrated at El Vergel I heard that Sacramento was in our hands and the main body of the Zaragoza, Hernández, Cuauhtémoc, Madero, and Guadalupe Victoria brigades was coming to join me. In Sacramento the enemy had suffered some three hundred casualties, and forty men, armed and equipped, came over to our ranks. The action had cost us one hundred wounded and fifty dead, among these Lieutenant Colonel Cipriano Puente. In flight the enemy tried to take a strong position at El Porvenir, on the line from Torreón to Monterrey, and our forces defeated them there, took their supply trains, and forced them to retreat toward Gómez Palacio. Aguirre Benavides destroyed the track from Jameson to San Pedro de las Colonias and had Colonel Toribio V. de los Santos occupy San Pedro de las Colonias and immediately continue the destruction as far as Hipólito so as to close the road to reinforcements from Monterrey.

That same night Aguirre Benavides' forces camped in Jameson. I sent him orders by an officer to join me at my camp the next morning. I also sent him, Don Rosalío, and the forces which had fought with them messages of commendation. That night I received the report that Herrera had just taken Ciudad Lerdo, which was the other triumph that I needed.

About eight the next morning Aguirre Benavides and Hernández joined me with their 3,500 men. Soon afterward Herrera brought me a report of his action of the day before.

While we were regrouping and our trains were occupied with the repair of the track I saw the enemy soldiers leaving the field of the previous day's combat. In midmorning they tried to bombard us on the pretext of interrupting our repair, but perhaps to entice our artillery into replying and revealing our new emplacements. We ignored them, as the fire was not bothering us, but soon afterward, encouraged by our inaction, they gave indications of preparing to move forward again. I advanced my escort and five hundred of Aguirre Benavides' men, and thus succeeded in thwarting the move.

Our attack would pose difficulties, and it was urgent that it be conducted according to plan. I called a meeting of my generals. We decided upon these measures: General Domingo Arrieta would aid us with the forces he had in Santiago Papasquiaro; Generals Calixto Contreras and Severino Ceniceros would move their troops from Pedriceña

to Avilés; General José Isabel Robles would bring his brigade, encamped at Picardías in Durango, to La Perla; the track between Parras
and Torreón would be cut, to sever enemy communications in that area.
Considering the strength of Velasco's positions, our objective was to surround him in Torreón and weaken him by wearing out his men and
exhausting his provisions. It was necessary to prevent him from receiving assistance or reinforcements from anywhere and I was sure I could
accomplish this, for I had cut his communications with Mexico City at
the beginning of our operations; I had just cut them with Monterrey;
and next I would see that they were cut between Parras and Saltillo.

CHAPTER 17

In Stupendous Assaults Villa Takes Half of La
Pila Hill from Velasco.

Ambulance Trains. Santibáñez' Batteries. Flashes of Gun-
fire. Cannon for La Jabonera. Gonzalitos. Gustavo Bazán.
Maclovio, Rodríguez, and Urbina on La Pila Hill. The
Delay of Eugenio and Rosalío.

Throughout the afternoon and the next morning
we and the enemy watched each other very calmly. They were probably
busy fortifying their positions and gathering up their wounded. I was
busy putting ours onto trains for Jiménez, Santa Rosalía, and Chihuahua. Under Dr. Andrés Villarreal it was a marvel the way our
wounded were gathered and taken north in good ambulance trains. In
the lull we were placing our artillery in position to be of more value
to us in the first two days of battle. Felipe Angeles said, "We must move
our cannon up, my General—so close that the shells can penetrate armor
plating."
  "And when will we do that, Sr. General?"
  "When we take La Pila hill."
  "Then this same night, Señor, I will take La Pila hill, or damage the
fortifications so much that you can unleash your full power."

The attack was to be made in the following manner: the right, formed by the Villa and Juárez brigades, would advance until it routed the enemy front between Gómez Palacio and Lerdo; its objective would be to take La Pila. The center, formed by the González Ortega and Guadalupe Victoria brigades, would move on Gómez Palacio from both sides of the railroad; it was to protect the artillery up to points from which our cannon would cause great damage, and draw part of the enemy fire away from our right. The left, formed by the Hernández and Zaragoza brigades, would march against Gómez Palacio from the east; it was to perform the final operations, which should end in taking the town when, with La Pila silenced, we could launch ourselves upon the three enemy fronts.

We had not paused a moment in the work of repairing the railroad and by three that afternoon I sent out our first scouting train. It drew the Federals' fire from the time it was within three kilometers of them. This was between four and four-thirty as our forces were pushing up and El Niño was finding its targets on La Pila.

At five, when the fight was getting hot, Urbina appeared with an escort of 160 men. He had sent the rest of his two thousand on ahead from Las Nieves. Without wasting time in talking, he proceeded at once against La Pila, where the forces of Rodríguez and Herrera were already engaged.

At dark, when the action grew general, Severino Ceniceros arrived with an escort of two hundred men and word that the rest of his forces were advancing upon Avilés and that Calixto Contreras was on his way and would make his entrance at Ciudad Lerdo. I instructed him to support the action of my center, since the left was dragging. Unless the center could offset this, the entire attack might fail. Without my knowing why, Rosalío Hernández and Aguirre Benavides were showing no signs of life east of Gómez Palacio, the sector assigned to them. My mind was uneasy, suspecting that they would arrive too late for concerted action.

On my right front I had more than 4,200 men, on my center more than 2,500 men and on my left front more than 2,300 men. The fighting increased. We were dominating everywhere but with great losses. Under protection of darkness our artillery had moved to points from which according to General Angeles, our bombardment would be effective. I saw that the batteries commanded by García Santibáñez were hitting their marks on La Pila, and cannon nearer Gómez Palacio, to the left and right of the track, were supporting the action of the troops of Toribio Ortega and Miguel González, which were advancing there.

We must not fail in the attack on Gómez Palacio that night, and I was overlooking no point on the battlefront. I reconnoitered them all, joined often by General Angeles, who would hurry back to his cannon, but when he happened to be near me would ask my opinion or give his advice, frankly and intelligently.

It was nine that night when Maclovio, Urbina, and Rodríguez began to throw their troops against La Pila. Supported by the action of my center and the extreme right and the bombardment of our artillery, they cleared the level ground of all obstructions, their progress marked by flashes of gunfire, which only wavered when they began to climb the hill, where they seemed to lose bits of conquered ground and then recover them. Every inch of ground gained was an inch of ground swept by machine guns, rifles, and cannon. The flashes of gunfire overpowered the mind. Señor! It took brave men to assault those positions! It was an honor to be in that battle, and a greater honor to have assembled that army of free men.

While reconnoitering a stretch of the line on the north I met a group of men marching to the rear. My escort halted them and brought them before me. They told me they belonged to Ortega's forces and were looking for me to ask for artillery needed to attack La Jabonera where the enemy was beginning an advance. I immediately took their words on faith and, carried away by impulse, did not find out for certain whether our troops were in control where they said artillery was needed. I went over to a battery nearby and ordered two officers to take two cannons and go to the support of La Jabonera. One of these, by the name of Gonzalitos, was a boy in Angeles' confidence. The other, Bazán, was the one I had taken on my horse at El Vergel.

I soon found out that the men had deceived me. It was not true that the enemy was about to take La Jabonera or that an advance in that area would permit us to use artillery. Gonzalitos and Bazán, with all their energy and daring, could not even approach the positions to which I had sent them.

Luckily, General Angeles appeared. He said he had just come from the section where the cannons were advancing and it was impossible to make such an advance. I had him order the withdrawal of the two pieces of artillery. But I had put them in a dangerous situation and had virtually sent Gonzalitos and Bazán and their soldiers to their death. But the men who had deceived me I would recognize by the look in their eyes, and I would have them convicted of falsehood and shot.

It must have been nine-thirty at night when the assault on La Pila came within reach of the fortifications at the top, thanks to bombs and damaging fire from García Santibáñez' artillery. Fighting increased all along the front, except on the left. There the absence of the Zaragoza and Hernández brigades permitted the defenders to rest, and let them concentrate on the other lines. The enemy knew, as we did, that the fate of Gómez Palacio was being decided on the hill. They were dying in order to save those positions; we were dying in order to seize them. An hour and a half after the assault began, Maclovio, Urbina, and Rodríguez reached the highest point of the hill. Fully exposed to machine guns and entrenched riflemen, my men reached through loopholes to disarm their opponents and with fire and sword took everything within reach. It was of no help to the usurping forces to make such a heroic defense and lose hundreds of soldiers and officers. At ten-thirty that night on March 25, 1914, we gained possession of two of the five fortified positions on La Pila. We had possession of half the hill.

And as that gave us control on our right, I took my measures to make the triumph complete. I sent Herrera to rout the enemy between Gómez Palacio and Lerdo. If he succeeded, and if Aguirre Benavides and Hernández arrived on time, Gómez Palacio would be ours at dawn. Within a short time he had executed my order: he drove the forces which extended to Ciudad Lerdo back into Gómez Palacio. Thereupon we intensified our fire on the other fortifications on La Pila, and strengthened the attack on La Jabonera and La Casa Redonda and the houses on the northern side of the town. For more than two hours we kept this up, without relaxing our efforts, as we waited for the Hernández and Zaragoza brigades to arrive on the east. But as they did not come until one in the morning, when they began their action the right was already exhausted, and the center, although it had received less punishment than the right, was too weak to lend decisive aid to the attacks of the left.

It angered me to see a part of our victory slip away from us, but I was uncertain as to whether the blame should fall on Hernández and Aguirre Benavides, who had made a slow march in order to keep in contact on their roundabout approach, or on me for not realizing in time that the delay might occur. The chief must foresee every reasonable event that might prevent compliance in a subordinate, and the subordinate is not responsible if, under the circumstances, he complies as far as possible.

CHAPTER 18

After a Stubborn and Heroic Defense the Federals Surrender Gómez Palacio to Villa's Troops.

Contreras' Two Thousand Men. El Niño and El Chavalito. The Federal Counterattack on La Pila. Ricardo Peña. Eduardo Ocaranza. A Federal Charge. General Felipe Angeles. José Isabel Robles' Fifteen Hundred Men. Villa's Measures. The Silence at La Casa Redonda. Gómez Palacio. A Telegram to the First Chief.

At dawn I received a report that Calixto Contreras and his two thousand men had already passed Avilés. I had them supplied with ammunition at once, and ordered them to advance and help us take the other half of La Pila. I ordered the rapid repair of the track on which we were then approaching the station at Gómez Palacio. The Federals, intending to drive us back and protect themselves against El Niño and El Chavalito, which I was moving forward as fast as the repairs were made, were interrupting our progress with their cannon.

Battle broke out on top of the hill very early that morning, and moments afterward assumed major proportions. The enemy, realizing the danger there, were concentrating their greatest strength against it and were determined to recover by daylight what we had taken away by night. My only recourse was to hasten the march of Calixto Contreras' troops. Nothing would help as much as reinforcements on other fronts, which would require the enemy to weaken his resistance on the hill. Our assistance did not arrive with the necessary promptness. We had to prepare for the new struggle with the added disadvantage of the enemy's being able to bombard us better with his good artillery.

Even so, that action was not easy for them; in attempting it they ran the risk of great losses. They had to climb to assault the fortifications we had won, and we were facing them fully armed from the top and sides of the hill. As the struggle spread it grew into a battle almost as terrible as that of the previous night, and since we now had the protection of fortifications and trenches, which a few hours before had been theirs, they were taking the worst of the punishment. In the struggle they lost General Ricardo Peña, a man of very great valor; and General Eduardo Ocaranza, another good military man, was wounded.

It went on for more than two hours. They were fighting with so much determination and with such good support from their artillery and they were throwing themselves on the fortifications in such large columns that my generals saw that Velasco's plan was to drive us from the hill at whatever cost. Certain of this, my generals decided to return the positions, rather than lose the best men in their brigades there. It was better to let them have their fortifications then and retake them by night and hold them the next day, thanks to the concerted help of other troops, for this would reduce our losses.

So we abandoned the top of La Pila and its slopes, taking the two or three machine guns we had captured, and carried the battle back to the plain. But again in possession of the hill, the enemy succeeded in paralyzing the action of my center and my left with his good artillery. Thus they thought to correct the difficulties which our occupancy of the hill had caused them. They began to leave their shelter, and at what they considered a propitious moment threw themselves upon our center with a cavalry attack which endangered the artillery commanded in person by General Angeles.

The cannon, which Angeles during the night had brought to within barely more than a kilometer from the enemy, had not been moved, perhaps with the good intention of not discontinuing firing or perhaps because the gunners mistakenly thought I had ordered the reinforcement of the troops on La Pila. A little later when the enemy cavalry got close, it seemed that nothing could save the cannon but a rapid withdrawal. Angeles then demonstrated how very brave a man he was. As soon as he noticed that the enemy was rushing him, he took his pistol from its holster and threatened his troops who were hesitating, so that the very last man would stay at his post. Then when the charge was on top of him he was able to divert it with his cannon and the help of some of our other forces. The enemy were stopped, and Angeles and his troops kept control of the field.

But this showed me how difficult it would be to maintain such advanced posts within enemy territory. I ordered the withdrawal of the artillery to El Vergel, and instructed the forces to conserve their lines as best they could and always under the protection of the cliffs. As part of my final plan, I sent El Niño and El Chavalito out to bombard La Pila, since the repair of the roadbed was going forward with each moment. The two cannons were soon hitting their targets, but an enemy battery hiding near La Casa Redonda so promptly concentrated on the two pieces and the repair crews that we had to stop the movement to save El Niño and El Chavalito from damage.

We were doing this when General José Isabel Robles appeared with an escort of 40 soldiers and the officers of his staff. He told me that the 1,500 men of his brigade were coming and would arrive in groups. I gave orders for the new troops to be supplied with ammunition. Then I added, "Compañero, I hope you come determined to conquer or to die."

He replied, "We come to die, my General."

After four that afternoon the enemy gave indications of risking an attack on our line. Their cavalry left Gómez Palacio and advanced to within eight hundred meters of our center. I was glad, for what I wanted most was to catch them away from the protection of their cannon in an open field. But they merely looked at us from their eight hundred meters of distance and soon withdrew. Their positions grew quiet, and I suspected Velasco of preparing some surprising action. I called a meeting of my generals and said, "Señores, we must not let the enemy draw their breath. They cannot afford another assault on La Pila. If they lose the fortifications again at night, they haven't enough troops for actions that cost them generals. We ought to make a furious attack on their lines tonight, and if we do not weaken, Gómez Palacio will be ours within two or three hours afterward."

They were all of that same opinion. I dictated my measures: at the center, the Morelos, Villa, Ortega, and Guadalupe Victoria brigades would advance under General Urbina, and most of the artillery under General Angeles; on the right the Benito Juárez and Cuauhtémoc brigades would advance under General Herrera, and part of the Juárez Brigade, with artillery commanded by Colonel Santibáñez; on the left the Robles, Hernández, and Zaragoza brigades would advance under General Robles.

When it grew dark we began the movement as ordered, although I suspected what was going to happen. I began to see that the enemy purpose had not been to recover La Pila for defense but only to keep me from using it to block their withdrawal from Gómez Palacio; they had sacrificed troops and even two generals to that end. As I approached La Casa Redonda, followed by my escort and several officers, there was no enemy to stop us; our fire went unanswered. I sent out scouts, and they drew no response. I ordered the scouting forces to approach the city with caution; the result was the same. My suspicion that the enemy was not in Gómez Palacio was confirmed. That morning they had carried away supplies and provisions and a large number of bales of cotton in order to leave a more free retreat for the main body of their forces at the moment when their cavalry attack had kept us quiet in our lines.

We entered Gómez Palacio before nine on the night of the twenty-sixth of March. There was no noise or confusion in the city, but there were signs of the violence of the three-day struggle. The streets were strewn with the bodies of men and animals, as were the fortifications, the hillsides, and all the places they had occupied. I thought to myself that the principal work was still to be done but we had already taken the first step toward a decisive triumph.

From El Vergel I sent Carranza a report of my operations: "Señor, after three days and nights of fighting, our troops have taken Lerdo and Gómez Palacio. I congratulate you, Señor, on another triumph in the cause of the people, as do General Angeles and General Urbina who are here with me. Francisco Villa."

CHAPTER 19

In His First Assault on Torreón Villa Takes Santa Rosa, Calabazas, La Polvorera, and El Cañon del Huarache.

The Federals' Sketch. Demand for Surrender. The English Consul. Huarache Canyon. On the Sands of the Nazas. Burying the Dead. Plan of Attack. On Santa Rosa Hill. La Polvorera. Calabazas. El Huarache.

The fourth day before Torreón began with the advance of our trains, repair of the tracks, and the clearing away of roadblocks. I spent part of the morning dictating orders and making a reconnaissance.

While reconnoitering we came upon a sketch, the Federal plan for the defense of Torreón. Later it turned out that the Federals were occupying the very positions indicated on the sketch and the battle developed exactly as outlined there.

At dinner in Gómez Palacio, Angeles and I agreed upon summoning Velasco to surrender, seeing that his position was hopeless. I said, "If he were defending the cause of legality, it would be his duty to fight to the last. But he cannot reconcile a vain expenditure of lives with his conscience." I knew he had continued to recognize Sr. Madero in his days of trouble and had not chosen to abandon him. At my request then, Angeles wrote the following summons to surrender:

Sr. General José Refugio Velasco:
At Bermejillo I asked you to surrender Gómez Palacio. You refused. Now that Gómez Palacio is already in my power, I again call upon you to surrender. Valor, Sr. General, is not blind determination to struggle but devotion to a worthy cause. Remember, Señor, your loyalty at Veracruz and consider how the ranks of the people are growing day by day. The government of Huerta is the government of treason, and if you, Señor, continue to support him, the people will never pardon you.

Francisco Villa
Gómez Palacio, March 27, 1914

As it happened, the English consul at Torreón, who came to see me at my quarters, offered to carry the letter to Velasco and did so.

That afternoon, when my men had just finished gathering up the corpses, the enemy began to bombard us at the station. Some of the shots were so accurate that they were interrupting the switching of the engines. They killed two soldiers and an officer, they wounded some of the citizens of the town, and finally we had to pull our trains out of reach. It was not a real attack. They were only trying to prevent the new deployment of my troops they thought was in progress; late in the afternoon, with the same purpose, their cannon at Santa Rosa began to bombard our nearest lines. This was when Calixto Contreras' forces were approaching the canyon called El Cañon del Huarache by way of San Carlos and nearing the enemy stationed at La Alianza pass. The rest of my troops had only tightened their line from Gómez Palacio to Lerdo, and on the left of Gómez Palacio up to the sands of the Nazas, and along the right margin of that river, north and east of Torreón.

The enemy were still fatigued, like our own troops, and their fire had no continuing purpose. In any case the darkness protected us. Such are the contrasts in war. We could see the flames from the piles of corpses my men were burning on top of La Pila. As I watched, I thought, "Señor! What a profound thing war is. Many men must die that others may live, and only at the cost of slaughter can the cause of the people progress."

The next morning the enemy returned to the luxury of bombarding us from Santa Rosa and Torreón. Since that fire was not hurting us, we let them continue to waste their ammunition until, understanding this, they fell quiet, and we could occupy the rest of the morning in search of positions for our artillery. At noon I called a meeting of my generals and brigade chiefs. I said, "Compañeros, the enemy has disregarded our demand. We have had two days of rest and the time has come to continue the battle." These were our measures: the Villa and Morelos brigades, which had suffered most the last two days, and the Ortega and Cuauhtémoc brigades, numbering about four thousand men, were to form our reserves; the brigades of Aguirre Benavides, Herrera, and Robles would advance on the east; Calixto Contreras' troops, with some forces from Durango and the support of Santibáñez' artillery in Lerdo, would lead the attack; at the center and on the north—that is, from Gómez Palacio to the Nazas—the rest of the division would hold the line, with the support of most of the artillery under the command of General Angeles.

The enemy had strong positions: in the center they were above us on Santa Rosa; to the west, on the hills Calabazas and La Polvorera, they dominated El Huarache canyon and La Alianza pass. Having no such elevation on the east, they had placed their artillery there in the heart of the city.

It was six in the afternoon of March 28, 1914, when our artillery began to bombard them. At seven I started toward Torreón with Urbina, Ríos, Luisito, and my escort to direct the action. At eight flames rose in the city, the result of Angeles' salvos. At nine it seemed that the enemy must have set a bridge on fire at the rear, near Noé, but when I sent officers to investigate this unlikely happening, it turned out that the fire was coming from bales of cotton ignited by sparks from a machine gun. At about ten there were indications that the new battle was intensifying. The enemy were bombarding La Jabonera at Gómez Palacio, and opposing the advance of Contreras at El Huarache and our attacks on the east at La Metalúrgica. I ordered my reserve to advance in the center, and the enemy perhaps suspected this, for they began to bombard the left bank of the river opposite Gómez Palacio.

While our lines were making a sustained advance in the center and on the east, the forces of our right had moved up on the west to El Huarache canyon, where they encountered the enemy artillery, placed at each side, and a powerful piece which was being fired from a train. They found the road mined with dynamite. At first they had to stop and retreat, but when supported soon afterward by Santibáñez' artillery they extended their attack to the north of Calabazas, the south of La Polvorera, and the side of Santa Rosa facing Lerdo, throwing themselves on the enemy in an irresistible assault.

It was a bitter encounter and for some time increased in fury, illuminated by the glare from other hills. At La Polvorera the enemy cannon continued to fire for about two hours, but finally gave up the position. On Calabazas brave gunners kept firing after their support had already abandoned them. And when our men arrived and took the area and the pieces and the machine guns, they saw that the officer in command was dead, along with his lieutenants and sergeants and a large number of troops.

Soon afterward, about two in the morning, a telephone in the position rang. One of our men took the receiver and heard a Federal officer talking with General Velasco.

The officer said to him, "Yes, General Velasco, I am here."

Velasco asked, "But haven't you retreated yet?"

The officer answered, "No, Señor. The entrance to the canyon is quiet. They only bombard me from Lerdo now and then."

Velasco ordered, "Then retreat immediately; Calabazas and La Polvorera are in the hands of the enemy. If you cannot leave with the train, take the locks from the pieces and destroy the ammunition.

CHAPTER 20

The Irresistible Pressure of the Northern Division Forces Velasco To Propose a Truce.

Velasco and Argumedo. San Carlos. The Alameda at Torreón. José Isabel Robles. Toribio V. de los Santos. Federal Reinforcements. Pablo González. Coyote Dam. The Slopes of Calabazas. The Torreón Market. Velasco. Mr. Carothers. Cunnard Cummins. Enrique Santos Coy.

At three in the morning the three hills had fallen into our hands, but before my troops had time to fortify themselves on Calabazas and Polvorera, Refugio Velasco and Argumedo were already leading the enemy in such strong assaults that we could hardly withstand them. Every piece of their artillery seemed to be bombarding us from the city and La Cruz. By seven we had lost two of the three positions gained during the night, and they were pushing us back to San Carlos in spite of Santibáñez' artillery.

Encouraged by this, they tried to take Huarache with their cavalry. But our men, rallying and taking the offensive once more, forced them back.

After eight the fighting increased all along the line to the west and the east, where the troops of Robles, Eugenio, and Maclovio were advancing on the city. These entered the Alameda, reached two of the enemy barracks, took some mules and equipment, and in the face of artillery, infantry, and cavalry dug in and held their positions. José Isabel Robles was wounded in this advance. I ordered him to retire to the field hospital. But he would not leave his men and only asked for artillery support and a doctor who could attend him under fire.

That was our situation when I learned from Colonel Toribio V. de los

Santos, holding the line between Hipólito and San Pedro, that three Federal trains on the way from Monterrey were already in Benavides. I sent two thousand of Ortega and Hernández' men to take over De los Santos' group and destroy the track if possible. I was alarmed at learning that Pablo González, after all his promises, had not cut the line. Only reinforcements and provisions could enable Velasco to stop me and force me into retreat.

To shorten the battle I sent the Villa and Morelos brigades, under Rodríguez and Urbina, against the center. The enemy shelled them from above, but Angeles returned the fire and silenced it. Soon afterward he brought up Santibáñez' artillery from Lerdo to Gómez Palacio. With my center supported and the fortifications on Calabazas and La Polvorera under the fire of our cannon, I ordered an advance on the west.

In the bloody struggle we could not break their resistance, and they could not throw us back. Cannon and machine guns seemed to come into existence in their defense, but neither their grenades nor their bullets stopped us. At three in the afternoon we climbed Calabazas again and captured a machine gun, prisoners, and boxes of ammunition, at the same time that my center was forcing them to concentrate at Coyote dam and the elevations above it. The firing grew general. I wondered whether it would ever come to an end. It was already the eve of the thirtieth, and our resources and energy might be exhausted before we could win. But my forces were irrepressible. That night some of them on the left penetrated Torreón as far as the market place and stocked themselves with supplies and then returned.

At five in the morning we began to dynamite their positions, after a night's rest that left us with renewed vigor. On the left we made a penetrating movement toward the center of the city, and on the right wing climbed Calabazas again. But the resistance was holding us back. Our attack on the center failed; and on the left, about ten in the morning of March 30, 1914, Herrera and Aguirre Benavides asked for artillery to drive the enemy from positions at the hospital. Angeles sent them what he considered necessary while I was reinforcing our artillery at Santa Rosa to ravage the heights of El Coyote, where they had built adobe trenches and other defenses.

With our pieces so close that the crews hardly had the protection of their armored aprons, at point-blank range, he was able to get results with the ammunition we were using. But they returned the fire from Santa Rosa so successfully, thanks to the superiority of their projectiles, that they almost silenced us before El Niño and El Chavalito brought an end to their excesses. Justice and superiority in numbers were on my side, but Velasco was resisting with superior arms and advantageous positions, and the courage of my troops was offset by their defensive skill.

At one that afternoon a courier came from the enemy with a letter for Mr. Carothers, the United States agent who was somewhere in the vicinity. It was from the English consul at Torreón, and when Mr. Carothers read it he imparted the contents to me:

I request you to ask an escort for me. Considering the sentiments General Villa expressed to me in our talk on the twenty-seventh, I propose, at General Velasco's suggestion, that we meet to discuss affairs of great importance. While the escort is on its way General Velasco asks that there be no military action. There are foreigners here who have taken refuge in the Banco de la Laguna, the Banco Alemán, the Buchenau warehouses, and in one or two private houses, and all are safe.

Cunnard Cummins

When I had studied the proposals with General Angeles, I ordered the firing to cease and dispatched Roque González Garza and Enrique Santos Coy to seek out the Consul.

At the railroad bridge over the Nazas they met a Federal officer, who informed them, through the din of their own firing from Calabazas, that the Consul was on the bridge and they might pass. But as it turned out he was not there, either because he had grown impatient or because they wanted Santos Coy to appear before General Velasco. Their officer said, "Since the Consul is not here, let's go on to General Headquarters."

"Yes, Señor, let's go."

"I must blindfold you and take your arms."

"You may blindfold me, Señor, but I won't go disarmed, whatever the rules of war require."

So it was. They blindfolded him but he appeared before Velasco fully armed.

CHAPTER 21

Villa Refuses Velasco's Truce and Resumes the Assault on Torreón.

Santos Coy at Enemy Headquarters. José Carrillo and the Arrieta Brothers. Velasco's Proposition. A Communication from Pancho Villa. Urbina's Advice. Villa, Angry but Calm. Dr. Raschbaum. General Chao's One Thousand Men. A Special Council of War.

Velasco asked, "Who are you?"

"An officer of General Villa's staff."

"What do you want?"

"Nothing, Señor. I come only in search of the English Consul." Then what did Villa want? And Santos Coy answered that I wanted nothing, that the Revolutionaries were there to fight, and it was the Federals who were asking for a parley.

"It would be best to observe an armistice for forty-eight hours and bury the dead and care for the wounded." Santos Coy replied that he was there without authority to treat of such matters, and with that he was blindfolded again and returned to the river.

Seeing that they had not stopped bombarding Santa Rosa, I ordered the artillery on my left to reopen fire upon the city, but my officers stretched their interpretation to cover a cavalry attack also, and fighting broke out again on all sides. On Calabazas the encounters were sharp. There General José Carrillo with his four hundred men and the Arrieta brothers with their eight hundred were contesting Federal control of the hill, and hour by hour and piece by piece succeeding in taking it. That afternoon a group of the enemy with their officers tried to join our ranks. As they approached, they were shouting and signaling, but as neither Carrillo nor his troops were able to understand them, they answered them with all possible hostility, pursuing them and taking fifty of them prisoner. I accepted their offer to join me.

The English Consul arrived in Gómez Palacio with the Federal proposals. I answered that Villa was a man with a heart. But he had no need of an armistice to care for his dead and wounded; his ambulance service was already doing that. The purpose of an armistice was for them to bring up the reinforcements they badly needed. He could tell the General that I did not agree.

The English Consul asked, "Then what do you propose?"

"Señor, I want them to surrender the place and their arms."

That afternoon I sent the Consul to carry my message to the enemy camp:

Sr. General José Refugio Velasco:

I will grant your request to end hostilities, but only at the price of Torreón and your forces, and under promise to respect the lives of your officers and men. In case you refuse to surrender now, I invite you to spare the blood of civilians and the property of innocent people by bringing battle outside the walls of the city.

Francisco Villa

The escort who accompanied the Consul waited at the outpost until they saw the English flag waving on the other side, the signal agreed on in case the Federals did not accept my conditions. My left had continued fighting, and now I gave the order to begin firing at all points. At eight the fighting increased. I ordered the infantry to advance in the center under Martiniano Servín, and Angeles' artillery to bombard the city. They answered with accurate shelling of Gómez Palacio, but this was harmless, for anticipating their accuracy I deceived them with confusing movements in the dark. Anxious to get their bearings, they set off rockets.

Our center reached the right bank of the Nazas, and we took possession of it before eleven at night. But General Carrillo's troops on the right not only failed to carry out my orders but let themselves be surprised, lost our gains on Calabazas, and cost us heavy casualties. Urbina said, "Compadre, José Carrillo and his troops and Mariano and Domingo Arrieta and theirs are not to be trusted. If I was in authority, Carillo and his brigade would do no more damage here."

"Compadre, José Carrillo and his officers will pay for their error."

I spoke calmly but I was furiously angry. Perhaps my quietness owed something to a foreign doctor, Dr. Raschbaum, who was traveling with me and had advised me to give up eating meat in order to reduce my angry outbursts. I was also calm that night, the more that General Chao was reinforcing me with one thousand of the troops I had left him in Chihuahua, all of whom, he said, he did not need.

The next day I moved slowly, owing to a setback in my health, but not for one minute did I neglect details of the battle. I began with re-supplying my soldiers in the front lines. I ordered Robles to extend the left farther south of the Saltillo railroad lest Velasco expect help from that direction. With the line from the south cut as well as the one from Saltillo, the one from Monterrey, the one from the north, and the one from Durango, I wanted him to see that he must yield or fight without reinforcements.

That morning I also had José Carrillo's case submitted to the Council of War. González Garza reminded me, "My General, the Council cannot pass judgment upon Carrillo, who is a brigadier. We need a special council of generals only."

"We can take care of those formalities. There is not a general here but will pronounce the death sentence." On the spot I named a special council: Generals Tomás Urbina, José Rodríguez, Calixto Contreras, Andrés Villarreal, with the lawyer Ramos Romero as advisor, and Colonel Roque González Garza as secretary. By five that afternoon Carrillo was making his declarations. At six he was a prisoner. His troops I sent to Gómez Palacio, and had them disarmed. Shamed by this, they would later redeem themselves under a good leader.

CHAPTER 22

The Fall of Torreón.

The Prolongation of the Battle. José Carrillo's Officers. The Fear Called Panic. An Exit for the Enemy. Luis Herrera. Martín López. The Arrieta Brothers. The Coyote Dam. Benito Artalejo. Eladio Contreras.

On the night of the thirtieth I suspended the attacks, wanting to rest my troops for the following day and to regroup the artillery. But the Federals kept at it and after eleven o'clock vigorous fighting broke out on the north and continued until nearly twelve.

At three the next morning, fighting had already begun at El Huarache and La Alianza and it spread in give and take until six, when I ordered my left to begin the attack but only with a view to keeping the enemy busy, for the grand attack was to come that night. Daylight always favored the Federals and I had decided to storm the heights under cover of night. The fighting had already cost me two thousand men; my supplies were getting low. I would take Calabazas and La Polvorera that night, while my advance on the left would make it seem we were already in the heart of the city, and at the center I would be ravaging El Coyote.

The enemy took the lull in our firing as an opportunity to bombard us. At eight in the morning their shelling of Gómez Palacio was stronger than ever before and they turned upon Santa Rosa as well. While we were conserving our ammunition, they were wasting theirs.

When I was notified that General Carrillo was sentenced to death, I went to inform his imprisoned officers of this and warned them that the penalty for cowardice was death, though I had no intention of executing them. Talking with me the night before, Angeles had said, "Even the best armies sometimes yield to panic." I answered, "True, Señor. But shooting is a cure for it." He continued, "Pardon them and give them a second chance."

"All right, Compañero. I will pardon them for your sake, but any that fail me tomorrow will die." I therefore told the officers that it was in their hands to acquit themselves honorably and save their commander's life.

On the afternoon of April 1, 1914, I consulted Tomás Urbina and Felipe Angeles, who agreed that in view of the stubborn resistance of the enemy it would be advisable to leave them a road of escape. I therefore ordered my troops on the left to take care, as soon as we were making good progress, to leave the road to Saltillo clear.

At six the eight hundred men of the Villa and Morelos brigades arrived from Chihuahua, under General Luis Herrera and his fine officers Lieutenant Colonels Benito Artalejo and Martín López. I was angry because Mariano and Domingo Arrieta had ignored my order to bring me their well-mounted and well-equipped troops from Durango. Señor, this amounted to treason. When the Laguna campaign was over I would go in search of them and shoot them.

At eight the new troops and those under Martiniano Servín left to take their positions. At nine my center opened fire, and at nine-thirty my right. By ten the bombardment was general and under cover of the guns on Santa Rosa we were nearing the center of the city. At the same time the brigades of Luis Herrera and Servín were moving on Coyote dam.

Before eleven our right started the climb up Huarache and by eleven-thirty had a foothold on the slopes. The fiercest action developed op-

posite El Coyote. Soon my center was fighting at the foot of the earth-
works there. In the first fire Benito Artalejo fell, a friend for whom I
wept. A number of other officers were either killed or wounded. Our
assault on El Coyote was made in such force that in less than two
hours the Federals caused us some one hundred dead and no less than
three hundred wounded.

While the men of my center were fighting and shedding their blood
here, the brigades on my left were advancing into the heart of the city,
and those on the right were pushing up the hills, the most important
objective of all. For the action of the left, I had ordered Robles to withdraw his troops from the Saltillo line and leave that exit open to Velasco. Robles' forces and those of Maclovio and Aguirre Benavides were
engaged in a very difficult operation. They fought from street to street
and house to house with hand grenades and gunfire, gaining ground
here and holding there with a spirit that discouraged and overwhelmed
the defenders.

On the right Miguel González reached the fortifications on Calabazas
by dawn, and Eladio Contreras, with the Juárez Brigade of Durango,
reached those on La Polvorera. The gains were to be of short duration
but they weakened the enemy's faith in their stronghold. They saw that
these positions would be seized for good just as soon as their losses grew
a little greater.

CHAPTER 23

Villa Drives Huerta from Torreón and Opens the Road to Revolutionary Triumph.

Grenades Fall on Urbina's House. Federal Resistance. A
Cloud of Dust. Evacuation. The Foreign Journalists. The
Telegram to Carranza. The Entrance to Torreón. Villa
Looks at His Dead.

On the next day I again ordered my troops to rest
in preparation for a night assault. The morning was quiet except for
their bombardment of Santa Rosa and Gómez Palacio, where four gre-

nades burst on the house where Tomás Urbina was staying. But Santibáñez returned their fire skilfully and put an end to their arrogance. Informed that we had over 550 wounded the previous night, I wondered what the losses must be in Velasco's camp, and when Felipe Angeles came to speak to me about the disposition of the artillery, we agreed that we must persevere in the attack at any cost. With reinforcements cut off from the enemy, Angeles had no doubt that we would take Torreón.

But about four that afternoon the wind blew up great clouds of dust that enveloped us and obscured the entire south horizon; and Velasco, who had abandoned El Huarache canyon and La Alianza pass and was in trouble on the left and knew I would continue attacking him in the center and would soon reach La Polvorera and Calabazas, must have seen the providence of God in those clouds of dust. At any rate, he began the evacuation toward which I was pushing him by leaving the Saltillo line open. At five his bombardment grew stronger and his cavalry was sallying out at El Huarache. Huge flames rose in Torreón, accompanied by loud explosions. Remembering how he had prepared for his retreat from Gómez Palacio, I sent word to the commanders on my left that orders about the Saltillo line still held good. In the dust and approaching darkness no effective countermoves could be made.

At seven no enemy cannon were any longer to be heard, and at eight hardly any gunfire. Maclovio, Robles, and Aguirre Benavides were entering the city from the east, and at ten the people from Torreón came to tell me that the Federals had abandoned the place, part of them in cavalry formation on the Mieleras road and the rest by train toward Viesca. I sent for the foreign journalists and the representative of the United States government to announce that Torreón was in the hands of the people. One of the journalists asked me how I felt, and I answered, "Señor, you may say I feel the kind of joy you think proper, but I am not happy, because we pay for victory in the blood of our comrades."

Before going to bed I wired Carranza news of my victory:

Gómez Palacio, April 2, 1914
Sr. First Chief of the Constitutionalist Army, Ciudad Juárez
    Señor, the enemy are in retreat from Torreón under cover of darkness. Tomorrow I will pursue them. In eleven days of fighting, we have no less than 1,500 wounded and our dead will reach a third of that number. The enemy dead must exceed a thousand and their wounded must be equally high. Gen-

erals Calixto Contreras and José Isabel Robles were wounded, and Lieutenant Colonel Benito Artalejo died last night in battle. The cost has been great and painful.

General Francisco Villa

We had won control of all the northern part of the Republic. I not only controlled this but could advance upon Mexico City.

My forces made their formal entrance into Torreón on April 3, 1914, at eight in the morning. Generals Maclovio Herrera, Orestes Pereyra, and Eugenio Aguirre Benavides, and Colonel Raúl Madero entered on the left. Tomás Urbina, José Rodríguez, Miguel González, and Carlos Almeida entered on the north. Crowning the tops of all the hills, the forces of Calixto Contreras entered on the west. At one my brigades filed through on the way to quarters.

When I myself entered I wept at the sight of hundreds of my men there quiet on the ground, and I was thinking, "These humble and lifeless men and those in our hospitals are the heroes of the war, not the learned men or the generals." I resolved that if it was in my power to assure it, the people should never lose what they had won.

BOOK **3** *Political Panoramas*

CHAPTER 1

Villa Rests in Torreón before Undertaking To Destroy Huerta's Northern Army of the Republic.

The Federals' Wounded. Two Thousand Grenades and 100,000 Bales of Cotton. Martín Triana. The Spaniards of Torreón. The Wealth of the Cities of La Laguna. José de la Luz Herrera. Félix Sommerfeld. Victor Carusoe. Silberberg's Jewelry Shop. The Gold of Batopilas. Cattle, Hides and Gambling.

When I entered Torreón the common people applauded, but very few of the other class were present; I do not know whether it was because they were in mourning over their loss or because they feared me for my reputation as a cruel soldier.

I appointed civil and military authorities and arranged for guarantees to create confidence and encourage work. It had already been necessary to stop the excessive looting. I also arranged for the gathering of the dead, whom the enemy had left in piles, and gave orders for the care of the wounded abandoned by Velasco in his precipitate flight. These wounded were in the hospitals with letters appealing to "the protection of General Villa and the foreign consuls."

In truth, I intended to treat everyone humanely, residents and prisoners alike, and for that reason permitted no reprisals except for the shooting of some officers seized when attempting to hide in disguise and some members of the Social Defense. We acted in accordance with Sr. Carranza's new Law of January 25; but, in my opinion, there had been killings enough in the eleven days of fighting.

In Torreón, we took two thousand cannon shells of foreign make, a piece of artillery, six machine guns, and several cars of unserviceable arms and munitions. The most important items, besides the shells, were 100,000 bales of cotton, already loaded on three trains, and many locomotives and other rolling stock.

By telegraph that afternoon I conferred with the First Chief, taking advantage of the occasion to explain my reasons for wanting to punish General Martín Triana. I had ordered him arrested for disobedience, conspiracy, and inordinate addiction to absenting himself from combat, and he had gone to Carranza for protection, carrying tales of my violent methods. My report was in clarification of an earlier message, but it would soon be seen that Carranza did not heed my words. Instead he took Triana under his protection and carried him everywhere he went, either because he considered my charges only one of my many angry outbursts or because he was already planning to win over whoever was fearful of my justice.

My forces were weary but about four that afternoon I dictated measures for the pursuit of the enemy. It was demanding much to send my men to fight again after eleven days of combat, but war is cruel, and the chief must be hard. With less than a day of rest, I sent troops in pursuit of Velasco and dispatched brigades and artillery to reinforce Rosalío Hernández and Toribio Ortega, who were already fighting with the Federals at San Pedro de las Colonias.

Another of my concerns that afternoon was deciding the fate of the Spaniards in Torreón. Knowing that they had supported Huerta with money and even arms, since they were listed with the so-called Social Defense, I had them imprisoned in the cellars of the Banco de la Laguna pending my decision. For several hours I could not decide whether to bring them to judgment or, as I chose at last, to sacrifice justice to international conventions and condemn them only to exile. "Be thankful," I told them, "that I am not going to shoot you, and reflect in passing that Pancho Villa, contrary to what you say and publicize, is not a cruel bandit. Prepare for the road. Take what possessions you can, for you will need them; and do not delay in your preparations. In forty-eight hours the train will be ready to take you to the frontier." A Joaquín Serrano, a Serapio Santiago, a Fernando Rodríguez and another whose name I forget were allowed to stay. I not only spared these men but said, "The people of Mexico are glad to shelter foreigners like you."

Fear of us soon disappeared, and late on the day of our entrance the streets were lighted and business was resumed. Banks and stores were guarded, patrols scouted the downtown streets, and order was maintained in the outer districts. It was important to relieve the uneasiness of the peaceful residents after eleven days of hard fighting. I wanted the good conduct of my troops to alleviate the memory of war, of which there were scars even in the center of town. Shells had left gaping holes in the Banco de la Laguna, the Hotel Central, and the "Puerto de Santander."

Our problem was to exploit a rich district and convert our booty into money. The thickly populated cities of La Laguna must pay taxes and furnish other aids. It would be useful to open gambling houses, like those in Ciudad Juárez, and put these under José de la Luz Herrera, Maclovio's father and a man I trusted. All this I did within a few days in the urgent need to supply an army. I could get no help from others, and it was clear that I must be supplied with the best equipment, since the final battles were to be won by my troops.

I now had the state of Chihuahua in good production and my agencies of supply were well organized. I placed a German Jew, Félix Sommerfeld, in charge of purchasing war materials. As he was able and loyal, he always delivered arms and ammunition on time and in good condition. From the very first I had confidence in him because of his devotion to Sr. Madero. I knew by experience that men devoted to that President could be trusted.

I contracted with a business firm in El Paso, Haymon Krupp and Company, to outfit the troops. The manager of the firm, a Jew named Victor Carusoe, an intelligent businessman, gave me extensive credit and supplied me with everything. He knew our cause would triumph. He made money in dealing with me but he deserved it for his confidence in me and our cause when all the nations of the world were publicly branding our men as a gang of robbers and me, Pancho Villa, as their ringleader.

When the gold from the Banco Minero was spent, I put the Batopilas mines into operation under Gabino Durán, a trustworthy man and a good friend of mine. He made weekly deliveries of gold which sold through a firm in El Paso, some jewelers named Silberberg, Jews like the others.

My agencies likewise undertook to export herds of cattle and cargoes of hides, for which they had to get around the obstacles created in Texas by the Terrazas and other hacienda owners of Chihuahua. But I said, "Keep the price down and someone will buy," knowing from experience that, however just your cause, you must always sell illegal possessions cheap. What greater justice could there be than to sell in support of the people what the people had created by their labor?

My next greatest sources of money were the gambling houses in Ciudad Juárez and the horse races which flourished there. But all of this fell short of supplying the needs of my army; and I wanted to exploit the wealth of La Laguna.

CHAPTER 2

Villa Goes To Attack Velasco, De Moure, Maass, García Hidalgo, and Other Generals Whose Troops Are Concentrated at San Pedro de las Colonias.

Javier De Moure. Arnaldo Casso López. Eusebio Calzado. Troop Movements. Romero, Paliza, and García Hidalgo. Joaquín Maass. Huerta's Lies. Diebold. The Federal Troops. Domingo and Mariano Arrieta. Argumedo's Cavalry. Velasco's Convoy. Maass's Strategy. La Soledad. Measures for the Attack.

After Torreón it was urgent to defeat the enemy concentrated in San Pedro de las Colonias under Generals Javier de Moure and Arnaldo Casso López, who had wanted to aid Torreón, but were contained by the forces of Rosalío Hernández and Toribio Ortega after an attack at Bolívar. Seeing their position, they had asked Monterrey and Saltillo for help, and with the reinforcements they were receiving their strength was increasing. Their presence was a threat, for Velasco was near and retreating slowly. To overtake the crippled enemy in a favorable location held out less promise of decisive success than to attack San Pedro, and this move might force Velasco to halt his retreat.

The morning I entered Torreón I called upon Eusebio Calzado, my chief of railways, to figure out Velasco's movements and to provide trains for San Pedro. Not only did he put trains at my disposition that same day, after about three weeks without shops for his work, but he sent operators and telegraphers to follow Velasco with instructions on how to report. Observing the enemy with field glasses, these men communicated with me day and night, reporting on all they saw. Velasco was detained at the bridge on the Aguanaval River, where he rested until his trains caught up with him, and then continued by train and road to Viesca, after many stops.

For about a week after April 3, I was dispatching troops to San Pedro, some on foot and others by railroad. The Robles Brigade, Raúl Madero's troops, and part of Maclovio and Luis Herrera's forces went first, followed by almost all the rest as soon as these had rested and reorganized. The artillery accompanied the Zaragoza Brigade, except for the cannons El Niño and El Chavalito, which went on their platforms. Tomás Urbina, with his entire brigade, was entrusted with command until I arrived.

The enemy was continuing to receive reinforcements. In addition to the troops of Generals De Moure, Romero, and Paliza, the Federal Division of the North, under the command of General García Hidalgo, and men of the Bravo Division were in San Pedro. This last division, commanded by Joaquín Maass, had come from Saltillo to set a more decisive example, for Maass was considered one of their best generals. They were strong and determined to defeat me, for which reason they would be critically hurt by the loss of this engagement. As it was, Huerta found it necessary to deny abroad that I had taken Torreón. Five or six days after my entrance there, Diebold, an agent of his in the United States, was publishing a telegram in which Huerta declared that De Moure and Maass had joined Velasco after defeating me on the road, and that Romero and García Hidalgo had cut off my retreat. This is what they were saying in New York, in London, and in California.

Huerta was probably sure that his troops at San Pedro and those in retreat from Torreón could defeat me and recover the lost plaza. Under this illusion he was keeping the world deceived.

According to my information the enemy were composed of the following: 1,700 men with four cannons under General De Moure; 1,700 men with two cannons under General García Hidalgo; 1,300 men with four cannons under General Maass; 500 men under General Romero; and 800 under other generals and chiefs. That is, apart from the 5,000 or 6,000 retreating with Velasco, there were no less than 6,000 men and ten pieces of artillery and several machine-gun sections; all were well equipped and entrenched behind bales of cotton.

Before undertaking the action, I wanted to do something about the Arrieta brothers, Domingo and Mariano, who had deserted during my attack on Torreón. I thought it best to receive permission from Sr. Carranza, and requested it, informing him of their conduct. But just as in the case of Martín Triana, the First Chief disregarded my words and soon even aggravated the situation.

One after another my brigades were reaching San Pedro, where my generals incorporated them with those already engaged. Our line encircled the plaza from Santa Elena on the Hornos road, south to the railroad line at a point situated west of San Pedro, past Bolívar, and around on the north to some places below Las Carolinas. The brigades of Tomás Urbina, Rosalío Hernández, José Rodríguez, and Maclovio Herrera formed our center. Calixto Contreras, José Isabel Robles, Eugenio

Aguirre Benavides, and Raúl Madero led the right wing, that is, the one to the south. Those of Toribio Ortega, Miguel González, and Toribio de los Santos formed the left, to the north.

On April 5, with many of these troops in place, the advance began in the center, and before dawn of the following day our line was already less than half a kilometer from the railroad station and the nearby houses. There the Federals, from behind bales of cotton, succeeded in stopping us and holding their positions. While this was happening, Velasco, who was resting at Viesca, had detached Benjamín Argumedo's cavalry, with the purpose, as I at first thought, of beginning a general movement to join De Moure and the others. On the sixth, Argumedo reached San Pedro, after skirmishing with the advance troops of our right.

But the next day his intention was revealed: to return south, escorting a convoy of some thirty cars loaded with munitions and supplies. By now, however, our forces between Santa Elena and La Candelaria had him under view and sent their advance troops to halt him, with the result that, after an encounter, Argumedo had to retreat with a number of casualties. Cavalry and convoy sought shelter in the city.

Thus the enemy learned that they could not send out a convoy without masking the movement by a costly attack on our lines. Early on the morning of the eighth, therefore, a column of about two thousand men, supported by a battery, attacked our positions at Santa Elena. A bitter fight took place in which our artillery contained them with great skill and our infantry, from well-protected positions, stopped them quickly and soon forced them to withdraw in disorder. They were in danger of losing the artillery they had advanced, and in the fight lost no less than two hundred men. By three in the afternoon our cavalry was so close to surrounding them that to save them and cover their retreat another column of about one thousand men had to be dispatched.

General Maass led it, resolved to engage our entire right so that Argumedo and his convoy could get away. He succeeded, but only at the sacrifice of more than three hundred men in dead, wounded, and prisoners, and with the final effect of discouraging his troops, who would no longer resist except in strong defensive positions.

With half a million cartridges Argumedo's convoy reached La Soledad, between San Pedro and Viesca, and Velasco met them and was joined there by De Moure and Paliza, who had come with reinforcements. Thus supplied he prepared to march to the north. He started, as I remember, on April 9. That same day I reached San Pedro de las

Colonias with my other forces and the rest of the artillery. Tomás Urbina warned me that the operations would be long drawn out if Velasco arrived on time.

From the safety of the cliffs General Angeles and I reconnoitered the lines and decided that the battle had to be won within twenty-four hours. Some of our horses had carried saddles so long that their blankets were stuck to their backs, like the skin of their bodies, and few of our men had the rest they needed. To win in a day every man must be thrown into the battle. I ordered an assault on the town with fire and sword the next day at dawn.

CHAPTER 3

Villa's Triumph at San Pedro de las Colonias Gives the Revolution Control of the Northern Part of the Republic.

A *Viva* for General Ocaranza. April 10, 1914. The Pantheon of San Pedro de las Colonias. Velasco's Arrival. Raúl Madero. Two Armies. April 12, 1914. Argumedo and Almazán's Cavalries. The Federals in Defeat.

There had been a mix-up at La Soledad, between cavalry leader Juan Andreu Almazán, General Velasco's chief of vanguard, and De Moure, Argumedo, and Paliza, who were waiting for him to join them. According to my reports it occurred in this way. An officer who had fought at Torreón under Ocaranza was leading Almazán's advance troops, and as they began to file through the streets of the town at dark, he shouted by force of habit, "*Viva* Ocaranza," whereat De Moure's soldiers, thinking that they were hearing *vivas* for Carranza, began to fire. Later, as the struggle was spreading, Almazán discovered that the forces opposing him were not the enemy but Federal reinforcements and stopped the attack. In any case, De Moure and Paliza's troops not only failed to revive the courage of Velasco's men but after the forces joined it was evident that Velasco's were better soldiers and that their morale was only weakened by association with the others.

At dawn on the tenth, Holy Friday of that year, we began an operation for the total annihilation of the five thousand or so Federals in San Pedro. The battle was hard, directed from within by Maass, whose troops met our attack on the west and the north and at Las Carolinas, and by Hidalgo, who was defending the side of the Pantheon. Fighting quickly grew general and increased at such a pace that by midmorning we had driven them almost entirely from their frontline positions in spite of the strong defenses. Toward the Pantheon, which was the best-protected place, our advance proceeded slowly. On the station side, my left wing was in control and dominated their movements.

By three in the afternoon their casualties were no less than one thousand, most of these at the Pantheon, for our fire on the right wing was so skilful as to bereave Hidalgo of officers and staff. We were making progress, reducing the enemy, and encircling and controlling them. But our artillery, which Felipe Angeles had placed in good position above the Pantheon, exhausted its projectiles in the expectation that others would arrive soon, and this miscalculation brought about a delay in our final action. Velasco appeared in Buenavista soon afterward and we had to abandon our line at the Pantheon with the advantage we had won in ten hours of combat.

Velasco's vanguard reached San Pedro at six that afternoon. From then until nine or ten that night his forces were entering the town, always under fire, although we had no intention of disturbing the movement at the expense of the action we had already undertaken. Raúl Madero withdrew his forces and artillery in that part of the line, taking a short cut in order to avoid a serious encounter with Velasco.

It was sound military judgment not to prevent Velasco from joining the troops we already had under restraint in San Pedro. It is not necessarily a military axiom that two armies together are worth more than two separate ones, as we now demonstrated. Two armies were united in San Pedro—one which had failed to resist me in Torreón when in good positions, with great resources, and plenty of time to build up morale, and another which had failed to relieve that place when outfaced by two thousand of my men.

Velasco's troops were entering a city where the defenders were already starting fires to protect themselves from the inhabitants, who were considered Revolutionary, and he arrived condemning the conduct of the generals in command. Whether he was right or wrong, the Federals of San Pedro had certainly been unable to overcome my forces, and in order to send Velasco a convoy they had executed movements that cost them nearly five hundred casualties, while their defense brought their losses to more than one thousand men in wounded, dead and prisoners.

On April 12, two days after they had joined forces, I was ready for the attack. At three-thirty that morning our assault was so powerful that on our first thrust some of my men got within one hundred meters of the enemy's general headquarters. There, in a bloody struggle which lasted several hours, General Velasco was wounded and relinquished command of the troops. He offered it to General Romero, who refused, and then to General Maass, the most competent of his officers.

After the first hour of attack the defenders of several positions near the Pantheon deserted. One of their colonels, the chief of a non-regular regiment, committed suicide, disheartened by the loss of more than six hundred men in the first moments of the struggle. At the station we were able to get between the enemy infantry and their artillery. To avoid this danger they fired grapeshot but only increased their own casualties in the line.

By ten in the morning we had almost silenced enemy action, and the field was covered with their dead. Their withdrawal to buildings in the city and their trenches only cost them greater losses. With difficulty they sustained themselves until afternoon, when we again saw smoke from fires. Argumedo's cavalry attempted a move on the south and Almazán's on the north, and at the same time the fire from their artillery increased. They were covering evacuation. But we stopped Argumedo's advance, and he had to retreat in disorder; and we blocked Almazán although he moved with great skill. Some of the forces were leaving by train but most of them on foot, separated from their generals.

We entered San Pedro through heaps of wounded men and the ruins of burning houses. The enemy had abandoned artillery, impedimenta, grenades, cars of munitions, trains, and most of their locomotives. In one of the warehouses there were nearly six hundred wounded men, and the floor was running with blood. I, Pancho Villa, declare that the enemy were in such a hurry to retreat that hundreds of men were left behind, dispersed, not knowing where to turn. Many of our soldiers returned with four or five prisoners each.

That night I telegraphed a report of our new triumph to Carranza, listing the defeated generals: Velasco, Valdés, Maass, Casso López, De Moure, García Hidalgo, Paliza, Romero, Ruiz, Alvarez, Monasterio, Bátiz, Aguirre, Cárdenas, Corrales, Campa, Argumedo, Almazán, and others, and the captured stores. I numbered our own losses, 650 men, dead or wounded, none above a colonel in rank, and I asked for money to relieve the district and supply the needs of my 16,000 men.

The next day I confirmed my report, and General Angeles, with my approval, sent a telegram explaining how necessary it was for the Revolutionary forces of the northeast to aid us, saying that all of Huerta's trusted generals were defeated and discouraged, and their troops in such a state that only a miracle could help them. He added: "I believe that if the troops of General Pablo González and those of General Cepeda would march to Hipólito, they could totally annihilate General Huerta's forces at one time and bring this campaign to an end."

CHAPTER 4

Villa Participates in Diplomatic Talks on the Occupation of Veracruz. He Avoids War with the United States and Saves the Revolution.

Carranza. Don Pablo's Defeats. Manuel Chao. Carranza's Advisors. The North Americans Disembark in Veracruz. Carranza's Attitude. Obregón's Advice. Villa's Thoughts. Supper with Mr. Carothers. Villa Enters International Negotiations.

From La Laguna I returned to Chihuahua to be received by the First Chief. Chihuahua was my own territory. My base of operations was there. It was proper for me to go there to see Carranza, and if I had not done so before, it was because my military duties prevented. We met cordially. I think he was pleased with our victory.

His words were authoritative and calm. I felt soothed, knowing that our sacrifices and achievements were appreciated, and I praised not only my troops but my officers: General Angeles, a great artilleryman; my friend Tomás Urbina; General Maclovio Herrera; General Toribio Ortega; General José Isabel Robles; General José Rodríguez; General Rosalío Hernández; General Aguirre Benavides, and many others.

According to my memory our conversation took place before persons of his suite. But later, in private, I gave him my opinion of Alvaro Obregón's success in the west and General Pablo González' failure in the east, although I could not place the blame for this. Carranza answered that circumstances were not favoring González the way they were Obregón, and quoting from history he explained that in Benito Juárez' time there was a general who had always benefited the cause of liberty even in defeat. But he promised to see that Pablo González had sufficient resources, without which, he said, the best plans of the best of generals were of no avail.

In Chihuahua I saw that Manuel Chao was running the government wtihout due respect for my authority. I sent for him one morning and said, "You are governor of this state because of my deference to the authority of the First Chief, and because I have no time for this business. But I am the one in command, and I am going to shoot you on the spot to straighten out your ideas." I did not really mean to shoot him, for he was a man of much knowledge and good counsel, but I wished to cure him of his undesirable ways. An increasing number of Carranza's appointees had exaggerated ideas of their authority, thinking they received it from him alone and not understanding that he was governing there only because I believed it served the cause, and not because I would compliantly permit anyone to strew my path with obstacles. But Manuel Chao gave me reassurances. We parted friends, and I left him in charge.

This was the situation when some of Carranza's officers came to intervene in favor of Chao. Hearing how things stood, they reported to Carranza, who then asked me for an explanation. I repeated what I had done and said that, for whatever reason, Chao was behaving badly. Though the business ended there, I discovered that Carranza was surrounded by men who wanted to create dissension. I began to receive word that they publicly complained of my conduct. They invented tales of who knows what schemes of mine for killing Manuel Chao for his loyalty to Carranza. It was not enough to know my life or the numbers I had killed with just cause. They had to accuse me of what I had not done. As though they could stop me if I found Chao a menace to the cause.

The chocolate drinkers and sweet-scented friends of the First Chief were a greater danger to the Revolution than Huerta's armies. Carranza still seemed to be a sincere Revolutionary, but his choice of advisors was a weakness.

In any case there was a risk in having the Revolution guided solely by one man, who was flattered by those around him. As a result of some injury or other to American soldiers in Tampico, there was a break between Huerta and the United States; and the usurper, who saw that he could not keep on resisting us, tried to divert our attention and energies into a war with the United States. When his conduct caused the American Navy to disembark in Veracruz and open fire, Carranza was so carried away as to threaten to respond in the same manner if the foreign forces did not re-embark. In his well-meaning patriotism he was ready to interrupt the Revolution in order to attack the United States and even to further Huerta's designs.

My fear of these dangers increased when I learned that General Obregón, from Sinaloa, was advising Carranza to declare war if the Americans bombarded Mexican ports. I thought: If the United States should attack us, duty would require us to die as good Mexicans; if the United States should invade Mexico, duty would force us to unite with Huerta and take action together. But, in my opinion, the United States only wants to teach a lesson to a man who has committed offenses against them, and perhaps to help us in our war against the same man. To declare war on the United States, as Obregón wishes, is an act of insanity. To threaten them, as Carranza does, if they do not leave Veracruz, is good as a formula, but bad if we should attempt to carry out the threat.

I made a trip from Chihuahua to Ciudad Juárez, from where I called the American official, Mr. Carothers, and invited him to supper and asked him questions and told him things that Carranza in his role as Chief could not afford to ask or tell.

I asked, "Are these acts of war which the United States is committing against us?"

He replied, "They are not acts of war. They are words of President Wilson under the necessity of demanding reparations from Huerta. The Congress does not say that Wilson can declare war, but only that he can employ arms in exacting reparations."

"Then we Revolutionaries can continue to buy arms and ammunition in the United States?"

"You can continue to buy all the arms you want. The people of the United States do not wish to attack the people of Mexico and well know that the arms you buy will never be used against them."

"Very well, Señor, tell President Wilson that there will be no war between him and the Constitutionalists unless he declares it. In your reprisals against Huerta, commit no more acts of hostility. It was an error to disembark in Veracruz, but if your troops cannot yet abandon that port, we will not fight over that provided they stay there quietly. Tell him all this because it represents our true sentiments. Tell him that Huerta means nothing to us. He is a drunkard who, in order to save himself, does not hesitate to carry Mexico into a war which would destroy us. But tell him also that if his intentions are other, we will all fight."

The next day I gave the journalists a statement:

The American people helped us with their good offices in 1910, and they are doing so now. If Huerta wants war, neither we nor the United States will let ourselves be deceived. Sr. Carranza has given voice to the honor of our country, but he is not declaring war on the United States, and this is the true sentiment of all our Revolutionaries.

CHAPTER 5

Respecting Carranza's Orders, Villa Goes to Take Saltillo but Sees that This Will Interrupt the Course of His Triumphs.

Carranza, Villa, and Huerta. The True Law of Patriotism. Torreón. Huerta's Generals. Villa's Harsh Words. Zacatecas and Saltillo. Carranza's Will. A Supper without Villa. Durango. *Vida Nueva*. Ramón Puente. Luis G. Malváez.

My talk with Mr. Carothers had made Carranza very angry. He and many of his associates were accusing me of being a bad Mexican because I did not consider myself at war with the United States. I wondered, was I a bad Mexican because I wanted to prevent Mexico from shedding blood in a foreign war? The struggle against the Usurpation was for justice and the people, but what could we gain by going to war with a powerful nation which, far from wishing to fight with us, was helping our cause by merely favoring it?

As it turned out, when I returned to Chihuahua Carranza had only

kind words for my conduct. He merely asked me to keep silent there-
after on international affairs, which I cheerfully did, certain that my
words had helped to avoid the risks.

Today, after so long a time, I still think my reasoning was good. To
speak the truth, Carranza, by his answer to Mr. Wilson, brought us as
near to war as Huerta had done. Carranza, with his good aims, was
doing us as much harm as Huerta with his evil ones, and I, Pancho Villa,
intervened in the name of facts, not merely appearances and words.

My duty being to fight, not to discuss, I soon rejoined my forces, and
by May was already in Torreón making preparations to advance to the
South. There I received communications from Huerta's generals, calling
me to the defense of Mexico in the war with the United States. Among
the Huertista chiefs who opened these discussions there were Revolutionary men of earlier times who had been deceived or were prisoners
of reaction. I answered them, not in anger, but in reason, telling them
that Revolutionaries would never join hands with Huerta and entreat-
ing them to abandon the assassins of Sr. Madero. Those of another stripe
I rebuffed summarily, with accusations of treason, and if they had drawn
us into war with the United States they would have deserved still
harsher words.

Carranza soon made his trip to Torreón, accompanied by his many
followers. I staged a great welcome by the natives of the district and
my forces which were concentrated there. I did this to declare the
splendor of the Revolution and to attest to our unity. I wanted him and
his followers to feel that I was elevating him to the position of true
chief, in the center of my greatest power, and considering him my superior and showing my respect to every order of his in benefit of the
people. But I got a glimpse of what I might expect in my relations with
him. I saw that he distrusted me and was inclined to interfere with my
freedom of action, from secret impulse or at the instigation of those
around him.

When I was giving him an account of my preparations for the attack
upon Zacatecas, and the proposed route of advance, he disapproved
and told me that from then on I would submit my plans to a board of
generals over which he would preside, and the board would issue my
orders. And so it was. A meeting was called over which he presided,
and there he stated his opinion, which was different from mine and contrary to my knowledge of war, and spoke of his desires, not of military
necessities. That is, he told my generals that the next action of my troops
would not be an advance on Zacatecas but the taking of Saltillo in order

Far left, Enriqui Banda; *at motorcycle,* Pancho Villa; *behind Villa, with bandaged throat,* Javier Hernández.

Eugenio Aguirre Benavides; Pancho Villa; Alvaro Obregón; unidentified man *(in straw hat in center)*; Rodolfo Fierro; Dr. Raschbaum, Villa's personal physician; unidentified man *(in straw hat in background)*; General José Ruíz.

Revolutionary troops firing from a mountainside.

Second from left, General Máximo Castillo, President Madero's chief of staff, at Revolutionary camp, 1911.

A Revolutionary bugler.

Revolutionary gun emplacement on mountainside. Much of the bloody fighting took place in the mountains.

Federal leaders Emilio Campa and José Inés Salazar, quarreling during the battle of Juárez, February, 1912.

Revolutionary troops at the battle of Juárez.

Revolutionary troops boarding train.

Revolutionary troops beginning the attack at the battle of Juárez, which took place directly across the border from El Paso, Texas, and was witnessed from the International Bridge by many Texans.

Villa in civilian dress.

Revolutionary General Felipe Ángeles, whose skill and strategy were responsible for many of Villa's victories.

Victoriano Huerta, Provisional President of Mexico following his seizure of power from President Francisco I. Madero in 1913.

Revolutionary General Eulalio Gutiérrez, named Provisional President of Mexico in 1914 by the Convention of Aguascalientes.

Left, Revolutionary General José Isabel Robles, governor of Michoacan, 1913. *Right*, Don Luis Terrazas, owner of a large hacienda in Chihuahua, 1912.

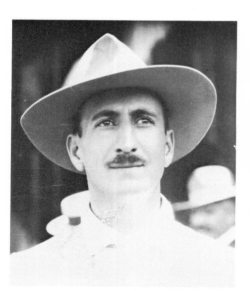

Left, Raúl Madero, brother of President Madero. Raúl fought with Villa's troops *Right*, Antonio Rojas, who, with Villa, liberated all the prisoners at Chihuahua Penitentiary on February 2, 1912. The prisoners had been arrested, illegally they claimed, on charges of stealing cattle from William Benton's hacienda.

U.S. General Hugh L. Scott and Pancho Villa in 1913. Scott, in civilian dress here, met with Villa a number of times to represent American interests.

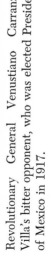

Revolutionary General Venustiano Carranza, Villa's bitter opponent, who was elected President of Mexico in 1917.

President Francisco I. Madero, leader of the successful Revolution against the regime of Porfirio Diaz. President Madero was always Villa's idol.

General Pascual Orozco, Jr., in Juárez. Orozco first fought with Madero but later turned against him.

ancho Villa in dress uniform.

In uniform in center, Juan N. Medina, mayor of Juárez.

evolutionary General Eduardo ay, who lost his right eye in the attle of Casas Grandes.

José Garibaldi (grandson of the Italian hero), who joined the Revolutionaries.

Revolutionary soldier firing from slope of mountain.

Revolutionaries firing cannon on hillside. The scarce cannons were extremely valuabl
Some were given affectionate names, such as "El Niño" (The Little Boy), "El Rorr
(The Baby).

raulio Hernández, secretary of state of Chihuahua; Abraham González, governor of Chihuahua; President Francisco I. Madero; Pascual Orozco.

Revolutionary soldiers.

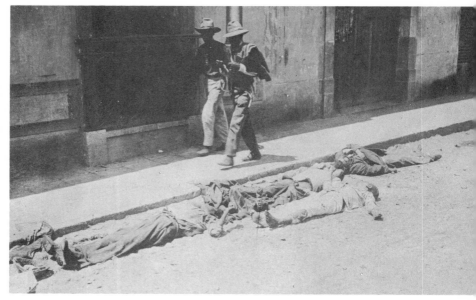

Dead persons in street of Mexican town following a battle.

A cartload of dead men.

Wounded Revolutionaries.

Villistas hanged along a public walk, by order of Federal General Murguía.

Section of destroyed railroad track. Blowing up tracks was a tactic used by all sides.

Rodolfo Fierro, Villa's longtime companion in arms; Pancho Villa; General José Rodríguez and Captain Juan García, both Revolutionaries, at Juárez, 1913.

Mexican Generals Alvaro Obregón and Pancho Villa with U.S. General John J. Pershing, commanding general at Fort Bliss, El Paso, at a meeting on the International Bridge between El Paso and Juárez, August 27, 1914.

to complete the conquest of the northern territory. A sharp discussion of the measure followed between him and Angeles, who gave very good reasons for opposing it. The Federals of the north were already a defeated enemy; they were fleeing from Laredo and Monterrey, and Pablo González could take Tampico and Saltillo and push them back to San Luis. But not wishing Carranza's authority to be weakened I acquiesced.

I wanted Carranza to see that I would obey him short of injury to my troops or the cause. But I saw that he was predisposed against me and trying to hold me back for the benefit of Alvaro Obregón, Pablo González, and other chiefs; or rather, my successes were irritating him, and he was trying to cut them short. This filled me with sadness.

Disinclined to attend the supper which my generals were giving him the next day, I sent Luisito to the Chief to excuse me, saying that I was not feeling well. Again, when Carranza decided upon a trip to Durango to meet Domingo and Mariano Arrieta, the two generals who had failed me in the battle of Torreón, I did not go along, although he invited me. From that date forward we were cool toward each other in the secrecy of our hearts. I even began to wonder, since he was going to Durango to honor generals whom I had accused of disloyalty, whether he had invited me to go along to make me ashamed, or had some other motive. By then I had begun to lose confidence in him, and could no longer feel at ease. But I, Pancho Villa, declare that even so I had no ill feeling for him. My attitude was friendly and respectful, since I considered him a capable man and a sincere Revolutionary. I ended by reflecting that I might have been partly to blame. I thought something might perhaps have come from the newspaper *Vida Nueva*, which a journalist by the name of Manuel Bauche Alcalde was publishing for me in Chihuahua. He was a well-informed and civilized writer, but given to flattery, and without delay I decided to remove him from the newspaper.

I spoke of my doubts to a doctor friend, Ramón Puente, who answered, "His paper will do you a great harm if it continues as now," and he recommended another Revolutionary journalist, Luis G. Malváez, whom I had known since the time of Sr. Madero. Malváez had never been disloyal to Sr. Madero. I telegraphed him to come to Torreón and when he appeared I said, "My friend, I am turning this newspaper over to you. Keep me and my victories out of it. Confine your writing to advancing the unity of our cause."

CHAPTER 6

In a Single Cavalry Engagement Villa Destroys Five Thousand Men Stationed in Paredón by Joaquín Maass.

Vito Alessio Robles. The March to Saltillo. Hipólito. Sauceda. Jesús Acuña and Juan Dávila. Five Thousand Men at Paredón. El Cañon de Josefa. The Railroad from Paredón to Saltillo. Zertuche. Angeles' Maneuver. Fraustro. Half an Hour of Combat. Ignacio Muñoz. Joaquín Gómez Linares. Francisco A. Osorno. Miguel Alvarez.

When dictating my measures for the march on Saltillo I said to Angeles, "General, we should carry all the artillery along, not because I think we will need it, but according to that theory of mine, that when large forces can be carried, a general should never carry small ones."

To aid him in moving our many cannon, I assigned him Vito Alessio Robles, who had come to Torreón to join me and to whom I gave the rank of colonel. He was in demand elsewhere but since he was a technician he would be most useful in the artillery. He had been loyal to Sr. Madero, and was brave in addition to being civilized. As we discussed the future of our cause and the ways of the First Chief, he made no secret of his thoughts, nor I of mine. I frankly declared, "Yes, if we let the grass grow round Carranza, the result will be of no benefit to the people. But we must go along with him until our final triumph. He is a good man, very firm in his ideas, and your ability to confer with him will be helpful. Our duty requires us to convince him of our sincerity in the name of the Revolution."

On the eleventh of May my troops began to move toward Saltillo along the Hipólito and Paredón line. Maclovio Herrera's brigade went as the vanguard. The next day our thirty-six cannon set out, and then the Villa Brigade, under José Rodríguez. Eusebio Calzado, our experienced railroad man, moved my convoys in good order. So by the fifteenth I was already in Hipólito with my staff and my escort and all the men and horses of the Zaragoza Brigade, the Robles Brigade, the Gonzáles Ortega Brigade, the Health Service Brigade, and my ammunition and supplies. We could not continue our march from Hipólito by train, not because of any error in my orders or on the part of Eusebio Calzado, but because the enemy, in self-protection, had destroyed the track beyond the Sauceda station.

By Carranza's order I was accompanied by Juan Dávila, a captain of his staff, and Jesús Acuña, a lawyer of whom I have spoken before. They were impressed by the great power of my forces, the number of my cannon, and the efficiency of all our operations. I could take Mexico City without Carranza's help.

Felipe Angeles, in command of the vanguard detained at Sauceda, had made scouting expeditions and sent Vito Alessio Robles to Hipólito, on May 15, to report that a force of five thousand men, with ten pieces of artillery, should be cut off and attacked there before they could retreat to Saltillo and destroy the railroad on the way. Commanding them were General Ignacio Muñoz, Francisco Osorno, and Miguel Alvarez. By reliable reports the total of the enemy forces in the district was more than fifteen thousand: five thousand at Paredón, two thousand posted in Ramos Arizpe under Pascual Orozco, and eight or ten thousand in Saltillo, all commanded by Joaquín Maass.

Alessio Robles had noted Angeles' remarks on a sketch. He added, "Look, my General, the line from Hipólito to Paredón and the line from Paredón to Saltillo are like two branches, not very open. At the junction of the said branches, to the north, is Paredón; at the point of one of them, here to the south, is Hipólito; at the point of the other, almost east of Hipólito, is Saltillo. In my General Angeles' judgment this must be our plan, unless you dictate other measures: the troops must disembark here in Hipólito and Sauceda; the infantry and the cavalry will advance, following the destroyed line from Sauceda to Fraustro, through the Cañon de Josefa; the artillery, which cannot pass through the canyon, will march from Sauceda to Fraustro, going around by La Tortuga, Treviño, Leona, and Las Norias; in Fraustro, we will assemble and fall on the five thousand Federals at Paredón, if they wait for us, and if they leave we must force them to a rapid withdrawal in order to save the track; by having two thousand of our horses go across from Hipólito to Zertuche, a station on the line from Paredón to Saltillo, we can save the track, for they will see that we have intercepted their retreat."

Felipe Angeles' plan appeared to be so wise that I at once began to dictate my orders. At three in the afternoon Alessio Robles had arrived. My three-thirty my men and horses were leaving the train. At four I called Toribio Ortega and gave him my orders to cross to Zertuche. And at five, with my troops already marching, some northeast toward Pa-

redón and others east toward Zertuche, I climbed into a motor car with
the chief of my trains and Rosalío Hernández and Alessio Robles.

The next day, May 16, the main body of my troops entered the
Cañon de Josefa while the artillery with its support went around by La
Tortuga, Treviño, La Leona, and Las Norias. On the seventeenth, at
six in the morning, we were all together in Fraustro, about fifteen kilometers from Paredón. I called the chiefs of my brigades, and dictated
my orders. Felipe Angeles said, "My General, if you approve it, I will
leave with the vanguard to choose the placements for my artillery."

I answered, "I approve, Sr. General."

In truth, I was thinking that the artillery was not going to be necessary. The five thousand men at Paredón were almost abandoned there,
ahead of our advance and without notice or suspicion of the breaking
of their line of communications with Saltillo. When I joined General
Angeles about three kilometers from Paredón, I did nothing more than
repeat the measures I had given before and arrange the signals for the
attack.

I said to my generals, "Señores, we are going to enter here in a great
cavalry spread against a conquered enemy. At the sound of an explosion
a few steps from here, the brigades will throw themselves on Paredón
in a cavalry assault and not stop until they have annihilated the enemy."

So it was. About ten that morning I ordered the signal given, and
thereupon no fewer than eight thousand of my cavalry rushed forward.
As I watched the wide formation, moving in faith, I thought of how the
brave deeds of war are worthy of watching, how a good beginning en-
tails a good end, and how truly the vigorous, well-conceived attack
holds the promise of victory. My men fell so suddenly on their objectives, the defenses built along the railroad and on a hill, that the enemy
hardly had time to reply, and their machine-gun fire was insufficient to
stop us, while our cannon, rapidly emplaced in a movement of great
mastery, were not needed at all.

Half an hour after we began our attack the enemy was retreating. The
Zaragoza Brigade, under Eugenio Aguirre Benavides and Raúl Madero, carried the struggle so far and with such fury that the Federals
lost all semblance of order. Their cavalry, withdrawing in good style,
attempted a flanking movement on our right, but it was of no advantage to them. Seeing it come, I rushed the troops of Maclovio and José
Rodríguez forward at a dead run, and the enemy horse faded from
sight.

The action of May 17, 1914, ended in the defeat of the enemy by my cavalry attack alone, and in their pursuit by José Isabel Robles. They had no less than 500 dead and 2,500 losses in wounded and prisoners. Only General Miguel Alvarez' cavalry succeeded in escaping to Saltillo, marching by way of Mesillas. In their precipitate flight, General Ignacio Muñoz, their chief, and Colonel Joaquín Gómez Linares were killed. General Francisco A. Osorno and I do not know how many other chiefs and officers were killed also. We took the enemy trains, their ten cannons, their munitions, and supplies. The defeat can best be summed up in saying that we took more than three thousand guns of the five thousand they had, and some of my men had the pleasure of bringing in fifteen or twenty prisoners each.

CHAPTER 7

After Victory at Paredón Villa Makes His Triumphant Entrance in Saltillo, Abandoned by Maass.

González García Is Wounded. The Bodies of Muñoz and Osorno. Rodolfo Fierro. Carranza's Orders. Humanitarian Sentiments. Dinner under the Mesquites. Two Prisoners. Jesús Acuña. Saltillo. Ramos Arizpe. The Government of Coahuila. Severiano Rodríguez.

At Paredón it happened that a piece of the grenade which was exploded as the signal for the attack wounded Roque González Garza; and as this was the result of imprudence on his part, I reprimanded him, though he was a good friend.

In the same battle I had to disarm José Bauche Alcalde and remove him and several of his officers from command. It happened in this way. When José Bauche Alcalde joined me, he was serving as chief of staff of the forces of General Manuel Chao. He considered it his duty to see that none of his men hung back from the fighting, as some soldiers do. In this he was correct. But when I noticed that he was doing this as an excuse to drop behind along with some of those near him, I knew not what to think: whether to consider it an act of cowardice, which hardly seemed possible, or to attribute it to ill will toward me because of my recent quarrels with General Chao. Since his conduct had a bad influence on my troops, I myself went to make an example of him, though not an irreversible one, since my judgment of him might be in error. On the spot I disarmed him and removed him from command, and put him under guard, but without ordering him shot.

The enemy Generals Ignacio Muñoz and Francisco A. Osorno were killed, as was Colonel Linares. When I had word of this one or two days later, I had Alessio Robles search for their bodies. He found the body of General Osorno in the bed of the Arroyo de Patos, and the bodies of General Muñoz and Colonel Linares at the top of San Francisco peak.

That morning my forces found another wounded colonel, or lieutenant colonel, whose last name I forget. Rodolfo Fierro wanted to shoot him, as Señor Carranza ordered in his new Law of Benito Juárez, but José Ballesteros, our chief who had captured him, said no, that he would not deliver him, that Felipe Angeles had ordered him to spare the lives of the wounded. I realized that Angeles was right and explained it to Fierro: Carranza's decree orders us to shoot all enemy chiefs and officers we take as prisoners. I obey the decree. But if a prisoner is wounded, the law of humanity orders us to cure him. I also obey that law. This is my decision: according to Carranza's wishes shoot all the enemy chiefs and officers who are in good health, but first cure all those you find wounded.

Before entering Paredón I was eating with a few companions under some mesquites when they brought in two captured officers and asked me what to do with them. Without leaving my dinner I said to shoot them on the spot, according to the decree. One of them, hearing my words, looked at me coolly and remarked that he had no objection, that we might shoot him whenever and wherever we liked, and if he had won the battle and we had been his prisoners, he would have done the same to us with pleasure, and with most pleasure of all to me, since he was a soldier and did his duty whereas I was only a glorified bandit living on booty.

Hearing this, I was unruffled, for his words, though untrue, were quiet in tone. I went on eating but signaled for my order to be carried out. I thought, "This is a brave man who is going to die. Why deprive him of believing that he dies for a good cause at the hands of a bandit?" But the other officer, overcome by great fear, did not follow his companion's road. He approached me and begged for mercy, getting down on his knees and weeping and swearing that he had been forced to serve Huerta and they had told him their forces were coming north to repel an American invasion, not to fight with the Constitutionalists, who also were struggling against the foreigners. I replied only that Carranza's law was our law and, in accordance with it, we would shoot them.

The escort made ready to shoot them. But the lawyer Jesús Acuña asked me not to do it there. "My General, spare us the sight of these deaths. We are eating; we are happy over our morning triumphs. Is it right to spoil our satisfaction with such sights?"

I answered sharply, for all to hear, "Why are you afraid to see the laws of the Revolution carried out? You chocolate-drinking politicians want to triumph without remembering the blood-drenched battle-fields." I repeated my order and the escort shot the prisoners before our eyes as we sat at dinner, and the bodies lay there throughout the meal. I watched Acuña showing his spirit by taking bigger mouthfuls than any of us.

The enemy abandoned Saltillo without fighting. José Isabel Robles' pursuing forces could hardly make contact with their rear guard, and by twelve on May 20, 1914, the plaza of Saltillo was already in our possession. I returned to Paredón. From Paredón I informed Carranza that we were masters of the capital of his state, thanks to my determined men.

My entrance into Saltillo that afternoon had all the aspects of a great occasion. With all, I kept my head. I remembered that I was only a soldier of the Revolution and that there were others who, perhaps, had performed greater deeds than mine, though without as great good fortune in concluding them. My first measures were to stimulate business and find work for the poor. The businessmen were no longer accepting Huertista paper money for fear I would not recognize it. So I ordered families of small means to exchange it for mine, of which I had great quantities distributed among the needy.

Carranza had instructed me to stay at the home of a rich man, Francisco Arizpe y Ramos, in Saltillo. I did so. He had told me to appoint Jesús Acuña governor. I did this. Also, I was told to appoint Severiano Rodríguez as chief of arms of Saltillo. Step by step, I was doing whatever Carranza ordered, not only because he was the Chief but because Coahuila was his state, where his wishes must prevail if the government was to be successful.

But some of Pablo González' generals were displeased with my arrangements. One of them, becoming excessively arrogant, said that he doubted the authority of my orders. I replied, "Carranza ordered it. If not, I did it. And Pancho Villa is accustomed to hanging soldiers and generals."

The opposition ended.

CHAPTER 8

Villa Remains in Saltillo Long Enough To Deliver the Plaza to Gonzalez' Troops.

The Rich Men of Saltillo. Jesús Acuña's Methods. The Friends of Vito Alessio Robles. José García Rodríguez. The Dance at the Normal School. "Jesusita in Chihuahua." The Destruction of Some Instruments. Maclovio Herrera and the Allowances. The Jesuits of Saltillo and the Mexican Priests.

I talked with Acuña about getting money from the rich men of Saltillo and he gave me a list of those to assess. Some of them, who had not escaped, were found and brought before me. I told them I would hold them prisoners until they delivered the aid we needed. Then it was that we saw the duplicity with which civilians in our Revolution threw upon military men the responsibility for acts which we all had agreed on. When the mediators approached Acuña, he disclaimed all responsibility and sympathized with them. This was the kind of help we got from the Chief.

A group of rich men wanted to clear themselves of having aided Huerta's troops. Fearing to provoke one of my fits of anger, they went to Vito Alessio Robles, also from Saltillo. Robles promised to introduce them, as former friends, but would not defend them or take offense at my decisions. He advised me of his conversations with them and I approved and agreed to see them at once.

One of them, José García Rodríguez, their spokesman, said, "Sr. General, the laws of war do not allow the defenseless man to be guided by his own wishes. We have helped Huerta's troops but we hope you will understand and excuse us." I answered that I forgave them and hoped that they would talk among themselves and voluntarily decide how much help they could give us. The next day they brought me 72,000 pesos.

In our honor the people of Saltillo gave a dance at the Normal School. I attended with my generals and aides. Pablo González' generals went also. That night there was much rejoicing. I danced with everybody and treated everyone in my best manner, even having a friendly conversation with General Francisco Coss, whom I had previously reprimanded for unbecoming conduct.

The ladies who organized the dance were very attentive. They said, "General, what piece would you like to have played?"

I answered, "*Jesusita en Chihuahua*, if you please." So the kind and attentive ladies danced to that piece and others I liked.

Several days after our entrance in the plaza, some of Maclovio Herrera's officers were still celebrating, against orders which the provost one night attempted to enforce. Maclovio's men resisted and a fight ensued, and in it some musicians lost their instruments, for which they then claimed payment. The provost put the disorderly ones in the guardhouse until the musicians should be paid.

I found them there the next day. They explained that they were responsible for the destruction of some instruments. I asked why they did not pay for these. They replied that they had no money. Where had their allowances gone so quickly? They had received none. If they had not yet received their Saltillo allowances, they should have something left over from those they got at San Pedro de las Colonias. They had not been given any allowances at San Pedro. Then from Torreón. They had received nothing at Torreón either.

In other words, I found out that Herrera had not given his men the allowances that I had ordered and paid for all my forces. I had the incarcerated officers released, promised to pay what they owed, and I went with them to Maclovio Herrera's quarters. "Why," I asked, "haven't these officers received their allowances?"

He answered, "My General, if the allowances are paid in town they lead to disorder."

"Then why haven't they received their allowances from San Pedro de las Colonias?"

"For the same reason, my General."

"And why didn't they receive their allowance at Torreón at the proper time?"

"For the same reason again, my General."

I could feel my anger pushing me toward one of my outbursts and held myself to saying, "I give you two hours, Señor, to come and report that the allowances have been paid and not a single officer or soldier among your troops has failed to receive the money that belongs to him. And you will give me an account of unpaid allowances from Torreón for those who died at San Pedro de las Colonias and from San Pedro de las Colonias for those who died at Paredón."

And I left to take care of my other duties.

In Saltillo I gave orders to round up all foreign priests and all Jesuits, both foreign and Mexican. I knew that these had supported the usurpers, besides which they were not good priests but enemies of the people. But this measure disturbed the people of Saltillo very much. Even Mexican priests, whom I wished no harm, came to mediate and explain that my act was unjust. I discovered that the Mexican priests were ignorant of their own interests and that the brotherhood was allowing foreigners to deprive them of their most productive posts.

CHAPTER 9

Villa Enters into Relations with Pablo González on Delivering the Plaza of Saltillo by Order of Carranza.

The Ladies of Saltillo. The Acuña Garden. Doña Gertrudis Morales de Rodríguez. Words That Soothe. Carranza, Natera, and the Arrietas. Pablo González and Villa. Antonio I. Villarreal. The Memory of Abraham González. A Walk in the Square. The Three Northern Armies. Don Pablo's Discretion.

I convinced the priests that my intentions were reasonable and kind and they returned to their churches. The Jesuits and foreign priests I kept under close guard pending further disposition. But the ladies of Saltillo were unwilling to respect my orders, although they always spoke to me in a friendly way. Away from me they complained and grumbled, and when they were near at hand they besieged me with messages. They were always saying, "Do not be cruel to our dear fathers, Sr. General."

The women were so well informed I realized it would be difficult to rid them of their ideas. I merely replied, "Señoras, I do this by mandate of the Revolution."

They tried to win me over by flattery and attention. They prepared a luncheon in my honor in a large garden, the Acuña Garden, and I attended without suspicion of their malicious intent. In the midst of things, when I was surrounded by the principal ladies, one of them, Doña Gertrudis Rodríguez, rose and addressed many compliments to me. She had served me with her own hands, and listening to her kind words, I felt soothed. But then she added something so different that I grew uneasy and regarded her in total disbelief. "You are so good to us, Sr. General Villa," she said, "and you have been so good in the past and you are going to be so good in the future that we are sure you will never deny us, the women of Saltillo, anything that we ask."

Now I saw through the show of affection. Not to let it pass, I answered, "Señora, your words are just, and I have the feelings you ascribe to me even if I do not find myself as good as you consider me. I respond to your words because your hearts are good and I will deny no request of yours provided it is nothing contrary to the welfare of the people. But do not ask me one thing, Señoras, because I will never grant it: the liberty of the Jesuits or the foreign clergy." The ladies did not change their friendly attitude, but they no longer persisted in their solicitations.

I had informed General Pablo González that my forces were being sent to take Saltillo by order of the Chief. I was in his territory and I had no wish to offend him. In Saltillo I again communicated with him and he replied that he would come to see me as soon as he could leave Tampico, which he had just taken by fire and sword.

I was making ready for my return to Torreón when these exchanges took place. Much time had passed, considering that I was very far from my intended theater of operations, Zacatecas, and I was getting reports that between entertainments on his trip to Durango and Sombrerete Sr. Carranza was encouraging the Arrieta brothers and Pánfilo Natera to take over my project. I discussed with Felipe Angeles the possibility of raising fresh troops for a move against Zacatecas, and he and Vito Alessio Robles and other officers immediately left for Torreón to form a regiment.

Pablo González came from Tampico to Saltillo, where I sent Generals Maclovio Herrera and Toribio Ortega and my secretary, Luis Aguirre Benavides, and some officers of my escort to welcome him at the station. When he was installed in quarters, I waited upon him and the persons who were accompanying him. We greeted each other with affection and entered into a conversation of no less than an hour about the course of the struggle against Huerta. Then we considered the future of our cause.

I saw that he was a good Revolutionary man, whose judgment was not as bad as it had seemed. But I saw too that he was of a gentle character that would help him little in the field. In war the chief has to drive, and if he does not, subordinates, at a time when obedience is necessary, will not expose themselves to the dangers of the campaign.

I then asked Pablo González why he had not come to help me in La Laguna. He said that he did indeed take steps to help, and I believed him. If his dispositions had come to nothing, the fault was not his but that of some subordinate or of circumstances.

He was glad to know me, and throughout our conversation treated me very cordially, although it seemed that we were verging upon a misunderstanding when I asked him about assistance. His military and civilian suite, some of them already friends of mine, likewise received me well. I rejoiced at this meeting of the Northern Division and the Northeastern Corps, and they responded in the same spirit. For General Antonio I. Villarreal, a Revolutionary from before the day of Sr. Madero, I had my warmest words. Our bond of friendship was the greatest for his reverence for the memory of Don Abraham González.

On the night of the twenty-seventh or twenty-eighth of May, 1914, González and his generals dined with me. At that time we agreed on the return of my troops to Torreón and on the manner in which his troops would enter Saltillo. The conversation was friendly. Afterwards González and I went for a walk in the square. A group of generals and officers followed at a short distance. We two continued talking. I told him that when I took Zacatecas, we all would have to come to an agreement, his forces and Obregón's and mine, to make the advance upon the capital in triumphant array. And he agreed, with obvious understanding and indications of good faith.

We were thus engaged when a boisterous group of soldiers appeared on the plaza. They shouted, "Viva Villa and down with all the rest," not being men for nothing, and added the gross words of which men are capable when not acting sanely. I pretended not to notice and continued the conversation. But soon another group appeared shouting in the same way and then another. And González, whether from anger or from discretion, could no longer refrain, but putting his hand on my arm, said, "Compañero, don't you think that the soldiers may make trouble?"

Still pretending not to notice, I replied, "Yes, Sr. Compañero, it could be. But you must believe me, between battles it is well to tolerate a little disorder." I stopped and called Rodolfo Fierro, who was following, and said, "Recall the troops to quarters."

CHAPTER 10

Returning to Torreón Villa Learns that the First Chief Does Not Want Him To Advance on Zacatecas.

Another Death Decree. The Federals in Hiding. Jesús or Luis Fuentes. Otilia Meraz. Darío Silva. Villa's Jealousy. Torreón. Carranza's Purpose. The Troops of Pablo González. The Advance to the South. Arms and Politics.

In Saltillo I received an order from Carranza to impose the death penalty upon any envoy of the usurpers who came to discuss the question of war with the United States. In Saltillo there were Federal chiefs and officers in hiding who wanted to speak with me and were sending me word by friends or by protected people. Before agreeing to see them I sounded a warning about our Chief's decree.

One officer, Jesús or Luis Fuentes, who had been with the troops of Joaquín Maass, sent several messages before coming to see me. He sent me this word, "I do not come to discuss the war or to surrender." I answered, "Then I will shoot you." He replied, "I surrender on one condition." I answered, "There can be no conditions." Again he replied, "I surrender with a request." Again I answered, "There can be no requests."

Being a very brave man, he did come to see me one night and said,

"Sr. General Villa, I come to surrender unconditionally, and I ask nothing in exchange, but I do have one hope."

I answered, "I accept your surrender, and as I do so in moments of peace, I do not apply Carranza's new Law of Benito Juárez. And now that your life is saved, what is your hope?"

He replied, "I hope, Señor, to serve with your troops and fight under your orders."

Fixing my eyes on him, I saw the true military spirit aglow in his face, and answered, "Very well, my friend. You are an officer of my escort as of today."

In those days I was threatened with a serious illness on account of violent attacks of anger provoked by a woman who was with me. It happened in this way. My forces were masters of the plaza of Torreón, and during a fiesta, I met a girl in Ciudad Lerdo named Otilia Meraz, who was satisfied with the propositions I made her. I discovered that she already knew much about love, and I saw how much it pleased her to eat at the same table with persons who came to see me or accompanied me. So I took her with me to Saltillo and the following incident occurred. One day she told me, I do not know why, that an officer sitting with us was a friend of hers before I took her. This was Darío Silva, one of my best friends and one of the eight men who had followed me since the beginning of the struggle, and I did not see how I could endure the revelation. Instead of blaming the woman who told me of her past when there was no remedy for it, or blaming myself for taking a woman who had belonged to others, I blamed Darío Silva, and I obeyed my impulse to punish him and humiliate him and make him understand that he should not have had the same woman as I, and show her that the men she had known before knowing me were nothing by comparison.

That day, when we were taking our places at the table, I said to Darío Silva, "You are not to eat with us; from now on you will be my errand boy. You will serve us at dinner."

And Darío Silva began to serve us as I had ordered, and seeing how he brought and took away my plates and brought and took away Otilia Meraz', so gently, so humbly, and so obediently—I do not know whether it was from fear that he appeared to be ashamed and showed indications of weeping, or from devotion—all my rancor melted away, and I felt as if an enormous weight had been lifted from me.

So it happened at that time. But reflection came with the passing days, and with reflection I realized how I had abused my power and authority. It was then that my anger rose against Otilia Meraz and I was overcome with such fury that I could hardly restrain myself from inflicting with my own hand the punishment she deserved. But I recovered and contented myself with throwing her out and calling Darío Silva to assure him of my friendship.

I left Saltillo for Torreón in the middle of the afternoon of the twenty-ninth or thirtieth of May, 1914, making a rapid trip and leaving General Toribio Ortega in Saltillo to remain until Pablo González made his advance. With words of mutual assurance Pablo González and I gave each other an embrace and said goodbye.

In Torreón I was told for reasons I could not understand that Carranza wanted Pánfilo Natera and the Arrieta brothers to make the attack on Zacatecas. But they must have been dreaming to think that the attack could succeed with only the resources of those three generals. I questioned Carranza's intention: it was as clear as the shining sun that even I, with the support of all my troops, and part of those from Durango, and those of La Laguna, had found it difficult to take Torreón. How then could the five or six thousand men belonging to Natera and the Arrietas be enough to face the enemy concentration at Zacatecas? So I was thinking, did he want to disgrace Natera and his men? Was he planning to close the road to my army and bring an end to my successes? Was he so anxious to leave me behind that he did not see the defeat ahead?

I pretended to know nothing and suspect nothing, and communicated with him regarding my future operations and those of the principal chiefs. I was hoping that if he knew my thoughts, he would reconsider. To this effect I sent him a telegram in code. I was anxious for him to understand that our advance southward should be made jointly. In my opinion, we were winning because the Federals did not know how to defend themselves, and some man with a better knowledge of war might happen to take command who would see that I was the greatest danger and would change his plan of action, abandoning the north and concentrating the main body of his troops at one point far enough south of Zacatecas to block my advance or fall on either Obregón or Pablo González on the march; and if that happened, I did not see what steps we could take unless we agreed on our movements and the agreement was made on a military basis, not a political one.

CHAPTER 11

To Preserve Unity Villa Does Not Await the Arrival of the Chief in Torreón.

Eusebio Calzado. The Civil Authorities of Torreón. The Wholesale Meat Business in Torreón. The Hunger of the Poor. The First Chief's Distrust. At the Casino de la Laguna. Felipe Angeles' Words. An Incident on the Railroad. José María Maytorena and Plutarco Elías Calles. Carranza's Duty.

I also learned in Torreón that Carranza wanted to relieve Eusebio Calzado of the management of the railroads I had taken, not seeing that Eusebio was very useful because of his skill and experience. He was trying to do the same with other persons I had appointed. I sent him a message giving my view of his dispositions, so that he might examine my words more closely. I did this in the hope that we could reach an understanding. It seemed to me that he should cooperate with us, the fighters, instead of being an arbitrary chief with power, which no man should be except in battle.

The wholesale meat business in Torreón was another point of discord between me and Carranza. Since Torreón was poorly stocked with meat, and the poor were suffering for lack of it, I did not want the business to be exploited, unless for the benefit of my troops. But Carranza's friends arrived and saw only their own interests and pretended to believe that I was trying to get rich from the business, not considering that the money was used in the war, and that if it was money I wanted I had only to hold out my hand.

And it is true that such distrust on the part of the Chief did not honor me or the men who were with me in the struggle, especially since I knew the persons he had around him in Durango were saying bad things about me. I said to myself, "If it causes no serious damage to our cause, we will make every sacrifice to obtain the people's triumph, and soon we will see what roads some take and what roads others take."

I decided to absent myself from Torreón on the days that Carranza would spend there on his way from Durango to Saltillo. I left for Chihuahua on the day he was to arrive with the chocolate drinkers who followed him and did not return until several days after he had passed through. I did this for fear some order of his or some word, born of the tales he had heard, would provoke me into one of my violent outbursts.

As I learned, Carranza reached Avilés at dark on the evening of June 4, 1914. He spent the night there—that is, he and his troops slept there in their trains—and at eight the next morning he entered Torreón without giving any notice of the time of his arrival, and so no one was commissioned to receive or greet him. But at noon that day he was honored with a banquet in the Casino de la Laguna, and Felipe Angeles and other generals were there to represent my division, and Angeles rose to say that we Revolutionaries of the Northern Division venerated the memory of Madero and were expecting such a legal government as Madero had given us and wanted no such usurping government as that of Huerta or tyrannical one like that of Don Porfirio.

They told me afterward that Carranza was not pleased with Felipe Angeles' words, and I did not then understand why. In any case, it was evident that he was already cool toward me and my men and that his jealousy or the bad advice he was getting was poisoning his mind against me. The next day, as he was leaving for Saltillo, the chief of his trains, Paulino Fontes, not being certain of his orders, failed to execute them on time, and bitter quarrels followed, and those who were mumbling in Carranza's ears investigated the situation and magnified it and said it was disrespectful to the Chief and they succeeded in getting the railroad man imprisoned. They even made an attempt to involve me. Me, Señor, when I was in Chihuahua and had left Torreón before the Chief arrived!

While Carranza was passing through Torreón I was receiving telegrams in Chihuahua from José María Maytorena, governor of Sonora, who was quarreling with Plutarco Elías Calles, chief of the forces in Hermosillo. Maytorena was calling on me to settle the quarrel. I was amazed to learn that Carranza, who had spent several months in Sonora, had permitted such dissensions to arise and had not foreseen the damage which would follow. It was Carranza's duty to settle the differences. He alone could end the dissension, and it was my duty as a Revolutionary to tell him the truth. I sent him a telegram without making gestures in favor of either José María Maytorena or Plutarco Elías Calles but acting only in the interest of our cause. This I did though Maytorena was my friend and had helped me at the outset of the war.

CHAPTER 12

Carranza Orders Villa to Reinforce Natera's Attack on Zacatecas but Villa Considers That A Mistake.

The Struggles in Sonora. Carranza and His Authority. Colonel Antonio Guerrero. The Troops Beseiging Guaymas. Natera at Zacatecas. The First Chief's Orders. Villa's Observations. Carranza's Silence. A Victorious Division. A Telegraphic Conference.

I do not believe Carranza wanted to end the struggles in Sonora. Obregón was advising the removal of Plutarco Elías Calles, a man of many grudges, and the chiefs of the troops besieging Guaymas wanted all the forces of the state, including those of Calles, placed under a single command. But Carranza disapproved of this arrangement; he wished to support Calles as a threat to Maytorena. It was a great error not to realize that Maytorena was a good Revolutionary from whom no harm could come if others respected his rights and dignity. And the error appeared the greater if the Chief had good reasons to distrust Maytorena, for he was letting the reasons grow instead of wiping them out once and for all.

What happened was that Calles remained in the north to antagonize Maytorena, who deserved better treatment, and another colonel, Antonio Guerrero, appointed by the First Chief to command in Hermosillo because he was in conspiracy with Calles, followed exactly the same course. As a result of Carranza's faulty measures things grew worse, until the chiefs of the besieging forces of Guaymas went to Maytorena's protection.

I left Chihuahua for Torreón with the intention of undertaking my advance on Zacatecas. In Torreón I learned that General Natera, following Carranza's plan, had already begun the attack, making it with only his own forces and those of Arrieta, Carrillo, and Triana. Carrillo was the man I had to disarm at the battle of Torreón. Triana was the one I had to accuse of misconduct.

Still I did not neglect preparations for my march. Inasmuch as Carranza had said nothing to me of his plans, and he well knew my own intentions, I had no reason to desist but rather to hasten. We were occupied with this on June 10, 1914, when I received a telegram. For the

first time Carranza spoke of Pánfilo Natera's movements: "As the chief
of the forces nearest to Zacatecas you will be ready to aid General
Natera if necessary."

I understood him to be ordering me to stay in Torreón while Natera
developed his operations and, though I knew the operations would fail,
I made up my mind to obey. The next day Carranza telegraphed me
again, saying: "Sr. General Francisco Villa: Yesterday I ordered you to
send reinforcements to General Natera for his attack on Zacatecas. If
you have not yet done so, have no less than three thousand men and
two batteries of cannon leave at once." I had no idea why Carranza,
who first had ordered me only to have troops ready, was now telling me
to set them in motion. Nor did I understand his peremptory tone. But
I bore it and went along with it. Still, I expressed my opinion, in respectful terms: "I believe it best, Señor, unless you think otherwise, to
move my entire division, in order to insure the success of the operations
and lessen as much as possible the sacrifice of lives."

So certain was I that he would not order otherwise that I renewed
my orders for the repair of the track on the Zacatecas line and dictated
other necessary measures. But he had no wish to accept my advice and
persisted in his idea of paralyzing my action while continuing to make
use of my resources in furthering the successes of other generals. He
replied, peremptorily again, as if I had told him nothing:

Sr. General Francisco Villa:
Yesterday I ordered you to send General Natera reinforcements consisting
of three thousand men and two batteries to consummate the taking of Zacatecas. Send them immediately under General José Isabel Robles. It would be
an error to lose what we have already gained now that only a little further
effort is necessary. Instead of the three thousand men you can send five
thousand, and if possible munitions also—Mauser and 30–30 guns.

Señor! I was the chief of a victorious division. After taking Torreón
and destroying the enemy in San Pedro de las Colonias I had explained
my intention to continue to Zacatecas, the next proper step. He had held
me back then, until Alvaro Obregón and Pablo González could catch
up, and I agreed to take Saltillo first. But while I, Pancho Villa, was ful-
filling my duty, the Chief, Venustiano Carranza, was intriguing against
me in Durango and Sombrerete, where he was looking for generals to
take Zacatecas behind my back. But, as if I counted as nothing in the
movement of our Revolution and as if the battles won by my men
signified nothing to him, the First Chief did not condescend to reply to

my message, perhaps because he considered himself too high above me.
He only repeated his orders and expanded them, indicating which of
my generals should go in command of the troops and expressing himself as if he knew all about war and I was obtaining my knowledge
from him. It was all very sad, but I endured it. I told him that I would
obey him, although I considered the order ill-advised.

According to my memory this happened on the night of June 12, 1914.
The next morning I made arrangements with Carranza for a telegraphic
conference.

CHAPTER 13

Faced With Carranza's Open Hostility, Villa Resigns His Command of the Northern Division.

Villa's Firm Decision. Carranza's Explanations. "You
Yourself Made an Error." The Attacks on Chihuahua and
Zacatecas. Villa's Resignation. Felipe Angeles. Maclovio
Herrera Loses His Temper.

When they notified me from Saltillo that Sr. Ca-
rranza was with his telegrapher, I sat down near mine and said, "Tell
him: Good morning, Sr. Carranza."

He answered: "Good morning, Sr. General Francisco Villa, and what
is the reason for the conference I have granted?"

I replied:

Señor, it will be five days before I can send assistance to General Natera because I cannot move my troops in less time than that. Who sent the men on
that job without the assurance of complete success? Didn't they know or you
know that I have here the needed resources? The problem you create for me
is difficult for the following reasons: first, José Isabel Robles cannot go because he is ill; second, if I send the troops with Tomás Urbina, nothing will
be gained because he will not deal with Arrieta. Tell me, Señor, if I go to

command the division, will it be under Arrieta or Natera, with them to take the credit?

Determined he should know the full force of my criticism, I added:

If you want some other person to take over my command, tell me who it is, and if I judge that he is capable of handling them, I will tell you so.

Carranza replied:

Now that the Zacatecas attack has begun, our men have taken the positions at Guadalupe and Los Mercedes and others near Grillo, but they have been driven back in their attempt to occupy La Bufa and La Estación. But this is no time to find fault. You yourself made an error when you attacked Chihuahua in November, 1913, and had to retreat after several days of fighting, nor would you have taken Torreón if I had not ordered Generals Robles, Contreras, and Urbina, and General Carrillo in command of the forces of General Arrieta, and others of lower rank, to put themselves under your orders. I do not wish to put you under the orders of General Natera but only to send a part of your forces to help him take the plaza and thus open your passage to the south. As for your separation from the command you now have, I do not consider it advisable; but if I have to make such a decision, I will act in the interests of our cause. I named General Robles to command the forces because of his knowledge of the terrain. But if he is ill, General Aguirre Benavides can go, or General Ortega, or General Contreras, or any other that you judge suitable. General Natera tells me that he can hold out two days more in the positions he occupies; there is time for the reinforcements to arrive.

It was hopeless to try to return him to reason. He no longer saw beyond forcing me to send reinforcements which would arrive only in time for their destruction. Why, Señor, should he maintain that my compadre Tomás Urbina's troops and José Isabel Robles' and Calixto Contreras' were not integral parts of my division but went with me only at his commands? If so, why didn't he order them directly to aid General Natera instead of having me send them? It was not true that I had made a mistake in attacking Chihuahua. If I could not take it then, my attack had nevertheless great military significance. Thanks to it, I could move without Mercado's detecting me, and take Ciudad Juárez by surprise and thus lure the Chihuahua forces out to the great defeat at Tierra Blanca, and even cause Mercado to abandon Chihuahua completely and flee to Ojinaga where I overtook and annihilated him.

I saw clearly that I no longer had anything to say to the man and could expect no order or measure from him which would benefit our arms. As they read me the last words of his reply, I added: "Señor, I resign command of this division. Tell me to whom to deliver it."

I did that, knowing that if Sr. Carranza was a good chief he would have to say, "Sr. General, then go take that plaza. Go with all your troops, with all your arms, with all your supplies, and be responsible to me for a victory."

I had Major Juan B. Vargas call Felipe Angeles, José Rodríguez, Maclovio Herrera, Eugenio Aguirre Benavides, Rosalío Hernández, Raúl Madero, and the other brigade chiefs.

When Angeles entered I told him to decide what to do with the forces. I was leaving them with him and going away. Those who had been with me earlier explained to him, saying that I had offered my resignation.

He remarked, "Carranza will accept your resignation immediately." His ideas agreed with mine. Some of the others were of a different opinion, but Angeles repeated his words. He came over as if to speak to me alone and said "Carranza will accept."

I answered, "I know it. That is why I tell you to take charge." And I added, "A month ago Carranza asked me to conquer the capital of his state for him, and I had barely left his presence when he began to consider the best ways to thwart me."

Maclovio Herrera, who heard what I was saying, turned to the telegrapher and said, "My friend, you will send the Chief this message of mine: 'Sr. Carranza, I am informed of your treatment of my General Francisco Villa. You are a son of a bitch. Maclovio Herrera!'"

He was so angry that he drew his pistol on the telegrapher in case the latter was reluctant to transmit the strong language. Felipe Angeles had to calm him and explain to him and the others that we do not settle misunderstandings and quarrels in this manner—that more than a dispute, the march on the enemy, was at stake.

"What do you want?" he asked. "To advance on Saltillo instead of Zacatecas?"

He quieted them and persuaded them to reflect.

CHAPTER 14

In Defense of Villa the Generals of the Northern Division Refuse To Elect Another Chief More Submissive to Carranza's Orders.

Toribio Ortega. A Letter about Villa. The First Chief's Decision. The Generals of the Northern Division. Manuel Madinabeitia. Villa and Venustiano Carranza. The Kindness of Felipe Angeles.

I learned that three days before those events, on June 10, 1914, Toribio Ortega had sent Carranza a letter expressing his loyalty to me. I had been rough with Ortega on several occasions, although always with reason, but he kept his faith in me and wanted to protect me against the chocolate drinkers.

When I heard what he had written about me, I thanked him but added, "If Carranza truly says what they say he says about me, he will never forgive me for being such a man as you picture me."

I could not have been mistaken. Carranza replied as Angeles predicted. He wired:

Sr. General Francisco Villa:

With the greatest regret I find myself forced to accept your resignation as chief of the Northern Division. I hope, Señor General, that you will now take charge of the government of Chihuahua, and accept the thanks I send in the name of our nation for the many services rendered by your arms in benefit of the Constitutionalist cause. I shall proceed now to appoint a chief to receive those forces, but first I wish you to speak with me from the telegraph office in the company of Generals Felipe Angeles, Eugenio Aguirre Benavides, José Rodríguez, Maclovio Herrera, Trinidad Rodríguez, Toribio Ortega, Rosalío Hernández, Calixto Contreras, Severino Ceniceros, Orestes Pereyra, Mateo Almanza, Martiniano Servín, and Máximo García. Send for them and advise me when they have arrived, as I wait for you here.

Venustiano Carranza

What he ordered had already been done, since many of the chiefs he named were there with me expecting the others. And why, Señor, wouldn't they be there, even though the Chief had not convoked them, since their hearts, even more than mine, were wounded by the misfortune. Many of them predicted that the division would be destroyed and it would be best for us all to return to the ravines of the sierra. Several of them were in tears.

At the same time that Carranza accepted my resignation, he sent the generals just listed a telegram to this effect:

Sres. Generals of the Division:
Please accept my sincere greetings. I advise you that at this moment I have just had a conference with Sr. General Villa, and since he has offered me the resignation of his command, I have considered it my duty to accept it. I now call you together, and I invite you to tell me which general, in your opinion, is your unanimous choice as interim chief. If there is any general there whom I do not know about, summon him to the meeting. I know that José Isabel Robles is ill and Tomás Urbina is absent. Inform General Robles of the purpose of the meeting and of my desire that your opinion be remitted in writing. If General Villa is present, inform him of the contents of this message.

But it was not possible to get all the generals together at once, and they agreed to postpone the meeting until the next morning. With this intention Manuel Madinabeitia wired:

Citizen First Chief of the Constitutionalist Army:
The generals gathered here have just withdrawn to eat. They request me to advise you that tomorrow morning at ten they will meet again to act on your proposal.
                                            Colonel and Chief of Staff

The next morning I assembled them and said, "Compañeros, you know that it is not Pancho Villa who calls this meeting but Carranza, First Chief of our Revolution. Even so I want to say, since it is good for you to know, that four days ago Carranza ordered me to send three thousand of our men to aid General Natera who, on his orders, has gone to Zacatecas with insufficient forces and is faced with failure there. Seeing the error in the order, I advised the advance of not three thousand men or five thousand but of the whole division, without which the operations will never succeed. He ignored my words and repeated his orders. I then asked for a telegraphic conference, and stated my reasons, which he did not choose to understand. So, confronted with a demand obliging me to execute orders contrary to the security of my troops and the good of our cause, I offered my resignation, which he accepted immediately. He now calls on you to name a substitute, who will command until he has made his own choice."

My words were hardly needed. I knew the day before that they had already decided not to yield to the Chief. But I reminded them that duty demanded that each one remain at his post and obey Carranza unless this meant useless sacrifice of men. I spoke thus because it was my opinion that one new chief after another would condemn the order to aid General Natera until Carranza was finally convinced of his error and would correct his orders.

And what happened was that my generals sent to him to request other orders, saying:

Señor, with greatest respect we ask you to revoke your decision to accept Villa's resignation; it would lead to a serious loss of morale and to trouble for the cause, not only inside our Republic but on the outside. Think like us in this matter, Señor, and appreciate the spirit that moves us.

Toribio Ortega. Eugenio Aguirre Benavides. Maclovio Herrera. Rosalío Hernández. Severino Ceniceros. Martiniano Servín. José Rodríguez. Trinidad Rodríguez. Mateo Almanza. Felipe Angeles. José Isabel Robles. Tomás Urbina. Calixto Contreras. Orestes Pereyra. Máximo García. Manuel Madinabeitia. Raúl Madero.

Sr. Carranza answered:

Sres. Generals of the Northern Division:

When I accepted the resignation of Señor General Francisco Villa as chief of those troops, I considered every situation that could result from it. I therefore order you to reach an immediate agreement as to who is to replace him and execute the orders I have given for the attack on Zacatecas.

Venustiano Carranza

Reading these words, most of my generals raged, like Maclovio Herrera, and declared that their only course was to offend Carranza irreparably, but Angeles again advised prudence and painted the dangers of a break in Revolutionary unity and explained that it is the law of politics to go along at times with men whose minds are closed to truth and justice. Angeles quieted them through his kindness and intelligence, and I believe he acted wisely.

CHAPTER 15

Restored to Command of the Northern Division by His Generals, Villa Prepares to Take Zacatecas.

The Generals Are Disobedient. Carranza's Answer. The Road to Dissolution and Rebellion. It was Impossible To Obey. The Three Corps of the Army. A Conference with Alvaro Obregón. Manuel Chao.

The second message from my generals to the Chief read:

Señor, we could all relinquish our commands, as General Villa has, and thus hasten the dissolution of our conquering troops. But we must not, and will not, deprive our cause of its most powerful element, the Northern Division. For this reason, Señor, we now declare to the Chief of the Division that it is his duty to continue the struggle, and we hope to convince him of this, and trust that we will see him again in command of these troops, as if today's unfortunate events had not occurred. Further, we advise and beg you, Señor, to proceed in the same manner since the one obligation we all share, you, he, and we, is limited to the destruction of our common enemy.

They did as they said. I was convinced by their arguments that I should not give up my post. They told me that it was my duty to remain in command and that they were the ones who had placed me there by their action at our meeting at the Hacienda de la Loma in September, 1913, and not Sr. Carranza.

But Carranza did not see their decision in the same light. He answered:

Sres. Generals:

I am sorry to advise you that I do not consent to reconsider the resignation of General Villa as Chief of the Northern Division. If I should do so, discipline would suffer, and with bad discipline all ranks would try to take over command. Three days ago I ordered General Villa to send reinforcements to General Natera and he has not yet obeyed me, although he was ordered not to send troops of the Northern Division, which is his, but those of Calixto Contreras, José Isabel Robles, Orestes Pereyra, Eugenio Aguirre Benavides, Máximo García, and José Carrillo, who do not belong to the division but are attached to it by my order. I call on you to do your duty as good soldiers, and I advise you to heed my orders. If contrary to what I expect, you have tried to reach some agreement in the presence of the general in question, I order you to meet alone and communicate to me the decision you make.

In the spirit of forbearance all my generals agreed on this answer:

Señor, our resolution to continue the struggle under the orders of our General Francisco Villa is unchanged. Furthermore, this is a well-meditated resolution, uniting us in our purpose, considered in the absence of the general. After adopting it as our own, we went to him and told him it was his duty and ours to comply with it, and he understood and accepted. He has decided to continue as our chief, and with him at the head of all our troops we are preparing to go south. To relieve you of all doubt, we declare that all the generals signing this telegram belong to the Northern Division and that all our forces form part of it.

And all my chiefs signed at the end of the message: Felipe Angeles, Tomás Urbina, Toribio Ortega, Maclovio Herrera, José Rodríguez, Rosalío Hernández, Trinidad Rodríguez, José Isabel Robles, Eugenio Aguirre Benavides, Raúl Madero, Martiniano Servín, Calixto Contreras, Severino Ceniceros, Mateo Almanza, Orestes Pereyra, Máximo García, and Manuel Madinabeitia.

Carranza should have acceded with good grace but he wired:

Sres. Generals of the Northern Division:
On ordering you to assemble for the purpose of naming a chief, I followed the impulse to avoid the difficulties which could arise if the chief of my choice did not please everyone. In view of the contents of your message I could decide immediately on that appointment. But I wish to proceed in harmony with you, and so consider it best for the following generals to be present tomorrow morning in Saltillo to discuss the affair with me: Generals Felipe Angeles, Tomás Urbina, Maclovio Herrera, Toribio Ortega, Eugenio Aguirre Benavides, and Rosalío Hernández.

Then we all grew angry together. "Not only," they thought, "did he despise our advice as soldiers but he cast reflections on our conduct as men. Where did he get the idea that we are incapable of thinking for ourselves and that these resolutions are not the work of our own minds? Does he imagine that General Villa walks over us and we dare not breathe? Does he think that there would be so many victories if that were so?"

This was all true. In the long period of my resignation I had no contact, either by word or deed, with the meeting at which my generals were counseling on my fate. I left this to their intelligence and will. If they then acted in concert in my favor and expressed their devotion, and came to ask me not to abandon them or their cause, it was because of their great knowledge of the war and the feelings in their hearts.

I then met with my generals and told them when Carranza had begun the persecution. I painted the hostility of his orders and his secret acts and the plot his favored men were contriving with Washington to stop my supply of arms and ammunition. On hearing this, they rose against Carranza with even greater anger than I felt, and in their indignation determined to express themselves in even harsher words. As I remember, Felipe Angeles, always so prudent, so calm, so discreet, grew angry and himself sent a telegram to the Chief telling him what they all thought and felt.

This was their answer:

Señor, from your last message we consider that you have not understood us or wished to understand. What we are saying, Señor, is that we do not accept your decision with regard to General Villa's resignation. We consider your measure a violation of both the laws of politics and war and the duties of patriotism. We inform you, Sr. Carranza, that we have convinced General Villa that his obligations to our country compel him to remain in command of this Division, as if you had never conceived the ill-considered idea of stripping him of the command which we recognize because he created it. We say further, that, among all those who defend our cause, General Villa is the chief with the greatest prestige, and if he should obey your order and retire, the people of Mexico would be right in blaming you and realizing your very great weakness, and they would accuse you of being the cause of a great loss. We say this much more, Señor: we know well that you were looking for the opportunity to stop General Villa in his action because of your purpose to remove from the Revolutionary scene the men who can think without your orders, who do not flatter and praise you, or struggle for your aggrandizement but only for the rights of the people. Before the interests and ambitions of the Chief come the sorrows and needs of the Mexican people whom we represent, and the people tell us that General Villa must not give up his command because his victories are still indispensable. By these words you will understand that it is our decision to march south at once and this means the generals you summon cannot be present in that city tomorrow morning.

Now, after so long a time, I see that this disobedience of my generals was justified by the events that followed it. When Carranza would not listen to them, two roads were open to him: either to resign his command and disband his troops which would result in serious damage to our cause, or to consider his order as nonexistent and continue in the service of the people, leaving the settlement of disagreements until later.

The thing we could not do was to obey, for that would lead to defeat and to the sacrifice of many thousands of lives. What would happen, Señor, if the Northern Division disbanded? By that alone the progress of the Revolution would be halted and perhaps reversed. What would happen if the five thousand men demanded by the Chief should leave to help Natera? They would be lost, with their arms and ammunition and supplies; and the enemy, encouraged by that triumph, would annihilate Natera and come to meet a Northern Division with its forces reduced and its morale lowered to where it could be defeated and completely routed. And what would happen if my generals decided to disobey a bad order and continued their march as if nothing had occurred? The chain of our victories would continue even though Carranza should grow angry because we won without his advice, his authorization, or his help. We recognized him as Chief in our cause, but we did not consider him the principal element of the Revolution, because the Revolution was being won by our arms and our blood.

Having decided to march south at once, I then thought to myself, "Won't my forces be the ones who win the Revolution as soon as they march to the center of the Republic? And to obtain that triumph, isn't it necessary that the troops of Alvaro Obregón advance toward the west and the troops of Pablo González to the east? Then it is only necessary that we, the three chiefs, agree on our movements and rid ourselves of the obstacles which the First Chief can create with his decisions."

I decided to communicate with the two generals and inform them of what had happened and ask them to participate in our action. But it was not then possible to talk with Pablo González, who was in Saltillo with Carranza; and Obregón, with whom I had a telegraphic conference from Torreón to Tepic, answered that he did not clearly understand me and was advising me to submit to all the measures of our First Chief.

On that night of June 14, 1914, General Manuel Chao arrived in Torreón. He was on his way to Saltillo to take command of Carranza's escort. As he got off the train, one of my generals went up to him and said, "Señor, look at this telegram the generals of the Northern Division have just sent to the First Chief."

When he had read it, he came over to me and said, "I am of the same opinion as the generals of the Northern Division."

Early the next day he went to the telegraph office to send this message to Carranza: "Señor, I fully approve and consider as my own the telegram sent you last night by the generals of this Division, which I again join with all my troops."

CHAPTER 16

By Villa's Order Urbina and Angeles March on Zacatecas and Form the Plan of Battle.

The Constitutionalist Treasury of Ciudad Juárez. Serapio Aguirre and Urbano Flores. Alberto J. Pani. Miguel Silva. Manuel Bonilla. Miguel Díaz Lombardo. Ramón Puente. Orders for Compadre Urbina. Orders for Felipe Angeles. San Vicente. Morelos. San Antonio. Veta Grande. Thirty-eight Cannons. Colonel Gonzalitos. Villa Approves the Plan.

The circumstances of my break with Carranza were not yet over when he began to commit hostile acts against me. His favored men were sending out telegrams which slandered me, saying, "Pancho Villa is a traitor: he renounces the Revolution and has no respect for our Chief. We advise that his reputation be subjected to the most scathing criticism." Carranza himself, with unjust words, called all Revolutionary chiefs to his aid, it was said, to protect himself from me and my men, and in this he was discrediting us. Besides, he ordered the port closed to munitions and arms which were coming to me from other countries, and neither he nor his envoys considered the efforts I would have to make to win a victory.

Seeing this, I wondered which would be better: to answer in like fashion or to ignore his acts. I understood the danger of showing too meek a face, which would encourage him to go to greater lengths. I decided therefore to take over his Treasury, which he had left in Ciudad

Juárez in charge of Serapio Aguirre and Urbano Flores. I ordered them imprisoned, and I also took over the office where the bills were stamped. This had been entrusted to the engineer Alberto J. Pani. I took all the stamped bills and those he was ready to stamp, which was all the Constitutionalist money in existence.

I worked thus, imagining that when Sr. Carranza found himself without money he would halt his hostilities and seek an understanding with me, which was important to our cause, not to me personally. But I thought too that the agreement would have to be provisional. By then nothing would appease his enmity toward me and other good Revolutionaries. In criticizing us he harped on the urgency of preparing men for government at the hour of triumph, men of law who would advise and guide us in the ways of justice and enlighten us in our reforms for the benefit of the people. I asked Angeles if he knew any men like that besides Don Miguel Silva and Don Manuel Bonilla, and he spoke of a man named Iglesias Calderón, who was then traveling with Carranza, and another named Miguel Díaz Lombardo, who was in Paris, and another, whose name I forget.

I called Dr. Ramón Puente and I said, "Ask my secretary for the money you need, and go to Paris to see Don Miguel Díaz Lombardo, an intelligent lawyer, whom we need here. Explain our situation to him, and bring him back at once." Dr. Puente left to carry out his mission.

Having decided to take Zacatecas, I dictated all the orders for our march on June 15, 1914. The next day my first trains left for Fresnillo.

I called my compadre Urbina and said to him. "Compañero, precede me in the development of this action. Advance with your troops and other brigades until you are near to Zacatecas. The next day I will send you artillery. The day after that the rest will leave. Today is the fifteenth. On the twentieth or twenty-first I will have no less than 22,000 men concentrated there, counting those of Natera and Arrieta, and no less than fifty cannons. The enemy will not withstand us. Study the terrain and decide with Angeles on the distribution of the troops. Take them close, and form your plan. On the twenty-second I will arrive, and if the plan is good, a thing which I shall decide, and if, as General Angeles promises me, the artillery fire suffices, I have no doubt that by the morning of the twenty-third we will begin the battle and that night we will sleep in Zacatecas, with the enemy annihilated.

My compadre considered the orders I had given him and left to fulfill his duty. Then I said to Angeles, "Sr. General, how is our artillery?"

"Completely organized, my General."

"Is it better than it was when we took Torreón?"

"It will be more effective than it was in the battle of Torreón."

"Is it better than it was when we took San Pedro?"

"It will be more effective than it was in the battle of San Pedro."

In view of this I added, "Very well, Señor. You will leave day after tomorrow with your artillery, behind the first trains of General Urbina, and at Zacatecas you will plan your action with him. Tell him that the battle will be supported by heavy fire so that our infantry and cavalry will not suffer. Choose the best location for your cannon. He will place the troops. General Urbina will understand and help you, Señor, for he knows the responsibilities of command. Today is the fifteenth. On the night of the twenty-first all our troops will be there, and all our munitions and supplies. On the twenty-second I will arrive. On the twenty-third we will fight until we enter Zacatecas. But I say only this: I expect your cannon to win this battle."

Angeles replied, "Señor, cannon win battles when the infantry does not fail to take advantage of the fire."

"I take that into account, Sr. General. Be responsible to me for the action of your pieces, and I will be responsible to you for the action of my troops."

The trains carrying the first brigades left on the sixteenth. Angeles left on the seventeenth with the five artillery trains. The trains carrying the rest of the troops left on the eighteenth, nineteenth, and twentieth. There were so many convoys that when the troops were unloaded, the cars had to be lined up all the way from Fresnillo to Calera station, about twenty-five kilometers from Zacatecas. According to my orders, Urbina and Angeles left their trains at Calera to proceed from there on exploring and scouting trips.

I found out later that on the nineteenth, soon after his arrival, Felipe Angeles had an encounter at San Vicente, when he and Manuel Chao were scouting Morelos on the heights that run from there to the hill called Loreta, just north of Zacatecas. Urbina sent the forces of Trinidad Rodríguez to help him, and Angeles employed them in pushing the enemy from Las Pilas and Hacienda Nueva, west of that hill, after which he succeeded in moving his cannon to Morelos that same day.

At the same time Maclovio Herrera and Manuel Chao, by orders of Angeles and my compadre Urbina, went forward with their brigades to Cieneguilla and San Antonio, two places southwest of Zacatecas, near the hill they call Los Clérigos. Thus the reconnaissance was being made, and thus the deployment of our troops began. The enemy, retreating before my men, were burning the forage without stopping to fight, leaving obstructions behind and retiring to the protection of their fortified positions.

I found out that on the following day Felipe Angeles, escorted by Natera and some of his men, carried their exploration as far as Veta Grande, a mine north of Zacatecas, opposite the hills they call El Grillo and La Bufa—El Grillo being west of that point of the city and La Bufa to the east—and that there he cut off the La Plata mine from the enemies and carried part of his artillery to Veta Grande in order to get it in position that night for the attack on the hills.

That day, the twentieth, my compadre Urbina ordered the troops of Natera and Arrieta, Triana, Contreras, Bañuelos, Domínguez, and Caloca to approach Zacatecas by way of Guadalupe, a town about seven kilometers to the east, and part of his forces and the Ceniceros Brigade and part of the Villa Brigade to advance beyond Veta Grande to support the artillery being placed there. That afternoon Angeles sent ten cannon to Herrera and Chao, who were already in San Antonio on the south. They were placing the cannon according to instructions which Angeles himself went to give them on the spot, and they were to stay quiet there until time for the attack.

All that day Angeles and Urbina made the explorations and movements for the location of the troops under fire of the enemy cannon from their fortified positions on El Grillo and La Bufa, but that did not disturb my men. They continued to perform their work, Angeles with his great intelligence and skill as a military man, and my compadre Urbina according to his good judgment and knowledge acquired in fighting for the people.

On the next day, the twenty-first of June, they finished placing the seven batteries on the north which were destined to break the enemy resistance there, and the ten cannons on the south which would give their support to the movements of Maclovio. These thirty-eight cannons were not to fire until the battle began and so they silently endured the enemy fire which was kept up all that day with the purpose of stopping the work or destroying or discovering the emplacements.

On that same day, by orders of Urbina, the forces of Martiniano Servín and Mateo Almanza took their position facing the hill called La Sierpe, west of the city; and the forces of José Rodríguez went farther toward the north on that same side, below the hill Tierra Colorada or Loreto, and next to the Cuauhtémoc Brigade, which had been there for two days. And thus we continued with our movements of approximation. Natera, Arrieta, Triana, and other troops were approaching the town of Guadalupe on the east. The troops of Herrera and Chao were moving toward Los Clérigos on the south. The Cuauhtémoc and Villa brigades were searching for better positions on the northwest. Angeles was placing most of his cannon on the north and improving the position of his supports and strengthening them with the infantry of Gonzalitos.

I got off my train at the Calera station at one the afternoon of the twenty-second. That morning the Ortega and Zaragoza brigades had arrived at Zacatecas. My compadre Urbina ordered Toribio Ortega's troops to march to San Antonio and remain there with those of Maclovio and Chao. He sent the Zaragoza Brigade, then under the command of Raúl Madero because Eugenio Aguirre Benavides was commanding the forces of José Isabel Robles who was ill, to Veta Grande to operate under the direct orders of Felipe Angeles.

When I arrived that afternoon at Urbina's general headquarters in the aforesaid town of Morelos, he looked at me and said, "Compadre, all your orders have been executed. The reconnaissance has been made, our troops have gone into position, and all is arranged as planned. As for the battle plan, it has been formed to the best of my ability and with the assistance of General Angeles. Unless you order otherwise, we will attack the enemy on its north front, which is defended by the fortified positions of El Grillo and La Bufa, and first we will have to take the hills called Tierra Negra, Tierra Colorada, and La Sierpe. That attack will be supported by the one we make on the south, on La Estación and on the the hill Los Clérigos. The enemy, driven from their positions, will not find shelter in the city because once we occupy these positions, the entire town will lie under our fire. The enemy will have no recourse except to leave by way of Guadalupe, and then our reserves there will cover their retreat and annihilate them. Most of our artillery, in the opinion of General Angeles, already occupies good emplacements, and will be ready to change to better ones tonight. Compadre, everything depends now on the chances of war and our courage. I am sure you bring plenty of munitions and supplies."

I answered, "Compadre, I think your plan is good. I only need to consider it from the standpoint of the terrain. I am going to see what my eyes tell me." And so it was. I left Morelos with my staff and advanced beyond Veta Grande.

As I approached the La Plata mine, Angeles appeared. We greeted each other with the warmest affection. He said, "My General, everything is ready. When you give your orders, the battle will begin."

I answered, "I know it, Señor, and General Urbina has already said that it is the plan that you developed."

He replied, "No, Señor, it is his. I have contributed only my advice for his consideration and for your revision if there should be some error."

Hearing him utter those modest words, I added, "Good, Señor. Whether it is your plan or his, I think the measures are good. I only want you to take me where I can view the field best."

He led me first to the batteries at the La Plata mine and the place where he intended to move them that night. From the site occupied by the battery of Captain Quiroz he showed me the field of battle, and he explained the value, in his judgment, of the locations and the reasons for the measures he and Urbina had taken.

I said to him, "It is all good, Sr. General. You and Urbina will enter under the protection of all these batteries. I will make a flank attack on the side over there on the right of Tierra Colorada while you attack in the center and on the left."

Considering the ravines and the hills and appraising the decisions of my compadre Urbina and of Felipe Angeles and the heavy employment of the artillery, I thought that it was going to be a great battle.

CHAPTER 17

Within Half an Hour after the First Shot, Villa Takes the First Line of the Enemy Defense at Zacatecas.

Eve of the Battle. Partial Combat. Natera and His Attacks on the Tenth. The Capes of the Troops. Placement of the Batteries. Villa's 23,000 Men. Major Saavedra. Major Jurado. Captain Quiroz. Medina Barrón's 12,000 Men. Colonel Tello and Pascual Orozco. Attack on Loreto and Tierra Negra. Infantrymen and Cavalrymen. Trinidad Rodríguez. Bazán's Aide.

The afternoon of the twenty-second I ordered the men of the Morelos Brigade to discontinue their support of the artillery at La Plata and join the Zaragoza Brigade on the left of that position.

I went with my officers to reconnoiter the front lines, and had my measures explained to all the brigade chiefs so that the battle could begin the next day at ten. To each of them I sent this word, "Our forces will move together at the hour. Nobody will enter one minute before or one minute later." I said this to avoid partial combats that might weaken us. Already, in only searching for good sites for our cannon and troops, the brigades had become impatient and had provoked encounters of such great fury that in one of them Maclovio Herrera was wounded in the arm, and two or three cannon were dismounted at Veta Grande and San Antonio, as Felipe Angeles told me, and some of our artillerymen were wounded and killed. But it is also true that those first assaults injured the enemy forces, who lost ground and retreated and took refuge in their fortifications, their only shelter, after having no rest since the first attacks by Natera and Arrieta on the morning of the tenth.

It began to rain, and the winds were chilling.

Felipe Angeles said, "The rain is heavy, my General. My soldiers are suffering from having to endure it without capes."

I answered, "Señor, this campaign will end, and soon afterward our equipment will be complete."

As we were discussing the change we would make that night in our artillery positions, he spoke the words of a great soldier, saying, "Count on surprise, my General. Dawn will come, the mist will rise, and they will discover that our cannon have disappeared from the visible positions where they are now. Then they will recognize the rule. Because, if possible, artillery is always situated out of sight of the enemy, not on the open hilltops where it can be seen. You see those cannon they have on El Grillo? They are badly placed, my General, although their troops imagine themselves well fortified."

"And are you confident that the new emplacements can be made in the rain and the dark?"

"You can be sure of it. We will even be aided by the lighthouse on La Bufa, which the enemy uses to explore our field, and if we aren't, I depend on the skill of my officers and the good advice my aides will give them. Major Cervantes, Major Bazán, and Captain Espinosa de los Monteros already have their orders." And that was what happened. The emplacements of no less than twenty-four cannons were changed that night.

The next day, June 23, 1914, all orders were dictated for the course of the battle. I had planned to begin at ten, with all the brigades entering in one single movement and all the batteries firing at the same time, each brigade, each battery according to its position.

This was the disposition of the troops: the troops of my compadre Tomás Urbina, and of Ceniceros, Aguirre Benavides, Raúl Madero, and Colonel Gonzalitos, would advance on the northeast and the north to attack Tierra Negra and Tierra Colorada hills from La Plata and Veta Grande. Those troops would be commanded by Urbina and Angeles, and they numbered 5,000 men in all. The forces of José and Trinidad Rodríguez and those of Rosalío Hernández, another 5,000 men, coming from Las Pilas and Hacienda Nueva, would advance on the northwest for the flank attack on Tierra Colorada hill or Loreto. Those forces would be under my command, and I would enter there with my officers and my escort. The forces of Mateo Almanza and Martiniano Servín, numbering 2,500 men, would advance on the west and on my right against the hill called La Sierpe. Those of Toribio Ortega, Maclovio Herrera, and Manuel Chao, no less than 3,000 in number, would advance on the southwest and the south, from San Antonio, on the fortresses of La Estación on the slope which runs in that direction from the top of El Grillo, and on Los Clérigos or El Padre. On the south and southeast, the troops of Natera, Bañuelos, Domínguez, Cervantes and Caloca, numbering more than 5,000 men, in a movement toward El Padre hill and another called El Refugio, would advance along these same hills. On the east, part of the forces of Arrieta, Triana, Carrillo, and other chiefs from Durango, numbering 2,000 men, would advance against Villa de Guadalupe and the elevation Grestón Chico, toward La Bufa. The other part of those forces would form our reserve.

That is, Zacatecas was threatened from all sides and by no less than 23,000 men and the artillery power of twenty-eight cannon on the north and ten on the south and the piece called El Niño, on its platform beyond Pimienta station, and twelve more cannon, also on the north but farther away. In their attack on Tierra Negra hill, my compadre Tomás Urbina, Ceniceros, Aguirre Benavides, and Gonzalitos would receive support from three batteries commanded by Major Saavedra. In their attack on Loreto hill, Raúl Madero and other forces would receive support from three batteries commanded by Major Jurado. My advance would be supported by the battery of Captain Quiroz, whom I mentioned before. In their attack on Los Clérigos and La Estación, Toribio Ortega, Maclovio Herrera, and Manuel Chao would receive support from the batteries on the south commanded by Major Carrillo. When we took Loreto and Tierra Negra hills, and then La Sierpe, we would go on to break the enemy's resistance on El Grillo and La Bufa, which was the most important, and then on the south Maclovio's attack on Los Clérigos and La Estación and Natera's on Refugio and Guadalupe would grow stronger, and all the defending forces would be defeated.

Señor! Was it possible that the enemy could resist our assault? According to reports that were arriving, they had 12,000 men and thirteen cannon with very good shells and fortified emplacements. The 12,000 men were distributed in their positions at La Bufa, Tierra Negra, Loreto, La Sierpe, El Grillo, La Estación, El Padre, Guadalupe, and Crestón Chico. There were thirteen cannon on La Bufa, El Grillo, and El Refugio, and one in movement on the track between La Estación and Guadalupe. We knew that General Luis Medina Barrón would be in command of the defense and that there were many other generals with him: Antonio Olea, Juan N. Vásquez, José Soberanes, Manuel Altamirano, Jacinto Guerrero, Antonio Rojas, Benjamín Argumedo, Jacobo Harotia, De los Santos, and others whose names I do not remember. Also, I knew that aid for Zacatecas was coming from the south. A Colonel Tello was already in the Cañon de Palmira with 1,000 men, and Pascual Orozco was much nearer, having passed the town of La Soledad with another 1,000 men.

Considering how close these new troops were, I ordered Sr. General Natera to be on the alert, in confirmation of orders which he had already received from General Angeles. I said to him, "Sr. General, in this battle your men are to give us help on the south line from Los Clérigos, or El Padre, to El Refugio and Guadalupe. You will be in action there, ready for the annihilation of the enemy when they retreat. You will cut the railroad line at those places and any other road by which the enemy might hope for reinforcements.

It was all done as ordered. At exactly ten, on that morning of June 23, 1914, the fighting broke out all along our lines. We then had twenty-four cannons above the enemy positions without their location being known, and as they began to thunder on the north and northeast, Carrillo's batteries were thundering on the southeast side in support of Maclovio Herrera, and on the south and southeast the sharp sound of shooting was coming from Natera's attack.

With the Villa and Cuauhtémoc brigades I left my positions at Hacienda Nueva and advanced on Loreto hill on the side facing me. From Veta Grande the battery of Quiroz was supporting me with devastating fire. On the other side of the hill and beyond roared the artillery thunder of the batteries hidden in the yards of the La Plata mine and of those which Angeles had ordered placed at the end of our line, to the left of La Bufa. I can still hear the great roar reverberating as if the hills would sink or crumble. The enemy pieces were answering from La Bufa and El Grillo, although without success in their attempt to stop our advance, since their infantry was withdrawing under the fire of our cannon, which their batteries were trying to silence, and our infantry, protected in that way, was pushing forward and was on top of the enemy positions before the attack could be contained. This happened again and again. I mean to say that the shells of our cannon were always exploding in front of us, sweeping obstacles from the field or preparing it for our advance. I was thinking to myself, "In truth, Felipe Angeles is a great artilleryman and also a military man who knows how to make use of his officers."

I do not think our enemies understood or appreciated our great skill in the use of the cannon. Because they had theirs placed in such high positions, they could not fire on our men as they advanced but only on or beyond our rear guard where our artillery was thundering. And when they saw how their infantry was paralyzed by the action of our cannon and how we were moving forward, they concentrated their effort on silencing the pieces that were causing them so much damage. And they did not know that this was what Angeles was striving for and what he was achieving.

Angeles had said, "It is necessary to draw their shells on our pieces so that our infantry can advance. When their artillery succeeds in dismounting one cannon of ours, we will already be entering their positions."

And in truth it went so. At the time my men were advancing on the hill, while that enemy infantry was hidden and without action, I was watching the enemy shells explode on the batteries of Veta Grande and La Plata where Angeles was. The fighting was increasing. There, as I soon learned, the enemy fire was dismounting a piece of artillery, and was killing our artillerymen and mules. Here, our men, masters now of the first trench, were crawling on to conquer the second, which the enemies were abandoning also, first overwhelmed by our cannon and then without the spirit to face the furious onslaught of our infantry. Or rather, their lines were breaking up and they were quickly disappearing toward the protected part of the hill.

In this way, the first step of the battle was consummated within half an hour after the fighting had begun. In twenty-five minutes Loreto hill, on the right, was ours, and La Tierra Negra, on the left and in front of La Bufa, was ours. The Villa and Cuauhtémoc brigades climbed this side of Loreto, and the Zaragoza Brigade under the command of Raulito climbed the other side. The forces of Urbina, Aguirre Benavides, Ceniceros, and Gonzalitos took Tierra Negra hill. In the assault on Loreto hill Trinidad Rodríguez received a fatal wound in the neck. I heard this with tears, for he was a fine Revolutionary, with a brave and generous heart. Other good soldiers of the people died or were wounded there. The enemy forces abandoned these two hills in defeat; they were annihilated by our shells, our machine guns, and our rifles; some of their men were running down the ravine there toward the plaza, and others were going to seek shelter on El Grillo or La Bufa.

At eleven that morning our infantry and our cavalry were already safe and in formation on Loreto hill. I went then in search of General Angeles to give him my advice with regard to moving our batteries to the new positions. He galloped up on horseback, followed by his staff. I said to him, "Sr. General, the benefit of these triumphs rests on the rapidity of our movements. It is necessary to move the artillery to Loreto hill, unless you think otherwise, in order to aid Servín's infantry which, by my order, is advancing now on the slopes of La Sierpe."

He answered, "Your orders are executed, my General. The cannons have already been moved."

We went with our officers toward a big house there on the hill which seemed to belong to a mine. The enemy began to fire on us, and although we galloped, we were unable to escape the machine gun and rifle bullets. Major Gustavo Bazán's aide and his horse were wounded there.

CHAPTER 18

After Taking La Sierpe and Crushing El Grillo, Villa Has the Plaza of Zacatecas at His Mercy.

At the Loreto Mine. Servín's Infantry. "Señor, Where Is Your Cannon Fire?" Gustavo Durón González. The Slopes of La Sierpe. Attack on Refugio, Los Clérigos, and La Estación. El Grillo. The Men of the Escort and the Staff. On the Pile of Rocks. Rodolfo Fierro. Federico Cervantes.

From the house at the Loreto mine I could see that Servín's infantry was not advancing but had stopped and was almost in trouble. I dictated orders for his assistance.

In truth our artillery was late in arriving although Major Federico Cervantes was already there giving Felipe Angeles a report on their proximity and Angeles was passing it on to me. I ordered machine-gun fire on the enemy lines which were holding Servín back on the slope of La Sierpe.

Felipe Angeles was a brave man. When I was dictating these orders, he climbed up on the roof of the house with one of his officers to observe the situation and drew much of the enemy fire upon himself and the officer. I called him back. "Señor," I asked him, "where are your cannon?" It was clear that Servín would be driven back in spite of our machine-gun fire. The enemy took courage when they saw that our guns were thundering at La Estación and on the other side of La Bufa but not against the front, and they began to leave their trenches and push Servín's men downhill in disorder.

Angeles, seeing this as plainly as I did, gave his orders to the officer who had climbed down from the roof with him. "Major Cervantes, bring up a gun or two at once. We can turn them back."

The Major returned with a piece which he himself put into service. After him came a captain with an entire battery, and as the cannons began to fire on La Sierpe, other pieces were arriving and the fire increased. The enemy, so powerful a moment before, abandoned the attack and turned to defense. Servín's men followed them with renewed vigor. Our machine-gun fire picked up. Our riflemen pressed closer. The captain, Gustavo Durón González, as I remember, was directing his fire so effectively that he had the enemy pinned down helpless on the slopes of La Sierpe.

Señor, how sweet the cannons sound when they are firing on the enemy. The fire of the enemy was weakening, and they were leaving their defenses again, this time not to drive back my troops but to escape. They fell by the hundreds, and scattered in disorder on the slopes. Servín's men showed great and disciplined courage in not becoming demoralized when the enemy had them almost defeated. And Captain Durón González and his artillerymen in a mighty fifteen minutes of firing put that part of the enemy forces out of action.

At twelve in the morning our flag appeared on top of La Sierpe. At twelve-thirty I had word of the progress of Maclovio, Chao, and Ortega at La Estación, of Natera at Los Clérigos and El Refugio, and of Arrieta and Triana at Guadalupe.

Said Angeles, "My General, we have taken the second step. The first was capturing Loreto and Tierra Negra, the second was the conquest of La Sierpe. Now that we are in control here, El Grillo can not resist much longer."

I answered, "Now, General, have your cannon support my men in the third step. Cover Raúl Madero's forces and the Villa and Cuauhtémoc brigades on their way up El Grillo."

As Raúl Madero began to attack El Grillo on one side and the Cuauhtémoc and Villa brigades on the other, Angeles brought batteries from Loreto to locations favorable to the movement I had planned. But it was not going to be easy to break the lines of defense on El Grillo. The cannon must move up to places under deadly fire. Durón González, with my officers assisting him, had to drive his men at pistol point in getting the guns into the position he wanted. And while he was at this, Angeles and his aides were placing other cannon on the left, where the bombardment was heaviest.

From Tomás Urbina I got word that as soon as the enemies weakened on El Grillo, we could move in and finish Zacatecas. I sent orders to the reserves to move up within protection of our relocated cannon and organize for a concerted movement. But with them, as with the advancing artillery, it happened that the first advance onto terrain dominated by El Grillo and La Bufa was a terrible test. My officers and escort employed every ounce of their courage to keep up the spirits of these troops. The pace of fighting increased. Our artillerymen no longer thought of danger but only of reaching the target, and this under a concentration of counterfire. Shells were exploding around us; some were so skilfully directed that they were reducing the number of our gunners.

I climbed up onto a pile of stones to observe the effect of our fire and the course of our advance. The progress up El Grillo was painfully slow. I called Angeles and said, "Señor, your cannon must do more."

And at that moment an enormous explosion enveloped us. My only feeling, as I remember, was one of admiration for the enemy who were bombarding us with such accuracy. But when the smoke and dust cleared away we saw that no enemy shell had fallen on the pile of stones. Angeles, his aides and I were standing there unharmed. I looked toward the batteries, and I saw that the men at the nearest gun all lay on the ground, either dead or wounded. We ran to the spot and learned that a shell had exploded in the hands of a gunner as he was getting ready to fire it.

The other pieces had stopped their fire, the gunners terrified by the thought of holding death in their hands, and I went among them with words of encouragement. "This is only an accident," I said. "It won't happen again. I am here with you. I protect you."

And Angeles added, "Nothing has happened, or almost nothing. But something worse will happen if we slacken fire and the enemy defeat us. Then we will die to no avail. The order stands: 'Fire without interruption!'" They recovered and again the thunder of our cannon answered the batteries on El Grillo and La Bufa. But I was grieved to the depths of my heart to see my men wounded and killed by our own arms.

Angeles came over to me and I pointed to where our infantry were halted. The enemy seemed to have doubled the number of their cannon and the spirit of their resistance. They were bombarding us on the north and Maclovio Herrera and Pánfilo Natera on the south, and their infantry and cavalry showed no signs of weakening. I said, "General, our infantry are discouraged. My officers and escort have gone to the front. I need an aide to carry orders to the generals."

Angeles answered, "Their spirit is still strong, Señor. It is their bodies which are exhausted. It is inhuman to ask us to take so many positions in a single day against a determined enemy with better munitions than ours. For our artillery to be successful it has to stand so close that if the enemy were better gunners they would destroy it. They are fortified; we are not. They have taken shelter in their second lines without having to move their main defense. After the advances of these three days and the night movements, we have thrown ourselves in a single assault of short duration against hills, ravines, and mines."

"That may be so, but we have to win today. Transmit my orders."

Rodolfo Fierro appearing at this moment, I wanted him to carry the orders. But he had been shot in the leg and was dripping with blood. He said, "The wound won't stop me, my General."

"But it will. Go to the ambulance and have the doctors bandage your leg."

Angeles then suggested Major Federico Cervantes and when the latter appeared I said, "Major, go to the front and tell the generals the order still stands: The infantry must advance and take El Grillo."

Soon after this the enemy began to abandon their positions on El Grillo, and at the same time Maclovio Herrera's advance at La Estación and Los Clérigos and Natera's advance at Refugio and Guadalupe forced the batteries on El Grillo and La Bufa to concentrate most of their fire there, so that in our sector we were free to advance.

CHAPTER 19

Villa Destroys the Garrison at Zacatecas and Thus Obtains the Definite Triumph of the Revolutionary Cause.

The Big House at Loreto. Maclovio Herrera and Toribio Ortega at La Estación. Natera at El Refugio. Angeles Makes a Reconnaissance. Captain Quiroz' Battery. The Taking of El Grillo and La Bufa. El Padre Hill. Crestón Chico. The Guadalupe Road. The March of Eight Thousand Men. Luis Medina Barrón. Sacking the Town. Flatcars for the Dead. The Lawyers Miguel Alessio Robles and José Ortiz Rodríguez. Carranza and Villa.

It was about one-thirty in the afternoon when the enemy began to abandon El Grillo, or pretended to abandon it. The firing from La Bufa ceased, either as the effect of Saavedra's batteries, which were supporting Urbina's attack, or because they were ready to evacuate. I said to Angeles, "The enemy must be offering us a dinner-time truce." With other officers we began to eat at the big house at the Loreto mine, while our cannon went on firing, as did Saavedra's and those bombarding the enemy on the south.

Today I think the enemy already considered themselves defeated. With reason, for at that moment Maclovio and Toribio Ortega were attacking the station yards on the south, and Natera, coming from El Refugio, was in control all along their line and destroying cannon and equipment. But soon after we had eaten, El Grillo again made a show of resistance, as if reinforcements had arrived or the troops were fighting with renewed courage.

Seeing this, Angeles asked me if I wanted him to reconnoiter. I said yes, and he left with his aides while I remained in our position at Loreto and from there gave orders for the next phase of the battle. The fighting intensified; it rose to new heights of fury; we were pouring the full weight of our fire upon the enemy, and I, Pancho Villa, confess that the Federals were fighting with great valor.

Angeles sent word that things were going well in the positions he had inspected and that he was extending his inspection to our lines on the other side of La Bufa, to consult with Urbina and Ceniceros there. I said to the aide, "Señor, tell General Angeles to send me more artillery if he can. I need it to take El Grillo."

Angeles did what I requested. From Veta Grande he sent Captain Quiroz' battery, which added to the fire. Captains Quiroz and Durón González fired with such skill that we could see the Federal trenches weakening and the defenders recoiling from the impact of our infantry, which climbed the slopes furiously. We saw them fleeing downhill, out of reach of all but the grenades, and finally running to the houses in Zacatecas for protection.

This I was accomplishing from Loreto, with the support of Raúl Madero, Rosalío Hernández, José Rodríguez, Mateo Almanza, and Martiniano Servín, and at the same time Angeles and Urbina were bringing their cannon close to La Bufa on the left and almost silencing the Federal fire.

Herrera and Ortega had taken La Estación on the south. Our advance had been blocked by the batteries on El Grillo and La Bufa, which not only defended on the north and northeast but protected these positions as well. But as Angeles and Urbina intensified the attacks on La Bufa, and I, supported from Loreto, strengthened mine against El Grillo, the Federal gunners, with too much to do, concentrated on a single target. So Herrera and Ortega could clear the passage from the yards to La Estación and then occupy it under the protection of Carrillo's batteries.

Our assault on El Grillo was made about five-thirty in the afternoon. The enemy fled before us, and our artillery destroyed them. We saw an enormous cloud of smoke rising from the heart of the city. It did not seem to come from a fire. It was yellow and dusty as if caused by explosions. Were they burning their ammunition and other matériel?

I received a report that we were in possession of El Padre hill, and that Natera and Arrieta were mopping up after their victory on Guadalupe road, where they were already in control, and on Crestón Chico, where some of the enemy were trying to dig in. As our firing line was reaching the top of El Grillo, the whole enemy structure crumbled in tremendous defeat.

Señor! How the enemy scattered, without form, order, or plan! From our position we followed their panic-stricken efforts. My men were on the slopes of La Bufa, facing the city. In their fury they were descending the other side of El Grillo, while to the south, where we dominated the fortification of La Estación, our shells were exploding on the road from Zacatecas to Guadalupe.

The Federals wanted to leave by that route, as Angeles and Urbina had figured, and twice we saw them driven back at what they told me was the cemetery of Guadalupe. There they tried to escape toward Jerez, only to be driven back again. Finding themselves trapped, they moved toward Veta Grande, though they knew it was hopeless to resist us there, and then sought shelter under the heights of Crestón Chico, but since the troops of Triana and Arrieta were destroying them there, they ended by rushing back to the Guadalupe Road, to be decimated, reduced to nothing, swept from sight.

I calculate that at five-thirty in the afternoon no less than eight thousand of those enemy troops began to flee before our lines and seek refuge in the street near La Estación. Our troops were worrying them out of Las Mesas, La Ciudadela, Guadalupe, and all the houses there and the hills, and we worked such destruction that as the mass of their thousands poured out onto the road from Zacatecas to Guadalupe, then grew still, and then moved again, it grew smaller and smaller. By six-thirty in the afternoon the soldiers of that army were lying dead on the ground. Seeing this, I appreciated the skill with which our reserves had been stationed there, Angeles and Urbina being sure that the retreat would take that road.

Later reports confirmed my estimate that out of twelve thousand defenders of Zacatecas no more than two hundred escaped. All those thousands with almost all their officers, chiefs, and generals remained there, dead, wounded, or prisoners. They left us their cannon, their machine guns, and almost all their rifles. They left us their supplies and their munitions. The flight was so precipitate, so panic-stricken, that demolished warehouses had not been cleared of the dead.

Afterward I learned that Luis Medina Barrón and Generals Antonio Olea, Benjamín Argumedo, Juan N. Vásquez, Jacobo Harotia, and another whose name I forget, had escaped. But their flight was so aimless that they were still wandering from one side to another, surrounded by the thousands who were trying to save themselves when Natera and Chao had already reached the plaza and were killing and taking prisoners and pursuing and annihilating with their fire.

Our great victory was consummated in the morning and afternoon of June 23, 1914. The next day at nine in the morning I entered Zacatecas; and as I contemplated the battlefield and the streets, the magnitude of the holocaust was visible. Those who came out to meet me, men, women, and children, had to leap over corpses to greet me. Beside the enemy dead many of my soldiers lay resting, sleeping in pools of blood.

At headquarters I found Natera. He had come to see me and report. He said, "General, our troops are sacking the town."

I answered, "I know it, Señor. Form a patrol of your best men and see that all the property is returned. I understand the soldiers and their needs. But their conduct may bring dishonor upon our cause."

And I called Banda and said, "See that no more sacking occurs and that what has been taken is returned. This is my only order: the death penalty for those who disregard your measures."

I gave orders to protect business and the lives of the people. They were terrified on realizing that the number of our soldiers was almost equal to that of the inhabitants, and they were still suffering from the shock of the bombardment. I wanted to win their confidence for the benefit of our cause, and for that reason had the dead gathered up and thrown into the shafts of the abandoned mines and covered with dirt. I sent out a train with flatcars to collect the piles of corpses blocking the seven kilometers of road between Zacatecas and Guadalupe, and the dead horses, since there were so many, and had the bodies which could not be buried quickly carried away and burned.

On the morning I entered Zacatecas two lawyers from Torreón were there to talk with me. They represented Pablo González and his Northeastern Division and came to settle my differences with Carranza. They were well-mannered persons and, I believe, good Revolutionaries. Their names were Miguel Alessio Robles and José Ortiz Rodríguez. When they explained their mission in Torreón, I said, "I have no grudge against Carranza. He is the son of all who support Revolutionary action. But as I understand it, since we have given birth to him, we have to train him and not let him follow his wilful impulses. We need a First Chief, and that chief can be Sr. Carranza, especially since a man who has more authority than all the others is always useful in the business of politics. But, Señores, this is not a point that I can decide alone. This must be done by the generals of my Division, who guide me with their advice. Come along on the attack upon Zacatecas, and there you will see us all together and can talk with them and with me."

I told them this, and then in Zacatecas they said, "Sr. General, it would help settle the differences if you would render Carranza a report on this new triumph as an act of respect."

I answered, "I think like my generals that Carranza is hiding his motives in these negotiations, wanting me to believe that it is all the work of the Northeastern Division. But for the report, why not? Our defiance of Carranza's bad military orders does not mean that we refuse to recognize him. Carranza will continue being our Chief as long as he listens to reason."

I said that to them, and it was the truth because I then rendered a report on that battle of Zacatecas just as if none of the disputes at Torreón had happened.

CHAPTER 20

To Avoid Fighting with Carranza, Villa Gives the Fruits of His Magnificent Victory at Zacatecas to Other Generals.

Federals in the Hospital. The Rules of War. Dr. López de Lara. Doctors, Assistants, and Nurses. Juan B. Vargas. Banda's Escort. The Road to the Cemetery. Damián. The Dismissal of Angeles. Seven Brigades to Aguascalientes. Don Pablo's Envoys. Dr. Miguel Silva. Jesús or Luis Fuentes. The Coal from Monclova. The Munitions from Tampico. Course North and Course South. Consequences of the Disaster at Zacatecas.

On the afternoon of that same day, June 24, 1914, I received a report that the doctors and nuns of our hospital were hiding several Federal chiefs and officers among the wounded. I do not accuse them, but such acts violate the rules of war. It is the purpose of hospitals to cure enemy men, not to hide them by pretending that they are wounded, or to cover up or favor the movements of those who fight.

I went in person to punish the violators of the new Law of Juárez. I called on the director, López de Lara, as I remember, and said, "Sr. Doctor, which are those chiefs and officers?"

He answered, "There are no chiefs and officers here."

I called the doctors and attendants, and said, "Señores, which are those chiefs and officers?"

They answered, "There are no chiefs and officers here."

Anger surged up in me. So many negatives were pure fabrication. I thought of having the beds and wounded examined, to find out which ones were truly wounded, and to make sure of the nature of the wounds. But that might be cruel to the ill and suffering, who would be paying for the faults of their fellows. Only the doctors and nuns could be to blame, so I decided to punish them. I said, "Esteemed Señoras and Señores, I regret very much what is going to happen to you, but war brings affliction to all; it is bad for the soldiers who fight but also for civilians who overstep the limits in their conduct. Make your decision. Do you know these chiefs and generals I am asking about? If you do, indicate them to me one by one and their fate will be in my hands. And if you do not know, find out and tell me. If nobody has identified them within the time it takes for an escort to arrive from Headquarters, all of you, nuns and doctors, will be shot today."

I said this not because I meant to carry out the threat, but to get the truth, or make them suffer the fear of death to atone for their offense. Seeing that they said nothing, I asked the medical director whether he had decided to tell me. He answered no, that I might shoot him if it suited me. I asked the medical assistants, who also answered no. Then I sent Vargas for an escort and added, "Señoras and Señores, prepare yourselves for death."

When the escort arrived and Banda presented it, I dictated my orders for the shooting. Banda, in execution of my orders, took nuns, doctors, and attendants on the way to the cemetery, believing that they were going to be shot; the doctors walked silently and the nuns prayed. But one of the nuns, I was told, did not devote herself entirely to her prayers but interrupted them to speak about me to her companions, or to those who were following. She said she was the niece of a famous soldier, González Ortega, and would know how to die; and she encouraged one of the doctors who was frightened, saying, "Be brave, Señor. If you die like a martyr, you will be received into the arms of the Redeemer."

Nevertheless, the pretended execution had a good result. Soon after that procession departed there were plenty who offered to bring me the information I needed. By the time I sent Damián, my chauffeur, to remand the sentence, the chiefs and officers I sought had already fallen into my hands.

As I said, Pablo González' two envoys and other chiefs of the Northeastern Army Corps came to Zacatecas to settle my difficulties with Carranza. I had agreed to call a meeting of my generals to discuss the problems and restore harmony. But it looked as if the meeting might not take place. The day after I entered Zacatecas, Angeles informed me that he had received a communication from the First Chief removing him from

the office of Minister of War and cashiering him, saying he was unworthy as a Revolutionary and a soldier to be at the head of our army
and did not deserve our confidence.

On hearing that I thought, "So, Señor, it stains the reputation of our
army to have at its head a general who helps me annihilate the usurpers?
What acts has Angeles committed, since he joined me in April, except
to demonstrate his loyalty and employ his skill in the aid of my forces?"

This I knew was the result of our disobedience at Torreón. Then why
did Carranza not strip me of my command, or remove Angeles from the
command of my artillery or dismiss the generals of my brigades? It was
evident that he was fixing the blame upon Angeles only as a Minister of
War, where we could not interfere.

I said, "Don't let this trouble you, Señor. I will settle it."

He answered that it did not trouble him at all, although the communication had reached him in the midst of the battle, and he had not come
to discuss this with me but to ask for four brigades for an attack upon
Aguascalientes. In proof of my confidence and esteem, I answered, "Not
four, Sr. General. Seven brigades, and before four days have passed our
cause will triumph at Aguascalientes."

I immediately dictated orders for putting seven cavalry brigades under Angeles, with their trains, their services, their supplies, so that he
could march on Aguascalientes the next day and execute the movement
alone. But I did not get over my anger at his dismissal. I sent for the
two envoys and let them know how angry I was. "Are these the examples
of friendship that you bring me?" I asked.

Feeling the onset of one of my angry outbursts, I would not hear their
words, although, as I now think, their own intentions were good. Dr.
Miguel Silva, a gentleman whom I esteemed highly, came to their aid,
not to protect them, for I was not trying to harm them, but to persuade
me to favor an agreement and to hold me to calling the meeting at which
the lawyers hoped to make their proposals to my generals.

In Zacatecas a bad turn of events ended in my ordering the Federal
officer shot who had run such grave risks to join my forces in Saltillo.
This officer, Jesús or Luis Fuentes, had joined my escort. My men welcomed him warmly, and their relations were good, since he was brave
and intelligent. But he was addicted to drinking, and was what they
call a quarrelsome drunk. In his cups everything went wrong because of
his disposition. After our victory at Zacatecas he went on a drunk and
hunted up another member of the escort against whom he had grievances and shot and killed him.

There was nothing for it but to give orders to apprehend and shoot him. At the place of shooting, when it was time for him to die, he pretended that his affliction was very great, and began to weep, and without a word he softened his executioners with his sobs alone. The chief of the escort, in a stifled voice, asked him what his last wish was; he redoubled his weeping, and said yes, he had a last wish but would not express it because he knew it would not be granted. And as the chief of the escort insisted that he express it, promising that it would be granted if possible, Fuentes had him and the other soldiers swear to this, and then no longer looking stricken but joyful, declared calmly that in his opinion I was a son of a bitch and his last wish was for them to tell me so in his name, although I had befriended him.

So Jesús or Luis Fuentes died cursing me, not in tones of anger or desperation but smiling and content to show me at the edge of his grave that his code of courage had prevailed. When I learned of this deed, with no one daring to tell me the unmitigated truth, I sent for the officer of the escort and said, "My friend, if you swear to a dying man to fulfill his last wish, do so if it costs you your life. Why didn't you bring me the message?" And I added, "The next time you come across a man as brave as Jesús Fuentes do not shoot him, even though Pancho Villa orders it."

On the night of the twenty-fifth of June I received reports that in Monclova Carranza had halted the carloads of coal I needed to move my trains south. He was also halting the passage of arms and munitions coming to me from Tampico. I accepted with bitterness the fact that I must continue south faced with the possibility of exhausting my resources and perhaps losing control of my base of operations, or turn back north with my troops and let other chiefs, unhampered by Carranza's machinations, benefit from the moment when the enemy, the backbone of his resistance broken by my men, was fleeing before our armies in defeat. Because it was clear that Zacatecas, the battle which Carranza did not want me to undertake, had destroyed the morale of the usurpers and they were looking for nothing but shelter.

I said to myself, "I could march on Monclova and bring back the coal which the Chief denies me." But this would throw us into war within our ranks and encourage the enemy. To Angeles, who was ready for the march to Aguascalientes, I said, "Not the enemy but the Chief is closing the road to the south. We cannot proceed without coal. With matériel and all, lead back to Chihuahua those same brigades that I gave you for the attack on Aguascalientes."

He did it.

CHAPTER 21

In Reward for His Triumph at Zacatecas, Villa Remains a Brigadier General while Pablo González and Alvaro Obregón Are Promoted to Division Generals.

Don Pablo's Convoys. Dr. Silva's Words. A Law for the First Chief. Villa Is Frank with Obregón. Obregón Is Frank with Villa. Advice from Don Pablo and Villarreal. Cesáreo Castro. Luis Caballero. Carranza's Strategy. Villa, Brigadier General.

The day following my entrance into Zacatecas we held the meeting with the lawyers from the Northeastern Division. I knew by secret report that the mission was known to the Chief and even had his approval, although he said it all came from the good will of Pablo González and Antonio I. Villarreal.

My generals, or rather, Dr. Silva, our spokesman, told them: "We recognize Carranza as First Chief, but we want a law adopted by all the Revolutionaries defining the extent and limits of his authority. Sr. Carranza should act as Chief in our Revolution and lead it in an orderly way but not capriciously dispose of us, the men who shed our blood in the war, or direct the war to his private purposes in injury of the interests of the people. Let him be the Chief, but let him listen to us, not insult us, and let him perform his duties insofar as they are needed, no more and no less, and in that he shall have our respect without detriment to us and without neglect of our cause. Therefore, we propose that representatives of our divisions, the Northern and Northeastern, assemble in a conciliatory meeting in the city of Torreón, and come to an agreement there regarding what our First Chief is and what he should do for the cause."

He spoke for me and for the generals who were there. And those two lawyers, being good Revolutionaries and under good orders from Pablo González and Antonio I. Villarreal, agreed that our proposal seemed reasonable and immediately communicated with their generals, who also agreed to accept it.

I sent Obregón a telegram about my quarrel with Carranza. I knew he had crossed the Sierra de Tepic and was moving toward Ixtlán on his march to Jalisco. I said:

Señor, I inform you that I deeply regret the way the First Chief continues to block my advance to the south. I asked him for coal from the mines of Coahuila to move my trains when I had just taken Zacatecas and had resolved not to stop but to take Aguascalientes in three days and continue on my way. But he not only refuses me the coal, without which I am paralyzed, but prevents me from receiving it elsewhere even though General González, in our talks in Saltillo, favored my petition. I have bought and paid for ammunition that comes from Tampico and is indispensable to my troops, but Carranza is taking measures to keep this ammunition from reaching me, and his consuls and other favored men are working to see that I am not supplied with this or any other resource. You will understand that under these conditions I cannot go farther south. Without sufficient coal my marches would not be made in regular form and my contact with my base of operations would be in danger. Without shipments of ammunition, what I have now would be exhausted after two or three battles, and I would find myself inactive in the face of the enemy and exposed to hostile acts by Carranza. I say this because Carranza bears me much ill will and this alone can explain why he holds González' troops in Monterrey and Saltillo, determined not to support my advance but to await some obstacle to my action before releasing them. I have therefore decided to return to the north with my troops and abandon the campaign unless the difficulties are settled, and I communicate this to you as your compañero and friend. The Northern Division is not continuing its advance to the south and neither is that of General Pablo González, and you must take measures to see that your advance, if you make it alone, does not result in grave risk to our cause and your troops. Fortunately, we will soon have conferences in Torreón in which my Division and González' will be represented, and I expect that Carranza will be represented there; in these meetings we will try to settle our differences. Your Division too should send delegates. The matters to be discussed are of great importance and I consider it necessary for the principal chiefs, or their attorneys, to be present so that the agreement reached may be formal and definite and entirely to the benefit of our cause.

Francisco Villa

He answered:

Sr. General, I reply to your message regarding your disagreements with our Chief. It happens that the telegraph service is bad on account of heavy rains and I lack details of what is happening, but I believe that regardless of the cause of your bad relations with Carranza you should not be the judge in this case, which you would consider from your viewpoint, lest any error on your part, if there should be one, should injure not one man alone but our cause and our country. If Carranza commits errors or arbitrary acts, it is our obligation to point them out to him to be corrected or avoided, but it would not remedy the situation to leave the struggle or refuse to recognize him, since we ourselves have appointed him. This would cause a break with comrades who are fighting for the salvation of the country. If I could go there at this time, I would bring my help to the just settlement of the difficulties, but at this distance and with these bad communications I can do little, although I would like to do much. I say this, that we must bear all sacrifices necessary to making the meeting at Torreón a success and that representatives of this Division will not attend only because time does not permit and because my men and I believe that nothing must distract us until we consummate our first purpose, which is the complete destruction of the Federal Army. The points pertaining to the future development of our cause and to the reforms in benefit of the people are work to be done later, as soon as the triumph of the Revolutionary troops permits it. That is, when they can be discussed calmly before the greatest possible number of chiefs in order that all of them, each for his own district, and each according to his experience, may shed light on the road for which we are searching. I cannot halt my march to the interior of the Republic. I have crossed the Sierra de Tepic and the first districts of this state without meeting serious opposition. A few days ago I made contact with the Federal force coming from Guadalajara to attack me. Under these circumstances I have to continue my advance although I consider it a great risk if your Division and González' do not also advance to the center. If I do not continue, I expose my troops to the risk of being placed in difficulties that the enemy can create by bringing up the garrisons at Guaymas and Mazatlán, which until now have been occupied with the defense of those ports. For this reason, in my name and that of all my chiefs, I invoke the best sentiments of your patriotism, asking you to continue forward, subordinate always to our First Chief, and waiting until later to ask Carranza for a statement of his Revolutionary program. We will do it then in our own right.

Alvaro Obregón

This message revealed good intentions on Obregón's part. He considered the evil and was in favor of correcting it. He was aware of the dangers in our disagreements and advised us to keep them under control. I believed that if he were nearer and better informed of my situation he would have seen eye to eye with me, for, as I soon learned, he telegraphed Carranza and complained:

General Villa informs me that he will return to the north with his forces; as this will be very inconvenient to my Division which will then be venturing alone in its advance south, I ask you to advise me of the absolute certainty of this report.

He was saying that the detainment of my troops in the north was a serious military error, as in truth it was. Practical experience had been telling me, since my entrance into Torreón, that our armies had to move at the same time, each supporting the others, in a convergent march—mine at the center, Obregón's on the right, and González' on the left.

By then I knew that days before, when it was known in Saltillo that my generals had disobeyed the First Chief's orders for my dismissal, González and Villarreal had gone to see Carranza and had said, "Señor, this comes of the poor organization of your government, which gives reason to believe you wish to command without any curb on your will. Give us a good government, Señor; this is urgent, and we will feel that the controlling power is not caprice but the good counsel of Revolutionary leaders."

So, on receiving notice that Villarreal and two other generals, Cesáreo Castro and Luis Caballero, were to attend the meeting at Torreón, I knew that a settlement would be reached, and I had hopes that soon Carranza would no longer be able to trouble me or to work against the Revolution. But I also learned that when González agreed to call a meeting he went to Carranza for his opinion, and the Chief accepted our proposition and authorized naming delegates if it were not known that he had been consulted and, having been consulted, had agreed. Had he no other desire than to stop me and had he made up his mind to reject the agreement made by the delegates?

I turned over Zacatecas to General Natera, which was what Carranza wanted; I left everything to Natera, military and civil command, and returned to Torreón with my forces, bent on the success of the talks.

In Zacatecas I was informed that Carranza had promoted Obregón and González to division generals, and I thought, "I agree with the Chief. Obregón and González are division generals because each of them commands a division, and they have made those troops themselves, uniting them or giving them the elements they need. Carranza must give them that rank because they have earned it. They fight for the cause of the people and win battles or lose them according to their ability or the chances of war. But Señor! If they are given the rank of division general, why am I left with the rank of brigadier general? Isn't my army larger and better organized than either of theirs? Don't I have more brigades under my command? Haven't I won more victories and haven't they been greater and more costly to the enemy? I took Ciudad Juárez, I took Chihuahua, I took Ojinaga, I took Lerdo, I took Gómez Palacio, I took Torreón, I took San Pedro, I took Saltillo, I took Zacatecas. I won my great triumph at Tierra Blanca which gave all the state of Chihuahua to the Revolution; I destroyed Mercado in Ojinaga, which was the same as taking an entire army from Huerta; I destroyed Velasco and his twenty generals in San Pedro de las Colonias and that was the annihilation of another enemy army; I defeated another army in Paredón, and that gave another state to the cause of the people; six days ago I destroyed another Federal army in Zacatecas, and that ended all Huertista resistance in the northern part of the Republic. After all these victories, am I no more than a brigadier general in the eyes of our Chief?"

CHAPTER 22

Under Villa's Protection the First Aims of the Revolutionary Cause Take Shape.

Maytorena's Quarrels with Calles. Luisito Speaks for Villa. A Telegraphic Conference. Ernesto Meade Fierro. Miguel Silva, Manuel Bonilla, and José Isabel Robles, Roque González Garza. The Meetings at the Banco de Coahuila. The Misery and Humiliation of the Poor. Villa and His Delegates. The Agreements at Torreón.

While the generals of the Northern Division were trying to settle my differences with Carranza, he was making no effort to help the chiefs in Sonora settle theirs. There Alvarado's troops, the besiegers of Guaymas, were approaching insubordination in their requests for Plutarco Elías Calles to leave that territory and their demands of respect for José María Maytorena, the legal governor. But Calles, who was no longer harassing Maytorena from Hermosillo but had retired to Nogales, Naco, and Agua Prieta, kept up his intrigues by means of the telegraph, accusing Maytorena of being a traitor to our cause when the whole town was with that government. Carranza listened to the intrigues and encouraged them.

This is how Plutarco Elías Calles stopped threatening Maytorena in the streets of Hermosillo. When I was in Chihuahua after taking Torreón, and Carranza was passing through Torreón, Maytorena, as I have said, sent me a telegram in code stating his fears that Elías Calles would sacrifice him. I wanted then to give him the aid he was requesting; I not only telegraphed Carranza about the events but said to Luisito, "Luisito, go to the telegraph office in my place and have a conference with Calles and with your best words convince him that he must stop persecuting Maytorena, who is a close friend of mine and a good Revolutionary."

Luisito had the conference with Calles. He said to him, "Francisco Villa is speaking, Señor."

Calles replied, "How are you, my General?"

Luisito said, "All right, Señor, except for my anxiety over the occurrences in Sonora. It is reported that since your break with Maytorena you are committing acts of hostility against him and even have him surrounded in his government office. That is not good, Señor; Maytorena is the constitutional governor and everyone should respect him. I ask you to do something to end the disagreements and help the progress of our cause. If we divide and use our arms against each other, what future can we expect in the hands of the enemy?"

Calles answered, "What they tell you is not true, General Villa. Maytorena is a reactionary, as his wealth shows, and he brings dishonor to our cause. If you knew him, you would not defend him."

Luisito replied, still as if I were speaking, "It is you, Señor, who are mistaken. I know Maytorena well, and my ideas about him are very different from yours. Sr. Maytorena is a man whom I esteem very highly, one who deserves everyone's esteem, as his acts in favor of Sr. Madero and his acts within our Revolution have demonstrated. I ask you to leave him in peace; I ask it in all sincerity."

Calles answered, "I tell you Maytorena is a traitor and we must exile him from the Republic."

Then Luisito, following orders, threatened him with these words of mine, "Very well, Señor, I am sorry that you do not agree to follow my advice. Do as you please, but as of today you will be responsible for the consequences of your acts. I will not consent for you to commit hostilities against Maytorena."

What happened was that the following day Calles retired from Hermosillo to Nogales, without my knowing then or now whether this was the result of my threats or of some other circumstance. But he continued his intrigues and his telegrams to Carranza. Knowing of these, I wondered whether Carranza would settle a conflict in Torreón when he supported one in Sonora.

Generals Villarreal, Cesáreo Castro, Luis Caballero, and a man named Ernesto Meade Fierro, who was going to serve as a notary in the registry of the agreements, came to Torreón. We chose as our delegates Dr. Miguel Silva and the engineer Manuel Bonilla. Both were civilized persons and well informed about our cause. We also chose José Isabel Robles, a good Revolutionary soldier, inclined to moderation and to justice in all its forms. As secretary of our commissioners we appointed Roque González Garza, a loyal friend, devoted to the cause of the people. In my judgment, the commissioners came to the talks in good faith. To the delegates of my forces, who met with me in advance, I entrusted my fate and that of my men with only one condition: that nothing or no one should stop us, that is, stop the progress of our cause.

During the five days of meetings I never attempted to influence the minds of the delegates in any way. They had their meetings in the Banco de Coahuila, and in order to make them comfortable and treat them with courtesy I would wait until they finished their deliberations and then take them to dinner. At those dinners, interested as I was in the business they were discussing, I never once said a word about it. I spoke only of my life. I said nothing of the great things in store for us after victory; I painted only the miseries and humiliations of the poor which I had endured.

So I knew the progress of the talks only from the reports of our delegates who came to inform me of their own free will and not because I asked them, although I was always ready to listen and follow them in their thinking. They said to me, "Sr. General, the talks would have a better chance of success if you returned Sr. Carranza's Treasury and released the Carrancistas you are holding as prisoners."

I answered, "Señores, I put my will in your hands. If you advise me to do so I will free the Carrancistas I have in Chihuahua, but they are not prisoners, Señores, they are required only to remain in the city; and I will return his money-making machine to the First Chief, the bills he has already made, and his furniture and papers."

They also said, "Señor, it is best to settle the conflicts in Sonora. Sr. Maytorena is in the right there, and we must concede this; but if in upholding that right his government occasions dissension and conflict, it is our duty to advise him to put patriotism before everything else and withdraw of his own will and leave his post to a man who represents him but will end the struggles."

I answered, "Yes, Señores, if it benefits the cause for José María Maytorena to withdraw from the government of Sonora, he will understand and will agree to do it, especially since on departing in this way he will leave not as a conquered man but as a conqueror. I say this because I too will go and will leave all my resources to others if our cause will gain by this sacrifice."

And so on.

On the first day of the conference it was agreed that we generals of the Northern Division would recognize Sr. Carranza as our First Chief and I would continue to lead the troops I was commanding. It was also agreed that the First Chief's immediate obligation was to supply the Revolutionary divisions with everything necessary for the development of operations and leave to the judgment of the chiefs everything concerning their action, requiring only that they give an account of their acts to Carranza. On the second day it was agreed to ask Carranza to form a government, proposing for that purpose persons whom the Northern and Northeastern divisions should recommend, and making it mandatory upon him at the time of our triumph to become the Interim President of the Republic, subject to the decisions of a convention of representatives, all Revolutionary men, with each force represented in proportion to the number of its men, one for each thousand. The third day it was agreed to advise Carranza to intervene judiciously in the conflicts in Sonora, without injuring the rights of the government or attacking the person of Maytorena, who was the elected governor. It was also agreed to ask Maytorena to take a patriotic view of the advantages and disadvantages of maintaining himself in that government or of separating himself from it by his own will. The fourth day it was agreed to recognize the First Chief's authority to appoint employees of his government in all territories controlled by our forces. The fifth day it was agreed to declare that our Revolution was the struggle of the poor and the humble against the rich and powerful and to require a solemn promise that the Northern and Northeastern divisions would not abandon their arms until the army of the Federation was defeated or replaced by Revolutionary soldiers and until a democratic government was put into operation and the clergy, the protectors of the usurpers, were punished, and until direct measures were taken to relieve the laborers and the land was taken away from the *hacendados* and delivered into the hands of the laborers.

These were sound agreements, all the work of able Revolutionaries, all in benefit of the people. It is true that other questions of apparently little interest were agreed on, but as they pertained to the remedy of grievances, this made them also important. Both divisions asked the First Chief to raise the Northern Division to the same category as the troops of the Northeast and the Northwest and to make my rank equal to that of González and Obregón and to vindicate Angeles by retracting his dismissal and accepting his resignation, and to permit the shipment of supplies coming to me from Tampico, and to agree to a number of other such things which I do not remember.

CHAPTER 23

The Presence of Villarreal in Torreón Leads Villa To Expect the Settlement of His Difficulties with Carranza.

The Future Regulations of the Revolutionary Government. Harmony and Disunion. Villarreal's Words. Serapio Aguirre's Gold. Water for the Wounded. The Twenty Cars of Coal. Villa's Tears. Political Errors. Money for the Troops. The Troublemakers. Satisfaction for Carranza.

Sr. Carranza was not pleased with our desire to set up future regulations of the Revolutionary government. I did not know whether that was due to his ambition for long years of power, to his being bound to his own men, or to his fear of how our action might develop. For this reason my delegates failed to persuade his delegates to prohibit the choice of any chief of the Constitutionalist troops as president or vice-president.

Our delegates said, "No constitutional chief can offer himself as a candidate for president or vice-president of our Republic in the elections to be held on the consummation of our triumph, since we are not fighting to enable military men to win the offices of government, and the great force that controls these men is inimical to the liberties of the people."

But González' delegates, or rather Carranza's, since they were his, answered, "Señores, this is not a point to be decided now, and besides there are many good citizens who are engaged in the struggle. If this were not true, the prohibition could be considered an attack on Sr. Carranza's future, and if we have come together for the sake of harmony and not disunion, why raise the banners of discord? We are in favor, once the triumph is obtained, of a convention where the regulations of our Revolutionary government will be agreed on. Then, Señores, let the convention decide who may be and who may not be president and vice-president of our Republic."

Further, in obedience to Carranza's orders, González tried to obstruct the free decisions of his delegates in the conferences. So, while I left our delegates free to follow their own intelligence, Carranza, through the mediation of Pablo González, was trying to constrain the spirit and the counsel of his delegates.

Villarreal said:

Continue the harmonious work of these conferences. It is already agreed that our two divisions give Carranza lists of politicians from whom, if he so wishes, he can choose his advisors or ministers. It is also agreed that we propose the holding of a convention, when he takes his position as Interim President at the hour of triumph, to set the date for the election and to decide what reforms the government will make and what citizens can be president and vice-president, and other similar points. It has also been agreed that the convention is to be composed of representatives of all our Revolutionary troops.

Pablo González answered:

Señor, I have your message stating your propositions. They do not seem wise. Consider the fact that it is not our right to appoint Sr. Carranza's ministers or advisors; consider that the type of convention you propose is not democratic since it would only hear the voice of the army and not the voice of the people. Even if this were not so, remember that in the meeting of generals which named you as delegate of this Division, it was agreed to send you to settle the disagreements between the Northern Division and the First Chief. But it happens that now you are proposing programs of government and other reforms which only the people can decide.

Villarreal replied:

Señor, you misunderstand my attitude and that of the delegates. It is our duty to learn the true desire of the generals of the Northeastern Division and put it in harmony with the declaration of the generals of the Northern Division. We do not advise any reforms at this time, Señor. Nor is it true that we want to appoint Carranza's ministers or advisors. We propose a convention of the Revolutionary Army after the triumph is obtained in order that an agreement may be reached regarding the future government, and if the convention does not seem to be democratic, it would be less democratic not to have any convention and leave the course of things to the will of a single man or a group chosen by him alone. As regards the list of men suggested for ministers or advisors, Carranza is not obligated to consider it as a mandate; it is the expression of our interest and he can listen or not, according to his degree of respect for the Revolutionaries. Those generals gave us full authority to discuss the business, and I consider our decisions a work of patriotism since we want harmony to rule in furtherance of victory. We have only one light to guide us, Señor, the benefit of our country; and we have only one limitation, not to decrease but to increase the dignity we Revolutionaries see in the office of our Chief.

One morning Villarreal came to see me and said, "Sr. General Villa, in my opinion, and that of the generals of the Northeastern Division, our talks will not be completely successful unless you return the gold your men took in Ciudad Juárez from the treasurer general, Serapio Aguirre."

I replied, "Sr. General, the gold I confiscated is in the possession of my financial agency in Ciudad Juárez. Nobody has touched it; it is just as it was when I took it, and it is not more than 43,000 dollars. Must I return this money before we close our conferences and before the First Chief approves our resolutions? If so, I will do it, although Sr. Carranza holds me here without money for my troops, after sending the lawyer Luis Cabrera and Don Nicéforo Zambrano and I do not know who else with the story that I should cease issuing bills because he is going to supply me with all I need. But I place all my confidence and faith in you, and will order the gold returned. Surely this is not going to be the punishment for having listened to your advice."

I took him to my telegraph office, and in front of him dictated an order for the delivery of the 43,000 dollars.

Then I added, "Now, Señor, come with me to visit my hospitals. You will see how my wounded are suffering for want of coal which was not sent to me. Because the First Chief did not send us coal, the water does not run, and without water the one thousand wounded I have here must suffer." When Villarreal saw the wounded in my hospitals and understood that what I said was true, he returned to the telegraph office that afternoon, and sent a telegram to Pablo González advising the delivery of the coal.

And when Dr. Luis G. Cervantes, whom González had sent to talk to me, had telegraphed similar advice, I received a message the next day from the General which read:

Sr. General Francisco Villa:

I am taking measures to send you twenty cars of coal today. I beg you, in appreciation of this service, to send me my three locomotives and other rolling stock now in those districts, since I am halted by the scarcity of these materials, as you know. Will you also return the twenty cars after you have unloaded the coal. I assure you that within two or three days I will have the pleasure of supplying you with greater quantities of fuel. With my best regards,

Pablo González

I answered:

Señor, I very much appreciate your kindness in sending me the coal. I ask only that you send it immediately since the soldiers and local people are suffering privations. The locomotives and other materials you mention I am having sent, Señor, and I hope they will be of service. Accept my sincere regards.

When I received that telegram from González I went to see Villarreal, and said, "Sr. General, I am very happy about the way you have treated me and also about General González' generosity. Why aren't we all blessed with this kind of harmony? I promise you, Señor, that I bear no grudge against Carranza nor do I disregard his authority when he exercises it within reason, nor have I any ambitions other than the triumph of our cause. But is it just for him to harass me and my troops and to pass us by and insult my best officer? I am here without coal, without money, almost without munitions, and all because I would not consent for the Revolutionary troops to go to their defeat in Zacatecas. You know Felipe Angeles. He is devoted to the cause, as his loyalty to Sr. Madero proves, and he has military knowledge and ability. Is it just for Carranza to remove him from his post as Minister at the very time he was exposing his life in Zacatecas in command of my artillery, and only because he and I were of the same opinion?"

When I uttered these words I was in a state of great agitation. We embraced, and I wept with him, and he understood my grief over all that was estranging me from Carranza without my deserving it. In answer he said, "These are political errors, my General, which confuse men. But you can be sure that everything will be brought into the clear and corrected. We generals of the Northeastern Division are here to make up for mistakes and to avoid a repetition of them. But do not blame all that has happened on Carranza, who also works as best he can. Consider how many men, both near and far, deceive him and poison his mind in the same way that others come to you intending to deceive you and poison your mind, and in the same way that others sow discord behind your back."

I answered that it was certainly true and that there were men near me too who were engaged in plotting, but good judgment told me to disregard their remarks. And he explained to me then how it was not always possible to keep a calm mind and troublemakers could sometimes succeed in their schemes, and for that reason it was necessary for others, in their desire for conciliation, to intervene. Then he added that Sr. Carranza had agreed to give me the money I needed for my troops, but in order to do it, he was waiting to receive the bills and machines I had taken from Serapio Aguirre because that was all the money he had and he could give me none of this without stamping it legally.

"Very well, Señor. The money and the machines are ready to be sent back, under the agreements in these conferences."

"Now, Sr. General Villa, so you may see how such disagreements are born, read this telegram from Pablo González."

The telegram went as follows:

Sr. General Villarreal:

I am told that Villista men have gone to American territory and to our principal Revolutionary chiefs for the purpose of discrediting the First Chief and creating enemies for him. This is detrimental because it widens our rifts in benefit of Huerta. Inform General Villa of this so that it can be corrected and prohibited and the aforesaid Villista agents can be withdrawn.

I replied, "Well, Señor, this is a very novel report. I have no idea who these Villista agents are or under whose order they are doing things I consider of no benefit to me. We will go to the telegraph office, and you can send González a telegram in my name, asking him to make a careful investigation of the complaint and give me the names of the said agents, whom I will send for and punish."

As I say, on July 8, 1914, the conferences at Torreón were closed. It was agreed lastly that to nullify their telegram of the fourteenth of June, my generals would send Sr. Carranza a statement of recognition and vindication. They said:

Sres. Delegates, we authorize you in our name to give Don Venustiano Carranza, the First Chief of the Constitutionalist Army, the fullest satisfaction for the language of our telegram of the fourteenth of June, which we withdraw in its entirety.

They all signed the letter: Toribio Ortega; Manuel Chao; and José Rodríguez, for whom I signed; Maclovio Herrera, whose father José de la Luz Herrera signed for him; Eugenio Aguirre Benavides; Felipe Angeles; Tomás Urbina; Máximo García; Rosalío Hernández; Orestes Pereyra; Severino Ceniceros; Calixto Contreras; Mateo Almanza; and Raúl Madero. The only one who did not sign was José Isabel Robles, and this was because he was one of the delegates to whom the letter was directed.

CHAPTER 24

While Carranza Repudiates Almost All the Agreements Made at Torreón, Villa Proceeds To Comply with Them to the Letter.

The Good Settlements at Torreón. Villa's Uneasiness. Serapio Aguirre and Urbano Flores. Federico González Garza. Herminio Peréz Abreu. Vicente Ramírez. Carranza's Answer. Ciudad Juárez. Alberto J. Pani.

My generals and González' made a good settlement in Torreón. It brought my quarrels with Carranza to an end and provided a way to prevent their recurring. In addition to this the conferences afforded an expression of popular desire, since the two divisions of the North and the Northeast would promise not to abandon their arms until the poor were protected against exploitation and government by law was obtained, until the hacienda lands were given to the peons who cultivated them, and until the weight of Jesuit and other religious powers was lifted from the minds of the people.

I was relieved as to the status of my forces and the future of our cause. That very day I received a telegram from Obregón, who had just triumphed in Orendain and was urging me to move south. I answered calmly:

I am glad to say my delegates and those of the Northeastern Division have reached a patriotic and completely satisfactory agreement and I can honorably continue my march to the interior. But I will not be able to start for a month yet, because I must supply myself with indispensable matériel. In the interests of a single unified effort I will advise you, Señor, of the course of my preparations. I send you my affectionate greetings.

I said this thinking I would hardly need to advance, with the enemy no longer having the spirit to resist. That was clear in the progress made by Pablo González and Eulalio Gutiérrez in San Luis, and the successes of Alvaro Obregón and Lucio Blanco, who were ready to take Guadalajara.

On the conclusion of the conferences I returned to Chihuahua, where the main body of my troops had already gone; if the settlement was good it would still be best for Pablo González to let no distrust of me delay him or injure Alvaro Obregón, who was already deep in enemy territory and in danger of a rear guard attack.

Determined to keep promises made at Torreón, I called Serapio Aguirre and Urbano Flores, Carranza's treasurer general and his accountant, the day after my arrival in Chihuahua and said, "Señores, the First Chief and I are friends and not enemies; we struggle in the same cause. Continue in your efforts for the poor without being discouraged by this incident, and stay with Sr. Carranza, or join me as you choose."

I called upon Silvestre Terrazas, secretary of the government of Chihuahua, and Federico González Garza to aid them. I freed Herminio Pérez Abreu, Vicente Ramírez, and other Carrancistas I had seized at the outbreak of my differences with the First Chief, and also offered them money and employment.

I made a trip to Ciudad Juárez to deliver Carranza's Treasury by my own hands. But in truth I knew he would reject most of the points agreed upon at Torreón although he had pretended that he approved of them. I saw this in the telegram he had Pablo González send to my delegates:

On the whole, I approve of the agreements and I speak only of the points to which I cannot consent, as I will discuss or accept the rest in due time. The idea of a convention is good, but on taking over the Presidency of the Republic I will call a meeting of the generals of the Constitutional troops and the governors to decide upon the reforms to be made and upon everything concerning future elections. I disapprove of your commitment to not abandoning your arms until laws are dictated for the liberty and welfare of the people, since this does not enter into our disagreements. Nor do I believe that the

Northern Division should be raised to the category of an army corps, since this division forms part of the Northeastern Army Corps even though it is independent in military action. Nor can I promote Brigadier General Villa to the rank of division general, nor need I now explain why. Neither can I consent to return General Angeles to his office of Minister of War, or even permit him to merely resign. I do accept in its entirety the letter in which the generals give me full and complete satisfaction for their words of the fourteenth of June.

That is, Carranza respected none of the agreements made to solve my generals' problems and my own, but did accept vindication, which proved him a man of small mind, a chief with little consideration for his subordinates, and a politician who abused the patriotism of the people to preserve himself in office and satisfy his own grievances.

A few days before my departure for Ciudad Juárez I was informed that the engineer Alberto J. Pani was in El Paso waiting for the return of the money and machines of the Treasury. He was the man who had come to see me with Martín Luis Guzmán the day after my troops had taken Ciudad Juárez. I knew him to be a trustworthy person and when I reached Ciudad Juárez sent for him. I said, "Venustiano Carranza is a man who breaks his word. But I am not like that. If I give my word, I keep it though it costs me my life and that of many men. You may take these machines and bills, but on condition that you tell Sr. Carranza what I think of him."

The engineer would not admit the truth of my charges and defended his Chief in a very civilized manner. He said, "Sr. General, you are mistaken. I promise you Carranza is a man who keeps his word, and if he is not keeping it now, as you say, it is because he was not bound to comply with the propositions brought to him by the generals of Pablo González. He only had to listen to them in order to decide which were good and which were bad. Perhaps the generals went beyond their instructions; and when you say that Carranza intrigues and deceives, you are mistaken in that too, Sr. General. Our First Chief is a good Revolutionary, struggling for the victory of the people."

I said, "My boy, Carranza does not struggle at all. He only reaps the reward for himself and his favorites while we do the dying."

"No, Sr. General, Sr. Carranza has no favorites. He prefers those who support him to those who disagree with him; he chooses them and trusts them; and these are the ones the people call his favorites although in reality they are not."

"Boy, who tells you that Sr. Carranza is the one to carry our cause on a course no one dares discuss? We had been struggling for a long time against the exploitation of the poor when he was still serving that tyranny."

"Even so, Carranza is our First Chief, and since we have elevated him to this office, we must obey him."

Hearing this I felt my anger rising, but I reflected that his statements should please, not anger me, since his purpose was only to inform me. I only said, "Very well, my boy. You have your own ideas, which are bad, and I have mine, which are good. We will part as friends and I will deliver the money and machines to him so that he will have the resources to declare war on me."

CHAPTER 25

Villa Considers the Revolution Won and Considers What Must Be Done for the Poor.

One Million Pesos. Villa's Scruples. Words in Code and Words in Christian. Alberto J. Pani's Report. Carranza's Reply. The Remittance of the Treasury. The Bank for the Poor. Pani's Advice. José Santos Chocano. A Discussion Between Chocano and Villa. The Return of Juan N. Medina.

I went to the station with the engineer Pani and there delivered what the Chief wanted, saying, "I am returning all of this without one bill missing, at a time when I need money badly for my troops, who are not yet tired winning battles."

"Sr. General Villa, with your approval I will stamp a million pesos of the money right now and leave it here to relieve your needs."

I believed he was trying to gain my good will with a million pesos, and said, "No, Señor. Take it all. If you leave me the million, Carranza will shoot you, and I don't want such deaths on my conscience."

But he said no, that he would be taking no risk, that he had the authority to leave me some of the money and had only to report it to the Chief.

"All right, my boy, but don't forget that it is by your own choice. In Torreón my generals agreed that it should all be delivered and I will not deviate an inch from what they promised."

We went to the telegraph office; and when I saw him beginning to write the contents of his message in code, I stopped him, saying that I had men who could put it into Christian.

"Good, Señor. As I have nothing to hide, I will communicate in Christian."

So it was. In his own language he communicated with the First Chief, saying that it was advisable to leave me a million pesos, and Carranza answered that it was all right to leave it and that he would soon send me another million from Monterrey or Saltillo. We returned to the car for boxes of bills and two stamping machines, and then and there he dictated his order for the million to be delivered the next morning, stamped and in legal form. He asked for an escort, an officer, and trustworthy men, to carry the Treasury to Saltillo or Monterrey.

"Why through my territory instead of the United States?"

"Because, my General, Pancho Villa is a great Revolutionary and his territory is the safest road."

The next morning he delivered the million pesos he had promised and prepared to leave. At this point I told him that I was planning to open a people's bank in Chihuahua and was looking for persons with financial knowledge who could enlighten me about it. I showed him the sample of the bills they were going to make for me in New York and added, "My boy, I want you to advise me in this."

"Sr. General, you are taking very great risks if you open this bank in Chihuahua. If you do, the Revolutionaries of Coahuila, of Sonora, of Sinaloa, and of all the other states will do the same thing. This, Señor, is contrary to one good purpose of our cause, which is to concentrate the manufacture and handling of bills in one single bank for the entire Republic, under the supervision of the government. There must not be many small banks that make bills; there must not be confusion or groups of men who make their profit by lending the people the bills they manufacture, which have value only because the people accept and use them. The profits made on the bills must favor the nation because it is the nation that produces these profits, and the movement of the bills, like the movement of the wealth of which we men of Mexico dispose, must aid not only the rich districts but also the poor ones; and all this cannot be done, Sr. General, unless we have only one strong bank working for the welfare of all, which takes care of all our needs and does not exist solely for the benefit of its owners."

I knew that he was right, for I remembered how the Banco Minero de Chihuahua had existed only for the enrichment of governing families, and I said I would not open my bank then but wait for the arrival of our government in the capital of the Republic and see what Carranza did with respect to those ideas.

Reflecting, I added, "But you can be sure, my boy, that if Carranza does not open such a bank, I will. And I will do so unless his bank assumes all the duties of assisting the poor, or if he uses it as a crutch for dominating the Revolutionary men who are not his favorites."

In Ciudad Juárez I received a letter from José Santos Chocano, who wrote:

Sr. General Francisco Villa:
I deeply regret your differences with Sr. Carranza. Mexico has two men who are the salvation of all Mexicans and who serve as an example for the other countries of America: you are one, Sr. General, and the other is Venustiano Carranza. Without Vinustiano Carranza, the great victories of Pancho Villa would be of no advantage to the people.

I answered:

Señor, I like your words about the fulfilment of our duty and about the progress and consummation of our cause depending on mine and Sr. Carranza's future action. I am willing to consider Venustiano Carranza as our First Chief provided that he does not block my men or ignore or harass them, and always provided that he does not dictate measures that will bring ruin to our cause. Unfortunately, Señor, this business is not going very well in spite of the fact that I submit to much unpleasantness in obedience to my duty.

In Ciudad Juárez many Mexicans and foreigners spoke of Juan N. Medina. "Medina is a loyal and useful man and a good Revolutionary. Justice demands that he return, now that Carranza no longer decides on anybody's fate in this territory."

I sent for Carlitos Jáuregui, one of my men who was saying such things, and I said, "Carlitos, go to the Hotel Sheldon in El Paso, where Medina lives, and bring him to me."

Medina was not afraid to come although they told him my compadre Tomás Urbina would not forgive him on account of old quarrels, and it was true that when one of my former secretaries returned to Torreón and I pardoned him, Urbina seized him and shot him behind my back.

But Carlitos brought him. I saw him. I embraced him. We talked to each other in the following style:

"I am at your service, my General."

"Do you want to be governor of Chihuahua?"

"I do not want to be governor."

"Do you want to be commandant of Ciudad Juárez?"

"I do not want to be military commandant."

"I see that you do not wish to serve me."

"I came to serve you, my General."

Then he told me that in his opinion I should avoid a break with Carranza, as we were being pushed to it, without our knowing it, by capitalists in the United States. Also that it was time to construct a strategic railroad from Matamoros to Ciudad Juárez, and on from Ciudad Juárez to Lower California. I asked him how much the railroad would cost. He said 180 million pesos. Where would I get such a great sum of money? We would make paper money. Had he drawn up his project in good form? Yes. And then I said, "Very well, Señor. Go to see Don Juan Brittenham, who knows a lot about such business, and if he tells you the railroad is a good thing, I will consider it and find the means to build it. But my order is: take over the government of this town because I need a man like you here."

And I called Luisito and said, "Luisito, appoint Colonel Medina the municipal president of Ciudad Juárez." In compliance with my orders, Medina decided to remain in that capacity.

BOOK **4** *The Cause of the Poor*

CHAPTER 1

Expecting the Final Triumph of the Revolution, Villa Prepares for the Probable Break with Carranza.

Medina's Three Conditions. Confiscations. Villa Foresees the End of the Struggle against Huerta. Martín Luis Guzmán. Carlos Domínguez. Carranza, Villa, and Villarreal. War among the Revolutionary Men. González and Obregón. Lucio Blanco. Jesús Dávila Sánchez. Andrés Saucedo. Ernesto Santos Coy. Eulalio Gutiérrez.

Medina said, "My General, before I agree, make me three promises."

"What are they?"

"First, no more confiscations. Second, no repetition of the Samaniego case. The men in Samaniego's family were bringing his wife's body across the river to bury it in Mexican soil. They were stopped on the bridge and brought before the Council of War as enemies. Third, Señor, I want the income from the gambling houses, which now goes to meet military demands, to be left for me, at least in part, to take care of sanitation and upkeep."

"If campaign needs do not prohibit, I will give you not only a part of the income from gambling but all the money you need for the adornment of this place. As for your second condition, consider it granted also. No one will be molested who comes to mourn at a family funeral. When I was a boy one night I saw candles burning in the distance over my mother's body and could not go near to shed my tears because I was being persecuted by Don Porfirio's *rurales* and the *acordadas* of those towns and haciendas. But with regard to your first condition, we will leave that pending because confiscations are the business of government and I first have to consult my compadre Fidel Avila, the governor."

"Then you will have to excuse me, my General. Unless you promise this, I cannot accept the office."

"Very well, Señor, then I will agree, although it exceeds my authority. I will issue a decree forbidding confiscation here or in any other district in my territory, except where the law rules otherwise."

"Now, my friend," I went on, "I want you to enlighten me on some other business. In my opinion, our struggle against Huerta is about to end. The victory of my men at Zacatecas has paralyzed him. The triumph of Alvaro Obregón in Orendain and that of Lucio Blanco in El Castillo have confirmed that great victory. The triumph of our cause in the field is near and the Chief and his favorite generals have an open road to the capital, and we will be watching to see whether he follows the desires of the people or betrays our cause. This disturbs me. I think it my duty to take measures against Carranza's plans before the evil spreads. For this I need a man who can go to the capital, approach the chiefs, and speak for me as if I myself were speaking to them."

"My General, I understand what you want. I know the man you need, or better said, the two men, because in my judgment, you ought to send at least two to perform that commission, especially since these two men of whom I speak almost always work together and they would make a perfect team. One is a lawyer named Martín Luis Guzmán, the other is a colonel named Carlos Domínguez. They come from Sonora; both are very civilized men and both are very devoted to the cause of the people."

I was the more inclined to follow Medina's advice because a little earlier I had mentioned my doubts to Carlitos Jáuregui, and he had made the same answer and had recommended the same men and expressed the same opinion of them.

On the afternoon of July 18, 1914, I sounded out Guzmán, who said, "As a Revolutionary I am at your service." And I sent for Colonel Domínguez, who made the same reply.

They both declared, "Sr. General Villa, you are the true chief of all who struggle for justice," and in answer to a question about the rift with Carranza, Guzmán said, "Sr. General, in my opinion there is no longer any cure for your disagreements. You can seek an understanding with him; he will accept your solicitude in rancor; you will comply and he will always deny the agreements. I do not say, Señor, that he is unpatriotic, but he thinks that there is no patriotism in others unless they embrace him as Chief. I do not deny that he considers himself a good Revolutionary, but he considers himself the only one who knows the scope of our Revolution, and thinks only the flatterers around him have the right to reflect on what our Revolution might be and express how it must be developed when it triumphs.

"Besides this he is a hard, skilful, and deceiving politician. Consider what he has just done with Villarreal. He sent for him, along with Cesáreo Castro and Luis Caballero; he had them meet together. He said to them, 'Señores, go and settle my differences with Villa, who is a dangerous man with his numerous troops and his military deeds.' And Villarreal came to Torreón in good faith and settled the differences. But now Carranza ignores Villarreal's words and rejects the compromises he proposed. It will always be like this, Sr. General. Carranza will complete the break he encouraged in Sonora and Sinaloa and tried to bring about in Chihuahua and instigated in Durango and attempted in Zacatecas, and he will end by causing a war among Revolutionaries, which will last until he is annihilated or until the only ones with any strength left are those with the same view of the future as his."

"Come, come, that is a very black picture."

Not that my ideas differed from his but because I wanted to know how far his reasoning led him, I added, "Perhaps you err. It is evident that the Chief is not the only other man behind our cause. There are Pablo González and Alvaro Obregón."

He answered yes, that González and Obregón were very good Revolutionaries and had followers who loved the cause, but that I should not be misled. Carranza would find a means of winning all the generals over. "And even though General González does not always think like Carranza, he will be submissive because it is not in his temperament to disagree. And as for Obregón, I say the same. He is interested in advancing our cause and will try to preserve harmony, but when the time comes he will join the Chief. This is my answer, Sr. General Villa, and this is my advice: If you find a way to agree with Obregón, nobody can break the unity of our movement, but if you and Obregón do not unite against Carranza, Carranza will lead us into war with Obregón and González. You must be prepared for this, Sr. General. Get the Revolutionary men of the south on your side."

I asked him if he and his compañero were willing to undertake the assignment. He answered yes, and explained, "Sr. General, I will approach Alvaro Obregón's men, since they are the ones I know, and Colonel Domínguez will approach Pablo González'."

"To which of Obregón's men will you carry my message?"

"I expect the most of Lucio Blanco, who has done a great deal for the people, as when he ordered the distribution of land in Tamaulipas which nobody thought could be done and which caused Carranza to dislike him."

I asked Colonel Domínguez which of González' men he would approach.

"Señor, I will speak with General Jesús Dávila Sánchez, General

Andrés Saucedo, and General Ernesto Santos Coy. But I also expect to
see General Eulalio Gutiérrez, since I have commanded his forces and
I believe him to be your friend."

And thus the lawyer and the colonel came to terms with me.

CHAPTER 2

Carbajal Wants an Understanding with Villa on the Delivery of the Government and the Surrender of the Federal Troops.

Huerta Flees. Francisco Carbajal. The Surrender of the
Federals. Villa's Telegram. New Threats of a Break. A
Meeting of Civilians and Soldiers. The Manifesto for the
People. Carbajal's Envoy. Conditions Imposed by Carranza and Demands Made by Villa. Luis Aguirre Benavides. Felipe Angeles. Federico Cervantes. The Telegram for Arturo M. Elías.

The government of the usurpers ended on July 23,
1914. Seeing himself already defeated by our great armies, Huerta relinquished his post on that day and appointed Francisco Carbajal as
his substitute, and the latter entered into talks with us.

I was in Chihuahua when Carranza telegraphed me that Carbajal
wanted to send him delegates to receive conditions of surrender. He
told me that he was against naming conditions; the surrender should
be unconditional. All soldiers and civilians who had given aid to the
usurpers should surrender on that basis, and he ordered our chiefs to
accept any surrender which was made to them but to guarantee the
life of no enemy ranked above a colonel. He wanted me to go and confer
with him about it.

I answered:

I congratulate you, Señor, on the position you have taken in regard to conditions. I too believe that we must have unconditional surrender of the Federal
armies and wreak justice upon the soldiers and civilians who caused the death

of Sr. Madero. The thirty thousand men under my command think the same thing, Señor, and will not lay down their arms until they see the triumph of our cause. In obedience to the orders I have received, I am continuing my preparations for the advance to the south at whatever time you indicate, and am glad to say that at present my only need is to receive the munitions on the way from Tampico. You can be sure that I will present myself as soon as business here permits.

That was my telegram but in reality I did not think Carranza wanted to impose the death penalty upon all Federals above a colonel. He only wanted credit for pardons; and I thought him insincere in his invitation to me to go to Monterrey or Saltillo. I was getting many reports of his growing distrust of me and his efforts to turn Maclovio Herrera, Manuel Chao, and other chiefs against me, and his communications to other generals to whom he was saying that I would betray him. The threat of separation between my troops and Carranza was so great then that I found it necessary to call a meeting of my chiefs and some civilians and tell them what was happening.

What happened was that my men, military and civil, decided to make a declaration to the people of what had occurred between the First Chief and the Northern Division. To formulate the document we chose the engineer Manuel Bonilla, the lawyer Emiliano Sarabia, the lawyer Francisco Lagos Cházaro, and another by the name of José Quevedo. To write what we had to say we appointed the lawyer Federico González. And it was done.

I was engaged in this when an envoy from Francisco Carbajal came to see me. Speaking in a confidential capacity, he said, "Sr. General Villa, I come to talk with you in the name of Sr. Carbajal, President of our Republic. In his opinion, now that Huerta is absent, there is no reason for Mexicans to struggle with one another. The justice you Revolutionaries seek will prevail, but it is time for peace. Sr. Carbajal wishes to deliver the government to the Revolution. For this purpose he seeks an understanding with the Revolutionary chiefs. Tell me, Sr. General Villa, what are your conditions?"

"You should not ask me to state them. I am only the chief of the Northern Division, not the chief of all the Revolutionary Army or the head of our government. Sr. Carbajal must go to Sr. Carranza, and from him he will learn our conditions."

"Carbajal has already spoken with Carranza, knowing that he is your Chief. But the conditions he imposes are very hard, and since Sr. General Alvaro Obregón will not enter into direct negotiations, General

Refugio Velasco and Sr. Carbajal come to you in search of the understanding which is proper and favorable to all."

"Tell me, what are Carranza's conditions?"

"The unconditional surrender of all Federal troops and the agreement of the Federal Army to disband and pass out of existence. We
come to you, certain that your conditions will not be so severe."

"My friend, the surrender of the Federals has to be unconditional,
with no security except that of life. If Carranza and Obregón say this,
be sure that I agree. In regard to the dissolution of the Army, perhaps
I have other ideas. I do not think we should dissolve the troops; I think
we should purify them by punishing the guilty and unite them afterward with our own forces to form a single army in defense of the people
and the nation. But I am too far removed for my voice to be heard,
especially since I am on bad terms with Carranza, although I recognize
and respect his authority.

"My men and I wish for nothing but the return of justice and law. If
I were the chief of all our forces, and occupied a position which authorized me to make agreements, and if other circumstances permitted,
I would tell the lawyer you represent, 'Señor, I am a man who came into
this world to fulfill my duty. Wealth is not my ambition, nor do I seek
the reward of repose. I am in this struggle to realize the cause of the
people.

"'Therefore, Señor, not being sure that it is to our advantage to deliver the presidency of our Republic into the hands of Carranza, I propose that you place under my command all the Federal troops who
want us to triumph and who respect and honor our cause, and with
those troops and mine, which are all the Revolutionary troops, I will
support you until legal elections can be held and you deliver the power
to a president named by the people. And if I, Pancho Villa, am not a
suitable commander for the troops you have, do not deliver them to me,
Señor, but to Felipe Angeles or any other Revolutionary who pleases
you better, always subject to my approval, and provided that those
chiefs and generals commit themselves in writing to follow and obey
him.' That is what I would say, my friend, and what I would do. But I
am not the chief nor in a position to make agreements."

These were my words, but as he insisted, I finally said yes, that I
would give him a list to take to Carbajal but I must first consult with
Angeles.

He asked me whether he could use my telegraph service to communicate with Arturo Elías, consul of the Mexican government in El Paso,

Texas. I answered yes. He asked whether I would authorize him to
transmit what we had said to Carbajal. I answered yes. He asked
whether I would be in favor of guaranteeing the lives of civil and military men who had given aid to Huerta. I also answered yes, that I would
guarantee the lives of all except those responsible for the death of Sr.
Madero and Don Abraham González.

I sent for Luisito to attend to sending the telegram. Luisito came,
although it took quite some time to find him, since it was past ten at
night. And when he read the telegram, he came over to me and said,
"My General, I do not think that telegram should be sent."

"Why, Luisito?"

"Because, Señor, it may have serious consequences and because it
damages your prestige."

He was right, and when I read over the words of that message I
agreed. But I had authorized the envoy to send it. So I had it given
to the telegrapher, but at the same time sent him a secret order not to
transmit it.

Felipe Angeles came. I said, "Sr. General, an envoy from Refugio
Velasco and Francisco Carbajal is here. He is asking for my conditions
of surrender. I want your good advice, Señor."

"My General, the Federals should surrender unconditionally, with
no other security than that of life and the integrity of their persons."

I answered, "Very well, Sr. General; write out these conditions and
send them to me tonight for delivery."

It was done. Angeles wrote the conditions and sent them at midnight by Luis Aguirre Benavides, Federico Cervantes, and another officer whom I do not remember now. He had them tell me that he knew
of the telegram which Carbajal's envoy sent to Arturo Elías, and, thinking it dangerous, had ordered it held for my reconsideration. I answered
that I approved of withholding the message, but without telling them
that I had already given the order to hold it. I left each one to his
thoughts.

The next day I ordered the conditions delivered to the envoy. On
reading them he must have been surprised, for he evidently expected
something else after our conversation, according to the message he
meant to send to the Huertista consul in El Paso, which read:

Sr. Arturo Elías, Consul of Mexico in El Paso
Señor, send a direct special wire to Sr. Francisco Carbajal saying that
Pancho Villa will not recognize the Presidency of Venustiano Carranza. He

advises you to hold elections and promises to support you until the said elections are held, and he asks only that the Federation and its generals recognize him or Felipe Angeles as its chief. Villa promises to respect the life of all soldiers and civilians who gave their help to Victoriano Huerta.

That was what he had written.

CHAPTER 3

With the Revolution Triumphant, Villa Tries To Keep Discord from Causing the Failure of the Reforms for the Poor.

The Advance on the Capital. Carranza and the Generals of the Northern Division. Accusations against the First Chief. Maytorena, Riveros, and Buelna. Maderista Revolutionaries and Carrancista Revolutionaries. The Need for Responsible Ministers. Mr. Wilson and Mr. Bryan. Advice about Harmony. Warnings about Recognition. An Invitation from Compadre Urbina.

Obregón and Pablo González were continuing their march to Mexico City and my generals and I and our thirty thousand men were watching the advance from the districts within my territory.

I thought, "We should all arrive together, just as we undertook this struggle together and are concluding it together. But perhaps it is my destiny to win the greatest battles of the war so that other generals may receive the honors of victory."

It was clear that the Chief could no longer maintain friendly relations with my generals. It was clear that he was still angry, though he had said that he was pleased to accept the satisfaction my generals had proffered, but his animosity persisted because of what they had written when we disobeyed him and marched on Zacatecas. It is true their words were harsh, though they contained nothing but the truth.

My generals had said:

Sr. Carranza, the impending struggle in Sonora, caused by friction between
the chief of the regular troops and the governor, forces us to write and ask
you for assurances of the success of our cause. The discord between the
Pesqueiristas and Maytorenistas of that state was aggravated when you gave
support to the enemies of Maytorena through Alvaro Obregón, without considering that Governor Maytorena was only exercising the authority vested in
him by the people, and that it was incumbent upon the troops to respect and
support him instead of being hostile.

When you left Sonora, Maytorena asked you in writing not to abandon him
unprotected among forces commanded by his enemy but you delivered the
command not to chiefs in favor of harmony but to Colonel Calles, the most
cruel, arbitrary, and unscrupulous enemy of Maytorena, and thus the state is
now threatened with an armed struggle which will delay and damage our
cause. Because of your conduct, the Revolutionaries are as divided in Sinaloa
as in Sonora, and if the threat of war seems less there, it is not owing to your
good measures but to the firmness of General Juan Carrasco, who was determined to rebel with all his troops if Felipe Riveros was not respected as the
elected governor. Furthermore, the dissension in Sonora and Sinaloa has
spread to Tepic, where it appears in acts of disrespect and hostility against
General Rafael Buelna. The chief of the Northern Division kindly invited you
to come to Chihuahua to mingle with the Revolutionary people and see how
they supported your authority as Chief; and you came intending to create
discord, and when you arrived among us we began to perceive in Chihuahua
the evils that troubled the men of Sonora and Sinaloa.

In other words, Sr. Carranza, we see your dislike for all Revolutionary men
who call themselves Maderistas because of their love for Sr. Madero, and we
note your inclination to favor and support your partisans. We know this is
why you are antagonistic toward Maytorena and Riveros and Buelna and
Angeles, and that for the same reason you carry on open and concealed hostilities against the Northern Division and its chiefs, knowing that these generals
venerate the memory of Francisco I. Madero and struggle for the cause of the
poor and will not consent to another dictatorship or another tyranny and are
determined, they and General Villa, not to lay down their arms until the great
triumph for which we are fighting is obtained.

Being committed to the fulfilment of our duty and being men always ready
to die or suffer for the sake of our ideas, we tell you exactly what we think:
We see, Señor, that your ways brand you as the chief of a dicatorial government, not a government concerned with the ideals of the Revolution; you
bring us discord instead of harmony; you repel independent Revolutionaries
and welcome only Carrancistas; and as you are carrying us to perdition, we,

the generals of the Northern Division, call upon you to take measures to guarantee our cause.

Señor, we want you to exercise your authority as Chief, not according to your personal caprice, but through ministers with authority and responsibility, whom you will appoint with the approval of the majority of the governors of Sonora, Sinaloa, Chihuahua, Zacatecas, Durango, Coahuila, Nuevo León, Tamaulipas, and Tepic, and of the chiefs of the forces who have conquered these regions. We want these ministers to begin the immediate application of the ideals for which we are struggling. Accept, Sr. Carranza, the respect and loyalty we owe you as our Chief.

Thus my generals put their principal ideas into writing and sent them to Carranza in a paper signed by Calixto Contreras, Tomás Urbina, Trinidad Rodríguez, Severino Ceniceros, Eugenio Aguirre Benavides, Mateo Almanza, Orestes Pereyra, José Rodríguez, Maclovio Herrera, Martiniano Servín, José Isabel Robles, Rosalío Hernández, Toribio Ortega, Felipe Angeles, and Máximo García.

I was following the uncertain situation, as were Felipe Angeles and my other generals, and the government of the United States was calling it to my attention. Those men knew how Carranza was treating me and were apprehensive of my violent character and sudden attacks of anger.

Mr. Bryan sent word to me through his consuls:

It will be an act of patriotism, Sr. General Villa, to devote your good intentions to the prevention of a break in the Constitutionalist forces. The cause of a people must not be crippled by personal jealousies, rivalries, and quarrels. You have won the battles of the war. Do not darken the triumph. Now that Victoriano Huerta is gone, the changes in your country must be made without further suffering. Be assured, Sr. General, that Mexico's future is a glorious one, and desiring this, President Wilson is anxious that there be no delay in realizing the reforms for justice and the welfare of the people. Since you, Sr. General, are responsible for the victories, our President trusts that you will work to maintain utmost harmony among all the Revolutionary armies.

Mr. Carothers brought me another message from Mr. Bryan, who said:

Sr. General Villa, our President Wilson believes that the disagreements between you and Carranza are not as great as certain sordid rumors make them appear. If this is true, do not consider the discord a sufficient reason for a disastrous break which would obstruct or paralyze the cause for which you are fighting. We believe it would be wise for you and Carranza to arrange to discuss the situation, since there are only two of you, and if this were done, your own opinion could be heard, and were you two determined to consider your problems from the standpoint of patriotism, you would be sure to come to an understanding. Mexico, Sr. General, is such a great land that every man who seeks to benefit the people can work there to achieve his noblest ambitions.

Thus in his name he sent me the kind message of Mr. Bryan and the President, Mr. Wilson, and it was sent to Carranza by other consuls, as I learned from Mr. Carothers. Our neighbors were giving us proof of their friendship and their interest in our cause. If they had wanted to harm us, and not to help us, they would have tried to add to our discord instead of relieving it as they were doing.

I thought, "Señor, what a pity that it is too late for this advice to do us any good." I doubted very much whether the Chief and his favorites would forget their enmity toward me and my forces—something that was confirmed when I learned that the lawyer who represented Carranza was plotting against me in Washington and throughout the United States many things were being said about me and Angeles and other men of mine by Sr. Alfredo Breceda, the lawyer Luis Cabrera and others close to the Chief.

Mr. Wilson and Mr. Bryan also sent me a message in regard to our final triumph. They told me what we had to do if we wanted their government to recognize our Revolutionary government in Mexico.

They said:

Sr. General, the world is watching you in your hour of triumph, at the moment when the change in your government is going to occur in Mexico City, and it is watching to see whether the steps you take will be good or bad for the government you are going to establish and good or bad for the poor, for whom you have been fighting. We say this, General Villa, with the friendly intention of helping Mexico in her sorrows.

From necessity we speak in the name of the world, and in our opinion the United States will be the first major power to say whether the government of the Mexican Revolutionaries should or should not be recognized. We are guardians of all the countries of America, and it is for us to answer for what these countries do by virtue of the Monroe Doctrine.

You must consider that everything your chiefs do in the future and everything revealed by the spirit in which you express your triumph and the reforms to which you are committed will be taken into account as the basis for recognizing or not recognizing the government you establish. This is our advice:

In the first place, give consideration to all acts touching the persons and lives of foreigners, their rights and property and the payment of the legitimate debts which Victoriano Huerta's government contracted with other nations. Unless you devote your closest attention and wisest intentions to these points, you can run into very serious complications. Already you and your forces have ceased to be Revolutionaries who overturn everything in your struggle against tyranny and usurpation; you are now responsible for the duties of government.

In the second place, do not be angry and merciless in your punishment of military or political enemies. Consider that if you do not offer general pardon or amnesty, you will lose the good will of the world and the people of the United States who are now good friends of the Revolutionary Constitutionalists.

In the third place, avoid violence against the Catholic Church, for you can be sure that the world will be horrified if you wreak your vengeance or vent your anger on the priests or the ministers of any religion. The United States government, President Wilson, and I take liberty of warning you and all the Revolutionary chiefs about this particular point in your treatment of an affair of such great importance.

We say then, Sr. General Villa, that all that you propose to do and all that your associates propose to do will succeed or fail according to your attitude toward these questions. Do nothing in the spirit of anger and proceed with deliberation. Be careful to do nothing that can prevent the recognition of your government by ours, which never recognized the government of Huerta because it did not deserve recognition. As friends, it is our duty to state these things clearly and firmly. In the same spirit, Sr. General, we sent you other messages motivated by our sympathy and also our responsibility to Mexico, ourselves, and the world around us.

Listening to those words from Washington and considering my relations with Carranza and his with me and my men, I decided to proceed in such a way that I would be, even from afar, the cause or excuse for no disturbing situation in the happy hour of triumph. I ordered the declaration of our grievances to be kept secret; and when my compadre Tomás Urbina invited me to visit him in Las Nieves, I made arrangements to go there and spend several days.

I did this with the thought that it would be useful to go through Hidalgo del Parral, since rumors were coming from there about Carranza's schemes to turn Herrera and other generals of mine against me.

Villa Visits Herrera in Parral and Urbina in Las Nieves; He Gets a Rest and His Trip Has Political Significance.

Invitation from Urbina. A Priest Serves as a Bishop. Parral. The Name of a Famous Conqueror. Don Pedro Alvarado's House. Herrera and His Father. Sacrifices and Joys of the People. A Conversation about Riches. Eulogio Ortiz. A Baptism in Las Nieves. Shining Instruments. The Future. Medina. Emilio Madero.

The trip to Las Nieves was one of international convenience, useful from the standpoint of politics, but restful too. As forces, other than my escort, I carried part of the Villa Brigade, under José Rodríguez, and a few other men. Accompanying me were Luisito, Pablo Seáñez, Rodolfo Fierro, Uriel Loya, and others. I took the priest I had in Chihuahua to replace a decamping bishop. I needed the priest in Las Nieves to sprinkle water on Tomás Urbina's child, which was going to be baptized, the occasion to which I was invited.

In Parral the fields were green and the inhabitants glad to see me again, as they usually were. Women, young girls, and children brought me flowers and fruit and cheese and other gifts. Each one of them said, "They are for you, Pancho Villa, all for you." I knew that they expressed the gratitude of the people. Maclovio Herrera and his troops welcomed me with demonstrations of joy and affection, and I saw that they were loyal and faithful, though the rumors ran to the contrary and something else might have been expected of the efforts of the conspirators, who were criticizing my relations with Carranza.

My chiefs and officers and I went to stay at the home of a rich friend of mine, or rather, one who had been rich. He was Pedro Alvarado—the name, they say, of a famous conqueror of Mexico who once saved his life by leaping over an irrigation canal with his lance. In Alvarado's mansion there were many pianos and strong boxes, either in memory of his past wealth or for other reasons. He treated us in a civilized manner which never varied.

Herrera and his father, Don José de la Luz, then planned the very best of fiestas and entertainments in my honor. They knew my favorite amusements, and they provided everything that pleased me most. Every day and every night they had horse races, cockfights, dances, and the *tertulias* we enjoy.

Seeing that the people of Parral were in full attendance at the festivities, and understanding that not only were they all glad to be near me but were also enjoying the fiestas, I thought, "Señor, it is the duty of the Revolutionary to demand sacrifices of the people in order to carry on the struggle for their welfare but it is also his duty to bring them joy every time a truce permits."

I spent a good deal of time in profitable conversation with Don Pedro Alvarado, who said, "I was once very rich, Sr. General Francisco Villa, and now I am not. But I have the satisfaction of knowing that I did no harm with my money."

I replied, "Señor, the man who is truly rich is simply the one who has always complied with his duty. In my opinion, money does not belong to the rich, although they have it, but to the laborers who produce it, and the rich have it not to please themselves but to alleviate the needs of those who suffer."

Don Pedro answered, "Pancho Villa, you are right. As to the accidents of fate which bring wealth or poverty to men, they are so certain that I say only this: I came upon the outcroppings of La Palmilla, the mine by that name and the source of my wealth, while relieving certain needs which it is best that I do not mention, and it was only good luck that the mine turned into a bonanza, and then it was bad luck that it later turned to mud. That is, only by good luck did I amass riches, which I did not produce but which came to me from the bosom of the earth, for no man's hands have ever been able to produce such wealth. So l looked upon finding this wealth as a sign that I should distribute it, and paid good wages in the mine, and not wanting a great increase in wages to corrupt miners and workers, I decided against increasing wages further, and gave away part of my gains. So on Saturdays, after paying the workers, my wife would empty sacks of money over the balcony for the needy, and later, as my wealth kept increasing, I tried to help all Mexicans by taking the debt of our nation off their shoulders and paying it myself, although I knew that my luck would not reach quite so far."

I answered, "Señor, I revere the memory of Don Francisco I. Madero, a rich man who bore the suffering of the poor in mind. I honor and respect you, and consider your former wealth and what you now have as sacred because you shared it with others instead of getting more and

more, and never attempted to grow richer by increasing the poverty of
those around you."

While I was in Parral differences arose between Maclovio Herrera
and Eulogio Ortiz, a colonel by that name, who commanded a regiment
of the Benito Juárez Brigade. As I remember, the said differences arose
from Ortiz' boasting that his only chief was Manuel Chao and not
Herrera, who had command of the brigade. One night when Ortiz was
seated at a table in the restaurant where he was accustomed to eat,
Maclovio, Luis Herrera, Pedro Sosa, Colunga, and another officer happened to enter and seized Ortiz and gave him a beating, and since he
would not knuckle under, they disarmed him and took him prisoner.
Vargas and other men of my escort saw what happened and came to
tell me. Friends of Ortiz came for the same reason, afraid it would end
in a shooting. I pretended to be angry. I was seizing upon the excuse
to show my authority and end the tales about Maclovio's intention of
defecting; it would be seen that in the midst of his troops, I could order
him to surrender his enemies to my protection.

I called Don José de la Luz, his father, and told him to have his son
release Ortiz and bring him to me at once, to be sent back to Chihuahua
to await investigations. I spoke to José de la Luz instead of Maclovio,
knowing that Don José held authority over the whole family and was
said to direct all of Maclovio's acts and even to be the principal instigator of his son's plan to desert me in my struggle with Carranza. Certainly Don José exercised such authority over his sons and inspired
such respect in them that although they were generals and Maclovio
commanded a brigade, they dared not smoke in front of him or reveal
any other weakness or vice. Don José carried my orders to Maclovio and
he obeyed it immediately, without my knowing whether he did it from
loyalty to me or to hide his deception or in fear of one of my violent
outbursts.

After three or four days in Parral I left for Nieves. There my compadre Tomás Urbina received me with the greatest affection. In Las
Nieves too we had fiestas and dances and horse races and cockfights,
all the things I like so much. The day of baptism of my compadre's child
the activity increased. Señor, how astonished those men, women, and
children were to see that my musical instruments were bright and
shining, like silver, and how all those people enjoyed the good music
they heard and all the entertainment I was giving them!

Thus several days passed, how many I do not remember, and I

amused myself and rested, hardly giving a thought to my cares. I was determined to make no movement and speak no word that could cause Obregón and González any trouble in their advance to Mexico City. I wanted them and the First Chief to be responsible for their acts and to consider them well and not alienate the favor of the United States, which was observing the final movements of our victory and waiting to accept or reject it as the representative of all the world.

As I remember, only once in all those days did my compadre and I speak of the future of our cause and our troops. I said to him then, "Compadre, here I am, so well-remembered in the first difficult hours of war and so forgotten today in the moments which bring tidings of peace. Carranza finds us a blot in his political panoramas."

Urbina answered, "Yes, Compadre; but we must be like hawks, which hover about and never scream. I say only this: be ready for the break; in my judgment there is no help for that. Carranza is waiting to annihilate you, Compadre."

"I understand; but the cause of the people comes first. Wait until our triumph is achieved, and then if Carranza is deaf to what the people say or denies them what they want, it will then be time to decide which road to follow. I think we will come to bullets again, and I have thought out some measures. The time will soon come to march upon Mexico City. For that it will be best for us to move our base of operations to La Laguna and have a skilful man in Torreón to supply us with everything from there. I already have Medina in Ciudad Juárez again. What do you think, Compadre, of Don Emilio Madero for La Laguna?"

He answered, "Compadre, I think that Don Emilio Madero is a good man for any office that you assign him."

CHAPTER 5

Villa Awaits the Taking of Mexico City with His Thoughts Centered on God, Religion, and the Priests.

The Herreras. Manuel Chao. José Ballesteros. Uriel Loya. The Theater at Parral. Duties of a Godfather. Good and Bad Priests. Jesuits. Revolutionaries Are Also Children of God. Bustillos. Doña Luz Zuloaga de Madero. Thou Shalt Not Kill. Thou Shalt Not Steal. San Sulpicio.

I learned in Las Nieves that Maclovio and Luis Herrera and their father, Don José de la Luz, were continuing to oppose me in my struggle with Sr. Carranza. I was told they were saying, "Venustiano is our Chief, he is a man of law and knowledge: he will realize the cause of the people in good form. Pancho Villa, who was born and raised a bandit, will continue to be a bandit until he dies although he has won many victories and has many soldiers under his command." The informers told me these words expressed Manuel Chao's ideas rather than the Herreras', but that even so Maclovio would not hesitate to abandon me and support Carranza.

Maclovio Herrera was a man close to my heart and a Revolutionary of great valor. I had heaped favors on Don José de la Luz. If these men were estranged, they could soon be won back, persuaded that the defenders of our cause must stay with me, since I was the one who worked for the people. But on the way from Las Nieves, a red-flag signal at a Y in the track stopped my train and a man got on. He wanted to introduce himself to Uriel Loya who was accompanying me; he was, he said, Major José Ballesteros, second chief of the 7th Regiment of the Benito Juárez Brigade, the force which until a few days before was commanded by Eulogio Ortiz, and he had decided to desert, since he disagreed with Maclovio and Don José de la Luz, who thought the troops should leave me if I did not recognize Carranza.

Uriel Loya reported this and, as I wanted more details, he talked with Ballesteros again, who then told him what had happened. While I was in Las Nieves, Maclovio and Luis Herrera had called a meeting of the chiefs and officers of the brigade at the Hidalgo del Parral Theater and they had discussed my disagreements with Carranza and had declared that they would abandon me and fight against me if, instead of giving

the First Chief my fullest respect, I was going to war with him. Ballesteros did not know whether the Herreras intended to take advantage
of my trip and immediately carry out their evil designs against me or
if they were only feeling out their troops for future action.

I did not then change my attitude toward the men who commanded
my forces in Parral. I continued my trip, reached the station there, got
off the train, and spoke with Maclovio and Luis Herrera, who came to
greet me. I observed that they had their troops extended way beyond
the station but did not know whether it was because they planned to
render me honors if I remained in Parral or for other reasons.

I made the trip to Santa Isabel, Bustillos, Guerrero, and other towns
in the district, where my sister Martina lived. She wanted me to be
present for a baptism, and the priest who, as I said before, was performing the bishop's duties in Chihuahua, went with me. That priest was a
man who had his own ideas, though he was also my friend. And knowing that I followed no religion, and was especially opposed to the ways
of the Jesuits, he discussed the protective doctrines and teachings of
the Church with the intention of influencing me.

"Sr. General, as you have consented to contract the duties of godfather, you do recognize the laws of our Catholic Church, as God dis-
poses; you live under the mantle of our Holy Religion, and you are
therefore obligated to follow its decrees and practices and to obey it
insofar as it commands us to live and die as its good sons."

"Señor, to contract the duties of godfather does not imply recognizing
any laws in this world or any other. Men are compadres by virtue of the
bonds of friendship and custom. That is, if a man consents to take on
himself the tutelage of the child of another in case the other man fails or
dies, this is not because of religious doctrine but because the duties that
unite us with our fellowmen require it, and this is true although the
believers believe something else, seeing that the Church intervenes in
these deeds to sanctify them. However, I do not deny belief in God. I
affirm it and certify to it since it has comforted me and all men in many
of life's crises. But I do not consider everything sacred that is covered
by the name of religion. Most so-called religious men use religion to
promote their own interests, not the things they preach, and so there
are good priests and bad priests, and we must accept some and help
them and prosecute and annihilate others. The bad priests, Señor, like
the Jesuits, are the worst men in the world because it is their duty to
teach what is good by means of sacrifice but instead they dedicate

themselves to the fulfilment of their passions in ways that are evil. I think they deserve greater punishment than the worst bandits in the world, for the bandits do not deceive others in their conduct or pretend to be what they are not, while the Jesuits do, and by this deception they work very great hardships on the people."

The priest said, "Sr. General, the bad priests will be punished in their time, but while they walk on earth they deserve our respect. God puts them here among us, and if He does it, He knows why."

"No, Señor. If I, as a Revolutionary, arise to punish rulers who fail to fulfil their duty to the people, I must extend the punishment to religious men who betray the cause of the poor. And our punishment is beneficial to the churches in warning the clergy to be charitable and useful, not greedy and destructive, just as the punishment of a bad soldier is beneficial to the military. I understand your reasons, Señor, for thinking God has good and bad priests in this world. He knows why, and He will reward them afterward or punish them according to the conduct of each. But you can be sure, Sr. Priest, that God has many ways, as you religious men preach in your sermons, and that one of the punishments He can impose upon bad priests is the punishment we mete out. God has us, too, the Revolutionaries, and if He permits us to struggle for our love of the people in the way we do, He knows why."

The priest replied, "Yes, Sr. General, Revolutionaries are also sons of God. For that I bless them, as I do all creatures. Those men who die or suffer for their fellowman are not untouched or abandoned by the hand of God. But He has His ministers here to prevent these men from exceeding the limits in their passionate impulses, and the law of God does not entitle the Revolution to deny sacred ministers and annoy and persecute them instead of listening to what they preach."

"Remember, Sr. Priest, that our Revolution is the struggle of the poor against the rich, who thrive on the poverty of the poor. And if in this struggle we discover that the so-called priests of religion, or most of them, are on the side of the rich and not of the poor, what faith, Señor, can the people have in their advice? In my opinion, our justice involves such holiness that the priests and the churches who deny us their help have forfeited their claim to be men of God."

On the trip we went to the Hacienda Bustillos, which belonged to one of the richest families in Chihuahua. The owner was a lady by the name of Doña Luz, who was married to an uncle of Sr. Madero's. As a friend of mine in former times, she welcomed us and treated us cordially. She asked us to stay in her house, which was grand and elegant as a palace. The meals prepared for us were excellent. She did her best to make us comfortable. And, in truth, we had a happy time there.

She too spoke for religion, giving me advice on my duties to God. She did it every time she spoke with me, and I consented to it because she was agreeable, and really very kind, and closely related to Sr. Madero, but principally because she was a woman of great beauty. I enjoyed looking at her while she was speaking about God, and I answered yes to everything or argued only to get her to say more, and did everything she recommended unless it conflicted with my own sacred duty.

With a smile or a reproach she passed judgment on my conduct. Each time we saw each other, she said, "General Villa, you are a very sinful man; your hands are stained with much blood; in thought and act you have committed many other crimes. Put yourself in God's graces and He will pardon your sins."

I said, "Sra. Doña Luz, I have never killed anybody without reason."

She answered, "I believe you, Sr. General. But God says, 'Thou shalt not kill,' and He does not say with or without reason."

I said, "Señora, to kill is a cruel necessity for men who are at war. If we do not kill, how can we conquer? And if we do not conquer what future is there for the cause of the people? Death is an accident in the course of our struggle, and we all either kill or die."

She replied, "Not all your deaths have occurred in war, Sr. General."

I said, "Sra. Doña Luz, for me the war began when I was born. I am a man whom God brought into the world to battle with I do not know how many enemies."

She answered, "Moreover you have committed many robberies, Sr. General Villa, and God says, 'Thou shalt not steal.'"

I replied, "I have never stolen, Sra. Doña Luz. I have taken from those who had much in order to give to those who had little, or nothing. For myself, I have never taken anything belonging to another except in a situation of the most urgent necessity. And he who takes food when he is hungry does not steal, Sra. Doña Luz. He only complies with his duty to sustain himself. It is the rich who steal because, having everything they need, they still deprive the poor of their miserable bread."

She answered, "That may be true, Señor, but why do you persecute the Church and its ministers? Some day you will need them for the salvation of your soul, and if you continue in your ways the tortures of hell will await you after your death."

I said, "I will do what you command, Sra. Doña Luz. Since you are so good, your advice cannot be harmful to me. And I say this much more to you: while I listen to you, I am not bothered by the threats of hell, but only by the fact that I deserve your reproaches."

I said that to her knowing that she would suffer if she thought I was going to condemn myself, because she was so religious that she wanted to save the souls of all who were near her, and she prayed to God for all of them in the chapel of the hacienda. That chapel was large, very fine and beautiful, and had cost much money. It was a replica, they say, of San Sulpicio, the church by that name in Paris.

By August 20, 1914, Carranza was already master of the capital. Carbajal had fled to other countries, unwilling to consent to the conditions of peace we Revolutionaries imposed upon him. So the Usurpation had no government, and the Federals, the troops already conquered by us in every district of Mexico, and José Refugio Velasco, their chief at that moment, conquered by me in Torreón and San Pedro de las Colonias, signed an agreement of unconditional surrender with Alvaro Obregón and Lucio Blanco. Thus they delivered the capital of the Republic and other cities which were still in their possession to the Revolutionary forces, and surrendered their arms and promised to dissolve their army and retire to private life, and acknowledged our triumph and recognized our government.

CHAPTER 6

Villa Agrees To Go with Obregón To Settle the Difficulties in Sonora.

A Telegram from the First Chief. Armed Conflict in Sonora. Carranza's Intentions. Villa's Advice to Maytorena. Reports from Calles. Obregón in Chihuahua. Obregón's Fair Words. The Future President. The Federals' Arms. Maytorena's Case.

While Carranza was entering Mexico City I received a telegram from him in which he notified me that Obregón was coming to Chihuahua for us two to discuss the rebellious acts they were imputing to Maytorena in Sonora. Carranza's telegram read:

Sr. General Villa:

There are difficulties between Governor Maytorena and part of the regular troops. I do not know whether the governor likewise opposes my authority as Chief, as he indicates in his disregard for my orders and as some of his subordinates are saying, or whether his quarrel is only with Colonel Calles and General Alvarado whom he has already imprisoned. Whatever the case, Sr. General Obregón is coming to see you in Chihuahua so that together you may investigate the matter and agree on the way to settle it. I beg you, Sr. General Villa, if the care of your troops does not prevent, to go to Sonora with General Obregón as my delegate for the purpose of convincing Maytorena that the difficulties must come to an end and with the intention of dictating your measures to that effect.

Venustiano Carranza

In my opinion, he was not very sincere in his desire for an understanding between Maytorena and the regular troops in Sonora, since he was supporting Calles in his action and supplying him with arms and other matériel which encouraged and inspired him, but I am uncertain as to whether he was doing this because he thought Calles was right in his warnings that Maytorena meant to rebel or whether he had already taken his measures to bring the government of Sonora to an end. In any case, he no longer intended to let Maytorena govern in peace. If he was sending me there with Obregón, it was not because of his desire for us to find some means of conciliation but to compromise me so that I could no longer encourage Maytorena with my sympathy. For he believed, as a result of reports from Calles and other informers, that I was favoring Maytorena, and this would prove troublesome to him.

In Sonora, Calles kept up his acts of hostility toward Maytorena and prevented him from governing. Calles was trying to deprive him of his office, which was legitimate and supported by the people; and Maytorena, seeing that Calles and his men and Salvador Alvarado were unwilling to grant him recognition and respectful treatment as a result of the advice and threats I was sending from my territory, or in response to the demands of the forces besieging Guaymas, took measures to protect himself. He got these troops to aid him after imprisoning Salvador Alvarado and all his staff, and they prepared for a struggle with Calles.

Being aware of the aforesaid situation, since Maytorena was informing me of everything he did, I had not wished to intervene any further than to give Maytorena my advice and offer my aid if his actions were justified. But knowing then that Obregón was coming so that together we two might prevent those struggles and that Maytorena was already advancing to attack and take Nogales, I asked him by telegraph to suspend all movement if possible.

I wired:

Obregón and I will leave here in several days. Wait until we arrive. Avoid fighting in your advance on Nogales. We will have a conference on our arrival, and you can be sure that your rights will be granted and nobody will obstruct the work of your government.

I gave him this advice because I was afraid that good Revolutionaries would be sacrificed in Sonora. I knew, from the telegrams to Calles and other Carrancistas on the frontier, which my agents in El Paso were intercepting, that the troops there were preparing to advance.

Calles informed the Chief:

Señor, from Santa Ana my men advise me that Maytorena's rebel troops, which are advancing north in several trains, are already in sight. As no peaceful measure will remedy this situation, I am dictating orders for the force under my command to meet the enemy. Maytorena is not only a rebel, but a traitor to our constitutional cause.

Obregón arrived in Chihuahua, where I met him at the station accompanied by several of my generals and with some of my troops ranged from the station to my house in barricade formation in his honor. He responded in friendly fashion, as did the officers with him.

That afternoon when we were alone, we talked of political affairs and

the future. I asked him whether he thought Carranza was taking measures to turn our triumph to the benefit of the poor. He answered that
the Chief would not betray our ideals. I asked him whether he considered Carranza's methods were autocratic, or contrary to what the
Revolutionaries were struggling for. He answered no, that in his opinion
Carranza also was a good Revolutionary, and if he was not, then he and
I and the other Constitutionalists were there to see that he followed the
right road, each one of us determined that the people's cause must not
be thwarted. I asked him whether he would agree to unite with me and
all mine, just as in Torreón my generals had already united with those
of Pablo González, to ask Carranza to form a government of the people,
to govern not by the caprice of a single man but according to the law
of our victory. He answered yes, that he would join us in such petitions,
which also represented his desires, and that since we and our troops
were the conquerors, Carranza would have to satisfy our wishes.

He was speaking fair words and I thought they were sincere, which
reassured me as to the future. As I listened to him I was moved by my
best feelings and got up to embrace him, saying, "Compañerito, I am a
man loyal to the cause of the people and the poor, for which Mexicans have died and suffered since Huerta assassinated Sr. Madero. You
too are a loyal man. We will not permit our cause to suffer or go astray.
If Carranza departs from his duty, we will punish him, and in less than
a second make the reforms and enact the laws the people expect. We
have very civilized and skilful men for the business of government.
Felipe Angeles could be our President, or Fernando Iglesias Calderón
who, they say, has good democratic ideas, which is to be expected from
his lineage. With us supporting them, the men governing will find no
obstacles to enacting their laws, a task for which we fighters are ill-
fitted; but our strength will not permit the people to be deprived of
protection and justice. I speak for myself, Compañerito, and other obscure chiefs like me. We have many who are intelligent, and any of
them, and you too, would be good to govern as our President."

I asked him, "Do you have faith that Carranza will make no bad use
of the arms and munitions and other matériel left in his hands after the
surrender of the Federals?"

"Feel no concern over that, Sr. General. I promise you that Carranza
will not betray us, and if he should, you and I, with our forces, would
defeat him."

We went on to discuss the question of Sonora. He said, "Maytorena
is very much in the wrong, Sr. General. Nobody wants to remove him

from his post or deny him the respect that is due him. When Huerta turned traitor, Maytorena did not try to lead the people of Sonora in the cause of justice but asked to be relieved of his duties as governor and went away and abandoned us, and he has since lost the esteem and the affection of many Revolutionaries. He takes this as disrespect for his authority, and this leads to disagreements which conspirators use to their advantage in promoting discord."

I answered, "Compañerito, your good intentions deceive you. Maytorena knows, and I know too, that Calles and other chiefs are conspiring against the authority of the government and the person of the governor."

"If so, the wrongs can be corrected and punishment can be administered. I have asked our Chief to recall Calles from that command. But if Calles stays and Maytorena thinks that his enemies are counting on Carranza's aid to overthrow him, he is wrong about that. Sr. Carranza does not want the constitutional life of that state to be disturbed."

"Compañerito, you are in error on that point too. The Chief is encouraging Calles in his war against Maytorena."

"Then, Sr. General, that is because Maytorena's acts have made him suspicious, and for that reason Carranza has had to take measures to protect himself. But if Maytorena redeems himself for having abandoned the cause of the people in the first place, he will soon find that nobody will attack or repudiate him."

"Compañero, you say that Maytorena abandoned you. But it is my opinion he did not leave his post by his own will but because you obliged him to leave, not wishing to recognize his jurisdiction."

We continued like this all afternoon, that night, and many hours of the following morning, afternoon, and night, with the added topic of a telegram to Obregón saying that Maytorena had entered Nogales on the twenty-fourth of August, his soldiers wearing hat bands that said "Viva Villa."

"How do you explain that, Sr. General?"

"Compañerito, it must be due to their enthusiasm for our cause. I see no other reason."

CHAPTER 7

In Villa's Presence Obregón Admits that Maytorena's Complaints against Calles Are Justified.

Consideration for Obregón. Medina and Tomás Ornelas. The Orders of Mr. Bryan and Mr. Wilson. Zach L. Cobb. Samuel Belden. "I Will Protect You if It Costs Me My Life." Nogales. Villa, Emissary of Peace. At Maytorena's House. Obregón Speaks. Villa's Reflections. Plutarco Elías Calles. Salvador Alvarado. Francisco Urbalejo. José María Acosta.

On the twenty-sixth or twenty-seventh of August, 1914, we left for Sonora on the Juárez and United States line. With us were our officers and my secretary, Luis Aguirre Benavides.

In Ciudad Juárez, Medina, Tomás Ornelas, and other authorities gave us a cordial reception. They not only came to greet me, as was their duty, but demonstrated that they were honoring General Obregón, which I noted with pleasure. On his trip through my territory, I wanted him to see the high regard my men had for him.

As we crossed the International Bridge to El Paso the Americans also demonstrated their sympathy. Many came to welcome us, and the authorities were glad to speak to the two principal chiefs of the Revolution, and were friendly, in obedience to orders from Washington.

We were there greeted in the name of their government by Mr. Zach L. Cobb, who had Medina forward the supplies and munitions I needed in the battle of Tierra Blanca. A Mr. Samuel Belden brought us the good wishes of the Mexican residents of those frontier districts. He represented Carranza there, but I did not know whether he was a Texan, an American, or from our country. As I remember, he spoke as if he was very close to our First Chief, and Obregón showed him special consideration.

By then Maytorena had already made his advance from Hermosillo to Nogales, the frontier town, and Calles' troops had abandoned it to take refuge in the region of Cananea.

In our trip on the United States railroads, Obregón said, "Nogales is now in the possession of Maytorena, Sr. General; but when we reach the line, I will cross over to our territory. Since I am their chief, his troops will not deny me, still less attack me."

But knowing the strong feeling against him in Sonora, since he was judged responsible for acts against Maytorena and the sovereignty of the state, I advised him to let me go first. "Sr. Compañero, you neither authorized nor instigated the conduct of Calles. You say that, and I believe you. But Maytorena and his men consider you are responsible for what is happening. If you go among them without first offering a new agreement, your life is in danger, or at least you are risking your dignity and involving my good name with what might happen to you. I am making this trip, Compañero, not only as a mediator in Sonora but as a protector of your person. Coming with me, you will be safe although it costs me my life. You can soon cross over without anything happening to you and talk with that Governor and either convince him of his error or be convinced by his reasons if he has any."

"Then I ask only one thing, Sr. General: for you and Maytorena's men, Colonels Acosta and Urbalejo, to be present at the meeting. You and the Colonels will be witnesses to the soundness of my reasoning."

"Very well, Sr. Compañero."

So it was agreed and so it was done.

We arrived in Nogales, on its United States side, at midnight of the day we left El Paso, and spent the night there. The next morning I crossed to Nogales, Mexico, with Luisito and my officers. Waiting for me there at the line were Maytorena and the colonels of his forces, the troops drawn up in my honor, the people anxious to welcome me— men, women, and children eagerly crowding around.

We spoke very frankly with each other.

"Sr. Governor, I have come as the envoy of the First Chief. I come to persuade you to end the quarrels that are disrupting Sonora and now approaching the point of bloodshed. With me is Compañero Obregón, who says he has no wish to harm you but only to get a true picture of the things that are happening here. Receive him in good faith, Señor, and let the differences be settled to the benefit of the people."

"You keep bad company, Sr. General Villa. Alvaro Obregón is a deceitful and disloyal man. You know how Carranza poisons minds and sows dissatisfaction and dissension wherever he goes. Well, Obregón is worse. He has betrayed everyone. Do you know why he brings you along? To deny and abandon me. He wants only to be served by all and then to forget all. On the road from Chihuahua to Nogales he must have given you his opinion of me, knowing you to be a Revolutionary excusing no obstacle in the path of the people. Do not be hood-winked by his words, Señor. He does not come to make peace."

On hearing him my doubts revived. I reflected, "He has had political dealings with Obregón. There must be something to it. Maytorena is neither unreliable nor given to libel and slander. But political rancors engender passions, and when passions enter the judgment goes astray."

"Very well, Sr. Governor. I accept what you say and grant his motives. But I cannot abandon him unless I discover that he is involved in treason. Since we are all here together let us try to settle the difficulties. Hear him out and take measures for his safety while he is in your territory, and have Colonels Acosta and Urbalejo and your other chiefs present at our talk."

Maytorena generously consented, though against his judgment. "General Villa, if this is what you wish, I will do it, but Obregón will lead us on with his words, with ruses we fail to detect. He will make promises he will never keep, for this is his method, and he is very skilful in it. Even so, bring him here, and be assured that nothing will happen to him while he is in my territory. But I say be prepared for cunning and deceit."

So it was. I brought Obregón over at noon and took him at once to Maytorena's house. We all sat down with Luisito, who accompanied me. I explained our reasons for being there, adding, "General Obregón is here only to punish offenders and avert a struggle by just and equitable means."

Then Obregón spoke. He asked Maytorena whether in truth his government was injured by disturbances which the regular forces had created. Maytorena answered yes. Obregón asked what the disturbances were. Maytorena said that they were offenses committed by Plutarco Elías Calles, Colonel Antonio Guerra, Lieutenant Colonel Arnulfo R. Gómez, and others, and explained them all specifically. Obregón asked him why he had apprehended General Salvador Alvarado and staff, who were besieging Guaymas. Maytorena explained, stating fairly how the General and his officers refused to recognize the sovereignty of the state or respect its authority.

Maytorena's answers clearly showed that he was right, and Obregón had to concede this. He interrupted to say, "Señor, in my opinion your complaints are justified, and I recognize the necessity of your measures. Continue to hold General Alvarado and his staff, as they deserve. I will appoint Colonel Urbalejo or Colonel Acosta or you yourself chief of all the forces of the state, for I have complete confidence in you three."

This was moving in the right direction and I added my encouragement, "Sr. Maytorena, I think you should be able to do this." But Maytorena, still suspicious, asked on what conditions Obregón would give
him command of the troops, and Obregón answered in a calm and
conciliatory manner, "Sr. Maytorena, I consider you a loyal Revolutionary. I make only one condition: recognize me as your chief, as I
am the general of the Northwestern Army Corps. I will leave you at the
head of the military in this state provided you consider yourself a soldier
under my command."

Maytorena replied, "Sr. General, if you have faith in me, I will trust
you. I accept, and General Villa is our witness that we have made this
agreement."

"Yes, Sr. Maytorena, and lest the doubts of the past confuse us, tell
me now, in the presence of General Villa, what offenses I have committed against you in your role as governor. You have the telegraph,
you have the mail, you have the customs, and other federal offices. Have
you had any order from me that is hostile to you in any of these
agencies? Colonels Acosta and Urbalejo are in your confidence. Have
I ever given them the least suggestion that they should disregard you?"

Maytorena made no answer. I think now he considered that we had
reached a good settlement and he was trying to avoid further recrim-
inations. I urged him, for Obregón to see my impartiality, to answer.
But he contented himself with remarking, "I would have to speak very
deliberately about that. Why go on if we are agreed on the essentials?"

CHAPTER 8

Villa Tries in Vain To Settle the Conflict in Sonora; by Agreement with Obregón He Succeeds Only in Declaring a Truce.

Obregón's Questions. Acosta and Urbalejo Answer. Villa's Reflections. A Compromise. Papers That Bring Discord. Obregón's Life and Villa's Responsibility. A Truce. Benjamín Hill. Maytorena's Good Wishes. A Letter from Mr. Bryan. The Answer of Obregón and Villa. President Wilson.

Obregón was not satisfied with this and continued with his questions, determined to justify himself. He addressed his questions to Colonels Acosta and Urbalejo.

"Sres. Colonels, I respect your word and always rely upon it. Tell me, before General Villa, whether I have ever tried to turn you against the government of Sr. Maytorena."

"No, my General; you have never done this."

"Have I ever told you that we must respect this government, whether we like it or not, as the constitutionally established one?"

"Yes, my General. You have told us that."

And so he went on with further questions, getting favorable answers, either because of his great authority over the Colonels or because in truth he had conducted himself correctly or had appeared to do so. In my opinion, it meant nothing for Maytorena's partisans to admit that he had made no such efforts, and his referring to Maytorena's government as one both liked and disliked may have been a ruse to lead them into revealing hidden thoughts. In any case, when the questions and answers were over, we drew up the agreement between Maytorena and Obregón, which the two of them signed with Acosta and Urbalejo. I too signed as a delegate of our Chief, and even Luisito signed.

The document read:

The offenses of Plutarco Elías Calles against the sovereignty of Sonora and the authority of its government are recognized; in view of these, Sr. General Alvaro Obregón and Sr. Governor José María Maytorena agree in the presence of General Villa on the following rules for maintaining peace in this territory, with the certainty that the offenses against the aforesaid sovereignty will be corrected and the honor of the men making these decisions will not suffer.

First—The forces of Colonels Francisco Urbalejo and José María Acosta respect Sr. General Alvaro Obregón as their chief and as chief of the Northwestern Army Corps, of which they form a part.

Second—General Obregón, by his authority as chief of these troops and in the name of Sr. Carranza, who is in command here by virtue of his commission, designates the Constitutional governor Don José María Maytorena as commandant of the forces of Sonora, to be removed from this command only when the new government of our Republic is formed.

Third—The troops of Plutarco Elías Calles, now in Agua Prieta, Naco, Cananea, and other districts of Sonora, will be under the command of Sr. Maytorena.

Fourth—Sr. Maytorena will bestow federal offices now at his disposition upon men chosen by him and General Obregón, and together they will secure the First Chief's approval of these men pending creation of the new government.

Those were terms that would have remedied the ills we sought to correct, for Maytorena was acting in good faith, and Obregón, I thought, was governed by mandate of his own good faith.

But the next day offensive and threatening papers were circulated against Compañero Alvaro Obregón in Nogales, and he came to speak to me with one of them in hand and showed it to me and announced that since it broke the agreement, he had already removed Maytorena from the new command.

"Señor," I said, "if there are men in Nogales who attack and vilify you, it is our duty to punish them for their acts but not, on the strength of their words, to nullify a pact we made under our signatures."

He answered, "Sr. General, yesterday I made the pact thinking to end these differences but intending also to establish the general corps headquarters in Hermosillo. Being there in person and dictating my measures, Maytorena would not injure my friends, just as my orders would not injure his. But in view of this attack, I should not go to Hermosillo, as I first planned, nor should I expose myself here in Nogales, especially since it is my duty not to damage your prestige as the mediator and my protector."

He added, "To convince yourself that I am speaking the truth, read the message I have already sent to Carranza." The message was indeed joyful. He told of the termination of difficulties, said he would make a trip to Hermosillo the next day to establish his general headquarters and review the troops, and said perhaps he ought to go on to Guaymas and the district of Alamos.

I also read the circular he brought, and considered the threats serious:

Sr. General Obregón, your command has injured the town of Sonora which furnished you with forces and equipment for your victory; you have disregarded our sovereignty; you have proscribed good Revolutionaries. And since you are the author of these crimes, the town and the Army have decided that you should be punished. Not one minute longer will you walk these streets as a free man. Prompted by justice, we received General Villa with our utmost affection because he is indeed a great soldier who wins battles to bring happiness to the people, not suffering. Today, by mandate of the same justice, we say that we will not tolerate violators of our liberties in Sonora and we, town and Army, have decided to rid our state of traitors and assassins who flout our sovereignty and the authority of our government.

I asked Obregón whether he really believed his life to be in danger. He answered yes. Was he not sufficiently protected by my presence and the agreements with Maytorena? No, because he saw Maytorena as the sole author of the threats and insults. What was there to do then? Nothing. Maytorena would not let us accomplish our mission as envoys of the First Chief.

But I, Pancho Villa, could not consider Maytorena responsible as Obregón did. It did, though, appear that he was unable to prevent such deeds from happening in his territory and I agreed to the nullification of the pact. "Very well, Señor, I understand your reasons," I said. "But must we allow the struggle to continue and Revolutionary men to shed their blood?"

"Sr. General Villa, I will remove Calles from the command of the forces and replace him with General Benjamín Hill, who is not only a man I trust but one of Maytorena's good friends. I will order Hill not to move his troops or provoke hostilities in any way. If you will obtain as much from Maytorena, we can avoid trouble."

When I explained to Maytorena that the pact was annulled as a result of the threats against Obregón, he assured me he was not implicated and that Obregón himself had begun to sow new discord. Still, when I pointed out the dangers of abandoning the man in the midst of so many enemies and his reluctance to consent to another pact under the circumstances, he ended by agreeing to hold his own troops in quarters if neither Benjamín Hill nor any other chief attacked him.

Immediately, to inform Maytorena and Calles of the extent of our arrangements, Obregón and I wrote and signed the new pact, which declared:

Generals Francisco Villa and Alvaro Obregón recognize that Sr. Maytorena's partisans commit acts of hostility against the chief of the Northwestern Army Corps. They also recognize that without discipline the former agreement cannot be consummated. Therefore, General Obregón withdraws Sr. Maytorena's appointment as chief of the forces of Sonora. But, understanding that peace must be maintained until the difficulties are settled, the aforesaid Generals together, in the name of Sr. Carranza, issue these orders to Plutarco Elías Calles and Governor Don José María Maytorena:

The forces now under Sr. Maytorena will continue to recognize him as chief and obey his orders.

The forces now under Plutarco Elías Calles shall recognize General Benjamín Hill as their chief.

These forces shall remain where they now are, without attempting to move or advance or further the breaking out of hostilities in any way.

The railroad, telegraph, and mail service shall be opened again throughout the state in benefit of the people.

If Governor Maytorena or Colonel Calles or General Hill disregard the order to maintain peace, they will be attacked immediately by the Northwestern Army Corps commanded by General Obregón and the Northern Army Corps commanded by General Villa and punished for their disobedience.

We left Nogales for Chihuahua on August 31, 1914. From Tucson, Arizona, Obregón notified Carranza by telegram of the termination of our trip and the decisions made. The next day we were in El Paso, where Mr. Zach L. Cobb delivered us a letter from Mr. Bryan congratulating us on the good results of our mission. It was a friendly and complimentary letter. We answered in words of friendship and appreciation:

Señor, we are very glad to have the letter congratulating us on our efforts. We ask you, Señor, to tell Mr. Bryan and Mr. Wilson and their entire government and city that we appreciate their interest in seeing these exhausting struggles brought to an end. They can be sure that their wishes will not be wasted, for we are making progress in our efforts to bring peace and prosperity to the people. Tell them also, Señor, that in this great work we can rely on the support and devotion of almost all Mexicans because of their great love of liberty and justice, and we and our Revolutionary government and all the people of our Republic appreciate the kindness with which the Washington government and the frontier authorities have supported the Revolutionaries in their struggle.

Our letter, I soon learned, pleased Mr. Bryan very much. He sent us word by Mr. Carothers. This was his message:

This Department of State is pleased to receive the expressions of friendship from Sr. General Villa and Sr. General Obregón, and their letter is being sent to President Wilson for his information and approval.

CHAPTER 9

In Perfect Accord Villa and Obregón Submit Their Proposal for the Direction of the Revolution but Carranza Refuses It.

Understanding between Villa and Obregón. General Juan G. Cabral. Pledges. Villa's Former Advice to Maytorena. Obregón's Opinion of Villa's Rank. Proposals for Carranza. Felipe Angeles. Miguel Silva. Miguel Díaz Lombardo. The First Chief's Reply.

All the way back to Chihuahua Obregón discussed the situation in Sonora and the trials the people would face if we did not succeed in maintaining peace. "If you and I, Sr. General, do not find a remedy for the situation in Sonora, it will grow worse and drag us all into who knows what conflict." He added, "Maytorena is not a man to be controlled in his anger over the insults he has received."

"No, Señor, you are wrong. Maytorena wants only the good of the people, and if you see him inclined toward war, it is only to protect his rights as governor, which his enemies violate and which he defends as the rights of the people who chose him for that office."

"That may be, Sr. General. Maytorena may accept the conditions of a settlement, but his principal partisans will not, as we have just seen."

"Yes, Compañerito, but what do you advise?"

"I think, Sr. General, that as long as Maytorena and his men dominate the government, there will be no peace there unless my forces and I outlaw ourselves from our own state. We must replace him with a good Revolutionary acceptable to him but uninvolved in his enmities."

"Compañerito, I support Maytorena because I consider his cause the cause of the people. But if that cause suffers, he himself will understand it and withdraw and leave the state to someone who has his confidence and keeps the peace. If you have a capable man whom Maytorena can accept, tell me who he is, and I will send for him, and he and I will go to Hermosillo or Nogales, and I will convince Maytorena that he must leave the government for the sake of the people. But prove your good intention by moving the forces of Plutarco Elías Calles and Benjamín Hill to Chihuahua."

Attentive to my words, Obregón answered, "The man you and I can send to Sonora is General Juan Cabral, and if Maytorena accepts him he will take the proper measures to settle all differences."

In Chihuahua we pledged ourselves in writing to bring the struggle to an end:

Francisco Villa, general in chief of the Northern Army Corps, and Alvaro Obregón, general in chief of the Northwestern Army Corps, pledge themselves under their signatures to terminate the difficulties in Sonora in the following manner: Don José María Maytorena will voluntarily leave his post as governor and receive as his substitute General Juan Cabral, a man in his confidence who will likewise command all the troops in that state.

Plutarco Elías Calles' forces will cross into Chihuahua, where they will encamp according to orders dictated to them and remain until the new commandant of Sonora asks them to return. It is further agreed that men who volunteered their aid to Calles and others in the struggle against Maytorena may be released and return to private life if they desire.

It will be the obligation of General Cabral to protect the person and interests of Sr. Maytorena and see that the laws are enforced, and he shall hold municipal elections until gradually constitutional government is re-established.

Three copies of this agreement will be made, all three signed by Sr. General Villa and Sr. General Obregón. Each General will keep one copy, and the other will be sent to Mexico to Sr. Venustiano Carranza, Interim President of our Republic.

I signed because I was sure of Maytorena's good intentions and believed the political convenience of a single man or of several men should not prevent the success of our cause, and also because months before, at the beginning of the troubles in Sonora, I had already telegraphed Sr. Maytorena a message of sound advice, saying: "Sr. Maytorena, would it not be advisable for you to voluntarily leave the government of Sonora in the hands of some man in your confidence?"

Obregón and I discussed everything in friendly terms and accord. He had said from the beginning, "Sr. General, you are right in your differences with Carranza. He should not have halted you before Zacatecas." And again, "Your troops, like mine, form an army corps." In fact, my forces were always referred to as a corps in the papers we were sending to Carranza, not as a division, and this though Carranza had declared that he could not raise them to that category.

Obregón further said, "Because of your many great victories, no one in our armies is entitled to a higher rank than yours. When we had only brigadier generals you were the best of our brigadier generals. Now that we have division generals, you are the best of our division generals. If the Chief still refuses to recognize your rank, that will soon pass."

"Sr. Compañero, the victories are not mine; they belong to my men, who won them with their lives."

Thus we confided in each other.

Trusting in Obregón's apparent good will, I asked him whether he did not think our cause would suffer from the form of government Carranza had invented in order to maintain himself forever in his post. He answered yes, that he saw very great risks in it, although Carranza was a good Revolutionary. I asked him then if he would join me, as my generals and Pablo González' had done, in a petition against the proposed form of government and in favor of choosing the best one at the time of final triumph. Again he answered yes, he would sign with me, and if I would bring him the document, we would revise and sign it together. I asked him for a few hours to put it in a form worthy of his examination. I called Felipe Angeles and Dr. Miguel Silva and the lawyer Miguel Díaz Lombardo, and other men who were advising me in matters of law, and asked what kind of petition Obregón and I should make, in the light of previous discussions. They brought me written petitions, and Obregón and I considered them, and after careful examination and corrections we signed. On his return to Mexico he was to deliver them to Carranza, and Dr. Silva and the lawyer Díaz Lombardo were to go with him to make the delivery.

The contents of those petitions were as follows:

General Francisco Villa and General Alvaro Obregón request the First Chief of the Constitutionalist Army to consider the following proposals:

First—The Citizen First Chief of the Constitutionalist Army will immediately become the Citizen Interim President of the Republic, as agreed in the Plan of Guadalupe, and will govern with a cabinet composed of citizen ministers or citizen secretaries of state.

Second—The Interim President and his ministers will immediately appoint judges of the Supreme Court of Justice and other federal judges. At the same time the present governors of the states will confer with their *ayuntamientos* in order to designate the magistrates and judges needed in each state.

Third—A month later, as the system of justice begins to function, the governors of the states, the Federal District, and the territories will elect *ayuntamientos,* and the week these elections are held the new *ayuntamientos* will take over the government of the cities and the towns. Also, the governor of each state will immediately convoke a meeting of representatives of all districts in his territory and have them study and decide on the delivery of lands to the workers.

Fourth—As soon as the new *ayuntamientos* are installed, the Interim President will hold elections for deputies and senators of the federation, and the governor of each state will hold elections for governor and local deputies and judges, with the understanding that these elections must become effective in the month in which they are held and that a man who has held the office of provisional governor cannot be governor.

Fifth—The new federal congress and the new local deputies will immediately take up the constitutional reform of our laws. They will declare that the chiefs of our Constitutionalist Army cannot hold the office of President of the Republic or governor of any state unless they have given up their commands six months before the election is held. They will see that new laws are enacted to benefit the poor: providing work, guaranteeing liberty and justice, and fostering education by means of schools and books.

Sixth—When the reforms of our Constitution are approved, the Interim President will hold elections for the new President of the Republic, excluding from this post the Interim President. The election of judges of the Supreme Court of Justice will be held at the same time as that of the President.

General Francisco Villa
General Alvaro Obregón

As discussed, so written and signed. Compañero Obregón returned to Mexico, and Dr. Silva and the lawyer Díaz Lombardo accompanied him as my representatives. The three agreed to discuss the business with Carranza and leave our petitions in his hands.

As I remember, we sent the proposals to Carranza in the early days of September; and a week or a week and a half later he replied:

Sres. Generals Alvaro Obregón and Francisco Villa

Señores, I have carefully considered the proposals you present in the name of the Northwestern Army Corps and the Northern Division. I believe that such matters should not be approved by a small group of men but should be laid before the entire nation. I believe, as you do, that we must form a truly national government which assures the triumph of our cause by establishing the reforms the people want. Of the proposals you submit I can approve only the first and a part of that which pertains to the election of *ayuntamientos*. All the rest must be presented to an assembly composed of representatives of all the men of our country. I am now dictating my measures to call together in Mexico City on the first day of October a body of Revolutionary men to study not only your proposals but many other matters of great importance to the people.

                                                                    Venustiano Carranza

CHAPTER 10

Villa Discovers that Obregón Is Treacherous and That Causes Him To Look on Everything with Deep Distrust.

Carranza's Methods in Occupying Mexico. Revolutionaries of the South. Cabrera and Villarreal, Ambassadors. Carranza and the Plan of Guadalupe. Madero and the Plan of Ayala. Villa Is Promoted to Division General. Maytorena and Benjamín Hill. Juan Cabral. Villa's Orders. Obregón's Remarks. The Evacuation of Veracruz.

In my opinion, Carranza was not wise in his way of occupying the capital with his armies. Being anxious to take over resources, in order to make immediate use of them for his own convenience, he arranged for only Obregón to take part in the advance. He brought neither me nor Pablo González in, nor did he even summon Emiliano Zapata and his Revolutionaries from the south, who had warred ceaselessly and now occupied much territory.

Thus the First Chief offended Pablo González who refused to accompany him on the day of his triumphal entry. He offended me and my chiefs further, when we already had grievances. As for Zapata and his men, seeing that they were treated as strangers and enemies, they developed a very deep distrust of Carranza and the Carrancista principles. The Revolutionaries of the south said to my envoys: "We are not proud, Señores; we do not claim to have won the Revolution. But we find unfriendliness in Mexico City. The Constitutionalists did not have an understanding with the other liberating armies. We consider it an act of hostility that they have replaced their advance forces with Federal troops who were our enemies. We consider the so-called First Chief's silence suspicious. He says nothing about the political future and hasn't a word about the distribution of lands. He enjoys his power without the consent of many chiefs and has continued to punish Lucio Blanco for his agrarian reform in Tamaulipas."

Wanting, at the time, a reconciliation with the Revolutionaries of Morelos, Carranza sent the lawyer Luis Cabrera and General Antonio I. Villarreal to see them. But Zapata insisted on strong conditions, answering, "An armistice must be signed between the armies of the north and those of the south to halt hostilities between the advance forces; Xochimilco must be delivered to us as a pledge of harmony and good will; our Plan of Ayala must be adopted by Carranza and his men since the Plan of Guadalupe cannot be relied on; a convention of Revolutionary chiefs must be assembled to name the Interim President; and, until the convention meets, Carranza must have one of my delegates there to advise him and take note of all his important measures."

Zapata's intelligent advisors wisely persuaded him to make these demands. In no other way could they be sure of Carranza's actions, but they went too far in holding out for all of their Plan of Ayala and not just the part which provided for the poor. Zapata had fought against Madero, thinking that the promises of the glorious Plan of San Luis would not be kept; he had recognized Pascual Orozco as his chief, without considering that Orozco was only a traitor, as he proved by throwing his aid to Huerta. These things being true, the Revolutionaries of the north could not adopt the complete Plan of Ayala, but I learned from my talks with Zapata that if Carranza had accepted his principal conditions, Zapata would not have imposed on him or on our Constitutionalist chiefs the points of the Plan of Ayala that were contrary to Sr. Madero's views.

But Carranza worked here as he did when my generals and González' had reached an agreement and sent him their conclusions, and as he had just done with the proposals Obregón and I formulated in Chihuahua. He accepted nothing that would lessen his power as First Chief or interfere with his political plans. He answered no to everything and immediately imprisoned Zapata's emissaries, and that ruined him forever with the men of the south.

I, Pancho Villa, say that Carranza committed a serious error in his dealings with the Zapatistas, as he did through his enmity for the forces of Chihuahua and his hostility toward the government of Sonora. It seemed that he was determined to cause war among the Revolutionaries. His mistakes appear the greater if we remember that not all the enemies of our cause were defeated. Benjamín Argumedo's forces, Pascual Orozco's, Higinio Aguilar's, Mariano Ruiz', Juan Andreu Almazán's, and those of many other chiefs went on struggling in disregard of the Conventions of Teoloyucan and inciting the inhabitants of many districts with stories to the effect that we, the Constitutionalists, were traitors to our country under orders from Washington, and criminals who were seeking to change the laws and the Constitution to serve foreign nations.

At the time of the break between the Chief and the Revolutionaries of the south, Jacinto Treviño wired: "Sr. General Villa, as chief of this staff, it is an honor to inform you that on this date the First Chief of the Constitutionalist Army has seen fit to confer on you the rank of division general. I am holding the dispatch until I receive your orders." And while reading that message, I thought this would be at the suggestion of Obregón or González, who knew how little the hierarchy of rank impressed Revolutionaries as long as I was left outside.

My only answer was: "Sr. Colonel Treviño, I have your message informing me of the honor of my recognition as a division general by Sr. Carranza. I acknowledge your notification and you may send me the dispatch you mention."

Obregón had left Chihuahua for Mexico around the fourth of September. Well then, within two or three days after that date, Hill had already joined Calles in the task of creating more trouble for Maytorena, and they were harassing him with new threats. It was urgent to settle these problems, and I communicated with Obregón, saying: "Sr. General Obregón, no doubt many important duties delay General Cabral in Mexico City, but I urge you to hasten his trip for it is imperative for him to settle affairs in Sonora according to our agreement."

He answered: "Sr. General Villa, I understand the just desires you express in your message. I promise you that as soon as General Cabral makes delivery of the office under his orders, he will leave for Chihuahua in conformity with our pledge."

But meanwhile things grew worse in Sonora, with Hill and Calles succeeding in their strategy of pushing Maytorena into war, and on the strength of the plans that Obregón and I had agreed on, I ordered Hill to move his troops to Casas Grandes. When he failed to obey me, I ordered him again, feeling that our measures authorized me; again he ignored the order and again I made it. When he did not move, I wired Obregón: "Sr. General Obregón, in accordance with our agreements, I have several times ordered Benjamín Hill to take his troops to Casas Grandes to avoid the aggravation of the problem in Sonora. If things continue as they are, I will encounter great difficulties in my efforts as mediator. Urge Benjamín Hill and his troops to retire to Chihuahua, and delay Juan Cabral's trip no longer."

Obregón answered: "Sr. General Villa, I understand your message, but we must not move my troops from Sonora until Juan Cabral takes command. These troops will be of great assistance to us if complications arise there on the application of our plans."

That is, it was no longer his intention to obtain a peaceful settlement. Nevertheless, I wired once more for the support of his authority: "Sr. General Obregón, if Hill and his troops remain in Sonora, we are asking for very serious trouble. I urge you to dictate your orders for the immediate withdrawal of those troops to any place in my territory. I send you my most cordial greetings."

He answered: "Sr. General Villa, I insist that it is not necessary to move Hill's troops before Cabral takes charge of the posts we have assigned to him. Working in any other way, we run the risk of great surprises in the progress of our action and we might never accomplish our purposes. Have patience. I will hold the chiefs of those troops responsible if they do not respect our orders for peace."

At this time Obregón sent me a telegram relative to the occupation of Veracruz by American troops, saying:

I inform you, Sr. General, that everything is progressing satisfactorily. In my conversations with Revolutionaries who come to the capital I find almost all of them with the same ideas we have and ready to give us complete cooperation. The only thing that worries us is the presence of American troops in Veracruz. It is contrary to our patriotic sentiments to have a foreign flag flying over our territory now that our struggle against Huerta has ended and the army that protected him is no longer in existence. The only flag that can wave over Mexico is the tricolor, the flag for which our dead have fallen and our wounded have shed their blood. I suggest then that we both write to Carranza telling him to ask the government at Washington, in terms appropriate to the dignity of Mexico, for the withdrawal of the troops that occupy Veracruz today.

I answered:

Sr. General, it is with the greatest joy that I read your report on the state
of our affairs and on the willingness of almost all the chiefs to give their support to our ideas for the benefit of the people. I am also glad to hear you say
that we should both express our sentiments to Carranza regarding the American troops in Veracruz. I consider, as you do, that the government of our
Republic and that of Washington must agree on the withdrawal of these
troops, and I feel that it is humiliating to allow the banners of invaders to fly
over our land. I authorize you, Sr. General, to write to Carranza as your good
judgment dictates and sign my name with yours. Please accept my sincerest
regards.

That was my answer. But the next day, knowing by reports from the
American gentlemen who were with me that Mr. Wilson's government
had already decided on the departure of the troops, I thought it would
be a good step to verify the report before asking for anything. I again
telegraphed Obregón, saying: "I beg you, Señor, to wait several days before writing to Carranza with regard to the evacuation of Veracruz. I will
state my reasons for this request as soon as you make your trip to this
plaza."

He replied: "Sr. General Francisco Villa, I have your message dated
today, and must tell you that the patriotism you expressed yesterday led
me to communicate your statements to our newspapers. Tell me
whether or not I must also have your latest sentiments published. Alvaro Obregón."

Señor! On reading this, how could I keep from raging. I began to
know the true mind of Obregón.

Villa and Obregón in Chihuahua Discuss the Meeting of Generals and Governors Convoked by the First Chief.

The Government of Durango. The Arrietas and Tomás Urbina. Punishment by Pancho Villa. Carlos Domínguez and Martín Luis Guzmán. The Presidency of the Republic. Felipe Angeles. Juan Cabral. "I Will Suggest to Carranza that We Depart This World." The Meeting of Generals and Governors. Villa's Doubts about Obregón.

While Compañero Obregón was still in Mexico City I had correspondence with Sr. Carranza about the government of Durango. The Arrieta brothers were disregarding law and order in those districts; they ran the government for their private interests, not for the people. And seeing that these evils increased when Domingo Arrieta was appointed governor, I took the measure of sending Tomás Urbina's troops to aid in establishing order and securing a governor friendly to our cause. Domingo Arrieta knew that my troops were coming to overthrow him and complained to the Chief, and the Chief communicated the complaints to me. He asked me to explain. I informed him:

Señor, my men from Durango, like me and my compadre Tomás Urbina, want only a just settlement of affairs in that state. But the Arrieta brothers, with intrigues and cunning, are creating confusion instead of harmony. I beg you, Sr. Carranza, to advise the Generals Arrieta to be guided by patriotism and love of the people; that is, to come to an agreement with the other chiefs in Durango on the appointment of a governor. You can be sure that if there is no agreement or the opinion of the majority at least is not respected, it will soon be difficult to have peace in Durango. I send you, Señor, my most cordial greetings.

And as messages brought no results, and the problems grew worse, I decided to punish the men who thus were blocking our Revolutionary way, although I did not wish to do it by force of arms. Instead, I gave orders to suspend the movement of trains between Torreón and Durango so that the Arrietas were left without communications. I did this knowing that they were oppressing the railroad men whom they did not consider theirs.

Next, Domingo Arrieta complained of this to Carranza, and again Carranza reprimanded me, and again I telegraphed my reasons, saying:

I assure you, Señor, that I took the measure of suspending railroad traffic between Durango and Torreón because of the lamentable situation in that state, which is oppressed by the Arrietas. The railroad employees there have had to leave because neither their persons nor their interests were respected, and they refuse to return, fearing vengeance. Sr. General Obregón has given me his advice in regard to these occurrences, and in agreement with him I have decided that the traffic in that state shall remain interrupted unless you issue better orders. I believe, Sr. Carranza, that if the injury which this measure of mine causes to the people of Durango is great, the need to impose order on certain troublemaking individuals is greater.

About that time the lawyer Martín Luis Guzmán and Colonel Carlos Domínguez returned to Chihuahua. I had sent them to Mexico City to talk with the other Revolutionary chiefs in my name. For some time I had wanted to find out which forces were inclined to protect the political views of the Northern Division against Carranza and what thoughts the chiefs had on popular reforms, candidates for the presidency, and so on.

I found that almost all the Revolutionaries wanted to hear the thoughts of Northern Division chiefs. Guzmán said, "Carranza proposes autocratic forms of government; but the soldiers of the people will not consent to anything but a legal government." When I asked him what was thought of Obregón's trips to Chihuahua and the bonds of friendship between him and me, he responded, "Many think that this friendship can be valuable, but if not, we must rely on Lucio Blanco, chief of cavalry of the Northeastern Army Corps. Blanco is a good Revolutionary, he is a man of principle and intelligence and loyalty. He says he has the same ideas as the chief of the Northern Division and will not permit the birth of another tyranny." And Carlos Domínguez added, "Other good men for this work, my General, are Eulalio Gutiérrez, my General Jesús Dávila Sánchez, my General Andrés Saucedo, and my General Ernesto Santos Coy, judging from the talks which we have had about the desires of the Northern Division. Venustiano Carranza will try to outwit us by extending his term of office as First Chief, but now all the generals say that they must hold a convention and make the political laws for the future."

I asked them if the said chiefs were saying who should be the new President. They answered yes, that most of them wanted a civilian, like

Fernando Iglesias Calderón or Dr. Miguel Silva, and others were saying that the President could be some Revolutionary chief who was intelligent and well informed.

I then said, "In my opinion, Felipe Angeles should be our new President; he will reinstate Sr. Madero's form of government and distribute the lands and reform the laws for the benefit of the workers." More exactly, I told them that when they returned to Mexico City they should impress upon the chiefs that it was best to name Felipe Angeles.

But Guzmán objected. "Sr. General, if you order us to do this, we will. But hear my opinion: we will meet with many strong objections, for Felipe Angeles is not the man for now. He has bitter enemies, such as Alvaro Obregón, who would never accept him. Carranza does not want him; many other Revolutionary men are against him because they consider him still a Federal. If you want our ideas to triumph, Señor, choose a man who does not stir up enmity or appear to threaten anyone but is satisfactory to all." His words made me angry, I admit, but I could not tell why, whether because they contradicted my own thoughts or, being reasonable, they grieved me for Angeles.

Juan Cabral arrived in Chihuahua and we exchanged friendly greetings and words. I sent my car to bring him to my house and went to the door to welcome and embrace him. When we were alone, I frankly discussed the conflicts in Sonora and Durango and Carranza's treatment of me and all my troops.

"Sr. General, a break among the Revolutionary men would be a very great calamity." When I answered yes, that perhaps a break might mean failure for us, he continued, "If that case threatens, you and Carranza must leave our territory before the break occurs."

I thought highly of the man who uttered these words, and answered sincerely, "The solution you propose is sensible. If we cannot come to an understanding before shedding blood by his fault or mine, I am ready to propose not only that he and I leave our country but that we depart this world together." I said this, and I meant it. In my conscience I believe that if two men are unalterably opposed, both, however great they may be, should sacrifice themselves to save the cause at issue.

One thing I did not discuss then with General Cabral was the work that Obregón and I had assigned him in Sonora, for, being notified that Obregón would arrive in Chihuahua the next day, I thought it better to say nothing about it until he was there. I did not want General Cabal or Obregón to think that I was trying to settle the differences in Sonora for my own benefit.

Before Cabral reached Chihuahua, Carranza had summoned the generals and governors to a meeting in Mexico City on the first day of October. With him this body would make a study of the whole problem of the new government, but it was not the democratic assembly requested by my generals and González'. It was a meeting of persons whom Carranza appointed and chose. Neither I nor my officers were pleased to receive the summons, nor did we place much value in its words:

Sr. General, at the beginning of this struggle I promised all the chiefs participating in the Plan of Guadalupe that I would convoke a meeting of governors and commanding chiefs in Mexico City as soon as I occupied it and took charge of the government, and in that meeting we would agree on the reforms of our laws, the date of the elections, and other matters of interest to all the country. As I head the Executive Power in the capital, I have designated the first day of October as the date of the meeting, and I invite you to attend in person or by means of a delegate as is your privilege as a chief in command of forces.

Venustiano Carranza

It looked as if the Revolutionary chiefs were not asked to assemble because it was our right but only because Sr. Carranza had promised us this. Did it mean that those who did not know about the Plan of Guadalupe could not meet with us?

Obregón arrived in Chihuahua at dawn on the Sixteenth of September, the day dedicated to our Independence. He embraced me, saying that he brought greetings from Carranza, adding that he was determined to finish not only the business of the new government of the Republic and the business in Sonora which we had already discussed but the business in Durango as well, under a commission from Carranza.

After dwelling on this, he read and delivered the communications Carranza had sent me regarding the aforesaid points. The contents of one of these official papers ran:

Sr. General Francisco Villa
Chihuahua
My good friend and colleague:
You must realize the great importance of the meeting I have convoked for the first day of the coming month of October. I am confident that you will be present and I will have the pleasure of seeing you and greeting you in the capital. You can be sure, Sr. General, that even if I had not convoked the meeting it would give me pleasure to have you here with us, if only for a few

moments, not solely out of my desire to talk with you but for the benefit of your advice in these matters with which we are occupied. Accept, Sr. General, the best of greetings from your friend,

Venustiano Carranza

The other paper said:

Sr. General Francisco Villa:

I again have the pleasure of expressing my gratitude for your efforts to settle the conflicts in Sonora. Being aware of the way in which you and General Obregón have undertaken and resolved those questions, and knowing that problems similar to those in Sonora exist now in Durango, I am asking, Sr. General Villa, that you two go together to that state and settle the disturbances there; I authorize you to replace the interim governor with a man who will create the harmony necessary to the transaction of public business. I am sure that if you accept this commission, the problems will be solved, and being confident that you will accept it, I repeat that I am your good friend and servant,

Venustiano Carranza

I wanted to speak frankly with Obregón, but knowing now that he was not the dependable man I had thought he was, I thought, "He comes to all appearances with the purpose of settling the questions of Durango and Sonora, but what if this is only a pretense?"

CHAPTER 12

Convinced of Obregón's Deception, Villa Threatens To Shoot Him if Hill Does Not Retire to Casas Grandes.

A Military Parade. Angeles and Obregón. The Warehouse of Arms and Munitions. Carranza's Negatives. The Meeting of Generals and Governors. A Message from President Wilson. Affairs in Sonora. Juan Cabral. Warning from Maytorena. Villa's Anger. Obregón's Calmness. Felipe Dussart. A Supper and a Dance.

For the Sixteenth of September, the day of Obregón's return, I had arranged a parade of the troops I had in Chihuahua. I invited Obregón to watch it from the balconies of the Government Palace, and he accepted. We were there together after our conversation of that morning. I remember he was surprised by all my well-disciplined forces, with their complete equipment and their splendid horses. Men and animals showed that they had been trained in war, and the arms promised that we would be ready to fight again.

Knowing the reputation of my cavalry brigades, Obregón said, "These, Señor, are the fortunate forces which always carry you to victory."

I answered, "No, Compañero, these are the forces which make me fortunate, because they always bring me victory."

And as my cannon, in good formation, were passing in front of us, I added, "This, Compañero, is my great artillery, which left I know not how many thousands of Federal troops lifeless at Zacatecas, and the reason it is so good, Señor, and has served me so well is that it is under the orders of Felipe Angeles, an artillery general of the greatest skill."

I said this because he had belittled General Angeles in Sonora, but it was not my intention to offend him, only to let him know that Angeles had been a very useful man in our cause and could be expected to continue being useful.

The parade ended. It must have lasted three or four hours as there were so many brigades and they marched slowly, to display their good appearance. Obregón asked me, "And is your stock of arms and munitions as good, Sr. General?"

I replied, "You be the judge, Señor. Come with me, and I will show them to you."

And so it was. We went to the arsenal in the Federal Palace where I had more than seven million cartridges alone, and where we saw my stores of rifles and carbines in piles of boxes which had not even been unpacked.

He considered all this a while. Then he said, "Indeed, Sr. General Villa, the Northern Army Corps has very powerful resources." He congratulated me and embraced me, although I did not know at that time whether he was being sincere or only concealing his motives in learning my strength.

That afternoon we spoke of our main interests. Obregón expressed regret that Carranza had disregarded our plans for the legitimate realization of our triumph. He said, "Do not worry, Sr. General, about these negatives to which our First Chief is inclined. They annoy me as much as you and if I endure them quietly, it is only because of my great love of our cause. At the meeting of generals and governors we will find the means of insuring the triumph of all our ideas."

I answered, "Sr. Compañero, I am not troubled by Carranza's negatives, but I do see that the political prospects are confused and the time is coming when we must take up arms again. I have little to say about the meeting you speak of, except that it will be subject to the will of the First Chief, who convokes it in his own way and not in the way proposed by Pablo González' generals and mine, who are all of a single opinion. Believe me, Sr. Compañero, with Carranza, we Revolutionary men who are the protectors of the welfare of the people have no other road except that of bullets. Carranza is stubborn and crafty, a man moved by very great ambition."

But he answered no, that the meeting would really serve to teach the First Chief to respect us and would give constitutional shape to the government and work for the good of the poor. He asked me then if I would go to the meeting, and I answered that I could not yet say for sure. He asked me why, and I answered that it was something that had to be taken under consideration by my generals. He asked me if I thought my generals were inclined to go, and I answered that I did not know. And in this way, with his questions and my answers, I finally promised him to call my generals together to consider Carranza's summons to the meeting and to advise them that they ought to go to indicate their devotion to our cause. So it was. I called a meeting of the generals and resolved to study with them the best way to accept Sr. Carranza's invitation.

The next morning brought the good news that the President of the

United States had ordered the departure of the American troops from
Veracruz. I was happy to see his attitude toward the Revolutionaries. It
confirmed my opinion that he had not wished to harm our people but to
help them. As soon as I was sure of the order I sent Mr. Wilson a telegram expressing my gratitude, saying:

Sr. President of the United States:
   With the greatest pleasure I receive the report that the American troops
now have orders to leave our port of Vercruz. I offer you, Señor, congratulations in my name and that of the people of Mexico. Your action shows your
respect for our dignity as Mexican patriots and we recognize the good attitude
of your government toward our country. Accept, Señor, the regards of the
general in chief of this Northern Division of the Constitutionalist Army.

                                                            Francisco Villa

   I was joyful all that morning. I found another cause for happiness
when Obregón and I agreed on the steps to be taken in Sonora. He said
to me, "Tomorrow, Sr. General Villa, Cabral will leave for Sonora, and
you can be sure that when Calles and Hill receive my instructions, that
confusion will begin to disappear." But after we had eaten, I received a
telegram from Maytorena, who informed me that Hill and Calles were
moving to attack him. Obregón not only was not helping to settle the
conflicts but was making them worse, pretending to me to want to settle
them but actually egging Hill and Calles on.
   I seethed with anger on seeing through Obregón's conduct. I had
him brought before me. He came, accompanied by two of his aides,
whom I sent into another room. When we were face to face, I spoke to
him out of my great anger, showing him the telegram which they had
just brought to me, and shouting, "Compañerito, you are treacherous
and deceitful, but neither you nor Calles nor Hill can play with me like
this." In his surprise, he contemplated me silently, as if not understanding. I added, "Reconsider and correct your ways, or I promise I will
have you shot here and now."
   I ordered the captain at the door to go and bring an escort of twenty
men to shoot Obregón if he did not reconsider his treacherous acts. To
this, Obregón replied, "I don't know whether you really intend to shoot
me, Sr. General. But I say only this: by shooting, you do me a favor
and yourself great harm. I am in the Revolution to lose my life for glory
while you are not in it to lose your honor. And have no doubt that if you
shoot me, your honor will be lost."
   He said this calmly and without the slightest arrogance, trusting

perhaps that his words about honor would move me. But seeing that he was only trying to deceive me, inasmuch as my honor would not suffer if I shot a man who came to betray me in my own house, nor would he gain glory by dying as a traitor, I gave rein to my anger and spoke bitterly, while he heard me out with his arms crossed and in silence. Then I added, "Yes, I will shoot you on the spot unless you send a telegram to Benjamín Hill ordering him to retire immediately to Casas Grandes."

When he answered yes, that he would send the telegram, I called to Luisito who was in the next room, "Luisito, write the telegram in which this traitor orders Benjamín Hill, as of this day, to march toward Casas Grandes." The message was written and sent, but, still angry, suspicious of deceit even in Obregón's consent, I continued to revile him.

Men of mine in Luisito's office heard the uproar, among them Raúl Madero and Dr. Felipe Dussart, and now a new turn of events occurred. Dr. Dussart, either to win my affection or to show his enmity for Obregón, entered and voiced his approval of my furious words and even added others of his own; it was a despicable act and made me even more angry. If I was violently insulting Obregón and he was listening in silence with bowed head, it was not good for another man to enter and gloat over him, taking advantage of the circumstances.

Almost insane with anger, I turned on Dussart and to keep from drawing my pistol and shooting him as he deserved, I shouted, "Get out of here, you good-for-nothing clown, before I kick you out myself." And as this incident made me realize the danger of committing some irremediable act, I left in search of repose.

Half an hour later I withdrew the escort which I had requested. An hour later I withdrew the guards I had posted. An hour and a half later, I returned to the room where Obregón was. I went over to him. I sat down. I told him to be seated at my side, which he did, subdued but not frightened. Quite calm by now, I spoke sanely. "Compañerito, you are right. If I shot you, they could accuse me of being an assassin and they would no longer consider me a good soldier, especially since you are here as my guest and by commission of Carranza, and men of other countries have seen us here together on a peaceful mission. Listen, then, to what I say: Pancho Villa is not an assassin or a traitor. But don't try to deceive him, and in serving Carranza, don't do anything with the look of deceiving him." I had realized that perhaps he was not solely responsible for his acts but was obliged to go along with the First Chief.

And we talked further. I was warning him not to be deceitful; he was assuring me that he had not and would not commit any treachery against me. Then, calm and composed, we went to supper, and as he had arranged for a dance that night in honor of me and my generals, I promised to attend as soon as I had finished my work.

CHAPTER 13

Violent Orders from Carranza Cause Villa To Deny the Office of First Chief and Threaten Obregón's Life.

Hill's Reply. Cabral at the Station. Villa's Reasoning. Obregón Leaves for the Mexico Meeting. Orders for Natera and Villarreal. Disavowal of Carranza. A Dialogue about the First Chief. Those Who Want To Kill Obregón and Those Who Want To Save Him.

The day after my outburst, Hill sent an answer from Sonora: "I will not obey Obregón's orders as long as they come from Chihuahua, where he can not issue them unconstrained." Obregón, without my knowing how, had found a secret way to communicate with him. But I no longer confronted Obregón with his acts; I merely detached two thousand men to Sonora, by way of Ciudad Juárez and Casas Grandes, to help José María Maytorena.

On the night of that same day, when Obregón was at the station with Juan Cabral, who was on his way to Nogales to take over his duties, several men from Sonora came there to kill him to avenge old grudges. Cabral, an old acquaintance, called them aside and dissuaded them. I too reprimanded them severely, saying, "Señores, I can have Obregón shot if he deserves it. But if one of my men assassinates him, my reputation will suffer."

My officers and I had convened several times to consider Carranza's invitation to the meeting in Mexico City. We decided, further, to examine the First Chief's reply to the proposals Obregón and I had made to give the government a constitutional form. My generals had said,

"Carranza is neither complying with the Plan of Guadalupe nor being governed by the desires of our armies. Along with González' generals we proposed certain terms of settlement, and he answered no. We proposed another agreement, and again he answered no. Now he summons only a part of the Revolutionary chiefs and only the generals and governors he appoints, depending on them to impose his will."

But Obregón, who attended our meetings, insisted that this was not true, and that even if it was, and Carranza summoned us with that intention, our ideas would prevail there. We agreed then that Obregón and I, without commitments, would accept in everybody's name:

Señor, we have your answer to our proposals and your invitation to these chiefs to attend the meeting of generals and governors. We agree that the meeting should not be convoked, since it was not mentioned in the Plan of Guadalupe nor is it a convention of democratic character as solicited in the Pact of Torreón for the time when that plan is put into effect. The purposes for which the meeting is convoked are not stated, and this involves the risk that the establishment of a legal government of our Republic will be delayed and the distribution of lands, which is the greatest aim of our struggle, may not be considered there. This, then, is our answer: As proof of subordination and respect, the representatives of the Northern Division will attend the meeting, but on condition that the first thing to be considered is whether the First Chief is to continue in his post as Interim President, and then that the date of the elections is agreed on, and immediately afterward provision is made for the distribution of lands. The Northern Division is obligated to confer only on these three points.

Obregón and I signed.

That happened on the twentieth or twenty-first of September. The afternoon of that same day Obregón left for Mexico City with José Isabel Robles, Eugenio Aguirre Benavides, and other generals of mine, who went in my name to explain our decisions and inform Carranza that I would not attend in person but would send an authorized delegate. But that morning, as Obregón and my generals were leaving, I received reports that the Chief had ordered Natera to destroy the track between Zacatecas and Aguascalientes and attack my troops if they attempted to move south of Torreón, and that he had given the same orders between Torreón and Monterrey, with the purpose of isolating me and defeating me. I was very angry on hearing this—so much so that, anxious not to believe it, I asked my telegraphers to confirm it. When I received full and definite confirmation I was really angry but I confined myself to telegraphing Carranza for the cause of his action. He answered insolently that he had no reason to explain anything to me and instead of asking him questions I might explain my treatment of Obregón.

Seeing that he was looking only for excuses to begin the struggle against me, I sent for my generals and the civilians who were advising me and informed them of these occurrences. We agreed to disavow him as our Chief. I sent him this telegram:

Señor, in reply to your message, I notify you that General Obregón and several of my generals left Chihuahua last night for Mexico City to meet with you and settle the serious questions which confront us. In view of your action, I have now ordered them to suspend their trip and return to Chihuahua. My division will not attend the meeting; furthermore, we do not recognize you as Chief and leave you at liberty to work as you please.

Francisco Villa

From this moment my division denied his authority and I at once telegraphed Robles and Aguirre Benavides to return to Chihuahua and to bring Obregón. Obregón returned at dawn on the following day. I sent Luisito after him in my automobile. When he arrived I told him why I had ordered his train to return. He answered, "If things are as you say, our First Chief is momentarily confused, but as soon as he knows the truth he will reconsider and correct his ways."

"No, Carranza will not overcome his dislike for me or Angeles, or Maytorena, or Zapata, or any of the Revolutionaries concerned with the welfare of the poor, nor will you persuade me to change my ideas again, my friend, for you are not the master of your own mind but a creature of the First Chief's, committed to excusing and protecting him."

"Sr. General, I do not think I support the designs of Carranza, if it is true that he has them; I only desire, as you do, the triumph of our Revolution. But I maintain that as soon as I reach Mexico City everything will be settled, the First Chief will withdraw the orders he has given, and he will do justice to the Northern Division."

I then replied that nothing of the sort could happen, nor should it, since we were determined to deny Carranza's authority and drive him from his post. I gave him our telegram to read; and he read it with uneasiness, I believe, but without comment.

That morning there was a struggle between those who advised me to shoot Obregón and those who opposed this. Díaz Lombardo, José Isabel

Robles, Eugenio Aguirre Benavides, Manuel Chao, Roque González Garza, Luisito, and Raúl Madero said, "Obregón must return in safety; otherwise our honor is stained forever." My compadre Tomás Urbina, José Rodríguez, Manuel Banda, Rodolfo Fierro, Pedro Bracamontes, and Anacleto Girón argued, "This is not the time for hesitation or mercy; Obregón is a traitor." And Urbina added, "Compadre, I will take the responsibility; leave it to me."

CHAPTER 14

Having Broken Relations with Carranza, Villa Moves His Troops Toward Zacatecas.

Obregón Returns Again. Villa's Charges. Maytorena's Answer. The Arrietas' Answer. Juan G. Cabral. Zacatecas. Panfilo Natera. Herrera's Words. Villa's Grief.

That night, the twenty-second or twenty-third of September, I arranged for Obregón to return to Mexico City. I knew it would be difficult to save him if he remained in Chihuahua. I had Rodolfo Fierro make up a train and told Roque González Garza to accompany Obregón to the limits of my territory. When I informed him that he and his men could leave he answered, "I have committed no treachery, and I promise you that in Mexico City all these differences will be settled at the meeting." He said goodbye and left, relying upon safe-conduct.

But the next day they came to tell me that he had intrigued up to the last hour in Chihuahua, urging Maclovio and his forces to join Carranza and trying to lure José Isabel Robles, Raúl Madero, Eugenio Aguirre Benavides, and Luisito, and others away from me. Angry all over again, I telegraphed orders for the train to return to Chihuahua. But Roque González Garza, from the train, and José Isabel Robles and Aguirre Benavides, from La Laguna, asked me to withdraw my order, reminding me of the safe-conduct I had given. I acceded, but now, after so long a time, I consider that I did wrong.

I informed Governor Domingo Arrieta in Durango and Governor Maytorena in Sonora that Carranza was beginning hostilities against me and my men and that I had denied his authority. Maytorena and his men replied by renouncing the First Chief the next day after I had done so. In a manifesto, which they distributed throughout Sonora, they said:

Francisco Villa is right: he exerted the maximum effort to avoid this break; he offered his advice to Venustiano Carranza in order to save him from the mistakes he was making; he has not been unpatriotic; his acts are acts of love for the people, executed with the determination that the poor will conquer injustice. This State of Sonora supports him and rises up against Carranza with outspoken resentment.

But Domingo Arrieta, a general and a governor by the will of Carranza, would not listen to my words. He advised peace, seeing no good reasons for my acts and those of my generals. "I must have other reasons if I am to say whether I am with Carranza or with you. I advise you to be calm, to meditate, and to sacrifice yourself while waiting for the meeting which will soon be held." In their great fear of me, Domingo and Mariano Arrieta were not committing themselves.

And then there were men of good faith who were unhappy at seeing that Revolutionaries were going to fight among themselves, and many with the utmost determination to avoid another bloody war. Juan Cabral said to me, "Sr. General Villa, I inform you that I will not fight in the approaching struggle. I undertook to fulfill my duty, bearing arms against the tyranny of Huerta, but confronted with this I must cease to be a soldier and resume my rights as a citizen dedicated to a peaceful settlement of all these arguments."

Carranza had attempted to cut my communications south of Torreón and Zacatecas, fearing the rapid advance of my troops on the center of the Republic. He ordered Natera to destroy the tracks between Zacatecas and Aguascalientes, but the latter temporized, asking for reasons. Carranza answered that General Villa had wanted to shoot General Obregón, was storing up arms and equipment in order to rebel, had sent troops to Durango against the Arrietas, had persuaded Zapata not to recognize Carranza, had encouraged Maytorena in acts of rebellion, had made agreements with the Federals of Lower California. And Natera replied, "Señor, that may be true, but my men and I must be sure we receive only just orders, and we ask that you clarify these."

And what happened was that Natera telegraphed me that his ideas were the same as mine, and forty-eight hours after the break, Robles and Aguirre Benavides were already marching to Zacatecas with the troops I had in Torreón.

An incident occurred in my own division. Herrera, badly advised by his father Don José de la Luz, disapproved of our renouncement of Carranza and rejected it. This was probably the result of discord the Chief had spread in Parral in the first months of our struggle, and of the webs Obregón had woven around some of my men on his two trips to Chihuahua.

Whatever it was, Maclovio turned against me in the worst way, sending messages in extravagant language, saying that Carranza was a good Revolutionary and I was not, and he could carry our cause to triumph while I would go down in defeat, and so on. These were his words:

Sr. General Villa:
Until today I have belonged to the Northern Division, but in view of your leaving Carranza and no longer recognizing him as Chief, I withdraw myself and my men from the Division. Carranza is the incarnation of our Revolution, which he will carry through to triumph by his courage and great knowledge of all things. You are only an ambitious man; you will fall in defeat, surrounded and managed by political enemies of our country who would bring dishonor and failure to our cause if we good Revolutionaries followed in your misguided steps. Your life has branded you as an assassin and a bandit; and you are unworthy of the company of honorable men, or their consideration or pardon, for which I am as of this day ready to shoot you and all those who follow you, to save the sacred interests of our country. I bid you goodbye, informing you that I am here in Parral waiting to give you a fine welcome and prove to the world that you are worth nothing as soldier or man.

Maclovio Herrera

Maclovio Herrera was a man close to my heart, whom I had protected and carried to his greatest triumphs. After reading his telegram I wanted to weep as if he were dead. Señor! One man can follow another, hear his orders and execute them, suffer with him, and share his confidence and his affection and his admiration, and then suddenly for something that has nothing to do with robbery or killing, discover that he was nothing but an assassin and a bandit.

My sorrow increased.

CHAPTER 15

The Break between Villa and Carranza Converts the Meeting of Generals and Governors into A Convention.

The Generals' Warning. Lucio Blanco and Villarreal. Don Fernando Iglesias Calderón. The Federals of Lower California. A Telegram to Sr. Carranza. His Answer. Jiménez. Parral. Villa's Restraint and Herrera's Intemperance. The Meeting at Zacatecas. The Convention Is Agreed On.

I learned that when my break with Carranza was known in Mexico City the Revolutionaries grew alarmed over the war that was brewing. Meetings began, and the studying of ways to avoid it. From Lucio Blanco, Eduardo Hay, and others I received telegrams saying: "Sr. General Villa, there must be some means of settling these differences peacefully. It is your patriotic duty to advise us of these means, and you can be sure that we will make efforts to see that Carranza accepts them."

I called my generals and the civilians who were advising me, and since we wanted only to remove Carranza from his post, I asked them which man we should choose in his place. They replied that in their judgment we should choose Fernando Iglesias Calderón, because of his spotless record in political affairs. I therefore answered the telegram, saying:

If I repudiate the Chief of the Constitutionalist Army, it is because I believe him incapable of returning us to the democratic standards of government, and I want our country and the world to know it. But I agree that we should avoid armed struggle, and to achieve this I propose that Sr. Carranza turn his power over to Don Fernando Iglesias Calderón, a man in whom we have confidence, one who will hold elections and receive our patriotic support. All my acts are for the good of the people, not for my personal ambition, and I would not accept the Presidency or Vice-Presidency either in provisional or in constitutional form.

That was also my answer to Villarreal, who was appealing to me from Monterrey, asking me to refrain from force and wait for the meeting. To him I added, "I recognize your good intentions and great patriotism. Have Carranza deliver his authority to Iglesias Calderón pending the elections; trust in my disinterestedness."

I sought no struggle though I would be prepared for it. In seeking to complete our victory by peaceful methods, I had already made a settlement with the Federals in Lower California, who would give me political power in their territory and maintain a garrison in defense against filibusters. José María Maytorena, too, wanted peace, as did Zapata.

My generals and civilian advisors in assembly shaped the following message and wired it to the Chief:

Sr. Carranza:

The generals, chiefs, and officers of the Northern Division and the civilians who are its advisors regarding the laws, are moved by the patriotic words of our brothers and their request asking us to consider only the good of our country in the present crisis. Our ambition is to save the Revolutionary cause, and we are ready to make any sacrifice to this end. Sr. General Villa and this Division will abandon their hostile attitude if you will transfer the office of First Chief to Don Fernando Iglesias Calderón, who will maintain and defend our cause pending the holding of elections and the formation of a government. We urge you therefore to relinquish your command and save our Republic, by which you will prove yourself to be a great man and a shining example to the Mexicans of the future.

These were words, I think, which Carranza might well have accepted, but a day or two later he replied with offensive statements about my person and ignored their request:

Sres. Generals of the Northern Division:

I have your telegram asking me to abandon this office and call upon Don Fernando Iglesias Calderón to take my place. I feel inclined to give up all my posts, but if I do, I should place them in the hands of the chiefs who delivered them to me, those of our Constitutionalist troops. To that end I have convoked a meeting of generals and governors, which you should attend, like the other chiefs. Your petition proceeds only from Sr. General Villa's disobedience and lack of discipline. I would have believed you impartial had you asked him to leave his command before asking me to renounce this office. However, if the chiefs accept my resignation the first of October, I will retire happy and satisfied, having left only in compliance with my duty; but if the resignation should not be accepted, I will employ the same vigor with which I opposed the usurpation of Victoriano Huerta to overcome the reaction of Francisco Villa, who is the instrument of the Porfiristas we have just defeated, just as Pascual Orozco was when he led the reactionaries, who conquered Madero. I recognize the sentiment that moves you to make these efforts, and I want them to succeed; but if they fail and an armed struggle occurs, I trust you will be on the side of honor as good soldiers; it would be sad if after risking your life for your country you should risk it now for dishonor.

He insulted me through my generals, calling me another Pascual Orozco and declaring that there was no dignity or honor with me.

I was then in Jiménez, ready to send my troops against the town of Hidalgo del Parral and Maclovio Herrera. I invited Maclovio to engage in a parley by wire. He agreed and I had the telegrapher transmit greetings in spite of his many offenses, and then did my persuasive best to bring him to reflect and recognize his error. I was his friend; if he thought us unjust in our renouncement of Carranza, he could give me his reasons, which I would heed if they were good, but not insults, which I did not deserve. A short time ago, when he knew the struggle was threatening us, he had asked me to send him matériel by his father and I had done so, counting upon his loyalty. I reminded him of that day in Torreón when he was outraged by the Chief's stripping me of my command and had telegraphed him the worst insult one man can offer another.

But emboldened, I believe, by my placating words, he answered in still stronger language than in his telegram of five or six days before:

Neither my men nor I wish anything from you. The words I sent to our Chief from Torreón, words provoked by Villa's fault and not by Carranza's, I now apply to you and your conduct. I have nothing more to say except that I am waiting for you with five hundred soldiers at the Mesa de Sandías, a place you know, and if you are man enough, you can come to meet me with the same force.

I ordered Raúl Madero to go and take Parral.

The generals in Mexico City had another meeting, called by Lucio Blanco and Alvaro Obregón, and Obregón had hard things to say about me. Among my forces, according to him, there were chiefs of two classes: those with morals and those without, and the chiefs with morals would have to abandon me, as Herrera had already done. But the generals who heard him had no wish to follow his suggestion; they advised peace, and then decided to send a commission to confer with me and my generals in Zacatecas.

Obregón came as chief of the delegates; he was accompanied by very good Revolutionaries, like Ramón E. Iturbe, Ernesto Santos Coy, Andrés Saucedo, Eduardo Hay, and others. They dealt with Pánfilo Natera, Eulalio Gutiérrez, and Martín Triana, who were waiting there with José Isabel Robles, Eugenio Aguirre Benavides, and other men of mine; but they understood that nothing was to be agreed upon in my absence, and so sent for me and I went to talk with them, but not with Obregón, who withdrew to Aguascalientes. As a result we were of a single opinion regarding the dangers of another war and decided that the Constitutional chiefs should meet in a convention although Carranza opposed this. Hostile acts were to be suspended immediately, all movements of troops were to cease, the Constitutionalist generals would meet in Aguascalientes on the fifth of October and for a period of five days would make plans for a convention on the tenth of that month.

CHAPTER 16

Luis Cabrera Prevents the Conference of Generals and Governors from Accepting Carranza's Resignation.

Villa's Manifesto. Madero, Carranza, and the Convention. The Shooting of José Bonales Sandoval. Augustín Pérez. Luis Cabrera. Carranza at the Conference. Manuel Bonilla. Enrique C. Llorente. Martín Luis Guzmán. Carlos Domínguez. Abel Serratos. Luis G. Malváez. Oaxaca and Sonora. Villa and Zapata.

Before marching south I gave orders for my renouncement of Carranza to be published. The contents of this manifesto were as follows:

Francisco I. Madero followed the roads of democracy, of the justice the people are seeking. But Huerta by his infamous treachery caused the death of that illustrious apostle and we Revolutionaries of 1910 took up the struggle. When we were all in the war, each according to his resources and his deeds, Venustiano Carranza came and said to us, "I want to be the chief this Revolution needs." And in our good will we consented and adopted and signed his Plan of Guadalupe, trusting that when we were victorious he would restore the democratic government of Sr. Madero and make the legal reforms wanted by the people.

But as our cause progressed, he too was progressing toward disregarding his promises and weakening other Revolutionaries. And when he took the capital by force of all the Revolutionary arms, and not solely with the men who were accompanying him personally, he revealed his intention of never surrendering his post and governing with absolute power. Not wanting to submit to the laws, he would not name an Interim President or have ministers to advise him.

Realizing the danger at this point, the Northern Division and the Northwestern Army Corps asked him to submit to the regulations of an interim government pending the formation of laws, the distribution of lands, and the application of other reforms. He still insisted on the meeting he had convoked, and, though this meeting was merely designed to confirm his position, we agreed to send delegates with Alvaro Obregón, asking only for safeguards to keep things under control. When the delegates were already on the way, Carranza took violent offense at reports he accepted without investigation and suspended business in all the territory occupied by the Northern Division and opened hostilities against us to checkmate those who were demanding reforms.

In view of all this the Northern Division has resolved to disavow him as First Chief of the Constitutionalist Army and Representative of the Executive Power, in connection with which I declare that, like my generals, I am unmoved by ambition; none of us will accept the office of President of the Republic or Vice-President or governor in any form, but, together with the other generals, chiefs, officers, and soldiers of our army who give us their support, we will fight until we have a civil government which protects the people with liberal laws.

I signed and published this before marching south, already resigned to war, but in Zacatecas I attended the meeting with Natera, Eulalio Gutiérrez, and commissioners from Mexico City, and there retracted the manifesto in favor of holding a convention in Aguascalientes and gaining a peaceful settlement.

On the return to Jiménez another incident occurred. When my train stopped there, another one pulled in from Ciudad Juárez, and the lawyer José Bonales Sandoval got off and came to see me. He had defended me when I was imprisoned by Huerta and later had come with friendly proposals from Félix Díaz when I conquered Chihuahua. Knowing he was among those responsible for the death of my friend Gustavo Madero, I had wanted to punish him but did not wish to do so without Carranza's authorization. Inasmuch as he had defended me and assured me that he could bring in Félix Díaz if I wanted him, I preferred not to dispose of him myself, but said, "Señor, I have come into this world never to betray a cause I embrace. I have no wish to harm you, since you have defended me and you are under my protection by virtue of my reply to your letter. But I warn you of one thing; I want no dealings with Félix Díaz except to punish him for his crime against Sr. Madero. If he appears here, I will punish him." If I had punished Bonales Sandoval at the time, I would have been at fault. But now that he appeared again, and again proposed that I should have near my person a man who had contributed to Sr. Madero's death, the situation was different.

He argued, "It would be to your advantage to join with Félix Díaz in your struggle with Carranza. He will bring you the rest of the Federal Army and never fail to look on you as his chief."

"Señor, you are deceived, like the men of your profession. This time I do not pardon you. Don't you know that Carranza accuses me of being another Pascual Orozco, managed by Porfiristas? How dare you appear with these messages? I shall have you and your baggage searched, and if they find a single damaging paper, I will have you shot immediately."

So it was. They found letters from Félix Díaz about the affair and I had him shot then and there, with a compañero of his, an engineer named Agustín Pérez, who came to support him in his propositions. To seal their fate, Emilio Madero arrived on the same train on which they came, and thus the memory of Gustavo Madero suddenly revived my spirit of vengeance.

What I did was right, both in memory of chiefs assassinated only because of their love of the people, and in self-defense against conspirators. Two or three days later, when it was known in Mexico City that Bonales Sandoval was in Chihuahua, but not known that I had shot him, Luis Cabrera declared that I was in league with reaction, and that was why Bonales Sandoval was with me. I had the pleasure of replying that he was in error and that he might come to Chihuahua to see what happened to reactionaries who came to join me.

By then the meeting convoked by the First Chief had opened in Mexico City, and Carranza appeared before the assembly, announcing that he had come to resign and painting the blackest picture of the Revolutionary outlook. He now claimed credit for proposing reforms that we had been demanding. But he devoted most of his words to me and my men and to Maytorena, describing me, after his fashion, as I was not and accusing me of what I had not done. He declared, "Our work will be frustrated by the acts of Francisco Villa who renounces and threatens me and has his men demanding power in a way that takes us back to times when Mexico lost half of her territory. Can't you see reaction hiding behind him."

I thought, "Señor! Who are the Porfiristas who hide behind me? And when he speaks of cowards and ignorant men, does he mean Felipe Angeles, Miguel Silva, Miguel Díaz Lombardo, and others who have left him to be with me? And if they are worth so little, why did he seize and imprison several of them in reprisal for Obregón, for he knows well that nothing has happened to Obregón?" For he had put Manuel Bonilla, Enrique Llorente, Martín Luis Guzmán, Carlos Domínguez, Abel Serratos, and Luis G. Malváez, who were my men and very close to me, in the Penitentiary.

At the meeting Luis Cabrera spoke very strongly against me and in favor of Carranza, so that with no one there to defend me he succeeded in persuading the delegates to refuse the resignation of the Chief. To frighten them he declared, "Oaxaca is in the hands of Félix Díaz. Sonora supports the rebellion of Maytorena. Zapata refuses to recognize Carranza. Villa denounces him in his famous telegram without its being known whom or what he likes. The enemies of our cause are Villa, Zapata, and the men whom neither we nor Sr. Madero have succeeded in conquering. Whom do we have then? Who guides us if we too let Carranza go?"

Those were his words, and although none of the Revolutionaries believed what he said of me or Zapata, they let themselves be swayed momentarily and left the Chief in his post.

CHAPTER 17

Villa Discovers that the Gaucho Mújica Is Plotting against His Life; He Seizes Him and Applies the Laws of Justice.

The Work of the Commissioners. Cabrera's Predictions. Villa Names His Representative. Advice to Roque González Garza. "Do Not Think Me Ambitious." A Civilian as a Candidate. The Laws and Many Other Things. The Gaucho Mújica. The Prisoners in the Penitentiary. Pablo González. Cosío Robelo. Villa's Anger. Mr. Carothers.

The commissioners who had come to confer with me in Zacatecas won a favorable reception in Mexico City for our idea of changing the meeting in session there into a true convention, to be held not in Mexico City, which afforded no guarantees, but in Aguascalientes, halfway between my territory and Carranza's.

Luis Cabrera, who definitely wanted discord, not peaceful understanding, worked and talked against it, as he had done to keep Carranza in his post. In his efforts to incriminate me with his eloquence, he was accusing me of deeds I had not committed. "If we go to Aguascalientes, we will find the true assassins of Sr. Madero with Pancho Villa; we will find Ramón Prida and José Bonales Sandoval; we will find the Jew Félix Sommerfeld, who sows dissension and surrounds Villa with the bad Revolutionaries our First Chief rejected in Sonora and Sommerfeld carried to Chihuahua. We will find businessmen from the United States, and Don Ernesto Madero and Don Rafael Hernández and all their attorneys and the representatives of reactionary groups in San Antonio, Texas."

After painting me with the colors of men he said were around me, he added that I was in the struggle out of no sincere Revolutionary conviction but only to restore reaction, for what purpose I do not know, and therefore my generals and my forces were moved by no such noble aims as the rest of the Constitutionalist troops. But this time Cabrera failed to move the generals who wanted peace. It was decided that there would be a convention in Aguascalientes, barred to civilians like Cabrera, who were capable of confusing us with their forecasts of the future. I asked Roque González Garza, my most learned friend, to represent me in Aguascalientes.

"It is a very heavy responsibility to represent Pancho Villa. You must enlighten me, Señor, and tell me what image you want me to present and what purposes you expect to achieve."

"I have nothing to tell you except to work according to your conscience and interpret me with honor. You, my chiefs, my officers, and my soldiers know my ideas. My only aim is to have our success turned to the benefit of the people. The petitions we made in the conferences at Torreón I make now; the method Obregón and I proposed for guaranteeing the principles of our cause I again propose. I add only this: don't let your imagination represent me as ruled by ambition, but believe in my disinterestedness, or rather, in my interest in putting the cause of the poor above everything else and fighting for justice."

"I understand, my General. But in the matter of certain steps, such as designating the President of the Republic, how can I decide without your advice?"

"That is no problem to disturb the conscience. Support the appointment of a good Revolutionary civilian like Don Miguel Silva. This does not mean that I necessarily think ill of military presidents, for one like Felipe Angeles would serve our cause. But if our willingness to consent to government by a military man conceals the threat that all military men expect to govern us as a reward for their prowess in arms, reason tells us to avoid that evil, even at a personal sacrifice." I added that he should seek advice from Miguel Silva himself, who would be there, or from Angeles, or José Isabel Robles, or Miguel Díaz Lombardo, or Francisco Escudero. Clearly I, not being a man of knowledge or words, could not go to the convention where laws and such things would be discussed.

During the progress of the convention a man came to Guadalupe, Zacatecas, and offered to fight for the cause. I asked him his name. He said he was the Gaucho Mújica. I asked him where he was from. He said from the Argentine Republic. I asked him why, not being a Mexican, he wished to risk his life in our struggles, which meant nothing to his people. He told me that they did mean something to him. He had been among us a long time and he had been responsible for many deaths and had suffered for some time in prison. I asked him what deaths. He said those of some impresarios who had defrauded him. I asked him where he had been in prison. He said in Belén, from which he had escaped at the time of the Ten Tragic Days in order to lend his services to Sr. Madero, and later in another prison, where he was held by Huerta.

This one he had left to offer his service to the Revolution. I asked him what services. He said he had served in the Northeastern Army Corps under Pablo González. And as I then asked him why, if he wished to serve our cause, he had not remained in the army corps where he was, he said it was because he was expecting the struggle to break out between Villistas and Carrancistas and wanted to be with the Villistas, who were fighting for the people, and not the Carrancistas, who were seeking only their own gain.

I found him a person of good appearance and manners that seemed to come from acts of valor and I thought that he could be useful. So I said, "Good, friend. You are the kind of person I like. I will make you an officer of my compadre Urbina's forces. He will be glad to have you and will treat you well. But instead of remaining here I want you to carry out the following commission: Carranza has imprisoned several Revolutionaries, close friends of mine, in the Penitentiary of Mexico City. These are Manuel Bonilla, Enrique Llorente, Martín Luis Guzmán, Carlos Domínguez, Abel Serratos, and Luis G. Malváez. Give them a letter from me and inquire about their situation and tell them to escape if they can and ask if I can help them in any way from here. Then, depending on the answer they give, either return with their message or stay there to serve them."

Thus I took him into my confidence and, along with a letter that Luisito wrote for me, I gave him money for his own use and more to deliver to the men he was going to see, and in that way I showed him every consideration, which he accepted with pleasure.

But soon after this a boy named Cabiedes came to me in the name of my men in the Penitentiary. They wanted to warn me against a man of such and such description, the Gaucho Mújica, who would appear under the guise of friendship but was commissioned by Pablo González to kill me. Cabiedes explained that Carlos Domínguez and Martín Luis Guzmán had helped Cosío Robelo organize the police in Mexico City and knew agents who kept them informed of what happened outside. The wife of one of those agents, likewise an agent, had learned from the Gaucho Mújica's wife that he was hired by Pablo González to kill me, for which he had already received his money and been promised more.

I wondered, "How is it possible, Señor, that González is so ill disposed toward me? Have we not endured the sorrows of the Revolution together? Didn't he consider himself my friend and compañero?" I was troubled in my anger, uncertain whether it came of concern for myself or for the prisoners in Mexico City whom I had perhaps injured, or of my desire for the Gaucho Mújica to return and give me an opportunity to punish him.

A few days later the treacherous fellow did return. My agents found him, seized him, took his arms, his papers, and his belongings, and brought him before me. One of his papers was a card from González giving the Gaucho permission to go anywhere; a second was a credential signed by Francisco Cosío Robelo, and a third was a letter from that señor to several of the Carrancistas at the convention.

In uncontrollable anger I seized his pistol and struck him with it, saying, "So this is what you are, you good-for-nothing so-and-so. Well, here I am, Señor. You have me within your reach, where you can earn the money González has promised you."

Hardly trying to protect himself from the blows I struck, he answered, "No, my General, they have deceived you. I am incapable of killing a man like you. I am an honorable man. A loyal man."

"What about these cards, Don So-and-so? And these papers?"

"No, my General. I did not come here to kill you although I told your enemies I would. Who would have the heart to kill a man like you?"

"Any traitor would. No man goes away alive if he comes to kill me face to face, but a traitor, yes, or several traitors together, if they catch me unarmed. And that is what you are, a traitor."

"No, my General, I say this as a man who knows how to die and how to kill. I was deceiving them."

"Even if that is so, your crime is the same; you are still a traitor."

When I tired of beating him—he was bloody and humble by now—I sent for a rope and with my own hands tied him, putting the pistol on the floor. The men who had brought him carried him away, and then and there took him off my train and shot him. I did this in anger, but it was justice, and by advice of Mr. Carothers, who was with me, I had it put in writing that according to the man's confession he had received money for coming to kill me. I did this because the Gaucho Mújica was an Argentinian, protected in our country by international law.

CHAPTER 18

Carranza Refuses To Attend the Convention; Villa Goes and Is Acclaimed by the Delegates.

González Protests. Villa's Satisfaction. At the Convention. The Aims of the Northern Division. A Letter to Zapata. The Invitation to Carranza and Villa. Prisoners of Carranza and Maytorena. "I Have No Prisoners in My Territory." A Discourse by Pancho Villa. A Discourse by Villarreal.

Pablo González, camped in Querétaro with his forces, was publicly denying that he had wanted me killed. In the Mexico City newspapers he was saying:

Publications in the north and in the United States carry the report that I commissioned the Gaucho Mújica to murder General Villa. This is slander, and I refute it as a Revolutionary and as a general in command of an army corps of Constitutionalist troops. The only men I have killed have had rifles in their hands to defend themselves. I hate only tyranny; my only grudge is against the enemies of the people, and Pancho Villa is not an enemy but a protector of the people. I joined the armed struggle to consummate it with honor, without resort to dagger or the acts of assassins, nor do I stain myself with the crimes it has been my purpose to oppose and which I will oppose to the end.

I was glad to hear those words, since Pablo González was a man I admired, but I kept wondering why, if he had not ordered me killed, the Gaucho Mújica had so confessed, at the time of his death, to me and others, among them Luisito and Mr. Carothers. In any case it pleased me to know that González was protesting against the report and I thought that perhaps others had made the plot and ascribed it to him, since the ways of murder are devious when contrived by men who are incapable of meeting their enemies face to face.

By the middle of October, 1914, the Sovereign Convention of Aguascalientes was in the midst of its work. Roque González Garza went there to be his most eloquent in explaining to the delegates why my men and I had entered the struggle:

Sres. Delegates of the Constitutionalist Troops:

I come to speak in the name of my General Francisco Villa. It is his purpose to make his intentions known with respect to the business you are discussing.

He wants your minds to be uninfluenced by personal love or hate; he wants your conscience clear for the sole consideration of our country. He wants a provisional form of government resolved to maintain peace and turn our triumph to the good of the people—a government, that is, which delivers the land to the laborers in the field, forms just laws to protect the poor, and makes all preparations for the constitutional government to come. He wants a civilian to govern us, not a military man or a group of military men who intimidate the people. He wants a well-conducted election with the free naming of governors, the President, and the deputies, as in the time of Sr. Madero. He wants proper safeguards against another dictatorship like that of Porfirio Díaz and another usurpation like that of Victoriano Huerta.

In order that no one may accuse him of ambition or doubt his sincerity, he wants the laws reformed so that military men cannot govern the people; and in addition, since justice and the necessity of a good peace demand it, he wants this Convention to bring in our absent brothers who have fought in this struggle; he wants it to call and welcome and hear them, and in agreement with them to decide what must be done for our best success. This Convention must do nothing without the knowledge and consent of Emiliano Zapata and his Revolutionary men of the South, who, with their Plan of Ayala, fought for the same ideals that Sr. Madero was fighting for with his illustrious Plan of San Luis.

Thus Roque González Garza stated my aims, and in my judgment, he stated them well, as he stated everything that I sought or agreed to during those meetings of the Convention of Aguascalientes.

There were many men in the Convention who hated or distrusted me, and I hoped the meeting would end by making the best possible settlement of all matters. I wished nothing to be done without Zapata's delegates and forces of the south, and to invite them I sent Angeles with Calixto Contreras, Rafael Buelna, and other good Revolutionary men with a letter from the Convention itself so that Zapata would receive them and listen to them; and I gave them my own letter requesting that chief to send delegates. We said this to Zapata:

Sr. General and Compañero:
The Convention of Revolutionary chiefs is meeting in Aguascalientes. It has sovereign powers by virtue of the agreement between the body that met in Mexico City to preserve the peace and the generals of the Northern Division and the Northeastern and Northwestern Army Corps. The representatives of José María Maytorena and those of the central, southern, and eastern divisions of our Republic are here, but we lack your delegates, Señor, and those of all the troops under your command, without whom we feel inadequate to carry

through the work that brings us here. We therefore beg the generals of the Liberating Army to send their delegates. We invite you as our brothers and we address you with our greatest esteem. We need you here to know, consider, and resolve the serious problems that confront us and to join with us in good will, so that nothing can delay our progress.

That Convention invited me and Carranza to honor it with our presence at least once. They did this, in my opinion, with the intention of committing us to the Convention's agreements. But Carranza refused to come, either from arrogance, from fear of being separated from his partisans, or from reluctance to join issue in a neutral place, where thoughts could be freely expressed. He showed little respect for the Convention, as was particularly evident on two occasions. They sent word to him to fly our flag in honor of the opening of the session, and after considering the question of my men whom he held as prisoners, they ordered these released. As regards the first, he asked just why that Convention was considered sovereign and on what its sovereignty was based; as regards my men, he declared that before he set them free, Maytorena and I would have to do the same with the Carrancistas we had seized.

Accordingly the Convention ordered me to release the political prisoners I was holding and I answered that there was not a single political prisoner in all my territory and that if anyone could name me one I would obey. To a second order to Carranza to release my men, he paid no attention, but decided to send them to be executed under the authority of a General Nafarrate, and they were saved only by the intervention of Villarreal, whose forces in Monterrey detained the train and brought it to Aguascalientes under strong escort of his men and those of Gutiérrez.

I shunned the example of Carranza. Out of respect for the Convention I went before it as soon as they requested my presence. As I remember, I arrived at Aguascalientes on that sixteenth of October between four and five in the afternoon, and the next day appeared at the theater where the delegates were holding their meetings. I entered and went to sit with the delegates who were occupying orchestra seats; but on seeing this, Villarreal, who was presiding, spoke to me from the platform, "Sr. General Villa, we welcome you to this Convention as one who honors us with his presence. I beg you, in the name of all these delegates, to take your seat at the executive table."

I answered, "Sr. General, I am the one who is honored, and I will be as pleased to sit here as in the place you indicate, which in my opinion is for men of greater intelligence and knowledge."

But as he insisted, I acquiesced, to the applause of all. Then they came and asked me to speak before the delegates, and I answered that I would say what was in my heart, and although I could not enlighten them, because of my ignorance, my obscure origin, my background, and my want of schooling, still I could declare my love for the people, my loyalty, and my intention to subordinate everything to the good of our cause. I rose and spoke, saying,

Compañeritos, Sres. Generals and Officers who performed your highest duty by making it possible for all of us together to overthrow the tyranny of Victoriano Huerta:

I cannot guide or enlighten you in any way, and you will hear the words of a man who comes before you with a total lack of culture. But if there are men of sound mind here who understand the meaning of patriotic duty and brotherly feeling, Francisco Villa will not make these men ashamed of him. Señores, I ask nothing for myself; I joined the struggle only to do my duty. I want nothing in benefit of my person or in payment of my services. I want everything for the good of the people and the relief of the poor. I tell you, I want to see my country happy and safe, because I have suffered much for it, and I refuse to allow other Mexicans, my brothers, to suffer what I have suffered, or the women and children to suffer what I have seen them suffer in the mountains, the fields, and the haciendas.

In your hands you hold the future of the country, the destiny of all Mexicans, and if that is lost, the entire responsibility will lie upon you people of law and knowledge.

I was overcome with emotion while I was talking and wept, and when they heard the feeling with which I spoke, they too were moved and applauded me. There were cheers and shouts, and they came to congratulate and embrace me. I thought, "Señor, why isn't Carranza here too to speak his words? Why doesn't he come before these men and take inspiration from them? Why can't we all embrace and continue our work together for the good of the country?"

Villarreal, touched by my words, rose and made a very fine speech. Addressing himself to me, he said:

Sr. General Villa, delegates of this Convention put their faith in you; the men of our country have confidence in you. We know that in coming here you show that you intend to comply with the settlements here agreed upon, and to see that others comply. I say more, Sr. General, for myself and in the name of the delegates who are listening: you are a Revolutionary of very great courage; fragile as crystal, you can weep, and strong as bronze, you can resist, and for that reason we understand you and praise your gentleness and your deeds; because in your gentleness, General Villa, we see the emotion with which our people feel their sorrows, and in your fortitude and the strength of your arms, we recognize the vigor with which our people struggle against injustice.

Again they applauded and acclaimed me; and while they were applauding I went to the table to take the oath to fulfil and enforce the dictates of the Convention and to respect its sovereignty, and I put my signature on the flag, which was evidence to all that we had taken the said oath.

Soon after, when the work of the meeting had already begun, General Chao rose to ask permission to go to Parral where he was called by the serious illness of one of his sons. But I intervened and said no, that such permission should not be granted. These were my words, "Sr. General Chao, the interests of our country come before the family."

CHAPTER 19

As a Condition of His Resignation as Chief, Carranza Demands that Villa and Zapata Retire to Private Life.

The Course of the Convention. Rincón de Romos. The Struggle in Sonora. Colonel Manuel Manzanera. The Arrival of the Prisoners from Mexico. Emiliano Zapata's Delegates. Paulino Martínez. Antonio Díaz Soto y Gama. Zapata's Message and Villa's Response. Carranza's Reasons and Conditions. Villa's Reflections.

There were many obstacles in the course of the Convention; some were the result of Carranza's intrigues with the chiefs he considered most devoted to him; others sprang from the distrust many of those delegates had for me and my men. I could not move, my

forces could not move, without a discussion by all and without incrim-
inations from many. That was what happened when it was known that
my compadre Tomás Urbina's troops had advanced north of Aguascalientes to the place called Rincón de Romos, as was necessary to do
in search of pasturage and food. The more our own delegates explained,
the less the rest believed; so it was that, considering we were not guilty
of the bad intentions they were attributing to us, Roque González Garza
assured them of our sincerity and proposed in my name and that of the
Northern Division that no general should have any troops in the entire
state of Aguascalientes.

The same thing was happening in the war in Sonora, which Maytorena's men were waging against those of Calles and Hill. Obregón and
other delegates submissive to the First Chief wanted no fault to be
found with Hill's acts; they wanted the blame to fall on Maytorena,
without considering that perhaps there was fault on everybody's part
when passion engulfed us all, and not on the part of one single faction
alone.

I must admit that my troops committed some acts which were disrespectful to the Convention, and, as luck would have it, their consequences were serious. I refer to the death of Colonel Manuel Manzanera,
a delegate of one of the Arrietas. As my compadre Urbina was a bitter
enemy of his, for some treachery on the part of the said Colonel, he
secretly ordered him seized and tied and brought to Zacatecas and shot,
in spite of my advice not to involve us. This was reported to the Convention, and deliberated on while my compadre was present, although I
little know what he and the other representatives of my forces may have
said in his defense. The case is that since the delegates considered the
charge against us very serious, they decided that they could do nothing
with so little information, finding it vague, and believing it necessary to
wait for more definite reports; for this reason, and thanks to the difficult
business before the Convention, the death went uninvestigated, which
was a great relief to me. I confess today that if the truth had been known
and the Convention had ordered me to punish my compadre Tomás
Urbina, in obedience to my duty and after the oath I had taken on the
flag and the signature I had put there, I could have found no way to
avoid putting the punishment into execution.

Colonel Manzanera died bravely, asking only that some day they
deliver to his mother a small card on which he had written these words,
"Mama, at twelve tonight they are going to shoot me." He wrote that
the card was for his widowed mother, Doña Virginia Salas, who lived

in Mexico City at No. 12, Londres Street. Some days later, this lady, who appeared to be a very cultured person, came to see me in Guadalupe, Zacatecas, and said that she was appealing to my sense of justice, since her son's only crime had been to leave Urbina's troops and join Arrieta's. I was distressed to see her weep, listened to her with great respect and calmed her as best I could, leaving her in the comfort of ignorance and not telling her that my compadre Urbina's anger was due to more serious causes.

My men from the prison in Mexico City arrived in Aguascalientes. All of them, Bonilla, Llorente, Guzmán, Domínguez, Serratos, and Malváez, came to my general headquarters at Guadalupe and told me the story of their confinement, of Venustiano Carranza's intention to execute them, of Obregón's efforts in their behalf, and of Lucio Blanco's protection.

I said, "Señores, in enduring this injustice you have aided our country."

In truth these men, at the risk of their lives, had done good work in Mexico City. They had saved me from death at the hands of the Gaucho Mújica, and one of them, Guzmán, brought Blanco to visit me one night and tell me he approved of the aims of the Northern Division and would aid me against Carranza as long as I did not abandon the interests of the people.

Zapata's delegates and other chiefs from the south arrived. They agreed to talk with me before joining the Convention. At noon of the day after they reached Aguascalientes they were eating with me at Guadalupe, Zacatecas. Among them were a couple of lawyers, Paulino Martínez and Antonio Díaz Soto y Gama, civilized and well-informed men. They said, "Sr. General Villa, we know your great love for the memory of Don Francisco I. Madero, and you know, as we do, that to protect the purity of the Revolution, since we considered the Treaties of Ciudad Juárez premature, we continued to fight against the government of that apostle of democracy and proclaimed our Plan of Ayala, which, to our way of thinking, discredited him. But we assure you, Sr. General, that the men of the prairies of the north and those of the mountains of the south who have overthrown the usurpation by Huerta are the same ones who supported the struggle against the dictatorship of Porfirio Díaz in 1910, and that the two men who represented the desires of the people then and who represent them now are still alive and standing after all the assassinations committed by the usurpers. These men are Sr. Francisco Villa in the north and Emiliano Zapata in the south. Guided and protected by them, we are determined to see that our Revolution is no longer led astray. From now on we want things to be done not for the sake of appearances but for the true benefit of the poor."

I answered, "Sres. Delegates of the Revolutionary Chiefs of the South, in my judgment all of us who joined in the struggle against Huerta are brothers, and in our triumph we seek no establishment of a new tyranny but the advent of just laws. You have done well to respond to my request and come to the Convention and you will do well to protect it by your decisions, whatever they may be, since the Convention is being held for the purpose of blocking the new tyranny and seeing that the men who enlighten us in the business of politics form a good government and prepare for the application of the laws which our justice demands."

At this time Carranza sent a message to the Convention stating why he was not coming and explaining the motives of his conduct and the conditions on which he would give up his office if we demanded it. The contents of that message, which revealed his ill will toward me, were as follows:

Señores of the Military Convention:

I have your invitation, and I reply that I cannot come because of the dangers which prevail in the city of Aguascalientes. It is not prudent to commit acts which could leave the government of our Republic without its Chief. Besides, in order to settle the differences between this office and Sr. General Villa, it is best for neither of us to appear there. Even if I wished to go, I would not; if I presented myself as Chief, the assembly could not work freely, and if I presented myself there as a general or governor, I would reduce myself to the rank of the others and that would handicap me as Chief.

Still, I consider it my duty to write you that I wish to contribute to the settlement of all the differences. In my judgment, the true cause of those differences lies in the reactionary elements which, in order to wreck our cause, have begun to surround the principal Revolutionary chiefs and whisper words which stir their ambitions. Nobody should assume that I have personal ambitions or wish to govern or seek to command; but if anyone does assume it, my acts will speak better than words, since time reveals as much as it conceals.

In regard to the military chiefs who come as my enemies, I say that their sole motive is ambition, which they prove by saying that they renounce the presidency of the Republic without referring to their powerful military command which they wish to preserve forever. There is an ambition greater than that of being President of the Republic, and it is military power, which allows one man alone to make or unmake presidents and hold the authority of government. This is obviously true of General Villa, in view of the fact that he does not desire to renounce the command of the Northern Division which he esteems an omnipotent thing, and in view of his aims of putting the Constitution into operation and of naming a civilian president, by which the aforesaid chief aspires to be the creator of all the future of Mexico, and the one who makes the laws and revokes them, and the one who names presidents and deputies and judges and the one who controls the power of the Republic. What I say of Pancho Villa, I also believe of Emiliano Zapata, although in truth I do not know what the pretensions of the other General are.

With respect to me, I add that your causes for demanding my departure from this office of First Chief are not yet known to me. However, I am not opposed to leaving my post as First Chief or as Representative of the Executive Power or to leaving the country, but I will do so only if the Convention considers it necessary and if it takes measures to make good use of the sacrifice it imposes upon me. Thus I want that Convention to tell me if it considers my departure necessary to re-establish harmony and secure our final victory, and if my presence in those posts is an obstacle to the attainment of our ideals.

The Convention must make this appraisal, and if it decides that I must go, then I will go, but only in case the following conditions are also fulfilled: a provisional government is formed, charged with instituting Revolutionary reforms before our Constitution is again put into effect; General Francisco Villa renounces not the presidency of our Republic, since no one offers it to him, but the command of the Northern Division; he and I retire to private life; he leaves our territory if the Convention decides that I also must go. I also ask that Zapata renounce his command of the forces of the south and retire to private life and withdraw to another country. If these conditions are met, I will retire; if they are not, I will not retire because I am unwilling for the Convention to deliver our Republic over to the personal ambitions of certain chiefs or to the representatives of the reactionary forces.

Carranza seems to have made his proposals with the intention of blocking any kind of settlement. He well knew that Zapata and I were in league with no reaction, but on the contrary were seeking immediate reforms for the benefit of the people, and that if he himself was now beginning to express himself on such reforms and declare that he supported them, he was echoing our demand, not of his own wishes but because he had grown uneasy on discovering that all the Revolutionaries shared our views.

If there had been no other reason for removing Carranza from office, the tone in which he addressed the Convention would have been reason enough.

CHAPTER 20

Uneasy before the Decisions of the Convention, Carranza, in His Struggle With Villa, Makes the Possibilities of Settlement More Remote.

The Railroad Workers' Circular. Maclovio Herrera and Sóstenes Garza. Dawn at Parral on October 23. The Guanajuato Barracks. Major Sarabia and Major Ballesteros. Eight Hundred Prisoners. Order and Counterorder by Villa. Carranza's Reply to Villa's Manifesto. Carranza's Advice to the Convention.

Señor! Carranza was so blind in his hatred of me that he halted traffic on all the railroads of Mexico on learning of a circular in which the railroad men supported me. It read as follows: "The Union of the Constitutionalist Railway Workers resolve to circulate as widely as possible General Villa's Manifesto. Railway workers, we are guardians of our Revolution; we must comply with our duty; we must be prepared to suffer if necessary for the welfare of our country!"

For one whole day Carranza halted the work on every line, and finally, to pacify him, his favorites had to persuade him it was not certain whether the signatures on the circular were genuine or its contents true.

It was now that Maclovio Herrera committed an act of treachery against me. I had sent the forces of Chao and Hernández to Parral, and as a result of our advance, Maclovio and Luis Herrera had withdrawn to a place called Mesa de Sandías. The day after my troops arrived, Sóstenes Garza, second-in-command of Chao's forces, communicated with Maclovio and explained that while the Convention was working to avoid war they should respect its orders, all the more since Maclovio and Luis Herrera had delegates at the Convention. And as Maclovio sent word that he agreed and would not fight unless attacked, a truce was agreed upon, pending the work of the Convention. My men at Parral, trusting the Herreras, grew careless while waiting, and their innocence favored Maclovio's designs. One day at dawn, I think on the twenty-third of October, Maclovio deliberately attacked and killed many of my men while they were asleep and resting unarmed near their wives and continued his work of destruction until they drove him back and defeated him.

Let me tell you about that combat. I had over a thousand men in Parral. Maclovio too had over a thousand, whom he brought in by way of the Materanas Hills to fall upon us by surprise. The enemy had moved so silently that at the first moment they were able to reach the interior of a large corral where sixty of Chao's men were guarding the horses, and killed these men and their wives without mercy; at the second moment a fierce attack raged along the streets as my men rushed out of their lodgings in alarm and, not knowing how to meet the assault, died in many cases in front of their own houses, among these one of Manuel Chao's brothers-in-law and other good Revolutionary men. The struggle grew more and more one-sided, they were pushing us back from our protected spots and Hernández' men were abandoning most of the points they occupied. By the time Maclovio entered Parral the only strong point was held by three hundred of Manuel Chao's men in the Guanajuato Barracks, and while the rest of our forces were trying to retreat in safety or were scattering in the darkness, Maclovio threw the main body of his troops against the barracks, determined to surround it and take it. He succeeded in surrounding it but did not take it because the chief who commanded there, Major Sarabia, was a man of such great courage that he did not even withdraw the guard from the door or try to fortify his position but dominated the street with rifle fire, and as fast as men fell replaced them with others, and thus and with the help of Major Ballesteros, who was guarding the bridge to keep the enemy from using it in their attack, they succeeding in holding their positions until sunup.

What happened then is easy to believe: with the light of day, whether because Hernández appeared or for some other reason, the troops that had fled in panic in the darkness of the night returned to throw themselves on Maclovio's troops encircling the Guanajuato Barracks; and the enemy, caught between two fires, was demoralized and routed, with so much disorder in their ranks that disaster followed and Maclovio abandoned the field and fled, leaving I know not how many dead and wounded and eight hundred men who surrendered their arms on seeing that they were fighting against their brothers.

Maclovio Herrera, Chapoy, and others, I learned, fled toward Jiménez and did not stop until they had reached the Sierra Mojada in the state

of Coahuila. Luis Herrera, with no more than forty men, fled toward
Sinaloa. And that was the end of Maclovio's treachery at Parral, which
brought death to many of our men.

By telegraph I promoted Major Sarabia to lieutenant colonel, and I
did the same for all the chiefs and officers who assisted in that feat of
arms. It is also true that being furious over what had occurred I ordered
the prisoners shot, but was persuaded to reconsider by persons I had
with me, among them Llorente and Guzmán.

At this time Carranza published a reply to our Manifesto. He said:

There are lies in Francisco Villa's renouncement which I shall answer with
the truth. He expresses his great love for Madero but he forgets that he and
Pascual Orozco, after the taking of Ciudad Juárez in 1911, tried to overthrow
him by force of arms, for which Villa was then in danger of being shot.

He says that I refused to accept the democratic settlement proposed by the
conferences of Torreón but forgets that I did not promise to accept the result
of those conferences. He declares he could have no confidence in the meeting
of generals and governors I convoked, since only the governors and generals
I named would attend it, but fails to consider that those men would act
honorably.

He accuses me of wanting to remain in my office of First Chief but forgets
that the Plan of Guadalupe, which he recognized, obligates me to take over
the Executive Power on entering the capital and to hold it until peace is
established and the new government is elected on the date that I announce.
He is sure that this reveals my ambition, but he does not look ahead and see
that I would belie it immediately, renouncing my offices of First Chief and
Representative of the Executive Power as I renounced them before the meeting of generals and governors, a renunciation which the generals and governors unanimously rejected. He affirms that I have objected to calling myself
Interim President in order not to be bound in the acts of government, but he
forgets that the Plan of Guadalupe did not require me to take this title and
that since Huerta destroyed all lawful order there is nothing else which requires me to do it.

He condemns me for making the functionaries and employees of my government promise to preserve and to have preserved the articles of the Plan of
Guadalupe instead of the mandates of our Constitution, but forgets that he has
disposed of the haciendas of Chihuahua without respect for the owners, whom
he has had shot, and that he killed the Englishman William Benton without a
thought of the international objections he would provoke. He says that I
have refused to choose ministers to enlighten me with their advice in the
dispatch of business, but he does not consider that in the absence of laws

obliging me to make the appointments, I have no reason to do it, especially since I have government functionaries, and they advise me as well as ministers.

He declares that I have combined in my person the three powers of government, the legislative, the executive, and the judicial, not considering that the Plan of Guadalupe prescribes this and that it is the natural course of our Revolution; nor does he see that in Chihuahua, to which my authority does not extend, the lives and interests of nationals and foreigners are in his inept and unrestrained hands, guided by men who did away with Francisco I. Madero and by Felipe Angeles, a Federal soldier who was with me but soon went there to exercise his worst influence.

He accuses me of offending the sentiments of the people by prohibiting the use of churches and punishing the practice of religion, but he forgets that he has expelled Catholic priests from almost every place his troops have occupied, and that he has closed churches, and has vented his fury on the foreign priests of Zacatecas, three of whom have never been heard of again.

He reproaches me for having issued 130 million pesos in paper money, but does not say that he has issued 12 million and that he has spent another 10 million that I sent him, and now, I am told, is ready to issue 30 million more, so that the Northern Division alone costs our nation more than the Northeastern and Northwestern Army Corps together.

He accuses me of having committed hostilities against him, ordering the suspension of the railroad traffic between Aguascalientes and Zacatecas and between Monterrey and Torreón when he attempted to shoot General Obregón in Chihuahua, but he does not say that when I asked him for an explanation of his conduct, he answered me with a threatening message, declaring that his generals would not attend the meeting I had convoked and denying my authority as Chief, which act, and not mine, would begin the war. By reason of this, I say that his accusations against me are unjust and unfounded.

Thus he disdainfully replied to our reasonable motives for denying his authority. The truth is that he damaged his position with the message in which he laid down his conditions for retiring. By reports that reached him the next day he learned that almost all the delegates felt inclined to remove him from his post. Then he sent the second telegram, in which he declared that he had not resigned his office and would not unless the conditions he imposed were fulfilled beforehand.

CHAPTER 21

Villa Proposes to the Convention that He and Carranza Be Shot in Order To Avoid Another War.

"If Villa Could Only Write." Carranza's Knowledge and Villa's Ignorance. Luis Cabrera's Writing. The First Chief's Message. Decisions of the Convention. Eulalio Gutiérrez, President. Carranza in Puebla. Francisco Coss. Pablo González. The Commission of Villarreal and Obregón.

Carranza condemned me for not being the author of published documents which carried my signature. He did this in his passionate desire to belittle me, not to discuss the thought in the written words. He would say, "If Pancho Villa could write, if Pancho Villa could read what others write." And I thought, "Why is it a crime for a man not to know how to write laws when he could not learn that or anything else because nobody ever taught him? Am I to blame for knowing little when I have to learn that little without help or guidance or instruction? Isn't it worse for Carranza, born into a rich family, and schooled since childhood, to get someone else to compose the messages he sends to the Convention? We do know that many of his papers are written by the lawyer Luis Cabrera, but we do not stoop to say that they are not Carranza's or look down on him for not writing them himself. If he were a well-meaning and highly intelligent man, he would not point this out to ridicule me, because it is to my credit that the school of suffering alone has enabled me to go farther than some men who have had the benefit of long study."

Although it is true that Carranza was complicating things with his message, most of the delegates considered his removal good for our cause and for peace; and in order to show no favoritism they likewise decided to remove me from my command. They adopted the following resolution:

It is to the advantage of our Revolution to remove Venustiano Carranza from his position as First Chief and remove General Francisco Villa from his position as chief of the Northern Division.

It is to the advantage of our Revolution to appoint an Interim President.

It is to the advantage of our Revolution to recognize Citizen Venustiano Carranza as a division general and to thank him and Citizen Francisco Villa for their patriotism and their many and great services for the good of our cause.

It is to the advantage of our Revolution to abolish the offices of chiefs of the Army Corps, and generals who now hold them will remain, with General Villa, under the orders of the Minister of War of the new government.

Regarding General Emiliano Zapata, the reply to Citizen Carranza is that nothing can be decided in this case since the Revolutionary men of the south do not yet recognize the sovereign authority of this Convention.

When those decisions were known in Aguascalientes, Felipe Angeles and some of my men had a telegraphic conference with me. Angeles said:

Sr. General Villa:
In his message to this Convention, Carranza makes it a requisite for his retirement from the office of First Chief that you also retire from your position as chief of the Northern Division. I advise you, my General, to accept this for the sake of peace. If you agree with me, telegraph General Robles, who is here with me, and authorize him to declare that you will give up your command.

I answered:

I propose not only that the Convention retire Carranza from his post in exchange for retiring me from mine but that the Convention order both of us shot.

They were so surprised that they telegraphed to ask if they could draw up a formal act stating what I had just told them and read it to the Convention along with Carranza's answer. I said yes, they might draw up whatever act they wished, with all the signatures and seals necessary, and publish it if they saw fit, and then come and see that I kept my promise.

The third of November, the Convention, with my delegates and Zapata's concurring, resolved to choose Eulalio Gutiérrez as President of the Republic and to inform Carranza that he had ceased to represent the Executive Power and me that I had ceased to be the chief of the Northern Division. At this meeting they read the statement in which I submitted to all the measures of the Convention and advised that Carranza and I should be shot as the best guarantee of the peace. I assume, from what they told me later, that nobody then doubted my patriotism or my love for our cause, for my words were heard to great applause.

Juan G. Cabral, General Martín Espinosa, and others were commissioned to tell me that I was no longer chief of the Northern Division and that I was to deliver my forces, my arms, my munitions, my warehouses, my railroads, and my territory to the government of Gutiérrez. I received the commissioners in my best manner, and in reply to their message and the paper they delivered I had Luisito write an official communication of acknowledgment.

This was my answer:

Sres. Generals and Governors of the Convention:
I am informed of the removal of Carranza from his position as First Chief and your decision to retire me from the command of the Northern Division. I accept your decision and await your orders.

It was sad to think how lonely and quiet I was going to be, but since my retirement would benefit the cause, I looked on it as no punishment but a reward, and if Carranza's retirement was obtained only so, it was one more battle I had won. But Carranza, bent upon resistance rather than obedience, slipped out of the capital on the pretext of going to reconnoiter his new territory. In Puebla, among his favorites, with the troops of Francisco Coss at hand, he encouraged the General, who was also the Governor, to rebel against the Convention. Coss telegraphed:

I have a report that the Convention has dismissed Sr. Carranza as Representative of the Executive Power of the Republic and appointed General Eulalio Gutiérrez to replace him. I consider this decision invalid, and withdraw from the Convention, and as governor of this state of Puebla and military chief of five thousand men who obey me, I recognize no Constitutionalist First Chief or President of our Republic except Venustiano Carranza.

I cannot tell, after so long a time, who was more to blame for the rebellion, Carranza who instigated it or General Coss who yielded to his instigation. The two of them, one in his desire to command, and the other in his readiness to follow, renewed the war, creating discord among the other generals and governors in Aguascalientes. But if the blame was equal, the dishonor was greater on the part of Coss, who was violating a sacred promise made on the flag of the Convention, at which he still had his representative.

Pablo González, in Querétaro, also decided to reject the agreement. Learning that the forces of José Isabel Robles, Gutiérrez' Minister of War, had entered Aguascalientes, he addressed the Convention with these words:

I have received messages that the troops of Robles have entered the city of Aguascalientes by permission of the Convention. I consider that this violates the neutrality of that city, and do not recognize any of the agreements made there.

But the day after he sent the telegram, he changed his mind: he accepted the presence of Robles' troops in Aguascalientes, also the agreements, including the one abolishing the offices of chief of the army corps.

Carranza telegraphed his refusal on the same date, saying:

As that Convention has not complied with the conditions on which I agreed to relinquish the Executive Power, I refuse to recognize Eulalio Gutiérrez as President in my place. My act has the approval and support of Generals Pablo González, Francisco Coss, Francisco Murguía, and other chiefs of the Northeastern Army Corps, and when it is known, I will be joined by other generals of the Constitutionalist Army, who will give me their aid and renounce everything that Convention has done against me.

Venustiano Carranza

He was throwing us into armed struggle without having the least certainty of what the Convention had done. And further, knowing that Villarreal, Obregón, Aguirre Benavides, and other delegates were coming to talk with him in the name of the Convention, he would not see them at once, as I had received Cabral's commission, but ordered González to have them wait in Querétaro for a new order. In other words the commissioners had to hold a long telegraphic conversation with him and promise that if he listened to them he would be under no obligation to answer, and only after this would he agree to let them pass. Even then he disdained to wait for them in Puebla, where he was, but went on to Córdoba to show them how little regard he had for them as representatives of the Convention, having already slighted and offended them by stopping them on the road and pronouncing their commission illegal, so that he could receive them as friends but not as envoys.

CHAPTER 22

Carranza Does Not Recognize the Sovereignty of the Convention. The Convention Declares Him a Rebel and Prepares To Fight Him with the Aid of Villa.

Telegraphic Conferences. Obregón and Carranza State Their Purposes. President Gutiérrez. Orizaba and Córdoba. Obregón, Hay, and Villarreal. Carranza's Answer. The Plan of Guadalupe and the Sovereignty of the Convention. The First Step toward War.

From Querétaro the delegates wired:

Señor, we commissioners of the Convention of Aguascalientes are waiting for your permission to proceed. We bring the answer to your request, and beg you to order González to let us pass.

He answered:

The action of the Convention has been unfavorable to me. For that reason it is imprudent to allow you to advance. Wait until I finish the business that keeps me here and then I will come to Querétaro.

They replied:

Señor, there is no time to wait. The Convention is in session and must know the result of our mission to conclude its business. Other commissioners went to talk with Sr. General Villa, who received them and gave them a satisfactory answer. We insist upon the urgency of our business and its importance to the future of our cause.

He answered:

My interests will not permit me to change my decision as to the time and place of our meeting, and I say this knowing that your commission is composed of my best friends. For me you are an instrument of the Convention which must not cause trouble in my territory at a time when I am occupied with the evacuation of Veracruz, from which the American troops are ready to depart.

They explained:

Señor, as a condition of the resignation of your command, you required that Pancho Villa should resign from his. The Convention accepted the condition; it has not worked without regard for you but has accepted your offer believing it to be inspired by patriotism and knowing how often you had spoken to your friends of your willingness to retire if General Villa would do so at the same time. Now that your offer has been accepted and acted upon, we cannot understand your readiness to bring war upon us.

And he argued:

I cannot say by telegraph all that should be said regarding the agreements at the Convention, but we shall discuss everything when I find time to talk. I am still ready to retire, but must first settle political matters which you and other chiefs entrusted to me when you put yourselves under my orders. The Convention has offended, scorned, and attacked me, unmindful of the dignity of my position, yet I remain calm, as I ask you to be, so that with minds at ease we can put our thoughts into words.

They said:

Señor, we wish only to deliver the paper sent by the Sovereign Convention; it is not our purpose to demand an immediate answer; nor do we consider you obligated to answer us except at the time and place you find convenient. We beg you then to let us pass and not to hold us responsible for the offenses of the Convention, although in our patriotism and our willingness to support Gutiérrez we will be the ones to choose the President of the preconstitutional government.

He then answered:

Very well, Señores, if this is your intention, you can follow until I have time to settle this business.

So the commissioners followed him from Querétaro to Puebla, but he did not wait for them there. They went on to Orizaba; but he sent word to Orizaba that he was called to Córdoba. They proceeded at serious risk to their personal safety, for Carrancista soldiers in Orizaba attempted to kill them, and in Córdoba some of Carranza's favorites openly protested against the Convention and its agencies.

When at last they overtook him in Córdoba, he gave them a very cool reception and entered into a discussion in which he told them that he would not relinquish his authority until he was convinced that I had given up mine and was certain that a form of government was set up that would guarantee the objectives he sought for our cause. In view of later actions of three of those envoys, Obregón, Eduardo Hay, and Villarreal, I now believe that he convinced them the agreements of the Convention were unwise, but I don't know whether he won them over or whether, though intelligent men, they were confused.

When Gutiérrez was named President, the Convention directed these words to the people:

Mexicans:

We are assembled in Convention to settle all differences between the Revolutionaries and to create a government of law, not tyranny. This is a Sovereign Convention, for it embraces the men who achieved the defeat of the usurpers and is concerned with the future of our people. We have appointed a Provisional President to govern us and make the reforms the people expect; and we have promised to support him and free him from obstacles raised by rebellious men.

In reply to these words, President Gutiérrez delivered his own message:

Mexicans:

I have taken an oath before the Convention to fulfill the agreements we make here, and the nation can be sure I will spare no effort or sacrifice to keep that oath. The mandates of the Constitution are not now in force, having been annulled by the usurpers, and only the Convention of Aguascalientes can dictate the rules of the new government. I count upon receiving the help of all the people and hope that all Revolutionaries will come to my aid.

As for Carranza, this was his answer:

Citizen Chiefs and Governors:

The errors of the Convention are great, and I cannot respect its decision to have me deliver my command and government over to Eulalio Gutiérrez. I have not renounced my command; I have only stated the conditions under which I would renounce it, and in appointing a President to take my place the Convention has committed an act of insubordination and disregard for the commitments of the Plan of Guadalupe. Without enacting a law to regulate the acts of the future government you decide that I should deliver my authority to that government in which there is danger of dictatorship or anarchy.

I agreed to resign after General Francisco Villa, but you decide that he and I should leave together, which shows a lack of respect for me. The Convention agreed that General Villa and I were to retire on the sixth of November, and it is now the eighth and it is certain that Villa is still in possession of his command, his customs houses, his post offices, his telegraphs, his railroads, and everything embraced within the limits of his jurisdiction.

I agreed to retire only after Emiliano Zapata also retired, but the acts of the Convention serve only to strengthen Zapata.

Since you have chosen Gutiérrez as President, many generals and governors

have protested. Nevertheless, rather than have you accuse me of not complying with my promise I propose the following in my sincere desire to save our
Republic from further bloodshed:

I, Venustiano Carranza, will deliver the authority of the nation to the
President named by the assembly for the entire period which is called preconstitutional, or for the time it takes, in my judgment, to effect the reforms
our people want; I, Venustiano Carranza, will make this delivery when the
new President has received authority from you and when the Northern
Division is in his control, with its military offices, government offices, railroads,
and matériel.

Everyone saw that Carranza's answer was that of a great schemer
who only wanted to keep the Convention involved in never-ending
work. He answered with arrogance, laying down his own conditions;
his arguments were false; he was even a traitor, for at the same time that
he bargained with the Convention he was publishing proclamations
against it in his newspapers and calling the Carrancistas to arms, declaring that the Convention would bring us to ruin. His reply disgusted
the men of the Convention. Still, Gutiérrez wired to convince him of his
error and point out the responsibility he would incur if he pushed us
into a new war.

Eulalio said:

Sr. General Carranza:

The Convention has appointed me President of our Republic and relieved
you of your authority. For that reason you cannot continue in that office
pending the acceptance of new conditions.

You may be sure, Señor, that I have not solicited this office; but having
been appointed to it, I will comply with my oath. It is not true, as you believe,
that I will cease to be President within twenty days. Until the Convention
elects a successor I will continue to be the President. I am the legitimate
authority in our country, which you must respect and obey as representing all
the Revolutionaries and not a single group only. I insist upon your recognizing
me as your superior and promise that your services to our cause will always be
appreciated.

You will note that I have no Villistas or Carrancistas or Zapatistas with me
but only men who support the national government and are concerned with
the general welfare, and among whom you should figure, for if our differences
are not resolved we are going to have the bloodiest civil war we have ever had,
and not for principle, as in the war just ended, but solely out of personal
ambition. General Villa has already relinquished the command of the Northern
Division and I have already named representatives to receive his offices and
papers; since yesterday his forces are under my orders, and if the said offices

and papers have not yet been received and General Villa is still here, it is because we are waiting for your decision. Once you manifest your respect for the resolutions of the Convention, General Villa will complete his act of resignation by retiring.

Gutiérrez could not have spoken better. I had already put all my troops under the orders of José Isabel Robles, Minister of War of the new government, and I intended to retire without even evoking the memory of the great command I had held. But Carranza answered no, that he did not recognize Gutiérrez or the authority of the Convention to name a President and would surrender power only in conformity with methods and laws he considered good. If Gutiérrez was a patriot and a disinterested party he would himself retire; the Convention was not sovereign inasmuch as he had not granted the sovereignty; it was false that I had retired; perhaps I was there in the telegraph office giving Gutiérrez bad advice; and all the Revolutionaries in convention assembled could not annul a single law nor did they have the right to reject the conditions he fixed for leaving, for there was no law but the Plan of Guadalupe, according to which he was the First Chief and Representative of the Executive Power and would continue to be until he renounced his responsibilities.

With this Gutiérrez ended the telegraphic conference and read Carranza's message to the Convention, which decided that Carranza was a rebel and leading us into war.

CHAPTER 23

Villa Is Appointed General of the Convention's Troops and Obregón and González Decide To Fight against Him.

Villa's Submission. Obregón's Message. Telegrams from González. The Evacuation of Veracruz. Bryan Addresses Villa, Carranza, and Gutiérrez. The Difficult Situation of the Provisional President. The Convention's Orders. José Isabel Robles. Eulalio Gutiérrez Makes His Last Effort.

When I learned of Gutiérrez' appointment I sent him a message of compliance, without being asked or advised by anyone. I said: "Sr. President of the Republic: You have my greatest respect, Señor, and I am ready to obey your orders."

At the very moment I was doing this, Carranza issued orders from Córdoba for the chiefs at the Convention to leave and resume their commands before six in the afternoon of November 10, 1914, under pain, otherwise, of being replaced by others. He declared the acts or mandates of the Convention were to be disregarded and only his orders to be obeyed.

The next day Obregón sent me this message:

Sr. General Villa:

I am informed that the Northern Division is advancing south of Aguascalientes. It is time, Sr. General, to prove by deeds and not by words that you are a patriot who considers only the cause of the people. Retire from your command and I promise you that Carranza will retire from his when the new President is elected in this capital. If you cooperate in this way, you will save our country from the approaching struggle and figure in history as one of our great men, of whom there are so few. If you do not, the curse of our country will fall upon your head although you have achieved great glory by your arms and have been acclaimed a patriot. Be guided by your conscience.

He was telegraphing all my generals to a different effect, saying that most of my victories were due to them and so I was obligated to listen to their advice and that if they came to me and asked me to accept his proposal surely I would do so if only to please them.

González and other chiefs were telegraphing to the men of the Convention: "Señores, in the name of patriotism we ask that Convention to exclude Villa from any part in the military and political life of our country. We promise to try to persuade Carranza to go also." To their First Chief they were telegraphing: "Sr. Carranza, confronted by the dangers of another war, we think it necessary that you retire; but if you do not retire, and if Gutiérrez and the Convention do not satisfy our desire for Pancho Villa to leave now and forever, we declare that with the greatest pleasure we will fight on your side for law and justice."

Obregón was wiring to his generals—the Arrietas, Juan Dozal, Jesús M. Ferreira, Pablo González, and I know not how many others—that if I would not retire, he was determined to fight against me with all his forces and expected them to do the same. He should have told them that he would first fight Carranza or would fight him too.

In his answers to the Convention Carranza claimed to be engaged in the serious and difficult business of getting the United States to withdraw their forces from Veracruz. But the truth was that the Convention had already accepted American proposals for withdrawal and authorized Carranza to meet them at the moment when he ostensibly accepted them solely on his own authority as First Chief. Mr. Bryan then informed the three of us, Gutiérrez, Carranza, and me, that measures had been dictated for the evacuation of American troops from Veracruz on the twenty-third of November.

When the Carrancistas kept insisting that only Villa should leave, not Carranza, Gutiérrez saw what was happening: they wanted him to risk facing the consequences of my departure without the advantages of having Carranza leave at the same time. In view of this the Convention decided, with Gutiérrez' approval, to appoint me as the general of the Convention troops until Carranza agreed to resign his post. This done, Gutiérrez answered González and Obregón:

Sres. Generals:
In reply to your messages regarding the retirement of General Villa, I inform you that he was relieved of his command according to the orders of the Sovereign Convention and I notified Sr. Carranza in the hope that he too would retire for the common benefit. But since in our judgment his refusal to do so makes him a rebel against my legitimate authority and obliges us to subdue him by force, the Convention and I have decided to entrust to the aforesaid General Villa the command of operations to be developed under my orders or those of my Minister of War. You may be sure that once Sr. Carranza respects the mandates of the Convention, General Villa will retire again, and I will be personally responsible for his retirement inasmuch as he respects my authority.

González answered:

Sr. General Eulalio Gutiérrez:

As of this moment I sever allegiance to the Convention of Aguascalientes and commit all my forces to the struggle against the Villista bandits.

Upon this, José Isabel Robles commented, "My General, the war can no longer be averted. González is threatening us with his advance troops in Lagos and León, and in Mexico City Obregón and other chiefs are making preparations for the struggle."

I replied, "Sr. General, our responsibility is great, and it is clear that the situation will grow worse. Your ministers of government must get the Carrancistas to persuade Carranza to respect our resolutions and retire, as I have agreed to do."

Gutiérrez arranged to have a personal talk with González at a place north of San Francisco del Rincón, where the track had been destroyed to stop our advance, and there the two conferred.

Gutiérrez declared, "Sr. General, I am the legitimate President elected by the Convention, and it is my duty to execute the orders of the Convention and bring Revolutionaries into harmony. You know that Villa has agreed to retire provided that Carranza does also. I beg you then to see Carranza and, in the name of all, convince him of his great error in leading us into this struggle. Tell him that I guarantee that Villa will retire at the same time he does and that it is only necessary for him to say he is ready to comply with the orders of the Convention."

But González did not wish to believe this and said that he was not sure that I would agree to go. But when Eulalio convinced him that I was sincere and demonstrated that he was determined to be a strong President, he finally yielded and promised to go to Córdoba and convince Carranza. In return he asked the Convention to move no troops while he was carrying out his commission. It was agreed to give Carranza time to decide; a truce was arranged to last until an answer was received from Pablo González.

As I remember, on the fourteenth of November Gutiérrez sent Carranza a telegram in which he granted him a period of twenty-four hours to declare his respect for the government of the Convention and warned him that it would be a serious error to bring on war and that the responsibility would be heavy for whoever was to blame. The next day Carranza replied that he had communicated his final answer to Pablo González. On his way back from Mexico City, González wired Gutiérrez that the answer was favorable, and that Sr. Carranza would surrender his authority on condition that he and I, Pancho Villa, left the country. Relieved to learn this, he notified Obregón and other generals that he was pleased to accept Sr. Carranza's last requirements.

But the next day Carranza, again through Pablo González, retracted what had been telegraphed the night before and declared he would surrender his authority only to a man like González, in whom he had complete confidence, and that I should deliver my command to Gutié-rrez, whereupon González, Gutiérrez, and the Convention would meet in Mexico City to appoint a President, and immediately he and I would leave the Republic together and be in La Habana on the twenty-fifth of November. Gutiérrez replied that the acceptance of those conditions was not in his hands, and he telegraphed the same to Alvaro Obregón.

CHAPTER 24

Seeing Pancho Villa at the Head of the Convention's Troops, Carranza's Men Revile Him Unmercifully.

The Federals Hiding in Guadalajara. Teodoro Elizondo. The Retreat of the Northeastern Army Corps. Villa, According to González. Villa, According to Obregón. Villa, According to Salvador Alvarado. George C. Carothers. The Impartiality of Wilson and Bryan.

I saw that Carranza's ambition was leading us into a hard and bitter struggle and began to study measures for strengthening the government of the Convention. I sent orders to my financial agency and Juan N. Medina in Ciudad Juárez to hasten the purchases of arms and matériel and took into my ranks whatever officers of the old Federal army came to offer their services in recognition of our victory and in the same way I attended to all the rest.

I remember that some of the Federal officers who came to join me had been in hiding in Guadalajara; they had supported Huerta, they told me, out of military duty, not that they loved the usurpers, and now, with that government conquered and its army nonexistent, they were free to adopt the Revolutionary cause, in which they saw that I was struggling for the welfare of the people while Carranza was making the same mistakes that our Revolution had just overcome. I found sincerity in their words and thought too that a man should not be damned forever for having been a Federal soldier under Huerta. I accepted them and told them to go after their compañeros, and gave them official papers so that they could put themselves under the orders of Julián and Jesús Medina, who were in San Juan del Teul in the state of Zacatecas.

The war began with an enveloping movement and the sudden capture of a division González had placed under the command of Teodoro Elizondo at San Francisco del Rincón. This first step was due solely to the impulsive force of our advance. It seemed to indicate that González' other troops would be overcome, for many of his chiefs abandoned him and gave their support to the Convention, and others followed him hesitantly in the retreat he ordered.

They retreated from León to Silao, from Silao to Querétaro, from Querétaro to San Juan del Río, and from San Juan del Río to Tula, without my knowing whether he intended to make a stand at some point or whether his withdrawal was only imposed upon him by events as they occurred during his march.

Step by step as he abandoned that territory to me, he reviled me in the newspapers in Mexico City. He said:

I fought against Porfirio Díaz' tyranny and Victoriano Huerta's usurpation, and I am now determined to fight against Pancho Villa's reaction. The Northern Division is made up of soldiers without honor. The neutrality of Aguascalientes was agreed on, and Francisco Villa broke it. A truce was agreed on between my troops and the so-called government of Eulalio Gutiérrez, and Francisco Villa broke it in the surprise advance of a traitor. Mexicans! The assassins of Sr. Madero are with Francisco Villa and intend to bring ruin to our country; but Venustiano Carranza will challenge them.

In great bitterness other Carrancistas were publishing horrible things about me. Obregón was saying:

Mexicans, that monster of treason and crime called Pancho Villa rises up to devour the cause that has cost us so many lives. He is united in a trinity of hate with Maytorena and Angeles. The three are deformed creatures who celebrate the agony of our country in a dance of death. It is time for Mexico's good sons to know that the devotees of waste, revelry, and licentiousness are with Pancho Villa and that we, the devotees of sorrow and privation, are with

Carranza, and on our death will leave to our children the sole heritage of an honored name.

Let us look at our native land: in agony she is searching to see how many of her good sons remain. Let us look at Pancho Villa, who preaches patriotism but exudes poison through his eyes and calls it tears of love for the people. Mexicans, our native land implores us to resist the reign of evil and struggle until we conquer or convert our country into a vast cemetery, for otherwise the fiendish ministers of Evil and Crime will govern us and infect and corrode and poison us.

Mexican mothers, Mexican wives, Mexican daughters, kneel at the altar of our country and condemn Francisco Villa, the monster of reaction, and call your children, your husbands, and your fathers to duty lest the traitors who form the Northern Division continue to twist their dagger in the vital organs of our native land!

And Salvador Alvarado was proclaiming:

Venustiano Carranza is a great man and a patriot, as he demonstrated by consenting to exile provided his sacrifice would serve to free Mexico from Pancho Villa, who is worse than Victoriano Huerta. If Huerta was a disgrace to Mexico which we Mexicans had to wash away with blood, Pancho Villa is a still greater disgrace who repeats Huerta's crimes, and we will have to rid ourselves of this evil man although it requires still greater bloodshed.

Pancho Villa did not win the battles that made him famous; another general won them for him, a great Revolutionary and a great soldier named Maclovio Herrera. Pancho Villa murdered William Benton and horrified the world; he has committed other crimes which are still worse; he is the bandit Doroteo Arango who hides in the uniform of a chief of the Northern Division; he is the minister of Cain and Caco, as his countenance betrays; he is the caveman who nourishes himself upon bones and raw flesh and the roots of trees. Pancho Villa's mind seethes with perverse thoughts. His evil conscience makes him an eternal robber, eternal traitor, eternal assassin.

Mexicans, if Pancho Villa triumphs in this war, think of what that will mean for our native land. Brave men and patriots will die; women will be dishonored; children will never know the light of goodness; and all for the sake of Pancho Villa's orgies and robberies and assassinations. He has soldiers like Felipe Angeles, Tomás Urbina, and Rodolfo Fierro, and listens to the advice of Manuel Bonilla, Miguel Silva, González Garza, Castilla Brito, and many other charlatans and prevaricators like the nefarious relatives of Sr. Madero who were the principal cause of that apostle's death.

They were painting me as they knew I was not, and I could not comprehend the true reason for their enmity. González knew that I did not violate the neutrality of the city of Aguascalientes. He knew that I did not break the truce which he and Eulalio Gutiérrez agreed upon, for the truce was supposed to end when Carranza's answer was known. He knew that the assassins of Sr. Madero and of his brother Gustavo were not with me and that I had been the first to wreak my vengeance on them and their instigators, as I showed by shooting Bonales Sandoval.

I thought, "Why, Señor, does he accuse me of crimes I have not committed? Obregón knows I would not celebrate the agony of our country with any dance because there are many and positive proofs that my men and I are committed to the fulfilment of our duty. What daggers do I drive into the vital organs of our native land? Am I the Minister of Evil for not wanting to abandon the people to the evil designs of the Chief? Am I the monster of treason because Carranza would not surrender his command when I was ready to surrender mine? What are the orgies I indulge in, being always concerned with the care of my troops, and what are the orgies of my men who have won the greatest battles of our cause?

"And Salvador Alvarado, who was always congratulating me on my triumphs over the usurpers, knows that I am not worse than Huerta. He knows that I entered this struggle for the people to fulfil my duty, not to hide past crimes, for I wished to hide nothing, and have nothing to hide. Those crimes were the result of my ignorance or inexperience when I was struggling against tyranny."

A few days before they were telegraphing me that I would go down in history along with our great men if I consented to retire, and now they were declaring that from the moment of my birth I was a man brought into the world as the Minister of Evil. At the same time they were saying that the true instigators of all the evils were the group of men who were guiding me by their advice. They were saying, "Mr. George Carothers appears in the White House before President Wilson and declares that Villa is the greatest man in Mexico, and then he returns to our country and whispers to our Revolutionary chiefs that President Wilson will recognize no government that does not have the support of General Villa. Secretly he convinced the Convention of Aguascalientes that its decisions would receive aid from Washington. Secretly he works to create disagreements in our Mexican family and thus invites the intervention of the United States in our affairs."

They were saying all this to discredit the Convention, accusing it of being an instrument of the United States while themselves fishing for foreign sympathy and while the lawyer Rafael Zubarán was in Washington for that purpose.

But I, Pancho Villa, say that they were doing a very great injustice to Mr. Carothers, to Mr. Bryan who kept him near me, and to Mr. Wilson, who decided what that government would do in consequence of reports it was receiving. That was evident when Veracruz was finally evacuated and Mr. Wilson's words to the commanding officer were: "Señor, carry out the evacuation without implying recognition of Venustiano Carranza or any other chief."

CHAPTER 25

Villa Endures the Displeasures of Politics in Public and Suffers the Agony of His Passions in Secret.

Weaknesses of Great Men. The *Tertulias* and Dances at Jiménez. Conchita del Hierro and Her Aunt. "It Is a Pity You Are Married, Sr. General." A Conversation about Love. The Letter of Promise. Jacobo Velázquez. Martín López. Villa's Disappointment. A Talk With Luisito.

Chiefs of great armies are only men. They cannot always control their impulses or unworthy purposes. I make this reflection because I was in a disturbed state of mind during the days of the Convention of Aguascalientes and knew that my unrest was the effect of my passions, not of fears arising from the state of our affairs. I was unable to master my feelings for the better performance of my duty, and they plagued me more and more as we advanced toward the city.

What was troubling me was this: in Jiménez, where I had been many times, I had met a very nice family by the name of Del Hierro, an aunt and two nieces—Anita, the older, and Conchita, the younger. They were well-bred persons who attended the *tertulias* and dances given in my honor; and as Conchita was beautiful of body and eyes and coloring,

I was attracted and soon fell in love with her. It happened that Conchita's aunt was always coming to talk with me about the vicissitudes of life and the great need in which they found themselves. I felt sorry for them, and sympathized and tried to help them. And one time the aunt said she knew of my love for Conchita and added, "It is a pity that you are married, Sr. General!"

"Why is it a pity?"

"Because as I see it, Sr. General Villa, Conchita was destined to fall in love with you."

"It happens, Señora, that marriage is one thing, and love is another."

So we continued talking, she, I imagine, with the purpose of discovering my true intentions, and I, with great interest in what she was revealing and in knowing something of Conchita's thoughts.

Then we had another talk. She asked whether in truth I was a good man, as might be inferred from the money and other assistance I brought them. I answered yes, that Pancho Villa was considered a good man. She asked me whether, being a good man, I would fall into the error of abandoning a woman who loved me but suffered some misfortune. I answered no, that I considered it my duty to take care of all who bestowed their affection upon me, especially if they were women. She asked me if my being married would prevent me from making another woman happy. I answered that I did not know, nor could I, since the woman's happiness would depend on her as well as me, and on the serenity of her mind and her devotion to me and her intention, if her love was true, of causing me no trouble.

She meditated on my answers and then spoke quite frankly, saying, "Very well, Sr. General Villa, Conchita loves you but she is ashamed, thinking that if you are married you cannot honorably take another woman. But I want her to be happy, and I shall try to convince her that her affection is pure because God wills it, and I shall tell her that yours is true and advise her to accept your protection, just as a wife accepts the protection of a husband. But on one condition, Sr. General; swear that if she comes to you, you will look on her as a man looks on the woman who is his own and will never abandon her or those she loves."

These were the conditions on which she made her offer. I swore to do as she requested, and took that oath with the honest intention of keeping it, for I was longing for that Conchita; and in proof of my sincerity, I asked the lady about her present and future needs and those of her nieces, and gave her all she requested and more. And as I was very anxious to consummate that union she was describing I insisted that she should make her promises good that very day, but she informed me that she could not do so and asked me to be patient for a few days since it was an affair that could not be hurried. She said, "Be calm and restrain yourself, Sr. General. These are not acts of war which men perform whenever their arms permit. They are problems of the conscience and the heart, which travel other roads. Even so, you can be sure that my promises are as sure as the light of day and you and Conchita will know the happiness I have planned for you."

Afterward, when I was in Guadalupe, Zacatecas, I received a letter from the lady informing me of the success of her efforts. She wrote:

Sr. General Villa:

This matter is now arranged according to your desires and mine, and as it is favorable to the future of my niece Conchita, she responds amiably to your noble attitude and accepts the agreements you and I have made in our talk. We are here at your orders, Sr. General, to welcome you whenever you come, or if you wish, you may arrange for Conchita and me to visit you in Guadalupe.

I felt so much satisfaction in merely reading her letter that I called Jacobo Velásquez, my engineer and a man in whom I had complete confidence, and said, "Amigo, take an officer of my escort and an engine and caboose and go to Jiménez to bring some lady friends of mine who are coming to discuss some business matters with me."

I called Martín López and repeated my instructions with regard to the train. I also told him that he was to bring Conchita safely to Guadalupe and that it was his responsibility to see that she received the most considerate treatment on the road with her every request gratified. He was to bring her as quickly as possible.

They left with these orders. And the next night Conchita del Hierro and her aunt arrived at my headquarters in Guadalupe. Wishing to receive them with the greatest courtesy, I went in person to meet them at the train. As Conchita greeted me with friendly words and a smile I knew that she was offering me her affection. I felt as if she belonged to me, and put my arm around her in a protective manner. And so we walked together with her aunt and Martín López to the car.

That night when Conchita's aunt and I were alone she said, "Sr. General Villa, as you see, I have kept my promise; and it is time for you to keep yours. Conchita is yours, and solely because she trusts in your affection." But a little later I began to wonder, and by the next day I was in a state of great confusion, doubting that the lady had told me the truth and suspecting that perhaps she had deceived me as to Conchita's consent. It was possible too that Conchita had come willingly, only to repent more and more each hour.

She talked of nothing but her dishonor, and when not telling me she let me understand it in other ways. She locked herself in the room we were occupying and wept all day, determined that nobody should see her or know of her presence or hear her speak. Only by night, when she was protected by darkness, would she go out walking for a few minutes, with her face covered. I thought, "Very well, Señor. This business has turned out different from what we expected, but time will take care of it."

But Conchita's grief increased instead of diminishing. Many days and nights passed in this way: she weeping and bemoaning her shame and dishonor, and I searching my conscience for proof of my crime. Although I realized that Conchita was hurting me by her conduct and I saw how much I displeased her and how much she disliked me, I was not angry with her but with myself. Nor did I reproach her or condemn her for her offenses, but I reproached myself, without knowing whether my meekness was due to affection or to my determination to win her.

I asked Luisito, "Luisito, what does this woman have in her soul? I offered my love, she accepted it, and it was decent and fine and honorable and religious. Señor! She came here on her own feet! Why does she offend me with her tears and wish to die? What have I done except to love and caress her?"

He answered, "Those are difficult things to say, my General."

"Whatever you think, speak."

"I do not think this woman loves you, my General."

"Very well. There may be women who do not love me. But if this one came to me, and I accepted her, why does she regret her acts and look on me as the cause of her unhappiness? I love her, Luisito, I really love her, and I tell her so, and demonstrate it with all sincerity. What more can she ask? Am I not good enough for the best of women of my people?"

"You are a married man, my General."

"Yes, Luisito, but marriage is one thing and love is another."

"For some women there is no love without honor, my General."

"Isn't it honor enough that Pancho Villa, being married already, chooses a woman and loves her and wins her and cherishes her? Marriage, Luisito, is contracted only for fear that love will end, and you can be sure that it is no honor to a woman for a man to be true to her only because religious and civil laws compel him. A man honors every woman he loves and protects with his affection."

"Your wife is in Chihuahua, my General."

"Good, Luisito, the honor of my marriage is there, and the honor of my love is here."

"It is as I said before, my General: if Conchita does not give you her affection, she finds neither honor nor love with you."

We two talked in this way for a long time. I was trying to overcome my bitterness. I wanted to be certain I was not to blame and I wanted Conchita to stop looking at me in horror.

BOOK **5** *The Adversities of Fortune*

Villa Leaves Aguascalientes and Undertakes His Advance to Mexico City as González and Obregón Abandon Him.

Gutiérrez' Problems. A Commission of Lawyers. Julio Madero. Luis Aguirre Benavides and Rodolfo Fierro. Carranza's Propaganda. A Letter for Emilio Madero. Celaya. Gertrudis G. Sánchez. Villa's Doubts about the Forces of Michoacán. "Who Are You To Demand More Help?" Acts of Generosity.

Eulalio Gutiérrez questioned the advisability of leaving me in command of the Convention's troops, free now for the struggle against Carranza and the chiefs who supported him; and many of our men and I questioned that same thing; perhaps it was my duty to retire to private life even though Carranza did not, and if I took up the struggle in support of the Convention, my promises to leave might be generally considered false. But later Gutiérrez and I deliberated and agreed that I should remain as chief. I would be of great assistance to the troops and the disadvantages of my separation outweighed those of my presence. With this thought, Gutiérrez left for San Luis Potosí to begin the organization of his government, and I began my march to the south.

To Irapuato came some lawyers by train from Mexico City. They were looking for Gutiérrez to propose a settlement and, learning that I was there, they asked to board my train and greet me; among them were Don Fernando Iglesias Calderón and other men well versed in law. I answered I would be honored by their presence and glad to talk with them.

They said, "We come here, Sr. General, in an effort to avoid the outbreak of war. The Revolutionary chiefs have been holding meetings in Mexico City, and all are in favor of supporting Gutiérrez provided the agreements of the Convention are observed."

On my asking them which of the agreements had to be observed, they answered, "Sr. General Villa, they ask you to retire so that Carranza will also agree to retire."

"Señores, if I am not mistaken, you propose the same old thing. It is not a question of having me leave to see whether Venustiano Carranza will also leave; Carranza must go, and to obtain that I am willing to go too, which was his condition. But if Carranza does not go but stays, and if he does not obey the orders of the Convention but ignores and defies them, why should Gutiérrez' legitimate government weaken itself by depriving me of my command? I was ready to go with Carranza, and I am still ready. Carranza says that he does not accept, that he will not go when I go but after I have gone, and that before he goes the Convention must name a President to his liking, and before he delivers authority to that President, the Convention must pass a law not according to Convention wishes, but as he conceives and dictates it. Who can fail to see in all this that Carranza will never consent to go?"

The lawyers understood that their trip in search of Gutiérrez would get nowhere and asked me to authorize their return to Mexico City, which I did. While their train was switching at the side of mine, one of the cars was left standing even with my headquarters, and Julio Madero appeared at one of the little windows. He belonged to Obregón's staff and was the officer who, in the days when I was having my talks with that General, had gone to El Paso with secret messages telling Benjamín Hill not to obey the orders that Obregón and I were sending from Chihuahua. Luisito and Rodolfo Fierro saw him from my car, and as they were friends, the three of them fell to talking. Madero said, "I came with the commission to seek an interview with Gutiérrez."

Fierro answered, "The commission should have its interview with Carranza."

"No, Señores, the interview will be with Gutiérrez over removing Villa from his command."

Luisito answered, "My General Villa has said many times that he is willing to go."

"Yes, he says it, but it is not true. The only true things about Pancho Villa are his criminal record and his ambition, which will bring us ruin. He is an assassin and a traitor. He wants power to revel in the banditry that made him famous in Durango. For this reason he hates Carranza and attempted to shoot Obregón in Chihuahua."

Fierro smiled at these words. He answered, "Leave your General Carranza and your General Obregón and come with us. General Villa will teach you the ways of men."

I had entered the room where they were talking, and they, absorbed in what they were saying, did not notice my presence, nor did Julio

Madero. I heard it all, thinking calmly, "The boy is repeating the propaganda they are spreading against me. He is to blame for his words but not for his thoughts and deserves only to be corrected and turned from the wrong road."

I approached to where he could see me, and he was alarmed. "So, my little friend," I said, "is this what you think of Pancho Villa? Your words offend the memory of your brother, the apostle Francisco I. Madero, who seated me at his table because he considered me a Revolutionary, not a bandit, and you offend your brothers Emilio and Raúl, who have joined me and recognize me as their chief and respect me as their general." He showed signs of being grieved, but he was not ashamed or cowardly, and in moderate terms, very different from his insults, he declared that I ought to leave my post for the good of the Republic—if I did not soon withdraw, our cause would be lost.

Considering his case a family affair, I said, "Luisito, write a letter to Don Emilio Madero in Torreón, telling him of this incident. Say that I am sending the boy there to be reprimanded. They must rid him of these ideas of his, or if not, send him to the United States with orders to proceed to Veracruz, from where he can continue to fight against us, and I will treat him as an enemy and not as a brother of Sr. Madero." To the boy himself I said, "My friend, here is a letter committing you to the custody of your brother Emilio, who is in command of Torreón. This is the officer who will take you there and protect you on the road. Go with God, and know by these acts of mine that Pancho Villa is not a reckless criminal. Your brother Emilio will judge you."

General Gertrudis Sánchez came to Celaya by train from Morelia, accompanied, as I remember, by Juan Espinosa Córdoba, Joaquín Amaro, and other chiefs of his and an escort. They were saying that they supported the government of the Convention, but I doubted their sincerity and had little opinion of their abilities, for I knew of no great battles Gertrudis Sánchez had fought or just how he had contributed to destroying Huerta's armies.

He came to see me with enormous requests for arms and money, "Sr. General, I respect the government of the Convention, and I recognize your position as chief. Michoacán is one territory in which neither Carranza nor any of his favorites will tread. But, Sr. General, I lack matériel, and I need money. I come to you, Señor, as our general in chief, asking you to supply me until the government of the Convention is organized and provides me with the necessities." Partly because I doubted him and partly to see what kind of man he was, I answered,

"Very well, Compañero: I will order 50,000 cartridges and 100,000 pesos delivered to you."

"That is very little, Sr. General. If you cannot give me more, I think it better to give me nothing."

I answered in anger, "Who are you to demand more help? And why do you want arms and munitions if you do not know how to use them? What battles did you fight in the war against Huerta? Don't you realize that if I give you all the money and ammunition you ask for, I run the risk of having the Carrancista forces take them away from you? Don't you know that Francisco Murguía is in Toluca and that if he is pushed out by Zapata he will perhaps seek an exit through Michoacán? Do you consider, Sr. General, that you and your chiefs have the strength to sustain yourselves with the supplies you request?" And seeing that he made no answer, I added, "I am ordering your escort disarmed, and as of this moment you are my prisoner."

He answered, "I came for aid because the two of us serve the same cause, and I did it in the spirit of an inferior addressing a superior. But if you consider that I do not deserve the command, I respect that judgment too." He was calm and humble, so that I was disturbed and retired to one of my rooms, and later sent for him and embraced him, saying, "If you know how to obey as you are obeying now, you also know how to command."

And I called Luisito and said, "Luisito, deliver 500,000 cartridges and one million pesos to General Gertrudis Sánchez."

CHAPTER 2

Villa and Zapata Celebrate in Xochimilco and Seal Their Union in Defense of the Cause of the People.

Carranza's Withdrawal. Advance of the Northern Division and the Army of the South. Pachuca. Veracruz. Azcapotzalco and Tacuba. Angeles' Proclamation. Counterfeiters. Lucio Blanco. San Gregorio. The Flowers of Xochimilco. The Men of the North and the Men of the South. Secret Pacts. A Dinner.

At that time, when my advance troops were following González, we knew that Obregón was leaving Mexico City and Zapata and his men of the south were approaching step by step. Carranza was waiting to receive the port of Veracruz from General Funston, in order to take shelter in those rich districts and waters, and González was withdrawing from Tula to Pachuca, with the intention of taking refuge in the same port, along with Carranza and Obregón.

The movements of the Carrancista troops revealed which were really remaining with Carranza and which were recognizing the authority of Gutiérrez, and there was great confusion among the chiefs who commanded them. Obregón succeeded in leaving Mexico City with only his infantry and his artillery, augmented by the artillery the Federals had delivered to him there, for his cavalry under Lucio Blanco took the road to Toluca, being inclined to respect the government of the Convention. González left Pachuca so precipitately that my advance troops dispersed his rear guard and, broken in this way, neither they nor he could reach the road to Veracruz but fled toward the Huasteca district, leaving us arms, munitions, money, their trains, and some cannon and machine guns. It was the greater disaster for him because many of his chiefs, recognizing the government of the Convention and not wishing to be Carrancistas, came with their men to join me.

As I remember, I reached Mexico City, or rather the municipalities of Tacuba and Azcapotzalco, on the second of December, 1914. I left my headquarters, expecting to consult with Gutiérrez on the way to enter the city, since he had just arrived, as had José Isabel Robles and the Convention delegates. Zapata's forces and my vanguard under Felipe Angeles were already there.

I had said to Angeles, "Señor, your troops will occupy the capital, and you will be in command of all the vanguard. My intention is not to disturb the peaceful inhabitants in any way or permit the slightest disturbance of order; this is especially important in the presence of foreign diplomats, who will praise or condemn us according to our acts." He consequently published a military order prescribing the death penalty for infractions of public order. The day after my arrival they brought me five or six prisoners accused of counterfeiting our money and defrauding the poor; I had them tried immediately by my court martial and when they were sentenced to death, I ordered them shot the next morning at ten. The counterfeiters were sons of good families. Many ladies urged clemency, but I refused, thinking robbery by the rich an unpardonable crime.

I made my entrance on the third of December with Gutiérrez and the members of the Convention. Accompanying Gutiérrez were his ministers of government among whom were numbered, as I remember, many good Revolutionaries like Robles, the lawyer Paulino Martínez, the engineer Felícitos Villarreal, the lawyer José Vasconcelos and other civilized men, like the engineer Valentín Gama, who was a relative of the lawyer Antonio Díaz Soto y Gama, one of Zapata's envoys at the Convention. Gutiérrez had made good appointments, and I was confident that he would create the government necessary to our cause while I carried on my shoulders the responsibilities of war.

Eulalio arranged for some of his envoys to talk with Lucio Blanco, then encamped with his forces in the state of Mexico; and to persuade him to delay no longer in recognizing the government of the Convention, I proposed a conference with Zapata, who had not waited for us but had returned south uncertain of the day of my arrival. When he immediately accepted, we arranged to see each other the next day at Xochimilco.

So it was. I went there accompanied by José Isabel Robles, Roque González Garza, Luisito, and some other men of mine. In the barrio of San Gregorio, while waiting for Zapata, I had to dismount to acknowledge the greetings of the inhabitants and receive their flowers and caress their children. Señor! If the whole town welcomed me with such affection, how could I do less? It was then that I saw Emiliano Zapata approaching, surrounded by his retinue. I went forward to greet him and presented him with one of the bouquets they had pressed upon me.

"Sr. General Zapata, today I realize my dream of meeting the chief of the great Revolution of the South."

"And I now realize that same dream regarding the chief of the Northern Division."

I thought, "It is not chance but justice that I, Pancho Villa, who was persecuted as a boy and man by the rich and powerful, should come in person to unite the north and the south in their struggle for the cause of the poor. For Zapata embodies the struggle of men here as I do that of men yonder." Emiliano Zapata and I, Pancho Villa, entered Xochimilco together, with all the town awaiting our passage through the streets and women and girls applauding us. So many were the bouquets and wreaths that our men could not carry them and our horses were walking on them while we rejoiced in our hearts.

Our interview took place in the Municipal School, or the Municipal Palace. Acting with me were the men I have mentioned, and with Zapata were his brother Eufemio, General Manuel Palafox, Professor Otilio Montaño, a woman named Prudencia Cassals, Paulino Martínez, Alfredo Serratos, Serafín Robles, and several others whose names I do not remember. Likewise present were Mr. George Carothers, the representative of Mr. Bryan, and Mr. Leon Canova, the representative of Mr. Wilson.

Where we were talking many people were listening, so that we could not prudently reveal our purposes, and I suggested that we continue our talk in privacy. In an inner room we conferred for more than an hour, at the end of which time he promised me the assistance of all his forces, and I promised him mine. Two days later we would enter Mexico City together so that all might know where the strength of the people lay, and I offered him munitions for his advance on the Carrancistas in the state of Puebla—and thus with many other topics.

Upon the conclusion of our agreement, we went with the Mexicans and foreigners who accompanied us, to attend the dinner the authorities had prepared. It was all very cordial. And I, Pancho Villa, say that Emiliano Zapata offered me a drink, which I accepted although in truth it was not my habit. "Compañero, I accept this drink solely for the pleasure of joining you, for the truth is that I never drink liquor." I drank it. I remember also that one of the American journalists approached us during dinner and asked us to answer his questions. I told him what I thought the men of the north had done for the Revolution; but Zapata, in response to the same question, said something quite different. "Señor, tell the readers of newspapers in the United States that the Revolution of the South was won with no help but that of our mountains. Our arms are what we have collected in our territory; our ammunition, what our

land has furnished us or what our hands have produced; our money, the
silver which we took from our mines or from our enemies."

I took no offense, though we in the north had fought with arms and
ammunition from the United States and with paper money we made in
our printing shops, not with silver we took from the mines. Since it was
true that Zapata had sustained himself as he said, why should I grow
angry at his boasting of it? Could he have resented it if I had declared
that the men of the north alone were responsible for the destruction of
Huerta's armies? How could he, Señor, when it was true?

CHAPTER 3

The Armies of Zapata and Villa Parade in Triumph through Mexico City while Carranza Makes Preparations in Veracruz.

La Calzada de la Verónica. The Acclamation of the
People. Zapata's Hat. A Banquet in the Palace. Pancho
Villa, Orator. The First Ministers of Gutiérrez. A Meeting
in the Palace. Carranza and Obregón. Zapata to Puebla.

On the day after our interview, Zapata and I had
a telephone conversation about our parade in which we agreed that he
would start from San Angel and Mixcoac and I from Tacuba and its
vicinity. We also agreed that his staff would come to the Calzada de la
Verónica, where I would wait for him, and from there we would continue to the doors of the National Palace. And so it was. The next
morning, December 6, 1914, we began a parade through the streets of
Mexico City which lasted until five that afternoon. My men maintained
a very orderly formation which showed off their discipline and our
arms to good effect. The people of the city welcomed us all with the
greatest enthusiasm and affection: Gutiérrez, Zapata, Angeles, and me
and the Convention delegates and other chiefs. Señor! How the young
ladies showered us with their flowers! They made a little basket of
Zapata's hat until the bouquets bent the brim with their weight and

overflowed. The diplomatic corps saw and estimated the Revolutionary troops and their praise was warm.

That same day Gutiérrez had an official banquet at the Palace in honor of the armies, the ministers of the government, the members of the Convention, the diplomats, and others. Placing me on his right, Gutiérrez said, "You are here at my side, Sr. General, because your troops are the strongest protection of our cause." And placing Zapata on his left, he said, "And you are at my side, Sr. General Zapata, because the Revolutionary spirit of the men of the south will keep the ideals of the people alive."

Then we sat down and ate. It happened that José Vasconcelos was on my right. He was the young boy who told me in Chihuahua that I would be the hero of the Revolution. Now he talked to me at length, saying, among other things, "Sr. General, with Pancho Villa and Emiliano Zapata together at the table the union of the people is consummated, and the day of justice has dawned."

I answered, "Señor, justice will come when you incorporate the welfare of the people in our laws and we sustain it with our arms."

A day or two after the parade we had a ceremony in honor of Francisco I. Madero, José María Pino Suárez, and Aquiles Serdán. Street placards that the people had dedicated to them had disappeared when Carranza's troops left Mexico City, without its being known what criminal hands were responsible. To make reparation the authorities requested that I be the one to replace the names with my own hand. At ten in the morning on the seventh or eighth of December, I went with Rodolfo Fierro, other men of mine, a military band, and I do not remember how many people, to where the shop called La Esmeralda was situated. I climbed an improvised stairway and at one corner of the shop unveiled the replacement of Sr. Madero's name, and at another unveiled the name of Sr. Pino Suárez. The band was playing our national hymn, all the soldiers stood at attention and all the civilians removed their hats. We then went to another corner where I unveiled the name of Sr. Madero again and from there to a plaza to unveil that of Aquiles Serdán.

At the conclusion of these ceremonies Zapata and I were accompanied by General Felipe Angeles, José Isabel Robles, Raulito and Dionisio Triana, and many other soldiers and civilians to the pantheon in which the remains of Sr. Madero rested. Together we dwelt upon the memory of that great apostle of the people's happiness, and laid our wreaths on the marble stones, and delivered our speeches. Dr. Miguel Silva made so beautiful a speech on Sr. Madero's martyrdom and his dreams for the good of our country that we were very deeply touched. When he had finished speaking to us, they urged me too to speak, and, unable to refuse such solicitude, though knowing how poor my ideas were and how badly expressed, I consented.

I said, "Mexicans: I have no words to utter the sentiments of my heart. Sr. Madero was a good man, a just man, who wanted to end the suffering of the poor forever. Unworthy Mexicans, ambitious men, betrayed him and assassinated him. Then, conscience-stricken, the honorable men of the North took up arms against Victoriano Huerta, and the honorable men of the South did the same. We went into the struggle determined to persevere until we had punished the authors of the crime. And now, Señores, we are here, men of the North and the South, our duty fulfilled. But even so, standing beside this tomb, our hearts grow sadder, for Sr. Madero died not only at the hands of his enemies but because his friends gave him little or no support, and this includes us all."

As I spoke I was overcome by my grief, and as I pronounced these last words my sorrow rose in my throat and I could not continue for sobbing. On seeing me weep, they wept with me, and our tribute to Sr. Madero was the tears that fell on his tomb.

At that time the first ministers appointed by Eulalio Gutiérrez took the oath. These were not all he intended to choose but only José Isabel Robles, Felícitos Villarreal, Valentín Gama, the lawyer Miguel Alessio Robles, who had brought me the message from González during the battle of Zacatecas, the engineer Rodríguez Cabo, and José Vasconcelos, also a lawyer. After the oath, the ministers held a council in the Palace, and soon after that Emiliano Zapata and I met with Gutiérrez and José Isabel Robles to discuss the distribution of command and the plan of operation against Carranza and his chiefs.

Not only were the Carrancistas in control from Puebla to Veracruz and in the Isthmus, Yucatán, Jalisco, Tepic, and Sinaloa, but they were growing strong in the northeast, which a little earlier had been controlled by Pablo González, and where Luis Caballero and Antonio I. Villarreal were already in arms, with Maclovio Herrera who had joined them. Nor was it yet known which side Lucio Blanco would support in the states of Mexico and Michoacán nor Luis Gutiérrez in Coahuila. The latter was Eulalio Gutiérrez' brother, but he had not agreed to recognize our government.

The confusion was great, and a furious struggle awaited us. We knew that Obregón was organizing troops in Veracruz, Tlaxcala, and Puebla and seeking communications with Mazatlán from Salina Cruz in an effort to make contact with Manuel Diéguez in Jalisco and Iturbe's forces in Sinaloa, where Felipe Riveros had not succeeded in establishing his authority. We knew also that Carranza was building his resources and creating agencies to discredit us with civilized nations and writing letters and messages to the Convention chiefs to turn them against us. Under cover of the confusion, the Carrancistas were fighting a vicious war of slander. Obregón was publishing his lies in papers in Veracruz, which he was sending to dishonor me in my own territory. He said:

Pancho Villa is a traitor, an assassin, and a robber. He betrayed Sr. Madero in Ciudad Juárez and tried to assassinate him, and there he began a life of constant treachery. He tried to betray Huerta when this traitor was still faithful to Madero. He assassinated the good Revolutionary García de la Cadena. He assassinated the Englishman William Benton. He tried to assassinate General Manuel Chao. He tried to assassinate me for not agreeing to unite with him in treason against Sr. Carranza. He seized millions of pesos and dollars which were in our Treasury at Ciudad Juárez. He made a traitor of José María Maytorena. He assassinated Colonel Manzanera, Domingo Arrieta's enemy at the Convention of Aguascalientes. He exploits gambling in his territory for the purpose of living a sinful life and squandering money on himself and his family. He tried to conspire with José Refugio Velasco to keep the Federals from surrendering Mexico City to me on the consummation of our triumph over Huerta. He tried to assassinate Lieutenant Colonel Julio Madero, who was passing through Irapuato on the discharge of a commission. He has made a pact with the Federals of Baja California, which is treason to the Revolutionary cause.

With me he was slandering Maytorena and Angeles, calling us the Unholy Trinity, the head of the reactionary movement, and he asserted that everything we three did was a work of assassination and treason and if the Convention triumphed, Mexico would be ruled by the government of three traitors.

On the day we visited the tomb of Madero, Zapata and I went to talk with Gutiérrez, who was ill. As already agreed with Robles, we named Zapata chief of operations in the states of the south, and laid down the plan of campaign his men would carry out. According to this, once he had Puebla, which his forces were already threatening to take from Salvador Alvarado and other Carrancistas, he would advance on Veracruz and then attack and take Oaxaca. I would leave for the north, where urgent business was calling me, and make arrangements at Irapuato for the departure of my troops, who would destroy Diéguez in Jalisco and then go on to Colima and Tepic.

I had doubts of Zapata's ability to overcome Obregón in Puebla and Veracruz or to face his attacks. But Zapata saw that as his line of advance and I wanted to respect it. I thought, "We must wait for the results of the first encounters. Zapata is a good Revolutionary and a brave man; if he fails to conquer, he will still be able to maintain himself in his territory, as he has done for years. And if he needs my help, he will ask for it. Why should I volunteer it at the risk of his taking offense?"

I limited myself to supplying arms, munitions, and advice, and undertook the trip north immediately after dictating my measures for the column that was to leave for the conquest of Jalisco.

CHAPTER 4

The Day after the Convention Troops Enter Mexico City, Villa and Gutiérrez Begin To Disagree.

Guillermo García Aragón. David Berlanga. Rodolfo Fierro. At the San Cosme Barracks. Don Hilario Lozoya. Nicolás Fernández. Don Sabás Lozoya. An Envoy from Robles. Paulino Martínez. Manuel Palafox. Antonio Díaz Soto y Gama. To Chihuahua. Carranza's New Law.

In my first conversations with Zapata he had said, "Sr. General Villa, among the generals of the Convention there is one who is disguised as a good Revolutionary but in truth is only a very bad influence. This is Guillermo García Aragón, and according to my reports Gutiérrez has chosen him as governor of the Palace. Deliver him to me, Señor. I won't take him by force since you are charged with protecting the delegates of the Convention."

I accepted his opinion, for he was as good a judge of men and their deeds in his territory as I was in mine. That afternoon I had General García Aragón held as a prisoner and the next day some of Zapata's men came to take him away. When Eulalio Gutiérrez knew what had happened, he sent me a message asking me to free García Aragón who, besides being a delegate to the Convention, was his Palace governor. I replied that the prisoner was already in the hands of Zapata.

Another delegate, David Berlanga, a schoolteacher with the rank of lieutenant colonel, was going around at all hours abusing me in the streets and cantinas and restaurants, where he was telling everyone that I was a bandit and a menace to the country. I instructed Rodolfo Fierro to watch him and if there was real harm in what he did or said, to seize him. The next day Fierro said, "My General, I have Berlanga imprisoned in the San Cosme Barracks. He was accusing all the men of the Northern Division last night, and his worst accusations were against you."

"What did he accuse me of?"

"You and the Northern Division will be our ruin unless Gutiérrez relies upon good Revolutionaries instead of being supported by bandits like Pancho Villa and Emiliano Zapata." I went to the Barracks with Fierro, Luisito, and others to examine Berlanga. He attempted to justify himself and prove the purity of his intentions. I gave orders for him to be shot at once and he heard them calmly and courageously.

Today I can see how difficult it was for me to restrain my anger when men were trying to estrange Gutiérrez and me. Another man, Hilario Lozoya, who had been governor of Durango in the days of Huerta, was a prisoner in the same barracks. I ordered him brought before me and berated him. He became restive as he listened and began to weep; and when he realized that they were going to shoot him, he got down on his knees and wept again and caught hold of my legs and begged for mercy. But I would not let him justify himself and ordered them to shoot him. They were on the point of doing this, but as we were leaving the barracks, Nicolás Fernández called Luisito aside and whispered in his ear; and then Luisito approached and said, "My General, Nicolás Fernández says that a mistake is being made."

"What mistake, Luisito?"

"In shooting Don Hilario Lozoya, my General."

"No, Luisito, there is no mistake. The men who supported the crimes of Huerta must be shot."

Then he explained that the man was not Don Hilario Lozoya at all, but a brother of his, Don Sabás, owner of the hacienda in Durango called Agua Zarca. "Nicolás Fernández, who was his foreman there, confirms it." My anger subsided and I called Nicolás Fernández to straighten the matter out. Greatly disturbed in thought, I revoked my orders and even wanted to release Don Sabás but, considering the gravity of the error my sudden anger had led me to commit, I decided that he should remain there to await justice.

Gutiérrez knew of the deaths of Guillermo García Aragón and David Berlanga. After meeting with his council of ministers he sent to inquire whether I was responsible and to notify me that the attitude of the Convention had greatly changed.

I answered, "Señor, I can tell you nothing about the death of General García Aragón, who was alive when my escort delivered him to Zapata's men. As for David Berlanga, it was necessary to shoot him so no one would think for a minute that you and I are at odds." This happened when I was about to leave for Irapuato to establish headquarters for the campaign against Manuel Diéguez, in Jalisco, and at the time nothing more was said about the affairs.

In Irapuato the next day an envoy of Robles came to say, "General Robles sends you word that Zapata is exposed to influences that may lead to disunity in the government. This is the work of the journalist Paulino Martínez, General Manuel Palafox, and the lawyer Antonio Díaz Soto y Gama. General Robles believes it urgent for you to check this before it spreads."

By chance another man I trusted, Don Luis de la Garza Cárdenas, arrived that day from Torreón. He brought the worst of reports on Paulino Martínez who, as the *Voice of Juárez* printed, had been a merciless enemy of Sr. Madero's. Paulino Martínez, I thought, and perhaps General Manuel Palafox, Zapata's secretary, and the lawyer Díaz Soto y Gama, his advisor, deserved no consideration. I sent Fierro back to Mexico City to confer with Robles, saying, "If it is best to shoot Paulino Martínez or General Palafox or the lawyer Díaz Soto y Gama, shoot them."

And what happened was that the next night, December 14, 1914, Fierro called Martínez from his house on the pretext that Robles requested his presence at the Ministry of War, and took him to the San Cosme Barracks and shot and buried him. He did this in obedience to my orders and by advice of Robles; and in my judgment we did well to defend the cause of the people in this way, when we were surrounded by intrigues. Still, as would be seen, I could not thus free myself from the entanglements in which men were trying to involve me with their plots, nor was I to free Robles, who would soon be misled and abandon the path of duty.

With my headquarters established in Irapuato, I made a trip to

Chihuahua. Reports reached me there of the new plan that Carranza was announcing in Veracruz. These were his words:

In the army organized for the struggle against the Usurpation, the divisions of the Northeast, the Northwest, the Center, and the South always respected orders from my office, and great harmony resulted. This was not the case with the Northern Division under Francisco Villa, who soon revealed his personal ambitions and ended by refusing me his obedience. When the triumph of our Revolution was consummated, I was prepared to organize the new government and wanted to make the new laws that the public demanded; but everything failed before the obstacles created by the Northern Division, which conspired with reactionaries to prevent the development of our constitutional ideals.

I convoked a meeting of generals and governors in Mexico City to institute the laws of the new government and the needed reforms and to fix a date for the election of new leaders; but the said meeting had to be moved to Aguascalientes, where it lost its freedom of action, subjected to the dictates of the Northern Division and General Villa; for that reason many of the chiefs gathered there repudiated it and returned to follow my leadership. This has brought about our present struggle in which my role is to protect the welfare of our country and see that the truth is known.

The men that support Villa are those who blocked Madero's efforts on behalf of the people; Villa is a reactionary, determined to obstruct our constitutional triumph; it is the duty of the Revolution to carry on the same struggle against him that we began against Victoriano Huerta.

For this purpose, acting in accord with my generals and governors, I order the continuance of the Plan of Guadalupe which recognizes me as the First Chief of our cause and calls for maintaining the office of Chief until the enemy is conquered and peace is established. In that time I plan to make the laws I think necessary and carry out agrarian, labor, tax, judicial, municipal, religious, and military reforms and any other reforms the people want. I will organize and command our army; appoint and remove ministers of government, military chiefs, governors, and all employees of the federation, the states, and the municipalities; print money; make loans; authorize expenditures; keep account of them; and take over properties; and so on. That is, I will be the sole authority until we triumph.

As I remember, this was the new law by which Carranza authorized himself to command without interference for I know not how many years. But in truth he was promising reforms that my generals and I, and Antonio I. Villarreal and other chiefs of González' had demanded in the conferences at Torreón but which Carranza did not then accept. While accusing me of reaction, he was paying me the compliment of adopting my program.

He had tried to be a tyrant without regard for the aspirations of the people. Seeing that he could not, he now promised within the framework of tyranny the things we were seeking within the framework of liberty.

CHAPTER 5

On Entering Guadalajara, Villa Senses Gutié-rrez' Uneasiness from His Conversations with Juan Cabral.

A Letter from Obregón. The Manifesto of Luis Caballero. Angeles' Plan of Attack. Zapata's Route and Villa's Fears. A Warning from Emilio Madero. Villa's Plan of Attack. Manuel Peláez. Estación Corona. Guadalajara. The Churches and the Welfare of the People. Juan G. Cabral's Mission.

While Carranza was announcing his political plans against my person, many of his generals were supporting him with words as well as arms. Obregón was condemning Gutiérrez for joining me. Through the newspapers he said to him:

Sr. General Eulalio Gutiérrez:
    Confess that on many occasions in Aguascalientes you declared before me, José Isabel Robles, Manuel Chao, and Eugenio Aguirre Benavides that Francisco Villa was a bandit and assassin, and a threat to the future of our Revolution. Confess that you deplored the efforts other good Revolutionaries and I were making in the interests of harmony, and said to us, "Pancho Villa is a man who understands nothing but bullets; Pancho Villa is a man who must be removed." I ask you only this: Did Villa cease being a bandit by the sole fact of your calling him to protect you in your war upon us, the honorable chiefs who refused to serve his ambitions? Did you forsake your honor, Señor, to conspire with Villa and go to war against your best compañeros? I say all this, General Gutiérrez, because it pains me to see you turned into an instrument of treason.

Obregón was trying to alienate Gutiérrez and me, and me and Robles and Chao and Eugenio Aguirre Benavides. Obregón was a man who used the lie whenever it suited him in the circumstances of the struggle. If Gutiérrez had thought what Obregón said, would he have chosen me as chief of the Convention armies?

Many of Carranza's chiefs were publishing such things. Luis Caballero said:

I call to arms again the honorable men who followed me against Porfirio Díaz and Victoriano Huerta. We combat a new tyranny. Revolutionaries of Tamaulipas: nourished in the heart of our Republic is a cursed and unrighteous trinity headed by the bandit Francisco Villa; duty demands that we go forth to annihilate him.

Angeles had said when he arrived in Mexico City, "My General, we must not allow the enemy to reorganize or let him flee to the districts of Veracruz. Carranza is a relentless politician; Alvaro Obregón is a soldier of great malice and many resources. If we give them time they will organize and fortify themselves. Carranza will create difficulties in Washington through Rafael Zubarán and Eliseo Arredondo, who represent him there; Obregón will weaken us with slander and bring discord among us and damage to our prestige. Throw the Northern Division against Veracruz at once and stop only when we have defeated the enemy and pushed him into the sea."

I answered, "Sr. General, the cause of the people follows many roads to its triumph. We cannot refuse Emiliano Zapata the route of his arms, which is that of Puebla, Oaxaca, and Veracruz. If we fall into the error of disappointing him, how can I convince him of our disinterestedness? How can I keep him from losing faith in me? Especially, Sr. General, with other and greater dangers lying in wait for us. There is Manuel Diéguez in Jalisco, with Iturbe in Sinaloa; there is Luis Gutiérrez in Saltillo, with Villarreal and Maclovio Herrera in Monterrey, and with Caballero in Ciudad Victoria, and with I know not what other forces in Tampico and on the San Luis line; there is Lucio Blanco at Acámbaro whose attitude I do not understand; and Zuazua in Salvatierra, and other chiefs who have not yet given me their confidence."

"I understand you, my General; but those lesser dangers will disappear when the great danger that Carranza represents has passed. These other chiefs are like hats hanging on a rack; the rack is Carranza, and the best use of our forces is not to pick off the hats one by one but to topple the rack, because then all the hats will fall."

Considering that he could be right, I said, "Sr. General, if Zapata does not withstand the first encounter with Obregón, we will make an irresistible advance to the beaches of Veracruz. With this in mind, have your seventy-seven cannons ready, and I will have my men prepared to follow you."

But I received a report from Emilio Madero on the preparations of Villarreal and Maclovio Herrera for an attack on Torreón. Their purpose was to cut off my base of operations, and I understood that I must no longer delay my plan to destroy the enemy that threatened my rear guard. I informed Angeles, Urbina, and Robles, "Señores, my base of operations is threatened by forces moving to attack Torreón. We cannot ignore this danger. These are my measures: with headquarters in Irapuato, I will lead troops to defeat Diéguez in Jalisco; you, General Angeles, will go with a column to take Monterrey, and you, General Urbina, will prepare to take the line that runs from San Luis to Tampico."

Angeles declared, "This is not a good plan, my General. Now that we have the capital of our Republic, our base of operations should be here, provided we obtain control of the Veracruz line. If we give Carranza time, he will grow stronger and save himself because he can count on the resources of the oil-producing districts. If we go against him first and defeat and annihilate him now while his forces are few, it will be easy to recover all that we have lost in the North."

I answered, "No, Señor. I have forty thousand Mausers, seventy-seven cannons, and sixteen million cartridges, with which I have no doubt we can reach Veracruz and penetrate all that territory, but think, Sr. General, what will become of me if I lose control of the north and the part of the frontier that favors me? What future awaits me without Torreón, Chihuahua, and Ciudad Juárez? Reflect on it, Sr. General Angeles; my resources and organization are there. With the control of only the most remote part of that territory, we have succeeded in reaching here once; with that control we will return again. The good road is the known road. And do not be alarmed about the resources of the oil fields, Señor. I am now making a deal with General Peláez to keep them out of Carranza's hands."

Angeles listened and made no objection to the orders I was dictating for the departure of my columns.

I entered Guadalajara the seventeenth of December, with all the inhabitants applauding my men, who had arrived almost without a struggle. Diéguez, after offering some resistance at Estación Corona, had scarcely drawn a breath in his retreat from Guadalajara to Zapotlán and from Zapotlán to the other side of Tequila, a place on the road to Manzanillo. I appointed authorities to protect laborers at their work, merchants in their business, and property owners in their rights. I authorized no punishments except for just cause.

A group of religious men and women came to see me; they said, "Sr. General Villa, we know nothing of war or politics or revolution, although we would like to know about these things in order to pray for the triumph of the armies that fight for justice. But, Sr. General, while we do no harm to anyone with our prayers, which are words of love for our fellowmen, as the God who illumines us commands, General Diéguez ordered our churches closed. For that reason, Sr. General Villa, we come to ask you: what harm can the candles on our altars and our sacred images do the cause of the people?"

I answered, "Señores, I agree in general with your reasoning. The relief that the sad implore cannot harm the people. But behind the altars that the poor erect you must admit that bad priests are often hidden. It was wrong for Diéguez to close your churches and I am going to open them, although he closed them to appear a great Revolutionary and by opening them I will appear to be an instrument of reaction. But if I find the clergy exploiting and deceiving the people under the protection of the churches, especially if they are Jesuits, I will not pardon them; I will punish them as I have punished them in other cities, because the church that shelters the poor under its mantle is one thing and the church that shelters itself under the mantle of the poor is another."

General Juan G. Cabral came to talk with me in the interests of Eulalio Gutiérrez. I saw him in the distance while I was giving my orders to open the churches and sent word for him to join me. "What brings you to this part of the country, Sr. General?"

"They have sent me here as a spy, Sr. General."

I laughed, because I knew it could not be true, and answered, "Soon you will know my innermost secrets. As soon as I finish this business, I will talk with you." When we were alone I asked him on what commission Gutiérrez had sent him and he replied that he was commissioned to discover my true intentions. About what? About my attitude toward the presidency. I said to him then, "Señor, Gutiérrez is the President of our Republic, and we must all respect and obey him as good Revolutionaries."

"But, Sr. General, Gutiérrez seems to doubt whether you really approve of the measures of his government and accept and support and execute them."

I expressed my attitude and obedience as best I could. "Señor, tell Eulalio Gutiérrez that as a man born to command, I know when it is time to obey; tell him that I am a disciplined chief and will honor, respect, and obey him."

And Juan Cabral, convinced of my sincerity, asked permission to return to Mexico City with my message, and I granted it, glad that he was the agent to explain my purposes. Juan G. Cabral, besides being a good Revolutionary, understood the nature of my justice and my unselfish aims, having witnessed them when he called on me to help the women and children of the three thousand Mayan Indians under his command, a point on which I will say more later.

CHAPTER 6

Ready To Give All His Support to the Government of Gutiérrez, Pancho Villa Returns from Guadalajara and Installs Himself in Mexico City.

The Families of Three Thousand Mayan Indians. The Word of Juan G. Cabral. Pancho Villa's Generosity. Complaints from Mr. Bryan and Mr. Wilson. Messages from Gutiérrez. Martín Espinosa and the Flag of the Convention. The Struggle in Naco. No. 76, Liverpool Street. "Send Your Sons to School or I Will Have you Shot." The Cashier at the Hotel Palacio. Ministers of France and Brazil.

Let me relate what happened to the families of three thousand Mayan Indians.

When Obregón undertook his advance from the districts of the northwest, Cabral, commanding one of his brigades, wanted to spare the women and children of his soldiers the hazards of such a long journey. They insisted that they must accompany him, fearing to be left helpless in the absence of their husbands, but he assured them they would not be helpless and gave his word he would always send them half the pay of the men at the very moment they were paid. He had been doing exactly that.

But afterward, when armies were divided as a result of the struggles of the Convention and when the Convention chiefs in Aguascalientes were planning the form of the new government, Obregón left Mexico and took the three thousand Mayan Indians who belonged to Cabral. So when Cabral returned to the capital of our Republic, he had no troops, no paymaster's office, and no money, but he was still committed to sending half-pay to three thousand women who were waiting in Sinaloa, trusting in his word.

In his difficulty he went to see José Isabel Robles. But Robles answered that the government had no money for such expenses. He went to Gutiérrez, but he too refused. As a last resort he came to me and told me his trouble, adding, "Sr. General Villa, these three thousand Mayan Indians will now fight against your cause. But is it right for their families in Sinaloa to be left in misery?"

"No, Señor, it would not be right, and has no place in my scheme of justice." The envoys of the three thousand women were there. I called Luisito and said, "Luisito, give them the money they expect." To Cabral I said, "Sr. Compañero, you can count on this same help whenever your obligations demand it."

In Guadalajara I had complaints from Mr. Bryan and Mr. Wilson about the executions that the struggle had required. They sent word through their consuls:

Señores, we are disappointed in these deeds. Do not kill political prisoners; exile them from your territory in order to keep them harmless. We urge this in no tone of censure, for these are acts not definitely understood at this great distance, but with the desire to give you our counsel, advising you that if you respect the lives of political prisoners, you will win the good will of the great civilized nations, a thing of advantage to your government in avoiding obstacles in the future settlement of international affairs.

Mr. Bryan and Mr. Wilson were warning us, and, thinking over their words, I said to myself, "Señor, I do not know what such struggles may have been like in other times and countries but here in Mexico politicians must lose their lives for the people."

Robles came to see me in Guadalajara with a message from Eulalio Gutiérrez about this. Eulalio's message was: "It is the duty of my government to stop these excesses. Therefore, I consider it urgent for you to return and for us to agree at once on measures that must be taken and the kind of support you must give my orders."

While I was in Guadalajara the President of our Convention, General Martín Espinosa, had fled with two of the secretaries and the flag on which we Convention chiefs had signed our oath, and the papers containing the proof of our legality. Eulalio Gutiérrez informed me that this flight occurred because my chiefs and Zapata's had killed several delegates.

There was another incident. A struggle had broken out in Naco between Maytorena's troops and those of Plutarco Elías Calles and Benjamín Hill, a thing which promised trouble and danger for the inhabitants on the American side of the frontier and brought objections from Washington. So Robles came to discuss this. He and Gutiérrez would need the support of my orders, for Maytorena disregarded those the Convention government was giving him. After hearing him out, I answered with the greatest respect, as I had responded to Juan Cabral. "Señor, Eulalio Gutiérrez is the President of our government and you are its Minister of War. You can both be certain, as I have said already and repeat now, that I will obey you with the utmost submission, for I do not believe you will ever dictate orders contrary to the welfare of the people."

In evidence of obedience I quickly terminated the business at Guadalajara and returned to Mexico City with Robles to aid Gutiérrez in solving his problems. This time I did not live in my train as I had done before but stayed in a house in Colonia Juárez, at No. 76 on Liverpool Street. I did this to show that I intended to remain in Mexico City and support the government; and if I took a house in a rich neighborhood it was not for the love of the neighborhood but out of friendship, for a close friend of mine had offered it to me and I could not refuse.

A few days before I set out for Guadalajara I had talked with a child of about seven or so at the Hacienda de los Morales, where part of my forces were. He was following my footsteps, or, rather, those of my horse, and watching me as he walked along peeling the piece of cane he had in his hands and sucking and chewing on the peelings. He came so close that I turned to him, took his cane and bit off a piece, and with a friendly smile said, "The bandit Pancho Villa is going to steal your cane. Don't you know that Pancho Villa came into the world to rob and kill?"

"Señor, I am following your horse just because I like to look at you."

"And why do you like to look at me?"

"I do not know, Señor."

I asked him how much his cane had cost and he said two cents. I asked him if he wanted me to return it or to buy it from him; he said no, he preferred to give it to me and he wanted me to eat it. Then I took two pesos and offered them to him, saying, "Take this from Pancho Villa for a piece of your cane." I added, "What will you do with the money?"

"I will take it to my mother, Señor."

"You have a mother?"

"Yes, Señor."

"You have a father too?"

"A father too."

"Does your father send you to school?"

"No, Señor."

"Why not?"

"Because I help him with the work on the farm, Señor."

Then I said, "Well, go and tell your father that Pancho Villa says to send you to school tomorrow or I will find him and shoot him." I said this thinking to myself, "This child, without knowing who I am, watches and follows me and even wants to give me what he eats. Why does he do this unless he sees me as a man who struggles for the salvation of the poor?" The child, I thought, was destined to grow up to help his brothers and it was a crime to let him fail for want of schooling.

When I came to my house on Liverpool Street, the father was there waiting for me; and when he saw me, he said, "Sr. General Villa, I am the father you threatened to shoot because my son was not going to school. If I send him to school, how can I gather the corn for him to eat?"

"I know nothing about your corn, Señor. But you can be sure that my men will hunt you out and shoot you if that son of yours and his brothers do not go to school. Don't you know that we are fighting the Revolution so that every Mexican child may go to school? If the greed of the rich deprived you of schooling, as it did me, and so you are unable to support yourself or your family, then steal, Señor, steal whatever you need to send your son to school. If you steal for that reason, I will not shoot you, I will reward you; but if in not stealing you allow your son to stay away from school and follow the road of misfortune and crime, I will shoot you for that." With this I ordered them to give him five hundred pesos and had some of my officers go out on the streets to gather up the poor children and bring them to me, so I could send them to Chihuahua and have them put in school.

One morning I went to have breakfast at the Hotel Palacio where Gutiérrez was staying and discovered that the cashier was a very pretty woman. When I went to pay my bill and that of my officers, I made some friendly remarks, which she answered with a very amiable smile. The following day I returned for breakfast and the same thing happened; I returned the next day and the day after that. Each time I went I talked at greater length until on the third or fourth day when I paid, I handed her a note in which I expressed my good intentions. "Señorita," I wrote, "as you seem not displeased with my desire to see you and talk to you, let me know when and where I can meet you alone and we can talk at liberty."

But the next day when I went back for breakfast, she was not there, and a different cashier occupied her place. At this, I grew angry; and when I saw the owner of the hotel, who was not a Mexican but a French-woman, whispering to the other woman and laughing, I accosted her and said, "Señora, where is the real cashier? I think you have hidden her, and I see that you are making fun of me with all your smiling and whispering." Instead of offering an explanation, she turned away to the stairs, just as if to leave me a laughingstock before I know not how many people. In sudden anger I started after her. My officers followed, and we caught her and took her out to my automobile and carried her to my house on Liverpool Street, where I locked her up in Luisito's room, intending no harm but resolved to keep her confined a day or two and mend her manners.

A great outcry followed in governmental and diplomatic quarters. My violent attacks of anger were held up to horror and I was reviled without quite knowing whether it was because of what I had really done or because they imagined that I had carried the woman away in response to base impulses.

The next night the Minister of France and the Minister of Brazil came to see me, the latter representing the United States as well as his own country. They asked me for the woman. They said, "Is it true that a Frenchwoman is confined here and you have brought her here to dis-honor her? In the name of France and Brazil and the United States, we ask you to set her free, Sr. General Villa."

I answered, "Yes, Señores; that woman who laughed at me is a pris-oner here. But I promise you, though it does not enter into the case, that nothing has happened to her or will happen, and when her term of punishment is over, I will set her free as you desire."

And so it was.

CHAPTER 7

In Spite of the Differences Which Separate Them, Villa and Gutiérrez Decide To Work Together for the Good of the Government.

Conversation with Luisito. 200,000 Pesos for the Hotel Palacio. Conchita del Hierro. Stefanini's Jewels. The Sincerity of Lucio Blanco. Three Thousand Men for Cabral. The Captain of a Japanese Warship. Mexico and the Wars of the United States. Gutiérrez' Complaint. The Renouncement of Miguel Alessio Robles. Aragón and Berlanga. Kidnaping and Ransom. Eulalio's Appeal.

When my guard released the French proprietress of the Hotel Palacio, I called Luisito and said, "Luisito, it is being said on the streets that I kidnaped the cashier of the Hotel Palacio and brought her here to enjoy her without risk. You know that this is slander, Luisito. The one I brought here was the owner of the hotel, not a young woman, and I brought her not to satisfy my desires but because she laughed at me. What should I do? If she wants it believed that I dishonored her or attempted to, what good will a denial do when all who hate me will say I forced her to speak in my defense?"

Luisito answered, "I can offer you no advice, my General. If you, a man of experience with the habit of command, do not know what to do, what can I say who knows so little of such problems?"

"Good, Luisito. If nothing can be done to free me from the slander, I cannot let her remain in the country as a living evidence that Pancho Villa does violence even to women he has no desire for. See her at once and give her my order to leave Mexico. Say that it is punishment for her offense. Since I have no wish to damage her interests or turn the episode into an international affair, tell her I will buy her hotel at a just price and that you are authorized to draw up the papers in my name and have the money to pay her."

I gave him 200,000 pesos to make the purchase and required him to terminate it in the best way possible and without adding encouragement to the accusations. I did this considering that when men fall into the hands of a woman they must silence her, or appease her with money, since she will always yield to this, or if she does not, will soften. It is the same whether the trouble she has caused comes of a serious love affair or of any other occasion.

I had done the same with Conchita del Hierro, the girl who troubled me so much as I advanced from Guadalupe to Mexico City. When my trains arrived at the capital, I began to wonder what the outcome could be, for Conchita not only failed to respond to my affection but looked on me with horror; as she was a woman of delicate spirit, who easily gave way to tears when she was wounded, I had no opportunity to tell her that I wanted to make amends and come to some agreement, giving whatever she wanted provided she stopped hating me and left with kindly feelings for me and returned to the protection of her sister and her aunt, the lady who had brought her to me by deceiving us both. As it happened, on my arrival in Mexico City an Italian named Stefanini came to the train to see me and offered to sell me a matching set of jewelry. I had Luisito make the deal and pay for them, fifty thousand pesos as I remember, and when he delivered them, I placed them in Conchita's hands without opening the case and said, "Conchita, accept this little gift and whenever you look at it, remember what a horrible fellow I am." When several days had passed and she had not returned the gift, my conscience was at ease, and I had no scruples about sending her home, which I did.

I attended to many important political matters in the house at No. 76 Liverpool Street; but I do not believe that I can remember them all, and if I remembered them I could not tell in detail all that happened. I do remember that General Lucio Blanco was among the first chiefs who came there to see me and that Martín Luis Guzmán, whom I sent to Robles as his advisor, brought him, just as he had brought him earlier, in Aguascalientes.

Lucio Blanco spoke very favorably, saying that he was inclined to accept the office of Minister of the Interior which Gutiérrez offered him but only if I was pleased with the appointment. He added that the twenty thousand men in his forces were unanimously in favor of supporting the Convention government and, being stationed in Michoacán and El Bajío, one part of them could go with the move against Manuel Diéguez in Jalisco and Colima, another could go on to Tepic, and another prepare for the campaigns in the north. I believe now that he was speaking in all sincerity that day, for the week following that interview Gutiérrez ordered Cabral to leave for Sonora to support Maytorena, and, as Cabral had no troops, Gutiérrez ordered him to take three thousand of Lucio Blanco's forces and Lucio delivered them in the spirit of good comradeship.

The captain of a Japanese warship also came to see me. He told me at once that his government had sent him to talk to me about the unfriendly relations between the United States and Japan and the possibility of a war between those two countries; he added that Japan's armies and her fleet were already preparing for it. I said nothing but looked at him in distrust as he continued to reveal his thoughts, saying, "Sr. General Villa, we Japanese have to take a great deal from the leaders and citizens of the United States. They are an ambitious nation; they wish to dominate everywhere for their own aggrandizement, always driven by expediency, here in America as on the maritime routes among the archipelagos of Asia. We Japanese know you as the greatest soldier in Mexico and I ask you therefore, Sr. General, in the name of the government of Tokyo, what your sentiments are toward the American nation. I hope that you will tell me beforehand where your sympathy and that of the Mexican nation will lie when our war with the United States breaks out. I think you know what the United States is, Señor. You have already endured injuries, in Texas, in California, and I know not how many other districts taken away from Mexico. You need no one to rouse your patriotism."

I answered, "I do not know what resentment Japan feels over the conduct of the United States. I know my own country only. But if the American people go to war with another country, and I am in a high position in the government, the people of Mexico will refuse the United States nothing they may ask in the way of materials of war. The government in Washington is our good friend and American citizens favor our Revolutionary cause. As for the remote events you speak of, much rain has fallen on the land since then and right now there are other fruits to be gathered."

I think he was disappointed in my answer and, hearing it, withheld other things that he had come to say. I made a mistake in expressing myself so frankly, not remembering that in international affairs it is always good to learn everything the others have to say, especially if it relates to war. Still, my answer was sound, for Mexico could not afford to endanger her future by promising aid to an enemy of the United States or even being willing to make the promise later.

In my talks with Eulalio Gutiérrez at that time, we discussed what should be done, in view of the political situation, to prevent murders and other excesses.

Gutiérrez said, "These excesses must stop, Sr. General; even members of my government are beginning to leave me, as happened a week ago in the case of the lawyer Miguel Alessio Robles, my undersecretary of justice, who says he will not run the risk of being accused later, as we are now accusing Rodolfo Reyes and others who agreed to crimes in the time of Huerta."

I answered, "The excesses, Sr. President, were not committed for love of tyranny but for the cause. If we let bad elements divide and weaken us, would it not be the same thing if we did not kill on the battlefield but surrendered our positions to the enemy?"

He observed, "But men like Guillermo García Aragón and David Berlanga are not bad elements, Sr. General. Berlanga was a good Revolutionary and devoted to the cause of the people."

I answered, "Señor, Berlanga was injuring and weakening us in his mistaken ideas about our cause. Am I to blame because he was biting at my heels and was condemning and reviling my forces on whom you and our government have to depend? What was I to do, Señor, however sincere he was in his love for our cause? In war and politics the errors of intelligence are punished as well as the sins of intention. David Berlanga made a mistake and paid the penalty, and since he paid it, his death will prevent others from following that same course."

Eulalio answered, "But harmless people are abducted, Sr. General Villa; rich men are taken from their homes or from their offices, and held for high ransom, and are not released until they deliver the money that is demanded."

It was true that some wealthy men, enemies of our cause, were hiding in Mexico City and secretly working for our defeat, as they had worked for Huerta before; my compadre Tomás Urbina discovered this, and I authorized our troops to be sent to imprison them and force them to contribute as much to the cause of the people as they were willing to give to destroy it. I therefore answered Eulalio, "It is true. But if your government, being legal, cannot authorize such just and beneficial punishment, isn't it well to leave it to us and for your government and the Revolution to reap the benefit of our misdeeds and blame us for committing them?"

We went on—he reproaching me with the acts my forces and Zapata's had committed, and I trying to get him to understand my reasons, as I understood his. What happened was that he insisted I was forcing him to make a public protest against the crimes, letting it be known that he wanted them to cease and appealing to the chiefs for cooperation. To which I said, "Very well, Señor. Publish whatever you think necessary, and you can be sure that I will respect and uphold what you say as long as it does not obstruct the progress of this war."

That same afternoon I had a telegraphic conference with Zapata, already in control of Puebla, about my discussion with Gutiérrez, and the next day Eulalio announced in newspapers that after a friendly talk with me he found I was willing to execute his orders and he would leave me in Mexico City to protect him. But a day later he published his protest against the crimes. In his proclamation he said:

Generals of the Convention Armies:

The government knows that our society is suffering from a panic caused by the disappearance of men who are assassinated in the dark of night or kidnaped and held for ransom. I remind you, on accepting appointment as Provisional President I trusted that none of my compañeros in arms would refuse their aid in forming a government of authority, justice, and honor. Must I consent now to murder without any form of judgment or abduction and extortion in violation of the laws, although this is done by order of the chiefs of certain groups and those groups are the most powerful? Generals of the Convention, I am opposed to the continuation of these crimes; they lower the prestige of my government and the forces which support it. For that reason, I ask all of you, as great patriots, to support the laws which protect us.

It seemed to me that Gutiérrez was right in wanting legal respect for his government, but it was also true that this was not the time for a normal government but for war.

The foreign nations were so glad to see Gutiérrez' proclamation that the next day Mr. Bryan and Mr. Wilson sent us congratulations through their consuls. The Minister of Brazil said to me, "Sr. General, in the name of my government and the government of the United States, I wish to say that the order published by the government of Mexico is good. It strengthens the said government. Do you intend to respect it and see that your men respect it?"

I replied, "Señor, I respect the orders of the government of Mexico just as you respect the orders of the government of Brazil."

CHAPTER 8

To Avoid Foreign Intervention in Naco, Villa Accepts the Pact Proposed by General Scott.

General Juan N. Banderas. José Vasconcelos, Minister of Education. "Leave Your Office." Maytorena and Hill. Rafael Zubarán. Mr. Bryan. George C. Carothers. General Bliss. Hugh L. Scott. Roberto V. Pesqueira. Enrique C. Llorente. The Pact of Naco. Congratulations to Villa.

A general of Zapata's forces, Juan Banderas, nicknamed "The Cripple," also came to see me on Liverpool Street. He was convalescing from a wound he had received, I think, in a fight in the Hotel Cosmos. It was over an automobile and cost the life of another general, Rafael Garay.

"I have come here to talk to you, Sr. General Villa, about an old business which is being revived. Señor, I want you to explain this miracle in which we good Revolutionaries are fighting so that unconscionable lawyers can climb to the top as ministers and govern us with their black arts."

I answered, "Sr. Compañero, I am responsible for the fortune of our arms, and Eulalio Gutiérrez for the acts of the government. But even so, tell me which ministers are exploiting the people, and I promise you they will be punished."

He answered, "It is a burden to the Revolutionaries to have that lawyer José Vasconcelos as Minister of Public Instruction, and we regret to see that you protect him and take him into your confidence. Vasconcelos, Sr. General Villa, is an intellectual without a soul, an intellectual of very great duplicity."

"And why, Sr. Compañero, do you accuse a minister in this way? Sr. Vasconcelos is a good Revolutionary, and devoted to democracy, welfare, and justice."

It was true that when I was in Guadalupe, Zacatecas, Vasconcelos used to come and talk with me, as he had taken a strong liking to me. He appeared to be a very intelligent man with a knowledge of many things, in addition to his great love for Sr. Madero. I too had noted a lack of prudence in his torrent of words, but I considered that Gutiérrez had made a good choice when he appointed him as minister and I certainly did not think it proper for Banderas to criticize him now.

But he added, "I accuse him of disloyalty, Sr. General Villa. When I was a prisoner in the time of Sr. Madero, they recommended him to me as a very good lawyer. Well, he came to see me in jail and, pointing out the value of his services and his influence, requested a large sum in advance for getting me out of the presidio. After an enormous amount of trouble and effort, I paid him what he asked. But then, with the money received and spent, he forgot all about me and left me to face the judges alone. I ask you only this, Sr. General, can such a man be a minister of the government of the people, especially in education, where everyone has to learn from him and then follow in his steps and imitate him? No, Señor, I will get hold of this lawyer and break him as he deserves, and it will be a good thing for our young people who are soon to be men and must not grow up under that kind of teachers."

I could see his point of view but did not want to agree with him, lest the affairs of the government suffer; therefore, going along with him, I said, "You need not break the lawyer, Sr. Compañero. I will order my Treasury to give you right now the amount of money you paid him, plus interest for the period covered, and you can be sure I will find a way for him to repay it and suffer the penalty he deserves."

But he replied, "Sr. General, I see that you are mistaken in your good intentions. I am not after money. I want retribution. What I do not consent to is for such a man to be a minister in our Revolutionary government, and I come to tell you this in proof of my respect and to ask you not to protect him with your authority so that I can get my hands upon him and punish him and save our country from his schools."

We two continued our conversation: he, determined to break Vasconcelos; I, advising against it. Finally, seeing that I could not convince him, and understanding his grievance, I suggested that he wait a few days until I could execute my own justice. I said, "Sr. Compañero, I think you are right; but we must not make the future of our struggle darker by the death of a minister. Leave the settlement of this affair to me, and I promise you that Vasconcelos will not be Minister of Education or any other department."

As he answered that he would wait, trusting in my intervention, I sent next day for Vasconcelos and explained to him the value of prudence, saying, "Señor, Juan Banderas intends to kill you in satisfaction of a grudge over some business which you did not attend to very well when he was a prisoner. I invite you to leave your office of minister, Señor, for the sake of your life and the good of our cause. Juan Banderas is a brave man; he has just killed Rafael Garay in the Hotel Cosmos, and he will kill you too if you do not succeed in killing him first or if you do not avoid the encounter."

He answered, "What kind of times are these, Sr. General, if a minister of the government must hide to keep a general of the army from carrying out the threat to kill him?"

I said, "My friend, this is a question of war, not of law. When we were at peace, you sowed a bad seed; today when we are at war it falls on you to reap the fruit. Listen to good advice. Give up your office and leave the capital. If you feel that you must have a position in the government, I will give you a letter instructing Felipe Angeles to make you secretary general of one of those states in the northeast which will soon be in control of our forces." Vasconcelos seemed to appreciate my advice and the offer I made him. He left me intending, as I then thought, to follow the road I had recommended.

The international conflict over damages caused in United States territory by Maytorena's struggle to take Naco from Calles and Hill broke out at that time. Rafael Zubarán, Carranza's representative, was saying in Washington, "Señores, the Convention forces are to blame. Their shooting causes damages on the other side of the line, but they persist, knowing that the women and children of our chiefs and soldiers have sought shelter there."

Our representative was saying, "Señores, how can we avoid the consequences of our firing if Hill defends himself on the very frontier in order to lessen the force of our attacks?"

On hearing these explanations, Mr. Bryan and Mr. Wilson sent me word to dictate measures halting the damage; they communicated with Gutiérrez and Carranza to the same effect. They said:

Sr. General Villa, the struggle at Naco has cost us many wounded and dead in the territory of the United States and we do not know whether these unfortunate events occur because the chiefs of the troops there do not try to avoid them or because the soldiers do not obey the orders they receive. However this may be, the injuries must cease, and you will understand that if the governments of Mexico do not correct them the American government will do so by means of military action.

Carranza answered, as they informed us:

Señor, if you employ force to prevent the damage of which you speak, you will antagonize Mexico by an act of intervention and promote the designs of Villa and Maytorena, who know the weakness of their attacks upon Naco and are only trying to develop the struggle into an international conflict.

Aware of the danger of foreign intervention, I answered:

Señor, we are not to blame for misfortunes which occur in the United States because of the struggle for the conquest of Naco. These are effects of war. But I promise you that I am now giving orders to prevent our bullets from reaching the American side of the line.

Gutiérrez answered:

Señor, the United States is a nation to which we are bound by the friendliest of ties. You can be sure that Maytorena already has orders not to repeat those injuries and to cease hostilities if necessary.

But the truth is that the answers were worth nothing. The struggle continued as before, the number of American dead and wounded increased, like other damages and disturbances. Mr. Carothers, by order of Washington, went to Naco to bring the enemy armies to some agreement, and through him I sent word to Maytorena advising him to find a way to avoid international risk.

Mr. Carothers saw Maytorena. Maytorena said to him, "Señor, I am ready to withdraw my line to where my fire cannot reach frontier cities. But if I do this, is it right for the enemy to remain in control of the place, thanks to which they receive supplies from across the line? Close the line, Señor, so that Hill cannot get arms, ammunition, or supplies, and when I besiege him from the distance he will have to abandon the place in search of supplies." And Carothers admitted that Maytorena was right, and the American General Bliss, there on the same mission, admitted it also. This being the truth of the situation, another general, Hugh L. Scott, came to Naco representing the American War Department and had very long talks with Maytorena, Calles, and Hill, and a youth named Roberto V. Pesqueira, representing Carranza, to all of whom he proposed a pact which would free the frontier towns from the ravages of war.

The terms of the pact were these:

First—General Hill's troops will evacuate the frontier town of Naco, Sonora.

Second—Maytorena and Hill agree not to occupy the aforesaid place in any manner; it will be considered neutral and closed to foreign trade.

Third—The forces now fighting in Sonora agree to respect the frontier town of Nogales, which will remain under the control of the Convention troops of Governor Maytorena, and the frontier town of Agua Prieta, which will remain under the control of the Carrancista troops of Hill.

Fourth—In support of this agreement Maytorena's troops will retire to Cananea and not interfere with the evacuation of Naco by General Hill's troops or with their march to Agua Prieta. It is also agreed that during the aforesaid operations General Hill's troops will not attack or molest those of Maytorena.

But with the agreement accepted and already signed by Hill, Calles, and Pesqueira as the representative of Carranza, Maytorena was disinclined to commit himself without being authorized by Gutiérrez and me. And when he stated his position to Hugh L. Scott, that General said he understood very well and asked then if he might be the one to request my consent, to which Maytorena answered yes, and that he would respect any orders I gave him. Therefore, the Minister of Brazil arranged to present to me in Mexico all papers covering the matter along with a message from General Scott; and Enrique C. Llorente, my consul in Washington to represent our government, telegraphed me the same.

This was my reply:

Señor, I have read the agreement made in Naco to protect the frontier towns from damage by war. Tell the United States government that I give my approval of the pact and advise Maytorena to sign it and respect and enforce it. But I also say that later we will have to attack Hill and Calles in Agua Prieta or in some other place which they choose for the battle, for we have to defeat that enemy.

This was my answer, and I had Llorente tell them the same thing in Washington. The next day the Minister of Brazil expressed the thanks of Mr. Bryan and Mr. Wilson for my good offices in the affair.

CHAPTER 9

Knowing that Gutiérrez Is Trying To Abandon Him, Villa Goes to the Convention To Prevent It.

The Northern Generals. Martín Espinosa. Villarreal's Proclamations and Letters. Tomás Urbina. Rodolfo Fierro. Roque González Garza. The Sins of Villa and Zapata. The Men of the Convention. Pánfilo Natera. Vito Alessio Robles. Felipe Riveros. Gutiérrez' Guard. Villa's Decisions and Questions. "I Will Even Ride a Burro To Get Away."

I received reports that while I was in the north and while I was taking Guadalajara, Eulalio Gutiérrez was having conversations and telegraphic conferences with Luis Gutiérrez, Luis Caballero, and I do not remember what other generals regarding the promise of their support in return for removing me from my post. I learned also that Gutiérrez had informed the foreign consuls at the same time that in his judgment many Convention chiefs were strongly opposed to me, and that all those with troops north of San Luis Potosí promised to support him if he would relieve me of my command. Along with these rumors, I received news that the President and the secretaries of the Convention who had fled to Saltillo and Monterrey with our flag and our signatures were plotting against me.

Those who came to talk with me were saying, "Martín Espinosa is not acting on his own initiative or as President of our Convention; it is Eulalio Gutiérrez who is disloyal." Unable to believe what my men were saying, I answered that if Gutiérrez was hoping to obtain the union of Revolutionary chiefs by promising to deprive me of my command, which he himself had conferred on me, then he considered it his duty to follow this path. But I thought, "If Gutiérrez makes the mistake of imagining he can defend himself against Carranza and Obregón without my aid, experience will show him his error." And I, Pancho Villa, say that I endured the bitterness of this situation calmly, though it made me sad to know that great Revolutionaries like Antonio I. Villarreal were ridiculing me in their proclamations and in letters and telegrams to our chiefs. Señor! Hadn't Villarreal been with me at the conferences of Torreón? Didn't he know my thoughts?

He was writing, and they said he was saying:

Pancho Villa is a wicked man and a traitor; Pancho Villa is the most serious threat to our cause. We must get rid of him before he gets rid of us; he is strong and astute, merciless and disloyal; he has distributed his troops well, with the intention of conquering us all one by one while we, the true Revolutionary men, destroy ourselves in search of harmony.

He wrote this or telegraphed it to Lucio Blanco, Carrera Torres, the Elizondos, Samuel de los Santos, Eduardo Hernández, the Cedillos, Salvador González, and many others.

This was the situation when at daybreak one day one of my generals came to inform me that Gutiérrez was getting ready to abandon Mexico City, having decided to take his government and troops and join his brother Luis, and in that way get rid of me and Zapata and the authority of the Convention, which he would consider dissolved since its true President and the flag and our signatures were no longer in Mexico City.

I called my compadre Tomás Urbina and said to him, "Compadre, Gutiérrez wants to strip us of our legality by abandoning the capital of the Republic and resorting to treason. Take your measures, Compadre. See that Gutiérrez does not leave Mexico City, nor any of the ministers nor any of the men they have under their command."

I called Rodolfo Fierro and said to him, "Friend, assemble the men of my escort and give them orders to scout the entire city and keep a close watch at all points, and wherever they find Convention soldiers or employees in the act of abandoning or betraying me, to shoot them down."

I called Roque González Garza, my representative in the Convention, who had been chosen to replace Martín Espinosa as President, and said to him, "My boy, do whatever is necessary, but this morning I have to talk with the men who carry on the business of the Convention. Don't you know, Señor, that our President Eulalio Gutiérrez, along with all his government, is trying to abandon us, leaving Zapata and me without authority?"

When giving my orders I was unable to control my violent anger over the conduct of Gutiérrez, who was conspiring against my person, trying to abandon me, and threatening to bring down the cause of the people. I saw things in this way: "We are at war with Carranza and his favorites, who want to make a dictatorship of our triumph. Our Convention worked against that future in Aguascalientes, and for that reason chose Eulalio Gutiérrez as President of the Republic and me as chief of all our Convention armies. Then how can he abandon me? Didn't he accept the position? If he accepted it, isn't it his duty to fulfil it, not to betray it or betray the men who have given him their respect and the support of their arms? What have I done, Señor, for him to strip me of my legal standing, except to cleanse the capital of the Republic of evil elements, enemies of our unity, and add the districts of Guadalajara to the Convention territory, and prepare for the conquest of the states of the north? What has Emiliano Zapata done, except to advance on Puebla, which he has already taken, and to lead his men to the struggle that Obregón and Carranza are preparing for him at Veracruz, and to suffer and shed blood in that struggle? And if we act in this way, dedicated only to the triumph of the people, am I now to let Eulalio abandon us?"

As I was thinking this, I gave way to one of my most violent attacks of anger. If the life of Eulalio Gutiérrez had not been so necessary, I would have seized him at that very moment and had him shot. But my reason returned, and seeing that the road to triumph was that of prudence not anger, I regained my composure, though determined to prevent the departure of Gutiérrez and his fellow conspirators. I would go to see him and talk face to face with him while my men were talking with the members of the Convention.

By six in the morning on that twenty-seventh of December I had reports that no member of the government had left the city nor was it possible for anyone to leave. By nine the cavalry of José Rodríguez and my compadre Urbina was extended along the Paseo de la Reforma, where Gutiérrez' house was located. At ten I went to deliberate with the principal chiefs of the Convention or, rather, of the Permanent Convention, who were waiting for me in the Green Room of the Chamber of Deputies.

They gave me a friendly welcome. I said, "I come here, Señores, to make a serious complaint against Eulalio Gutiérrez who at dawn this morning was preparing for flight and was near to effecting it, in order to rob us of legal standing. I say only this, am I a puppet to be handled in this way? Does he look on the men of the Convention as playthings? You, Sr. General Natera, and you, Sr. General Márquez, and you, Sr. General De la Vega, and you, Sr. General González Garza, and you, Sr. Colonel Piña, and you Sr. Colonel Alessio Robles, are you, in your good judgment, weighing the gravity of the situation that threatens us? You can be sure that I am going in search of Gutiérrez to make him change his mind, and if I do not succeed, I promise you that when I leave him he will no longer be able to abandon and betray us."

Then General Pánfilo Natera observed, "Sr. General Villa, in my opinion you must measure your steps carefully before going to talk with Sr. General Gutiérrez."

And Colonel Vito Alessio Robles said, "My General, we hear and understand your reasons. But remember your anger and consider how dangerous it is to our cause for you to enter into this discussion with Gutiérrez."

General Felipe Riveros, who had come there with me, said, "Sr. General, the delegates are speaking with prudence and letting you know their misgivings. Listen to them."

And González Garza said, "Consider, my General, what we all say and predict. It is only our love for the cause that guides us."

I saw that they were opposed to my going to see Gutiérrez because they feared what my words might provoke, and they were so considerate in their advice that I promised them that I would postpone the interview and wait until they settled the question and informed me of the result. I left with my compadre Urbina, Felipe Riveros, Rodolfo Fierro, José Rodríguez, and other men of mine, who accompanied me to my headquarters.

But the truth is I began to wonder what the Convention delegates would do to convince Gutiérrez of his error. I knew they had not the strength to impose their will upon him but ran the risk that he would impose his upon them, which would make our future still darker. I asked myself, "Must I let others be responsible for the fulfilment of my duty?" And I called upon my compadre Urbina, José Rodríguez, and Rodolfo Fierro to advise me in the matter. I asked them, "Señores, do you think the delegates are men enough for the case?"

My compadre Urbina answered, "Since they do not have their own forces to protect them, they are not the men for the case."

Again I asked, "Do you consider it dangerous for me to settle this affair with Eulalio Gutiérrez?"

Rodolfo Fierro answered, "My General, we never kill without reason. If the life of Gutiérrez is in danger, it is because that is what is best for us. When have we ever assassinated the defenders of the people?"

With them and other men of mine to cover us, I went at once to Gutiérrez' house, changed his guard for another that obeyed me, and when this was done, entered to talk with him, José Isabel Robles, and others who accompanied him, and the Convention delegates, who had also gone there.

I said to Gutiérrez, "Is it true, Sr. General, that you wish to leave our Convention Revolutionaries in order to deprive us of our legality? Is it true that you are trying to persuade chiefs in San Luis and Coahuila and Tamaulipas and Nuevo León to support you and fight against us?"

He answered, "Señor, I do not wish to destroy this legality. I only want to be surrounded by subordinates who obey me and respect their duties and the law."

I replied, "Then wherever you go, I will follow you with my whole division. Don't you know, Señor, that you are the President of our Republic, and my troops and I are charged with protecting you? Where would you be without me if you run the risk that nobody will respect you?"

He observed, "I want to be a long way from you and Emiliano Zapata, Sr. General; I want to free my conscience of the crimes the Villistas and Zapatistas are commiting under my government."

"Very well, Señor, but I will not let you go. I have already stopped the departure of all trains."

"If I have no trains at my disposal, I will even ride a burro to get away from you."

My first impulse was to draw my pistol and shoot him. But, determined not to give way to anger, and remembering that after all he was our President, I restrained myself. With the greatest calm, I said, "Tell me, Señor, what complaints you have against my person, and I promise to correct them."

"Your men assassinated Berlanga, who was a good Revolutionary."

"I have told you, Señor, that his death was in our best interests."

"You interfere with my ministers and advise them to leave my government."

"With which ministers of yours do I interfere, Señor?"

"With Vasconcelos, Sr. General, whom you warned to leave if he did not wish to be killed here."

Truly, hearing all that Eulalio charged me with, my mind was beset with doubts considering how our government converted my good deeds into evil ones and invented excuses to incriminate me.

CHAPTER 10

In View of the Dangers of the International Situation, Villa Leaves Mexico to Confer With General Scott in El Paso.

Vasconcelos. Eulalio's Questions and Villa's Answers. An Escort. José Isabel Robles. A Close Watch on Telegraph Offices. Lucio Blanco. Manuel Palafox. Carranza's New Laws. The International Question. Maytorena's Envoy. The Friendship of the Washington Government. Mr. Carother's Actions. Interviews with General Scott. A Telegram to Governor Maytorena.

Calming myself out of a sense of duty, I waited a few moments, as if thinking, and then said, "Sr. President, I promise you that Vasconcelos is lying. Some time ago he deceived Juan Banderas, whom others call "The Cripple," taking his money for a service which he never performed. Now Banderas wants to kill him. He says, 'Do you think I am going to accept as Minister of Public Instruction a man who will corrupt the people with the worst kind of teaching?' And I, Sr. President, called the lawyer and said to him, 'Señor, Juan Banderas intends to do this. Why don't you save yourself from death by taking refuge with some of my troops? You will not be without a position, Señor, for I will give you letters recommending you as a secretary in the north.' I said that to him for his own good and for the good of our government. Was this a bad act? Furthermore, if Vasconcelos is opposed to going or you are opposed to letting him go, you have only to request an escort, and I will give him one so large that nobody can come near him or even see him."

Eulalio answered, "I am the one to give escorts, Sr. General, not you."

I said, "Yes, Señor, and I say that you have only to order me to give him the said escort. I am your subordinate, I am loyal, and I know how to obey."

He asked, "And why, if I wish an escort, must I ask you to grant me one?"

I asked him, "And why, Señor, should I not transmit your orders to the troops if you yourself made me chief of your armies?"

We continued in this fashion: he insisting that he had to part with me, I explaining that we had to stay together for the benefit of the people and should not separate until our final victory. But seeing that my efforts at persuasion were unavailing, I turned to Rodolfo Fierro, who was accompanying me at this critical moment, and said, "Replace the guard of this house with your troops."

Then I addressed Gutiérrez, "So now you know, Señor. You are not leaving this house."

What then happened was that on hearing my order, several of those present intervened and succeeded in composing our differences, thanks to their conciliatory words. José Isabel Robles took the responsibility for seeing that Gutiérrez would remain in Mexico City and complete his government the first day of the following month, and I consented to retire the guard I had placed there. The business appeared to be settled. But I had little faith in the firmness of the arrangement and stationed my troops in the telegraph offices to keep a close watch, and took other precautions.

A few days after my arguments with Gutiérrez, he completed the formation of his cabinet, naming Lucio Blanco and Manuel Palafox as ministers, and some lawyers whose names I do not remember. I talked with Juan Banderas again about Vasconcelos, who was also a minister, and advised him to respect his life and leave him in peace. But my recommendations were unnecessary, for Vasconcelos had gone to take refuge with the forces of a general operating near Pachuca.

At that same time the men of the Convention went back to their meetings, determined to continue with the work of making the laws to realize our Revolutionary principles. They were saying, "The laws must not be delayed. Why permit Carranza to pose as a friend of the people, announcing reforms that he would not accept in the conferences of Torreón or on other occasions when we proposed them?"

This was spurring them on because Carranza was going to announce measures pertaining to municipal liberty and to divorce in unfortunate marriages and other progressive steps. I saw that they were proposing such measures to prove that they were more Revolutionary than we were; but I was thinking too, "Very well, Señor. Whoever proclaims the laws, the people will benefit from them."

We were occupied with that when international affairs called me to the north, the conflicts at Naco being still unsettled. I left for Ciudad Juárez to have talks with General Scott, who was waiting for me there. I arrived at Chihuahua. I stopped there. From Chihuahua I went on to the north. Beyond Chihuahua an envoy from Maytorena boarded the train and he said, "Sr. General Villa, I bring you a message from the governor of Sonora. He thinks that the pact General Bliss and General Scott arranged with Calles and Hill should not be recognized or signed. If we almost have Naco in our possession now and have almost conquered its defenders, who are the enemies of our cause, why should we agree to save that situation for them solely for fear of international dangers? Let General Scott and General Bliss close the frontier, Señor, and you can be certain that Calles and Hill will yield when their matériel is exhausted, and if not, they will come out to fight in an open field where Maytorena's forces will defeat them."

I answered, "Señor, I understand Maytorena's messages and agree with his reasons. Trust me to settle the business without prejudicing our cause. But the important thing in our war is not to take a town or two from the enemy or defeat an army or two but to keep the good will of those who can leave us an open road to victory if they desire, or put obstacles in our way and cause us to fail if they desire that. Don't you know what Juan Sarabia and other Carrancistas are doing on the frontier to make their cause look good and ours look bad? Haven't you been informed that Rafael Zubarán and Eliseo Arredondo are trying to do the same thing in Washington, criticizing and slandering me so that civilized nations, as they are called, will turn against me?"

I answered him so because I knew through Llorente, who represented our government in Washington, and other agents who represented me, that Carranza and all his envoys were trying to poison the minds of Mr. Bryan and Mr. Wilson and General Scott and other authorities who favored me, and because at each step I was aware of the many problems I faced as I tried, without knowledge of international affairs, to prevent my enemies from succeeding in their purpose.

In Ciudad Juárez I called my civilian advisors and said, "Señores, what do you think of the international situation?"

To which they answered, "It must be settled."

And I called Medina and other military men, and said, "Señores, what of our chances if this conflict at Naco is not settled?"

And they answered, "They will not be good,"

And what happened was that on the same day I arrived in Ciudad Juárez, Mr. Carothers and I discussed General Scott's proposal to Maytorena, which Maytorena did not want to accept. He asked me whether I considered it an easy settlement and I answered no, I considered it difficult, although I was in favor of it. It would be difficult to persuade Maytorena to abandon Naco when he was so near to winning and had made such great sacrifices. He asked which I thought better, the defeat of Calles and Hill in Sonora or the friendship of the United States. I answered that I valued the friendship very highly but my duty required me to help Maytorena defeat his enemies, who were the enemies of our cause, and to protect him in every way. He then asked me which was better for me, the triumph of Maytorena in Sonora or the friendly attitude of the Washington government. I answered that it was always best to fulfil one's duty, especially since no friendship was good if it required us to betray other friendships. He asked me whether I was willing to go to El Paso and talk with General Scott whenever necessary. I answered yes, that I was ready for any talks necessary but that if there were to be many we should hold them on the International Bridge where I would meet General Scott each time that he came to wait for me there.

He said, "Very well, Señor, I see that these settlements will not quickly be made although I feel sure they will be made. For everything to be done with true respect for your dignity and General Scott's, I am going to ask Mr. Bryan to have the General cross into Mexican territory to talk with you, and you, too, will come over into United States territory to talk with him. I trust that if you talk with each other when necessary, all difficulties will be overcome." It was done as agreed. General Scott and I and another chief who accompanied him, whose name I do not remember, talked several times. He visited me in the Mexican town of Ciudad Juárez and I visited him in the American town of El Paso.

With Mr. Carothers acting as interpreter, General Scott said to me, "It is wrong for the struggle over Naco to cost the United States so many lives."

I answered, "Señor, it is God's will that you happen to be next door to this war."

He said, "Señor, God is not responsible for evils that can be remedied."

I replied, "Sr. General, what in your opinion is the remedy for the evils that now afflict us?"

It happened that in those talks I was accompanied by Maytorena's envoy, the one who had come to meet me. And with the good intention of protecting Maytorena and helping me, he was answering General Scott. Since he was well informed on the situation at Naco, his words were enlightening and I let him talk. But I soon noticed that he and not I appeared to be the person with whom General Scott was treating, and the latter could not support this but spoke to me in the following man-

ner, "Sr. General Villa, I have come here to have an understanding with
you, not with this man who is always answering me. If you do not care
to talk, Señor, please tell me and I will get up and leave."

He said this, I think, with perfect right, and to calm him I answered
with very much concern, "I have good reasons for permitting Maytorena's representative to express himself. What good would it do us, Sr.
General, to make a settlement the Governor could not accept? Let the
representative give his reasons, and when he has stated them I will permit him to talk no longer."

So it was. When I thought the man had told me everything he knew,
I ordered him to be quiet and not disturb my thinking, and from then
on Scott and I continued to talk without interruption. And seeing that
Scott came to treat with me with candor and respect in the name of Mr.
Bryan and Mr. Wilson, I gave him the answer that I had already communicated to Minister Cardoso de Oliveira in Mexico: I would advise
Maytorena to sign the agreement. This is what I said, "Sr. General Scott,
as a good soldier you will understand the sacrifices we are making out
of friendship with the United States. If we were not considering the
safety of the frontier, Naco would already be in our possession, and if it
were not for the agreement you propose, we would soon take Agua
Prieta, and with control of these two places we would have no more
enemies in the entire state of Sonora. Carranza will be grateful to you,
Señor; but I trust that the reasons you have given me for the settlement
are true, and hope that when the time comes to show me your friendship, you and the Washington government will act in the same spirit in
which you approach me now."

I called a clerk from my secretary's office and told him to send Maytorena a telegram ordering him to accept, sign, and comply with the
pact. For further assurance I sent a copy of this telegram under my own
signature. This was my message:

Sr. Governor Don José María Maytorena:

In conferences in El Paso, Texas, and Ciudad Juárez, Chihuahua, Sr. General Scott and I have concluded after long discussion that you should accept
the agreement proposed for the security of that frontier. I expect you to sign
in the interests of our cause.

Afterwards I called the Governor's envoy and told him it was best to
sign and fulfil the agreement, concerning which he should transmit my
recommendation to Maytorena and see that it was made good.

Angeles' Great Victory at Ramos Arizpe Uncovers the Plot of the Gutiérrez Government.

Scott's Kind Words. Villa's Confidence. Two Million Pesos for Cabral. Angeles Advances. San Pedro de la Colonias and Estación Marte. Emilio Madero. Parras. General Cepeda. Saltillo. Ramos Arizpe. Monterrey. Martiniano Servín. Villarreal's Archives. Gutiérrez' Plans. José Isabel Robles and Eugenio Aguirre Benavides. Dealings with Alvaro Obregón. Eulalio's Manifesto.

My talks with General Scott were useful; they brought harmony and even close friendship. He spoke of the sympathy of Washington with our cause and I expressed our good opinion of Mr. Bryan and Mr. Wilson.

I said, "Señor, Japanese envoys have come to seek a military alliance against the United States."

He asked, "And what is the attitude of Mexico toward these overtures?"

"I informed the envoy who came to me to make the proposal: 'Señor, in case of war between the United States and Japan or between your country and some other nation than Mexico, the United States can count upon our resources.'"

On my way to those interviews or on my return, I no longer remember which, I received a visit from Juan G. Cabral in Chihuahua. Gutiérrez was sending him to Sonora with an order for the delivery of two million pesos of my money, which I respected and countersigned so that my treasury would issue it to him, a thing I mention to show how well I obeyed the orders of our President.

At that time I was receiving reports on Angeles' campaign in the northeast. With the main body of his troops he went from Torreón to San Pedro de la Colonias on the International Railroad, which is the Monterrey line but with a branch line from Paredón to Saltillo. As he was moving from Marte in this way he ordered Emilio Madero to advance from Torreón to Viesca, on the direct railroad from Torreón to Saltillo, and from Viesca to Parras, which Emilio took by fire and sword; and then he was to go on from Parras and threaten the place called General Cepeda on the road to Saltillo.

It seemed to the enemy that Angeles was advancing on Saltillo by the Paredón line, as I had done when it belonged to Huerta's government, or that he was going on to attack Monterrey; therefore most of the defensive troops, commanded by Maclovio Herrera and Antonio I. Villarreal, were concentrated on this side of Paredón, ready to give battle there. But Angeles, very good at maneuvers, diverted them with the pretense of cavalry attacks, which the enemy hastened to meet, thinking that the battle was about to begin, and while they were doing that, he abandoned his line by night and by forced marches, and without their knowing it, crossed over to Emilio Madero's line with the main body of his troops. At the same time he ordered Emilio to continue his own advance, also by forced marches, and attack the garrison at General Cepeda; joined by Orestes Pereyra, Raúl Madero, and Máximo García, he fell furiously upon the town, defeated the enemy, and took many prisoners, one of them the general in command, Ignacio Ramos.

I, Pancho Villa, consider this maneuver of Angeles' a very great military feat. By it he disappointed Villarreal and Maclovio Herrera in their plans to fight in the place of their choice and obliged them to move their front to the Saltillo-Monterrey line, so that he was able to take Saltillo without a struggle. The garrison there, commanded by Luis Gutiérrez, abandoned their positions when threatened by the large number of forces thrown against them.

As I remember, the action at General Cepeda took place on January 5, 1915. The next day Angeles made his march on Saltillo. The day after that he was in Saltillo and on the afternoon of that same day drove back attacks by enemy forces under Maclovio, which were taking up positions on the new line from Saltillo to Monterrey, and those of Luis Gutiérrez, which were retreating. Finally, the next morning, under the protection of a thick fog, Angeles threw himself on Maclovio and Villarreal, who were having difficulty in concentrating their forces in Ramos Arizpe in order to block the Monterrey road. He struck with such force that he defeated the army, took thousands of prisoners and seized their trains and munitions and all other matériel except the artillery, which was saved only because it had not yet arrived on the field. In other words, in Ramos Arizpe, Felipe Angeles won one of the greatest victories of the war and put himself in a position to control all the states of the northeast if supplies and men were available to him. Soon after this triumph, he occupied Monterrey without more fighting. In the battle of Ramos Arizpe ten thousand of my men fought against fourteen thousand or fifteen thousand of Villarreal's and I lost General Martiniano Servín, a very good Revolutionary who had accompanied me in my greatest triumphs and for whom I wept.

When Angeles had made his report on the progress of his victories, I received another message from him in Chihuahua, the conferences at Ciudad Juárez now being over. He told me that among the enemy spoils he found papers of Antonio I. Villarreal which revealed that Gutiérrez and the men of his government and other chiefs of our Convention forces were betraying me and making a deal with the Carrancistas, this time not to unite with them on the promise of removing me from my post, but to fight jointly against me and destroy me as a bandit. Angeles added, "My General, you must have these documents immediately; I will remit them today under close and secure guard. After reading them, dictate your best measures, for we are threatened with betrayal on all sides."

So it was. I left Chihuahua for Torreón, where I found Jesús Aguilar waiting for me with the documents. On considering them at length, aided by one of the clerks in my secretary's office and other men who accompanied me, I found to my fury that I was being abandoned and betrayed by Gutiérrez, José Isabel Robles, Lucio Blanco, Eugenio Aguirre Benavides, Mateo Almanza, and other chiefs who were encouraging and supporting them.

Gutiérrez was plotting in this way:

Señor, my ministers and I believe that honor and patriotism force us to carry forward our present intention to fight and annihilate Francisco Villa and Emiliano Zapata, who are bandits and criminals. Those of us who had refused to recognize Carranza as our Chief, since he was blocking the triumph of the people, are unwilling for this triumph to fail in the hands of Pancho Villa and the chiefs who support him in his crimes. We ask you, Señor, to stop your attacks on the well-disciplined and obedient forces of the Convention government and to give us time to prepare the plan of campaign we will pursue against Villa and Zapata. We are conducting talks with Obregón and the forces of the center of our Republic; have no doubt that the plan we have in mind will be realized in benefit to the people.

I studied Gutiérrez' words and the plans he was making against me, and I thought, "I may have been a bandit and a criminal, but am I any more of a bandit now than when I stood at Madero's side? Am I any more of a criminal than I was when the Convention of Aguascalientes ended its work? And if Gutiérrez accepted me then, saying, 'Sr. General Villa, take command of our armies and enforce the Convention's orders,' why does he denounce me now?"

I was much more deeply hurt by having José Isabel Robles and Eugenio Aguirre Benavides desert me, for they had learned the art of war at my side. Of Robles I remembered, "He counseled prudence when Eulalio wanted to leave Mexico City. He made himself responsible for holding Eulalio there. Then why does he join him now in his treachery? Robles is good, but he is young; they have deceived him."

In any case, Gutiérrez and his generals were now coming to an agreement with Obregón, just as he had been trying to do in the northeast on the day when Martín Espinosa, the President of the Convention, fled to San Luis and Saltillo by his order. This must have been known then, judging by the newspapers of Mexico and the United States, according to which Gutiérrez, on the seventh of January, sent Obregón and Cándido Aguilar a draft of the document in which he stated his reasons for renouncing our relations.

His manifesto said:

Our Revolution triumphed when Constitutionalist troops occupied the capital; but the triumph was frustrated by Carranza's determination to perpetuate himself as First Chief. Then came the Convention of Aguascalientes as a result of disagreements between Sr. Carranza and the chiefs who would not support him; and there it was decided to separate from the First Chief, Francisco Villa, and Emiliano Zapata; I was named President of the Republic with the duty of making the reforms that the people demanded.

But the Carrancista chiefs neither approved nor respected the agreements, and I had no forces to support my legality except my own and General Villa's, whom I re-established in his command for my protection. We left Aguascalientes for Mexico City and the day following our arrival, Villa and Zapata entered upon a career of crime and disobedience. Zapata ordered the arrest and assassination of General Guillermo García Aragón, Vice-President of the Convention. Villa ordered the arrest and assassination of Colonel David Berlanga, one of my secretaries.

In a meeting of my Council of Ministers we unanimously agreed to reprimand Villa and Zapata for their outrages, but without heeding our complaints they left the city, Zapata to take Puebla and Villa to take Guadalajara. As a result of the murders many delegates of the Convention decided to flee to San Luis, and Villa, hearing of this, issued an order for them to be apprehended and shot; they escaped by putting themselves under the protection of Antonio I. Villarreal. Besides this, Generals Villa and Zapata have obstructed me in my government work; they have disobeyed my orders; they have all offices and authorities in their territories under their command; they appoint commandants and governors without my authorization; they proceed with their military operations without order or knowledge of the Minister of War; and so it goes with all the rest. As for General Villa, he has control of almost all our railroads, he renders no accounts of the paper money he prints for his expenses, he interferes in international affairs, and on top of it all he is responsible for kidnapings, robberies, and assassinations which his forces commit in Mexico City and Pachuca, and in who knows how many other places, throwing our society into panic.

Knowing that I disapproved of his crimes, he called a secret meeting of the Convention members who support him and made agreements which are unknown to me, and after the meeting came to see me with a pistol in his hand and accompanied by ten or twelve of his men. With another two thousand surrounding my house, he changed my guard, insulted me, and accused me of trying to abandon him to save the good name of my government. I ask then for a consideration of these circumstances and the entire situation, which I cannot allow and cannot change as long as Villa always answers by saying that these are the ways of war.

It will be understood, then, why my government and I are determined to dissociate the cause of the people from robbery and assassination. For that purpose, by my authority as President, I announce the following points:

First—General Francisco Villa will surrender his command of the Northern Division and all the forces which are or have been under his orders.

Second—Generals Tomás Urbina and Rodolfo Fierro will likewise give up their commands.

Third—General Emiliano Zapata will give up his command of the loyal forces of the Convention.

Fourth—No chief of the loyal forces of the Convention will obey orders other than those dictated by this government through its Minister of War.

Fifth—These agreements will be made known to the forces which now refuse to recognize my government and their help and protection will be requested.

Eulalio Gutiérrez

CHAPTER 12

Determined To Separate from Villa before His Return to Mexico City, Gutiérrez Escapes to San Luis with His Troops.

Alberto Carrera Torres. El Ebano and Ciudad Victoria. Hipólito Villa. A Telegram to Robles. Luisito Returns Villa's Money. Aguascalientes. Victor Elizondo. Reports from Roque González Garza. The Flight of Gutiérrez. Querétaro. Lázaro de la Garza. Teodoro and José V. Elizondo. Francisco Murguía and Manuel M. Diéguez. Calixto Contreras and Rodolfo Fierro. The Security of the Convention.

On my way to Mexico City I learned that forces of General Alberto Carrera Torres were threatening the enemy in control of Tampico. He had reached the canyon El Ebano, and with the rest of his troops he was attacking Luis Caballero in Ciudad Victoria, a place which he had occupied for two days, with great havoc to the defenders, who wore themselves out in recovering it. As Angeles' troops were advancing in the north, and other troops of mine were undertaking their march from San Luis at this same time, I considered Carrera Torres' movements very skilful.

I proceeded on my way south determined to quell disloyalty there; and now I received new warnings of Gutiérrez' plotting. My brother Hipólito sent me this message from Ciudad Juárez: "The reports here say that Gutiérrez is sending envoys to Obregón to propose concerted action against you."

Seeing how such acts were weakening us and destroying our legal position, I would not believe that José Isabel Robles knew of them and approved, although my reports told me otherwise. I sent him a telegram informing him of what I had learned and recommending that he keep a grip on things until I arrived. I was worried not only about José Isabel Robles but about Luisito Aguirre Benavides too, who had remained in Mexico City to purchase the Hotel Palacio but, unable to do this since the building did not belong to the Frenchwoman who was operating it, had returned the money to my paymaster's office. This made me think, "Is Luisito unwilling to be the guardian of my money even? Has his brother Eugenio persuaded him to leave me?"

We arrived in Aguascalientes. Knowing from Gutiérrez' papers that the chief of the plaza was one of the generals working against me, I ordered him seized and brought before me. He declared that he knew nothing of the treachery.

"You know nothing here in front of me, but you know it all behind my back. Don't these papers prove it, Sr. General?" I showed him the documents but he answered, "I know nothing of what they say. If I did, I would say so. There is more than one man in this world, my General." He remained firm in his answers, unyielding and unafraid, but I was convinced of his guilt and delivered him up to my escort to be shot. They were going to shoot him, but on contemplating what awaited him, he sought another way out by cutting his veins. My men could only finish what he had begun and throw his body from the moving train.

That same afternoon, moving south from Aguascalientes, I stopped the train for a telegraphic conference with Roque González Garza, in response to his urgent call from the capital. He said, "I must inform you, my General that today at dawn Gutiérrez and several of his ministers and other officials left the city under protection of José Isabel Robles, Mateo Almanza, Lucio Blanco, and Eugenio Aguirre Benavides, and their forces. The Convention does not know why Gutiérrez has abandoned the government, especially since we confirmed his appointment as President until December 31, 1915. The Convention was continuing its work under his supervision; he had appointed a representative to attend the sessions; with Robles he was studying the new law relating to the government authority. He should be in Pachuca by this time, perhaps with the intention of going on to San Luis. The troops of Madinabeitia and Agustín Estrada, about five thousand in number, remain here faithful to the cause, along with three thousand Zapatistas. As president of the Convention I have taken charge of the government pending approval by the honorable delegates, who are giving this their intelligent consideration. I hope you will see that I had no choice. Only in this way has our status been saved for the good of the people. Order reigns; the civil and military authorities are already in their new positions. At the moment we are waiting only for the Convention to appoint a new Representative of the Executive Power.

I asked him what matériel Gutiérrez carried with him. He answered that he took whatever the Almanza, Robles, and Zaragoza brigades had and part of what belonged to Lucio Blanco's division. I asked him about money and he answered that he took all the funds in the Treasury except four million which he had been unable to carry. Had he taken measures to pursue the disloyal forces? Yes, he had taken such meas-

ures with Manuel Madinabeitia and Agustín Estrada. What laws had
he dictated in such a serious situation? He had declared martial law.
Finally, I approved all his acts and informed him that I would return
and aid in the settlement of our great difficulties, that I would respect
and protect the Convention and would remain loyal to its mandates. I
added, "Señor, inform that Convention that I share their anxieties, and
that any man they choose to replace Gutiérrez will be the man I listen to
and respect and obey without question."

At dawn the next day my train stopped in sight of Querétaro. While I
was dressing, one of my officers came and said, "My General, a column
of about one thousand men is leaving Querétaro, and it looks as if it
may be withdrawing to escape from us." Lázaro de la Garza, my financial agent in Ciudad Juárez, also appeared. He volunteered the opinion
that the troops in question might be those of Teodoro Elizondo, whose
attitude last night was reported to be suspicious, and who must have
known the government was going to abandon us.

I struck at once. Leading the men of my escort and the soldiers of
my scouting train, I fell on the rear guard of the column, and the surprise was so great that we paralyzed it and disarmed it by our verbal
orders alone, and did the same with the forces going on ahead, and then
with others, and others. All of them were brought to a standstill, more
than a thousand, their officers prisoners, their arms captured, their
horses turned loose, and the only ones able to escape were Teodoro and
José V. Elizondo with their staff and a few men following them.

In Querétaro I received reports that Francisco Murguía and Manuel
M. Diéguez were moving against our forces in Guadalajara. I stopped
and ordered the trains transporting the troops of José Rodríguez and
Pablo Seáñez to come closer and those carrying horses and forage to
return. The next day, confronted with the danger that operations at
Guadalajara were not developing successfully, I established my headquarters in Irapuato. There I received news of the defeat of Rodolfo
Fierro and Calixto Contreras, who had been unable to protect the territory I had left them. Señor! Were they dreaming? Had they no eyes
and ears to inform them of the movement against them? Hadn't they
enough experience to know how to stop it? Or did they lack the courage of good soldiers, which is not the courage to die but the courage to
resist until the enemy yields and is broken?

This is how they lost Guadalajara. Francisco Murguía, who was
somewhere around Toluca when the troops of the Convention entered
Mexico, had succeeded in getting across to Morelia, where Gertrudis

Sánchez met him and let him pass, the two insisting that they were for neither Carranza nor the Convention. Then Gertrudis Sánchez ordered Joaquín Amaro and Anastasio Pantoja to make a surprise attack on Murguía's rear guard. But, despite the surprise, Murguía succeeded in getting to Michoacán and entering southern Jalisco. There Diéguez was waiting for him; they united in Tuxpan and together planned a skilful move against Guadalajara of which neither Rodolfo Fierro nor Calixto Contreras had an inkling.

Diéguez and Murguía joined forces in Tlajomulco. Moving their center from there to Orozco, they extended their right wing to Atequiza, threatening the Irapuato line, and their left to the vicinity of our positions beyond the Colima line. The movement of their ten thousand men was so accurate that on the first afternoon of the battle, without the support of artillery, they broke the defense of our left and took El Castillo, cutting the Irapuato line; the next morning they broke our right defense, and soon after, in their push at the center, our men suffered final defeat and lost four hundred men, and trains, cannon, and machine guns. General Melitón Ortega was killed there.

The battle of Guadalajara was fought on the seventeenth and eighteenth of January, 1915. When I heard about it I was grieved, for my forces had suffered a great loss in men and matériel and prestige. My anger was for Rodolfo Fierro and Calixto Contreras. As their scattered forces began to arrive in Irapuato, I received and reorganized them.

Around the twentieth of January, Roque González Garza summoned me to another telegraphic conference. He already knew I was not continuing my journey to Mexico City, and the Convention had already appointed him Chief of Government. He asked me to leave him the five thousand men under Manuel Madinabeitia and Agustín Estrada for the defense of the city. I answered no, that the forces of Zapata were enough to defend it and my troops would have to join me in my struggle in the center and the north. If the Zapatistas could not defend the capital they should abandon it.

He opposed my decision, saying, "It is important to our prestige to keep the capital from falling into the hands of the enemy."

"It is important to win battles in war and then let the battles provide the prestige and deliver the cities."

"The Convention needs forces to protect it."

"The Convention was not created to fight. If you want to be safe, go to any of my cities in the north."

I ordered my troops to join me, knowing that I had good opportunity for a double action. It was urgent to defeat the enemy which, as a result of the flight of Gutiérrez, was concentrating in San Luis and endangering my line at Aguascalientes, and I must prepare for a second conquest of Guadalajara.

CHAPTER 13

Villa Returns from Irapuato and in Aguascalientes Prepares To Take San Luis and Guadalajara.

The Convention Confirms Villa's Appointment. "I Will Never Fail To Serve the Cause of the People." Aguascalientes. The Advance on San Luis and Guadalajara. The Train of Agustín Arroyo Ch. Martín Luis Guzmán. Rodolfo Fierro. Eulalio Gutiérrez. José Isabel Robles. Lucio Blanco. Supper with Villa. Generous Acts. The Meeting in Saltillo. Felipe Angeles Replies to Eugenio Aguirre Benavides.

In Irapuato on the nineteenth or twentieth of January, 1915, I received a telegram from Roque González Garza confirming my appointment as general in chief of our Convention forces. He said:

Sr. General Francisco Villa:

The Presidency of the Sovereign Convention knows what great service you have performed for the cause of the people in times of our deepest anguish. Considering this, and finding myself entrusted with our Executive Power by order of the delegates, I have seen fit to confirm your appointment as general in chief of Convention armies and commandant of all our military operations, certain that the nation puts its faith in your support of the Revolutionary principles and that you will succeed in realizing these, as well as all the dispositions and decrees of the Convention.

I answered:

Sr. President of the Sovereign Convention:

I have your telegram regarding my new appointment as chief of the Convention forces and director of our military operations. You can be sure, Señor, that I will never fail to serve the cause of the people, but will follow it, as I have all these years, devoted to the fulfilment of my duty. I promise you, besides, that the ideals of our Revolution will reach their full development under my command and that the decrees of that Sovereign Convention will be respected and executed.

I remained two or three days in Irapuato, receiving and reorganizing the men who had fled after Rodolfo Fierro's defeat in Guadalajara. I then marched to Aguascalientes to take my measures for the reconquest of Guadalajara. In Aguascalientes I summoned my compadre Urbina and said, "Compadre, Angeles is already gaining control of the districts of the northeast; Cabral is carrying aid to Maytorena, who will dominate the northwest; the north is mine from the frontier to Torreón; the center belongs to me from Torreón to Querétaro. While I organize my column here for the taking of Guadalajara, organize yours, take San Luis and then threaten and attack Tampico. Take the forces of the Morelos, the Melchor Ocampo and the Chao brigades. Take the infantry of the Reza brothers and whatever matériel you need."

So it was. Tomás Urbina began preparations for his departure to San Luis, and I for mine to Guadalajara. I was occupied with this when the postal service train arrived from Mexico City. A Convention man named Agustín Arroyo Ch. had arranged to transport this office. Knowing that Martín Luis Guzmán, the youth whom I had sent to advise José Isabel Robles, was coming on the train, I sent some troops to bring him to me. But he presented himself that afternoon as I was returning from my camp without knowing that my men were looking for him. I welcomed him with greatest affection, giving him a warm embrace and saying, "I knew you would not leave me. From today on we will never be separated; I cannot have you associating with traitors." I added, "Luisito is leaving me. From now on you will be my secretary."

I took him by the arm and led him to my headquarters. And it happened as we were entering the car that I saw Rodolfo Fierro seated there. He rose to greet me, not having seen me since I left him with Calixto Contreras in Guadalajara. And as I wanted to punish him for the bad reports he was bringing me, I anticipated him, saying, "No, Señor, tell me nothing about your defeats."

Without stopping, I went straight into my office with Martín Luis Guzmán and closed the door. When we were alone, I said, "My friend, I want you to give me an account of Gutiérrez' departure and all that you know about it."

"My General, Eulalio left as he had already planned to do, and it was all because of the political situation and the advice he was receiving."

"Yes, my friend; I know how Eulalio let himself be influenced by José Vasconcelos and Eugenio Aguirre Benavides and others who were pushing him on, but how is it that José Isabel Robles supported their plans? How could he let them deceive him? Didn't I entrust Robles to you? Didn't I send you there to guide him?"

"Robles, Sr. General, was working as my superior and did not confide his secrets in me. He showed no signs of abandoning you but only of going along with Eulalio's inclinations in order to show him the error of his ways. Wasn't he still in communication with you? Didn't he come to Guadalajara to see you and return with instructions for the death of Paulino Martínez? Didn't he make himself responsible for keeping Eulalio with our Convention government, and didn't you entrust him with that? Under the guise of serving the Northern Division, wasn't he giving me orders to deprive Zapata of all help, so that the Zapatistas would fail in their defense of Puebla?"

"Why, Señor, did you bring me no reports on all this?"

"Because you put me with Robles to enlighten him with my advice, my General, not to spy on him."

"It is not spying, Señor, for a subordinate to tell a superior what the subordinate discovers and learns within the service; and if it is spying, it is for the cause of the people. Don't I have to kill to fulfil my duties?"

He added, "That may be true, my General, but twice Robles and I went to talk with you and neither time was it discovered that he was betraying you. Robles appeared to be obedient and loyal; he took your orders, he respected them, and he executed them."

"And the document in which the government denounced me, why did you let Robles sign it?"

He answered, "I knew nothing about that paper, Sr. General."

"My friend, I see that you bring me very bad reports on everything. Didn't you promise me that Lucio Blanco would join me and be faithful? Didn't you ask me to give him my pistol in proof of my friendship, and didn't he accept it? You see where his loyalty is now."

"Lucio Blanco is a weak man, my General. First, he could not decide whether to follow Carranza or abandon him; then he was uncertain as to whether to remain with the Convention or not; and now I cannot tell whether he will remain with Gutiérrez or turn his steps in some other direction."

We two continued talking: I, expressing my doubts; he, explaining what had actually happened. And as I soon saw that he was not really to blame for events, or that if he was, he repented, I asked him to have supper with me alone and continue telling me what he knew about things in Mexico City.

After supper, which was served in the same room, I said, "Very well, Señor. They have deceived Robles about me. If he came now, I would pardon him, as I would pardon Luisito, and now pardon you. But there will be no pardon for Gutiérrez, Eugenio Aguirre Benavides, Mateo Almanza, or that lawyer Vasconcelos, who turned against me for trying to save his life when Banderas wanted to kill him. My men will have orders to shoot them wherever they catch them." I again expressed my desire for him to remain with me and fill the post vacated by Luisito, and I ordered a private room prepared for him in my car. But he remarked, "My General, I am very pleased to accept the office you offer me. I only ask that you grant me a few days leave. Two weeks ago my family left Mexico City for the north. I do not know whether they have reached El Paso, which is where I sent them, or are in Chihuahua, or still in Torreón. Permit me, Sr. General, to go look for them, and I promise that as soon as I find them and put them in a safe place, I will be back with you, always at your orders."

That was what he said, and wanting to believe him I quieted my doubts and consented for him to leave as he requested. I said, "My boy, your troubles grieve me; go in search of your family and return as soon as you find them. But mind you: don't abandon me or follow the others, who leave because they fear my punishment or because they are not men enough to oppose my acts." I gave him one thousand pesos of my paper money to help him with the expenses of his trip; and thinking that if he went to El Paso, he would need United States money, I gave him an order for two hundred dollars to be paid by my financial agency in Ciudad Juárez. After that, I took him to the train and commended him to the chief of the escort and to the conductor. I thought, "If he wants to return, my kindness will dispel his uneasiness; and if not, my good treatment will win him over."

It is certain that he reached Torreón; from Torreón he went to Chihuahua; from Chihuahua to Ciudad Juárez; and from Ciudad Juárez he crossed to El Paso, all of which I knew by the telegrams he sent me. But five or six days after his arrival at El Paso he wrote me a letter of apology, telling me that he could not return. He said,

Sr. General Villa:

I am already in the territory of the United States, where I have my family, and I feel that I must retire from the struggle. Believe me, my General, when we said goodby in Aguascalientes I did not intend to deceive you; I was sincere in promising to return and work at your side for the good of the people. But I realize now that all the men of my preference are your enemies. Blanco is your enemy, my General, and Robles, Gutiérrez, and Villarreal, and certainly I have no wish to fight against them, just as I have no wish to fight against you. This is especially true now, when the new struggle is no longer a struggle for our cause but one over designating the powers of the government. I am going far away from our country, to lands where my acts can appear hostile to neither you nor my other compañeros; and in sacrificing myself in this way, I will show you the loyal spirit that separates me from all sides.

On reading his words I was stricken with sadness, "Señor, do I protect the cause of the people so badly that everyone abandons me?"

Again, at this time it happened that Eugenio Aguirre Benavides reached San Luis where Blanco's troops were stationed and from there asked Emilio Madero for a safe conduct to Saltillo. In Saltillo he called a meeting of my generals who were there and in Monterrey, to persuade them to abandon me and defend Gutiérrez. But they all answered no, that they would not abandon me in my struggle, much less aid the cause of Gutiérrez, who was conspiring with Carranza and Obregón. But believing, since he did not see Angeles at the said meeting, that the latter would be favorable to him, he sent him a telegram making the same proposals, which Angeles scorned out of his great wisdom.

Aguirre Benavides said to him:

You made a mistake in not attending the meeting I held in Saltillo with Emilio and Raúl Madero, Orestes Pereyra, and Santiago Ramírez. You, Sr. General Angeles, being a good Revolutionary and a politician, cannot want our country, after four years of struggle, to fall under the tryranny of a man like Francisco Villa. Tell me then what you think, Señor, since I know a man of your good faith will not defend a new tyranny but will support the cause of the people, which we represent.

Angeles answered:

I remember, Sr. General Aguirre Benavides, our oath at Aguascalientes and its consecration on the flag of the Convention, and I say that Gutiérrez is not a loyal President. We were struggling in defense of his government, and he in the meantime was negotiating a plan for the enemy to advance on us from

Saltillo and Monterrey and from Tampico and San Luis, all of which we learned on capturing the archives of Villarreal in Ramos Arizpe. Do not be deceived, then, or expect us to be deceived. I see you now as the same man who conspired in Chihuahua with Obregón, and your own error will teach you a lesson. General Villa is a great man and a patriot, and if he were not, your acts would be enough to make him seem so.

Felipe Angeles

CHAPTER 14

The Convention Government Abandons Mexico City and Villa Assumes Civil Authority in the North.

Villa's Reprimand for the Defeat at Guadalajara. Measures for the Attack on San Luis. Agustín Estrada. Miguel M. Acosta. Manuel Chao. Rincón. La Quemada. The Zaragoza Brigade. The Hacienda del Cubo. A Report from Manuel Banda. A Conference with Estrada. Juan B. Vargas. Political and Military Power. Villa's Manifesto.

In all the fury of my anger I reprimanded Rodolfo Fierro for the defeat he had suffered. I said, "Señor, were you dreaming? Did I send forces to conquer the place, only for you to lose it afterwards? War has its laws, Sr. General Fierro, and following them, good generals either win battles or lose them with little harm if the chances of the struggle dispose their loss. Don't you know that a good general cannot permit such rearguard movements as the one Diéguez made against you at La Capilla and El Castillo? And what do you have to say about Bazán's artillery which you ordered to move without support? Cannon are used to cripple the enemy, Señor; you don't win battles just by firing them."

But Fierro said no, it was not lack of skill that caused his defeat but lack of good means to avoid it, for the combined forces of Murguía and Diéguez had more power than he could withstand, especially since

Calixto Contreras and Julian Medina were not fighting with much spirit, or with the spirit of real brigades of the Northern Division. He therefore had to choose between defending Guadalajara, at the risk of very serious defeat, and abandoning it before the action in order to withdraw to a position where he had control of his line and movements.

To which I answered, "If that was so, Señor, why didn't you conserve your forces and hold out in Guadalajara until I came to assist you?"

I kept on reproaching him and pointing out his lack of skill, not that I had decided to punish him, for Fierro was a very good Revolutionary who had performed many brave deeds, but with the purpose of teaching him a lesson from that defeat; nor did I wish to humiliate him too much, as he might become too cautious, which is paralyzing in time of struggle. In the end, then, I pardoned him with a few kind words. I said, "Very well, the defeats also are battles."

These were the measures to be taken for the attack on San Luis Potosí: as my compadre Urbina was advancing from Aguascalientes, where I stood, other men of mine under Agustín Estrada and Fernando Reyes, and the forces of Bañuelos and Francisco Carrera Torres, soon to join them on the road, would march on the line from Querétaro to Dolores Hidalgo in a movement to immobilize the enemy within the plaza of San Luis or bring them out to meet defeat.

As it happened, these forces, formed of Blanco's division in Acámbaro, part of the Zaragoza Brigade and part of the Robles Brigade, saw the threat in my maneuver. To the north the way was closed by Angeles' troops; to the east by Magdaleno Cedillo and Alberto Carrera Torres; to the west by my compadre Urbina's advance; and to the south by the column of Agustín Estrada and Fernando Reyes. Miguel M. Acosta, their general, had to choose among the four dangers that threatened him or consent to face all four of them at once. Unwisely, I believe, he chose the danger on the south, perhaps thinking less of the column advancing there, or being eager to join Obregón. He disregarded his best exit, which was on the east toward Tampico, especially since all his forces were cavalry.

He moved south then; and beyond San Felipe, near Rincón, his vanguard had an unfortunate encounter with Estrada's column and he withdrew in defeat to the town of San Felipe, sometimes called Torres Mochas. The next day, informed that Urbina's vanguard, under Manuel Chao, was continuing its advance and passing every obstacle on the road, he again moved south, now with the main body of his troops, presumably intending to overtake Estrada's rear guard and take them by surprise on two sides, for the Zaragoza Brigade, Robles' brigade, and another three thousand men would be in San Felipe under Gonzalo Nova, while he, by secret roundabout, marched behind the sierra.

He came very near to succeeding, although he was unable to overtake the rear guard of my troops and make his attack with Nova coming in from the north. He did succeed in engaging them in a furious struggle at La Quemada; and when my men appeared to have him surrounded, the troops he had left in San Felipe appeared on the north, causing such surprise and confusion in our ranks that some of the men considered themselves defeated, like Manuel Banda, whom Estrada ordered to leave with the trains.

The forces from the north were not all of Nova's men but only the Zaragoza Brigade, and when they saw that they were fighting against forces of the Northern Division, not Carrancistas, they first withheld fire and then supported Estrada, not Acosta. In the midst of great confusion, theirs and ours, Acosta's troops were almost defeated but turned back to the north and found shelter that night in San Felipe once more. This was of little advantage to them, however, for the next day, when they attempted to go east toward San Diego de la Unión, by way of the Hacienda del Cubo, my men overtook them and treated them so roughly that most of them, formerly some 12,000 to 14,000 men, either fled or were destroyed. Only Acosta and 1,000 or 1,200 of his men succeeded in reaching El Cubo, while some retreated to Tierra Nueva by a roundabout way and others surrendered, with the loss of their supplies and control of San Luis Potosí and its territories. Manuel Chao occupied the city and then detached columns in pursuit of the rest of the enemy.

I learned afterward about the battles of San Felipe Torres Mochas, as they are called, although in truth none took place there. At that time, I think it was the first or second of February of that year of 1915, it was reported that we had been defeated. I was at headquarters in Aguascalientes when Manuel Banda appeared suddenly and reported: "The news is, my General, that they defeated us yesterday, but I was able to save the trains, which I have brought with me."

"Where did they defeat you, Friend?"

"On the other side of Dolores Hidalgo, toward San Felipe. The fiercest combats took place yesterday, my General. With our forces in disorder and almost defeated, Agustín Estrada ordered me to save the trains, which I have here at your service."

I refused to believe him, my mind being unresigned to these repeated blows of adversity. I thought, "after the flight of Gutiérrez, which is the same as losing the line from Puebla to Veracruz, and after the defeat of Fierro in Guadalajara, which is the same as losing the Colima-Tepic line, am I now to suffer Estrada's defeat, with the loss of my line from Querétaro to Irapuato?"

In the midst of these doubts and fears, I was notified that Estrada was calling me to a telegraphic conference. I began to talk with him, and he communicated the circumstances of his great triumph. I should have rejoiced over Estrada's report, but instead I was seized with a sudden attack of anger at what Banda had just reported, even though his words had turned out to be false. Señor! Could panic bring a soldier to report a defeat when, in truth, he should have reported a victory? In the course of the conference Estrada added: "I ordered Banda to move to the rear to protect my trains, but he understood he was to withdraw them, somewhere or other, and here I am on foot."

I called Juan B. Vargas and said, "Friend, summon an escort and have Banda shot at once." I intended for the order to be carried out, knowing that Banda's action could have upset my plans, but then I remembered how loyal he had always been and how many great tasks he had performed for the cause of the people. I pardoned him and ordered Vargas to set him free.

The Convention and its government had abandoned Mexico City and Obregón had made his entrance with ten or twelve thousand men. Roque González Garza telegraphed me:

It is impossible for the men of the south to defend the capital. I think we should abandon it and let them have the burden of defending it. Then we will come close, harass it, paralyze it, and cause great havoc.

I answered:

Yes, Señor. That is a good plan. Keep Obregón diverted there, content with being in the capital even though he does not control it; and while you carry out that measure, I will go on with the campaigns in the center, the east, and the west that promise us triumph. I ask only that you men break the lines of communication between Mexico City and Puebla, Mexico City and Apizaco, Apizaco and Pachuca, and Pachuca and Tula in order to keep them from building up their strength, or if they do build it up to prevent them from bringing aid to the center before I have brought these campaigns to a successful conclusion.

But I saw afterward, as did my legal advisors, that with the men of the Convention incommunicado we would be without the protection of a government and stripped of all legality. So these advisors came to confer with me, and when I imparted my doubts to them, they spoke of their own. They gave me intelligent advice, all being of the single opinion that I should take over political authority in my territory, just as I had taken over the military authority, and appoint ministers who, with me, would attend to public affairs while we were without communication.

Having settled that point, I said to them, "Now my enemies will say that they were right about my ambition to become President."

They remarked, "They will not say it, Sr. General, and even if they do, it is done for the good of the people."

But as I still insisted that I wanted the point clarified to keep our motives clear, they agreed to write a manifesto, which I signed and published on January 31, 1915. Its contents were the following:

Citizens of Mexico:

Venustiano Carranza, who violated his own Plan of Guadalupe in order to make himself a dictator, was renounced for his obstinacy by the generals of the Northern Division and afterward replaced by our Convention of Aguascalientes. This Convention also legalized the new government, removed the chiefs who commanded divisions from their posts, and named General Eulalio Gutiérrez Provisional President.

But as it happened then that Carranza refused to obey and several of his generals threw themselves immediately into the armed struggle, Gutiérrez, to protect himself, appointed me as Chief of the Convention Army and gave me orders to begin the war. I took my troops to Mexico City, where Zapata joined me with the men of the Liberating Army of the South, and then, as Zapata took possession of Puebla and I took possession of Guadalajara, the government and the Convention began to realize the triumph of the people, considering new laws to govern us.

Then, unfortunately, politicians with ambition or more love for intrigue than for the future of our cause rose within the government, and knowing that Gutiérrez was a weak President, afraid to meet the exigencies of the struggle, and that his Minister of War, José Isabel Robles, was young and inexperienced, confused the two with bad counsel and pushed them into renouncing and abandoning the Convention and fleeing from the capital. For this reason the Convention has had to recover the executive power, which it exercises through the person of its President, General Roque González Garza, who has confirmed my position as general in chief of the Convention armies.

It occurs, however, that by force of circumstances the armies are now separated and even without communication, a part of them concentrating in the north under my orders, with headquarters in Aguascalientes, another part in the south under Zapata, and the President of the Convention with general headquarters in Cuernavaca—all of which now obliges me to take over the civil authority, which I will not exercise personally but through three offices situated in the city of Chihuahua. The first of the said offices will be concerned with justice and international affairs; the second, with communications and the business of internal government, and the third, with the treasury and the development of industry. But I, Pancho Villa, declare that the new authority circumstances force me to assume will be no authority of dictatorial form but only that of the man who, in his devotion to the people, has already expressed his ideals of redemption, the authority of the man who swore to be faithful to the Convention, to respect and obey its orders, and to recognize whatever government it might establish.

After the manifesto I published the first decree under my new authority, designating the chiefs of the three offices of government which had been created.

CHAPTER 15

After Taking Guadalajara Villa Pursues Murguía and Diéguez and Makes Them Wait for Him at Cuesta de Sayula.

Miguel Díaz Lombardo. Luis de la Garza Cárdenas. Francisco Escudero. Manuel Bonilla. Carranza's Laws and Those of the Convention. The Lawyer Blas Urrea. Doctor Atl. The Post Office Funds. Arroyo Ch. Rubén Eudeber López. Angeles' Warnings. Fierro and Seáñez. La Barca. Guadalajara. Santa Ana Acatlán. Zacoalco.

My three chiefs, or ministers of government departments in my territory of the North were: Miguel Díaz Lombardo, that great lawyer whom Dr. Ramón Puente, by my order, had brought from Paris; Luis de la Garza Cárdenas, who revealed the cruel attacks that Paulino Martínez made upon our apostle of democracy; and Francisco Escudero, the man sent by Carranza to Ciudad Juárez when my forces took that town, the man who offended me there by making light of my valor and that of my troops.

Besides these men I had others in Chihuahua to write the laws for the realization of our Revolutionary triumph. Don Manuel Bonilla was writing those for the delivery of lands to the laborers in the fields, and others were writing them for laborers and skilled workmen in cities and towns. So we were attending to these things too and not only the war; and I, Pancho Villa, say this to show that the accusation with which the Carrancistas began to discredit me and my troops was utterly false and malicious. They were reviling us as reactionaries, but to prove their statements they began to write many laws in Veracruz, like the divorce law, the agrarian laws, the laws affecting land and oil, and others I do not remember. We were not reactionaries nor could we be, and our acts were forcing Carranza to turn into a true Revolutionary and to propose laws like those our Convention had under study and my men wanted to issue in the north and Zapata in the south. But deceiving everybody, and misrepresenting us, whose arms had done most to bring about the defeat and fall of Huerta, the Carrancistas maligned and defamed and slandered and vilified us in the theaters of Veracruz and the newspapers which Carranza's intellectuals were publishing there.

The lawyer Luis Cabrera, whom others called "Blas Urrea," said:

Pancho Villa is a deceitful and disloyal politician. At the beginning of the Convention he used his influence on all the chiefs to create trouble and darken the future. He whispered in their ears, saying, "Compañerito, you want me for President of the Republic," which he did in his determination to confuse them while he was gaining time and support for his intrigues.

The writer everyone called "Dr. Atl" said:

Pancho Villa is a ferocious man, an animal of the quaternary ages. Díaz Lombardo, a Jesuit lawyer, a coward, and a lover of extravagance, advises him. Angeles guides him with the deceit and cunning of a soldier trained under Porfirismo. Villa is a politician who employs treachery in everything he does. He has succeeded in bewitching Zapata, whom he disorients and betrays.

And so on with the rest.

The train transporting the post office from Mexico City passed through Aguascalientes and in it arrived the young Convencionista called Agustín Arroyo Ch., accompanied by another, Eudeber López, whose first name I forget. Informed that funds were coming on the train, I instructed the young men to render an account and deliver the money to me.

They answered, "Sr. General, we have no money. We bring account books, furniture, and two million pesos in postage stamps."

"And the capital that you draw on, where is it?"

"The post office draws on no capital. What is credited on one side is marked paid on the other, and if anything is left, it goes to support the government."

They not only explained that they brought no money, nor could, but convinced me of their need, or, rather, the need in the office their chief Eusebio García Martínez was opening in Torreón. Without some 500,000 pesos the office could not continue to operate, and with that amount operations would still be difficult. I understood their position and then and there ordered the delivery of 750,000 pesos, so that the people of La Laguna might have the convenience of the post office and the prestige of our cause would not suffer. I did this, and relate it now, to show that my ways and those of the Convention government were judicious even when faced with the most serious demands. At the time there was little enough money for all the arms, munitions, equipment, and supplies I had to buy and pay for.

In Aguascalientes preparing for the advance on Guadalajara, I was notified of a surprise attack made there by Julian C. Medina and other chiefs of mine. In it, according to my reports, our men almost reached the center of the town but were driven back. This confirmed my judgment that the troops of Diéguez and Murguía were neither skilful nor numerous. I pressed on with my preparations, anxious to reconquer those districts and the line I had to control to annihilate the enemy operating in Sinaloa and southern Sonora.

By then I knew that Pablo González was threatening Monterrey. Angeles telegraphed me:

Sr. General Villa:
    General González is coming by way of Cadereyta to attack Monterrey with his maximum strength. Maclovio Herrera, at Topo Chico, is threatening our line to Laredo; Villarreal threatens the Matamoros line at Apodaca; González threatens the Ciudad Victoria line at Guadalupe. I will resist the attacks and repel them, but I need your aid to destroy the enemy protected by our northern frontier.

I answered:

Sr. General Angeles:

My compadre Urbina is already in San Luis and moving from there on Tampico. His advance will alleviate the threats you speak of. Hold your positions, Señor, and extend your control if, as I predict, part of the enemy troops go to the aid of Tampico or try to defend themselves from attacks on that side. It is important for me to recover Guadalajara; after that, the center of our Republic will belong to us, and we can go on to destroy the enemy troops commanded by Ramón F. Iturbe and Juan Carrasco in Sinaloa and those that Angel Flores is organizing and training in southern Sonora. Rafael Buelna is advancing by way of Tepic, but he can do little or nothing unless we bring him aid from Guadalajara.

I telegraphed this message determined and confident that I would defeat and annihilate the forces of Diéguez and Murguía in Jalisco, and certain also that I would gain control from Colima to Manzanillo and from Guadalajara to Tepic.

These were my measures for retaking Guadalajara: order General Estrada to return from San Felipe to Querétaro and cover the line to San Juan del Río, always with an eye on advances by Obregón; order the brigades of José Rodríguez, under Fierro and Pablo Seáñez, and that of Contreras, all cavalry, to undertake their march on foot toward Encarnación, San Juan de los Lagos, and Arandas until reaching Degollado and the railroad line from Irapuato to Guadalajara; order the infantry and the artillery to depart by train to Irapuato and from there to the west until joining the cavalry at Yurécuaro, one-third of a day's journey from La Barca.

The five thousand men of my cavalry left on foot. Another four or five thousand of my infantry and artillery left by train with other cavalry forces and my staff and escort. By the eighth or ninth of February I was already near Yurécuaro, and Murguía had retreated from La Piedad. José Rodríguez was in Degollado with his brigades, and I sent him an order by an airplane I had with me to continue his advance to La Barca where, according to my information, the Carrancista advance troops were stationed.

José Rodríguez made his entrance into La Barca that night. I arrived with the main body of my troops and my artillery at dawn the following day. The morning of that same day I called a meeting of my generals and I said, "Compañeritos, this enemy is not prepared to give us a very strong battle. I believe they will abandon Guadalajara and all the districts of Jalisco, knowing their inability to resist. Murguía and Diéguez leave it to us to pursue them until our breath gives out. These are my orders for destroying them: "You, Sr. General Fierro, and you, Sr. General Seáñez, will march behind Murguía, south of Lake Chapala, to Pajacuarán, Jiquilpan, Manzanillo, Concepción, and Atoyac; and while you cover that distance, I will go with the main body of my troops to Las Juntas, or La Junta, and after entering Guadalajara, will march south in pursuit, with you, my Generals, following to halt them or force them to retreat farther, or even, if possible, to cut off all retreat."

We left that afternoon to put the plan into effect. Fierro and Pablo Seáñez fought in Pajacuarán with Murguía's rear guard, which retreated and fought at other places and continued their march, as I had ordered, to Atoyac and Techaluta, a district where the enemy abandoned trains and some impedimenta in their rapid retreat. I reached Las Juntas, cleared the camp, still strewn with the dead of the previous battle, and continued the pursuit of Diéguez who, according to my predictions, had not waited for me but had retreated to Zapotlán. I entered Guadalajara accompanied by my aides and my escort only, ordering my forces to await my return in Las Juntas. I did not want my troops to seek the amusements of the city. The celebration of our victory might distract them for several days.

My re-entrance into Guadalajara was on the twelfth or thirteenth of February, 1915, and the people were happy to see me again. I was welcomed by the ringing of bells, by women with their flowers, and by men and children with friendly greetings, all in the midst of arch-covered streets. While I was in the Palace to deliver the government to Julian C. Medina, the crowds were cheering me and calling me to speak. I went out on the balcony to express my friendly feelings and spoke of my hopes for the triumph of our ideals. Señor! I saw that these were good people, with no hatred in their hearts but only the desire for peace, not war! They must have been pleased with my words, too, for when I went out into the street again, the humble ones surrounded and followed me and smiled at me, and even the powerful people greeted me. I could not help thinking, "However much Carranza's favorites abuse me, these people know that Pancho Villa is not a bandit without a conscience or a wild beast. They love me for my deeds, in spite of slander."

I hurried back to Las Juntas to give the enemy no rest. The next morning I ordered an advance to Santa Ana Acatlán, which we reached after an engagement between our vanguard and the enemy's rear guard under the command of Enrique Estrada. We continued on to Zacoalco. There I waited for my artillery; and hearing that the brigades of Fierro and Seáñez were already in Atoyac, where Fierro had overtaken the enemy and taken prisoners, among them an engineer, Colonel Amado Aguirre, I ordered my brigades to join those of José Rodríguez in Techaluta and Atoyac.

The track from Guadalajara had been destroyed, so that my vanguard and the main body of my troops had to advance on foot, which we were doing when my scout service advised me of the position of the enemy, drawn up and waiting on the slopes of the sierra called Cuesta de Sayula.

CHAPTER 16

Villa Defeats Diéguez and Murguía at Cuesta de Sayula; Then Returns to the Northeast To Assist Angeles.

Reflections at Sayula. The Troops of the Two Armies. Dispositions for the Battle. February 18, 1915. The Heights of the Sierra. Enrique Estrada. The Weakness of the Center. At One O'Clock. At Six O'Clock. The Last Resistance of the Right. Final Defeat. Fierro's Shootings at San Nicolás. Zapotlán. Tuxpan. Angeles and Villa Differ. Guadalajara.

Diéguez first intended to remain in Sayula, where he was entrenched, and then, changing his mind, abandoned it and retreated to La Cuesta, to wait for me there. He was no longer master of his own will but merely acting in response to mine.

My headquarters, my center, and my artillery were at the Hacienda Amatitlán; my left was on the line from Atoyac to the beginning of the sierra; and my right was alongside Sayula. In number my troops were some eleven thousand men. The enemy had about twelve thousand. Diéguez pitched his left a long way off, without my understanding why, on the Cerros de Tecolote. He put his right on the heights of the sierra, in the mistaken notion, I think, that such a position would give him an advantage and that I would never be able to dislodge him.

At dawn on February 18, 1915, we were already engaged in a hard struggle. My left under Fierro and Seáñez moved from Atoyac to the top of the sierra, where the enemy fell back after suffering great losses. Aware of what was occurring there, I turned my cannon on the center, and with this under fire, the presence of my right, in advance from Sayula, kept their left under restraint; as I said, it was too far from their center to receive support.

The fighting increased from dawn until nine or ten in the morning. At that time Murguía and Diéguez discovered that I was turning their right and they would be unable to hold in the center; therefore they reinforced that side with all the cavalry forces of Enrique Estrada. The fight grew hotter there as they endeavored to recover their positions, and as Fierro and Seáñez continued advancing. It was the decisive moment when Estrada attempted to regain control of those positions, for he had to face enormous losses to do it. It was good tactics for Fierro and Pablo Seáñez to let him weaken himself, which he did.

Diéguez was employing no less than three thousand men, or perhaps four thousand, in bolstering his right while another two thousand were immobilized on his left; then I saw the weakness of his center, bombarded by García Santibáñez' artillery, which was firing with great accuracy. I sent my infantry against it, with the cavalry carrying the firing line up to the front under cover of a bombardment which the enemy cannon could not silence. At one the struggle on my left redoubled, where Estrada's men, after the losses they had suffered in their counterattack, were now being pounded by Fierro and Pablo Seáñez. At two I saw that the center could resist me no longer and threw most of my troops into the assault. It was four when the enemy began to waver in the lines. Then as they appeared ready to abandon their positions, my cannon fire grew stronger and my infantry launched its assault; at the center my cavalry threw them into disorder, and with that the fury of our attack increased, their resistance broke, and we drove them back in retreat.

While this was happening Diéguez' right wing was so wrapped in struggle with the brigades of Fierro and Seáñez that it could have done nothing in support of his center, even if it had tried and meanwhile his left, commander, I believe, by Rómulo Figueroa, was abandoning the line and withdrawing to Zapotlán.

Thus our complete triumph and the complete defeat of Diéguez and Murguía began. At six in the afternoon their right was still offering some resistance, but my cavalry and a part of Fierro's were already in pursuit of most of the defeated, who were dispersed or overtaken and killed, wounded, or taken prisoner. The battle of Sayula cost Diéguez and Murguía no less than one thousand men, dead and wounded, and the flight of I do not know how many thousands, and for the second time gave me control of the state of Jalisco.

That night I reached San Nicolás with my forces. I learned that Fierro was ordering all prisoners shot, not out of military necessity but to punish troops that had defeated him before. I sent Juan B. Vargas to say—"Discontinue this shooting, since every man killed is one less to work on repairing the railroads." Fierro complied, as I could tell when the firing ceased. I thought to myself, in the silence that followed, "If the men who were about to die knew why the order was changed, they would run all over the world denying the cruelty my enemies attribute to me."

At dawn the next day I advanced on Zapotlán. The enemy had left us their trains and several cars of ammunition, and also the same artillery taken from Fierro when he was defeated on the eighteenth of January. From Zapotlán I notified Angeles of my victory. In reply he congratulated me, saying, "I won't be able to equal that triumph, Señor. My men are as brave as yours but they do not have as great a leader." His words showed his modesty.

From Zapotlán I continued my march to Tuxpan. Seeing that the enemy was still retreating, I called a meeting of all my chiefs—and asked whether they considered it best to continue the pursuit. The others agreed with Fierro that we should continue until we pushed Diéguez and Murguía into the sea. They reasoned that if we seized the few trains Diéguez and Murguía still had, their infantry would be halted, and away from Manzanillo there would be no port to assist them or routes by which Carranza could supply them.

But while I was still in Tuxpan Angeles telegraphed again and said:

Diéguez and Murguía will need much time to reorganize. Come north with the main body of your troops. Together we can take all this territory from González. Then combining my attack with that of Urbina, who is advancing from San Luis, we can also take Tampico.

I answered: "Wait until my men here annihilate the enemy."

You will never annihilate them if they are intelligent, considering that they have shelter in all the districts of Michoacán and Guerrero. Dictate measures for holding Guadalajara, to insure the line from there to Irapuato, and then come north, Señor. Once we are masters of the northeast, the north, and the frontier, we can safely move to the center and end the western campaign. But with the enemy in Sinaloa and Sonora and me resisting the attacks on Monterrey with too few forces, a campaign as far away as that offers no solid results.

I accepted his opinion and returned to the north with the main body of my troops, leaving Julian Medina to cover the line from Zapotlán to Tuxpan, and Fierro, Contreras, and Seáñez to guard Jalisco.

CHAPTER 17

Without Interrupting His Trip to Monterrey, Villa Tries To Send Troops to All the Regions That Favor Carranza.

Obregón's Movements. Doctor Arroyo. A Communication from Eulalio Gutiérrez. Rafael Buelna and Juan Carrasco. Escuinapa. The Martyrdom of Mexico City. Federico Cervantes. José I. Prieto. Acuitzio. Tacámbaro. The Death of Gertrudis Sánchez. Luis Gutiérrez and Maclovio Herrera. Rosalío Hernández. Manuel Peláez. Manuel Chao and Emiliano Sarabia. San Mateo. The People of Cedillo.

Either the twenty-fourth or twenty-sixth of February, 1915, I learned of movements some of Obregón's forces were making from Pachuca and Tula and of his attempts to approach San Juan del Río. I learned too of the arrival of Gutiérrez and the rest of his government at Doctor Arroyo, a town situated in the south of Nuevo León, where he had fled after the defeat of his forces at San Felipe Torres Mochas.

From Doctor Arroyo he sent agents to communicate with Villarreal and other Carrancistas of the northeast, asking them to join him and protect him. He said:

It is not my intention to perpetuate myself in supreme command in opposition to the good chiefs who elected me, but I advise the immediate reunion of the Convention, to deliberate on public matters and again choose a capable chief. In the meantime it is urgent for my government to reach some frontier town where it can communicate with the rest of our country and with foreign governments. I hope your patriotism will induce you to sustain this legitimate government, which is yours, and that you will grant it safe passage. Believe me, as I have removed Villa and Zapata from their posts, so I will remove Carranza from his, according to the mandates of the Convention.

He was marching farther down his road of errors. To defend himself against Carranza he once had my protection, which alienated Carrancistas; then to protect himself from me, he sought an understanding with the Carrancistas, who had left him; and now without the support of either, he wanted to be protected by all and to struggle against all. Señor!

As I remember, it was then I received reports from Sinaloa of Rafael Buelna's fierce battle with Juan Carrasco, whom he had defeated at Escuinapa, and of other actions in the struggle with Ramón F. Iturbe, who was dominating the region of Mazatlán. In admiration of Buelna's fighting spirit, which carried him deep into enemy territory without means of supplying himself with munitions and other stores, I was thinking to myself, "With control of the northeast, according to Angeles' plan, it will not be difficult to take Sinaloa and the southern part of Sonora. That advantage we will owe to this bold youth Rafael Buelna."

From my couriers and from reports by Roque González Garza, who was in Cuernavaca, I also learned of measures Carranza and Obregón were taking to overcome Mexico City, which they considered hostile. They had decided not to occupy the capital but were seeking to destroy its commerce; instead of helping the inhabitants and providing them with relief, they were secretly trying to starve them. Their purpose was to induce those of the people who were not Carrancistas to join the new army they were organizing for their struggle against me and Zapata. They made loud outcries, saying that the rich had to help the poor, publishing orders and decrees to that effect, but in truth they wanted no such help nor were they encouraging it but were quietly opposing it.

Obregón said, "The Zapatistas have cut off the water supply from the springs in Xochimilco. I lack the forces to recover the springs."

Carranza said, "Villa left the city flooded with his paper money. I do not recognize it."

Luis Cabrera said, "Mexico City is a white elephant. We need not protect and feed it."

And they carried their iniquity so far, as I learned, that Federico Cervantes and other Convention men finally went from Cuernavaca to

Xochimilco to restore the water; Obregón, forgetful of his duties, never attempted this.

Mr. Bryan and Mr. Wilson, knowing what was happening, sent diplomatic notes to Carranza and Obregón appealing to their humane feelings and saying that the great city of Mexico deserved a better fate, and that if they felt they could protect and sustain it, they should keep it, but not otherwise. I learned this in a message from Llorente, the consul who was representing me in Washington.

Before undertaking my trip to the northeast I sent a column under José I. Prieto to advance on Michoacán and pursue and annihilate Gertrudis Sánchez. I did this knowing that Sánchez had refused to obey the Convention and was leaning to Carrancismo.

Later those troops of mine and others from Michoacán united and attacked Sánchez in full force. He abandoned Morelia and Pátzcuaro. They overtook him and defeated him in Acuitzio and pursued him farther. Soon they overtook him and defeated him again at Tacámbaro, capturing all he was carrying, and from there they followed him to San Antonio de las Huertas, where they defeated the rest of his troops and wounded him. He fled, almost alone, and in Guerrero took refuge with his troops, who pretended they would protect him but murdered him.

Before that I had received reports from Emilio Madero and Angeles on the movements of Luis Gutiérrez and Maclovio Herrera who were approaching Chihuahua, coming from the region of Monclova. In support of the plan to gain control of the northeast, I dictated orders for Rosalío Hernández to move from Camargo to Jiménez in northern Coahuila, going by way of Sierra Mojada, and to fight until he defeated the Carrancistas there.

And so he did. By the first days of March, 1915, he had already advanced from Sierra Mojada to Cuatro Ciénagas. Luis Gutiérrez retreated, whereupon Hernández moved from Cuatro Ciénagas to Monclova, and again Gutiérrez retreated, but this time Hernández overtook him and Maclovio Herrera in Sabinas and defeated both of them. After this, by advancing from Sabinas to Allende, very near Piedras Negras, he forced them to abandon that place, and Villa Acuña, and other frontier points.

Tomás Urbina was on his way from San Luis to Tampico—a march for the conquest of the oil fields, a source of great income to Carranza. As it happened, there were soldiers already there who recognized my authority, for example, Manuel Peláez, who was imposing loans and duties on the oil companies in the district of Tuxpan. But as they neither controlled the territory nor had any of its ports, their demands caused only a small deduction from Carranza's collections. On the other hand they were confusing the international situation, especially since they were not officially my men.

Mr. Carothers asked me, in the name of Mr. Bryan, "Is it true, Sr. General Villa, that General Peláez represents you in the field of Temapache in the state of Veracruz? Is it true that you have ordered him to exact loans from the oil enterprises? If it is not true that you support him in such demands, do you have the authority to order him to withdraw them? Is it true that you have ordered him to grant protection to some oil enterprises and not to others?" To which I answered, "Señor, tell Mr. Bryan that the forces of my compadre Urbina are now advancing upon the oil fields of Tampico and Tuxpan; that I cannot be expected to issue orders not knowing whether they can be executed; and that once I have taken Tampico, justice will be fully imposed in the fields." And knowing that the advance was in fact taking place, the consuls waited for me to follow and make my decisions good.

The advance was made in this way: Urbina had occupied San Luis Potosí and sent some of Manuel Chao's forces under Emiliano Sarabia to overtake Miguel M. Acosta. This they did in Las Tablas. To make contact with the forces of Magdaleno Cedillo, who was in Ciudad del Maíz, Chao soon left San Luis for Rascón. Going down to Rascón, the Cedillos and Alberto Carrera Torres joined forces. From Rascón, Chao set out for Micos. Alfredo Rueda Quijano, Meave, and some troops of the Morelos Brigade joined him there. He continued from Micos to San Mateo. On the way the enemy, under the command of General Lárraga, came out to meet him. At the first encounter, the troops of the Cedillos, who formed a vanguard of about five thousand men, retreated, leaving the Chao Brigade and part of the Morelos Brigade and other troops to sustain the attack and repulse the enemy. From San Mateo, Chao proceeded to Valles and Bañito. In Bañito he fought for no less than three days; then he met Lárraga again, this time occupying positions. Having artillery now, he dislodged the enemy. With his opponents forced to retire toward Tampico, Chao marched beyond Las Palmas, Guerrero, and Auza, where he found the bridges destroyed and the railway track razed. In spite of this, by March 5, 1915, he was engaged in combats of great fury, opposite the hill and woods they call El Ebano, where the enemy had fortified themselves.

CHAPTER 18

While Villa Undertakes the Northeastern Campaign with Angeles, Diéguez and Murguía Defeat Fierro and Seáñez in Jalisco.

Angeles in Monterrey. González' Attacks. "They Flee at the Jingle of My Spurs." Los Ramones. Los Herreras. Cerralvo. The Plan of Campaign. Cadereyta and San Juan. Laredo. Evasions at Washington. Funston and Scott. Fierro's Defeat in Tuxpan.

In reporting his struggle in Monterrey, Angeles said:

Sr. General Villa:

It is an honor to communicate to you that the division under my command is repelling all attacks of the Carrancistas along the Laredo, Matamoros, and Ciudad Victoria lines. González has had to retire to Cadereyta, Villarreal to Los Ramones, and other troops of his, under José E. Santos, to Villaldama. The enemy forces are not powerful enough to move me from here, but neither am I strong enough to go out and destroy them. The column with which I won at Ramos Arizpe now protects the Torreón-Saltillo line and the Saltillo-Monterrey line and garrisons both Saltillo and Monterrey. So I am here with less than four thousand men.

When I reached Monterrey, I saw that Angeles was not exaggerating, but it was also true that he was too much concerned with protecting the place. Part of the cavalry were even serving in the firing line, which did not appear good to me. In talking with him I said, "Why don't you attack, Señor? Just by putting in an appearance I terrify the enemy. Taking advantage of that, I make a sudden attack, break through although it costs me losses, then I attack again and defeat them."

"Sr. General," he answered, "I am not as much on the defensive as it may seem. I cannot pursue all three enemies at once. So I wait, let the enemy come within reach, then strike. It is different now you are here." So it was. We advanced on Villarreal the next day at Los Ramones. He retired but we overtook his rear guard. I said, "You see, Sr. General. These Carrancistas flee at the jingle of my spurs."

After destroying Villarreal's rear guard and taking part of his trains I detached troops to follow him to Los Herreras and Cerralvo. There he abandoned impedimenta and his artillery. Seeing this, we planned the northeastern campaign. José Rodríguez would advance on the same line and take Matamoros. Máximo García and Severino Ceniceros would march on Ciudad Victoria. Another column, under Orestes Pereyra, would leave for the Piedras Negras and Laredo lines, to overtake Maclovio Herrera and Luis Gutiérrez. After the attack on Matamoros and Ciudad Victoria, Angeles would go to the attack on Tampico, which Tomás Urbina would take with his aid, and I would go to direct the campaigns at the center and in the west. By March 20, 1915, the column sent to Ciudad Victoria had defeated González in Cadereyta and was pushing him back to San Juan. By the twenty-first or twenty-second, Villarreal had retreated to Matamoros with all his forces, and Maclovio Herrera had abandoned Coahuila and Nuevo León and was taking refuge in Nuevo Laredo, while Luis Gutiérrez was hiding in the Sierra de Arteaga.

We were occupied with this when I received notice I was needed in Monterrey to attend to international affairs. Through Mr. Carothers, Mr. Bryan advised me of dangers to the American towns on the frontier. These were his words:

The government in Washington is informed that Maytorena's forces are ready to attack Agua Prieta, and Convention troops under Juan Cabral are advancing on it from Chihuahua; we know further that Carrancista troops will attempt some action against Naco and Nogales. As this means danger to the lives and property of our frontier towns, we invoke your prudence, sure that you will enforce observance of the agreement signed by Maytorena and Calles which establishes the neutrality of Mexican cities situated on the frontier. Only in this way can you avoid serious measures that this government will take to defend the lives and property of our citizens.

I informed Mr. Bryan that it was my intention to respect the agreement, though circumstances might some day require us to attack frontier towns. In conference with Miguel Díaz Lombardo by telegraph, I asked: "Señor, to avoid injury on the other side of a frontier, does an army have to leave frontier towns in the hands of the enemy forever? Study this question, Señor, and see to it that international law, which I do not wish to violate, does not obstruct our operations."

Several days later I had reports of his talks with Mr. Carothers and his letters to Mr. Bryan. He had argued:

Señores, our Convention government considers your attitude inconsistent with the laws of neutrality, inasmuch as you hamper our freedom of action at the frontier while arming and supplying, and thus encouraging, the enemy who have taken refuge there. We propose, gentlemen, that the same principles should apply as govern naval attacks on seaports. That is, provided our armies or those of Carranza can surround a frontier plaza and prevent the arrival of reinforcements, supplies, money, or other aid, as in a blockade, your government will declare all trade with the place suspended; in which case the defending troops will have to surrender or struggle in the open field.

But Washington would not accept, answering that they were not trying to prevent attacks upon Matamoros or Nuevo Laredo but only to safeguard their frontier towns, and had already warned the chiefs at Laredo and Matamoros to conduct the war in the proper manner. General Funston and General Scott wanted to hold a conference, but I knew the danger of such talks and pleaded a lack of time.

In Monterrey I learned that Fierro had been defeated again, in Jalisco, where I had left him with Julian C. Medina and Pablo Seáñez. This filled me with gloom, for I saw that we would lose the fruit of my victory at Cuesta de Sayula. In Manzanillo, Diéguez and Murguía found a ship with several cannon and a good supply of shells; and three or four weeks later, when Angeles and I were developing our plan in the northeast, another ship arrived with I know not how many million cartridges that Carranza was sending them from Salina Cruz. Well-armed and well-equipped, they made the march from Manzanillo to Tuxpan. Fierro, being an impetuous man, made the mistake of letting them wait for him in good positions, instead of being the one himself to wait. He found Pablo Quiroga's infantry well fortified, and Diéguez' artillery so well located that it could fire on him with great effect. Their troops numbered six thousand, ours five thousand. Their bombardment broke Fierro's ranks as they advanced on level ground, and Fierro, anxious to correct his error, weakened himself by launching cavalry charges that yielded nothing. He fought in this fashion all day on the twenty-first of March and the twenty-second, and on the morning of the twenty-third, with his attacks still unsuccessful, could not face counterattack. His resistance broke. By ten that morning he was defeated; by twelve, routed and almost dispersed, he had to retreat to Zapotlán; by three he had withdrawn to Sayula; and by dark on the following day was back in Guadalajara. There he reorganized and regained some strength when he incorporated reinforcements I sent him from Irapuato. He then returned to Zacoalco and halted Diéguez and Murguía at Zapotlán. In Fierro's defeat in Jalisco, my forces lost no less than two thousand men and eight hundred horses and a large amount of arms and ammunition for guns and cannon.

CHAPTER 19

Learning of Obregón's Advance at Querétaro, Villa Abandons the Northeastern Campaign and Moves South Again.

Merchants, Manufacturers, and Bankers of Monterrey. The Fruits of Labor. Corn and Beans. Peón. Nopala. Cazadero. Manuel Chao in El Ebano. Jacinto B. Treviño. Bryan and the Peaceful Inhabitants. Carranza's Reply. Roque González Garza. Obregón's Advance. Angeles' Advice. Villa's Decision.

The businessmen of Monterrey hastily assembled and planned to entertain me. They said, "Sr. General, we have the honor to welcome you in the name of this city, its trade, industry, and banks. We know that you are liberal, just, and a good Revolutionary and we come to say the city of Monterrey is also devoted to liberty, justice, and the well-being of all its inhabitants, great or small, rich or poor."

I answered, "Men of business and industry, be rich in good sentiments and not in property only; take pity on the poor and needy and help them. Consider that the wealth of our Republic is the fruit of toil and of intelligent men whom toil supports. So it is not justice to look on anything you have as your own or to use it for your sole benefit."

They answered that I was right, that without the labor of the people nothing would be produced and nothing would endure. But, as they added that they wanted to invite me to a banquet, I asked them whether the entertainment would be as splendid as they pictured it. They answered yes. I asked how many persons were coming to honor me. They answered that everyone in business, industry, and banking would be there. I asked them what they expected to spend on the fiesta. They answered, no less than thirty thousand pesos. At this I said, "I accept your invitation, Señores, but considering that I do not eat so much and neither do the persons who invite me, I propose that the fiesta be given for the benefit of the poor. I always have my dinner at headquarters; you always have yours at home. Why feed us those thirty thousand pesos when there are so many poor and miserable families in Monterrey?" I turned to Raúl Madero and added, "Sr. Governor, collect thirty thousand pesos and spend them on corn and beans. Open places at the four corners of the city and every day give each woman who comes a quart of corn and a quarter-pound of beans for her family."

Hearing this, they accepted it in good spirit, but as they still wanted to entertain me with some kind of fiesta, they arranged for a bullfight with tail-twisting and other feats, to which I agreed on condition that the people be permitted to enter free.

Obregón could not lift the siege of the capital. He was attacked and almost surrounded by the forces of Benjamín Argumedo, Juan Andreu Almazán, Juan M. Banderas, Manuel Palafox, and others. By the beginning of March he was searching for an exit to the center by way of San Juan del Río, or to Veracruz by way of the Hacienda Otemusco. As the quicker, he chose the first of these roads and prepared to march on San Juan del Río. I believe he was pushed into this by Carranza, both of them being worried by my earlier advance against Diéguez and Murguía and my present one in the northeast. They saw it would not be easy to contain my action against the frontier towns and Tampico and that once I was in control of them my material resources would be greatly increased.

In any case, by the sixth or seventh of that month of March, 1915, Agustín Estrada, Fernando Reyes, Joaquín de la Peña, and Martínez y Martínez were halting the Carrancistas at Peón, south of San Juan del Río, and making them retreat toward Nopala and Cazadero. But Estrada notified me in Monterrey that Obregón was abandoning Mexico City and advancing on Querétaro with all his forces, clearing our advance posts and threatening to move on with a vast number of troops, since the corps that had belonged to Acosta or Sánchez were joining him. I gave Estrada orders to fall back from San Juan del Río to Querétaro and from there to Celaya, and told him to hold on that line and wait for the aid I would send.

As I remember, this happened at the time I received news of the defeat of Fierro and Seáñez in Jalisco. It was then too that a struggle in the district of El Ebano stopped Manuel Chao's advance on the port of Tampico. Many of González' forces were entrenched there under Jacinto B. Treviño, who was Carranza's chief of staff when he came from Sonora to Chihuahua. Treviño had constructed strong defenses there to wear down any troops that attacked him. Chao tried to take the lines by assault, and his men did him honor in the difficult task. But the enemy yielded not one foot of ground, though machine-gun fire decimated them. As their trenches extended I know not how many kilometers, their lines were protected by ditches two meters wide, their cannon and machine guns were well placed, and they were making use of an armored train on the track and many other devices, the assault lasted three days and nights without gains.

I was concerned with this when I received another telegram from Mr. Bryan about protection for foreigners and peaceful Mexicans who were exposed to injury in Mexico City. He sent word through Mr. Carothers that it would be wise to declare the city a neutral zone, not subject to control by any of the combatants but respected by all of them. I wanted to avoid being compromised by international talks, and when Mr. Carothers asked me what answer I would give him if he presented the message in official form, I answered, "Mexico City is under the control of Roque González Garza and Emiliano Zapata. My advice, Señor, is to have Mr. Bryan send them the message, and I promise you that they will take it under consideration."

Apparently this was a good reply, for Mr. Bryan made the proposal to González Garza, who assented. He said: "For humanity's sake I agree to leave Mexico City and consider it a neutral zone if and when Carranza does the same." But Carranza answered that he would not agree to the neutrality, that foreigners who were suffering should leave, and he would facilitate their passage through Puebla and Veracruz; if they remained, it was by their own choice and they would have to suffer along with the Mexican inhabitants. I now think that Carranza gave a very good answer, an answer that I too would have given if necessary, just as I had done earlier on the neutrality of Naco and Agua Prieta when I had said I could not consider a situation eternal just so that foreign interests should not suffer.

With new reports on Obregón's advance to Querétaro, I decided to go there without loss of time, anxious to halt him on his march. I did it knowing that Obregón represented the greatest danger.

Angeles said, "Do not let Obregón distract you from your plans, Sr. General. He only makes those movements to draw off troops from the campaign against González. His resources are limited, for otherwise he would have driven off the Zapatistas who besieged him in Mexico City. Order our troops to block the road and divert him and harass him, by which he will be delayed, and in the meantime we will win control of all the north."

"No, Señor, you are mistaken. If I let Obregón advance and organize and grow stronger, it will cost me much blood to bring him down to his present dimensions. Consider, Señor, I would not listen before for fear of losing our base of operations, which is the north, and now he is

coming there with no less than twelve thousand men. If I let him rest
for another three months, he will have more than twenty thousand
troops."

Angeles observed, "Obregón is cautious Sr. General. He never attacks
unless he is sure of superiority in men and materials. Let him advance
but harass him in his march. Draw him away from his base. Make him
weaken his line of communications. If he goes west or comes to attack
us here we can defeat him. Don't fall into his trap, don't move south."

"You are wrong, Sr. General. Zapata's men will never control the line
from Pachuca to Veracruz or from Pachuca to Tula. Concentrate most
of the available forces here, for me to take with me. I will make an all-
out assault and he will yield."

CHAPTER 20

With the Fury of a Hurricane Villa Drives Obregón's Forces from El Guaje to the Edge of Celaya.

Torreón. Munitions and International Affairs. Hipólito
Villa. Irapuato. Rumors. Obregón's Troops and Villa's.
Salamanca. Measures for the Attack. El Guaje. Fortunato
Maycotte. Crespo. Embankments and Ditches. Fighting
Spirit. Yaquis and Machine Guns. Villa's Horse. Skirm-
ishing in the Night.

In Torreón I learned that the munitions we were
expecting had not arrived. These were necessary to the battles we were
going to fight, since my men were carrying very few and the store in
Guanajuato would still be insufficient. I wired my brother Hipólito, who
was in charge of procurement, and asked what had happened. He answered that our agents had bought and paid for large quantities, but
there were difficulties in getting them into Mexico as Washington was
not so favorable as before. He had hopes but no assurance, and meanwhile would send me some 200,000 cartridges he was expecting at that

moment. As for greater quantities, he would do what he could, though he promised nothing.

Obregón was already falling on Celaya in very great numbers. I brought my forces to Irapuato by train and had them concentrate in Salamanca. Being informed that Obregón had sent spies to learn my movements and the number of my forces, I spread the report that I was going to Jalisco in pursuit of Murguía and Diéguez, but the next morning, the fifth of April, 1915, I prepared to make a rapid and concerted movement of my brigades against Obregón.

I did this with full knowledge of the number of his forces, which exceeded twelve thousand, and the number of mine, which hardly reached eight thousand. With my men engaged everywhere—in the northeast, the northwest, the west, the east, the center, and the south— with intrigues in Washington moving to cut off my supplies, could I let Obregón hold me inactive, even though he had twelve thousand men, fifteen cannons, and one hundred machine guns? It was my duty to throw myself on Obregón and defeat him. With this in mind and knowing that Obregón was adding to his forces with every train that came from Veracruz by way of Pachuca and Tula, I was even unwilling to wait for José I. Prieto, José Ruiz, César Felipe Moya, and Pablo López, whom I had ordered to come from Michoacán.

I gave my orders: at the center, on the railway line and the road nearby, the infantry of José Herón González, Dionisio Triana, Pedro Bracamontes, and San Román and the six batteries of José María Jurado and Gustavo Durón González would march in a line; on the left the cavalry of Agustín Estrada and Canuto Reyes and Joaquín de la Peña would attack from Cerro Gordo; on the right the cavalry contingents of the Morelos Brigade and those of Calixto Contreras, under Abel Serratos, would advance by La Cal.

And so it was. The next morning my troops left Salamanca in high spirits, and at nine my vanguard was already engaged with Obregón's. By ten my cavalry on the two wings had defeated part of the opposing forces, which had taken shelter in fortifications at El Guaje. At eleven, already broken and defeated, these forces, the two thousand men of Fortunato Maycotte, fled in fear, leaving their dead and wounded, and their arms. Not half of them escaped. At twelve the main body of the enemy, knowing they had lost about one thousand men in less than three hours and seeing their vanguard disappearing, tried to protect what was left of Maycotte's cavalry, in support of which Obregón sent out other cavalry columns and an infantry train with machine guns from

Celaya. But those new troops could not withstand the onslaught of my men, and all had to retreat together, the other cavalry defeated like Maycotte's and the train pursued by my swiftest horses, which were near to overtaking and surrounding it.

So my extreme vanguard reached the Hacienda Crespo, where Obregón's men tried to reorganize and resist, but failed. We passed Crespo and reached the farms and fields just out of Celaya, after a pursuit of more than fifty kilometers in which the enemy cavalry was routed and their infantry found no way to stop us. In the shelter of embankments and ditches that run there on both sides of the railroad, Obregón fortified himself and began to offer strong resistance. He used his cannon and machine guns, and the fighting increased. Now that the enemy had the protection of the city, my cavalry could no longer overwhelm them as they had done in the open field, but still we caused them great losses. To gain time, Obregón sent out another column of cavalry, to flank us, and it was met by Agustín Estrada, who quickly repulsed and scattered it, leaving no less than five hundred casualties.

This happened about five in the afternoon. At six, with my forces concentrated near the line of fire that protected the enemy, I gave orders to hold, and prepared for an assault the next day. But I could not curb my men. They had found nothing to stop them in El Guaje or Crespo and now they crossed embankments and fields from which came the fire of Yaqui infantrymen and machine guns; and they kept on going when they saw that the enemy cavalry had sought shelter in the city. Señor! What an error it was for my troops to rush ahead, without artillery protection or the aid of infantry, against an enemy who, if they were suffering great losses, were inflicting still greater ones.

I planned my assault the next day as follows: the infantry of Bracamontes and the cavalry of Joaquín de la Peña and other forces would attack on the left; the infantry of Dionisio Triana and the cavalry of Canuto Reyes and other contingents, in the center; the infantry of José Herón González and San Román and the cavalry of Estrada and that of Contreras and other forces, on the right. The entire line, which extended over the space of five or six kilometers, would have the support of twenty-two cannon, which José María Jurado distributed in the following manner: two batteries on the right wing, commanded by Fraire and Perdomo; two in the center, commanded by Durón González; two on the right, commanded by Ortega and a chief whom I do not remember.

The enemy bombardment was so strong as I was dictating this order that my horse became frightened and had to be held by hand to keep him quiet in his place, this while all the cannon and machine guns were firing at once. Our own pieces, already in position, answered from the edge of the city. Again the fighting increased, and again the boldness of my men carried them to the first enemy lines, where they were driven back with losses which may have diminished their ranks but did not break their spirit. When one of our lines had to retreat momentarily, it quickly returned to the offensive and, with the same impetus as before, undertook to regain its last position.

We continued fighting until the early hours of night, Obregón withdrawn into the shelter of the city and I facing it with my lines extended; Obregón hidden behind the defenses he had prepared and I with my men spread out on the other side of embankments that chance provided.

Night and dawn passed with nothing but the bombardment and from time to time a burst from machine guns and rifles on their side. Considering my own scarcity of ammunition, but with faith in our triumph, I thought, "Does Obregón have so much ammunition that he uses it for illumination?"

It seemed evident that the enemy could not resist us, and I was even surprised to find him still there. But it would be hard to say whether my faith came from the valor of my troops, who had immobilized Obregón with their vanguard alone, doing it in ten hours of combat with no less than two thousand casualties, or from knowing that I represented the cause of the people. Be that as it may, I slept little. Every half hour my chiefs came with their fears. They said, "My General, find us more ammunition; what we have may not be enough." And I ordered them to go to the trains, some four kilometers away, for all the ammunition possible. But I calmed them too, adding, "You will not use much this morning. The city will fall under the fury of our first assault, and if not then, under the second."

CHAPTER 21

Eager To Conquer Obregón, Villa Exhausts Himself at Celaya, and the Enemy Drives Him Back.

Bombardment at Dawn. Fraire and Jurado. Machine Guns and Yaquis. Obregón's Lines. The Assault. Reinforcements from Acámbaro. Obregón's Maneuver. Villa on the Left, the Center, and the Right. Gustavo Durón González. The Casualties on Both Sides. Obregón's Reports.

According to my orders of the night, at four the next morning the battle raged again, more bloody, I think, than in our attacks on the sixth. On the north side, where I had placed my headquarters, our artillery fire was so heavy that soon after dawn the enemy was hardly able to answer. Fraire, a very good artilleryman, and José María Jurado, who was in command and equally good, were concentrating our fire with so much skill that our shells fell in the midst of Obregón's ranks with a deathly roar. This much is true; but it is also true that it was evident that morning that our projectiles were not very good. In the campaign of Jalisco and the northeast we had already used the foreign shells Angeles had taken from Villarreal, and now our cannon were firing those my workmen had manufactured, with a shortage of all kinds of elements, in my shops at Chihuahua. Even so, the vigor of our attack did not diminish; at first it increased without my knowing whether it was because of the valor of my men or because the artillerymen had followed Angeles' advice about handling poor projectiles and had put the batteries up so close to the enemy that the shells could not fail.

At dawn my infantry began to move on the enemy in firing line; and Obregón's one hundred machine guns and the Yaqui Indian riflemen in the shelter of dugouts were firing with such deadly accuracy that we were hardly able to advance before we were decimated and broken; we had to withdraw to reorganize; again we returned to the encounter and again we suffered the same havoc; again we were driven back, once again to reorganize and attack.

Viewing the daring with which my men marched without cover to attack positions which it seemed impossible to reach and against concealed troops whom our fire could not harm, I knew I must defend them against their own temerity if they were to achieve their purpose. I ordered them to advance only when the fire from our cannon was strong. I had the cavalry relieve them by carrying them behind their saddles to the points where they could be effective. It was sad to see them fall as they took the first step from their positions. Moreover, I had all my cavalry charge with greater force than ever while the infantry was supporting the line.

We began the struggle at dawn on the seventh of April, 1915, and I, Pancho Villa, say we were defying the dangers of the attack at such close range that during the first hours of the morning the fire of enemy machine guns was ringing on the armor plating of our cannon. Obregón had extended his infantry in a line that crossed the railroad track west of the city. He had his artillery behind the center of these positions and some cavalry at the extreme right, toward the north, and on the extreme left, toward the south, with other corps situated in the center near his cannon.

It was seven when our shells caused their artillery to cease firing, and soon they abandoned their positions, the artillerymen and their supports afraid they could not face the assaults my men were making on their first lines. I wondered, "Señor, do these Carrancistas retreat so soon before my attack? What would become of them if we were using good shells like theirs?" The infantry that Obregón was keeping in the shelter of his positions at the center also seemed to be unprotected and weakening in its defense; it began to break and leave the trenches and embankments which had covered it since the previous afternoon. I perceived the weak point in the line and calculated where I could break it and destroy it quickly, for I saw that the center was paralyzed under the attacks of my infantry and my artillery fire. I sent officers of my escort to give the chiefs of all sectors my measures for a general assault at nine.

My officers were beginning to execute the order when suddenly something happened that no one could have expected. As Agustín Estrada's column and the troops following him launched the attack in one great onslaught, the fields they were crossing began to overflow; perhaps these were already inundated without our knowing it. The assault slowed down and gave the enemy time to bring up reserves. A great part of our effect in the center was lost. It happened too that when my troops were almost in the streets of the town, several of their chiefs were fatally wounded, and the men became confused and abandoned the points they had overrun in their attack.

In spite of this, the fighting increased until eleven, we keeping up our furious attempts, each time greater, to drive them from their positions, and they persisting in their resolution, each time stronger, to hold the positions and even die defending them. We were exhausting ourselves in the struggle, all of it bloody since the early hours of the previous day, or rather, we were exhausting our resources, not our valor or our energy, while their resources seemed to increase without my knowing whether this was due to Obregón's superiority in numbers, which allowed him to have reserves, or to other causes. I say this because, as I learned later, Obregón had received new cavalry troops at Acámbaro, no less than two or three thousand in number, who brought him aid when he needed it most. With all that, the battle raged again; in spite of our fatigue I was determined to give the enemy no rest but to continue attacking them, hoping they would break.

Obregón's cavalry reinforcements attacked me about twelve that morning in a flanking movement from positions on the extreme left. I was still considering the danger and the way to meet it without halting my main effort, when another column of cavalry appeared on our right, in a maneuver like the one they were executing on the other side.

Obregón, this clearly indicated, judged the situation now good enough to throw his whole force against me. I hoped to demonstrate that he was mistaken, but my right wing, fatigued by the long battle and perhaps fearing the enveloping movements, failed to repel the attack, or repelled it in part only and with their forward positions surrounded, they had to abandon them. With this chance to move forward, the enemy now dominated the approaches to the next line, which in turn my men had to abandon, and so on. Very soon the entire flank was first pushed back, then broken, and finally defeated. My center, now unsupported, had to retreat in the same way and abandon the ground we had taken; and with my center withdrawn, my left also withdrew without resisting the cavalry column which, if it had not been for that, would have failed to gain its objective. It was a situation that threatened destruction, and my inner voice told me not to re-form my lines and continue the attack but to save my troops from serious danger. They were exhausted, most of them were short of ammunition, many of their chiefs and officers were either wounded or dead. For the time I dropped the determination to defeat Obregón. I accepted the reverse, with the intention of correcting it when my strength permitted.

With my escort I went to the aid of the right, where there was danger of a disbanding that would leave my men defenseless against cavalry; this remedied, I went to support my center, which was beginning to suffer though it had not been routed. I rallied the lines in ranks for an orderly withdrawal to the train, from which they could retreat further; next I would have gone to the support of my left, except that this was unnecessary. My men on that side were slowly retiring, with battalions, regiments, and batteries in good shape.

The chief of the batteries in the center, Gustavo Durón González, brought his guns safely out, in spite of being wounded, and I went to praise and encourage him. This happened about two in the afternoon, and it was then I discovered that part of the enemy cavalry were surrounding several cannon which had been on the right. Seeing this, I had no thought but to reunite the troops nearest me, some four hundred or five hundred men, all cavalry, and took command and led them against the enemy. We engaged them fiercely and drove them back half-defeated, while our cannon were being withdrawn. Afterwards I learned that this squadron of the enemy was the rest of Fortunato Maycotte's cavalry, who had hoped to vindicate themselves for the defeat at El Guaje. I think that my artillerymen and their support had committed no error in letting themselves be surrounded. The boxes and cannon must have bogged down, since the road was muddy and several mules were missing.

For the rest, we continued our retreat until dark. We abandoned our dead; we collected our arms; we gathered our wounded and carried them to the trains of my health service, where they were taken aboard and sent to my hospitals in the north.

In this battle of Celaya, on the sixth and seventh of April, 1915, my forces caused the enemy no less than 2,500 casualties, dead and wounded, prisoners and dispersed, of which I am sure, not because I counted them but from practiced estimate. My own losses were 2,000, including Agustín Estrada, a very good Revolutionary for whom I wept. Francisco Natera and other chiefs and officers of very great valor were killed; many other men were wounded, dead, or taken prisoner. Obregón, several days later, published official reports in which he claimed that I had no less than 30,000 men, of whom 2,000 were killed, 3,000 wounded, and I know not how many made prisoners. He also said that I had been the first to flee and that he had pursued us after our defeat, which was not true because he neither defeated nor pursued us.

One word more: a week after the combat, Obregón was still in Celaya and I attacked him again.

CHAPTER 22

At His Headquarters in Irapuato Villa Prepares To March on Celaya Again.

Gold Mines. Francisco Escudero. *Vida Nueva*. Mr. Bryan's Complaints. "These Are Not the Times of Porfirio Díaz." Treviño's Resistance at El Ebano. Word from Urbina. Emilio P. Nafarrate. José Rodríguez. Saúl Navarro. The Return of Victoriano Huerta. Enrique C. Llorente.

Though occupied with the war, I found time for the business of government and the settlement of international conflicts. I learned from the lawyer Escudero, who was in charge of my Treasury and public works, that the gold mines of Chihuahua and Durango remained idle. He explained that contributions were paid as if the mines were being worked, but the operators claimed the work could not proceed in war time.

When I declared this illegal he wrote a decree making it obligatory to work the mines or lose them. I signed this for publication in our newspaper *Vida Nueva* in Monterrey, and when the owners of the mines learned of it some were willing to comply but others not. For that reason, about the time of my withdrawal from Celaya to Irapuato, international complaints began; most of the mine operators being English, American, or French, they went to their consuls for protection.

Mr. Carothers reminded me that the law of Porfirio Díaz under which the owners obtained their concessions did not require them to work the mines but only to pay their taxes, and that they expected their contracts to be honored. I answered that these were not the times of Díaz, that the mines belonged to the people and must be worked and worked well for the benefit of the people.

He asked, "Who will decide, Sr. General, which mine is worked well and which is not?"

"My officials will make the decision, Sr. Consul."

"But, Sr. General, consider the position of the owners who do not agree to the loss of their mines. Mr. Bryan thinks the question should be decided by a judge."

I thought he was right, and said, "Very well, Señor. When my impending battle with Obregón is over I will provide for the office of a judge. Tell Mr. Bryan and Mr. Wilson there will be no serious international disagreements over this."

From Irapuato I wired Urbina that it was urgent to win at El Ebano and then take Tampico and the oil fields quickly, after which we could unite at least some of our forces. He replied that he was doing his best, but the fortifications, the barbed-wire entanglements, the searchlights, and the airplanes made it the hardest fighting of the war. He himself needed reinforcements; he would win but it would not be easy.

I encouraged him, but my words failed to express the thoughts that raged in the back of my mind. Carranza was succeeding in his defensive warfare. And I could not see where I had committed my error in the struggle: whether in paying no heed to Angeles when he advised me to destroy Obregón and Carranza in Veracruz; whether in heeding him in Jalisco when he advised me to abandon the pursuit of Diéguez and Murguía and come to his aid in the northeast; or whether in disregarding his entreaty to continue with the campaign in the northeast, without interrupting it for Obregón at Irapuato or even at Aguascalientes or Zacatecas.

I also had reports of José Rodríguez' bad luck in his march on Matamoros. Those reports said:

The enemy forces occupy good positions, with the protection of twenty machine guns, and the frontier to supply them. For two days my assaults have been unsuccessful, and I have withdrawn to Rosita to reorganize and prepare for a new attack. The enemy have no less than 1,200 men here under Emiliano P. Nafarrate, reinforced with Villarreal's troops.

A few days later, emboldened with new reinforcements and encouraged by having resisted us there, the enemy silently sallied out from Matamoros and in a surprise attack fell on our troops with great fury, slew Saúl Navarro and other good Revolutionaries, and rid our men of any idea of taking Matamoros.

In Irapuato I received notice from Llorente that Victoriano Huerta was on his way from Spain to New York. To this I answered: "I have your warning, but I promise you that Huerta will never come to Mexico, which grieves me deeply because I would like to have the opportunity of sentencing him to pay for his sins by hanging."

CHAPTER 23

Villa Continues To Attend to International Affairs while Reorganizing Troops for the Advance on Celaya.

Vasconcelos in Washington. Llorente. The Clamor of the Foreigners. Duval West, Mr. Wilson's Envoy. Contributions and Loans. Mr. Carothers. Foreigners in a Civil War. The Chinese in Sonora. Mr. Bryan's Complaints. The Widow of McManus.

Llorente wired that Vasconcelos was in Washington trying to undermine the prestige of our cause. I showed Mr. Carothers the telegram and he said, "Sr. General Villa, I do not know what messages Vasconcelos carries to Mr. Bryan. But I assure you, everything that happens here is known there. Besides this, our Department of State passes judgment only on the clear and calm reports of its envoys in Mexico. For that reason Mr. Canova was with Eulalio Gutiérrez, Mr. Silliman is with Carranza, and I am with you."

This was a time when rich Mexican families incited foreign residents to increase their outcries against the Revolution and condemn everything we Revolutionary men were doing, and carry their petitions to Mr. Wilson, hoping he would take measures to protect them and other peaceful people against the alleged destruction we were causing, and the great hunger—they were even saying this—which our armies would bring if Washington did not prevent. Foreign residents said such things in their messages to Mr. Wilson not from love for the Mexican people, as they pretended, since they had always conspired with rich Mexicans to exploit them, but from hatred for the cause of the poor. Moved by their protests, Mr. Wilson sent his envoy Duval West to the capital to find some way to make peace between us.

I had to attend to this and more in Irapuato, without neglecting the reorganization of my forces, who were now ready for a second advance on Celaya. And I, Pancho Villa, say that if a problem like this is difficult for lawyers, then how much more difficult was it for a man like me, with no learning but what he acquired in the line of duty and the service of the poor!

Agents from the chiefs I had fighting in all the districts of my territory came for money for their troops, for munitions or equipment, and I had to satisfy them all. I did not always have the money or the supplies they requested, and advised them to search for resources in the districts under their control. Authorized by these words, they took loans or collected contributions, which some foreign businessmen would not agree to pay. When my chiefs or governors then required them to make payment, under threat of confiscation, they complained to Mr. Bryan, and Mr. Carothers came to protest to me.

I answered, "Sr. Consul, foreigners live here by choice. If they come to enjoy our riches it is only just for them to share our misfortunes as well. If a flood devastated Mexico, would the foreigners demand to be specially saved?"

"But foreigners are not citizens; it is not their duty to give help in a civil war."

"For that reason, Sr. Consul, we do not ask them for their blood, but only for their money. Their wealth comes from the people and if the people need it for their well-being, they can take it back."

Mr. Bryan and I disagreed on other things than money; at times he complained of assassinations that my men had committed, or he solicited my intervention to prevent other chiefs from committing them. Such was the case in Sonora. Chinese there were refusing to help the cause and, being disliked for this reason as well as others, were persecuted by some of the chiefs.

Mr. Bryan telegraphed me:

Sr. General Villa:

Troops in Sonora are inflicting great injury on the Chinese who live there. According to my reports, Maytorena has given orders to respect them but the orders are not obeyed, without my knowing whether that is because he lacks authority over his chiefs or the chiefs lack authority over their subordinates. I ask you, Sr. General, to order the generals in Sonora not to commit the acts complained of or let their men commit them. I urge you to consider our humanitarian duties and also the diplomatic protests from China.

I answered:

Señor, your reports about the Chinese in Sonora grieve me, although I believe that whatever happens to them comes of their own conduct. However, I have ordered Sr. General Sosa, Sr. General Acosta, Sr. General Morales, and Sr. General Urbalejo to prevent a repetition of the offenses. You can be sure that they will do so, since neither Maytorena nor I want to provoke an incident.

Like Zapata and Roque González Garza, we had reason to avoid international trouble. An American named McManus was assassinated near

Mexico by Zapatista forces. González Garza and Zapata's generals decided they would neither conceal the act nor discuss it. They asked the widow of the murdered man what amount of money she would accept in compensation; she requested 160,000 pesos for herself and her sons. It was paid, and no quarrel followed with her or Washington. González Garza acted well, for Carrancistas were denouncing us on all sides as robbers and assassins. By such means, blind to the harm they did our Revolution, they were trying to secure recognition in Washington.

CHAPTER 24

In Spite of the Numerical Superiority of Obregón's Forces, Villa Decides To Attack Him Again.

Salamanca. A Letter to Obregón. Preparations for the Advance. The Brigades of Prieto and Ruiz. Troops from Jalisco, Natera, and Serratos. The Number of Villa's Troops and the Number of Obregón's. Crespo. Three Advance Columns. Combat Orders. The Battle of the Fourteenth.

In those four or five days when my forces were concentrating for a second advance on Celaya, I was now in Irapuato, now in Salamanca, where the troops were being equipped and supplied.

In Salamanca on the tenth or eleventh of April, I had talks with representatives of foreign consuls regarding the security of residents in Celaya during my next attack; and as a result I wrote a letter to Obregón inviting him to come out and fight in the open instead of protecting himself behind the women and children and peaceful men of the city. Ignoring me he replied to the consuls and their men: "I have your letter regarding the protection of peaceful citizens from the enemy attacks on this plaza. We Mexicans do not accept the intervention of foreign consuls in the fulfilment of our duty. Furthermore, I do not consider Francisco Villa's words sincere."

In Irapuato I incorporated the few forces that could come to my aid. The brigades of José I. Prieto and José Ruiz and the troops of César Felipe Moya arrived with about two thousand men from the districts of Michoacán. Some infantry, cavalry, and artillery arrived from Jalisco. I received contingents organized by Abel Serratos and other forces from Francisco Carrera Torres, Natera, and other chiefs whose names I do not remember. I also received shipments of cartridges from my brother Hipólito in Ciudad Juárez. As these additions came, I dispatched them to Salamanca. My staff, escort, other chiefs, officers, and I finally followed them with the last of the new troops. Seeing me go, the people cheered and expressed hope for my victory.

In Salamanca on the morning of April 12, 1915, I held a review. There were not many men to enter the new battle and most of these had not yet recovered from their fatigue; munitions as well as forces were scarce, and I considered the situation with uneasiness. My men would have to perform heroically to triumph over Obregón. He had considerably more forces and equipment than before, and while I was organizing in Irapuato and Salamanca the forces of Amaro, Novoa, Porfirio González, Juan José Ríos, Gabriel Gavira, and other chiefs had joined him. With these the number of his men now exceeded twenty thousand—eight or nine thousand of infantry and nine or ten thousand of cavalry, besides artillerymen. Only in cannon were his forces inferior to mine; according to my calculations he was relying on eighteen or twenty pieces; I was relying on thirty-four or thirty-six. But to offset our cannon, they had more machine guns than we had.

But, knowing all the risks, I knew also that our future would not be improved by retreating, and although there was danger of defeat, as always in war, we had to face the odds. Such is revolution, or, rather, the cause of the poor: the main thing is not immediate victory, however desirable, but final triumph through the will of the people to persevere after every defeat. The truth is I knew our best chance in this war was to achieve some great military feat, assisted by good luck, because Obregón would never fight unless he was fortified and entrenched and I would have to conquer him like that or let myself be conquered. But although conquered many times I would never surrender, and perhaps in this way the people might triumph.

I marched from Salamanca to Celaya the morning of April 13, 1915. At Crespo I left my trains because the enemy had destroyed the track from that point forward. At noon we advanced on Celaya. Part of my cavalry was sent to occupy positions which would form my right wing, and other cavalry to form my left wing; the infantry, the artillery, and another part of the cavalry went to form the center in the same positions we had occupied in the combats on the sixth and seventh.

About three that afternoon my forces were in their lines opposite the enemy. At four I reconnoitered, anxious to encourage my men. On the right, the side of the La Laja River, the Guerrero Brigade would attack under Cruz Domínguez and Fernando Reyes, and with it the Queré-taro Brigade and other forces under Joaquín de la Peña. In the center, the four brigades of infantry and the troops of César Felipe Moya would make the attack. On the left, cavalry would advance. The batteries of Fraire and Perdomo would support the movement there, and those of Gustavo Durón González and Licona would support the right. So, except for some lines being farther away than the other time and some being in places which others had occupied previously, the measures for battle were almost the same as before. This was likewise true of Obregón's lines; under the protection of his trenches he expected to resist my at-tacks until he exhausted me, as he did before.

At five in the afternoon my right began their approach to the enemy positions. By eight our cannon were ready and most of them never ceased firing, and neither did the enemy cannon and machine guns. At ten, under cover of darkness my infantry moved into positions within five hundred meters of the trenches. At twelve my right was in touch with the enemy rear guard, on the La Laja in the direction of Apaseo. The next day, at six in the morning our right again provoked the fight-ing. Very early I sent an officer with orders for these troops to cross the river. It was done. As they were forming on the other side, my officer encouraged them, and they cheered and advanced as one man on the positions they had to take. My other officers were similarly at work in the center and on the left.

All the morning and the afternoon we had no rest. We had to throw ourselves upon them to take their positions. There was nothing else I could do except besiege them and reduce them to hunger. Our attacks were thin and weak, but a single instant of weakness at a single point in the enemy line might give us a chance. But my cannon, though skil-fully directed, were not giving us support. Again it was the bad quality of our shells.

CHAPTER 25

Defeated by Obregón at Celaya, Villa Retreats to León and Aguascalientes To Reorganize His Troops and Supply Them with Ammunition.

The Night of April 14. Orders for the Next Day. Cesáreo Castro's Cavalry. Villa's Efforts. The Enveloping Movement on the Right Wing. Retreat to Crespo. The Skill of the Railroad Men. Loss of the Artillery. Manuel Bracamontes. Joaquín Bauche Alcalde.

That was a night of heavy rain. The troops of my right returned to the near side of the river, afraid the rising water might cut them off. Thus they were back in the positions they had occupied in the morning, losing all they had gained. The same night, considering that the defenses seemed to grow stronger each moment instead of weaker, and that our few remaining munitions would be exhausted soon, I gave orders to increase the pressure on the rearguard. Seeing this new turn in the attack, Obregón would be forced to move troops to where I wanted them.

So it was. The struggle was renewed with our attack on their rear guard and the action of one or two batteries which Jurado sent there under the orders of Durón González. As the new attacks were bitter and the cannon fire more effective, the enemy positions began to break at some points, and the infantry of my left, perceiving this, redoubled the force of their assaults. For an hour we carried our lines up to their positions and beyond San Juanico; we overcame strong resistance there, since Obregón's reinforcements did not come out. I hoped for the chance I was waiting for, inclined to think that there were many indications of it, since my forces on the right had crossed the river again and reoccupied the positions they had left during the night.

I asked myself, "Señor, where is Obregón's cavalry? Is it all fighting as infantry?" The answer was that it must be, but as I was absorbed in these thoughts I saw the cavalry I was wondering about. They had begun an enveloping movement on my extreme left. For the two days of the battle, most of them had waited with great cunning in mesquite thickets close to the rear guard.

The movement began quietly, but I saw it increasing and dispatched officers with orders to resist while I organized a column and went to break it up. The cavalry, however, was composed of no less than five or six thousand horsemen and their advance was so well concerted and decisive that my extreme right could not withstand it, even by sacrificing everything. Nevertheless I took command of officers at hand, my escort, and other troops, and we left at full gallop to repel the advance. In our first impetus we broke the advance to some extent, and, as I was hoping, our ranks revived and threw themselves into the struggle behind us. With my left and my right united, we stopped Cesáreo Castro and Fortunato Maycotte and routed part of their line, and they began to withdraw and scatter as my men grew bolder.

But now the infantry of their right and center came to assist the cavalry; our formation was broken, and we had to defend instead of attacking. Then it happened. A mass of no less than ten thousand men overwhelmed us with their weight. I had no way to remedy the situation, my numbers allowing no reserves for such a critical moment. My flank and part of my center broke, my infantry retreated, my artillery supports fell back, and my cannon were left surrounded, beyond saving.

Cesáreo Castro's enveloping movement began about nine in the morning; we succeeded in containing it about ten; they rallied and drove us back about eleven. More or less at this last hour my right wing perceived another cavalry movement like the one on the left. Favored by the small number of troops covering my line there, they were already on my flank and had it routed and defeated while my troops and cannon and my rear guard were still holding on the left. Many were killed or wounded there, but my men finally left their positions on the river, abandoned the field, and fell back along the bank.

But I, Pancho Villa, now declare that my right, my left, and my center displayed great valor in fighting as they did, although I was then very angry and berated them. After two days of constant fighting my forces had exhausted their munition and with fewer cartridges than a soldier keeps for his retreat, stayed there until the last, suffering and dying.

I learned that Obregón had received reports of the scarcity of my munitions at the beginning of the battle and had counted on my exhausting these in the two days of combat, ready to overwhelm me then with his numbers, and sure that I would destroy myself. And in truth it almost happened, for, seeing my lines yielding, broken by fatigue, and without ammunition, my impulse was to urge them on. But I soon realized that little could be gained in this way. It was best to acknowledge defeat and aid in the retreat of the forces that were able to move.

At two in the afternoon most of my left was already withdrawing to the hills of Crespo, pursued by cavalry. It was three when my right was flanked, and part of it retreated toward Cerro de la Gavia on the road to Salamanca or Irapuato. I was trying to save the infantry on the left, the center, and the right who fought till the last moment and, no longer having an exit, were unable to break through the encirclement and were taken prisoner. At four I was leading the retreat of the troops we had succeeded in reaching with our orders.

In the skilful hands of my railroad men my trains moved from Crespo to Salamanca, despite efforts to obstruct them. Some artillery was saved by retiring it at the center next to the railroad line and some got through the brakes of the La Laja. But most of it was lost. The batteries of Fraire and Perdomo and those of Cortina and Quiróz were lost, like that of Rodríguez, Ortega, and Cuesta, from all of which, I hardly remember now from which, only some of the boxes and one or two cannons were saved, in addition to all of Licona's battery. I had carried thirty-four or thirty-six pieces of artillery to Celaya. Twenty-eight were left in the hands of the enemy.

In those three days of combat my forces lost 3,000 or 3,500, dead, wounded, prisoners, and dispersed. Pedro Bracamontes was wounded and he lost his hand from the wound he received. His brother Manuel was taken prisoner, as were Joaquín Bauche Alcalde, a very intelligent youth, and other good Revolutionaries. Obregón ordered them shot, not in the name of justice but to quiet the terror many of the Carrancistas felt on being informed of my advance. The executioner, as I learned later, was a German colonel named Maximilian Kloss, a chief whom Obregón had wanted to shoot when he retreated with his artillery in the combats on the sixth and seventh of April.

This was the second battle of Celaya, fought on April 13, 14, and 15, 1915. Some call it the "second fight at Celaya," without reason I think, since, in the proper language of war, it was a battle not a fight. However that may be, I suffered a very serious defeat there, which so greatly relieved Carranza's favorites that they began to publish Obregón's exaggerated reports with great joy.

CHAPTER 26

While Villa Reorganizes His Troops in Aguascalientes, Obregón Continues His Advance to the North Step by Step.

Salamanca. Irapuato. The Retreat of Fierro and Seáñez. León. Abel Serratos. Aguascalientes. "The People Will Benefit and We Will Return to What We Were." The Death of Maclovio Herrera. The Advance on Ciudad Victoria. Urbina and El Ebano. Talks with Angeles.

At Salamanca, with my trains lined up in retreat, I was surprised to see the night close down to protect us and the sun rise without Obregón's cavalry anywhere in sight. "Obregón," I thought, "is so overjoyed he cannot move. What else could keep them from taking advantage of my great danger?" At eleven the next morning, April 16, 1915, I was still in Salamanca making the best possible arrangements for my march to the North and the concentration of my troops in Aguascalientes.

In Irapuato I received reports from Fierro and Seáñez on their departure from Jalisco, which I had ordered them to abandon before Obregón could attack their rear guard. In Silao, Fierro informed me that he had passed Irapuato with no enemy to stop him, and, according to his reports, César Castro's cavalry had just entered Salamanca. I ordered him to follow me to León, serving as my rear guard, and to remain there with half his troops and send the other half to me at Aguascalientes.

The people of León welcomed me as if I was returning in great triumph, not in defeat. Women and children brought me bouquets of roses; men tried to come close to greet me. Abel Serratos, whom I had left in Guanajuato as governor and military commandant, was waiting at the station to receive my orders. He asked me to rest in León but I answered no, that I was not seeking rest and only wanted to go on with the struggle. It was necessary to reorganize in Aguascalientes, a strategic point. Canuto Reyes and Fierro would remain as my rear guard while I prepared to return, which would be soon if my efforts to purchase munitions did not fail.

I wanted everyone to understand that the main thing was not glory but perseverance in the struggle for justice. To make them understand me better, I sent wives of chiefs and officers away to Chihuahua, as I was sure this would make them more apt to fulfil their duty. Every morning and afternoon, after dictating my measures and disposing of business, I would leave my train, accompanied by my chiefs, and with an axe split wood, saying, "The people will benefit, and we will return to what we were."

In Aguascalientes I heard of the death of Maclovio Herrera, the good Revolutionary who had turned renegade and gone over to the ranks of Carranza. According to one report his death occurred near Nuevo Laredo, at a place threatened by the forces of Orestes Pereyra, Jr., advancing by the Monterrey line, and those of Rosalío Hernández, approaching Piedras Negras. Maclovio had ordered a change of flags to keep his troops from being confused with those of Hernández, but the troops of a scouting train, not knowing about the change, failed to recognize him and his escort. A skirmish followed, in which Maclovio and some of the men with him were killed. Others assured me that there was no such skirmish but that Maclovio died at the hands of one of his officers. In either case, he was a brave man and a skilful soldier, who met the death he had to die, killed by his own troops and far removed from glory, at the end of the road down which his errors had carried him.

Severino Ceniceros and Máximo García were marching on Ciudad Victoria. They defeated César López de Lara at Puerto del Aire, pushed Luis Caballero back to the district of Padilla, and after causing the enemy to abandon most of the region, marched to Victoria and took it without resistance.

I received reports on the fighting at El Ebano. Urbina telegraphed of the difficulties: the underbrush, the entrenchments, the bomb-throwers, the airplanes. He was making slow progress and called for help. I answered that I was in the same predicament but promised to send help as soon as I could.

While in Aguascalientes, I had talks with Angeles, who repeated his objections to the developments of the campaign. How could our troops face the enemy without uniting again when the enemy had superior numbers and supplies, received munitions and equipment from Matamoros, Manzanillo, and Veracruz, and were favored by some in Washington?

I answered that this might be true, but if we were divided, so were they.

Angeles repeated, "We must reunite the forces of this corps and one by one defeat the several enemy corps that attack us."

I replied, "If that is what you want, take charge of the campaign and dictate your measures, which I will respect and execute. But I make one prediction: you will gain nothing, Señor, or you will gain less than I do. If you concentrate to annihilate Obregón, the enemy will come from Tampico to San Luis and from the northeast to La Laguna. If you and all your troops go to El Ebano to take the oil fields, Obregón will occupy Torreón and cut off your base of operations; and the same will happen if you devote everything to the sole conquest of the northeast. You can retreat to La Laguna and defend the territory between there and Chihuahua, but you will lose the war before the battles begin, because Carranza will control almost all the Republic and the international situation will favor him. We can win this struggle by one road only, though we may lose it by the same one, and that road is to keep trying to defeat Obregón at the center while the rest of my forces sustain our lines in the northeast and the northwest until we can aid them."

I think I convinced him. He was then willing to give me his good advice on my orders for new operations.

CHAPTER 27

Fearing that Dionisio Triana Is Disloyal Villa Listens to the Insinuations of His Generals and Shoots Him.

A Carrancista Courier. Dionisio and Martín Triana. Villa's Judgment. Angeles' Ring. Silao, León, and Guanajuato. Obregón's Movements and Villa's Preparations. Nápoles, Romita, Los Sauces, and Sotelo. An Appeal to Urbina. Mexican Reactionaries Abroad.

I learned that a courier from the Carrancista camp had brought a message from Martín Triana, one of Obregón's generals, to Dionisio Triana, his nephew and a general of mine. Martín Triana was advising his nephew to support Carranza instead of me and to deliver his forces to Obregón's army. He had added: "Pancho Villa is an assassin and a bandit, and now a leader of reactionary forces. You and your officers will find great advantages here. When you decide to come, we will send you the password, and see that you have no difficulty in reaching our lines."

This was the message, but, hearing it and considering Dionisio Triana a good Revolutionary, I thought, "Señor! Let Martín Triana send all the messages he wishes. Is Dionisio responsible for what his uncle writes? I myself might get such messages from González or Obregón." I decided to do nothing about it.

The next morning, however, most of my generals came to me and said, "We hear ugly rumors about the conduct of Dionisio Triana. We know he has been a good Revolutionary, but can he face our reverses? What if he betrayed us in battle?" I saw that they had lost confidence in him. It was true that he was holding important positions in our lines with the good infantry that Angeles had organized. In case of treason, this could be a very serious danger. I reflected, without changing my mind, but said, "Señores, all the responsibilities must not fall on me. What do you want me to do with Dionisio Triana?"

They answered, "Sr. General, relieve him of his command, let his men serve under other chiefs and officers, and distribute his chiefs and officers among loyal corps."

I did what they proposed. I assembled the Dionisio Triana Brigade with other forces forming a square around it; part of it, without chiefs and officers, was incorporated into the Gonzalitos Brigade, and the other part remained under orders of Macario Bracamontes, commanding in the absence of his brother Pedro, who was wounded at Celaya.

But returning from this ceremony I met Dionisio himself as he was going to his train, and he neither spoke nor looked at me although he was close. Seeing this, I felt sorry and spoke a word of sympathy, saying, "I wish this hadn't happened, and wouldn't have consented to it if several of my generals had not requested it."

When he still made no answer, I added, "Now you are going to Chihuahua. You will take your horses, officers of your confidence, and any aides you wish. You will be there for some time and soon everything will be explained and settled. If we have made an error in removing you from command, we will correct it, and if you have been harmed or injured, we will make amends."

He looked at me and said, "I don't want to go to Chihuahua; it would be better to send me to the United States."

"To the United States? Why? Isn't this the best offer I can make you?"

He stood looking at me and I saw in his glance that he was a traitor. I ordered him disarmed and put under guard, though still without thought of further punishment. A few minutes later the generals returned. They said, "This will be a good lesson to our troops, who know he was in communication with the enemy, and when he is punished it will serve as an example."

I asked, "And what punishment does he deserve?"

"The death sentence, my General."

I turned to Juan B. Vargas and said, "Have an officer and five men take Dionisio Triana to the cemetery and execute him. Go with them to witness the shooting, and come back to report."

And so it was. Vargas went, it must have been at five in the afternoon, and a half hour later returned and said, "He has been shot, my General. He gave me this gold topaz ring and these keys to open his locker and get another ring of platinum and diamonds that Angeles gave him. And he wrote this note."

"Did he die bravely?"

"Yes, my General."

"Did he himself give the order to fire?"

"Yes, my General."

"Did he make any dispositions?"

"None, my General."

"Did he say who was to receive the note?"

"No, my General."

I took the note and read it. It said: "I don't care whether I live or die, but I am glad to be going to a world where perhaps I will find neither executioners nor tyrants."

To concentrate and reorganize my forces to the best effect I had ordered my vanguard withdrawn from Silao and Guanajuato. Knowing this, Obregón extended his lines to these places on the twenty-second or twenty-third of April, 1915. About the twenty-fourth, my advance troops made scouting excursions from Trinidad to Los Sauces and Nápoles. Obregón, carefully avoiding our rearguard action, was moving little by little and reinforcing his right as far as Guanajuato. He knew that I dominated the National Line from San Luis Potosí to San Miguel Allende and saw the danger of moving from Silao to León when I could move forces from Dolores Hidalgo to Guanajuato and attack his rear guard in Silao. I had thought of this and was in favor of it as soon as Obregón took the offensive in his advance on León, and with this in mind I was expecting assistance from Pánfilo Natera's brigades then occupying this line.

On the twenty-sixth Obregón extended his left to Romita and his right to Los Sauces and Sotelo. According to my orders, my forces allowed him to advance, intending to let him take the offensive and to draw him away from the defenses he was constructing everywhere. Then, when fighting started, they would drive him back. In this fashion they defeated his right between Sotelo and Nápoles, his center beyond the station at Nápoles, and his left between La Sandía and Romita. These were strong attacks which my forces made when he was expecting to advance, and his losses and injuries were great, especially at the center where he himself was and on his left where Murguía's cavalry, almost surrounded, had to disperse and abandon their wounded and leave I know not how many prisoners.

So Obregón was trying to advance and we were letting him, hoping to lead him on and make him take the offensive near León in order to attack him in a rear guard action at Silao and cut his line of communications to the south. But I had decided not to give battle until I had reunited sufficient elements, knowing that now, as in Celaya, I had fewer troops than he.

I continued to dispatch men and equipment from Aguascalientes to León, and the enemy continued to make trial movements north of Silao, as I wanted them to do. Obregón again advanced on our right to Santa Ana del Conde and points near Trinidad, and on the left to the vicinity of the Hacienda de la Loza. In these new advances my men were giving him strong resistance, setting up obstacles to delay him until my artillery was rehabilitated, munitions arrived, and other forces joined me.

I telegraphed Urbina: "Sr. General, take the positions at El Ebano and go on to Tampico in a hurry. If I cannot rely on most of your forces, it will be impossible to halt Obregón's march."

My compadre answered: "I am doing what I can, Sr. General Villa, in woods that hold us back and against an entrenched enemy, but in two or three days I hope to leave here victorious."

Meanwhile Miguel Díaz Lombardo informed me that Carranza was trying to secure recognition from Washington by promising not to carry out the reforms the people wanted, and Mexican reactionaries in the United States were spending their money to defeat the Revolutionary cause. I asked him where they got the money and he answered that they got it by selling their property from abroad. I then ordered him to write me a law to nullify such sales in my territory and all the territory of the people's government, and to bring it for me to sign and publish abroad in every nation. When it was remitted to Mr. Bryan and Mr. Wilson, perhaps the reactionaries would think twice about their intrigues.

CHAPTER 28

Villa Does Not Listen to Angeles, Who Wants To Resist in Aguascalientes; He Prepares to Fight Next between León and Trinidad.

Vida Nueva. Don Francisco Escudero. Carranza's Agrarian Law and Villa's. Promises in Exchange for Recognition. Messages from Obregón and Diéguez. Francisco Murguía. Benjamín C. Hill. Pablo González. Ramón F. Iturbe. Aguascalientes and León. Angeles' Plan. Villa's Plan. Juan N. Medina.

Don Miguel Díaz Lombardo wrote the law and brought it to me in Aguascalientes. I signed it and had it published at once in *Vida Nueva*.

I asked the lawyer Don Francisco Escudero what we should do to offset Carranza's propaganda, and he answered, "Whatever the turn of events, we can insure the hopes of the people by hastening to publish the laws we have written for the hour of triumph."

"Very well, Señor. Bring me these laws to sign. Let them be published and applied." I added that the most important law was the one concerning the land. There would never be peace in Mexico while the haciendas were cultivated to benefit a few families and not to remedy the miseries of the people. In a few days he sent me the law, and I signed it and ordered it published and enforced.

The provisions were as follows:

I, Francisco Villa, announce the following points: First, most Mexicans, being day laborers in the fields, are slaves of the *hacendados*. Second, because of this servitude, it is impossible for Mexicans in the fields to overcome their misery and ignorance, which serve the interests of the rich. Third, exploited in this way, and with their children mistreated and their wives and their daughters dishonored, the people have no recourse but to resort to arms and throw themselves into the struggle for justice. Fourth, to give land to the poor is the greatest aim of our Revolution. For that purpose the Convention government proclaims the following law:

First—From this date forward no Mexican or foreigner can possess in Mexico any amount of land greater than he can work without oppressing other Mexicans. Second—Leaving to each owner the fields to which he is entitled, the haciendas will be distributed among the rural laborers. Third—The land needed by the inhabitants of the towns and ranches for their existence will be taken from the haciendas and distributed. Fourth—Jointly with the land, the water that corresponds to it, the animals, the tools, and the buildings will be given to the rural laborers when distribution is made. Fifth—Payment for the lands taken for the laborers will be made by means of bonds called the Agrarian Debt, and the price paid will cover only just value. Sixth—The laborers who receive land will pay the same price that the government has to pay in Agrarian Debt bonds, plus expenses. Seventh—Each laborer will lose the land he receives if he fails to cultivate it within two years, except for causes beyond his control.

Francisco Villa

That was the law that Don Francisco Escudero wrote for me, and in my judgment it was good.

Carranza's promises in exchange for recognition were damaging the cause so much that even some Carrancistas themselves would not accept them. Strong statements were made, and many chiefs and governors definitely opposed the announcement and execution of the promises. I was receiving reports of this from my consuls and other informers, but could not reveal it, though it was the vilest treason, because the reports were secret and I had to protect my informants.

Llorente telegraphed: "Eliseo Arredondo and Mr. Douglas and Mr. Lind are framing a compromise to obtain recognition of Carranza. They are studying the laws the Carrancista government must enact to receive American support."

Obregón, they said, expressed himself as follows, "Sr. Carranza, the compromise you are making to secure recognition from Washington is in benefit of rich families, the enemies of the people. Señor, the chiefs and troops under my command join me in asking you not to enter into any such compromises."

And Manuel M. Diéguez said, "Señor, Mexican reaction is hiding behind the American government, through which it attempts to obtain the renewal of its former dominion and the return of its riches. As the representative of my men, I hope that you will not let the Revolution fail. Recognition is not worth that much."

Murguía said, "Sr. Carranza, this is a struggle for the ideals of the Revolution, which permits no understanding with the reactionaries now protected by government. Such a compromise will frustrate the triumph of the Mexican people. If you offer to indemnify the rich for their losses in our struggle, they will be richer and more powerful, and the war will have to go on or a new one will have to begin. Señor, do not let yourself be trapped and dominated by the same reactionary forces that try to take advantage of Pancho Villa."

Benjamín C. Hill said, "Señor, your compromises with the Washington government are a hard blow to our cause. If you do not accept confiscation, you fail to fulfil the most important of our ideals. Don't you know, Señor, that confiscation is the only way to rid ourselves of the true enemy of the people?"

Pablo González said, "I suppose, Señor, you must have very serious reasons for making compromises with Washington; but no compromise surpasses the one the men of the Revolution have made with our people."

Ramón F. Iturbe said, "Señor, we who fight are far away and cannot appreciate the urgency of an understanding with Washington. In my name, Señor, and that of the chiefs who accompany me, I say you must not darken the hopes of the people; do not pay too high a price for recognition."

In other words, most of the Carrancista chiefs, even his favorites, opposed the agreements. He ignored them and went ahead with his proposals and promises.

So went the political problems. Meanwhile, Obregón kept up his attempts to advance on León, and my troops were trying to lead him on and then attack. Seeing the advance, Angeles observed, "Obregón is coming here to entrench himself and make us take the offensive, as he did at Celaya. I suggest, Sr. General Villa, that we abandon León and Lagos and fortify ourselves in Aguascalientes, where it will be Obregón who comes to us. Then we will force him to undertake offensive operations to dislodge us. If we do it this way, Obregón's thirty-two thousand men will weaken and break before our twenty thousand, and soon, when it becomes difficult for him to supply himself from his base of operations, which is very far away, the time will come for us to make our assault and destroy him."

I answered that the plan he proposed might be good. He and his officers began making a sketch of the best battlefield, and Angeles came and showed it to me. But the truth is I considered his plan too slow and my own for León and Silao better. So I said, "Sr. General, your plan is good but remember that most of my cavalry are now fighting with the Carrancistas between Silao and Trinidad; remember that the inhabitants of León and its district trust me. If I withdraw and bury myself here after struggling there for four or five days, what then will inspire the troops who are still depressed by what happened in Celaya? I am a man who came into the world to attack, and if I am defeated by attacking today, I will win by attacking tomorrow."

Thereupon Angeles went to León to decide on the location of infantry lines and artillery emplacements, each according to the order in which they arrived.

Juan N. Medina arrived in Aguascalientes before I left. He came under guard of Fidel Avila, governor of Chihuahua, who knew that Medina was making contemptuous remarks about the methods of that government. Several months before I had issued a passport to a man named Silvano Montemayor for his return from the United States to Ciudad Juárez. He had been political chief there in the time of Porfirio Díaz. But Avila, knowing that Montemayor was once more involved in political intrigue, had him imprisoned. Then Medina, who was protecting him, lost his temper and gave vent to angry words, and the commandant had him apprehended also.

Because of this, I called Medina to Aguascalientes, not to punish him but to assign him some duty to which he was suited. On his arrival I said, "Amigo, I don't want you in a civil post but in a military one. Tomorrow you will take command of the Guerrero Brigade, which is without a chief since Agustín Estrada was killed in Celaya."

He answered, "What is the good of a chief who is held for I know not what crime, and all because he respected a passport you had issued?"

I knew what he wanted to tell me and answered, "Silvano Montemayor will be released, and you will take command of the Guerrero Brigade."

The next day I had Montemayor released and ordered Medina, with the rank of general, to take charge of the military commandant's office in Torreón, for which he left immediately.

Publisher's Addendum

The rest of Pancho Villa's story is yet to be told by Martín Luis Guzmán, author of this volume.

In the eight years more he was to live, Villa continued his flamboyant and reckless career. Defiant in the series of defeats he suffered in his war with Carranza, he at last defied even the United States when it recognized Carranza. Determined to demonstrate his control of northern Mexico, he executed some U.S. citizens there and raided on both sides of the border. He daringly attacked Columbus, New Mexico, leaving it in flames and with many casualties. When Brigadier General John J. Pershing led a force into Mexico to capture the rebel leader, Villa—in terrain he knew so well, and aided by the common people of Chihuahua, among whom he was enormously popular—proved to be uncapturable.

For five years he remained a rebel, continuing to harass Carranza, at times even taking some of the large North Mexico cities. When Carranza fell from power, in 1920, Villa made his peace with the government, which gave him a large ranch near Durango. There for three years he lived the peaceful life of a country gentleman. In 1923, on his way to visit in the town of Parral, where he had lived as a boy and fought as a supporter of the Revolution, he and all in his car were ambushed and shot down. The assassin or assassins were never apprehended.

INDEX

Acámbaro, México: 86, 387, 430, 458

Acosta, José Mariá: in Maytorena-Obregón meeting, 293–297 *passim*; mentioned, 463

Acuña, Jesus: objects to executing prisoners, 199; appointed Coahuila governor, 199; mentioned, 195

Agua Prieta, Sonora: neutrality of, 404, 414, 447, 451; mentioned, 97 249

Aguascalientes, Aguascalientes: railroad of, 317, 322, 347, 424; reason for holding convention in, 331; mentioned, 327, 337, 341, 386, 418, 420, 425, 428, 430, 431, 434, 435, 436, 461, 470, 471, 475, 479, 480. SEE ALSO Aguascalientes Convention

Aguascalientes Convention: approved by Revolutionaries, 331; Zapatistas in, 337, 349; Sonora war discussed in, 340; on shooting of delegate by Urbina, 340; on movements of Villa's troops, 340; Herrera breaks truce of, 344; appoints Gutiérrez Interim President, 348, 349; abolishes offices of chiefs, 348–349; González rejects agreements of, 350–351; to people on Gutiérrez appointment, 354; and withdrawal of American troops, 358; Gonzáles severs allegiance to, 359; accused of being instrument of U.S., 363; Blanco supports, 376, 396–397; Carrancista troops defecting to, 375; Gertrudis Sanchéz' support of, 373; Maytorena's disregard of, 392; purpose of, 406–407; Gutiérrez' abandonment of, 406, 421–422; chiefs of, on Villa-Gutiérrez meeting, 407–408; forms laws, 411; González Garza assumes charge of, 421; troops remaining faithful to, 421; troops requested to protect, 423; leaves Mexico City, 432; reform laws of, 435, 477–478; mentioned 328, 376, 378, 381, 391. SEE ALSO González Garza, Roque; Gutiérrez, Eulalio; Villa, Pancho, against Carrancistas (with Convention forces)

— and Carranza: opposes convening of, 327; creates obstacles to, 339; ordered to release Villa followers by, 337; attendance at, 337, 338, 342; on opponents' motives in, 342–343; on conditions for resigning, 343, 346, 347, 352–353, 354–355, 359–360; removed as President by, 348, 349; dealings with commission of, 351–353; Gutiérrez encourages Carranza to respect, 359–360; encourages Coss's rebellion against, 350; refuses to recognize Gutiérrez' appointment, 351, 356; works against, 355; refuses to recognize, 356, 357; recalls chiefs from, 357; considered rebel by, 358; prepares for war against, 359, 381; retracts resignation agreement with, 360; Carrancistas villify supporters of, 381

— and Villa: agrees to, 328; appearance at, 332, 337–339; instructs representative to, 332; aims stated at, 335–336; on Zapatistas at, 336–337, 342; ordered to release political prisoners by, 337; praised at, 338–339; swears to respect, 339; on obstacles in, 339–340; confers with Zapata delegates to, 341–342; removed from command by, 348–349, 350; on agreement to retire, 349, 350; recognizes Gutiérrez as President, 357; as head of forces of, 358–359, 371, 402–404, 405, 419, 424–425; accused of breaking truce of, 361; plot against, in, 405–411, 417; version of history of, 433–434

Aguascalientes (state): Villa's attack on, 243, 246; Robles' troops enter, 350–351; neutrality of, 361–362

Aguilar, Cándido: 418

Aguilar, Higinio: 306

Aguirre, Amado: 439

Aguirre, Serapio: as Carranza's treasurer, 223, 255, 257, 259

Aguirre Benavides, Adrián: 124

Aguirre Benavides, Eugenio: advises Villa on strategy, 109; in battles, 109,